SRIMAD-BHAGAVAD-GITA

ŚRĪMAD-BHAGAVAD-GĪTĀ

(The Scripture of Mankind)

The Text in Devanagari with Transliteration in Roman letters, Chapter summaries, Word-for-Word meaning in Prose Order, Translation, Notes and Index of first lines.

BY

Swami Tapasyananda

SRI RAMAKRISHNA MATH
16, RAMAKRISHNA MATH ROAD
MYLAPORE :: MADRAS-600 004

Published by :
© The President,
Sri Ramakrishna Math,
Mylapore, Madras 600 004.

Sixth Impression
VI-5M 3C-10-94
ISBN 81-7120-094-X
ISBN 81-7120-449-X

Printed in India at
Sri Ramakrishna Math Printing Press,
Mylapore, Madras 600 004.

Contents

Preface

Ever since Sri Śankaracharya's time, the *Bhagavad Gītā* has been recognised as one of the three authoritative and basic source books (*prasthāna-traya*) of Vedic religion. Though Sri Śankara's Introduction to his commentary on the *Gītā* bemoans the misinterpretation of this Text by others, we have no extant commentary or any kind of writing on the *Gītā* that precedes him. So it is reasonable to surmise that it was Sri Śankara who for the first time lifted it up from the vast ocean of Mahābhārata literature, and fixing its verse-contents at seven hundred, wrote an authoritative commentary on it, which is still studied with respect even by those who do not subscribe to his interpretation of it. We may also surmise that it must be he who gave recognition to it as an Upaniṣad and as Brahma-Vidya—a scripture that shatters ignorance and gives the knowledge of Brahman—, as it calls itself in the colophon.

It is customary to discuss the date and authorship of Hindu texts in their modern publications. We are not doing so here, as it is a futile exercise - a veritable counting of the leaves in place of eating mangoes after entering a mango garden. Discussing all the numerous modern views on these questions, Robert N. Minor, a learned and impartial modern exegetical commentator on the *Gītā*, concludes: "In summary, then, in the current state of *Gītā* studies there is no solid evidence to show that the *Gītā* is other than a basic unity. On the other hand, as many such as Edgerton and Zaehner have shown, the *Gītā* when understood in its own terms, is quite consistent and its parts on further study are inter-related. However, it is also not possible to identify the *Gītā*'s author with any probability, and then another question in the introductory matter remains unsolved." And regarding the date of the *Gītā* from the modern point of view, he concludes after taking into account all existing speculative theories: "We must tentatively date the *Gītā* to 150 B.C. *without much evidence*." Under the circumstances, the Indian tradition on these subjects remains intact, and it consists in this: the *Gītā* is a revelation given by Sri Kṛṣṇa, the Pūrṇāvatāra, to humanity through his friend and disciple Arjuna at a critical moment of his life, and it has been put into its present form by Kṛṣṇa Dvaipāyana Vyāsa. As the well-known Sanskrit couplet says: "The *Gītā* is the most excellent nectarine milk, drawn by the cowherd's son Kṛṣṇa as its milker, from the cow of the *Upaniṣads,* using Arjuna as the calf. All men of purified intellect are the consumers of that milk."

Presenting as it does a credible world-view and a faith that is both broad and inspiring, its appeal is to the conscience of spiritually sensitive sections of humanity everywhere, irrespective of their religious affiliations. We have therefore described it as the Scripture of Mankind. It is for this reason that it has become one of the most oft-translated works, English itself having more than fifty translations, besides others in all the Indian languages and in some of the other foreign languages as well. A recognition of this universality of the *Gītā* is made in a slightly garbled form by Farquhar, the well-known Christian missionary-scholar of conservative views, when he says that 'Jesus is the reality of which the *Gītā* gives an imaginative picture'and that 'the author of the *Gītā* would have been a Christian, had he known Jesus.'[1] Far more correct it would have been to say that had the author of the *Gītā* and the deliverer of the Sermon on the Mount met, they would have recognised in each other a kindred spirit teaching an identical message, only with modifications as necessitated by variations in time and place.

The *Gītā* teaches man the goal to be attained by him and the means for attaining it. The goal is the Supreme Personal-Impersonal Brahman and the means, the paths of knowledge, work, psychic control and devotion. Differences in the interpretations of the *Gītā* among the Ācāryas ,both ancient and modern, have arisen due to their varying perceptions on the relations between Brahman and the Jīva and on the relative importance of the four paths.

[1]As quoted by Geoffrey Parrinder in his *Avatār and Incarnation.*

Critics may find in this a vein of inconsistency and unreliability that stands in the way of recognising the value of the Gītā as a guide to man and as a universal scripture. It is, however, forgotten by such critics that a universal scripture must contain in it several strands of teachings suited to men of different stages of development. These varying strands are not mutually contradictory or incompatible. They are the visions of the same Reality from the points of view of Jīvas at different stages of development, dominated by different dispositions. The presence of this feature, in place of being a disqualification, is a proof of the genuineness of the inspiration behind this Text. For, God's gifts are not for a few only but for all who have need of them, and everyone can understand something from them provided one has spiritual sensitivity. That is why the *Gītā* has several interpretations coming from Ācāryas representing different spiritual traditions. In spite of their differences, they have to be accepted as embodying the varied views included in the inspired literature that is the Gītā.

In the annotations given in the present volume, comments have been confined to technically important verses for limiting the size of the volume. The comments have got only the Text as such in view, without identification with any particular school of thought. But help has been sought from classical interpretations as well as from the modern exegetical commentators like Zaehner and Minor. The overall point of view adopted is what is contained in Swami Vivekānanda's famous restatement of the Vedānta in the following aphoristic dictum:

Every soul is potentially Divine.

The goal of life is to manifest this Divine within by controlling Nature, external and internal.

Do this either by work, or worship, or by psychic control, or philosophy, by one or more or all of these—and be free.

This is the whole of Religion. Doctrines or dogmas, or rituals, or books, or temples, or forms are but secondary details.

Amidst the numerous extant translations of the *Gītā,* a new edition of it like the present one may not in any way look very significant. It has, however, this much significance: it provides an *economy edition* of the Text, with all facilities for serious students to study the verses—these facilities being introductory summary of each chapter, the Text in Devanagari, its transliteration into Roman script, the prose order with word for word meaning in Roman script, running translation and annotations wherever necessary. It is hoped that this edition will meet the need of a large cross section of spiritual enquirers who want to study the Gītā in the original.

RAMAKRISHNA MATH,
MADRAS.
1-1-1984.

Publisher

Meditation on the Gītā

पार्थाय प्रतिबोधितां भगवता नारायणेन स्वयं
व्यासेन ग्रथितां पुराणमुनिना मध्येमहाभारतम् ।
अद्वैतामृतवर्षिणीं भगवतीमष्टादशाध्यायिनी-
मम्ब त्वामनुसंदधामि भगवद्गीते भवद्वेषिणीम् ॥

Om pārthāya pratibodhitāṁ bhagavatā Nārāyaṇena svayaṁ
vyāsena grathitāṁ purāṇamuninā madhyemahābhāratam:
advaitāmṛta varṣiṇīṁ bhagavatīm aṣṭādaśā'dhyāyinīm
amba tvām anusandadhāmi bhagavad-gīte bhavadveṣiṇīm.

Om : Om *Nārāyaṇena svayam* : by Nārāyaṇa Himself *Pārthāya* : to Pārtha or Arjuna *pratibodhitām* : imparted *purāṇamuninā* : by the ancient sage *Vyāsena* : by Vyāsa *madhyemahābhāratam* : in the middle of Mahābhārata *grathitām* : recorded *advaitāmṛtavarṣiṇīm* : showering the nectar of Advaita *bhagavtīm* : Goddess *aṣṭādaśā'dhyāyinīm* : consisting of eighteen chapters *bhavadveṣiṇīm* : destroyer of Samsāra *amba* : Mother, *bhagavad-Gīte*: O Bhagavad-Gītā *tvām* : Thee *anusandadhāmi* : I meditate upon.

Om! O Blessed Mother Bhagavad-Gītā, Thou Goddess! Who was imparted to Arjuna by Nārāyaṇa Himself. who was recorded amidst the Mahābhārata by Vyāsa the ancient sage, who showers the nectar of Advaita, who is composed of eighteen chapters—I meditate on Thee, the destroyer of Samsāra!

नमोऽस्तु ते व्यास विशालबुद्धे फुल्लारविन्दायतपत्रनेत्र ।
येन त्वया भारततैलपूर्णः प्रज्वालितो ज्ञानमयः प्रदीपः ॥

Namo'stu te Vyāsa viśāla-buddhe
phullāravindā'yata-patra-netra:
yena tvayā bhārata-taila-pūrṇaḥ
prajvālito jñāna-mayaḥ pradīpaḥ.

Viśālabuddhe : Of gigantic intellect *phullāravindā'yata-patra-netra* : having large eyes resembling the petals of a blossoming lotus *Vyāsa* : O Sage Vyāsa! *yena tvayā* : Thee by whom *bhārata-taila-pūrṇaḥ* : brimming with the oil of Mahābhārata *jñāna-mayaḥ* : of the nature of wisdom *pradīpaḥ* : lamp *prajvālitaḥ* : was lit *te* : to Thee *namaḥ* : salutations.

Salutations to Thee, O Vyāsa of mighty intellect, Thou whose eyes are large like the petals of a full-blown lotus! It was Thou who lit the wisdom-lamp which brims with the oil that is the Mahābhārata.

प्रपन्नपारिजाताय तोत्रवेत्रैकपाणये ।
ज्ञानमुद्राय कृष्णाय गीतामृतदुहे नमः ॥

Prapanna-pārijātāya totra-vetra'ika-pāṇaye;
jñāna-mudrāya Kṛṣṇāya gītāmṛta duhe namaḥ.

Prapanna-pārijātāya : Who is a wish-yielding tree to the surrendered ones *totra-vetra'ika pāṇaye* : holding a cane for driving cattle in one hand *jñāna-mudrāya* : showing the sign of wisdom with the other *Gītā'mṛta-duhe* : milker of the nectarine milk of Gītā *Kṛṣṇāya*: to Kṛṣṇa, *namaḥ* : salutations.

Salutations to Thee Kṛṣṇa, who art a veritable wish-yielding tree to all surrendered ones, whose one hand holds a cane to drive cattle while the other is held in the Jñāna-pose, and who is famous as the milker of the nectarine milk that is the Bhagavad-Gītā.

सर्वोपनिषदो गावो दोग्धा गोपालनन्दनः
पार्थो वत्सः सुधीर्भोक्ता दुग्धं गीतामृतं महत् ॥

Sarvo'paniṣado gāvo dogdhā Gopāla-nandanaḥ;
pārtho vatsaḥ sudhīr-bhoktā dugdhaṁ gītāmṛtam mahat.

Sarvopaniṣadaḥ : All the Upaniṣads *gāvaḥ* : cows; *gopāla-nandanaḥ* : the cowherd's son i.e. Kṛṣṇa *dogdhā* : milker; *Pārthaḥ* : Arjuna *vatsaḥ* : calf; *sudhīḥ* : men of pure mind *bhoktāḥ* : drinkers; *mahat* : great *amṛtam dugdham* : nectarine milk *gītā* : the Gītā.

All the Upaniṣads are the cows; the cowherd's son Kṛṣṇa is the milker; Pārtha (Arjuna) is the calf; the nectarine Gītā is the milk; and the pure-minded are the drinkers of it.

वसुदेवसुतं देवं कंसचाणूरमर्दनम् ।
देवकीपरमानन्दं कृष्णं वन्दे जगद्गुरुम् ॥

Vasudeva-sutaṁ devaṁ Kaṁsa-Cāṇūra-mardanam;
Devakī-paramānandaṁ Kṛṣṇaṁ vande jagadgurum.

Vasudevasutam : The son of Vasudeva *Kaṁsa-Cāṇūra-mardanam* : The destroyer of Kamsa and Cāṇūra *Devakī-paramānandam* the bestower of supreme delight to Devaki *jagadgurum* : the world-teacher *devam Kṛṣṇam* : Lord Kṛṣṇa *vande* : I salute.

I salute Lord Kṛṣṇa, the son of Vasudeva, the bestower of supreme delight to Devaki, the destroyer of Kamsa and Cāṇūra, and the teacher of the world.

भीष्मद्रोणतटा जयद्रथजला गांधारनीलोत्पला
शल्यग्राहवती कृपेण वहनी कर्णेन वेलाकुला ।
अश्वत्थामविकर्णघोरमकरा दुर्योधनावर्तिनी
सोत्तीर्णा खलु पांडवै रणनदी कैवर्तकः केशवः ॥

Bhīṣma-droṇa-taṭā jayadratha-jalā Gāndhāra-nīlotpalā
Śalya-grāhavatī Kṛpreṇa vahanī Karṇena velākulā;
Aśvatthāma-vikarṇa-ghora-makarā Duryodhanā'vartinī
s'ottīrṇā khalu paṇḍavai raṇa-nadī kaivartakaḥ Keśavaḥ

Bhīṣma-droṇa-taṭā : With Bhīṣma and Droṇa as banks *Jayadratha-jalā* : with Jayadratha as water *Gāndhāra-nīlotpalā* : with the prince of Gāndhāra as the blue lotus *Śalya-grāhavatī* : with Śalya as the crocodile *Kṛpeṇa* : with Kṛpa *vahanī* : as current *Karṇena* : with Karṇa *velākulā* : as high waves *Aśvatthāma-*

Vikarṇa-ghora-makarā : with Aśvatthāma and Vikarṇa as terrible sharks *Duryodhanāvartinī* : with Duryodhana as the whirl-pool *sā* : that *raṇa-nadī* : battle-river *Pāṇḍavaiḥ* : by the sons of Pāṇḍu *uttīrṇā* :was crossed *khalu* : lo! *kaivartakaḥ Keśavaḥ* : (with) Keśava as ferry-man.

Lo! The battle-river of Kurukṣetra, with Bhīṣma and Droṇa as the banks; with Jayadratha as the water; with the prince of Gāndhāra as the blue water lily; with Śalya as the crocodile; with Kṛpa as the current; with Karṇa as the high wave; with Aśvatthāma and Vikarṇa as terrible sharks; and with Duryodhana as the whirl-pool—was crossed by the Pāṇḍavas because they had Kṛṣṇa as the ferry-man.

पाराशर्यवचः सरोजममलं गीतार्थगन्धोत्कटं
नानाख्यानककेसरं हरिकथासम्बोधनाबोधितम् ।
लोके सज्जनषट्पदैरहरहः पेपीयमानं मुदा
भूयाद्भारतपङ्कजं कलिमलप्रध्वंसिनः श्रेयसे ॥

Pārāśarya-vacaḥ-sarojam amalaṁ gītārtha-gandhotkaṭam
nānā'khyānaka-kesaraṁ Harikathā-sambodhanā-bodhitam;
loke sajjana-ṣaṭpadair aharahaḥ pepīyamānaṁ mudā
bhūyād bhārata-paṅkajaṁ kalimala-pradhvaṁsinaḥ śreyase.

Amalam : Stainless *Pārāśaryavachaḥ-sarojam* : born on the water of the words of the son of Parāśara *bhārata-paṅkajam* : the lotus of Mahābhārata *gītārtha-gandhotkaṭam* : having the message of the Gītā as its overpowering fragrance *Harikathā-sambodhanā-bodhitam* : which proclaims the glory of Śrī Hari *nānā'khyānaka-kesaram* : numerous narratives for its stamens *loke* : in the world *sajjana-ṣaṭpadaiḥ* : by honey-suckers constituted of virtuous men *mudā* : in great joy *aharahaḥ* : every day *pepīyamānam* : drunk again and again *kalimala-pradhvamsinaḥ* : of all who want to be free from the taint of the age of Kali *śreyase* : for the good of *bhūyāt* : may prevail.

May the stainless lotus of Mahābhārata, which was born on the waters of the words of Vyāsa, the son of Parāśara, which has the message of the Gītā for its overpowering fragrance, which contains numerous narratives proclaiming the glory of Hari as its stamens, and which is sucked again and again in great joy every day by the honey-suckers of virtuous men—may it prevail for the good of all who want to be cleansed of the taint of the age of Kali!

मूकं करोति वाचालं पङ्गुं लङ्घयते गिरिम् ।
यत्कृपा तमहं वन्दे परमानन्दमाधवम् ॥

Mūkam karoti vācālam paṅguṁ laṅghayate girim;
yat kṛpā tam aham vande paramānanda-mādhavam.

Yat : Whose *kṛpā* : grace *mūkam* : the dumb *vācālam* : eloquent *karoti* : makes, *paṅguṁ* : the lame *girim* : mountain *laṅghayate*: enables to cross, *tam*: Him *paramā'nandam* : supremely blissful *Mādhavam* : Mādhava (Kṛṣṇa) *aham* : I *vande* : salute.

I salute Mādhava (Lord Kṛṣṇa), the Supremely Blissful One, by whose grace a dumb man can become eloquent, and a lame person cross over mountains.

यं ब्रह्मा वरुणेन्द्ररुद्रमरुतः स्तुन्वन्ति दिव्यैः स्तवै-
र्वेदैः साङ्गपदक्रमोपनिषदैर्गायन्ति यं सामगाः ।
ध्यानावस्थिततद्गतेन मनसा पश्यन्ति यं योगिनो
यस्यान्तं न विदुः सुरासुरगणा देवाय तस्मै नमः ॥

Yaṁ Brahmā-Varuṇe'ndra-Rudra-Marutaḥ stunvanti divyaiḥ stavaiḥ
vedaiḥ sāṅga-pada-kramo'paniṣadaiḥ gāyanti yaṁ sāmagāḥ:
dhyānā'vasthita-tad-gatena manasā paśyanti yaṁ yogino
yasyāntam na viduḥ surāsura-gaṇā devāya tasmai namaḥ.

Yam: Whom *Brahmā*: the creator Brahmā *Varuṇaḥ*: Varuṇa *Indraḥ*: Indra *Rudraḥ*: Rudra *Marutaḥ*: the Maruts *stunvanti*: glorify *divyaiḥ*: by divine *stavaiḥ* : by hymns; *yam* : whom *sāmagāḥ* : singers of Sāman *sāṅga-pada-kramo'paniṣadaiḥ* : with complementary parts, sections and Upaniṣads *Vedaiḥ* : by Veda *gāyanti* : praise by chanting; *yam*: whom *yoginaḥ*: Yogins *dhyānā'vasthita-tad-gatena*: (with minds) concentrated in the state *paśyanti* : intuit; *yasya* : whose *antam* : limit *surāsura-gaṇāḥ* : the hosts of Devas and Asuras *na viduḥ* : do not know *tasmai* : to that *devāya* to the Deva (the Supreme Being) *namaḥ* : my salutation.

My salutations to that Supreme Being, whom Brahmā, Varuṇa, Indra and Rudra glorify by divine hymns; whom singers of Sāman praise by chanting the Veda with all the complementary parts, sections and Upaniṣads; whom Yogins intuit with minds concentrated in meditation; and whose limit neither the hosts of Devas nor of Asuras know.

INTRODUCTION

A Bird's-Eye View of the Gita Teachings

The Appeal of the Gitā

Among the world's scriptures, the *Bhagavad Gitā* is one of the most popular texts. Its popularity is demonstrated by the fact that next to the Bible it is perhaps the most widely translated of scriptural texts, and in several languages, both Indian and foreign, its translations are to be counted in dozens. This tremendous general appeal of the *Bhagavad-Gitā* was voiced forth in prophetic words by Warren Hastings, the first British Governor-General of India (1773-85)—a personality one would least expect to deal with such a subject. In his Introduction to the first-ever English translation of the scripture by Charles Wilkins (1784), Hastings has remarked that "works as the *Gitā* would live long after the British dominion in India has ceased to exist" and that it contains passages "elevated to a track of sublimity into which our habits of judgement will find it difficult to pursue."

In India it has attracted the attention of all the Ācāryas (teachers) of the Vedānta philosophy, of which it is recognised as one of the three source books, ever since the great Sankarācārya wrote his commentary on it. Following Sankara, all the Ācāryas of the different schools of Vedānta wrote commentaries on this great text, each interpreting it in support of his own thesis. It has been given the status of an Upanishad, a revealed scripture embodying the quintessence of the Vedic revelation, as enunciated in the following oft-quoted verse: "All the Upanishads are the cows, the cowherd boy Krishna is the milker, Arjuna is the calf, the pure-minded are the consumers, and the ambrosial *Gītā* is the delicious milk".

It is not the ancient Indian thinkers alone, but also the leaders of modern times, that have taken it as a text for the exposition of their highest thoughts. Thus we have got in modern times Tilak's *Gītā Rahasya*, Aurobindo's *Essays on the Gītā* and Mahatma Gandhi's *Anāsakti Yoga* as examples of the continuing preference and admiration of the Indian mind for this great scriptural text of seven hundred verses.

What is the secret of this tremendous appeal of the *Bhagavad-Gītā*? Probably it consists in the fact that it deals with a practical problem of life, namely, how a man could discharge his duties as a member of an imperfect social order and at the same time realise his highest spiritual destiny envisaged by the sublime metaphysics and theology enshrined in the Vedic revelation. The Gītā, therefore, begins with an ethical problem, and in solving this problem, a noble devotional philosophy is expounded.

The Ethical Problem in the Gītā

The ethical problem is graphically depicted at the outset through the predicament of Arjuna. Arjuna is the leader of the Pāṇḍava host, and his whole life has been a preparation to meet his cousins, the Kauravas, in battle, defeat them, and wrest from them the kingdom they had usurped from himself and his brothers. The Gītā scene is cast in the battlefield of Kurukṣetra where the armies of both the sides have gathered, and Arjuna is called upon to fulfil his historic mission by leading his men against the army of the Kauravas. Arjuna realises at this critical moment that it is a fratricidal war, and that its consequence will be the destruction of the very friends and relatives for the sake of whom men usually seek wealth and kingdom, as well as the social chaos consequent on the holocaust of the flower of Kaurava and Pāndava chivalry. A war-weariness and a world-weariness together come upon him with dramatic suddenness. Under their impact he forgets all his social and family obligations, and wants to take to an ascetic life instead of indulging in what he conceives to be a senseless carnage under the guise of duty

(Swadharma). He becomes a pacifist and a quietist all of a sudden.

The conflict here is between a sudden and purely personal inclination bursting on one's mind and a social duty, the avoidance of which under that inclination would have meant ruin to a whole community that had laid its trust in one. Sri Kṛṣṇa, though God incarnate, is Arjuna's friend, charioteer and spiritual counsellor, and he is called upon to resolve the conflict in Arjuna's mind and restore him to a sense of moral equilibrium by finding a new sanction for action.

Inevitability of Action in Life

In the protracted dialogue between the teacher and the disciple, the final answer to the problem is given only at the end, but the mind of Arjuna is prepared for it by a series of talks on the inexorable nature of work in the life of man and on the utter futility of Arjuna's resolve to withdraw from a life of action. Man's body and mind are parts of Prakṛti (Nature) which is dynamic in its constitution. As a product of Prakṛti, action is the law of life for the mind and the body, and the very process of living is impossible without it. And so its elimination can only mean practice of idleness according to one's convenience, and he who attempts it under a false impression of his spiritual greatness, will end in rank hyprocrisy and spiritual stagnation. Only one, who has overcome the body idea completely and is established in the sense that he is not the body but the immortal, ever-conscious and ever-blissful Atman, can be actionless; for, he no longer identifies himself with the body, the product of Nature.

Besides, from the ethical point of view, every one with body-consciousness has to remember that he is living in a community of similar beings governed by a cyclic law of mutual exchange of services and commodities. If he does not contribute his share to it by means of work but enjoys the benefits of others' work for the maintenance and comfort of his own body, he lives the life of an exploiter and a thief. He has no moral basis and hence no spiritual progress.

Even in the case of a person who has been emancipated from identification with the body, it is better that he works. He has not the compulsion of duty as in the case of the ignorant man, but he may feel the compulsion of love, which makes one work for *lokasamgraha* or world-welfare. His actions are not self-centred and so have no binding effect on him. Work therefore is the law of life for the ignorant, and an expression of love for the enlightened, the work of the former being self-centred and of the latter God-centred.

Doctrine of Niṣkama-Karma as the Panacea for the moral Conflict

But the two questions still remain: Actions like leading men in war have many evil consequences, though they may be part of one's duty. Is not avoidance of such duties better than doing them and incurring sin? How can their performance promote spiritual life at all? The ideal of the Sthitaprajña depicted in the *Gītā*—the ideal of a person who is absolutely indrawn and unperturbed, who is the master of the senses and mind—is so far removed from that of a soldier engaged in a form of dreadful action like war, that it looks incredible that Swadharma of that type can ever lead a man to that state of spiritual excellence. This doubt persists continually in Arjuna's mind in spite of Kṛṣṇaa's exhortation to action.

In answer to this Sri Kṛṣṇa propounds the doctrine of Nishkāma-Karma—the doctrine of actions done with detachment and in dedication to the Lord. Works in themselves are amoral, if we eliminate the self-centred agent from them. Nature's cataclysms with their terribly destructive effect cannot be classified as moral or immoral. They are amoral. All works are a mixture of beneficence and destructiveness as far as their effects are concerned. They are like the brilliance of fire, always accompanied by the obscuring cloudiness of smoke.

Work at the human level has various ramifications. There is work done under compulsion like slave labour, which may be characterised as sub-moral in its effect on the worker. Higher than that is work prompted by the profit motive (*kāmya-karma*), on which human civilisation as constituted today is based. *Kāmya-karma* can take two forms: On the one hand there is anti-social work which is technically denoted as *Vikarma* or

Adharma or *Niṣiddha-Karma*; on the other hand there is socially oriented action which is termed Dharma. Anti-social work is done by persons with demoniac nature. Everything they do is for ostentation and self-aggrandisement and no form of cruel exploitation and selfish indulgences is repugnant to them, provided their pleasure, profit and ambition are promoted thereby. Such anti-social beings are endowed with *Āsurī-sampat* (demoniac nature) characterised by pride, greed, passion and cruelty. Moral and spiritual degradation is the wage for their sins. In contrast are men with *Daivīsampat* (divine nature), who follow Dharma or socially oriented action. They too are self-centred and seek pleasure and power, the good things of life, but their pursuit of these is socially oriented and is regulated by norms that take others and their needs too into consideration. In return for what they seek and take, they are prepared to give away what is due from them. They observe the law of Yajna. They are *Dhārmikas,* men who too pursue pleasure and power but always subordinate such pursuit to a code of give and take based on a sense of collective good and of moral responsibility. When their sense of obligation to society dominates overwhelmingly over the demand for individual fulfilment, they become elevated into patriots, philanthropists, and votaries of similar other noble values of a collective nature.

Arjuna was in his early life a *Dhārmika* of this type, when he found himself all of a sudden in the predicament described earlier, wherein the old sanctions for action like Swadharma (or discharge of one's duty), socially approved pursuit of power and pleasure, communal welfare, patriotism etc., became meaningless as inducements for action. A new sanction had to be found if Arjuna were to take part in action, and this sanction, different even from the one applicable to the *Dhārmikas,* is expounded by the Bhagavān. It is the doctrine of *Niṣkāma-karma,* the doctrine of work without desire, applicable to men who seek only liberation (*Mumukshu*). In expounding it, a sublime theology and a devotional metaphysics are propounded as the spiritual rationale of such desireless action. For, then only the 'how' and the 'why' of desireless action will become clear. Without this spiritual basis, desireless action will only be an incomprehensible and a puzzling concept, as we cannot think of any action devoid of the prompting of some desire or other. The main thoughts of the *Gītā* in these respects are as follows :

The Metaphysics and Theology of the Gītā

All Jīvas (individual spiritual centres) are sparks from the fire that is the Divine Vāsudeva. Not the Jīvas only but all other categories too. So Vāsudeva is the 'All' (*Vāsudevaḥ sarva-miti*). How could that one Being be all and yet be Himself, His identity unimpaired? The Gītā theology answers this by the theory that the Supreme Being has two Prakṛtis or Powers of manifestation, which are aspects of Him, non-different yet distinct from Him. Power and Power-holder, though distinct, are not different. It is His Prakṛti that changes, not Himself. Speaking on this mystery of the Supreme Being manifesting as the universe of living and non-living beings, without himself undergoing any change, the *Gītā* says; "Earth, water, fire, air, ether, mind, intellect and egoism — this is Prakṛti Different from this, O mighty armed one, know that higher Prakṛti of Mine in the form of the individual soul (Jīva) for whose growth and salvation this world cycle is sustained. Know that all beings have these two for their origin. I am the origin of the entire universe as also its destroyer. Higher than Myself there is nothing else, O Dhanañjaya. In Me all this is strung like gems on a string" (VII 4-7).

Again adverting to the non-involvement of the Lord in the universe, in spite of His being its material and efficient cause, the Gītā says, "All this is pervaded by Me in My unmanifest form; all beings are in Me, but I am not in them. Nor are the beings in Me. Behold My divine mystery; though the sustainer and the protector of beings, I am Myself not in these beings. As the vast wind blowing everywhere ever abides in space, know that even so do all beings abide in Me. At the end of a cycle all beings, O son of Kunti, attain My Prakṛti , and at the beginning of the next cycle I again send them forth. Presiding over My Prakṛti, I again and again send forth this entire aggregate completely under the dominance of Prakṛti. These acts of creation etc., O Arjuna, do not bind Me, who remain unattached to them like one unconcerned" (IX 4-9).

While such is the cosmic stature of this Divine as depicted in the *Gītā*, He is also an intensely Personal Being, loving and beneficent, easily approachable through service and surrender. He is the same to all, and none is specially dear to Him or inimical. Those who cling to Him in adoration, they dwell in Him and He in them. Nor is He a far off being, a deistic God isolated from men and the world. He is the nearest of the near, being ever present in the hearts of all, vitalising their intellect, mind and body. "I am the father of this world," declares the God of the *Bhagavad-Gītā*, "the mother, the protector, the grandsire, the one object to be known, the supreme purifier, the sacred sound symbol Om and the Vedas. I am the goal, the sustainer, the lord, the witness, the abode, the refuge, the friend, the source, the destroyer, the support, the repository and the eternal seed. I give heat, I restrain and release rain. I am immortality as also death. I am both Being and Becoming (IX 17-19)"; "In whatever way a man adores Me, that way I bless him. The paths men adopt everywhere are paths leading to Me (IV. 11)"; "He who with devotion offers Me a leaf, a flower, a fruit or water, that devout offering of the pure-minded, I accept. Whatever you do, or eat, or sacrifice or give—whatever austerity you perform—that O son of Kunti, you do offer unto Me. Thus you will be rid of the bondage of action resulting in good and evil; being free and with your mind endowed with the Yoga of renunciation, you will attain Me. I am the same to all beings, there is no one hateful or dear to Me. But they who worship Me with devotion are in Me, and I also am in them. Even if a very wicked man happens to worship Me in deep devotion excluding all other loves, he should be regarded as righteous; for he has rightly resolved. He soon becomes righteous-minded and attains eternal peace. O son of Kunti, proclaim that my devotee never perishes." (IX 26-31)

The Theophany of the Lord

The God of love of the *Bhagavad-Gītā* is also the dispenser of death and destruction. For, creation, preservation, destruction and redemption go side by side. His theophany as Time the destroyer, of which Arjuna had the vision, is described as "Having many mouths and eyes, and containing many a wonderful sight, with many heavenly ornaments, wielding many heavenly uplifted weapons, wearing celestial garland and apparel, anointed with heavenly perfumes, wondrous, resplendent, infinite and having faces on every side. If the effulgence of a thousand suns were to flash in the skies simultaneously, it might compare somewhat with the splendour of that great form. There the son of Pāṇḍu saw the entire universe with its manifold divisions united in the body of the God of gods. Then awed and wonderstruck, Arjuna said, adoring the Lord with joined palms: 'In Thy body, O Lord, I see the Devas, as also all the hosts of various beings, Brahma, the ruler seated on his lotus-seat, all the heavenly sages and serpents. I see Thee with many hands, bellies, mouths and eyes possessing infinite forms on every side. O Lord of the Universe, O Thou of universal form! I see, however, neither Thy end, nor middle, nor beginning...O Viṣṇu! Seeing Thee touching the sky, blazing, of many hues, with open mouth and fiery eyes, I am frightened at heart. All these sons of Dhṛtarāṣṭra along with the hosts of kings, Bhīṣma , Drona, as also the charioteer's son (Karna) together with the principal warriors on our side are entering with a rush into Thy terrible jaws set with fearful teeth...As moths enter a blazing fire in a great hurry only to be destroyed, even so are these people also entering into Thy mouths with great speed just to be destroyed."

Overpowered, awe-struck and exalted, Arjuna asks that 'Ferocious Form' to reveal His identity, and the Lord replies, "I am terrible Time (Kāla), the destroyer of peoples, and am here proceeding to destroy them. Even without you, all these warriors in every division shall cease to be...By Me alone all these have been killed already; be you merely an instrument."

Arjuna's Attainment of a Cosmic World-view and Resolution of Conflict

The experience of the above described Cosmic Form of the Lord opens up a new dimension before Arjuna. It resolves the difficulty he is faced with. Till now his life has been like that of an individual cell in a body which thinks, out of ignorance, that it is an independent entity, functioning on its own, while in truth it has been only a part of a whole, for whose energy it has been but a conduit and in fulfilment of whose purpose it has been functioning. In the human body such a cell functioning apart from the life of the whole becomes a cancerous cell. Arjuna now feels that he has till now been such a cancerous cell in a spiritual sense, his outlook being based on self-centredness. He realises now that he is neither a solitary individual, nor merely a member of a society, but a cell in the mighty being of the Lord, with an apportioned piece of work to perform, not for his own sake, nor even for his community or country, but for the sake of Him to whom everything and everyone ultimately belongs — realises also that, residing within the hearts of all, He is turning the wheel of Time with all beings poised on it, and that to be in communion with this Cosmic Spirit with undivided devotion and to be discharging one's allotted functions without egotistic sense and in resignation to the Supreme Will, is the way to the peace of salvation.

In the light of this enlightened and enlarged world-view, work gains a new sanction and a new significance. Neither self-aggrandizement, nor even the service of any worldly cause is its ultimate purpose. The purpose is the spiritual development of man—to be freed from the hold of the body and realise one's kinship or unity with the Divine. For he, the Jīva, is a spark from the great Divine Fire, but identification with the body has effaced the sense of his inherent Divinity. This predicament of man, called ignorance, must be due to the will of the Divine, and only by the will or Grace of the Divine can he be redeemed from it. This grace descends on him who resigns himself to Him with his entire being—body, mind and soul. Discharge of the works that devolve on one as duty without any self-centred motive, but as an offering unto the Divine—to start with, of all results, and finally of agency too—is the way of this total resignation leading to enlightenment.

Works, too, cannot be accepted or shunned by any mere momentary considerations of their being good or bad, agreeable or disagreeable. All works, however good at first sight, carry some bad effects too, just as fire is always accompanied by smoke. In the Divine dispensation there are four character types, and the work appropriate to each of these types is called its Swadharma (natural duty). The four character types are called in the Indian tradition—Brāhmana, Kshatriya, Vaisya and Sudra. It has to be emphasised again and again that these are not castes as they are unfortunately looked upon today, but character types evolved according to the Divine dispensation, having nothing to do with caste and community based on mere birth in certain families. The Brāhmana is the introvert type, reflective, intellectual and self-restrained and with the dominance of the Sattva element of Nature. The Kshatriya is the extrovert, flamboyant, lordly, pugnacious, chivalrous and possessed of qualities of leadership and having the dominance of Rajas in him. The Vaisya is the acquisitive type, industrious, organising, enterprising and conserving, with the elements of Rajas and Tamas in him. And the Sudra is the dull type, without enterprise or initiative, requiring direction from others, and fit only for routine subordinate work, mental and physical. The element of Tamas dominates him.

Works and ways of living, suited to these natures and in the line of their evolution, are their Swadharma, irrespective of what some may consider good or bad elements in them. For, as already pointed out, every work in this world will have these two elements of favourableness or unfavourableness to some one or other, but irrespective of that, they fall within the scope of Swadharma, provided they have social acceptability and are in the line of one's nature dictated by one's stage of evolution. For one who accepts and contemplates on the Divine world-view and the destiny of man as presented in the Gītā, the performance of such Swadharma with detachment and as an offering to the Divine is a potent means to spiritual evolution. By the offering of the fruits of his works man's sinful tendencies born of physical nature are effaced, and when he is able to resign his sense of agency too to Him, he realises the Whole as the Divine, in which His will alone is functioning through all individual centres of consciousness (Jīvas) spread in His being.

This supra-ethical vision of life is stated thus in thrilling language in the Gītā: "From whom proceeds the activity of all beings, and by whom all this is pervaded, worshipping Him through one's Swadharma, a man attains perfection. Better is one's Swadharma, though defective, than another's duty, apparently well performed. Doing the duty ordained by one's nature, one incurs no sin. One should not, O son of Kunti, relinquish the duty born of one's nature, although it may be attended with evil; for all undertakings are covered by defects, as fire by smoke. He whose undertakings are unattached everywhere, whose mind is under control, who is bereft of desires, attains by renunciation that supreme state of freedom from action...Resigning mentally all actions, regarding Me as the supreme goal, and resorting to communion with your whole being, ever fix your mind on Me. Fixing your mind on Me, you will overcome all difficulties through My grace. But if from self-conceit you do not listen to Me, you will perish. If, indulging in self-conceit, you think, 'I will not fight', vain is that resolve of yours. Your nature will compel you to fight. O son of Kunti, what out of delusion you do not wish to do, you will do in spite of yourself, fettered by your own duty born of your nature. In the heart of all beings, O Arjuna, resides the Lord, whirling all of them by His Maya as if they were mounted on a machine. Take refuge in Him alone with all your heart, O descendant of Bharata. By His grace you shall attain supreme peace and the eternal abode... Fix your mind in Me; be devoted to Me; worship Me; bow down to Me. Then you shall come to Me. Truly do I promise you, for you are dear to Me. Giving up all other Dharmas, take refuge in Me alone. I will liberate you from all sins, do not grieve."

KEY TO TRANSLITERATION AND PRONUNCIATION

	Sounds like		*Sounds like*
अ	a-o in son	ट	ṭ -t in ten
आ	ā-a in master	ठ	ṭh -th in ant-hill
इ	i -i in if	ड	ḍ -d in den
ई	ī-ee in feel	ढ	ḍh-dh in godhood
उ	u-u in full	ण	ṇ -n in under
ऊ	ū-oo in boot	त	t -t in French
ऋ	ṛ-somewhat between r and ri	थ	th -th in thumb
		द	d -th in then
ए	e -ay in May	ध	dh -theh in breathe
ऐ	ai-y in my	न	n -n in not
ओ	o-o in oh	प	p -p in pen
औ	au-ow in now	फ	ph-ph in loop-hole
क	k -k in keen	ब	b -b in bag
ख	kh -ckh in blockhead	भ	bh -bh in abhor
ग	g -g (hard) in go	म	m -m in mother
घ	gh -gh in log-hut	य	y -y in yard
ङ	ṅ-ng in singer	र	r -r in run
च	c -ch (not k) chain	ल	l -l in luck
छ	ch-chh in catch him	व	v -v in avert
ज	j -j in judge	श	ś -sh in reich (German)
झ	jh-dgeh in hedgehog	ष	ṣ -sh in show
ञ	ñ -n (somewhat) as in French	स	s -in sun
		ह	h -in hot
			m-m in sum
		:	h -h in half

Chapter I

अर्जुन-विषाद-योगः

ARJUNA'S SPIRITUAL CONVERSION THROUGH SORROW

SUMMARY

The Significance of the Opening Chapter: The first chapter, depicting Arjuna's grief, is meant to show under what conditions man opens himself to the voice of the Spirit. A crisis is often required to make him turn his eyes to the spiritual reality. Often it is the impact of death, loss, disease, faithlessness of man, or any other such bitter experience of life that causes the awakening.

In the case of Arjuna, the hero who forms the central figure in this philosophical poem, it is not any of these but the naked display of man's cupidity and heartlessness that brings about the change of outlook. Trained to the profession of arms, and accustomed to the pursuit of power and pleasure, Arjuna has till now led the life of a respectable man of the world, seeking the good things of life and doing his ordained religious duties. Now when he is called upon to perform his historic duty of leading the armies of his clan against the usurping Kauravas, the moment of disillusionment comes to him on reflecting on the consequences of the fratricidal war and on the sordid and bloodstained prizes for which it is fought. He seeks shelter in his Divine Teacher Kṛṣṇa, who has been for him a friend and counsellor till now.

Arjuna on the Battlefield of Kurukṣetra: (1-47) The scene is laid on the battle-field of Kurukṣetra, also described as Dharma

Kṣetra, where the armies of the Kauravas and Pāṇḍavas are arrayed in battle formations to settle finally by the might of arms their respective claims to the common ancestral kingdom. After the first few verses, wherein a brief review of the leaders on both sides is made by Duryodhana, Arjuna appears on the scene in a chariot driven by Kṛṣṇa. Stationed in his chariot between the two armies, he finds on both sides close kith and kin and venerated persons like teachers and grandfathers standing ready to kill one another for the sake of power and pelf. The frightful consequences of a fratricidal war dawn on him in all vividness, and he feels it better to eat a beggar's food than enjoy wealth stained with the blood of persons related to him as sons, fathers, uncles, brothers-in-law, friends, grandfathers and teachers. Shocked at the prospect of a senseless carnage in which his own near and dear ones are going to be the victims, Arjuna decides to lay down arms, surrender the kingdom to the Kauravas, and even to court death at their hands, or, if he were to survive, to become an ascetic. He drops his weapons in a mood of depression caused by utter confusion as to what his duty is under such circumstances.

धृतराष्ट्र उवाच—

धर्मक्षेत्रे कुरुक्षेत्रे समवेता युयुत्सवः ।
मामकाः पाण्डवाश्चैव किमकुर्वत सञ्जय ॥ 1 ॥

Dhṛtarāṣṭra uvāca:

Dharma-kṣetre kuru-kṣetre samavetā yuyutsavaḥ ।
māmakāh pāṇḍavāścaiva kim akurvata, sañjaya ॥ 1 ॥

Sañjaya : O Sañjaya! *dharmakṣetre* : in the sacred field *kurukṣetre* : in Kurukṣetra *yuyutsavaḥ* : eager to fight *samavetāḥ* : assembled *māmakāḥ* : my people *pāṇḍavāḥ ca* : and the followers of the Pāṇḍavas *eva*: indeed *kim akurvata* : what did they do?

Dhṛtarāṣṭra said:

1. O Sañjaya! What indeed did my people and the followers of the Pāṇḍavas do after having assembled in the holy land of Kurukṣetra, eager to join battle?

सञ्जय उवाच—

दृष्ट्वा तु पाण्डवानीकं व्यूढं दुर्योधनस्तदा।
आचार्यमुपसङ्गम्य राजा वचनमब्रवीत्॥ 2॥

Sañjaya uvāca:

Dṛṣṭvā tu pāṇḍavānīkaṁ vyūḍhaṁ duryodhanas tadā ।
ācāryam upasaṅgamya rājā vacanam abravīt ॥ 2 ॥

Tadā : Then *pāṇḍavānīkam* : the army of the Pāṇḍavas *vyūḍham* : arrayed for battle *dṛṣṭvā*: having seen *rājā duryodhanaḥ*: king Duryodhana *tu*: indeed (for his part) *ācāryam*: the teacher (Droṇa) *upasaṅgamya* : having approached *vacanam* : word *abravīt* : said.

Sañjaya said:

2. Then seeing the army of the Pāṇḍavas arrayed in battle order, king Duryodhana for his part approached the teacher Droṇa and spoke to him the following words:

पश्यैतां पाण्डुपुत्राणा-माचार्य महतीं चमूम्।
व्यूढां द्रुपदपुत्रेण तव शिष्येण धीमता॥ 3॥

Paśyaitāṁ pāṇḍu-putrāṇām ācārya mahatīṁ camūm ।
vyūḍhāṁ drupada-putreṇa tava śiṣyeṇa dhīmatā ॥ 3 ॥

Ācārya : O teacher *dhīmatā* : talented *tava* : your *śiṣyeṇa* : by disciple *drupadaputreṇa* : by the son of Drupada *vyūḍhām*: drawn for battle *pāṇḍuputrāṇām* : of the sons of Pāṇḍu *etām* : this *mahatīṁ camūm*: great army *paśya* : behold.

3. O Teacher! Behold this great army of the sons of Pāṇḍu, arrayed in battle order by your talented disciple, the son of Drupada.

अत्र शूरा महेष्वासा भीमार्जुनसमा युधि।
युयुधानो विराटश्च द्रुपदश्च महारथः॥ 4॥

Atra śūrā maheṣvāsā Bhīmārjuna-samā yudhi ।
Yuyudhāno Virāṭaśca Drupadaś ca mahā-rathaḥ ॥ 4 ॥

Atra : Here *śūrāḥ maheṣvāsāḥ*: valiant bow-men *yudhi* : in battle *Bhīmārjuna samāḥ*: equal to Bhīma and Arjuna *mahārathāḥ*: great car-warriors *Yuyudhānaḥ*: Yuyudhāna *Virāṭaḥ ca* : and Virāta *Drupadaḥ ca*: and Drupada;

4. Here (in that army) are many brave bow-men of note who are equal to Bhīma and Arjuna in battle—great car-warriors like Yuyudhāna, Virāṭa and Drupada;

धृष्टकेतुश्चेकितानः काशिराजश्च वीर्यवान्।
पुरुजित्कुन्तिभोजश्च शैब्यश्च नरपुङ्गवः॥ 5॥

Dhṛṣṭaketuś Cekitānaḥ Kāśi-rājaś ca vīryavān ।
Purujit Kuntibhojaś ca Śaibyaś ca nara-puṅgavaḥ ॥5॥

Dhrṣṭaketuh Dhṛṣṭaketu *Cekitānaḥ ca:* and Chekitāna *vīryavān Kāśirājaḥ ca*: and the brave king of Kāśi *Purujit*: Purujit *Kuntibhojaḥ ca*:and Kuntibhoja *narapuṅgavaḥ saibyaṇ ca*: and Śaibya the best of men.

5. Dhṛṣṭaketu, Cekitāna and the brave king of Kāśi; Purujit, Kuntibhoja and Śaibya the best of men;

युधामन्युश्च विक्रान्त उत्तमौजाश्च वीर्यवान्।
सौभद्रो द्रौपदेयाश्च सर्व एव महारथाः॥ 6॥

Yudhāmanyuś ca vikrānta Uttamaujāś ca vīryavān ।
Saubhadro Draupadeyāś ca, sarva eva mahā-rathāḥ ॥6॥

Vikrāntaḥ: Powerful *Yudhāmanyuḥ*: Yudhāmanyu *vīryavān Uttamaujāḥ ca*: and the brave Uttamauja *Saubhadraḥ*: the son of Subhadra *Draupadeyāh ca*: and the sons of Draupadi *sarve* : all *eva* : indeed *mahārathāh* : great car-warriors.

6. The powerful Yudhāmanyu, the brave Uttamauja, the son of Subhadra, and the sons of Draupadi—all these are indeed noted car-warriors.

अस्माकं तु विशिष्टा ये तान्निबोध द्विजोत्तम ।
नायका मम सैन्यस्य संज्ञार्थं तान् ब्रवीमि ते ॥ 7 ॥

Asmākaṁ tu viśiṣṭā ye tān nibodha dvij'ottama ।
nāyakā mama sainyasya saṁjñ'ārthaṁ tān bravīmi te ॥ 7 ॥

Dvijottama : O best of Brāhmaṇās *asmākaṁ tu* : regarding our side *ye* : (those) who *viśiṣṭāḥ* : distinguished *mama* : my *sainyasya*: of the army *nāyakāḥ*: leaders *tān*: them *nibodha*: know. *Samjñārtham* : for your information *tān* : them *bravīmi* : I speak.

7. O best of Brāhmaṇās, I shall mention for your information the names of the distinguished leaders of our army.

भवान् भीष्मश्च कर्णश्च कृपश्च समितिञ्जयः ।
अश्वत्थामा विकर्णश्च सौमदत्तिर्जयद्रथः ॥ 8 ॥

Bhavān Bhīṣmaś ca Karṇaś ca Kṛpaś ca samitiñ-jayaḥ ।
Aśvatthāmā Vikarṇaś ca Saumadattir Jayadrathaḥ ॥ 8 ॥

Bhavān : Yourself *Bhīṣmaḥ ca* : and Bhīṣma *Karṇaḥ ca* : and Karṇa *samitiñjayaḥ* : victorious *Kṛpaḥ* : Kṛpa *Aśvatthāmā* : Asvatthāmā *Vikarṇaḥ ca* : and Vikarṇa *Saumadattiḥ* : the son of Somadatta *Jayadrathaḥ ca* : and Jayadratha

8. Yourself, Bhīṣma and Karṇa, the victorious Kṛpa, Aswatthāmā, Vikarṇa and Jayadratha, the son of Somadatta.

अन्ये च बहवः शूरा मदर्थे त्यक्तजीविताः ।
नानाशस्त्रप्रहरणाः सर्वे युद्ध-विशारदाः ॥ 9 ॥

Anye ca bahavaḥ śūrā mad-arthe tyakta-jīvitāḥ |
nānā-śastra praharaṇāḥ sarve yuddha-viśāradāḥ || 9 ||

Madarthe : For my sake *tyakta-jivitāḥ* : who are ready to give up their lives *nānā - śastra - praharaṇāḥ* : who fight with various types of weapons *anye ca bahavaḥ* : also many other *śūrāḥ* : brave men (*santi* : there are). *Sarve* : all of them *yuddha-viśāradāḥ*: skilled in war.

9. These and many more brave men, who are ready to lay down their lives for my sake and who fight with various types of weapons, are present here. All of them are seasoned warriors.

अपर्याप्तं तदस्माकं बलं भीष्माभिरक्षितम् ।
पर्याप्तं त्विदमेतेषां बलं भीमाभिरक्षितम् ॥ 10 ॥

Aparyāptaṁ tad asmākaṁ balam Bhīsm'ābhirakṣitam |
paryāptaṁ tv idam eteṣāṁ balam Bhīm'ābhi rakṣitam ||10||

Bhīṣmābhirakṣitam : Defended by Bhīṣma *tad* : that *asmākam* : our *balam* : army *aparyāptam* : inadequate; *Bhīmābhi rakṣitam* : defended by Bhima *eteṣām* : their *balam* : army *tu*: while *paryāptam*: adequate.

10. Though numerically superior, inadequate is the army of ours defended by Bhīṣma, while theirs guarded by Bhīma is adequate.

अयनेषु च सर्वेषु यथाभागमवस्थिताः ।
भीष्ममेवाभिरक्षन्तु भवन्तः सर्वं एव हि ॥ 11 ॥

Ayaneṣu ca sarveṣu yathā-bhāgam avasthitāḥ |
Bhīṣmam evābhirakṣantu bhavantaḥ sarvą eva hi ||11||

Bhavantaḥ sarve : All of you *eva hi* : even indeed *sarveṣu* : in all *ayaneṣu ca* : in divisions *yathā-bhāgam* : appropriate positions *avasthitāḥ* : remaining *Bhīṣmam eva* : Bhīṣma *abhirakṣantu* : protect.

11. Therefore do ye all protect Bhīṣma remaining in appropriate positions in your respective divisions.

तस्य सञ्जनयन् हर्षं कुरुवृद्धः पितामहः।
सिंहनादं विनद्योच्चैः शङ्खं दध्मौ प्रतापवान् ॥ 12 ॥

Tasya sañjanayan harṣaṁ Kuru-vṛddhaḥ pitāmahaḥ ।
simha-nādaṁ vinady'occaiḥ śaṅkhaṁ dadhmau pratā-pavān ॥ 12 ॥

Tasya : His (Duryodhana) *harṣam* : cheer *sañjanayan* : causing *kuruvṛddhaḥ* : oldest of the Kurus *pratāpavān* : valiant *pitāmahaḥ*: grand father *uccaiḥ* : aloud *simhanādam* : lion roar *vinadya* having sounded *śaṅkham* : conch *dadhmau* : blew

12. Cheering him up, the valiant grandfather Bhīṣma, the oldest of the Kurus, sounded a lion roar loudly and blew his conch-shell horn.

ततः शङ्खाश्च भेर्यश्च पणवानकगोमुखाः।
सहसैवाभ्यहन्यन्त स शब्दस्तुमुलोऽभवत् ॥ 13 ॥

Tataḥ śaṅkhāś ca bheryaś ca paṇav'ānaka-gomukhāḥ ।
sahas'aiv'ābhyahanyanta sa śabdas tumulo' bhavat ॥ 13 ॥

Tataḥ : Thereupon *sahasā eva* : suddenly *śaṅkhāḥ* : conchs *bheryaḥ*: kettle-drums *paṇavānaka gomukhāḥ ca*: and tabors, military drums and cowhorns *abhyahanyanta ca* : blared forth *saḥ* : that *śabdaḥ* : sound *tumulaḥ* : tremendous *abhavat* : was.

13. Thereupon, conchs, kettle-drums, tabors, military drums, and cowhorns all blared out suddenly, causing a tremendous sound.

ततः श्वेतैर्हयैर्युक्ते महति स्यन्दने स्थितौ ।
माधवः पाण्डवश्चैव दिव्यौ शङ्खौ प्रदध्मतुः ॥ 14 ॥

Tataḥ śvetair hayair yukte mahati syandane sthitau ।
Mādhavaḥ Pāṇḍavaś c'aiva divyau śaṅkhau pradadhmatuḥ ॥ 14 ॥

Tataḥ : Then *svetaiḥ* : with white *hayaiḥ* : horses *yukte* : yoked *mahati* : in the great *syandane* : chariot *sthitau* : seated *Mādhavaḥ* : Sri Kṛṣṇa *Pāṅḍavaḥ ca eva* : also the son of Pāṇḍu (Arjuna) *divyau* : celestial *śankhau* : conchs *pradadhmatuḥ* : blew.

14. Then Sri Kṛṣṇa and Arjuna, seated in a great chariot with white horses yoked to it, blew their celestial conch-shell horns.

पाञ्चजन्यं हृषीकेशो देवदत्तं धनञ्जयः ।
पौण्ड्रं दध्मौ महाशङ्खं भीमकर्मा वृकोदरः ॥ 15 ॥

Pāñcajanyaṁ Hṛṣīkeśo Devadattaṁ Dhanañjayaḥ ।
Pauṇḍraṁ dadhmau mahā-śaṅkhaṁ bhīma-karmā Vṛk'odaraḥ ॥ 15 ॥

Hṛṣīkeśaḥ : Sri Kṛṣṇa *Pāñcajanyam* : Pāncajanya *Dhanañjayaḥ*: Arjuna *Devadattam* : Devadatta *bhīma-karmā* : one of terrible deeds *Vṛkodaraḥ*:Bhīmasena *mahāśaṅkham* : great conch *Pauṇḍram*: Pauṇḍra *dadhmau* : blew.

15. Sri Kṛṣṇa blew his conch Pāñcajanya, Arjuna blew Devadatta, and Bhīma of terrible deeds sounded his great conch Pauṇḍra.

अनन्तविजयं राजा कुन्तीपुत्रो युधिष्ठिरः ।
नकुलः सहदेवश्च सुघोषमणिपुष्पकौ ॥ 16 ॥

Anantavijayaṁ rājā Kuntī-putro Yudhiṣṭhiraḥ ।
Nakulaḥ Sahadevaś ca Sughoṣa-Maṇipuṣpakau ॥ 16 ॥

Kuntīputraḥ rājā Yudhiṣṭhiraḥ : King Yudhiṣṭhira, the son of Kunti *Anantavijayam* : Anantavijaya *Nakulaḥ* : Nakula *Sahadevaḥ ca*: and Sahadeva *Sughoṣa-Maṇipuṣpakau*: Sughoṣa and Maṇipuṣpaka.

16. Raja Yudhiṣṭhira, the son of Kunti, blew his conch Anantavijaya, and Nakula and Sahadeva, Sughoṣa and Maṇipuṣpaka respectively.

काश्यश्च परमेष्वासः शिखण्डी च महारथः ।
धृष्टद्युम्नो विराटश्च सात्यकिश्चापराजितः ॥ 17 ॥

Kāśyaś ca param'eṣvāsaḥ Śikhaṇḍī ca mahā-rathaḥ ।
Dhṛṣṭadyumno Virāṭaś ca Sātyakiś c'āparājitaḥ ॥ 17 ॥

Parameṣvāsaḥ : Great archer *Kāśyaḥ ca* : and the king of Kāsi *mahārathaḥ* : mighty car-warrior *Śikhaṇḍī ca* : and Śikhaṇḍī *Dhṛṣṭadyumnaḥ* : Dhṛṣṭadyumna *Virāṭaḥ ca* : and Virāṭa *aparājitaḥ* : invincible *Sātyakiḥ ca* : and Sātyaki.

17. The great archer, king of Kāśi, the mighty car-warrior Śikhaṇḍī and Dhṛṣṭadyumna and invincible Sātyaki,

द्रुपदो द्रौपदेयाश्च सर्वशः पृथिवीपते ।
सौभद्रश्च महाबाहुः शङ्खान् दध्मुः पृथक् पृथक् ॥ 18 ॥

Drupado Draupadeyāś ca sarvaśaḥ pṛthivī-pate ।
Saubhadraś ca mahā-bāhuḥ śaṅkhān dadhmuḥ pṛthak-pṛthak ॥ 18 ॥

Drupadaḥ: The king of Drupada *draupadeyāḥ ca* : and the sons of Draupadī *mahābāhuḥ* : strong armed *Saubhadraḥ ca* : and the son of Subhadrā *sarvaśaḥ* : on all sides *pṛthivīpate* ; O King *pṛthak pṛthak* : again and again *śaṅkhān* : conches *dadhmuḥ*: blew.

18. The King of Drupada, the sons of Draupadī, the mighty-armed son of Subhadrā—all these, O king, sounded their conch-shell horns again and again everywhere.

स घोषो धार्तराष्ट्राणां हृदयानि व्यदारयत् ।
नभश्च पृथिवीं चैव तुमुलो व्यनुनादयन् ॥ 19 ॥

Sa ghoṣo Dhārtarāṣṭrāṇāṁ hṛdayāni vyadārayat ।
nabhaś ca pṛthivīm c'aiva tumulo vyanunādayan ॥ 19 ॥

Tumulaḥ : Tumultuous *saḥ* : that *ghoṣaḥ* : uproar *nabhaḥ ca* : and sky *pṛthivīm ca* : and earth *eva vyanunādayan* : resounding *dhārtarāṣṭrāṇām* : of the followers of Dhṛtarāṣṭra *hṛdayāni* : hearts *vyadārayat* : pierced.

19. That tumultuous uproar, resounding in the sky and over the land, pierced the hearts of the followers of Dhṛtarāṣṭra.

अथ व्यवस्थितान्दृष्ट्वा धार्तराष्ट्रान् कपिध्वजः ।
प्रवृत्ते शस्त्रसंपाते धनुरुद्यम्य पाण्डवः ॥ 20 ॥
हृषीकेशं तदा वाक्यमिदमाह महीपते ।

Atha vyavasthitān dṛṣṭvā Dhārtarāṣṭrān kapi-dhvajaḥ
pravṛtte śastra-sampāte dhanur udyamya Pāṇḍavaḥ ।
Hṛṣīkeśaṁ tadā vākyam idam āha mahīpate ॥ 20-21 ॥

Mahīpate : O King *atha* : then *Kapidhvajaḥ* : one with the monkey as the crest of his banner (Arjuna) *Pāṇḍavaḥ* : the son of Pāṇḍu *Dhārtarāṣṭrān* : the army of Dhṛtarāṣṭra *vyavasthitān* : drawn up in battle *dṛṣṭvā* : seeing *śastrasampāte pravṛtte* : as the clash of weapons began *dhanuḥ* : bow *udyamya* : holding *tadā* :

then *Hṛṣīkeśam* : Srī Kṛṣṇa *idam vākyam* : following words *āha* : said.

20-21. O King! Arjuna, the Pāṇḍava-leader with the banner crest of a monkey, on seeing the followers of Dhṛtarāṣṭra arrayed for battle and the clash of weapons about to start, held up his bow and said the following words to Sri Kṛṣṇa ;

अर्जुन उवाच—

सेनयोरुभयोर्मध्ये रथं स्थापय मेऽच्युत ॥ 21 ॥

यावदेतान्निरीक्षेऽहं योद्धुकामानवस्थितान् ।
कैर्मया सह योद्धव्य-मस्मिन् रणसमुद्यमे ॥ 22 ॥

Arjuna uvāca:

Senayor ubhayor madhye ratham sthāpaya me' cyuta
yāvad etān nirīkṣe' ham yoddhu-kāmān avasthitān ।
kair mayā saha yoddhavyam asmin raṇa-samudyame॥21-22॥

Acyuta: Acyuta! *me*: my *ratham*: chariot *ubhayoḥ* : of both *senayoḥ* : armies *madhye*: in the middle *sthāpaya*: station. *Yoddhukāmān*: desirous of fighting *avasthitān*: standing *etān*: these *yāvad*: while *aham*: I *nirīkṣe*: behold *asmin*: in this *raṇasamudyame*: eve of battle *mayā* : by me *kaiḥ saha* : with whom *yoddhavyam* : the battle should be fought.

Arjuna said *:*

21-22. O Acyuta! Please station my chariot between the two armies, so that I may have a view, on the eve of this battle, of all those standing ready to fight, and learn who all are the persons with whom I have to contend.

योत्स्यमानानवेक्षेऽहं य एतेऽत्र समागताः ।
धार्तराष्ट्रस्य दुर्बुद्धेर्युद्धे प्रियचिकीर्षवः ॥ 23 ॥

Yotsyamānān avekṣe' ham ya ete'tra samāgatāḥ ।
Dhārtarāṣṭrasya durbuddher yuddhe priyacikīrṣavaḥ ॥23॥

Durbuddheḥ : of the evil-minded *Dhārtarāṣṭrasya*: of the son of Dhṛtarāṣṭra *yuddhe* : in war *priyacikīrṣavaḥ* : desirous of favouring *ye ete*: all those *atra* : here *samāgatāḥ* : have arrived *tān* : them *yotsyamānān* : ready to fight *aham*: I *avekṣe*: let me see.

23. Let me see all those who have arrived to favour the evil-minded son of Dhṛtarāṣṭra in war and are standing ready to join battle.

सञ्जय उवाच—

एवमुक्तो हृषीकेशो गुडाकेशेन भारत ।
सेनयोरुभयोर्मध्ये स्थापयित्वा रथोत्तमम् ॥ 24 ॥

भीष्म-द्रोण-प्रमुखतः सर्वेषां च महीक्षिताम् ।
उवाच पार्थ पश्यैतान् समवेतान् कुरूनिति ॥ 25 ॥

Sañjaya uvāca:
Evam ukto Hṛṣīkeśo Guḍākeśena Bhārata
senayor ubhayor madhye sthāpayitvā rath'ottamam ॥ 24 ॥
Bhīṣma-Droṇa pramukhataḥ sarveṣāṁ ca mahī-kṣitām
uvāca Pārtha paśy'aitān samavetān Kurūn iti ॥ 25 ॥

Bhārata : O Bhārata (O King Dhṛtarāṣṭra) *Guḍākeśena* : by Guḍākeśa, conqueror of sloth (Arjuna) *evam* : thus *uktaḥ* : told *Hṛṣīkeśaḥ* : Hṛṣīkeśa, the conqueror of the senses (Kṛṣṇa) *ubhayoḥ* : of both *senayoḥ* : armies *madhye* in the middle *Bhīṣma-Droṇa-pramukhataḥ* : in front of Bhīṣma and Droṇa *sarveṣām* of all *mahīkṣitām ca* : kings *rathottamam* : the best of chariots *sthāpayitvā* : having stationed *iti* : thus *uvāca* : spoke *Pārtha* : O Arjuna *samavetān* : assembled *etān* : these *Kurūn* : Kurus *paśya* : see.

Sanjaya said :

24-25. O King Dhṛtarāṣṭra! Sri Kṛṣṇa, to whom Arjuna addressed these words, stationed that most splendid of chariots at a place between the two armies, confronting Bhīṣma, Droṇa and all those chiefs, and said: "O Arjuna! See these men of the Kuru horde assembled for battle."

तत्रापश्यत्स्थितान्पार्थः पितॄनथ पितामहान् ।
आचार्यान् मातुलान् भ्रातॄन् पुत्रान् पौत्रान् सखींस्तथा ॥ 26 ॥

श्वशुरान् सुहृदश्चैव सेनयोरुभयोरपि ।
तान् समीक्ष्य स कौन्तेयः सर्वान् बन्धूनवस्थितान् ॥ 27 ॥

कृपया परयाविष्टो विषीदन्निदमब्रवीत् ।

Tatrāpaśyat sthitān Pārthaḥ pitṛn atha pitāmahān
ācāryān mātulān bhrātṛn putrān pautrān sakhīṁstathā ॥26॥

Śvaśurān suhṛdaś caiva senayor ubhayor api
tān samīkṣya sa Kaunteyaḥ sarvān bandhūn avasthitān ॥27॥

kṛpayā parayā'viṣṭo viṣīdann idam abravīt

Tatra : there *ubhayoḥ* : of both *senayoḥ* : armies *api* : also *sthitān* : stationed *pitṛn atha* : and fathers *pitāmahān* : grandfathers *ācāryān* : teachers *mātulān* : uncles *bhrātṛn* : brothers *putrān* : sons *pautrān* : grandsons *sakhīn* : comrades *tathā* : and *śvaśurān* : fathers-in-law *suhṛdaḥ* : friends, *ca iva* : and *Pārthaḥ* : Arjuna *apaśyat* : saw *avasthitān* : stationed; *sarvān* : all *bandhūn* : relatives *samīkṣya* : having seen *saḥ* that *Kaunteyaḥ*: son of Kunti *parayā* : supreme *kṛpayā*: pity *āviṣṭaḥ* : filled *viṣīdan* : sorrowing *idam* : thus *abravīt* : said.

26-27. There he saw standing in both the armies—fathers, grandfathers, uncles, brothers, sons, grandsons, comrades, fathers-in-law and bosom friends. Seeing all these kinsmen arrayed, Arjuna was overcome with great pity, and said sorrowing:

अर्जुन उवाच

दृष्ट्वेमं स्वजनं कृष्ण युयुत्सुं समुपस्थितम् ॥ 28 ॥
सीदन्ति मम गात्राणि मुखं च परिशुष्यति ।
वेपथुश्च शरीरे मे रोमहर्षश्च जायते ॥ 29 ॥

Arjuna uvāca:
Dṛṣṭv'emaṁ svajanaṁ Kṛṣṇa yuyutsuṁ samupasthitam

sīdanti mama gātrāṇi mukhaṁ ca pariśuṣyati
vepathuś ca śarīre me roma-harṣaś ca jāyate ॥28-29॥

Kṛṣṇa : O Kṛṣṇa *yuyutsum* : eager to fight *samupasthitam* : standing *imam* : this *svajanam* : groups of relatives *dṛṣṭvā* : seeing *mama* my *gātrāṇi*: limbs *sīdanti* : give way *ca*: and *mukhaṁ* : mouth *pariśuṣyati* :is parching, *me*: my *śarīre*: in the body *vepathuḥ*: trembling *ca* : and *romaharṣaḥ* : horripilation *ca* : and *jāyate* : arises.

Arjuna said:

28-29 Seeing these relatives standing eager to join battle my limbs are giving way, my mouth is parching. I get trembling of the body and horripilations.

गाण्डीवं स्रंसते हस्तात्त्वक्चैव परिदह्यते ।
न च शक्नोम्यवस्थातुं भ्रमतीव च मे मनः ॥ 30 ॥

Gāṇḍīvaṁ sraṁsate hastāt tvak c'aiva paridahyate
na ca śaknomy avasthātuṁ bhramatī' va ca me manaḥ
॥ 30 ॥

Gāṇḍīvam : the bow Gāṇḍīva *hastāt* : from the hand *sraṁsate* : is slipping *tvak ca eva* : skin too *paridahyate* : is burning *avasthātum* : to stand firm *na śaknomi ca* : not possible *me* : my *manaḥ* : mind *bhramati iva ca* is reeling as it were.

30. My bow Gāṇḍīva is slipping from my hand. My skin too is burning. I find it impossible to stand firm, and my mind is, as it were, reeling.

निमित्तानि च पश्यामि विपरीतानि केशव ।
न च श्रेयोऽनुपश्यामि हत्वा स्वजनमाहवे ॥ 31 ॥

Nimittāni ca paśyāmi viparītāni Keśava
na ca śreyo' nupaśyāmi hatvā svajanam āhave ॥ 31 ॥

Keśava : O Keśava! *viparītāni* : adverse *nimittāni ca* : omens *paśyāmī* : I see *āhave* : in the war *svajanam* : one's own men (relatives) *hatvā* : having killed *anu* : afterwards *śreyaḥ* : good *na paśyāmi* : I do not see.

31. O Keśava! I see adverse omens. I do not feel that any good will come by killing all one's kinsmen in battle.

न काङ्क्षे विजयं कृष्ण न च राज्यं सुखानि च ।
किं नो राज्येन गोविन्द किं भोगैर्जीवितेन वा ॥ 32 ॥

Na kāṅkṣe vijayaṁ Kṛṣṇa na ca rājyaṁ sukhāni ca
kiṁ no rājyena Govinda kiṁ bhogair jīvitena vā ॥32॥

Kṛṣṇa : O Kṛṣṇa! *vijayam* : victory *na kāṅkṣe* : I do not desire *rājyaṁ ca* : neither the kingdom *sukhāni ca* : nor the enjoyments. *Govinda* : O Govinda *naḥ* : for us *rājyena* : with the kingdom *kim* what (is to be achieved)? *bhogaiḥ* : by enjoyments *jīvitena vā* : by even life *kim* : what (accrues)?

32. O Kṛṣṇa! I do not long for victory, or kingdom, or enjoyments. O Govinda! Of what use is kingdom, enjoyments or even life itself ?

येषामर्थे काङ्क्षितं नो राज्यं भोगाः सुखानि च ।
त इमेऽवस्थिता युद्धे प्राणांस्त्यक्त्वा धनानि च ॥ 33 ॥

आचार्याः पितरः पुत्रास्तथैव च पितामहाः ।
मातुलाः श्वशुराः पौत्राः स्यालाः संबन्धिनस्तथा ॥ 34 ॥

Yeṣām arthe kāṅkṣitaṁ no rājyaṁ bhogāḥ sukhāni ca
ta ime' vasthitā yuddhe prāṇāms tyaktvā dhanāni ca
|| 33 ||

Ācāryāḥ pitaraḥ putrāḥ tathaiva ca pitāmahāḥ
mātulāḥ śvaśurāḥ pautrāḥ syālāḥ saṁbandhinas tathā
|| 34 ||

Yeṣām arthe : For whose sake *naḥ* : by us *rājyam* : kingdom *bhogāḥ* : enjoyments *sukhāni ca* : and pleasures *kāṅkṣitam* : are desired, *te* : those *ācāryāḥ* : teachers *pitaraḥ* : fathers *putrāḥ* : sons *tatha eva ca* : and also *pitāmahāḥ* : grandfathers *mātulāḥ* : uncles *śvaśurāḥ* : fathers-in-law *pautrāḥ* : grandchildren *syālāḥ* : brothers-in-law *tathā saṁbandhinaḥ* : as well as relatives *ime* : these *prāṇān* : life *dhanāni ca* : and wealth *tyaktvā* : abandoning *yuddhe* : in battle *avasthitāḥ* : are stationed.

33-34. Those for whose sake kingdoms, enjoyments, and pleasures are desired,— those very teachers, fathers and sons, as also grandfathers, uncles, fathers-in-law and other relatives are here stationed in battle ready to give up their lives and possessions.

एतान्न हन्तुमिच्छामि घ्नतोऽपि मधुसूदन ।
अपि त्रैलोक्य-राज्यस्य हेतोः किं नु महीकृते ॥ 35 ॥

Etān na hantum icchāmi ghnatopi Madhusūdana
api trailokya-rājyasya hetoḥ kiṁ nu mahī-kṛte || 35 ||

Madhusūdana : O Madhusudana *ghnataḥ api* : even if killed (by them) *etān* : them *trailokyarājyasya* : for the three worlds *hetoḥ api*: even for the sake of *hantuṁ* to kill *na icchāmi* : do not desire *mahī-kṛte kiṁ nu* : much less for this earth.

35. Even for the sovereignty of the three worlds, I do not desire to kill them, though myself killed — how much less then for this earthly kingdom!

निहत्य धार्तराष्ट्रान्नः का प्रीतिः स्याज्जनार्दन ।
पापमेवाश्रयेदस्मान् हत्वैतानाततायिनः ॥ 36 ॥

Nihatya Dhārtarāṣṭrān naḥ kā prītiḥ syāj Janārdana
pāpam ev'āśrayed asmān hatv'aitān ātatāyinaḥ ॥ 36 ॥

Janārdana: O Janārdana (Kṛṣṇa) *Dhārtarāṣṭrān*: the sons of Dhṛtarāṣṭra *nihatya*: having killed *naḥ*: for us *kā*: what *prītiḥ*: joy *syāt*: there would be? *Ātatāyinaḥ*: murderous felons *hatvā*: by killing *asmān*: for us *pāpam*: sin *eva*: only *āśrayet*: will accrue.

36. What joy can there be for us by killing these sons of Dhṛtarāṣṭra? Though they are murderous villains, only sin will accrue to us by killing them.

तस्मान्नार्हा वयं हन्तुं धार्तराष्ट्रान् स्वबान्धवान्
स्वजनं हि कथं हत्वा सुखिनः स्याम माधव ॥ 37 ॥

Tasmān n'ārhā vayaṁ hantuṁ Dhārtarāṣṭrān svabāndhavān
svajanaṁ hi kathaṁ hatvā sukhinaḥ syāma Mādhava ॥ 37 ॥

Tasmāt: Therefore *Mādhava*: O Mādhava (Kṛṣṇa)! *vayam*: we *svabāndhavān*: own relations *Dhārtarāṣṭrān*: sons of Dhṛtarāṣṭra *hantum*: to kill *na arhāḥ*: not justified: *svajanam*: relations *hatvā*: having killed *katham hi*: how *sukhinaḥ syāma*: could we be happy persons.

37. Therefore, O Mādhava! it is not befitting that we kill our relations, the sons of Dhṛtarāṣṭra. How could one be happy by the slaughter of one's own kinsmen?

यद्यप्येते न पश्यन्ति लोभोपहतचेतसः
कुलक्षयकृतं दोषं मित्रद्रोहे च पातकम् ॥ 38 ॥

कथं न ज्ञेयमस्माभिः पापादस्मान्निवर्तितुम् ।
कुलक्षयकृतं दोषं प्रपश्यद्भि-र्जनार्दन ॥ 39 ॥

Yady apy ete na paśyanti lobh'opahata-cetasaḥ
kula-kṣaya-kṛtam doṣam mitra-drohe ca pātakam

kathaṁ na jñeyam asmābhiḥ pāpād asmān nivartitum
kula-kṣaya-kṛtaṁ doṣam prapaśyadbhir Janārdana
॥ 38-39 ॥

Janārdana : O Janārdana *lobhopahata cetasaḥ* : with the understanding destroyed by greed *ete* : these people *kulakṣayakṛtam* : due to the decay of families *doṣam* evil *mitradrohe* : in the persecution of friends *pātakam ca* : sin also *yadyapi* : though *na paśyanti*: do not see, *kulakṣayakṛtam* : done by the decay of families *doṣam* : evil *prapaśyadbhiḥ* : seeing well *asmābhiḥ* : by us *asmāt pāpāt*: from this sin *nivartitum* : to abstain from *katham*: why *na jñeyam*: not learn.

38-39. O Janārdana! Even if these people, with their intelligence overpowered by greed, do not see any evil in the decay of families and any sin in the persecution of friends, why should not we, who are aware of the evil of such decay of families, learn to desist from that sin?

कुलक्षये प्रणश्यन्ति कुलधर्माः सनातनाः ।
धर्मे नष्टे कुलं कृत्स्नमधर्मोऽभिभवत्युत ॥ 40 ॥

Kula-kṣaye praṇaśyanti kula-dharmāḥ sanātanāḥ
dharme naṣṭe kulam kṛtsnam adharmo' bhibhavatyuta
॥ 40 ॥

Kulakṣaye : By the decay of clans *sanātanāḥ* : ancient *kuladharmāḥ* traditions of the clan *praṇaśyanti* : perish; *dharme naṣṭe* : when tradition perishes *kṛtsnam* : entire *kulam* clan *adharmaḥ* : lawlessness *abhibhavati* : overcomes *uta*: indeed.

40. When a clan becomes decadent, its ancient traditions (laws) perish. When traditions perish, the entire clan is indeed overcome by lawlessness.

अधर्माभिभवात् कृष्ण प्रदुष्यन्ति कुलस्त्रियः ।
स्त्रीषु दुष्टासु वार्ष्णेय जायते वर्णसङ्करः ॥ 41 ॥

Adharmābhibhavāt Kṛṣṇa praduṣyanti kula-striyaḥ
strīṣu duṣṭāsu Vārṣṇeya jāyate varṇa-saṅkaraḥ ॥41॥

Kṛṣṇa : O Kṛṣṇa *adharmābhibhavāt* : by the prevalence of lawlessness *kulastriyaḥ* : the women of the clans *praduṣyanti* : become corrupt. *Vārṣṇeya* : O scion of the Vṛṣṇis! *strīṣu duṣṭāsu* : when women become corrupt *varṇa saṅkaraḥ* : mixture of classes (promiscuity) *jāyate* : arises.

41. O Kṛṣṇa! When lawlessness prevails, the women of the clans become corrupt. O Scion of the Vṛṣṇis! When women are corrupted, mixture of classes (promiscuity) prevails.

सङ्करो नरकायैव कुलघ्नानां कुलस्य च ।
पतन्ति पितरो ह्येषां लुप्तपिण्डोदकक्रियाः ॥ 42 ॥

Saṅkaro narakāy'aiva kula-ghnānāṁ kulasya ca
patanti pitaro hy eṣām lupta-piṇḍ'odaka-kriyāḥ ॥42॥

Saṅkaraḥ : Admixture of classes (promiscuity) *kulaghnānām* : of the destroyers of the clan *kulasya ca* : also of clans *narakāya eva* : for hell only. *Hi* : For *eṣām* : of these *pitaraḥ* : ancestors *luptapiṇḍodaka-krīyāḥ* : being deprived of Piṇḍas or offerings of rice balls and water *patanti* : fall.

42. Promiscuity results only in hell to those destroyers of the clans, as also to the members of the clan. For (being without legitimate progeny to perform obsequies), the spirits of their ancestors fall, deprived of the offerings of rice ball and water.

दोषैरेतैः कुलघ्नानां वर्णसङ्करकारकैः ।
उत्साद्यन्ते जातिधर्माः कुलधर्माश्च शाश्वताः ॥ 43 ॥

Doṣair etaiḥ kula-ghnānāṁ varṇa-saṅkara-kārakaiḥ
utsādyante jāti-dharmāḥ kula-dharmāś ca śāśvatāḥ
॥ 43 ॥

Kulaghnānām : Of the ruiners of clans *varṇasaṅkarakārakaiḥ* : causing promiscuity *etaiḥ doṣaiḥ* : by these misdeeds *śāśvatāḥ* : immemorial *jātidharmāḥ* : laws or traditions of communities *kuladharmāḥ* laws of the clans *ca* : and *utsādyante* : are destroyed.

43. By the misdeeds of these ruiners of clans and promoters of promiscuity, the immemorial traditions of the communities and clans are uprooted.

उत्सन्नकुलधर्माणां मनुष्याणां जनार्दन ।
नरके नियतं वासो भवतीत्यनुशुश्रुम ॥ 44 ॥

Utsanna-kula-dharmāṇāṁ manuṣyāṇāṁ Janārdana
narake niyatam vāso bhavatī'ty anuśuśruma ॥ 44 ॥

Janārdana : O Janārdana! *utsannakuladharmāṇāṁ manuṣyāṇām*: for men who have lost all their family traditions (ancestral religion) *narake* : in hell *vāsah* : residence *niyatam* : sure *bhavati* : is *iti* : thus *anuśuśruma* : we have heard.

44. O Janārdana! We have heard that residence in hell awaits men, the religious traditions of whose clans have been destroyed.

अहो बत महत्पापं कर्तुं व्यवसिता वयम् ।
यद्राज्यसुखलोभेन हन्तुं स्वजनमुद्यताः ॥ 45 ॥

Aho bata mahat pāpaṁ kartuṁ vyavasitā vayam
yad rājya-sukha-lobhena hantum svajanam udyatāḥ
॥ 45 ॥

Aho : Alas! *vayam* : we *mahat* : great *pāpam* : sin *kartum* : to commit *vyavasitāḥ* : resolved *yat* : that *rājyasukha lobhena* : by greed for the pleasures of kingdom *svajanam* : kinsmen *hantum* : to destroy *udyatāḥ* : prepared *bata* : also.

45. Alas! What great sin have we resolved to commit when we prepared ourselves to destroy our kinsmen out of greed for the pleasures of a kingdom!

यदि मामप्रतीकार-मशस्त्रं शस्त्रपाणयः।
धार्तराष्ट्रा रणे हन्युस्तन्मे क्षेमतरं भवेत्॥ 46॥

Yadi mām apratīkāram aśastraṁ śastra-pāṇayaḥ
Dhārtarāṣṭrā raṇe hanyus tan me kṣemataraṁ bhavet

Aśastram : Without arms *apratīkāram* : unresisting *mām* : me *śastrapāṇayaḥ* : armed with weapons *dhārtarāṣṭrāḥ* : the sons of Dhṛtarāṣṭra *raṇe* : in battle *hanyuḥ yadi* if they kill *tat* : that *kṣemataram* : far better *bhavet* : would be *me* : for me.

46. Far better would it be for me if the sons of Dhṛtarāṣṭra, with weapons in hand, kill me in battle, unarmed and unresisting!

सञ्जय उवाच—

एवमुक्त्वार्जुनः संख्ये रथोपस्थ उपाविशत्।
विसृज्य सशरं चापं शोक-संविग्न-मानसः॥ 47॥

Sañjaya uvāca:

Evam uktvārjunaḥ saṁkhye rathopastha upāviśat
visṛjya saśaraṁ cāpaṁ śoka-saṁvigna-mānasaḥ ॥47॥

Evam uktvā : So saying *śokasaṁvignamānasaḥ* : with mind overwhelmed by grief *Arjunaḥ* : Arjuna *saśaraṁ cāpam* : bow along with arrows *visṛjya*: abandoning *rathopasthaḥ*: in the car seat *upāviśat* : sat down.

Sanjaya said:

47. So saying, Arjuna, with his mind overwhelmed with sorrow, abandoned his bow and arrows and sat down on the chariot seat.

इति श्रीमद्भगवद्गीतासूपनिषत्सु ब्रह्मविद्यायां योगशास्त्रे
श्रीकृष्णार्जुनसंवादे अर्जुनविषादयोगो नाम
प्रथमोऽध्यायः ।

Iti Śrīmad bhagavdgītās'ūpanisatsu brahma-vidyāyām
yogaśāstre Sri Kṛṣṇā'rjuna-saṁvāde
Arjuna-viṣāda-yogo nāma prathamo'dhyāyaḥ

In the Bhagavad Gītā, which is an Upaniṣad, a text on Brahman-knowledge, a scripture of spiritual communion, and a dialogue between Sri Kṛṣṇa and Arjuna, here ends the first chapter named *Arjunaviṣādayoga* (Arjuna's spiritual conversion through sorrow).

NOTES

All the great Indian commentators of the past have taken the background events of the Gītā and the personalities involved in it as historical. The Kurukṣetra war is supposed to have been fought in about 1400 B.C. according to the latest archaelogical evidence as against the traditional date ascribing it to a time just before the beginning of Kali Era in 3102 B.C.

In modern times, however, there is a swing towards a symbolical interpretation of the background events. The most noteworthy among the modern upholders of this view is Mahatma Gandhi who opines: "The Gītā is not a historical discourse. A physical illustration is often needed to drive home a spiritual truth. It is the description not of war between cousins but between two natures in us—the good and the evil."

The Mahatma could not but take this view, as he was a total pacifist, and believed that love and suffering undergone by oneself should be the only means of converting the enemy, and never violence. However noble this view might be, there will always be another section of thinkers who will hold that a surgical treatment is necessary where medical therapy is found ineffective, that there are cancerous developments in the body politic which will carry the disease all over the organism unless removed from the system by radical measures. Sri Kṛṣṇa, and in fact most of the Divine Incarnations of the Hindus, are on the side of this view. From the practical point of view also Kṛṣṇa was not a warmonger. He tried to settle the dispute between the two factions through the arts of diplomacy and conciliation, to the best of his abilities, and only when the doors of justice were completely closed, did he allow the issue to be settled by the might of arms.

The symbolical interpretation is not, however, in any way opposed or contradictory to the acceptance of historical validity. If we accept a Divine mind behind the great developments of history, there is no harm in reading divine purposes into the great incidents of life. When the events are gone with the ebbing away of time, it is only the lessons learnt from them and the interpreted understanding of these events that last in the mind of man. These surviving ideological contents of events alone belong to the realm of eternal values, while the events themselves are their temporal and fleeting forms. So the Mahābhārata war of history may very well be interpreted as the illustration in space and time of the eternal idea of a struggle between the Good and the Evil, which the Cosmic Mind conceives as the pattern of human evolution. Symbolism and history can therefore be complementary and not conflicting.

There have been other symbolical explananations of the context of the Gitā. One popular explanation is that it is an extension of the symbolism of the chariot described in the Kathopaniṣad. The human body is compared to the chariot, in which the soul of man is seated as the master of the chariot with the Buddhi as the charioteer. The mind constitutes the reins, and the senses, the horses. The chariot is coursing through the battle-field of life, the Kurukṣetra. Stationed in that battle-field, the bewildered spirit of man represented by Arjuna occupying the chariot of the body, looks to the charioteer, the higher mind or the Buddhi,here represented by Kṛṣṇa, for advice, guidance and inspiration. The Gītā is the eternal dialogue going on between the ego and the higher mind in the personality of man struggling on the battle-field of life. There have been scholastic interpreters who give symbolic meaning to many of the principal interlocutors like Sañjaya, Dhṛtarāṣṭra, Duryodhana etc.

The significance of the chapter from the Vedāntic point of view, namely,that a thorough disillusionment with life as constituted in Nature is necessary for spiritual instruction to take effect, has been discussed in the summary at the beginning of the next chapter and in the general introduction.

Chapter II

सांख्ययोगः

COMMUNION THROUGH KNOWLEDGE

SUMMARY

Arjuna Seeking Refuge in Kṛṣṇa: (1-16): To Arjuna thus overcome with pity for his doomed kith and kin, Śri Kṛṣṇa administers a strong dose of reprimand, saying that his attitude befits only a eunuch and not a hero. But Arjuna's sorrow and confusion are so deep-rooted that the reprimand has no effect on him, and he continues in his attitude of self-pity, and finally takes refuge in Kṛṣṇa as a disciple, seeking solace and instruction.

The Immortal Atman: (17-25): Sri Kṛṣṇa recognises that Arjuna's recoiling from his duty of leading his forces stems from two presumptions in his mind. First, the people threatened with destruction are his own nearest kith and kin. This in turn has its basis in his blindness to the essential spiritual nature of man. Ignorance makes him equate man with his visible body, which in turn makes him think of death as total destruction. But the truth is that man's spirit is indestructible. Until man lives by this truth, there can be no abiding virtue in him. In order to bring this home to Arjuna, Kṛṣṇa, at the very start of his discourse, expounds the high philosophy of Ātman in the following words: You pretend to be a wise man in speech, but your behaviour is like that of the most ignorant. Your sorrow is for persons who are not in need of it. A wise man takes death as a trifle. For, he knows that the Essence in man is the Ātman, the birthless, the deathless, the eternal Spirit, whom weapons cannot cleave, fire burn, or air dry. Birth and death are only of the body and not of the Ātman, and the body in relation to the Ātman is like clothes one puts on and throws away; or like the passing stages of life like childhood, boyhood, youth and old age. Pleasant and painful experiences of life are passing episodes. A man who knows this and is never moved by pleasure and pain, by life and death, is alone wise and fit for spiritual freedom.

Death from the worldly Point of View: (26-39): Even from the point of view of a worldly wise man, you need not feel sorry for these men. Death is natural to all embodied beings, and there is no use in sorrowing for this unavoidable occurrence. From the Unknown, life comes; for a short time it remains in the field of the known; and to the Unknown it goes back again. Of what use is man's wailing over this eternal process? On the other hand, if you avoid your responsibilities in this righteous war—a veritable portal to heaven for the valiant Kṣatriyas—every one will say that you have tucked tail for fear of death and fled away for life like a coward. To survive with the stigma of cowardice is worse than a hundred deaths. Dead in the field of battle, you will attain heaven; victorious, you will enjoy the earth. So arise and fight! And if you can practise even-mindedness in pain and pleasure, in success and failure, you shall not incur any sin by slaughter in battle.

The Gospel of Dedicated Work: (40-53): Having reminded Arjuna of the real nature of man as the eternal Spirit, Sri Kṛṣṇa now proceeds to declare the disciplines by which one could gradually realise this Divinity inherent in oneself. For, it is a matter of realisation, and not mere talk. Sri Kṛṣṇa therefore teaches further as follows: "I taught you till now about the philosophy of the Ātman. Now hear from me about the doctrine of communion through work. This path is free from dangers and is easy to perform. It seeks to secure the one-pointedness of mind through detachment in work. Man is generally after many worldly enjoyments and ambitions, and, hearing that they could be secured through Vedic ritualism, he performs various ritualistic works, one after another, hoping for success. Though they may look like acts of piety, they are only expressions of pure worldliness. They make the mind restless and scattered. But if you can work without an eye on their fruits, your mind will get more and more ingathered and concentrated gradually. The more we are motivated by selfish gains in our work, the more we get steeped in worldliness; and the more we work in a spirit of duty without caring for gains, the more shall we get spiritually oriented. You have therefore got the right only to work as a matter of duty, and not to expect any selfish gain from it, if you want to evolve spiritually. But lack of interest in selfish returns should never make you lethargic or slipshod in work. For, communion through work (Karma Yoga) consists in maximum efficiency combined with detachment. It is for this reason that Karma Yoga is described as 'skill in action.' A man who discharges his duty in the manner described, acquires neither merit nor demerit, but evolves spiritually and becomes fit to realise his real nature as the immortal and impervious Ātman. He attains to liberation from the trammels of ignorance. When one is free from longings for worldly enjoyments, one gains spiritual conviction and one's intelligence is established in steadiness."

The Man of Steady Wisdom: (54-72): Arjuna thereupon asks Kṛṣṇa how he could recognise a man who has attained to the state of 'steadiness of intelligence.' Kṛṣṇa replies: "Such a person, having abandoned all desires from his heart, is ever satisfied with the bliss that is in his higher self. Nothing external attracts him. He is unperturbed in misery and happiness alike. He is free from all attachments, fear and anger. He has such control over his senses that he can withdraw them inward in the presence of the objects that excite them, as a tortoise withdraws its limbs into its shell. The hold of the senses on an ordinary man is very powerful. As a ship on the high seas is at the mercy of the winds, so is the intelligence of man at the mercy of sense objects. One who thinks longingly of sense objects develops attachment for them. Attachments, in turn, grow into strong desires and infatuation. Infatuation effaces man's sense of distinction between the proper and the improper, and he becomes a slave of his animal instincts—in fact he loses his rationality. So the control of the senses is the pathway to spiritual advancement, and the lack of it, to spiritual ruin. And he who is the absolute master of the senses—into whom the stimuli from sense objects can enter without causing any perturbation, as rivers into the brimming ocean—he attains to the peace that passeth understanding. This is what is meant by being established in Brahman-consciousness. Attaining to it a man is never reborn."

सञ्जय उवाच

तं तथा कृपयाऽऽविष्ट-मश्रुपूर्णाकुलेक्षणम् ।
विषीदन्तमिदं वाक्य-मुवाच मधुसूदनः ॥ 1 ॥

Sañjaya uvāca

Taṁ tathā kṛpayā'viṣṭam aśru-pūrṇākul'ekṣaṇam
viṣīdantam idam vākyam uvāca Madhusūdanaḥ ॥ 1 ॥

Tathā : Thus *Kṛpayā* : by pity *āviṣṭam* : one overcome with *aśru-pūrṇākulekṣaṇam* : with eyes full of tears and with a bewildered look *viṣīdantam* : sorrowing *tam* : him *Madhusūdanaḥ* : Sri Kṛṣṇa *idam* : this *vākyam* : word *uvāca* : said.

Sañjaya said:

1. To him who was thus overcome with pity and whose eyes were full of tears and bore a bewildered look, Sri Kṛṣṇa spoke as follows:

श्री भागवानुवाच—

कुतस्त्वा कश्मल-मिदं विषमे समुपस्थितम् ।
अनार्यजुष्ट-मस्वर्ग्य मकीर्तिकर-मर्जुन ॥ 2 ॥

Sri Bhagavān uvāca

Kutas tvā kaśmalam idaṁ viṣame samupasthitam
anārya-juṣṭam asvargyam akīrtikaram Arjuna ॥ 2 ॥

Arjuna: O Arjuna! *anāryajuṣṭam*: entertained by worthless men *asvargyam* : a bar to heaven *akīrtikaram* : bringing disrepute *idam* : this *kaśmalam* : loathsome stupidity *viṣame* : in this crisis *tvā* : you *kutaḥ samupasthitam* : whence come upon.

The Blessed Lord said

2. O Arjuna ! Whence has this loathsome stupidity come upon you in this crisis? It (this attitude) is unworthy of a noble personage; it is a bar to heaven and a cause of much disrepute.

क्लैब्यं मा स्म गमः पार्थ नैतत्त्वय्युपपद्यते ।
क्षुद्रं हृदयदौर्बल्यं त्यक्त्वोत्तिष्ठ परन्तप ॥ 3 ॥

Klaibyaṁ mā sma gamaḥ Pārtha n'aitat tvayy upapadyate ।
kṣudraṁ hṛdaya-daurbalyaṁ tyaktv' ottiṣṭha paraṁtapa ॥ 3 ॥

Pārtha : O Arjuna! *klaibyam* : state of impotency, unmanliness *mā sma gamaḥ* : do not attain to. *Etat*: This *tvayi*: in thee *na upapadyate* : is not fitting. *Kṣudram* : Base *hṛdayadaurbalyam* : faintness of heart *tyaktvā* : abandoning *paraṁtapa* : O dreaded hero *uttiṣṭha* : rise up.

3. O Pārtha! Yield not to unmanliness! It befits thee not. Abandoning this base faint-heartedness, rise up, O dreaded hero! [1]

अर्जुन उवाच—

कथं भीष्म-महं सङ्ख्ये द्रोणं च मधुसूदन ।
इषुभिः प्रतियोत्स्यामि पूजार्हावरिसूदन ॥ 4 ॥

Arjuna uvāca :

Kathaṁ Bhīṣmam ạhaṁ saṁkhye Droṇaṁ cā Madhusūdana ।
iṣubhiḥ pratiyotsyāmi puj' ārhāv arisūdana ॥ 4 ॥

Madhusūdana : O Madhusūdana *Bhīṣmaṁ Droṇaṁ ca* : Bhīṣma and Droṇa *saṁkhye* : in battle *aham* : I *iṣubhiḥ* : with arrows *katham pratiyotsyāmi* : how shall attack, *tau* : they two *pujārhau* : are worthy of worship *arisūdana* : O destroyer of foes!

Arjuna said

4. O Kṛṣṇa! How can I attack Bhīṣma and Droṇa in battle with my arrows? They are, indeed, worthy of worship, O destroyer of foes!

गुरूनहत्वा हि महानुभावान्
श्रेयो भोक्तुं भैक्ष्य-मपीह लोके।
हत्वाऽर्थकामांस्तु गुरूनिहैव
भुञ्जीय भोगान् रुधिरप्रदिग्धान् ॥ 5 ॥

Gurūn ahatvā hi mahā'nubhāvān śreyo bhoktuṁ
bhaikṣyam apī' ha loke
hatvā'rtha kāmāṁs tu gurūn ih'aiva bhuñjīya
bhogān rudhira-pradigdhān ॥ 5 ॥

Mahānubhāvān : Venerable *gurūn* : teachers *ahatvā*: without killing *iha loke* : in this world *bhaikṣyam* : food got by begging *api* : even: *bhoktum* : to eat *śreyaḥ* : leading to one's good. *Gurūn* : Teachers *hatvā tu* : if killing *iha eva* : here itself *rudhirapradigdhān* : blood-smeared *arthakāmān* : power and pleasure *bhogān* : enjoyments *eva*: even *bhuñjīya* : enjoy (will have to enjoy).

5. It is indeed better to live here in this world on a beggar's fare than to prosper by killing these venerable teachers. The enjoyment of pleasure and power obtained through the slaugher of these teachers and elders will surely be bloodstained.

न चैतद्विद्मः कतरन्नो गरीयो
यद्वा जयेम यदि वा नो जयेयुः।
यानेव हत्वा न जिजीविषाम-
स्तेऽवस्थिताः प्रमुखे धार्तराष्ट्राः ॥ 6 ॥

Na c'aitad vidmaḥ kataran no garīyo yad vā jayema
yadi vā no jayeyuḥ ।
yān eva hatvā na jijīviṣāmas te' vasthitāḥ pramukhe
Dhārtarāṣṭrāḥ ॥ 6 ॥

Yad vā : Whether *jayema* : we should conquer *yadi vā* : or that *naḥ* : us *jayeyuḥ* : they should conquer *katarat* : which of the two *naḥ* : for us *garīyaḥ* : better *etat* : this *na vidmaḥ*: we do not know. *Yān* : whom *hatvā* : having killed *na jijīviṣāmaḥ eva* : we shall not care to live at all *te dhārtarāṣṭrāḥ* : these men on the side of Dṛtarāṣṭra *pramukhe* : in front (arrayed against) *avasthitāḥ*: stand.

6. We do not know which of the two (alternatives) will be the better — the one that we should conquer them or the other that they should conquer us. The men on the side of Dhritrāṣṭra, standing arrayed against us, are the very people after killing whom we should not care to live.

कार्पण्यदोषोपहत-स्वभावः
पृच्छामि त्वां धर्मसम्मूढचेताः ।
यच्छ्रेयः स्यान्निश्चितं ब्रूहि तन्मे
शिष्यस्तेऽहं शाधि मां त्वां प्रपन्नम् ॥ 7 ॥

kārpaṇya-doṣ'opahata-svabhāvaḥ pṛcchāmi tvāṁ
dharma-saṁmūḍha-cetāḥ
yac chreyaḥ syān niścitaṁ brūhi tan me śiṣyas te'
haṁ śādhi māṁ tvāṁ prapannam ॥ 7 ॥

kārpaṇyadoṣopahata-svabhāvaḥ : One whose natural disposition has been vitiated by the sense of pity *dharmasaṁmūḍhacetāḥ* : one with a mind in utter confusion regarding one's duty (*aham* : I) *tvām* : you *pṛcchāmi* : ask. *Yat* : whatever *me* : my *śreyaḥ* : good *syāt* : is *tat* : that *niścitam* : for certainty *brūhi* : tell. *Aham* : I *te* : thy *śiṣyaḥ* : disciple, *tvām* : Thee. *prapannam* : taken sheltter *mām* : me *śādhi* : instruct.

7. My natural disposition is vitiated by a sense of pity, and my mind is in utter confusion regarding my duty. Lord, I beg Thee: tell me with certainty what will lead to my good: I am Thy disciple. Instruct me, who have taken refuge in Thee.

न हि प्रपश्यामि ममापनुद्याद् यच्छोक-मुच्छोषण-मिन्द्रियाणाम् ।
अवाप्य भूमावसपत्नमृद्धं राज्यं सुराणामपि चाधिपत्यम् ॥ 8 ॥

na hi prapaśyāmi mam'āpanudyād yac chokam
ucchoṣaṇam indriyāṇām
avāpya bhūmāu asapatnaṁ ṛddhaṁ rājyaṁ surānām
api c'ādhipatyam ॥ 8 ॥

Bhūmau : In the world *asapatnam* : without enemies *ṛddham* prosperous *rājyam* : kingdom *surāṇām* : of the Devas *ādhipatyam* : overlordship *avāpya api* : even attaining *indriyāṇām* senses *ucchoṣaṇam* : drying up *mama* : my *śokam* : grief *yat* : what *apanudyāt* : can remove *tat* : that *na hi* : do not *prapaśyāmi* : I see.

8. I do not find anything that can assuage this grief which numbs my senses. Neither the unchallenged lordship over a prosperous kingdom, nor even the overlordship of all the Devas can do so.

सञ्जय उवाच—

एवमुक्त्वा हृषीकेशं गुडाकेशः परन्तपः ।
न योत्स्य इति गोविन्द-मुक्त्वा तूष्णीं बभूव ह ॥ 9 ॥

Sañjaya uvāca

Evam uktvā hṛṣīkeśaṁ guḍākeśaḥ paraṁtapaḥ
na yotsya iti Govindam uktvā tūṣṇīṁ babhūva ha ॥9॥

Guḍākeśaḥ : Arjuna the conqueror of sleep *paraṁtapaḥ* : the scorcher of foes *hṛṣīkeśaṁ govindam* : Kṛṣṇa the master of the senses *evam* : thus *uktvā* : having said, *na yotsye* : I will not fight *iti* thus *tūṣṇīm* : silent *babhūva ha* : became.

Sanjaya said

9. Addressing Sri Kṛṣṇa, the master of the senses, Arjuna, though valorous and vigilant, said, 'I will not fight', and sat silent.

तमुवाच हृषीकेशः प्रहसन्निव भारत।
सेनयो-रुभयो-र्मध्ये विषीदन्त-मिदं वचः ॥ 10 ॥

Tam uvāca hṛṣīkeśaḥ prahasann iva Bhārata
senayor ubhayor madhye viṣīdantam idaṁ vacaḥ ॥ 10 ॥

Bhārata : O Dhritarāṣṭra *ubhayoḥ* : of both *senayoḥ* : armies *madhye* : middle *viṣīdantam* : sorrowing *tam* : him *hṛṣīkeśaḥ* : Kṛṣṇa *prahasan iva* : as if ridiculing *idaṁ vacaḥ* : this word *uvāca* : said.

10. O King! To him who was thus sitting grief-stricken between the two armies (instead of fighting), Sri Kṛṣṇa said as if by way of ridicule.

श्रीभगवानुवाच—
अशोच्या-नन्वशोचस्त्वं प्रज्ञावादांश्च भाषसे।
गतासू-नगतासूंश्च नानुशोचन्ति पण्डिताः ॥ 11 ॥

Śrī Bhagavān uvāca
aśocyān anvaśocas tvaṁ prajñā-vādāṁś ca bhāṣase
gat'āsūn agat'āsūṁś ca n'ānuśocanti paṇḍitāḥ ॥ 11 ॥

Aśocyān : Those who should not be moaned for *tvam* : you *anvaśocaḥ* : are moaning *Prajñāvādān* : words worthy of wise men *bhāṣase ca* : you speak too. *Paṇḍitāḥ* : wise men *gatāsūn* : the dead *agatāsūn* : living *ca* : and *na anusocanti* : bewail not.

The Blessed Lord said

11. You are moaning for those who should not be moaned for. Yet you speak like a wise man. The truly wise never weep either for the dead or for the living.

न त्वेवाहं जातु नासं न त्वं नेमे जनाधिपाः ।
न चैव न भविष्यामः सर्वे वयमतः परम् ॥ 12 ॥

Na tvevāhaṁ jātu nāsam na tvaṁ n'eme jan'ādhipāḥ
nac'aiva na bhaviṣyāmaḥ sarve vayam ataḥ param

aham : I *jātu* : at any time *na tu āsam* : did not even exist (*iti*: this) *na eva* : not indeed; *tvam* : you *na* (*āsīḥ iti*) did not exist *na* : not; *ime janādhipāḥ na* (*āsan iti*) *na* : it is not that these kings ever did not exist; *ataḥparam* : hereafter *sarve vayam* : all of us *na bhaviṣyāmaḥ* : shall not exist (*iti ca na eva* : it is not at all so.)

12. Never was there a time when I did not exist, nor you, nor these rulers of men. Nor shall all of us cease to be hereafter.

देहिनोऽस्मिन् यथा देहे कौमारं यौवनं जरा ।
तथा देहान्तरप्राप्ति-र्धीरस्तत्र न मुह्यति ॥ 13 ॥

Dehino' smin yathā dehe kaumāraṁ yauvanaṁ jarā
tathā dehā'ntara prāptir dhīras tatra na muhyati ॥13॥

Dehinaḥ : To the embodied soul *asmin dehe* : in this body *kaumāram* : childhood *yauvanam* : youth *jarā* : old age *tathā* : in the same way *dehāntaraprāptiḥ* change to another body. *Dhīraḥ* : A wise man *tatra* : by this *na muhyati* : is not deluded.

13. Even as the attainment of childhood, youth and old age is to one in this physical life, so is the change to another body (at death) for the embodied soul. Wise men are not deluded by this.

मात्रास्पर्शास्तु कौन्तेय, शीतोष्ण-सुखदुःखदाः ।
आगमापायिनोऽनित्यास्तांस्तितिक्षस्व भारत ॥ 14 ॥

Mātrā-sparśās tu Kaunteya śīt'oṣṇa-sukha-duḥkhadāḥ
āgam'āpāyino'nityās tāṁs titikṣasva Bhārata ॥ 14 ॥

Kaunteya : O son of Kunti (Arjuna)! *mātrāsparśāḥ tu* : contact of the senses with their objects *śītoṣṇa sukha duḥkhadāḥ* : producing cold and heat, pleasure and pain *āgamāpāyinaḥ* : now coming and now going *anityāḥ* : are impermanent. *Bhārata* : O Scion of the Bharata race! *tān* : them *titīkṣasva* : bear patiently.

14. Contact of the senses with their objects generates cold and heat, pleasure and pain. They come and go, being impermanent. Bear with them patiently, O scion of the Bharata race!

यं हि न व्यथयन्त्येते पुरुषं पुरुषर्षभ ।
समदुःखसुखं धीरं सोऽमृतत्वाय कल्पते ॥ 15 ॥

Yaṁ hi na vyathayanty ete puruṣaṁ puruṣ'arṣabha
sama-duḥkha-sukhaṁ dhīraṁ so'mṛtatvāya kalpate ॥ 15 ॥

Puruṣarṣabha : O leader of men! *ete* : these *samaduḥkhasukham* : unperturbed alike in pleasure and pain *dhīram yam puruṣam* : the enlightened one whom *na vyathayanti* : do not distress *saḥ* : he *amṛtatvāya* : for immortality : *kalpate hi* : is fit indeed.

15. O leader of men! That enlightened one who is unpertubed alike in pleasure and pain, whom these do not distress — he indeed is worthy of immortality.

नासतो विद्यते भावो नाभावो विद्यते सतः ।
उभयोरपि दृष्टोऽन्त-स्त्वनयो-स्तत्त्वदर्शिभिः ॥ 16 ॥

N'āsato vidyate bhāvo n'ābhāvo vidyate sataḥ
ubhayor api dṛṣṭo'ntas tv anayos tattva darśibhiḥ ॥ 16 ॥

Asataḥ: of the unreal *bhāvaḥ:* existence *na vidyate* : is not, *sataḥ* : of the real *abhāvaḥ* : non-existence *na vidyate* : is not. *Anayoḥ ubhayoḥ* : of these two *api antaḥ tu* the final end, (truth) *tattva-darśibhiḥ* : by philosophers *dṛṣṭaḥ* : seen.

16. The unreal can never come into existence, and the real can never cease to be. The wise philosophers have known the truth about these categories (of the real and the unreal). [2]

अविनाशि तु तद्विद्धि येन सर्वमिदं ततम् ।
विनाश-मव्ययस्यास्य न कश्चित् कर्तुमर्हति ॥ 17 ॥

Avināśi tu tad viddhi yena sarvam idaṁ tatam
vināśam avyayasy'āsyā na kaścit kartum arhati ॥ 17 ॥

Yena : By what *sarvam idam* : all this *tatam* : pervaded *tat tu* : that *avināśi* : indestructible *viddhi* : know. *Avyayasya asya* : of this immutable *vināśam* : destruction *kartum* : to effect *kaścit na arhati* : no one is able.

17. Know that Reality, by which everything is pervaded, to be indestructible. No one can cause the destruction of this immuble Being.

अन्तवन्त इमे देहा नित्यस्योक्ताः शरीरिणः ।
अनाशिनोऽप्रमेयस्य तस्माद्युध्यस्व भारत ॥ 18 ॥

Antavanta ime dehā nityasyo'ktāḥ śarīriṇaḥ
anāśino'prameyasya tasmād yudhyasva Bhārata ॥ 18 ॥

Nityasya : Eternal *anāśinaḥ* : indestructible *aprameyasya* : immesurable, unlimited *śarīriṇaḥ* : of the indweller of the body, spirit *ime dehāḥ* : these bodies *antavantaḥ* : with end, perishable *uktāḥ* : are said to be. *Tasmāt* : therefore *Bhārata* : scion of the Bharata race *yudhyasva* : do you fight.

18. What is said to perish are these bodies, in which the imperishable and unlimited Spirit is embodied. Therefore fight, O scion of the Bharata race!

य एनं वेत्ति हन्तारं यश्चैनं मन्यते हतम् ।
उभौ तौ न विजानीतो नायं हन्ति न हन्यते ॥ 19 ॥

Ya enaṁ vetti hantāraṁ yaś c'ainaṁ manyate hatam
ubhau tau na vijānīto nāyaṁ hanti na hanyate ॥ 19 ॥

Yaḥ : Who *enam* : him *hantāraṁ vetti* : know as the killer *yaḥ enam* : who him *hatam* : killed *manyate* : knows as *tau ubhau* both of them *na vijānītaḥ* : do not know the real truth. *Ayam* : He *na hanti* : does not kill *na hanyate* : is not killed.

19. He who thinks him (the Self) to be the killer, and who experiences him (the Self) as the killed — both of them know not. He (the Self) neither kills nor is killed.

न जायते म्रियते वा कदाचिन्नायं भूत्वा भविता वा न भूयः ।
अजो नित्यः शाश्वतोऽयं पुराणो न हन्यते हन्यमाने शरीरे ॥ 20 ॥

Na jāyate mriyate vā kadācin-nāyaṁ bhūtvā bhavitā vā na bhūyaḥ
ajo nityaḥ śāśvato'yaṁ purāṇo na hanyate hanyamāne śarīre ॥ 20 ॥

Ayam : He, this Self *kadācit* : at any time *na jāyate* : is not born *na mriyate* : does not die. *Ayam* : he, the Self, *bhūtvā* : once coming into existence *bhūyaḥ* : again *na bhavitā vā na* : does not afterwords cease to be. *Ajaḥ* : Unborn *nityaḥ* : eternal *śāsvataḥ* permanent *purāṇaḥ* : primeval *śarīre* : body *hanyamāne* : when killed *na hanyate* : is not killed.

20. He (this Self) has neither birth nor death. Nor does he cease to be, having been in existence before; unborn, eternal, permanent and primeval, he is never killed when the body is killed.

वेदाऽविनाशिनं नित्यं य एनमजमव्ययम् ।
कथं स पुरुषः पार्थ कं घातयति हन्ति कम् ॥ 21 ॥

Ved'āvināśinaṁ nityaṁ ya enam ajam avyayam
kathaṁ sa puruṣaḥ Pārtha kaṁ ghātayati hanti kam ॥21॥

Pārtha : O Arjuna! *enam* : this (Self) *nityam* : eternal *avyayam* : undecaying; *ajam* : birthless *avināśinam* : indestructible *yaḥ* : who *veda* : knows, *saḥ puruṣaḥ* : that person *katham* : how *kam* whom *hanti* : kills *kam* : whom *ghātayati* : causes to slay.

21. O Arjuna! know this self to be eternal, undecaying, birthless and indestructible. A person who knows him to be so — how and whom can he kill, how and whom can he cause to be killed?

वासांसि जीर्णानि यथा विहाय नवानि गृह्णाति नरोऽपराणि ।
तथा शरीराणि विहाय जीर्णान्यन्यानि संयाति नवानि देही ॥ 22 ॥

Vāsāṁsi jīrṇāni yathā vihāya navāni gṛhṇāti naro'parāṇi
tathā śarīrāṇi vihāya jīrṇānyanyāni saṁyāti navāni dehī

Naraḥ : Man *yathā* : as *jīrṇāni* : old *vāsāṁsi* : garments *vihāya* : abandoning *navānī* : new *aparāṇi* : other (clothes) *gṛhṇāti* : takes, *tathā* : in the same way *dehī* : the embodied self *jīrṇāni* : decrepit *śarīrāṇi* : bodies *vihāya* : abandoning *navāni* : new *anyāni* : other bodies *saṁyāti* : enters, assumes.

22. Just as a man gives up old garments and puts on new ones, so the embodied self abandons decrepit bodies and assumes new ones.

नैनं छिन्दन्ति शस्त्राणि नैनं दहति पावकः ।
न चैनं क्लेदयन्त्यापो न शोषयति मारुतः ॥ 23 ॥

Nainaṁ chindanti śastrāṇi nainaṁ dahati pāvakaḥ
na c'ainaṁ kledayanty āpo na śoṣayati mārutaḥ ॥ 23 ॥

Enam : Him *śaṣtrāṇi* : weapons *na chindanti* ; cut not; *enam* : Him *pāvakaḥ* : fire *na dahati* : burns not; *enam* : Him *āpaḥ* : waters *na kledayanti* : wet not; *mārutaḥ* ; wind *na śoṣayti* : dries not.

23. Him the weapons cleave not; Him the fire burns not; Him the waters wet not; Him the wind dries not.

अच्छेद्योऽय-मदाह्योऽय-मक्लेद्योऽशोष्य एव च ।
नित्यः सर्वगतः स्थाणु-रचलोऽयं सनातनः ॥ 24 ॥

Acchedyo'yam adāhyo'yam akledyo' śoṣya eva ca
nityaḥ sarvagataḥ sthāṇuḥ acalo'yaṁ sanātanaḥ ॥ 24 ॥

Ayam : He *acchedyaḥ* : is uncleavable; *ayam* : He *adāhyaḥ* is unburnable; *ayam* : He *akledyaḥ* : is unwettable; *aśoṣyaḥ eva ca* : and also undriable; *ayam* : He (is) *nityaḥ* : everlasting, *sarvagataḥ* : all-prevading, *sthāṇuḥ* : immovable, *acalaḥ* motionless, *sanātanaḥ* : eternal.

24. He cannot be cut or burnt. He can neither be wetted nor dried. Eternal, all-pervading, immovable and motionless, He is the same for ever.

अव्यक्तोऽय-मचिन्त्योऽय-मविकार्योऽय-मुच्यते ।
तस्मादेवं विदित्वैनं नानुशोचितु-मर्हसि ॥ 25 ॥

Avyakto'yam acintyo'yam avikāryo'yam ucyate
tasmād evam viditv'ainaṁ n'ānuśocitum arhasi ॥ 25 ॥

Ayam avyaktaḥ : He is unmanifest (to the senses), *ayam acintyaḥ* : He is inconceivable, *ayam avikāryaḥ* : He cannot be subjected to change *iti ucyate* : so it is said; *tasmāt* : therefore *enam* : Him *evam* : in this way *viditvā* : having known *anuśocitum* : to mourn for *na arhasi* : you are not fit (should not).

25. Knowing Him (the Self) to be unmainfest, inconceivable, and unmodifiable, it is improper to mourn for Him.

अथ चैनं नित्यजातं नित्यं वा मन्यसे मृतम् ।
तथापि त्वं महाबाहो नैनं शोचितु-मर्हसि ॥ 26 ॥

Atha c'ainaṁ nitya-jātaṁ nityaṁ vā manyase mṛtam
tathāpi tvaṁ mahā-bāho n'ainaṁ śocitum arhasi ॥ 26 ॥

Athavā : In the alternative *enam* : Him (Self) *nityajātam* : frequently born *nityam mṛtaṁ ca* : and frequently dying *tvam* : you *manyase* : think, *tathā api* : even then *mahābaho* : O mighty armed! *tvam* : you *evam* : like this *śocitum* : to mourn *na arhasi*. not proper.

26. In the alternative, even if you hold him (the Self) to be subject to constant births and deaths, there is no justification, O mighty armed, for your mourning for him.[8]

जातस्य हि ध्रुवो मृत्युर्ध्रुवं जन्म मृतस्य च।
तस्मा-दपरिहार्येऽर्थे न त्वं शोचितु-मर्हसि ॥ 27 ॥

Jātasya hi dhruvo mṛtyuḥ dhruvaṁ janma mṛtasya ca
tasmād aparihārye'rthe na tvaṁ śocitum arhasi ॥ 27 ॥

Jātasya : For the born *mṛtyuḥ* : death *dhruvaḥ hi* : sure indeed, *mṛtasya* : for the dead *janma ca* : birth too *dhruvam* : sure; *tasmāt* therefore *aparihārye arthe* : in the inevitable matter or situation *tvam* : you *śocitum* : to sorrow for *na arhasi* : do not deserve. (should not).

27. For the born, death is unavoidable, and for the dead birth is sure to take place. Therefore in a situation that is inevitable, there is no justification for you to grieve.

अव्यक्तादीनि भूतानि व्यक्त-मध्यानि भारत।
अव्यक्त-निधनान्येव तत्र का परिदेवना ॥ 28 ॥

Avyakt'ādīni bhūtāni vyakta-madhyāni Bhārata
avyakta-nidhanāny eva tatra kā paridevanā ॥ 28 ॥

Bhārata : O Arjuna! *bhūtāni* : beings *avyaktādini* : mysterious in their origin, *vyakta madhyāni* : clear in their middle, *avyakta nidhanāni eva* : mysterious or unmanifested again in the end *tatra* : in this *kā* ; what *paridevanā* : grief.

28. Mystery surrounds the origin of beings. Mysterious too is their end. Only in the interim between birth and death are they manifested clearly. Such being the case, what is there to grieve about?

आश्चर्यवत्पश्यति कश्चिदेनं आश्चर्यवद्वदति तथैव चान्यः।
आश्चर्यवच्चैन-मन्यः शृणोति श्रुत्वाप्येनं वेद न चैव कश्चित् ॥29॥

Āścaryavat paśyati kaścit enam āścaryavad vadati tath'aiva c'ānyaḥ
āścaryavad c'ainam anyaḥ śṛnoti śrutvā'py enaṁ veda na c'aiva kaścit ॥ 29 ॥

Kaścit : Some one *enam* : Him *āścaryavat* : as a marvel *paśyati* : sees, *tathā eva ca* : in the same way *anyaḥ* : another *āścaryavat* : as a marvel *vadati* : speaks *anyaḥ ca* : still another *enam* : Him *āścaryavat* : as a marvel *sṛṇoti* : hears. *Śrutvā api ca* : Even on hearing *na kaścid* : no one *veda eva* : knows at all.

29. Some have a glimpse of Him as a marvel, some speak of Him as a marvel, and yet others hear of Him as a marvel. Yet none understands Him in truth, in spite of (seeing, speaking and) hearing about Him.

देही नित्य-मवध्योऽयं देहे सर्वस्य भारत।
तस्मात् सर्वाणि भूतानि न त्वं शोचितुमर्हसि ॥ 30 ॥

Dehī nityam avadhyo'yaṁ dehe sarvasya Bhārata
tasmāt sarvāṇi bhūtāni na tvaṁ śocitum arhasi ॥ 30 ॥

Sarvasya dehe : In the bodies of all *ayaṁ dehī* : this embodied spirit (the soul) *nityam* : always *avadhyaḥ* : indestructible. *Tasmāt:* Therefore *sarvāṇi bhūtāni* : all beings *tvam* : you *śocitum* : to mourn *na arhasi* : does not befit.

30. At no time can the Spirit embodied in all beings be slain. Therefore there is no reason for you to grieve for any one.

स्वधर्ममपि चावेक्ष्य न विकम्पितु-मर्हसि ।
धर्म्याद्धि युद्धाच्छ्रेयोऽन्यत् क्षत्रियस्य न विद्यते ॥ 31 ॥

Svadharmam api c'āvekṣya na vikampitum arhasi
dharmyād dhi yuddhāc chreyo'nyat kṣatriyasya na vidyate ॥ 31 ॥

Svadharmam : One's own Dharma (duty) *api ca* : further *avekṣya* : considering *vikampitum* : to falter *na arhasi* :ought not *Kṣatriyasya* : for the Kṣatriya *dharmyāt yuddhāt* : than a righteous war *śreyaḥ* : good *anyat* : any other *na vidyate hi* : does not exist.

31. Further, even from the point of view of one's own duty, you ought not to falter. There is no greater good for a Kṣatriya than what a righteous war offers.

यदृच्छया चोपपन्नं स्वर्गद्वार-मपावृतम् ।
सुखिनः क्षत्रियाः पार्थ लभन्ते युद्ध-मीदृशम् ॥ 32 ॥

Yadṛcchayā c'opapannaṁ svarga-dvāram apāvṛtam
sukhinaḥ kṣatriyāḥ Pārtha labhante yuddham īdṛśam ॥ 32 ॥

Pārtha : O Arjuna! *Yadṛcchayā* : by chance *upapannam* : come *apāvṛtam* : opened *svargadvāram ca* : gate of heaven *īdṛśam yuddham* : a battle like this (*ye*) *Kṣatriyāḥ* : whichever Ksatriyas *labhante* : obtain (*te* : they) *sukhinaḥ* happy.

32. O Arjuna! That Kṣatriya must indeed be a happy man to whom comes unsought a war like this, which is an open gate to heaven.

अथ चेत्त्वमिमं धर्म्यं संग्रामं न करिष्यसि ।
ततः स्वधर्मं कीर्तिञ्च हित्वा पाप-मवाप्स्यसि ॥ 33 ॥

Atha cet tvam imaṁ dharmyaṁ saṁgrāmaṁ na kariṣyasi
tataḥ svadharmaṁ kīrtiṁ ca hitvā pāpam avāpsyasi ॥ 33 ॥

Atha : But *dharmyam* : righteous *imam* : this *sangrāmam* : war *tvam* : you *na kariṣyasi* : do not engage in, *tataḥ* : by that *svadharmam* : one's own duty *kīrtim* : reputation *ca* : and *hitvā* : abandoning *pāpam* : sin *avāpsyasi* : shall incur.

33. If you do not take part in this righteous war, you will incur sin, besides failing in your duty and forfeiting your reputation.

अकीर्तिश्चापि भूतानि कथयिष्यन्ति तेऽव्ययाम् ।
संभावितस्य चाकीर्ति-र्मरणा-दतिरिच्यते ॥ 34 ॥

Akīrtiṁ c'āpi bhūtāni kathayiṣyanti te' vyayām
sambhāvitasya c'ākīrtir maraṇād atiricyate ॥ 34 ॥

Api ca : Besides *bhūtani* : beings *te* : your *avyayam* : everlasting *akirtim* : dishonour *kathayiṣyanti* : proclaim. *Sambhāvitasya* : for one honoured *akīrtiḥ* : dishonour *maraṇāt* : than death *atiricyate ca* : exceeds.

34. Besides, every one will speak ill of you for all time. More poignant than death is disrepute to a man accustomed to be honoured by all.

भयाद्रणा-दुपरतं मंस्यन्ते त्वां महारथाः ।
येषां च त्वं बहुमतो भूत्वा यास्यसि लाघवम् ॥ 35 ॥

Bhayād raṇād uparataṁ maṁsyante tvāṁ mahā-rathāḥ
yeṣāṁ ca tvaṁ bahu-mato bhūtvā yāsyasi lāghavam ॥ 35 ॥

Mahārathāḥ : Great car-warriors *tvām* : you *bhayāt* : out of fear *raṇāt* : from battle *uparatam* : turned back *maṁsyante* : will regard. *Tvam* : you *yeṣām* : whose *bahumataḥ bhūtvā* : having been the object of respect *lāghavam* : lightness, *yāsyasi* : will receive.

35. The great car-warriors will consider you as having fled from battle out of fear, and you who have been the object of their respect, will be despised by them hereafter.

अवाच्य-वादांश्च बहून् वदिष्यन्ति तवाहिताः ।
निन्दन्तस्तव सामर्थ्यं ततो दुःखतरं नु किम् ॥ 36 ॥

Avācya-vādāṁś ca bahūn vadiṣyanti tav' āhitāḥ
nindantas tava sāmarthyaṁ tato duḥkhataraṁ nu kim ॥ 36 ॥

Tava : Your ***ahitāḥ*** : enemies ***tava*** : your ***sāmarthyam*** : ability, prowess ***nindantaḥ*** : slandering ***bahūn*** : many ***avācyavādān*** : improper words ***vadiṣyanti*** : will speak; ***tataḥ*** : than that ***duḥkhataraṁ kim nu*** : what is more painful?

36. Your enemies will indulge in derogatory speeches against you, belittling your prowess. What is more painful than that?

हतो वा प्राप्स्यसि स्वर्गं जित्वा वा भोक्ष्यसे महीम् ।
तस्मा-दुत्तिष्ठ कौन्तेय युद्धाय कृतनिश्चयः ॥ 37 ॥

Hato vā prāpsyasi svargaṁ jitvā vā bhokṣyase mahīm
tasmād uttiṣṭha Kaunteya yuddhāya kṛta-niścayaḥ ॥ 37 ॥

Kaunteya : O son of Kunti! ***hataḥ vā*** : if killed ***svargam prāpsyasi*** you will attain heaven, ***jitvā vā*** : if victorious ***mahīm*** : the kingdom ***bhokṣyase*** : you will enjoy. ***Tasmāt*** : therefore ***yuddhāya*** for battle ***kṛtaniścayaḥ*** : having resolved ***uttiṣṭha*** : arise.

37. O son of Kuntī! If killed in battle you will attain heaven; if victorious you will enjoy the kingdom. Therefore arise, resolved to fight.

सुखदुःखे समे कृत्वा लाभालाभौ जयाजयौ ।
ततो युद्धाय युज्यस्व नैवं पाप-मवाप्स्यसि ॥ 38 ॥

sukha-duḥkhe same kṛtvā lābh'ālābhau jay'ājayau
tato yuddhāya yujyasva n'aivaṁ pāpam avāpsyasi ॥ 38 ॥

Sukhaduḥkhe : Pleasure and pain ***same kṛtvā*** : considering alike ***lābhālābhau*** : gain and loss ***jayājayau*** : victory and defeat (*same kṛtvā* : considering alike) *tataḥ* : afterwards *yuddhāya* : for battle *yujyasva* : be ready. *Evam* : Thus *pāpam* : sin *na avāpsyasi* shall not incur.

38. Treating alike pleasure and pain, gain and loss, victory and defeat, be ready for battle. Thus you will not incur any sin.

एषा तेऽभिहिता सांख्ये बुद्धिर्योगे त्विमां शृणु ।
बुद्धया युक्तो यया पार्थ कर्मबन्धं प्रहास्यसि ॥ 39 ॥

Eṣā te'bhihitā sāṁkhye buddhir yoge tvimāṁ śṛṇu
buddhyā yukto yayā Pārtha karma-bandhaṁ prahāsyasi

Pārtha : O Pārtha! *te* : to you *abhihitā* : declared, imparted *eṣā* : this *sāṁkhye buddhiḥ* : Truth according to the path of knowledge. *Yoge tu* :according to Yoga (the path of selfless action) *imām*: this *śṛṇu*: hear. *Yayā*: By which *buddhyā yuktaḥ* : endowed with conviction *karmabandham*: bondage of works *prahāsyasi*: abandon.

39. O Arjuna! What has been declared to you is the Truth according to the Sāṁkhya (the path of knowledge). Listen now to the teaching of Yoga (the path of selfless action combined with devotion)[5] by practising which the bondage of Karma is overcome.

नेहाभिक्रम-नाशोऽस्ति प्रत्यवायो न विद्यते ।
स्वल्पमप्यस्य धर्मस्य त्रायते महतो भयात् ॥ 40 ॥

n'eh'ābhikrama-nāśo'sti pratyavāyo na vidyate
svalpam apy asya dharmasya trāyate mahato bhayāt ॥ 40 ॥

Iha : Here, in this path of Yoga *abhikramanāśaḥ* : loss due to incomplete effort *na asti* : does not exist. *Pratyavāyaḥ* : sin due to failure *na vidyate* : does not accrue. *Asya dharmasya* : of this

Dharma *svalpam api* : even a little *mahataḥ* : from great *bhayāt* : fear *trāyate* : rescues.

40. In this path of Yoga — the path of selfless action combined with devotion — no effort is lost due to incompleteness and no contrary effect of an adverse nature is produced due to failures. Even a little observance of this discipline saves one from great fear.

व्यवसायात्मिका बुद्धि-रेकेह कुरुनन्दन ।
बहुशाखा ह्यनन्ताश्च बुद्धयोऽव्यवसायिनाम् ॥ 41 ॥

Vyavasāy'ātmikā buddhir ek'eha Kuru-nandana
bahu-śākhā hy anantāś-ca buddhayo'vyavasāyinām ॥ 41 ॥

Kurunandana : O Arjuna : *iha* : in this (path of selfless action) *vyavasāyāatmikā buddhiḥ* : the understanding or determinative faculty which produces conviction *eka* : rests in a single objective. *Avyavasāyinām* : In men without conviction (in the spiritual verity) *buddhayaḥ* : intelligence *bahuśākhāḥ* : many-branched *anantāḥ ca*: and endless.

41. O Arjuna! In those following this path, the Buddhi (the understanding) that has the nature of producing conviction, is directed towards a single objective. In those without any spiritual conviction, the understanding gets scattered and pursues countless ends.

यामिमां पुष्पितां वाचं प्रवदन्त्यविपश्चितः ।
वेदवादरताः पार्थ नान्यदस्तीति-वादिनः ॥ 42 ॥

कामात्मानः स्वर्गपरा जन्मकर्म-फलप्रदाम् ।
क्रियाविशेष-बहुलां भोगैश्वर्यगतिं प्रति ॥ 43 ॥

भोगैश्वर्य-प्रसक्तानां तयापहृत-चेतसाम् ।
व्यवसायात्मिका बुद्धिः समाधौ न विधीयते ॥ 44 ॥

Yām imāṁ puṣpitāṁ vācaṁ pravadanty avipaścitaḥ
vedavāda-ratāḥ Pārtha nānyad astīti vādinaḥ ॥ 42 ॥

Kām'ātmānaḥ svarga-parāḥ janma-karma-phalapradām
kriyā-viśeṣa-bahulāṁ bhog'aiśvarya-gatiṁ prati ॥ 43 ॥

Bhog'aiśvarya-prasaktānāṁ tayā'pahṛta-cetasām
vyavasāy'ātmikā buddhiḥ samādhau na vidhīyate ॥ 44 ॥

Pārtha : O Arjuna! *Vedavādaratāḥ* : those who delight in the eulogistic statements of the Vedas *na anyat asti* : there is nothing but that *iti vādinaḥ* : who argue like this, *kāmātmānaḥ* : who have their mind full of desires, *svargaparāḥ* : who look upon heaven as the highest end, *avipaścitaḥ* : (those) foolish men, *bhogaiśvarya gatim prati* : which are directed towards the attainment of enjoyments and power, *janmakarma phalapradām* : which yield rebirth as the fruit of actions, *Kriyā viśeṣa bahulām*: which are full of descriptions of ritualistic works *puṣpitām yām imām vācam* : whichever florid texts *pravadanti* : expatiate upon *tayā* : by them *apahṛta-cetasām*: with their minds stolen away *bhogaiśvarya-prasaktānām*: those who are full of cravings for enjoyments and power *samādhau* : in the mind *vyavasāyātmikā buddhiḥ* : steadfast wisdom *na vidhīyate* : is not established.

42-44. O Arjuna! There are people who delight in the eulogistic statements of the Vedas and argue that the purport of the Vedas consists in these and nothing else. They are full of worldly desires; paradise is their highest goal; and they are totally blind in a spiritual sense. They expatiate upon those florid Vedic texts which describe the means for the attainment of pleasure and power, which provide attractive embodiments as the fruits of actions, and which are full of descriptions of rites and rituals (through which these fulfilments are obtained). In the minds of these votaries of pleasure and power, addicted to enjoyments of the above description, steadfast wisdom (capable of revealing the Truth) is never generated. [7]

त्रैगुण्य-विषया वेदा निस्त्रैगुण्यो भवार्जुन ।
निर्द्वन्द्वो नित्य-सत्त्वस्थो निर्योगक्षेम आत्मवान् ॥ 45 ॥

Traiguṇya viṣayā vedā nistraiguṇyo bhavārjuna
nirdvandvo nitya-sattvastho niryogakṣema ātmavān ॥ 45 ॥

Arjuna : O Arjuna! *vedāḥ* : the Vedas *traiguṇya viṣayāḥ* : deal with the three dispositions (Guṇas) of Nature—Sattva, Rajas and Tamas, *Tvam* : you *nistraiguṇyaḥ* : beyond the influence of the three Guṇas *nirdvandvaḥ*:beyond the pair of opposites (like pain and pleasure, heat and cold etc). *nityasattvasthaḥ* : ever steady in purity *niryogakṣemaḥ* : unmindful of acquiring and preserving *ātmavān* : established in the spirit.

45. O Arjuna! The Vedas deal with material ends. But you be established in the Spirit, in the immutable purity of it, having abandoned all material values, attachment to possessions and concern with the contraries of life like pleasure and pain, heat and cold. [8]

यावानर्थं उदपाने सर्वतः संप्लुतोदके ।
तावान् सर्वेषु वेदेषु ब्राह्मणस्य विजानतः ॥ 46 ॥

Yāvān artha udapāne sarvataḥ samplut'odake
tāvān sarveṣu vedeṣu brāhmaṇasya vijānataḥ ॥ 46 ॥

Sarvataḥ : Everywhere *samplutodake* : flooded with water *udapāne* : in a small water receptacle (pond) *yāvān* : as much *arthaḥ*: use *vijānataḥ* : of the knowing *brāhmaṇasya* : for a Brāhmaṇa *sarveṣu Vedeṣu* : in all Vedas *tāvān* : that much.

46. What use a pond has got when a whole country is flooded, that much use only the Veda has got to a Brāhmaṇa who is full of wisdom. [9]

कर्मण्येवाधिकारस्ते मा फलेषु कदाचन ।
मा कर्मफलहेतुर्भू-र्मा ते सङ्गोऽस्त्वकर्मणि ॥ 47 ॥

Karmaṇy ev'ādhikāras te mā phaleṣu kadācana
mā karma-phala-hetur bhūr mā te saṅgo'stv akarmaṇi ||47||

Te : Your *adhikāraḥ* : competence *karmaṇi eva* : in action only *kadācana* : ever *phaleṣu mā* : should not be in fruits. *Karma phala-hetuḥ* : with fruits of action as the motive force *mā bhūḥ* : should not be. *Akarmaṇi* : in inaction *te* : your *saṅgaḥ* : **attachment** *mā astu* : let not be.

47. To work alone you have competence, and not to claim their fruits. Let not the longing for fruits be the motive force of your action. At the same time let not this attitude confirm you in indolent inaction. [10]

योगस्थः कुरु कर्माणि सङ्गं त्यक्त्वा धनञ्जय ।
सिद्ध्यसिद्ध्योः समो भूत्वा समत्वं योग उच्यते ॥ 48 ॥

Yogasthaḥ kuru karmāṇi saṅgaṁ tyaktvā dhanañjaya
siddhy-asiddhyoḥ samo bhūtvā samatvaṁ yoga ucyate ||48||

Dhanañjaya: O Arjuna! *tvam* : you *yogasthaḥ* : with mind steadfast in Yoga *saṅgam* : attachment *tyaktvā* : abandoning *siddhyasiddh-yoḥ* : in success and failure *samaḥ bhūtvā* : being alike *karmāṇi kuru* do actions. *Samatvam* : evenness of mind *yogaḥ* (*iti*) *ucyate* : is called **Yoga.**

48. Engage yourself in action with the mind steadfast in Yoga. Abandon attachments, O Arjuna, and be unperturbed in success and failure. This unperturbed sameness in all conditions is Yoga.

दूरेण ह्यवरं कर्म बुद्धियोगा-द्धनञ्जय ।
बुद्धौ शरणमन्विच्छ कृपणाः फलहेतवः ॥ 49 ॥

Dūreṇa hy avaraṁ karma buddhi-yogād dhanañjaya
buddhau śaraṇam anviccha kṛpaṇāḥ phala-hetavaḥ ||49||

Dhanañjaya : O Arjuna! *buddhiyogāt* : than action done with the Buddhi (intellect, mind) held in Yoga (evenness) *karma* : mere action *dūreṇa* : far *avaram hi* : inferior indeed. *Buddhau* : In unperturbed sameness of mind *śaraṇam* : refuge *anviccha* : seek. *Phalahetavaḥ* : One whose motive is the fruits of one's action *kṛpaṇāḥ* : pitiable.

49. O Arjuna, mere action (with attachment) is far inferior to action done with the mind poised in evenness. Seek shelter in this state of unperturbed evenness (which can arise only in a desireless mind in communion with the Divine). Those who work for selfish gains are indeed pitiable.

बुद्धियुक्तो जहातीह उभे सुकृतदुष्कृते ।
तस्माद्योगाय युज्यस्व योगः कर्मसु कौशलम् ॥ 50 ॥

Buddhiyukto jahātī'ha ubhe sukṛta-duṣkṛte
tasmād yogāya yujyasva yogaḥ karmasu kauśalam ॥ 50 ॥

Buddhiyuktaḥ : One endowed with unperturbed evenness of mind *ubhe* : both *sukṛtaduṣkṛte* : good and bad actions *iha* here *jahāti* : abandons. *Tasmāt* : Therefore *yogāya* : for this state of Yoga *yujyasva* : strive. *Yogaḥ* : Yoga *karmasu* : in action *kauśalam* : skill.

50. One endowed with this unperturbed evenness of mind abandons the effects of both good and bad actions even here itself. Therefore strive for this state of Yoga. Yoga is skill in action.

कर्मजं बुद्धियुक्ता हि फलं त्यक्त्वा मनीषिणः ।
जन्मबन्धविनिर्मुक्ताः पदं गच्छन्त्यनामयम् ॥ 51 ॥

Karmajaṁ buddhi-yuktā hi phalaṁ tyaktvā manīṣiṇaḥ
janma-bandha-vinirmuktāḥ padaṁ gacchanty anām-
ayam ॥ 51 ॥

Buddhiyuktāḥ : Those endowed with unpertured evenness of mind *manīṣiṇaḥ* : wise men *karmajam* : born of action *phalam* : fruits *tyaktvā* : having abandoned *janma bandha vinirmuktāḥ* : free from entanglement in the cycle of births and deaths *anāmayam* : free from sorrow *padam* : state *gacchanti* attain to.

51. Wise men, established thus in the unperturbed evenness of mind, abandon the fruits of action, free themselves from entanglement in the cycle of births and deaths, and attain to the state of freedom from all sorrow (liberation).

यदा ते मोहकलिलं बुद्धि-र्व्यतितरिष्यति ।
तदा गन्तासि निर्वेदं श्रोतव्यस्य श्रुतस्य च ॥ 52 ॥

Yadā te moha-kalilaṁ buddhir vyatitariṣyati
tadā gantā'si nirvedaṁ śrotavyasya śrutasya ca ॥ 52 ॥

Yadā : When : *te* your *buddhiḥ* : understanding *mohakalilam* : evil of delusion *vyatitariṣyati* : crosses beyond, *tadā* : then *śrotavyasya* : what has yet to be heard (i. e. experiences yet to be had) *śrutasya ca* : what has already been heard (i.e. experiences already undergone) *nirvedam* : indifference *gantāsi* : will attain to.

52. When you have overcome the delusions of your understanding sprung from self-centred attachments, then you will attain to a state of indifference towards all the past experiences and for the others yet to be had. [11]

श्रुति-विप्रतिपन्ना ते यदा स्थास्यति निश्चला ।
समाधावचला बुद्धिस्तदा योगमवाप्स्यसि ॥ 53 ॥

Śruti-vipratipannā te yadā sthāsyati niścalā
samādhāv acalā buddhiḥ tadā yogam avāpsyasi ॥ 53 ॥

Śrutivipratipannā : Distracted by various scriptural doctrines *te* : your *buddhiḥ* : intellect *yadā* : when *niścalā* : steady, firm *samādhau*: in Samadhi (introspection; Atman) *acalā* : unwavering *sthāsyati*: will remain *tadā* : then *yogam* : true Yoga *avāpsyasi* : will attain.

53. When your intellect, fed up with the bewildering scriptural doctrines and their interpretations, settles (finally) in steady and unwavering introspection (in the spirit), then you will attain to real Yoga.[12]

अर्जुन उवाच

स्थितप्रज्ञस्य का भाषा समाधिस्थस्य केशव।
स्थितधीः किं प्रभाषेत किमासीत व्रजेत किम् ॥ 54 ॥

Arjuna uvāca

Sthita-prajñasya kā bhāṣā samādhi-sthasya Keśava
sthita-dhīḥ kiṁ prabhāṣeta kim āsīta vrajeta kim ॥ 54 ॥

Arjuna said:

Keśava : O Kesava! *sthitaprajñasya* : of a man of steady wisdom *samadhisthasya* : of one of deep introspection *bhāṣā kā* :what is the description. *Sthitadhīḥ* : A man of steady wisdom *kim prabhaṣeta* : how does he speak? *Kim asīta* : how does he sit? *Kim vrajeta* : how does he walk?

54. O Kesava! What is the description of a person who has attained to steady wisdom and deep introspection? How does he speak? How does he sit? How does he walk? (How does he behave in life in general ?)

प्रजहाति यदा कामान् सर्वान् पार्थ मनोगतान्।
आत्मन्येवात्मना तुष्टः स्थितप्रज्ञ-स्तदोच्यते ॥ 55 ॥

Srī Bhagavān uvāca

Prajahāti yadā kāmān sarvān Pārtha mano-gatān
ātmany evātmanā tuṣṭaḥ sthita-prajñas tado'cyate ॥ 55 ॥

The Blessed Lord Said

Pārtha : O Son of Prithā! *yadā* : when *manogatān* : contained in the mind *sarvān kāmān* : all desires *prajahāti* : abandons *yadā* : when *ātmanā* : by the Atman *ātmani eva* : in the Atman only *tuṣṭaḥ* : satisfied, *tadā* : then *sthitaprajñaḥ* : a man of steady wisdom *ucyate*: one is spoken of as.

55. O Son of Prithā! When all the desires of the heart have been abandoned, and the Spirit finds joyous satisfaction in Itself (without dependence on any external factor) — then is one spoken of as a person of steady wisdom.

श्री भगवानुवाच—

दुःखेष्वनुद्विग्नमनाः सुखेषु विगतस्पृहः ।
वीतरागभयक्रोधः स्थितधी-र्मुनिरुच्यते ॥ 56 ॥

Duḥkheṣu anudvigna-manāḥ sukheṣu vigata-spṛhaḥ
vīta-rāga-bhayakrodhaḥ sthita-dhīr munir ucyate ॥ 56 ॥

Duḥkheṣu : In suffering *anudvignamanāḥ* : with mind not agitated, *sukheṣu* : in pleasure *vigataspṛhaḥ* : without desire, *vitarāga bhayakrodhaḥ* : devoid of attachment, fear and anger, *muniḥ* : a sage *sthitadhīḥ* : steady-minded *ucyate* is called.

56. Whose mind is not agitated in adversity, who is free from desire, and who is devoid of attachments, fear and anger—such a person is called a sage of steady wisdom.

यः सर्वत्रानभिस्नेह-स्तत्तत्प्राप्य शुभाशुभम् ।
नाभिनन्दति न द्वेष्टि तस्य प्रज्ञा प्रतिष्ठिता ॥ 57 ॥

Yaḥ sarvatr'ānabhisnehas tat-tat prāpya śubh'āśubham
n'ābhinandati na dveṣṭi tasya prajñā pratiṣṭhitā ॥ 57 ॥

Yaḥ : Who *sarvatra* : everywhere *anabhisnehaḥ* : without self-centred affections *tat tat* : whatever *śubhāśubham* : good and evil (favourable and unfavourable situations) *na abhinandati* : rejoices not *na dveṣṭi* : hates not *tasya* : his *prajñā* : wisdom *pratiṣṭhitā* : is firmly set.

57. Whoever is without self-centred affection for anything, who rejoices not in favourable situations and hates not in unfavourable ones — such a person's wisdom is firmly set.

5

यदा संहरते चायं कूर्मोऽङ्गानीव सर्वशः।
इन्द्रियाणीन्द्रियार्थेभ्य-स्तस्य प्रज्ञा प्रतिष्ठिता ॥ 58 ॥

Yadā samharate cāyaṁ kūrmo'ṅgāni'va sarvaśaḥ
indriyāṇi'ndriy'ārthebhyas tasya prajñā pratiṣṭhitā ॥ 58 ॥

Kūrmaḥ : Tortoise *sarvaśaḥ* : on all sides *aṅgāni iva* : like its limbs *ayam* : he *indriyārthebhyaḥ* : from objects of senses *indriyāṇi* : organs *yadā* : when *samharate ca* : withdraws *tasya* : his *prajñā* : wisdom *pratiṣṭhitā* : is firmly set.

58. When a person can withdraw his senses from their objects just like the tortoise its limbs on all sides, his wisdom is firmly set.

विषया विनिवर्तन्ते निराहारस्य देहिनः।
रसवर्जं रसोऽप्यस्य परं दृष्ट्वा निवर्तते ॥ 59 ॥

Viṣayā vinivartante nirāhārasya dehinaḥ
rasa-varjaṁ raso' py asya paraṁ dṛṣṭvā nivartate ॥ 59 ॥

Nirāhārasya : Of the abstinent *dehinaḥ* : embodied soul (Jīva) *rasavarjam* : barring the taste : *vinivartante* : fall away. *Asya* : His *rasaḥ api* : even taste *param* : the Supreme Truth *dṛṣṭvā* : having seen (known) *nivartate* : falls away.

59. From the abstinent soul sense objects fall away, but not the taste for them. When the Supreme Truth is realised, even the taste departs.[13]

यततो ह्यपि कौन्तेय पुरुषस्य विपश्चितः।
इन्द्रियाणि प्रमाथीनि हरन्ति प्रसभं मनः ॥ 60 ॥

Yatato hy api Kaunteya puruṣasya vipaścitaḥ
indriyāṇi pramāthīni haranti prasabhaṁ manaḥ ॥ 60 ॥

Hi : Indeed! *Kaunteya* : O Son of Kunti *yatataḥ* : the striving *vipaścitaḥ* : the discerning *puruṣasya* : of the man *manaḥ* : mind *api* : even *pramāthīni* : turbulent *indriyāṇi* : senses *prasabham* : violently *haranti* : draw away.

60. O son of Kuntī! The turbulent senses do violently draw away the mind of even a discerning person who is earnestly striving in the spiritual path.

तानि सर्वाणि संयम्य युक्त आसीत मत्परः ।
वशे हि यस्येन्द्रियाणि तस्य प्रज्ञा प्रतिष्ठिता ॥ 61 ॥

Tāni sarvāṇi saṁyamya yukta āsīta mat-paraḥ
vaśe hi yas'yendriyāṇi tasya prajñā pratiṣṭhitā ॥ 61 ॥

Tāni sarvāṇi : All of them *saṁyamya* : having controlled *yuktaḥ* : steadfast *matparaḥ* : wholly devoted to Me *āsīta* : should remain *yasya* : whose *indriyāṇi* : senses *vaśe hi* : are under control *tasya* : his *prajñā* : wisdom *pratiṣṭhitā* : is firmly set.

61. Having controlled them all, one should become entirely devoted to Me. He whose senses are under control, his wisdom is firmly set.

ध्यायतो विषयान् पुंसः सङ्गस्तेषूपजायते ।
सङ्गात् सञ्जायते कामः कामात् क्रोधोऽभिजायते ॥ 62 ॥

Dhyāyato viṣayān puṁsaḥ saṅgas teṣū'pajāyate
saṅgāt saṁjāyate kāmaḥ kāmāt krodho' bhijāyate ॥ 62 ॥

Viṣayān : Sense objects *dhyāyataḥ* : dwelling longingly in the mind *puṁsaḥ* : of one *teṣu* : for them *saṅgaḥ* : attachment, inclination towards *upajāyate* : arises, *saṅgāt* : out of inclination *kāmaḥ* : desire *saṁjāyate* : is born, *kāmāt* : out of desire *krodhaḥ* : anger *abhijāyate* : grows.

62. In one who dwells longingly on sense objects, an inclination towards them is generated. This inclination develops into desire, and desire begets anger.

क्रोधाद्भवति संमोहः संमोहात् स्मृतिविभ्रमः ।
स्मृतिभ्रंशाद् बुद्धिनाशो बुद्धिनाशात् प्रणश्यति ॥ 63 ॥

Krodhād bhavati saṁmohaḥ sammohāt smṛti-vibhramaḥ
smṛti-bhraṁśād buddhi-nāśo buddhi-nāśāt praṇaśyati ॥63॥

Krodhāt : Out of anger *sammohaḥ* : delusion, *sammohat* : out of delusion *smṛti-vibhramaḥ* : loss of memory, *smṛti-bhraṁśat* : from loss of memory *buddhi nāśaḥ* : ruin of the discriminative power, understanding *buddhināśāt* : from ruin of understanding *praṇaśyati* : one is destroyed.

63. Anger generates delusion, and delusion results in loss of memory. Loss of memory brings about the destruction of discriminative intelligence, and loss of discriminative intelligence spells ruin to a man. [14]

रागद्वेष-वियुक्तैस्तु विषया-निन्द्रियैश्चरन् ।
आत्मवश्यै-र्विधेयात्मा प्रसाद-मधिगच्छति ॥ 64 ॥

Rāga-dveṣa-viyuktais tu viṣayān indriyaiś caran
ātma-vaśyair vidhey'ātmā prasādam adhigacchati ॥ 64 ॥

Tu: But *vidheyātmā*: one with a disciplined mind *rāgadveṣaviyuktaiḥ*: devoid of attachment and aversion *ātmavaśyaiḥ indriyaiḥ* : with senses under one's control *viṣayān caran* : approaching sense objects *prasādam adhigacchati* : attains serenity, tranquillity.

64. A man of disciplined mind, who has his senses under control and who has neither attraction nor aversion for sense objects, attains tranquillity, though he may be moving amidst objects of the senses.

प्रसादे सर्वदुःखानां हानि-रस्योपजायते ।
प्रसन्न-चेतसो ह्याशु बुद्धिः पर्यवतिष्ठते ॥ 65 ॥

Prasāde sarva-duḥkhānām hānir asyo'pajāyate
prasanna-cetaso hy āśu buddhiḥ paryavatiṣṭhate ॥ 65 ॥

Prasāde : On attaining tranquillity (serenity) *asya* : his *sarvaduḥkhānām* : of all sorrows *hāniḥ* : end, destruction *upajāyate* : takes place. *hi* : for *prasannacetasaḥ* : of the man of tranquillity *buddhiḥ* : intellect *āśu* : quickly *paryavatiṣṭhate* : remains steady.

65. On attaining tranquillity all one's sorrows come to an end. For soon does the intellect of a tranquil person become steady.

नास्ति बुद्धिरयुक्तस्य न चायुक्तस्य भावना ।
न चाभावयतः शान्ति-रशान्तस्य कुतः सुखम् ॥ 66 ॥

Nāsti buddhir ayuktasya na c'ā yuktasya bhāvanā
na cā bhāvayataḥ śāntir aśāntasya kutaḥ sukham ॥ 66 ॥

Ayuktasya : Of the uncontrolled *buddhiḥ na asti* : faith or spiritual comprehension does not exist, *ayuktasya* : of the uncontrolled *bhāvanī ca na* : there is no meditation also, *abhāvayataḥ* : for the unmeditative *śāntiḥ ca na* : there is no peace, *aśāntasya*: of the one without peace *kutaḥ* : wherefrom *sukham* : happiness.

66. A man of uncontrolled senses has no spiritual comprehension. He has no capacity for meditation either. For the unmeditative there is no peace. And where is happiness for one without peace of mind? [15]

इन्द्रियाणां हि चरतां यन्मनोऽनुविधीयते ।
तदस्य हरति प्रज्ञां वायु-र्नावमिवांभसि ॥ 67 ॥

Indriyāṇāṁ hi caratāṁ yan mano'nuvidhīyate
tad asya harati prajñāṁ vāyur nāvām ivāmbhasi ॥ 67 ॥

Caratām : Moving, wandering *indriyāṇām* : among the senses *yat* : whichever *manaḥ* : mind *anuvidhīyate* : follows, *tat* : that *asya* : of that mind *prajñām* : discriminative power *ambhasi* : upon the waters *nīvam* : ship *vāyuḥ iva* : like wind *harati hi* : carries off.

67. The senses are naturally disposed to move towards their objects. Whichever of these senses the mind pursues, that sense carries away that mind as a gale does a ship on the high seas.

तस्माद्यस्य महाबाहो निगृहीतानि सर्वशः ।
इन्द्रियाणीन्द्रियार्थेभ्य-स्तस्य प्रज्ञा प्रतिष्ठिता ॥ 68 ॥

Tasmād yasya mahā-bāho nigṛhītāni sarvaśah
indriyāṇi'ndriy'ārthebhyas tasya prajñā pratiṣṭhitā ॥68॥

Mahābāho : O mighty Arjuna! *tasmāt* : therefore *yasya* : whose *indriyāṇi* : senses *sarvaśaḥ* : completely *indriyārthebhyaḥ* : from all sense objects *nigṛhitāni* : are restrained *tasya* : his *prajñā* : wisdom *pratiṣṭhitā* : is firmly set.

68. Therefore, O mighty Arjuna, he who could completely restrain his senses from pursuing their objects, has his wisdom firmly set.

या निशा सर्वभूतानां तस्यां जागर्ति संयमी।
यस्यां जाग्रति भूतानि सा निशा पश्यतो मुनेः॥ 69॥

Yā niśā sarva-bhūtānām tasyām jāgarti saṁyamī
yasyām jāgrati bhūtāni sā niśā paśyato muneḥ ‖ 69 ‖

Sarvabhūtānām : Of all beings *yā niśā* : what is night *tasyām* : in that *saṁyamī* : the self-controlled one *jāgarti* : is awake. *Yasyām* In what *bhūtāni* : all beings *jāgrati* : are awake *sā* : that *paśyataḥ* enlightened *muneḥ* : of the sage *niśā* : night.

69. What is like night to all ignorant beings, to that Atman-consciousness the self-controlled sage is awake; and the sensate life to which all ignorant beings are awake, that is like night to this illumined sage.

आपूर्यमाण-मचलप्रतिष्ठं-समुद्रमापः प्रविशन्ति यद्वत्।
तद्वत्कामा यं प्रविशन्ति सर्वे स शान्ति-माप्नोति न कामकामी॥

Āpūryamāṇam acala-pratiṣṭhaṁ samudram āpaḥ
praviśanti yadvat
tadvat kāmā yaṁ praviśanti sarve sa śāntim āpnoti na
kāma-kāmī ‖ 70 ‖

Āpūryamāṇam : Ever being filled, *acalapratiṣṭham* : immobile and steady *samudram* : sea *āpaḥ* : waters *yadvat* : in what way *praviśanti* : enter *tadvat* : in that way *sarve kāmāḥ* : all desires *yam* : in whom *praviśanti* : enter *saḥ* : he *śāntim* : peace *āpnoti* : attains, *na*: not *kāmakāmī* : one who longs for objects of desire.

70. He into whom all objects of desire enter (unsought and causing no perturbation), even like the ocean that is ever being filled by the rivers but still remains steady within its bounds — such a person attains to peace, not he who runs madly after objects of desire.

विहाय कामान् यः सर्वान् पुमांश्चरति निस्पृहः ।
निर्ममो निरहङ्कारः स शान्ति-मधिगच्छति ॥ 71 ॥

Vihāya kāmān yaḥ sarvān pumāṁś carati niḥspṛhaḥ
nirmamo nirahaṁkāraḥ sa śāntim adhigacchati ॥ 71 ॥

Yaḥ : Whichever *pumān* : man *sarvān* : all *kāmān* : desires *vihāya*: abandoning *niḥspṛhaḥ* : without longing *nirmamaḥ* : without the feeling of 'mine' *nirahaṅkāraḥ* : without the sense of 'I' *carati* : goes about *saḥ* : he *śāntim* : peace *adhigacchati* : attains.

71. Whoever has abandoned desires, and moves about without attachments and the sense of 'I' and 'mine' — he attains to peace.

एषा ब्राह्मी स्थितिः पार्थ नैनां प्राप्य विमुह्यति ।
स्थित्वास्या मन्तकालेऽपि ब्रह्मनिर्वाण-मृच्छति ॥ 72 ॥

Eṣā brāhmī sthitiḥ Pārtha n'aināṁ prāpya vimuhyati
sthitvā'syām antakāle'pi brahma-nirvāṇam ṛcchati ॥ 72 ॥

Pārtha : O son of Pritha! *brāhmī sthitiḥ* : state of dwelling in Brahman *eṣā* : this is. *Enām prāpya* : Attaining to this state *na vimuhyati*: is not deluded; *antakāle api* : even at the end of one's life *asyām* therein *sthitvā* : abiding *brahmanirvāṇam* : oneness with Brahman *ṛcchati* : attains

72. This, O son of Prithā, is the state of dwelling in Brahman. Having attained it, one is no more deluded. By abiding in that state even by the time of death, one is united with Brahman.

इति श्रीमद्भगवद्गीतासूपनिषत्सु ब्रह्मविद्यायां योगशास्त्रे
श्रीकृष्णार्जुनसंवादे सांख्ययोगो नाम
द्वितीयोऽध्यायः ॥

NOTES

1. *Vr.* 3: This is an exhortation following the Gospel of Spiritual Strength based on the philosophy of the immortal Ātman as the Essence in man. So long as man feels he is the body and nothing but the body, he lives in fear and sorrow. He stands up in real strength, shaking off all fear and sorrow, when his sense of individuality is shifted from the body to the Spirit. This verse expresses concisely the practical consequences of accepting the doctrine of the Ātman expounded in the succeeding verses of the chapter.

2. *Vr.* 16: This and the verses preceding it up to the 12th and those succeeding up to the 25th, deal with the topic of the immortality of the Ātman, the Essence in man. A general principle in support of the doctrine is laid down in this verse. If we take the words Sat and Asat as real and unreal, and Bhāva and Abhāva as existence and non-existence literally as logical contradictories, the sentence will only involve repetition, adding nothing to the problem posed. The Asat or the unreal cannot be totally non-existent like the horn of a hare which is only a wordy figment incapable of being experienced and there is no meaning in the denial of the 'coming into being' of such an entity. So the coming into being of Asat or non-entity, means the changing forms of things we experience. These forms are experienced but they disappear immediately and give place to new forms, which too disappear. These changing forms are called Asat, non-existent, in the sense that they have no ultimacy in themselves. They come and go, and if all the forms cease, they leave no residue, except Sat or Essence, the changeless Being, the substratum on which all forms appear. The Sat or Essence is Changeless Being, Awareness or Witness of change.

Now while a general philosophy of Being and Becoming can be spun out of the verse, the context limits the meaning of the term Sat to the Ātman in the human personality and Asat to the body-mind. The former is the changeless Awareness or Witness, the Essence in man, while the latter is the changeful body which the Ātman assumes when He is embodied. Now in the embodied state the Ātman appears to be one with the body, just as the light within several coloured glasses seem to be one with the glasses in spite of its distinct identity, or just as electricity appears as one with the field in which it manifests for the time being, in spite of its distinction from the field. After all man, when he thinks of himself, can do so only as a body-mind and nothing more. This is the state of ignorance, when man is not aware of his real nature as the Sat, the Ātman, but feels his self-hood entirely in the Asat, the body-mind. The *Tattvadarsī* (Truth-seer or philosopher) spoken of in the verse is the man of enlightenment who has succeeded in distinguishing between these and recognising his true identity with the immortal Ātman whose nature is graphically described in several passages as 'Him the weapons cleave not' etc. What is required of a *Tattvadarsī* is not a mere intellectual understanding but an intuitive conviction which is expressed in life as the capacity for detachment that is described in the section on Sthita-prajña or man of steady intelligence.

On the subject of the Asat or the body, one has to keep in mind the distinction between the Sukṣma-śarīra (subtle body) and the Sthūlaśarīra (the gross body). The gross body is the one that changes from birth to birth. So it is compared to changing of dress. The analogy is used to show the absolute discontinuity, the catastrophic break that marks physical death. But the other body, the subtle body or Sūkṣma-śarīra in which the Prāṇas (vital forces), mind, intellect, and the ego are integrated, survives, carrying all the Karma-efficiencies created in one life to the next. It is because of the Sūkṣma-śarīra that re-embodiment becomes possible. So in respect of Sukṣma-śarīra there is continuity from birth to birth. But when the enlightenment comes and the Jīva realises his real identity as the Ātman, the Sukṣma-śarīra also perishes. This marks the real Death which is the door to Immortality. Death in this sense is also catastrophic in that it brings enlightenment, whereas in physical death it is catastrophic at the physical level only; what follows is only another embodiment.

In these verses the Immortal Self and the Sūkṣma-śarīra continuing from body to body are indiscriminately alluded to, as they go together in the Jīva, the embodied being. Reference to this Immortal Self will be seen in verses such as 12, 19, 20, 21, 24, 25 etc., and the references to the continuing Sūkṣma-sarīra in verses such as 13 and 22.

In this context, the analysis of the human personality according to the Vedānta may be stated. The human personality has three bodies consisting of five sheaths or Kośas. These Kośas are: Annamaya-kośa or Gross body; Prāṇamaya-kośa or Vitalistic sheath; Manomaya-kośa or mental sheath; Vijñānamaya-kośa or intellectual sheath; and Ānandamaya-kośa, or the sheath of bliss. The Ātman, the spiritual Self, which is by nature Existence-Consciousness-Bliss, is clothed in these sheaths. It is the Ātman that endows the sheaths with the light of consciousness. Now these five sheaths are organised into two bodies — the Sthula-Śarīra, or the gross physical body, and the subtle body also known as the Linga-śarīrà. All the sheaths except the Annamaya-kośa, ensouled by the Ātman, constitute the Sukṣma-Sarīra, which parts from the gross body at death, carrying along with it all the tendencies and the merits and demerits acquired in life until it gets another embodiment in this earth-sphere or in any of the higher or lower spheres according to the Karma of the Jīva. The Jīva can enjoy the fruits of his Karma only with a gross body pertaining to this or any other sphere. In itself it is a carrier of the tendencies and merits and demerits acquired in previous embodiments. When enlightenment comes and the Ātman realises his spiritual nature as Existence-Knowledge-Bliss, he is freed from the union with the Sukṣma-śarīra, and the latter is dissolved into its elements. This is emancipation or Mukti.

3. *V.* 26-27: In these verses, the reference seems to be to some systems of philosophy like the Pūrva-mīmaṁsā which accepted an undying soul, the Ātman, but did not accept an ultimate Mukti or liberation for him. The Jīva acquires merits or demerits in this world, goes to heavenly or nether regions to enjoy their fruits and on the exhaustion of the merits or demerits comes again to the earth to acquire merits through Karma. He is never liberated. Enjoyment of heavenly felicities as a result of ritualistic and ethical actions done in life is the highest destiny of the Jīva. The continuity of the Jīva is accepted, as without it there will be nothing to conserve and enjoy the values generated by work. Arjuna is told that even if such a view of man different from that of the Vedantins is held, there is no cause for sorrow at death, as it will surely be followed by birth.

4. *V.* 28: This and the succeeding verse seem to refer to some school of naturalism, which accepts no immortal spirit. Death becomes a natural and no doubt a mysterious and unavoidable phenomenon.

5. *V.* 39. Sāṁkhya and Yoga are known in Indian philosophy as two allied systems having the same metaphysics but different methods of practice. Sāṁkhya is the intellectual analysis of the material categories, and the separating of Prakṛti from the Puruṣa, the spiritual monad. The system does not accept a God, a universal Being, who is the master of all spiritual monads and material categories. Salvation consists in the monad or Puruṣa getting isolation from the material categories with which it is integrated in the state of bondage. Intellectual analysis and reflection form the means for this. See Appendix for more information.

The Yoga has no metaphysics of its own but generally accepts the Sāṁkhya theory. But it concerns itself with various ways of inward concentration by which the ingathered mind can be made subtle enough to pierce the coverings of the spirit, and become aware of the spirit as distinct from its material vestments. Thus practically the Sāṁkhya, though having an identity of its own, is a metaphysics including the discipline of reflection or self-analysis leading to realisation. Yoga is the systematic practice of concentration by which the realisation of that metaphysical truth is attained.

In the Gītā passage under discussion, though this Sāṁkhya and Yoga nomenclatures are used, the words practically mean what in modern Vedandic parlance we call Jñāna-Yoga and Bhakti-mixed-Karma Yoga. So the verse has to be understood as meaning: I have given you the understanding, the conviction, which enlightenment (Jñāna or Sāṁkhya) gives of the real nature of man — of his Essence, the Atman. Now I shall declare to you another way of attaining it, the Yoga or Karma-mixed Bhakti, which consists in performing all actions without attachments as devoted offering to the Divine, and in practising love of Him and getting one's mind absorbed in Him through concentration (Samādhi). The idea is to cultivate devotion to God and dedicate oneself and all one's actions to Him, as His servant and devotee. If one practises this discipline in life, the Supreme Being bestows the knowledge of the devotee's true relation with His being—the awareness of being part and parcel of the Sat-chidānanda. Sri Ramakrishna illustrates this by an analogy. A very faithful servant serves his Master for long and pleases him immensely by his love and loyalty. The master, out of intense love and consideration for him, puts him on his own seat, saying 'You are myself; sit on it.' Just like that, supreme knowledge of one's spiritual identity (or intimacy) is what comes out of the Lord's grace for a Jīva who serves and surrenders to Him through love and service.

This surrender in early stages consists in cultivating the feeling that one is the servant of God and that everything one does is on His behalf and what accrues from it is His. Thus the purely self-centred motivation in life is changed with the aid of devotion. In the maturity of spiritual understanding even the sense of agency is given up and one is established in the conviction that one is a mere instrument and He is the real agent too. When surrender is complete, the Supreme Being bestows that illumination which makes the Sāṁkhya or Jñāna doctrine of man's spiritual identity as the Ātman, a real experience that one is the Spirit and not the body, and that death and all the infirmities of the body do not affect the Self. This experience may be interpreted as oneness with Him, or intimate kinship with Him.

5. *V.* 40: Spiritual practices may take a whole life-time or several lives to fructify as realisation. But an aspirant need not feel that the efforts he has put in this field are ever lost, unlike in agriculture and other such enterprises where one loses evey-thing if failure occurs due to drought or other causes. In the spiritual field the competence that one has acquired remains as tendencies in the subtle body, and in the next life one begins from where one left in the previous life.

There is another kind of defect in fruit-oriented action, especially of a ritualistic nature for the attainment of earthly or heavenly felicities. If they are done wrongly, one not only loses the fruits, but suffers adverse consequences, which are referred to in the text as *pratyavāya*. In the path of devotion, there is no such adverse effects for mistakes; for there are no mistakes or spiritual offences at all except want of faith. So *Srīmad Bhāgavata* speaks of this path of devotion as a well-paved high road along which one can even run blindfolded without any fear of fall.

6. *V.* 41: This gives the contrast between one who whole-heartedly follows the spiritual path and a wordly minded man who follows wealth, sensual satisfaction and ambition. A man who has a spiritual world-view, a firm faith in a Divine Intelligence based on the instruction of the scripture and the Guru, has got a fixed goal that does not vary. He is like a man who has a correct idea of the destination and has selected the correct road to it. He is therefore at peace, knowing, that he is on the right road. A worldly-minded man, on the other hand, may not often have a fixed world-view. He cares only for gains, enjoyments, and pursuit of ambitions. So without any conviction about the nature of the universe and his own destiny in it, he pursuses these diverse satisfactions, the objects of which change from time to

time. Hence the understanding of such a person gets many-branched, being engaged in the pursuit of several ends. His mental energies are thus dissipated, and he loses control of the mind and becomes a salve of the senses and their objects.

7. *V*. 42-44: The criticism offered here is intended to draw the distinction between the outlook of the new Gospel of Bhāgavata Dharma which Kṛṣṇa preached and the outlook of the Vedic fundamentalists who followed the philosophy of Vedic ritualism, which is known as the Purvamīmāṁsa system of thought. These ritualistic philosophers held that the purpose of the Veda is to induce man to perform rituals and fire sacrifices, which will gain him heavenly felicity. After death the Jīva will go to those heavenly regions where they will have the enjoyments of the fruits of the sacrifices they have performed. After the fruit-bearing effects of Karma are exhausted, the Jīva comes back to the earth to do more Karma enabling him to enjoy heavenly felicities again. Thus according to them, there is no salvation for the soul or getting out of Samsāra. The soul goes from embodiment to embodiment on earth and other spheres enjoying the fruits of his actions. Their outlook therefore multiplies man's desires and ambitions, and they justify this by quoting the Vedas as authority. In the nature of things, their mind becomes 'many branched' or divided by all kinds of passing desires. They have no conviction about the ultimate destiny of man beyond what has been stated. They are just like wanderers and vagabonds in the expansive field of life.

In contrast to them are the Sāṁkhyas and the Yogins. They have a spiritual world-view and a conviction regarding the ultimate destiny of man. They are free from desires. Their mind therefore gets unified following a single goal, unlike that of the ritualists whose mind becomes 'many-branched' because of their changing desires and objectives. That 'single goal' of the Sāṁkhyas and the Yogins is the realisation of one's spiritual nature as the Ātman and one's integral relation with the Supreme Being. The realisation of the truth puts an end to the transmigration of the Jīva and he becomes united with the Divine.

In this path of salvation also work as duty has a place. But all work, sacred or secular, has to be done as an offering to the Divine, and not for the attainment of heavenly felicities or any other type of enjoyments. The only result of it is purification of the mind and the dawn of the grace of God on the Jīva, by which he obtains illumination.

8. *V.* 45: In continuation of the thought of the previous verse the limitation of the philosophy of Vedic fundamentalists is again stated in the expression *traiguṇya viṣayāḥ* — connected with the three Guṇas of Prakṛti or Root-matter. Sattva, Rajas, and Tamas constitute Prakṛti or Root-matter. So the Veda as understood by the fundamentalists, deals only with matters material i.e. the life of the body, on earth and in heaven, as explained already. Arjuna is asked to accept the spiritual outlook *nistraiguṇya,* which sees in matter or Prakṛti, only the shadow of the Spirit. The implication of accepting the primacy of the Spirit is given in the second line of the verse.

It must be understood that these and similar verses are not a condemnation of the Veda but a criticism of it as understood and interpreted by the fundamentalists. Really the Bhāgavata Dharma which Kṛṣṇa teaches is included in the Vedānta, or the Upaniṣads, which teach the nature of Jīva and Brahman and the way for realising the Brahman and attaining release from Samsāra, which is identical with the teachings of Kṛṣṇa. But the fundamentalists reject the Upaniṣads or interpret them as subsidiary to the ritualistic philosophy. So Kṛṣṇa's criticism is directed against that way of thought, and his Bhāgavata Dharma is the correct re-statement of the Upaniṣadic thought with an emphasis on the practice of devotion and dedicated work as the royal road to God's grace and salvation.

9. *V.* 46: This a continuation of the criticism of Vedic fundamentalism. The bliss of Brahman attained through Jñāna and Bhakti, for which the Upaniṣads and the Bhāgavata Dharma stand, includes in itself all other fufilments like those that Vedic fundamentalism has in view, just as the lights of a few candles are

all included in the sun's light, or the waters of all the tanks in a place are merged in the water of a flood. Both candles and tank-water lose their significance in such situations.

10. *V.* 47-52: In these verses the ideal of Yoga as contrasted with the Sāṁkhya and the Vedic fundamentalism is stated. Sāṁkhya eschews work. Vedic fundamentalism advocates work for selfish purposes — the attainment of heavenly felicities. From here till the verse 52 is discussed the fundamental doctrine of the Bhāgavata Dharma, namely that of taking part in activities of life that form one's duty without desiring their fruits. This is unlike the attitude of Vedic fundamentalists and worldly minded people towards work. At the lowest level of the animal and the slave, work is the result of force or compulsion. At the higher level of a free man, it springs from profit motive — profit here or in other spheres in the hereafter.

When man grows out of his self-centred outlook, he gets a still higher motivation in occupations involving work for the community, country or humanity. But those who have a devotional outlook and want higher evolution, will find a satisfactory scheme of work only when work is dedicated to God, whether its immediate inducement is an individual or social concern. From the beginning to the end the Gītā teaches this scheme of devotion-oriented-work without desire for fruits. The fruits of work are offered to the Divine in the first instance and the sense of agency too at the maturity of spiritual life.

In reading this and the succeeding verses of the Gītā, it should be remembered that the even-sightedness or unperturbed state of mind is not to be had for the mere asking or wishing. It is the result of prolonged discipline and maturity of mind. It is an ideal state towards which we have to strive in our own imperfect way. Like an infant learning to walk, we may fail in our effort, but one has to persist in it in spite of such failure. Success will depend on the genuineness of our desirelessness, our discriminative endeavours, our earnestness to find a spiritual sanction for life, and our devotional fervour. As no hard and fast distinction can be made in spiritual life between the ideal and the actual, the end and the means, the ideal of Karma Yoga itself is stated at the beginning. The ideal of Yoga or absolutely unperturbed condition of mind can be actualised only when one has the realisation that one is the Ātman. This state and the state described by the Sāṁkhya — of being established in the Ātman that is not affected by any material change or impact — are identical. Thus it is seen how the Yoga shades off into the Sāṁkhya. Hence though they can be analysed into two disciplines, they are basically one. Their relation of mutual dependence is discussed in the 3rd chapter.

11. *V.* 52: This is the state of Vairāgya, the capacity to view objects of sense without any self-centred motives — capacity to view such objects suited for food, sex-enjoyment, possession etc., as they are in themselves, and not as objects catering to our needs. Unless we have this capacity to some extent at least, we shall be entirely under the grip of instinctive drives — a state of mind which is described here as delusion. To the extent we are free from this delusion or infatuation, to that extent our mind is fit for spiritual perceptions.

12. *V.* 53: Just as we should be free from the hold of the senses, we should be free from intellectual doubts of a dilettante nature, which result from casual reading and lack of a positive and serious intellectual attitude towards spiritual problems and scriptural study. Thus a moral and intellectual earnestness is the prime requisite for attaining that state of spiritual realisation described as the state of the Sthitaprajña or the perfect sage of steady understanding, described from verse 54 onwards.

13. *V.* 59: Keeping aloof scrupulously from objects of enjoyment is no ultimate remedy for the thirst for sensuous enjoyments. These instinctive urges and subtle hankerings continue to be in our mind and draw us away when they get the upper hand at some time or other. Only spiritual realisation, the experience that one is the Spirit and not the body, can uproot them completely. The word *Āhāra* also means food, and the passage can be interpreted to mean that a man who fasts may be

able to abstain from objects as the body becomes weak, but he cannot conquer the hankering for sense objects by such physical means. Spiritual enlightenment alone can do this.

14. *V.* 63: In this and the previous verses the cause of man's all-round degradation is pointed out. Giving oneself up to the cravings of the senses, without any effort to regulate, control and sublimate them, is that cause. Such a life reduces him to the level of animality, which is the meaning of *Buddhināśa* or loss of discriminative intelligence.

15. *V.* 66: Contrary to the popular view, sense control, and not sense indulgence, is the way to happiness. For, true happiness can be had only on a basis of peace, which one can have only through meditation on God or the Ātman. But meditation is impossible without control of the senses. For, sense indulgence strengthens the outward-going tendencies of the mind and prevents the mind from getting in-gathered and concentrated on the Ātman, who is the source of all joy.

Chapter III

कर्मयोगः

COMMUNION THROUGH ACTION

Summary

Conflct between work and Contemplation (1-2): Hearing the discourse on 'The Ideal of the man of steady wisdom', Arjuna's confusion only increases. If that state of inwardness and serenity depicted in the above ideal is the end for man to seek, how could its pursuit be reconciled with the life of action to which Kṛṣṇa has been simultaneously exhorting him, especially when that action is participation in a terrible holocaust like a fratricidal war? He therefore poses this question before Kṛṣṇa, and the rest of the chapter is Kṛṣṇa's answer to it.

The two paths : (3-8): Sri Kṛṣṇa said: Two ways of spiritual fulfilment have been revealed by Me — the Path of Knowledge (the Sāṁkhya) and the Path of Devotion-cum-Action (Yoga). They appear different, but as will be shown later, the difference is only apparent and they can be reconciled. But it is the Path of Action that now forms the subject of discourse.

By merely abstaining from actions, man does not gain that serenity of spirit, the unperturbed state of the *Sthitaprajña*. He will only be relapsing into idleness thereby. For one thing, it is impossible for any man to live for even a minute without any action; for, man is physically a part of Nature, and Nature is ever active. He is therefore compelled to act. So sitting quiet and thinking that one has attained to that unperturbed state of the spirit, will be rank hypocrisy. For, such a person's mind will be very busy thinking of the objects to which he is attached. So the way of spiritual development for him lies not in abstinence from action but only in action performed without attachments and under proper regulation of the senses.

The law of yajña: (9-18): God created man with the law of Yajña as the means for his worldly prosperity and for his higher spiritual evolution. Yajña means self-sacrifice — the offering of what one considers precious, for the service of God and one's fellow beings. If our fellow beings can be looked upon as the very tabernacle of the Divine — for God indwells everything and everything is, in that sense, the body of God — this service itself becomes the highest form of worship too. Yajña, at the lower levels, is one of give and take. Man lives in a community which can thrive only by the exchange of commodities and services among its members. Each gets certain services from others and gives back certain other services in return. One who fails to do his part of the work but insists on his getting his share of the good things of social life, is an exploiter and a thief. He violates the law of Yajña and gets morally degraded. Rights and duties therefore go together, and to claim the former without due insistence on the latter, begets corruption and decadence and leads to ruin ultimately. The Vedic fire sacrifice, where thanks-giving offerings are made to the Devas for the benefits that they have bestowed on man through Nature, is symbolic of this great law of life. Both the ritual Yajña, and Yajña in a social sense consisting in the discharge of one's duties to the body politic, are based on action. And one who gives up action will be abandoning Yajña too and thus violating the basic commandment of the Creator — the ethical law of a life of non-exploitation.

Enlightened Ones too should work: (19-26): There may, however, be some rare individuals who have risen above all personal wants. They may be able to withdraw themselves from society, and live a life of self-contentment without depending on the services of others. Even they should work without attachment or desire for the fruits of work. For, by so doing, one progresses spiritually and attains the Supreme Being. Just as socially-oriented work makes man ethical, work done without any thought of selfish gain, as an act of pure service of God and man, raises him to spiritual heights. Purely unselfish action without any thought of returns or obligations, is the higher aspect of the law of Yajña. So Janaka and other great Rajarṣis continued to be in the field of action and attained perfection through a life of disinterested action.

There is also another reason why all, including men of higher spiritual attainment, should work; for, otherwise they will be setting a bad example for unenlightened men, who, without a proper understanding of their mental state, would surely imitate their external behaviour, and relapse into abandonment of their duties, ending in pure idleness. A leader has always to be careful about the example he sets. Again look at Isvara Himself. He has no wants, but He is ever engaged in works for the sake of the Jīvas in Saṁsāra. So an enlightened man, though he might have risen above all considerations of self-interest, should work unattached and without any return in view, but at the same time evincing just the same zeal and energy with which a man desirous of selfish returns works. Otherwise he will be creating conflict of ideas and ideals among common people.

Wisdom is not to be confused with Inactivity: (27-35): The difference between the wise man and the ignorant man consists in this: the former is established in the experience that all actions that are supposed to be his, are only the movements of Prakṛti and that the 'real he', the Self, is only the uninvolved witness. The ignorant man, on the other hand, being absolutely involved in, and identified with, the movements of Prakṛti, feels that *he* is acting and enjoying. The way to attain detachment is not by keeping quiet without doing anything, but by discharging all one's duties, surrendering their fruits and the sense of agency to the Supreme Divine. Non-attached work (Karma Yoga) and discriminative understanding of one's basic nature as the 'unattached self' (Jñana Yoga) are not contradictory but complementary. For, non-attachment in work is impossible unless one practises simultaneously the understanding that one is basically the 'unattached self.' And, except in the case of a few rare aspirants, the practice of such discriminative understanding about the Self, without the support of unselfish work, will end only in pure idleness and failure to do one's duty. One who fails to do his duty and runs after ways of life that are alien to his inherent nature and aptitude, only incurs sin. For, to do what one ought to do, is virtue, and avoiding it out of idleness, or cupidity, or base passions, is sin.

What is Sin: (36-48) Arjuna thereupon asks the question why man commits sins, even though he may not want to. And Sri Kṛṣṇa answers: It is desire (lust) and anger that appear as sin and compel man to undesirable action. The seats of these passions are the senses, mind and intellect. So to avoid sin man must learn to control the senses first, but this cannot be achieved merely by suppression. One has to bring to bear the light of the Self, the Divine spark in one, on the intellect, mind and senses. Thus should one conquer man's great enemy sin, the combination of lust and anger.

अर्जुन उवाच—

ज्यायसी चेत्कर्मणस्ते मता बुद्धि-र्जनार्दन।
तत्किं कर्मणि घोरे मां नियोजयसि केशव ॥ 1 ॥

Arjuna uvāca;
Jyāyasī cet karmaṇas te matā buddhir, janārdana
tat kim karmaṇi ghore māṁ niyojayasi, keśava ॥ 1 ॥

Janārdana : O Kṛṣṇa! ***karmaṇaḥ*** than action ***buddhiḥ*** : discriminative insight *jyāyasī* : superior ***te*** : by you ***matā*** : considered ***cet*** if, ***tat kim*** then why *Keśava*: O Keśava ***ghore karmaṇi*** : in this terrible action (like war) ***mām*** : me ***niyojayasi*** engage.

Arjuna said :

1. O Janārdana, if, according to Thee, discriminative insight is superior to action, why dost Thou enjoin on me this terrible action (of engagement in war)? [1]

व्यामिश्रेणेव वाक्येन बुद्धिं मोहयसीव मे।
तदेकं वद निश्चित्य येन श्रेयोऽहमाप्नुयाम् ॥ 2 ॥

Vyāmiśrṇ'aiva vākyena buddhim mohayasīva me
tad ekam vada niścitya yena śreyo'ham āpnuyām ॥ 2 ॥

Vyāmiśreṇa : By conflicting *iva* seemingly *vākyena* : by words *me* : my *buddhim* : intellect *mohayasi* : you confuse. *Yena* : by what *aham* : I *śreyaḥ* : the highest good *āpnuyām* : attain to *tat* : that *ekam* alone *niścitya* : definitely *vada* : tell.

2. By seemingly conflicting words, Thou art confusing my understanding. Speak to me only about that which will definitely lead to my highest good.

श्रीभगवानुवाच—

लोकेऽस्मिन्द्विविधा निष्ठा पुरा प्रोक्ता मयानघ ।
ज्ञानयोगेन साङ्ख्यानां कर्मयोगेन योगिनाम् ॥ 3 ॥

Śrī Bhagavān uvāca :

Loke'smin dvividhā niṣṭhā purā proktā mayā'nagha
jñāna-yogena sāṁkhyānāṁ krama-yogena yoginām ॥ 3 ॥

Anagha : O sinless one! *asmin loke* : in this world *sāṁkhyānām* : for the sāṁkhyas (ascetic contemplatives) *jñānayogena* : by the path of knowledge *yoginām*: for Yogis (aspirants of an active nature) *karma-yogena* : by the path of action *dvividhā niṣṭhā* : twofold spiritual path *purā* : of yore *mayā* : by Me *proktā* : taught.

The Blessed Lord Said :

3. In times of yore a twofold spiritual path was taught by me, O sinless one — that of knowledge for Sāṁkhyas (who are pure contemplatives), and that of action for Yogis (who combine detached work with devotion). [2]

न कर्मणा-मनारम्भान्नैष्कर्म्यं पुरुषोऽश्नुते ।
न च संन्यसनादेव सिद्धिं समधिगच्छति ॥ 4 ॥

Na karmaṇām anārambhān naiṣkarmyaṁ puruṣo'śnute
na ca saṁnyasanād eva siddhiṁ samadhigacchati ॥ 4 ॥

Puruṣaḥ :Man *karmaṇām* : of actions *anārambhāt* : by non-performance *naiṣkarmyam* : state of egoless actionlessness (spiritual passivity) *na aśnute* : reaches not. *Saṁnyasanād eva* : by mere external abandonment (by merely putting on the garb of renunciation) *siddhim* : spiritual perfection *na ca samadhigacchati* : does not attain.

4. By non-performance of action a man does not gain the state of spiritual passivity (or the state of egoless actionlessness called Naiṣkarmya). By mere external abandonment (Saṁnyāsa), he does not attain to perfection.

न हि कश्चित् क्षणमपि जातु तिष्ठत्यकर्मकृत् ।
कार्यते ह्यवशः कर्म सर्वः प्रकृतिजैर्गुणैः ॥ 5 ॥

Na hi kaścit kṣaṇam api jātu tiṣṭhaty akarma-kṛt
kāryate hy avaśaḥ karma sarvaḥ prakṛtijair guṇaiḥ ॥ 5 ॥

Jātu : Ever *kṣaṇam* : a moment *api* : even *akarmakṛt* : one without any action *na hi tiṣṭhati* : does not indeed remain *hi* for *prakṛtijaiḥ* born of Nature *guṇaiḥ* : by Guṇas (impulses) *avaśaḥ* deprived of freedom *sarvaḥ* : all *karma* : action *kāryate* , are made to perform.

5. No man can ever remain even for a moment without performing any action. The impulses of nature deprive him of freedom in this respect and compel him to act.

कर्मेन्द्रियाणि संयम्य य आस्ते मनसा स्मरन् ।
इन्द्रियार्थान्विमूढात्मा मिथ्याचारः स उच्यते ॥ 6 ॥

Karm'endriyāni saṁyamya ya āste manasā smaran
indriy'ārthān vimūḍhātmā mithy'ācāraḥ sa ucyate ॥ 6 ॥

Karmendriyāṇi : Organs of action *saṁyamya* : restraining *yaḥ* : who *manasā* : by mind *indriyārthān* : objects of senses *smaran* : thinking of *āste* : sits *vimūḍhātmā* : deluded person *saḥ* : he *mithyācāraḥ* : hyprocrite *ucyate* : is called.

6. He who restrains the organs of action but continues to brood in his mind over the objects of sensual desire (enjoyed through them) — such a deluded person is called a hypocrite.

यस्त्विन्द्रियाणि मनसा नियम्यारभतेऽर्जुन ।
कर्मेन्द्रियैः कर्मयोगमसक्तः स विशिष्यते ॥ 7 ॥

Yas tv indriyāṇi manasā niyamy'ārabhate'rjuna /
karm, endriyaiḥ karma yogam asaktaḥ sa viśiṣyate //7//

Yaḥ tu : But who *indriyāṇi* : sense organs *manasā* : by the mind *niyamya* : controlling *asaktah* : unattached *karmendriyaiḥ* : by organs of action *Karma yogam* : communion through work *ārabhate* : begins, *Arjuna* : O Arjuna *saḥ* : such a man *viśiṣyate* : excels.

7. But he who, controlling all sense organs (by the power of his will) and becoming non-attached, lives a life of communion through dedicated action—such a person excels.

नियतं कुरु कर्म त्वं कर्म ज्यायो ह्यकर्मणः ।
शरीरयात्रापि च ते न प्रसिद्ध्येदकर्मणः ॥ 8 ॥

Niyataṁ kuru karma tvaṁ karma jyāyo hy akarmaṇaḥ /
śarīra-yatrā'pi ca te na prasiddhyed akarmaṇaḥ //8//

Tvam : You *niyatam* : prescribed *karma* : actions *kuru* : perform; *hi* : for *akarmaṇah* : to inaction *karma* : action *jyāyaḥ* : superior. *Akarmaṇah* : Of the inactive *te*: your *śarīrayātra api ca* : survival of the body even *na prasiddhyet* : would not be possible.

8. Perform your prescribed duties. For, action is superior to inaction. If you are totally inactive, even the survival of the body would become impossible.

यज्ञार्थात्कर्मणोऽन्यत्र लोकोऽयं कर्मबन्धनः ।
तदर्थं कर्म कौन्तेय मुक्तसङ्गः समाचर ॥ 9 ॥

Yajñ'ārthāt karmaṇo'nyatra loko'yaṁ karma-bandhanaḥ /
tad-arthaṁ karma Kaunteya mukta-saṅgaḥ samācara //9//

Kaunteya : O son of Kunti! *ayam* : this *lokaḥ* : world *yajñārthāt* for the sake of Yajña (God) *karmaṇah* : of action *anyatra* : in respect of others *karmabandhanaḥ* : are bound by action. *Tadartham* : for the sake of God *muktasangaḥ* : without attachment *karma*: work *samācara* : perform.

9. O son of Kunti! In this world all actions, unless they are done as an offering to God (or as Yajña), become causes of bondage. Therefore, work for the sake of God without personal attachments.

सहयज्ञाः प्रजाः सृष्ट्वा पुरोवाच प्रजापतिः ।
अनेन प्रसविष्यध्वमेष वोऽस्त्विष्टकामधुक् ॥ 10 ॥

Saha yajñāḥ prajāḥ sṛṣṭvā puro'vāca Prajāpatiḥ /
anena prasaviṣyadhvam eṣa vo'stv iṣṭa-kāmadhuk //10//

Purā : In the beginning *prajāpatiḥ* : the creator (Brahma) *sahayajñāh* : together with Yajña *prajāḥ* : beings *sṛṣṭvā* : having created *uvāca* : said, *anena* : by this *prasaviṣyadhvam* : shall you multiply *eṣaḥ* : this *vaḥ* : to you *iṣṭakāmadhuk* : a cow yielding all your wants *astu* : let be.

10. In the beginning Prajāpati, having created men together with Yajña (selfless work dedicated to God or Vedic sacrifice) as their duty, declared: "By this shall you multiply. May this be to you the Cow of Plenty yielding all your wants!"[4]

देवान्भावयतानेन ते देवा भावयन्तु वः ।
परस्परं भावयन्तः श्रेयः परमवाप्स्यथ ॥ 11 ॥

Devān bhāvayat'ānena te devā bhāvayantu vaḥ /
parasparaṁ bhāvatyantaḥ śreyaḥ param avāpsyatha //11//

Anena : With this *devān* : the Devās *bhāvayatu* : cherish, *te* : those *devān* : Devas *vaḥ* : you *bhāvayantu* : may cherish. *Parasparam* : Mutually *bhāvayantaḥ* : cherishing *param* : highest *śreyaḥ* : good *avāpsyatha* : shall attain to.

11. "You cherish the Devas with Yajña, and may the Devas in turn bless you (with rain and other desired gifts)!

Thus, mutually cherishing, you shall attain the highest good."

इष्टान्भोगान्हि वो देवा दास्यन्ते यज्ञभाविताः ।
तैर्दत्तानप्रदायैभ्यो यो भुङ्क्ते स्तेन एव सः ॥ 12 ॥

Iṣṭān bhogān hi vo devā dāsyante yajña-bhāvitāḥ /
tair dattān apradāy'aibhyo yo bhuṅkte stena eva saḥ //12//

Yajñabhāvitāḥ : Cherished by Yajna *devāḥ* : the Devas *vaḥ* : to you *iṣṭān bhogān* : desired enjoyments *dāsyanyte* : will bestow. *hi* : Therefore *taiḥ* : by them *dattān* : gifts given *ebhyaḥ* : to them *apradāya* : without giving *yaḥ* : who *bhuṅkte* : enjoys, *saḥ* : he *stena* : thief *eva* : verily.

12. Worshipped by sacrifices, the Devas will give you the desired objects of enjoyment. They are verily thieves who enjoy their gifts without giving their share in return.

यज्ञशिष्टाशिनः सन्तो मुच्यन्ते सर्वकिल्बिषैः ।
भुञ्जते ते त्वघं पापा ये पचन्त्यात्मकारणात् ॥ 13 ॥

Yajña-śiṣṭ'āsinaḥ santo mucyante sarva-kilbiṣaiḥ /
bhunjate te tv aghaṁ pāpā ye pacanty ātma kāraṇāt //13//

Yajñaśiṣṭāśinaḥ : Those who eat what is left after sacrifice *santaḥ* : virtuous men *sarvakilbiṣaih* : from all sins *mucyante* : are released. *Ye tu* : Whoever *ātmakāraṇāt* : for one's sake only *pacanti* : cook *te* : those *pāpāḥ* : degraded persons *agham* : sin *bhuñjate* : eat.

13. Those persons who eat what is left after sacrifice, are released from all sin. But those who cook food for the self alone (without sharing it with others), such degraded men eat sin.

अन्नाद्भवन्ति भूतानि पर्जन्यादन्नसंभवः ।
यज्ञाद्भवति पर्जन्यो यज्ञः कर्मसमुद्भवः ॥ 14 ॥

Annād bhavanti bhūtāni parjanyād anna-saṁbhavaḥ /
yajñād bhavati parjanyo yajñaḥ karma-samudbhavaḥ //14//

Annāt : From food *bhūtāni* : creatures *bhavanti* : are born, *parjanyāt* : from rain *anna-sambhavaḥ* : the origin of food takes place *yajñāt* : from yajña *parjanyaḥ* : rain, *yajñaḥ* : Yajña *karma-samudbhavaḥ* : is born of Karma.

14. From food (i.e., from reproductive power sustained by food) creatures are born. Food is produced by rain. Rain is born of sacrifice, and sacrifice originates from action.

कर्म ब्रह्मोद्भवं विद्धि ब्रह्माक्षरसमुद्भवम् ।
तस्मात्सर्वगतं ब्रह्म नित्यं यज्ञे प्रतिष्ठितम् ॥ 15 ॥

Karma brahm'odbhavaṁ viddhi brahmā'kṣara-samudbhavam /
tasmāt sarvagataṁ brahma nityaṁ yajñe pratiṣṭhitam //15//

Karma : Acts of sacrifice *brahmodbhavam* : originate from Veda *brahma* : Veda *akṣara-samudbhavam* : arises from the Imperishable Being; *tasmāt* : thus *sarvagatam* : all-comprehending *brahma* : Veda *nityam* : eternally *yajñe* : in sacrifice *pratiṣṭhitam* : is established.

15. Works of sacrifice have their authority in the Veda. Veda has been revealed by the Supreme Being. Therefore the all-comprehending Veda is established in sacrifice (that is, has performance of sacrifice as its fundamental teaching).

एवं प्रवर्तितं चक्रं नानुवर्तयतीह यः ।
अघायुरिन्द्रियारामो मोघं पार्थ स जीवति ॥ 16 ॥

Evaṁ pravartitaṁ cakraṁ n'ānuvartayatī'ha yaḥ /
aghāyur indriy'ārāmo moghaṁ Pārtha sa jīvati //16//

Pārtha : O son of Pṛthā! *evam* : thus *pravartitaṁ* : set in motion *cakraṁ* : wheel, cycle (i.e. the arrangement of mutual dependence and service) *yaḥ* : whoever *na anuvartayati* : does not follow *aghāyuḥ* : living in sin *indriyārāmaḥ* : delighting in the senses *saḥ* : that man *mogham jīvati* : lives in vain.

16. Vain is the life of that sinful and sense-indulgent person who fails to fulfil his obligations in this cycle of mutual

inter-dependence and service (which the law of sacrifice implies).

यस्त्वात्मरतिरेव स्यादात्मतृप्तश्च मानवः ।
आत्मन्येव च संतुष्टस्तस्य कार्यं न विद्यते ॥ 17 ॥

Yas tv ātma-ratir eva syād ātma-tṛptaś ca mānavaḥ /
ātmany eva ca saṁtuṣṭas tasya kāryaṁ na vidyate //17//

Tu : But *yaḥ* : whichever *mānavaḥ* : man *ātmaratir eva* : delights in the self alone *ātmatṛptaḥ ca* : and satisfied in the self *ātmani eva* : in the Ātman alone *saṁtuṣṭaḥ* : is content *tasya* : his *kāryam* : what ought to be done *na vidyate* : does not exist.

17. But whoever delights in the Self (Spirit) alone, and is content and satisfied in the Self, for such a person there is no obligatory duty to discharge.[5]

नैव तस्य कृतेनार्थो नाकृतेनेह कश्चन ।
न चास्य सर्वभूतेषु कश्चिदर्थव्यपाश्रयः ॥ 18 ॥

N'aiva tasya kṛten'ārtho n'ākṛten'eha kaścana /
na c'āsya sarva-bhūteṣu kaścid artha-vyapāśrayaḥ //18//

Tasya : For him *iha* : here, in this world *kṛtena* : by actions done *arthaḥ* : object *na eva* : does not exist at all *akṛtena* : by what is not done *kaścana na* : there is nothing to come by. *Asya* : For him *sarvabhūteṣu* : among all created beings *kaścit* : any *artha-vyapāśrayaḥ* : dependence for any object *na* : is not.

18. He has no object to gain here in this world by action. Nor does he lose anything by abstaining from action. For him, there is no dependence on any created being for any object of his.

तस्मादसक्तः सततं कार्यं कर्म समाचर ।
असक्तो ह्याचरन्कर्म परमाप्नोति पूरुषः ॥ 19 ॥

Tasmād asaktaḥ satataṁ kāryaṁ karma samācara /
asakto hy ācaran karma param āpnoti pūruṣaḥ //19//

Tasmāt : Therefore *asaktaḥ* : without attachment *satataṁ* : always *kāryaṁ karma* : work that has to be done *samācara* : perform; *hi* : for *asaktaḥ* : without attachment *karma* : works *ācaran* : performing *pūruṣaḥ* : man *param* : the Supreme *āpnoti* attains to.

19. Therefore perform action always without attachment. For, by working without attachment a man attains the Supreme.[6]

कर्मणैव हि संसिद्धिमास्थिता जनकादयः ।
लोकसंग्रहमेवापि संपश्यन्कर्तुमर्हसि ॥ 20 ॥

Karmaṇ'aiva hi saṁsiddhim āsthitā Janakādayaḥ /
loka-saṁgraham evā'pi saṁpaśyan kartum arhasi //20//

Janakādayaḥ ;Men like Janaka *Karmaṇā eva* : by work alone *saṁsiddhim* : perfection *āsthitāḥ* : attained *hi* : verily. *Loka-saṁgraham* : Good of society *sampaṣyan* : having in view· *kartum:* to work *arhasi* : you should.

20. Men like Janaka verily attained to perfection by work alone. You ought to work for the good of the world (having their example in view).[7]

यद्यदाचरति श्रेष्ठस्तत्तदेवेतरो जनः ।
स यत्प्रमाणं कुरुते लोकस्तदनुवर्तते ॥ 21 ।

Yad-yad ācarati śreṣṭhas tat-tad ev'etaro janaḥ /
sa yat pramāṇaṁ kurute lokas tad anuvartate //21//

Śreṣṭhaḥ : A noble person *yat yat :* whatever *ācarati :* does *tat tat :* that *eva :* only *itaraḥ :* other *janaḥ :* men. *Yat :* What *saḥ* : he *pramāṇam* : standard *kurute* : sets, *lokaḥ* : the world, ordinary men *tat* : that *anuvartate* : follows.

21. Whatever the noblest persons do, the ordinary man imitates. The standard they set, the ordinary men follow.

न मे पार्थास्ति कर्तव्यं त्रिषु लोकेषु किंचन ।
नानवाप्तमवाप्तव्यं वर्त एव च कर्मणि ॥ 22 ॥

Na me Pārthā'sti kartavyaṁ triṣu lokeṣu kiṁcana /
nānavāptam avāptavyaṁ varta eva ca karmaṇi //22//

Pārtha : O Son of Pṛithā! *me* : for me *kartavyam* : duty *na asti*: does not exist. *Triṣu lokeṣu* : In the three worlds *avāptavyam* : to be attained *nānavāptam* : impossible to attain *kiṁcana* : anything *na* : does not exist. *Ca* : Still *karmaṇi* : in action *varte* : am engaged *eva* : verily.

22. In all the three worlds there is nothing, O son of Pṛthā, that is binding on Me as duty. Neither is there anything that I have to gain, nor anything that I cannot gain. Still I am always engaged in work.

यदि ह्यहं न वर्तेयं जातु कर्मण्यतन्द्रितः ।
मम वर्त्मानुवर्तन्ते मनुष्याः पार्थ सर्वशः ॥ 23 ॥

Yadi hy ahaṁ na varteyaṁ jātu karmaṇy atandritaḥ /
mama vartm'ānuvartante manuṣyāḥ Pārtha sarvaśaḥ //23//

Pārtha : O son of Pṛthā! *aham* : I *jātu* : always *atandritaḥ* : unwearied *karmaṇi* : in action *na varteyam* : did not continue *yadi* : if, *manuṣyāḥ* : men *sarvaśaḥ* : all around *mama* : my *vartmā* : way *anuvartante* : would follow.

23. O son of Pṛthā! If I did not ever continue in action unwearied, men all around would have followed My way.

उत्सीदेयुरिमे लोका न कुर्यां कर्म चेदहम् ।
संकरस्य च कर्ता स्यामुपहन्यामिमाः प्रजाः ॥ 24 ॥

Utsīdeyur ime lokā na kuryāṁ karma ced aham /
saṁkarasya ca kartā syām upahanyām imāḥ prajāḥ //24//

Aham : I *karma* : action *na kuryāṁ* : do not work *cet* : if, *ime* : these *lokāḥ* : worlds *utsīdeyuḥ* : would perish; *saṁkarasya*: of confusion *kartā* : author *syām* : would be ; *imāḥ* : these *prajāḥ*: beings *upahanyām ca* : destroy also.

24. If I were not to work, all these worlds would have perished. I would have been the cause of confusion among men and of their ultimate destruction.

सक्ताः कर्मण्यविद्वांसो यथा कुर्वन्ति भारत ।
कुर्याद्विद्वांस्तथासक्तश्चिकीर्षुर्लोकसंग्रहम् ॥ 25 ॥

Saktāḥ karmaṇy avidvāṁso yathā kurvanti Bhārata /
kuryād vidvāṁs tathā'saktaś cikīrṣur loka-saṁgraham //25//

Bhārata : O scion of the Bharata race! *Karmaṇi* : to action *saktāḥ* : attached *avidvāṁsaḥ* : ignorant people *yathā* : as *kurvanti*: act, *tathā* : in the same way *vidvān* : the enlightened man *asaktah* : without attachment *lokasaṁgraham* : good of the world *cikīrṣuḥ* : desirous of *kuryāt* : should act.

25. O scion of the Bharata race! Just as ignorant men do action out of attachment, so let enlightened ones perform the same unattached, with the good of the world in view.[8]

न बुद्धिभेदं जनयेदज्ञानां कर्मसङ्गिनाम् ।
जोषयेत्सर्वकर्माणि विद्वान्युक्तः समाचरन् ॥ 26 ॥

Na buddhi-bhedaṁ janayed ajñānāṁ karma-saṅginām /
joṣayet sarva-karmāṇi vidvān yuktaḥ samācaran //26//

Vidvān : Enlightened man *karmasaṅginām* : attached to action *ajñānāṁ* : of the ignorant *na* : not *buddhibhedām* : unsettlement of the mind *janayet* : should create; *yuktaḥ* : with equanimity *samācaran* : doing everything *sarvakarmāṇi* : all actions *joṣayet* : should make them interested in.

26. An enlightened man should not cause confusion in the minds of ignorant people (by his conduct). Himself working with equanimity, he should make them interested in all activities.

प्रकृतेः क्रियमाणानि गुणैः कर्माणि सर्वशः ।
अहंकारविमूढात्मा कर्ताहमिति मन्यते ॥ 27 ॥

Prakṛteḥ kriyamāṇāni guṇaiḥ karmāṇi sarvaśaḥ /
ahaṁkāra-vimūḍh'ātmā kartā'ham iti manyate //27//

Prakṛteḥ : Of Prakṛti *guṇaiḥ* : by Gunas (dispositions) *sarvaśaḥ*: everywhere *karmāṇi* : actions *kriyamāṇāni* : are performed. *Ahaṁkāra-vimūḍhātmā* : man deluded by egoism *aham* : I am *kartā* : the doer *iti* : thus *manyate* : thinks.

27. Everywhere the dispositions (powers) of Nature perform all works. But deluded by egoism, man thinks, 'I am the doer.'[9]

तत्त्ववित्तु महाबाहो गुणकर्मविभागयोः ।
गुणा गुणेषु वर्तन्त इति मत्वा न सज्जते ॥ 28 ॥

Tattva-vit tu mahā-bāho guṇa-karma-vibhāgayoḥ /
guṇā guṇeṣu vartanta iti matvā na sajjate //28//

Mahābāho : O mighty armed *guṇakarma-vibhāgayoḥ* : of the division of the dispositions of Nature and of actions springing from them *tattvavit tu* : knower of the real truth about them *guṇāḥ* : dispositions of Nature as organs *guṇeṣu* : in dispositions as objects *vartante* : remain, *iti* : thus *matvā* : knowing *na sajjate* : does not become attached.

28. But those who know the truth that the dispositions of Nature and the actions springing from them are distinct from the Self, do not get attached, understanding that it is not the Self, but the dispositions of Nature as organs that settle on the respective objects, which too are products of the same dispositions.

प्रकृतेर्गुणसंमूढाः सज्जन्ते गुणकर्मसु ।
तानकृत्स्नविदो मन्दान्कृत्स्नविन्न विचालयेत् ॥ 29 ॥

Prakṛter guṇa-sammūḍhāḥ sajjante guṇa-karmasu /
tān akṛtsna-vido mandān kṛtsna-vin na vicālayet //29//

Prakṛteḥ : Of Prakriti (Nature) *guṇasammūḍhāḥ* : deluded by the dispositions *guṇakarmasu* : in works prompted by these dispositions *sajjante* : become attached; *akṛtsnavidaḥ* : who do not know the whole truth *mandān* : dull-witted *tān* : those *kṛtsnavid* : who know the whole truth *na vicālayet* : should not shake or unsettle.

29. Men, deluded by the dispositions of Nature, get attached to work prompted by these dispositions. Those who know the whole Truth should not unsettle these dull-witted men of imperfect understanding.

मयि सर्वाणि कर्माणि संन्यस्याध्यात्मचेतसा ।
निराशीर्निर्ममो भूत्वा युध्यस्व विगतज्वरः ॥ 30 ॥

Mayi sarvāṇi karmāṇi samnyasy'ādhyātma-cetasā /
nirāśīr nirmamo bhūtvā yudhyasva vigata-jvaraḥ //30//

Sarvāṇi : All *karmāṇi* : actions *mayi* : in Me *samnyasya* : offering or surrendering *adhyātma cetasa* : with mind in unison with the spirit *nirāśīḥ* : free from desire *nirmamaḥ* : devoid of egotism *vigatajvaraḥ* : with passion spent *bhūtvā*: becoming *yudhyasva*: fight.

30. Offering all your actions to Me, your mind in unison with the spirit and free from desires and egotism, you fight without the slightest touch of hatred or excitement.[10]

ये मे मतमिदं नित्यमनुतिष्ठन्ति मानवाः ।
श्रद्धावन्तोऽनसूयन्तो मुच्यन्ते तेऽपि कर्मभिः ॥ 31 ॥

Ye me matam idaṁ nityaṁ anutiṣṭhanti mānavāḥ /
śraddhāvanto'nasūyanto mucyante te'pi karmabhiḥ //31//

Ye : Whichever *mānavāh*: men *śraddhāvantaḥ* : having faith *anasūyantaḥ* : free from disparagement *me* : My *idam* : this *matam* : teaching *nityam* : always *anutiṣṭhanti* : follow, *te* : they *api* : also *karmabhiḥ* : by (from) Karma *mucyante* : are released.

31. Whoever follow this teaching of mine, with their minds full of faith and free from disparagement, they also are released from the bondage of Karma.

ये त्वेतदभ्यसूयन्तो नानुतिष्ठन्ति मे मतम् ।
सर्वज्ञानविमूढांस्तान्विद्धि नष्टानचेतसः ॥ 32 ॥

Ye tv etad abhyasūyanto n'ānutiṣṭhanti me matam /
sarva-jñāna vimūḍhāṁs tān viddhi naṣṭān acetasaḥ //32//

Ye tu : But whoever *me* : My *etat* : this *matam* : teaching *abhyasūyantaḥ*: disparaging *na anutiṣṭhanti* : do not follow *acetasaḥ* : senseless *sarvajñāna-vimūḍhān* : blind to all wisdom *tān* : them *naṣṭān viddhi* : know as lost.

32. But those who disparage this doctrine of mine and discard it, know such senseless men, blind to all wisdom, as lost.

सदृशं चेष्टते स्वस्याः प्रकृतेर्ज्ञानवानपि ।
प्रकृतिं यान्ति भूतानि निग्रहः किं करिष्यति ॥ 33 ॥

Sadṛśaṁ ceṣṭate svasyāḥ prakṛter jñānavān api /
prakṛtiṁ yānti bhūtāni nigrahaḥ kiṁ kariṣyati //33//

Jñānavān api : Even a wise man *svasyāḥ* : of his own *prakṛteḥ*: nature *sadṛśam* : in accordance with *ceṣṭate* : acts. *Bhūtāni*: Beings *prakṛtim* : nature *yānti* : follow; *nigrahaḥ* : repression *kim* : what *kariṣyati* : will do.

33. Even a wise man acts in accordance with his nature. All beings follow their nature. What can repression do?[11]

इन्द्रियस्येन्द्रियस्यार्थे रागद्वेषौ व्यवस्थितौ ।
तयोर्न वशमागच्छेत्तौ ह्यस्य परिपन्थिनौ ॥ 34 ॥

Indriyasy'endriyasy' ārthe rāgadveṣau vyavasthitau /
tayor na vaśam āgacchet tau hy asya paripanthinau. //34//

Indriyasya : Of the senses *indriyasya arthe* : in the object of the senses *rāgadveṣau* : attachment and aversion *vyavasthitau* : are naturally established. *Tayoḥ* : Of them *vaśam* : sway *na āgacchet*: let not come, *hi* : for *tau* : they *asya* : his *paripanthinau* : enemies.

34. It is natural for each organ to feel attraction or aversion in respect of objects pertaining to each sense. Do not come under their sway, for they are enemies (of all spiritual aspirants).

श्रेयान् स्वधर्मो विगुणः परधर्मात्स्वनुष्ठितात् ।
स्वधर्मे निधनं श्रेयः परधर्मो भयावहः ॥ 35 ॥

Śreyān svadharmo viguṇaḥ para-dharmāt svanuṣṭhitāt |
svadharme nidhanaṁ śreyaḥ para-dharmo bhay'āvahaḥ //35//

Svanuṣṭhitāt : Well performed *paradharmāt* : than the duty of another *viguṇaḥ* : imperfect, not glamorous *svadharmaḥ* : one's own duty *śreyān* : leading to the good. *Svadharme* : in one's own duty *nidhanam* : death *śreyah* : leading to one's good. *Paradharmaḥ* : Another's duty (duty alien to one's growth) *bhayāvahaḥ* : conveying fear.

35. One's own Dharma (duty), even though not glamorous, is better than duty alien to one's growth (Para-dharmaḥ), however well performed. For even death in doing one's duty leads to one's good, while a duty alien to one's growth is burdened with the fear of downfall.[12]

अर्जुन उवाच

अथ केन प्रयुक्तोऽयं पापं चरति पूरुषः ।
अनिच्छन्नपि वार्ष्णेय बलादिव नियोजितः ॥ 36 ॥

Arjuna uvāca:

Atha kena prayukto'yaṁ pāpaṁ carati pūruṣaḥ |
anicchann api Vārṣṇeya balād iva niyojitaḥ //36//

Vārṣṇeya : O scion of the Vṛṣṇi race! *atha* : then *ayaṁ pūruṣaḥ* : man *anicchan api* : even unwillingly *kena* : by what *prayuktaḥ* : prompted *balād* : by force *niyojitaḥ* : compelled to *iva* : as if *pāpam* : sin *carati* : indulges in.

Arjuna said:

36. What is that, O scion of the Vṛṣṇi race, prompted by which a man is forced, as it were, to indulge in sin even against his will?

श्रीभगवानुवाच

काम एष क्रोध एष रजोगुणसमुद्भवः ।
महाशनो महापाप्मा विद्ध्येनमिह वैरिणम् ॥ 37 ॥

Srī Bhagavān uvāca:
Kāma eṣa krodha eṣa rajo-guṇa-samudbhavaḥ /
mah'āśano mahā-pāpmā viddhy enam iha vairiṇam //37//

Eṣaḥ : This *rajoguṇa-samudbhavaḥ* : born of Rajoguṇa *kāmaḥ* : lust, *eṣaḥ*: this *krodhaḥ* : anger *mahāśanaḥ*: insatiable *mahāpāpmā*: cause of great sin. *Enam* : This *iha* : in this matter (i.e. in man's spiritual life) *vairiṇam* as enemy *viddhi* : know.

The Blessed Lord said:

37. It is lust, it is anger, born of Rajoguṇa, insatiable and prompting man to great sin. Know this to be the enemy (in man's spiritual life).

धूमेनाव्रियते वह्निर्यथादर्शो मलेन च ।
यथोल्बेनावृतो गर्भस्तथा तेनेदमावृतम् ॥ 38 ॥

Dhumen'āvriyate vahnir yathā'darśo malena ca /
yath'olben'āvṛto garbhas tathā ten'edam āvṛtam //38//

Vahniḥ : Fire *dhumena* : by smoke *ādarśaḥ malena ca*: and mirror by dirt *tathā* : so *āvriyate* : is enveloped *garbhaḥ* : embryo *ulbena*: by the placenta *yathā* : as *āvṛtaḥ* : covered, *tathā* : thus *idam* : this (knowledge) *tena* : by that (lust) *āvṛtam* : covered.

38. As fire is enveloped by smoke, mirror by dirt, and the embryo by the placenta, so is knowledge overcast by lust.

आवृतं ज्ञानमेतेन ज्ञानिनो नित्यवैरिणा ।
कामरूपेण कौन्तेय दुष्पूरेणानलेन च ॥ 39 ॥

Āvṛtaṁ jñānaṁ etena jñānino nitya-vairiṇā /
kāma-rūpeṇa Kaunteya duṣpūreṇ'ānalena ca //39//

Kaunteya : O son of Kunti *jñāninaḥ* : of the knowing one *nitya-vairiṇā* : by the eternal foe *duṣpūreṇa* : difficult to appease *kamarūpeṇa* : of the nature of lust *etena analena* : by this fire *jñānam* : knowledge *āvṛtam* : covered.

39. Knowledge, O Son of Kuntī, is covered up by this eternal foe of the aspirant after knowledge—the insatiable fire of lust.

इन्द्रियाणि मनो बुद्धिरस्याधिष्ठानमुच्यते ।
एतैर्विमोहयत्येष ज्ञानमावृत्य देहिनम् ॥ 40 ॥

Indriyāṇi mano buddhir asy'ādhiṣṭhānam ucyate /
etair vimohayaty eṣa jñānam āvṛtya dehinam //40//

Indriyāṇi : Senses *manaḥ* : mind *buddhiḥ* : intellect *asya* : of it *adhiṣṭhānam* : seat *ucyate* : is spoken of as. *Eṣaḥ* : This (lust) *etaiḥ* : by these (organs) *jñānam* : knowledge *āvṛtya* : veiling *dehinam* : embodied spirit *vimohayati* : deludes.

40. The senses, the mind and the Buddhi are said to be its seat. With these it veils knowledge and deludes the embodied spirit.

तस्मात्त्वमिन्द्रियाण्यादौ नियम्य भरतर्षभ ।
पाप्मानं प्रजहि ह्येनं ज्ञानविज्ञाननाशनम् ॥ 41 ॥

Tasmāt tvam indriyāṇy ādau niyamya bharatarṣabha /
papmānaṁ prajahi hy enaṁ jñāna-vijñāna-nāśanam //41//

Bharatarṣabha: O scion of the Bharata race! *tasmāt* : therefore *tvam* : you *ādau* : at the very beginning *indriyāṇi* : the senses *niyamya* : controlling *jñāna-vijñāna-nāśanam* : destroyer of knowledge and of special knowledge (realisation) *pāpmānam enam* : this foul enemy *prajahi hi* : slay indeed.

41. Therefore, O scion of the Bharata race, controlling the senses at the beginning itself, slay this foul enemy, the destroyer of all knowledge and realisation.[13]

इन्द्रियाणि पराण्याहुरिन्द्रियेभ्यः परं मनः ।
मनसस्तु परा बुद्धिर्यो बुद्धेः परतस्तु सः ॥ 42 ॥

Indriyāṇi parāṇy āhur indriyebhyaḥ paraṁ manaḥ /
manasas tu parā buddhir yo buddheḥ paratas tu saḥ //42//

Indriyāṇi : The senses *parāṇi* : great *āhuḥ* : they say. *Indriyebhyaḥ param* : Superior to the senses *manaḥ* : is the mind, *manasaḥ tu* : than even the mind *parā* : superior *buddhiḥ* : is the intellect. *Yaḥ* : Who *tu* : even *buddheḥ* : than intellect *parataḥ* : superior *saḥ* : is He (the Ātman).

42. The senses are great, they say. Superior to the senses is the mind, and superior even to the mind is the intellect. What is superior even to the intellect is He, the Ātman.[14]

एवं बुद्धेः परं बुद्ध्वा संस्तभ्यात्मानमात्मना ।
जहि शत्रुं महाबाहो कामरूपं दुरासदम् ॥ 43 ॥

Evaṁ buddheḥ paraṁ buddhvā saṁstabhy'ātmānam-ātmanā /
jahi śatruṁ mahā-bāho kāma-rūpaṁ durāsadam //43//

Mahābāho : O mighty armed! *evam* : in this way *buddheḥ param* : what is superior to Buddhi *buddhvā* : having known *atmanā* : by the higher self *ātmānam* : the lower self *samstabhya* : controlling, *kāmarūpam* : in the form of lust *durāsadam* : difficult to conquer *śatruṁ* : enemy *jahi* : kill.

43. Thus knowing Him who is superior even to the Buddhi, and controlling the lower self with the higher, kill that tough enemy in the form of lust, O mighty-armed Arjuna!

ॐ तत्सदिति श्रीमद्भगवद्गीतासूपनिषत्सु ब्रह्मविद्यायां
योगशास्त्रे श्रीकृष्णार्जुनसंवादे कर्मयोगो
नाम तृतीयोऽध्यायः ॥ 3 ॥

NOTES

1. *V*.2: Arjuna's doubt would probably arise in the mind of every reader of the Gītā after going through the second chapter. The Lord is trying to prompt Arjuna to action as against his desire to give up an active life and become a pacifist and an ascetic. But beyond mentioning Karma Yoga and offering some criticism of the Vedic ritualism he gives no exposition of that theme, but speaks all through about the philosophy of the Ātman, about control of the senses and the self-satisfied state of a man of steady wisdom (*Sthitaprajña*). All this looks irrelevant and confusing, if the object of the earlier discourse is to prompt Arjuna to action. Hence Arjuna's query.

2. *V*.3: It would appear that the Lord accepts the validity of the criticism of Arjuna and, though not in so many words, he seems to suggest that in His first discourse, which is only preliminary, He has put all the issues together and that a clarification is therefore called for. He gives that clarification now in unambiguous language. He has promulgated two paths—the Sāṁkhya or the way of the contemplative philosophers, and Yoga or the way of the activists (Karma Yogins) for whom action performed with the proper attitude is a part of their spiritual discipline.

Much confusing controversy will be found in the writings of Vedāntic Ācharyas in the interpretation of this passage because of the difference in their basic views on the relation between action and pure contemplation. Two views are held on this question. One is Yoga—that work and contemplation should be combined all through one's spiritual life. The other is Sāṁkhya maintaining that action with devotional contemplation is applicable only up to a certain stage, i.e. till the aspirant gains *Chitta-suddhi* or purity of mind, which in practical life means the capacity to check the outward going tendency of the mind. Karma Yoga has no relevance afterwards and one should take to the life of a pure contemplative philosopher at that stage. The main reason given for this idea is that works of every kind go to emphasise the reality of multiplicity and the ego, whereas the pure contemplative's discipline consists in the denial of these and so at one stage work has to be abandoned. There is a clear support for this interpretation in the Gītā passage: 'For one desiring to attain to the state of equipoise (Yoga), work is the means. But for one who has attained equipoise (*Yogārūḍhaḥ*), quietude (*Śama*) is the means" (6.3). Again: "But the man whose delight is in the Self alone, who is content with the Self, who is satisfied with the Self, for him there exists no work that needs be done as duty." (3.17).

The Gītā is equally clear in the passage under discussion that these two paths are distinct paths, and each independently takes one to a goal that is common to both. "The Status which is obtained by the Sāṁkhyas (contemplatives) is reached also by Yogis who combine action with contemplation. He who sees that Sāṁkhya and Yoga are one, he sees truly" (5.5.) It is also said towards the close of the Gītā in favour of Yoga: "Acts of sacrifice, gift, and austerity are not to be relinquished but should be performed. For, sacrifice, gift and austerity are purifiers for the wise. But even these works ought to be performed giving up attachment and desire for fruits. This, O Pārtha, is my decided and final view" (18.6). It is also said: "Though performing all kinds of action all through, the one who is resigned to Me attains to the eternal and undecaying state by My grace" (18.58).

Besides, the Gītā quotes the examples of royal sages like Janaka, Asvapati etc., who, even after being enlightened, continued to work with the attitude characteristic of the enlightened ones. Arjuna, too, is exhorted to follow their example (3.20). Those philosophers who hold to the doctrine of incompatibility of contemplativeness with activistic devotion after a stage, look upon these royal sages as exceptions to the rule and not as a proof of the compatibility of the two disciplines. They attribute it to their *Prarabdha* or operative Karma. The Gītā text, however, does not say they are exceptions. On the other hand, in Chap. 4. 1-3, the Lord asserts that this tradition of Karma Yoga, was known to Rājarṣis from ancient times, but it has since become extinct and that He is reviving it through Arjuna.

In the light of the general teaching of the Gitā, the followers of the two ways may be held as two distinct types—the one discarding the combination at a certain stage, and the other continuing the combination till the end. The former, called in the Gītā as the Sāṁkhyas, following the path of knowledge, abandon all actions at the very start itself if they are qualified for it, or at a certain later stage, after being purified by Yoga discipline, when they take to a purely contemplative life. Through that discipline, they come to the recognition of all multiplicity as mere appearance and realise the unity of all existence in Brahman. The latter, called the Yogins, pursuing the path of combining devotion, contemplation and dedicated action, surrender the fruits of all their actions in the first stage of spiritual life and finally surrender their sense of agency also, to that Universal Will, Iśvara, whose expression the world of multiplicity is. They also attain to the Divine. The former approach may be described as ontological in setting, and the latter, volitional. The end is the realisation of the unity of all existence as Sat-cid-ānanda.

3. *V*.4: *Naiṣkarmya* is not mere worklessness—external passivity or idleness. It is the state of establishment in the experience that one is the Ātman, the pure spirit, the uninvolved witness of passivity as well as of activity of the body-mind. Wilful worklessness which is tantamount to idleness is not the aim. 'True worklessness' has been compared to that of a man sitting in a train. The train may move or stop but the sitter in the train, being distinct from the train, is not affected by these states, but none the less moves with the train. When one's ego identifies itself with the body and feels 'I am the body', he becomes an actor, one involved in works. When he feels 'I am the Atman', he remains as the spirit, the pure witness. That state is called *Naiṣkarmya,* or egoless passivity of the spirit. Spiritual perfection is never to be identified with self-willed passivity or idleness. So by mere external abandonment and adoption of the insignia of renunciation, perfection is not attained. Not only that, absolute passivity is an impossibility for any living being. That way even the process of living becomes impossible. One attempting it will turn a hypocrite. So what one is expected to do is to work controlling the senses by the mind and doing his duty in a dedicated way without caring for the fruits.

4. *V*.10: This and the succeeding verses up to V. 16 are put in the language of the Vedic sacrificial cult in which Yajña, the fire-sacrifice, is the central ritual. All old commentators comment on these in a literal sense, as Vedic ritualists conceived of a Yajña. Man can have a happy and prosperous life only if he lived in harmony with his environment, which consists of

Nature and the Divine agencies, the Devas, who control the forces of Nature. Man gets his progeny and his sustenance as the gifts of Nature and he has therefore got to be thankful to those Divine agencies whose expression these forces of Nature are. Man is required to make as offering of thanks-giving to the Devas, a share of the good things of Nature which he gets by their goodwill. This offering is made through fire which is the link between man and the Devas. So this thanks-giving takes the form of ritualistic fire sacrifices with offerings of commodities and utterance of Vedic hymns. Proper performance of these Yajnas by individuals and communities secures the goodwill of the Devas, and through that, worthy progeny and plentiful rain, on which man's survival and sustenance in this world depend. To partake of this gift of the Devas without being thankful to them and without making the offerings due to them is a form of theft, as the Gītā describes this, and a heinous sin. The relevancy of this in the Gītā context here is that such an essential duty imposed by the Veda on man in society as sacrifice will not be possible for one who abandons works and he will therefore be condemning himself to an unethical life, the life of a thief or exploiter.

While this simple ritualistic conception of Yajña is the plain meaning of these verses, it may be just a suggestion directed towards higher psychological and spiritual verities. Mahāviṣṇu, the Supreme Being, Himself is called Yajña and just as the Cosmos is His physical expression or body, the whole sacrificial set-up is considered a ritualistic form of His and the offerings to Devas and all adoration done are only the adoration of the One Supreme Being, whose parts all the Devas worshipped are. There is also the conception of the whole creative process as a sacrifice of Himself by the *Yajña-puruṣa.*

Besides, in Chapter 4 the Gītā itself speaks of Yajñas of several types, of which fire sacrifice described as *Dravya-yajña* or sacrifice of commodities, is only one. He describes Brahman-knowledge itself as Yajña and speaks of several forms of Yajña like sacrifice of commodities (*Dravya-yajña*), sacrifice of vital breath (Prāṇāyāma-yajña), sacrifice of austerity (Tapo-yajña), sacrifice of scriptural study (*Svādhyāya-yajña*), and sacrifice of knowledge (Jñana-yajña). Thus fire -sacrifice, a ritual commonly known and practised, becomes the symbol for all the moral and spiritual effort of man for his higher evolution.

Taking advantage of the symbolical value attached to the fire-ritual called Yajña in the Gītā, a modern student of the Gītā, who is a stranger to the fire-sacrifice as a ritual, can interpret these passages in terms of relevant factors of social life today. Production and distribution of consumable commodities is done through an exchange of services by capitalists, teachnocrats, labour, the distributor and the consumer. All these factors functioning with the good of the whole social order in view and contributing their respective services and receiving their due rewards without any party trying to take undue advantage of the others—may be called Yajña in the social sense. All this is based on work and a person who seeks all the benefits of society but keeps quiet and fails to contribute his share for social good can be described as an exploiter and a thief as the Gītā does. The difference in this interpretation is that, in place of the divine agencies, only the social environment is taken for mutual exchange of services and rewards. This explanation sublimates the ritualistic Yajña.

5. *V.*17: It is contended that a sage who remains fulfilled in his own higher Self and does not seek satisfaction from anything outside of him, and who has been described as a *sthitaprajña*, is free from the cycle of duties and obligations described earlier. He has no debt of any kind to pay to the Devas, as he has no interest even in the sustenance of the body. For he is fully satisfied with the Self in which he is absorbed. He has thus nothing to do (*Kāryam*) under moral compulsion. He is a free spirit. This is explained in the following verse.

6. *V.*19: The word 'therefore' here is very enigmatic, coming as it does after the description of a knowing one whose exclusive delight is in the Self, who is a free man without compulsion from any quarter to do anything. *Therefore* i.e. *for the above reason*, that he is free from the compulsion of duty, he should out of his free will work for the good of others, without any attachment for anything and without any sense of agency. This is the meaning of '*therefore*' from the point of view of those who hold that a kind of Karma-Yoga which combines Bhakti, Karma, and Self-knowledge is the message of the Gītā.

Those who do not accept this combination of disciplines would interpret this '*therefore*' as follows: "As you, Arjuna, is not endowed with the above-mentioned Self-Knowledge, but are at a lower stage of evolution, you have to follow the discipline of Karma in which alone there can be a combination of action and contemplation. After you have evolved into the state in which you are fit for pure contemplation, you can **abandon** all work, but not till then. *Therefore* you now perform Karma without attachment." It is obvious that this is an interpretative assumption unjustified by the context provided by the next verse.

7. *V.* 20—24 : The example of sages like Janaka appears to be given here to prove the self-sufficiency of Karma Yoga and in support of combination of the Sāṁkhya and Yoga — contemplation and non-attached action–till perfection is reached and thereafter. But those who oppose such combination describe these examples as exceptions. There is, however, nothing in the Gītā text to prove them to be so. They may be rare examples of perfection through Karma Yoga. But so too are perfect ones who follow pure Sāṁkhya. Both are rarities. The point to be noted here is that Kṛṣṇa considers Karma Yoga (which means action, devotion and contemplation combined) to be a self-sufficient discipline for attaining spiritual perfection. Welfare of the world (*lokasamgraha*), and not any self-centred objective, becomes the purpose of the action of such enlightened ones. Much more important than any individual example, the Gitā holds forth Iśvara Himself as the most conspicuous example of such disinterested work. Man is exhorted to follow the Divine example. This is a conclusive argument in favour of Karma Yoga.

8. *V.* 25: The distinction between the work of the worldly-minded man and the enlightened Karma Yogi is clearly indicated. The former is self-centred, while the latter has overcome self-centredness and still works for the good of all. If Karma Yoga can take one to such a state of selflessness, that goal must be the same universal Self to which the Sāṁkhya attains by abandoning all desires and the ego. The ways of the two may be different but the ultimate goal is the same. It is the Self which embraces all selves.

The object of such work is the good of the world. Apart

from the good directly proceeding from such work, the example it sets is itself of immense good. If the best men in society practised quietism, lesser men may imitate their example and lapse into idleness. So they too should work but with a different motive.

9. *V.* 27-29 : The distinction between the ignorant man and the enlightened one, whether he has reached that state through Yoga or Sāṁkhya, is stated here. The enlightened man has no sense of agency and is therefore free from bondage. The ignorant man thinks he is the agent and he has therefore bondage arising from the good and bad fruits of his work.

10. *V.* 30: Till now Karma Yoga was described as work without attachment and without desire for the fruits of action. But a more complete description of Karma Yoga is given here, where it is taught that all actions should be resigned to the Lord. This resignation has two stages. First all the fruits of actions are resigned to the Lord. The Yogi has still the sense of agency—the feeling that he is doing the work. At a higher level of perfection, the sense of agency also is resigned. It has been already stated in 5.27 that a wise man understands that in work, the forces of Nature work on objects that are Nature's creations. The sense 'I am doing' on the part of the worker is superfluous, having no foundation. It is born of ignorance. But here it is pointed out that higher than Nature even, is the Nature's Lord, Iśvara. Nature is only His executive force or His will and so His will is the only agency that performs all works. The individual will is only a distortion of the Divine will by man's egoism. When this distortion is overcome through devotion and resignation to the Divine will, complete peace and perfection is attained even in the midst of all work. Thus it is Bhakti that completes the Gita doctrine of dedicated and detached work. The Bhakti element is here stressed in the text for the first time. The doctrine of Bhakti is elaborated especially from the 7th chapter onwards.

11. *V.* 33-34: Verse 33 looks like a fatalist's dictum. But it is not so when it is read with the next verse 34. Prakṛti or Nature here means the manifestation in the present life of the mental tendencies, the character potential etc. formed by the virtuous and vicious actions done in past lives. It operates even on the knowing one. Prarabdha can include good and bad elements, but

since knowledge can arise only in a pure mind, evil tendencies in a knowing one will be very few and inconsequential. That all creatures are subject to their nature is a truism which none will dispute. But the dispute and doubt come when it is said: "What can *nigraha* (control or repression) do?" This question may be taken merely as raising an issue and not as a denial of the possibility of overcoming natural tendencies. *Nigraha* can be equated with the modern psychological concept of repression. It means, to forcefully suppress a desire or to try to eliminate it by forgetting in a fit of violent fear or shame. In either case the desire or the tendency is not eliminated, but only driven underground from where it will work havoc on the body and mind of man. So the question is asked: to what extent repression can succeed in overcoming nature? The answer is: 'Very little'.

The next verse gives the correct way of controlling nature. It is by cultivating awareness. It is given in 2. 66-68, how man gets infatuated with sense objects. He dwells on them longingly; that develops attachment; attachment develops into desire; desire generates animosities and infatuation; and infatuation makes him forget his moral and spiritual foundation. So if natural impulses are to be controlled it must be done at the outset, when they are just beginning to hold one's interest. This is possible only if one cultivates awareness of things and moods that entice one's mind, and then overcome them by discrimination and counter-suggestion at the start itself. So in verse 34 man is asked to remember always that there is a natural attraction between the senses and their objects and he is therefore exhorted to avoid exposure to their influence. If unavoidably exposed, one should exercise discrimination to protect oneself. The best way is to invoke the Divine aid through prayer and self-surrender. If this is not done at the very early stage and infatuation thus combated, then man becomes a helpless entity before the pull of the senses like an object that has been sucked into the vortex of a whirlpool. He could have avoided getting into it but having got in, it is difficult for him to escape.

Or the two verses may be understood as directly connected with Karma Yoga without drawing any of those psychological implications elaborated above. It may be thus stated: The

Prakṛti or the nature of man is to engage himself in all forms of activities with the body and the mind. To resist all this forcefully and to sit quiet like a stock or stone without doing anything as Arjuna wanted is an impossibility for any human being. Even a knowing one i.e. one who has realised his Ātmanhood and thus got detached from the body has to follow Nature's impulses in the matter of eating, sleeping, speaking, moving about etc., which are unavoidable for his physical and social survival. In Vedantic terminology even a knowing one is subject to his *Prārabdha* or Karmas that have led to the present embodiment until death destroys the body. That being the case, none, even a knowing one, can remain workless.

What is possible for an ordinary person is to practise discrimination, taking into account the fact that there is natural attraction for the senses to their objects and that these senses, if allowed to dominate, will cause the downfall of a spiritual aspirant. When a person is thus convinced of the danger posed by this attraction of sense objects, he will guard himself against the dominance of their influence. Non-attached work, and not forced withdrawal from all work, is the way of progress for man. For, to work is implicit in the nature of man and suppressing it by forcible means will only have adverse effects on him.

12. *V.* 35: The word Svadharma means, as understood by medieval Hindus, the duties sacred and social, that devolved on people according to their hereditary affiliations as Brahmaṇa, Kṣatriya, Vaiśya and Sūdra. People's birth in these different groups was supposed to be determined by their Karmas of the past marking the stage of their evolution. Each class had its own social functions and means of livelihood as laid down in the Smṛtis. That formed the Svadharma or one's own duty for each individual of that class or Varna. He was to follow it and not that of others, *Paradharma*.

This way of determining Svadharma is possible only in a society where class has become crystallised into castes based on birth. Where classes lose all rigidity and tend towards classlessness, determining Svadharma by birth becomes impossible. Svadharma will have to be described as work in line with one's mental constitution and higher development. While as a psychological criterion it is acceptable, it is not possible to determine it in actual life, and even if determined, one may not have the facility to pick and choose one's duty. In practical life one has to take it as the work that devolves on one as duty.

But here in this context Svadharma and Paradharma can be interpreted in quite a different way also, which perhaps is more appropriate too. Svadharma, for the vast majority of men, is a life of action. Arjuna is being exhorted to adopt Karma Yoga as his way of spiritual development, because a life of activity is the Dharma or way of life born of his own nature. Sāṁkhya or workless contemplation will be Paradharma, work alien to his nature, and therefore harmful to him. Paradharma may look attractive and one may, to a certain extent, succeed in pursuing it, but in the long run, one is sure to break down. The threat of this break-down will be always a cause of an obsessive fear within him. Workless contemplation will easily degenerate into sheer idleness in unworthy hands, and result in spiritual ruin. Svadharma or Karma Yoga may not be so glamorous, but it is safe, and will be found contributive to one's ultimate good.

13. *V.* 41: An aspirant is again reminded of the importance of controlling the senses, especially of tackling passions like lust, anger etc., at their very outset. If they are allowed to gather force, man will be at their mercy, and no control will be possible.

14. *V.* 42-43: In these two verses a psychological analysis of the human personality is given as an aid to the practice of the control of the senses spoken of earlier.

The senses, the mind, the intellect, and the Spirit (Ātman) are the four layers of human personality. The Spirit which is the ultimate foundation of man, is pure consciousness and the uninvolved witness of the modifications of these three layers. He alone is the conscious entity, and the three layers associated with Him are inert in themselves, but become living and conscious when His light of consciousness percolates through them, just as the dull shades of a lamp are illumined when the rays of the central light passes through them.

Now these appendages of the Ātman form the instruments of perception and the storage space for the memories of experiences.

So the impressions of the countless experiences of past lives are in them. The impressions of experiences they contain and convey are derived from repeated contacts with external objects for the enhancement of bodily life. These impressions have made the senses prone to look at these objects, only from the point of view of instinctive satisfactions. Thus when a man's eyes see a tasty food, he can think of it only as something fine to eat; when a person sees one of the opposite sex, he often thinks of the other as an object of sensual enjoyment; when he sees a tiger, he looks at it exclusively as a dangerous creature; when he sees a cow, he sees it as a creature useful for getting milk. This outlook generated by the senses colour the mind and intellect too. It is this tendency that is described in verse 41 as the foul enemy destroying man's discrimination and knowledge. They prevent a dispassionate view of the object, the view of the witness. On the other hand, they give a biassed interpretation of them from the point of view of the instinctive satisfactions they can give. This has been referred to in a less pointed and indirect way in 2.62 and 2.64. The purification of the intellect and the mind can be achieved only when their attention is drawn inward towards the Spirit, who is behind the intellect even, instead of being driven to external objects by the force of natural tendencies, causing attachment and entanglement.

Communion with the Spirit purifies the intellect, mind and senses. It liberates the senses from the earlier dominance of nature over them, and puts them in a position to view all sense objects from an impersonal point of view and thus gain mastery over them. That is why the practice of devotion is absolutely essential for success in the discipline of Karma Yoga. For, non-attachment can never arise until the mind is able to hold the attitude of the witness and not of one seeking enjoyment. This new capacity can develop only when the bias given to the mind and senses by nature or past experiences is eliminated. This in turn can be achieved only when through devotion and meditation, the immaculate purity of the Spirit is brought to bear on the psychic being of man.

Chapter IV

ज्ञान-कर्म-संन्यास-योगः

RENUNCIATION OF ACTION IN KNOWLEDGE

Summary

The Doctrine of Incarnation : (1-16) Sri Kṛṣṇa tells Arjuna: I have revealed this spiritual knowledge in different ages for the benefit of man. Whenever unrighteousness prevails I embody Myself as the Incarnate for the protection of the good and the destruction of the wicked. By contemplation on the deeds and teachings of these Incarnations man can attain salvation.

In whatever way men worship Me, I approach them in that very aspect. Those who have worldly desires, worship various deities who are aspects of the Divine. But true worship consists in reflecting on the Divine in oneself. I, the Supreme Divine, have created both the Orders of Nature and of Society (*Cāturvarṇya*) but I am not in the least affected by these actions, because I have no attachment to them. Those who contemplate on Me as the great Creator without any attachment, will themselves be freed from attachments and gain liberation.

The True Meaning of Actionlessness: (17-35) Non-action or Naiṣkarmya, which is the characteristic of the Ātman, does not mean inactivity. It means being established in pure awareness without involvement in any kind of change. Among embodied beings, he who has attained to that spirit-consciousness—by virtue of which he is ever established in this uninvolved Ātman-awareness and is free from any egoistic impulse even while his body and mind are carrying out all their characteristic movements, he is the really wise man, not the one who, by an effort of his will, keeps aloof from external action, but inwardly remains subject to attachments and egoistic motivation. The former is an enlightened man while the latter is a mere idler.

This state of actionlessness in the sense of non-attachment is attained only through long and steadily practised discipline of dedicated action, combined with the discriminative understanding of one's being basically the 'non-attached Self.' Such knowledge-based action is the highest form of Yajña in the Vedic tradition. Yajña can take various forms. It may be with material ingredients, or it may take the form of austerity, or of practice of concentration, or of control of the senses, or of control of Prāṇa, or of scriptural study, or of practice of discrimination. The peak of Yajña discipline is reached when an aspirant sees the acts, the means of actions, the things acted upon and the process of action as but different manifestations of Brahman. This is called attainment of Samādhi in action. All action has Jñāna or wisdom as its end—the wisdom that enables one to experience everything as resting in Me who form their innermost soul. This knowledge has to be sought by serving wise teachers.

The Power of Enlightenment: (36-42) This Jñāna is the most powerful of purifiers, so that it is said that even the erstwhile sinner becomes a saint instantaneously on its onset. This wisdom comes naturally to one who becomes perfect in the discipline of disinterested action. One who has attained this is no more bound by any action, as even in the midst of all action he is established in the sense that he is the pure, detached and unaffected Ātman. Doubts and delusions about his spiritual identity no longer assail him. Service of the teacher, faith, and control of the senses are indispensable aids to the acquisition of this wisdom.

श्रीभगवानुवाच

इमं विवस्वते योगं प्रोक्तवानहमव्ययम् ।
विवस्वान्मनवे प्राह मनुरिक्ष्वाकवेऽब्रवीत् ॥ 1 ॥

Sri Bhagavān uvāca:
Imaṁ Vivasvate yogaṁ proktavān aham avyayam /
Vivasvān Manave prāha Manur Ikṣvākave'bravīt //1//

Avyayam : Eternal *imam* : this *yogam* : Yoga *aham* : I *Vivasvate*: to Vivasvān *proktavān* : taught, *Vivasvān* : Vivasvān *Manave* : to Manu *prāha* : told, *Manuḥ* : Manu *Ikṣvākave* : to Ikṣvāku *abravīt* : told.

The Blessed Lord said:

1. I imparted this immortal Yoga to Vivasvān, Vivasvān to Manu, and Manu to Ikṣvāku.

एवं परम्पराप्राप्तमिमं राजर्षयो विदुः ।
स कालेनेह महता योगो नष्टः परंतप ॥ 2 ॥

Evaṁ paraṁparā-prāptam imaṁ rāja' rṣayo viduḥ /
sa kālen'eha mahatā yogo naṣṭaḥ Paraṁtapa //2//

Paraṁtapa : O scorcher of enemies! *evam* : in this way *paraṁparāprāptam* : handed down in succession from teacher to disciple *imam* : this *rājarṣayaḥ* : the Rājarṣis *viduḥ* : knew. *Saḥ* : That *yogaḥ* : Yoga *mahatā kālena* : by long lapse of time *iha* : here in the world *naṣṭaḥ* : was lost.

2. O scorcher of foes! This Yoga handed down from teacher to disciple in succession, was known to the **Rājarṣis** (royal sages). But owing to long lapse of time, it was lost to the world.

स एवायं मया तेऽद्य योगः प्रोक्तः पुरातनः ।
भक्तोऽसि मे सखा चेति रहस्यं ह्येतदुत्तमम् ॥ 3 ॥

Sa ev'āyaṁ mayā te' dya yogaḥ proktaḥ purātanaḥ /
bhakto'si me sakhā c'eti rahasyaṁ hy etad uttamam //3//

(*Tvam* : You) *me* : My *bhaktaḥ* : devotee *sakhā* : friend *ca* : and *asi* : are, *iti* : thus (thinking) *purātanaḥ* : ancient *saḥ eva* : even that *ayam* : this *yogaḥ* : Yoga *mayā*: by Me *adya* : now *te* : to you *proktaḥ* : has been told; *hi* : for *etat* : this *uttamam* : great *rahasyam* : secret.

3. You are My devotee and friend—thinking thus, I have today declared to you even that ancient Yoga. For, it is a

noble secret (imparted by a teacher only to a worthy disciple).

अर्जुन उवाच

अपरं भवतो जन्म परं जन्म विवस्वतः ।
कथमेतद्विजानीयां त्वमादौ प्रोक्तवानिति ॥ 4 ॥

Arjuna uvāca:

Aparaṁ bhavato janma paraṁ janma Vivasvataḥ /
katham etad vijānīyāṁ tvam ādau proktavān iti //4//

Bhavataḥ : Of Thee *janmaḥ* : birth *aparam* : is not distant, is later, *Vivasvataḥ* : of Vivasvān *param* : very distant, earlier. *Tvam* : Thou *ādau* : in the beginning *etat* : this *proktavān* : have taught *iti* : this *katham* : how *vijānīyām* : am I to understand.

Arjuna said:

4. Thy life-time is later, that of Vivasvān was much earlier. How then am I to understand that Thou didst impart this doctrine to him?

श्रीभगवानुवाच

बहूनि मे व्यतीतानि जन्मानि तव चार्जुन ।
तान्यहं वेद सर्वाणि न त्वं वेत्थ परंतप ॥ 5 ॥

Sri Bhagavān uvāca:

Bahūni me vyatītāni janmāni tava c'ārjuna /
tāny ahaṁ veda sarvāṇī na tvaṁ vettha paraṁtapa //5//

Arjuna : O Arjuna! *me* : for Me *tava* : for you *ca* : and *bahūni* : many *janmāni* : births *vyatītāni* : have passed through. *Tāni sarvāṇi* : All that *aham* : I *veda* : know, *tvam* : you *na vettha* : do not know *Paraṁtapa* : O scorcher of foes!

The Blessed Lord said:

5. O Arjuna! You and I have passed through many births; I remember them all, but you do not, O scorcher of foes![1]

अजोऽपि सन्नव्ययात्मा भूतानामीश्वरोऽपि सन् ।
प्रकृतिं स्वामधिष्ठाय संभवाम्यात्ममायया ॥ 6 ॥

Ajo'pi sann avyay'ātmā bhūtānām īśvaro'pi san /
prakṛtiṁ svām adhiṣṭhāya sambhavāmy ātma-māyayā //6//

Ajaḥ : Birthless *avyayātmā* : deathless *api san* : though being *bhūtānām* : of beings *īśvaraḥ* : Lord *api san* : though being *svām* : My own *prākṛtim* : Nature *adhiṣṭhāya* : governing, employing *ātmamāyayā* : by the mysterious power inherent in Me *sambhavāmi*: am born.

6. Though birthless and deathless, and the Lord of all beings as well, yet I (the Eternal Being) take birth by My inherent mysterious Power (*Ātma-māyayā*), employing the pure or Sattva aspect of My material Nature (Prakṛti).

यदा यदा हि धर्मस्य ग्लानिर्भवति भारत ।
अभ्युत्थानमधर्मस्य तदात्मानं सृजाम्यहम् ॥ 7 ॥

Yadā-yadā hi dharmasya glānir bhavati Bhārata /
abhyutthānam adharmasya tadā'tmānaṁ sṛjāmy aham //7//

Bhārata : O scion of the Bharata race! *Yadā yadā* : whenever *dharmasya* : of Dharma (righteousness) *glāniḥ* : decline *adharmasya* : of Adharma (unrighteousness) *abhyutthānam* : ascendance *bhavati* : takes place, *tadā* : then *aham* : I *ātmānam* : Myself *sṛjāmi* : send forth, manifest.

7. Whenever there is decline of Dharma and ascendance of Adharma, then, O scion of the Bharata race! I manifest (incarnate) Myself in a body.

परित्राणाय साधूनां विनाशाय च दुष्कृताम् ।
धर्मसंस्थापनार्थाय संभवामि युगे युगे ॥ 8 ॥

Paritrāṇāya sādhūnāṁ vināśāya ca duṣkṛtām
dharma-samsthāpan'ārthāya sambhavāmi yuge yuge //8//

Sādhūnām : Of the good *paritrāṇāya*: for the protection, *duṣkṛtām*: of the evil *vināśāya* : for the destruction *ca* : and, *dharma-saṁsthāpanārthāya* : for the establishment of Dharma *yuge yuge* from age to age *sambhavāmi* : I am born.

8. For the protection of the good, for the destruction of the evil, and for the establishment of Dharma, I am born from age to age.[2]

जन्म कर्म च मे दिव्यमेवं यो वेत्ति तत्त्वतः ।
त्यक्त्वा देहं पुनर्जन्म नैति मामेति सोऽर्जुन ॥ 9 ॥

Janma karma ca me divyam evaṁ yo vetti tattvataḥ /
tyaktvā dehaṁ punar-janma n'aiti mām eti so'rjuna //9//

Arjuna : O Arjuna! *me* : My *evam* : in this way *divyam* : divine *janma* : birth *karma* : actions *ca* : and *yaḥ* : who *tattvataḥ* : in their nature *vetti* : understands, *saḥ* : he *deham* : body *tyaktvā* : abandoning *punaḥ* : again *janma* : birth *na* : not *eti* : gets, *mām* : Me *eti* : gets.

9. O Arjuna! He who thus understands the truth about My embodiment and My deeds—he, on abandoning his present body, is not reborn, he attains to Me.[3]

वीतरागभयक्रोधा मन्मया मामुपाश्रिताः ।
बहवो ज्ञानतपसा पूता मद्भावमागताः ॥ 10 ॥

Vīta-rāga-bhaya-krodhā manmayā mām upāśritāḥ /
bahavo jñāna-tapasā pūtā mad-bhāvam āgatāḥ //10//

Vītarāgabhayakrodhāḥ : free from passion, fear and anger, *manmayāḥ* : ever absorbed in my thoughts, *mām upāśritāḥ* : dependent on Me *bahavaḥ* : many *jñānatapasā* : by knowledge and austerity *pūtāḥ* : purified *madbhāvam* : My state *āgatāḥ* : have attained to.

10. Freed from passion, fear and anger, ever absorbed in My thought, and ever dependent on Me—many have attained

to My state, being purified by the fire of knowledge and austerity.

ये यथा मां प्रपद्यन्ते तांस्तथैव भजाम्यहम् ।
मम वर्त्मानुवर्तन्ते मनुष्याः पार्थ सर्वशः ॥ 11 ॥

Ye yathā māṁ prapadyante tāṁs tath'aiva bhajāmy aham /
mama vartm'ānuvartante manuṣyāḥ Pārtha sarvaśaḥ //11//

Pārtha : O son of Pṛthā! *ye* : whosoever *yathā* : through whatever path *mām* : Me *prapadyante* : worship, *tān* : them *tathā* : in the same way *eva* : verily *aham* : I *bhajāmi* : accept. *Manuṣyāḥ* : men *sarvaśaḥ* : everywhere *mama* : My *vartma* : path *anuvartante* : follow.

11. O Pārtha! Whosoever worship Me through whatsoever path, I verily accept and bless them in that way. Men everywhere follow My path.[4]

काङ्क्षन्तः कर्मणां सिद्धिं यजन्त इह देवताः ।
क्षिप्रं हि मानुषे लोके सिद्धिर्भवति कर्मजा ॥ 12 ॥

Kāṅkṣantaḥ karmaṇāṁ siddhiṁ yajanta iha devatāḥ /
kṣipraṁ hi mānuṣe loke siddhir bhavati karma-jā //12//

Iha : In this world *karmaṇām* : of Karmas *siddhim* : results, fruits *kāṅkṣantaḥ* : those desiring *devatāḥ* : deities *yajante* : worship; *hi* : for *mānuṣe* : in the human *loke* : world *karmajā* : born of Karma *siddhiḥ* : fruit *kṣipram* : quickly *bhavati* : is attained.

12. In this world those who entertain desire for the fruits of pious works, worship the deities. For in this world of men such actions bear fruit quickly.[5]

चातुर्वर्ण्यं मया सृष्टं गुणकर्मविभागशः ।
तस्य कर्तारमपि मां विद्ध्यकर्तारमव्ययम् ॥ 13 ॥

Cāturvarṇyaṁ mayā sṛṣṭaṁ guṇa -karma-vibhāgaśaḥ /
tasya kartāram api māṁ viddhy akartāram avyayam //13//

Guṇakarmavibhāgaśaḥ : According to division of aptitudes born of Nature's dispositions (Guṇās) and works *cāturvarṇyam* : the division into fourfold Varṇās *mayā* : by Me *sṛṣṭam* : created. *Tasya* : Of it *kartāram* : originator *api* : though *mām* : Me *akartāram* : non-doer *avyayam* : unchanging *viddhi* : know as.

13. According to the aptitudes resulting from the dispositions of Nature (Guṇas) and works, the social order of fourfold division has been created by Me. Though I am their originator, know me to be not an agent but the spirit unchanging.[6]

न मां कर्माणि लिम्पन्ति न मे कर्मफले स्पृहा ।
इति मां योऽभिजानाति कर्मभिर्न स बध्यते ॥ 14 ॥

Na mām karmāṇi limpanti na me karma-phale spṛhā /
iti mām yo'bhijānāti karmabhir na sa badhyate //14//

Karmāṇi : Actions *mām* : Me *na* : not *limpanti* : affect, *na* : not *karmaphale* : in the fruits of action *spṛhā* : desire; *iti* : thus *mām* : Me *yaḥ* : whoever *abhijānāti* : knows, *saḥ* : he *karmabhiḥ* : by Karmas *na* : not *badhyate* : is bound.

14. Actions do not affect Me. Nor have I any desire for the fruits of action. Whoever knows Me to be so, is not bound by Karma.

एवं ज्ञात्वा कृतं कर्म पूर्वैरपि मुमुक्षुभिः ।
कुरु कर्मैव तस्मात्त्वं पूर्वैः पूर्वतरं कृतम् ॥ 15 ॥

Evam jñātvā kṛtam karma purvair api mumukṣubhiḥ /
kuru karm'aiva tasmāt tvam pūrvaiḥ pūrvataram kṛtam //15//

Evam : Thus *jñātvā* : knowing *pūrvaiḥ* : ancient *mumukṣubhiḥ* : seekers after liberation *karma* : action *kṛtam* : was performed. *Tasmāt* : Therefore *pūrvaiḥ* : by the ancients *pūrvataram* : from time immemorial *kṛtam* : performed *karma eva* : Karma itself *tvam* : you *api* : also *kuru* : perform.

15. Knowing thus, the ancient aspirants after liberation per-

formed works. Therefore you too do work as these ancients did from time immemorial.

किं कर्म किमकर्मेति कवयोऽप्यत्र मोहिताः ।
तत्ते कर्म प्रवक्ष्यामि यज्ज्ञात्वा मोक्ष्यसेऽशुभात् ॥ 16 ॥

Kiṁ karma kim akarm'eti kavayo'py atra mohitāḥ /
tat te karma pravakṣyāmi yaj jñātvā mokṣyase'śubhāt //16//

Karma kim : What is work, *akarma kim* : what is 'no-work', *iti* : thus *atra* : in this matter *kavayaḥ api* : even wise men *mohitāḥ*: are perplexed; *yat* : which *jñātvā* : knowing *aśubhāt* : from evil *mokṣyase* : you will be liberated, *tat* : that *karma* : action *pravakṣyāmi* : I shall tell.

16. What is work and what is 'no work', is a subject regarding which even the wise are perplexed. I shall therefore speak to you about work, by knowing which one is liberated from evil (or the life of bondage in Samsāra).[7]

कर्मणो ह्यपि बोद्धव्यं बोद्धव्यं च विकर्मणः ।
अकर्मणश्च बोद्धव्यं गहना कर्मणो गतिः ॥ 17 ॥

Karmaṇo hy api boddhavyaṁ boddhavyaṁ ca vikarmaṇaḥ /
akarmaṇaś ca boddhavyaṁ gahanā karmaṇo gatiḥ //17//

Karmaṇaḥ : (The truth) about beneficial Karma *api* : even *boddhavyam* : has to be understood, *vikarmaṇaḥ ca* : also (the truth) about baneful work *boddhavyam* : has to be understood, *akarmaṇaḥ ca* : (the truth) about 'no work' also *boddhavyam* : has to be understood, *karmaṇaḥ* : of Karma *gatiḥ* : the way *gahanā* : difficult to understand.

17. The truth about the nature of 'beneficial work' has to be understood, as also of 'baneful work' and of 'no work'. The way of work is difficult indeed to understand.

कर्मण्यकर्म यः पश्येदकर्मणि च कर्म यः ।
स बुद्धिमान्मनुष्येषु स युक्तः कृत्स्नकर्मकृत् ॥ 18 ॥

Karmaṇy akarma yaḥ paśyed akarmaṇi ca karma yaḥ /
sa buddhimān manuṣyeṣu sa yuktaḥ kṛtsna-karma-kṛt //18//

Karmaṇi : In work *akarma* : 'no work' *akarmaṇi karma* : in 'no work' work *ca* : and *yaḥ* : who *paśyet* : would see, *saḥ* : he *manuṣyeṣu* : among men *buddhimān* : intelligent; *saḥ* : he *kṛtsnakarma kṛt* : accomplisher of all work *yuktaḥ* : established in Yoga.

18. He who sees work in 'no work' and 'no work' in work, he is wise among men. Even while doing all work, he remains established in Yoga.[8]

यस्य सर्वे समारम्भाः कामसंकल्पवर्जिताः ।
ज्ञानाग्निदग्धकर्माणं तमाहुः पण्डितं बुधाः ॥ 19 ॥

Yasya sarve samārambhāḥ kāma-saṁkalpa-varjitāḥ /
jñān'āgni-dagdha-karmāṇam tam āhuḥ paṇḍitaṁ budhāḥ //19//

Yasya : Whose *sarve* : all ***samārambhāḥ*** : actions *kāmasaṁkalpavarjitāḥ* : devoid of desire-born objectives, *jñānāgnidagdha-karmāṇam* : whose actions have been burnt up by the fire of knowledge, *tam* : him *budhāḥ* : the wise *paṇḍitam* : sage *āhuḥ* : call.

19. Whose undertakings are devoid of self-centred objectives, whose works have been burnt up by the fire of knowledge—him the wise call a sage.

त्यक्त्वा कर्मफलासङ्गं नित्यतृप्तो निराश्रयः ।
कर्मण्यभिप्रवृत्तोऽपि नैव किञ्चित्करोति सः ॥ 20 ॥

Tyaktvā karma-phalāsaṅgaṁ nitya-tṛpto nirāśrayaḥ /
karmaṇy abhipravṛtto'pi nai'va kiñcit karoti saḥ //20//

Karmaphalāsaṅgam : Attachment for the fruits of action *tyaktvā* : having abandoned, *nityatṛptaḥ* : ever satisfied *nirāśrayaḥ* : free from calculations *karmaṇi* : in action *abhipravṛttaḥ* : engaged *api*: even *saḥ* : he *kiñcit* : anything *na karoti eva* : does not do verily.

20. Without attachment to the fruits of action, ever-satisfied and free from calculations, he is verily doing nothing, even though engaged in actions.

निराशीर्यतचित्तात्मा त्यक्तसर्वपरिग्रहः ।
शारीरं केवलं कर्म कुर्वन्नाप्नोति किल्बिषम् ॥ 21 ॥

Nirāśīr yata-citt'ātmā tyakta-sarva-parigrahaḥ /
śārīraṁ kevalaṁ karma kurvan n'āpnoti kilbiṣam //21//

Nirāśīḥ : Without desires *yatacittātmā* : with mind controlled *tyaktasarvaparigrahaḥ* : with no sense of ownership over possessions *śārīram* : physical *kevalam* : mere *karma* : actions *kurvan*: performing *kilbiṣam* : sin *na āpnoti* : incurs not.

21. One who is free from desires, whose mind is well-controlled, and who is without any sense of ownership, incurs no sin from works, as his actions are merely physical.

यदृच्छालाभसंतुष्टो द्वन्द्वातीतो विमत्सरः ।
समः सिद्धावसिद्धौ च कृत्वापि न निबध्यते ॥ 22 ॥

Yadṛcchā-lābha-saṁtuṣṭo dvandv'ātīto vimatsaraḥ /
samaḥ siddhāv asiddhau ca kṛtvā'pi na nibadhyate //22//

Yadṛcchālābhasaṁtuṣṭaḥ : Satisfied with whatever comes without calculation, *dvandvātītaḥ* : rising above the contrasting conditions of life, *vimatsaraḥ* : free from competitive spirit, *siddhau* : in success *asiddhau* : in failure *ca* : and ***samaḥ*** : alike, *kṛtvā api* : though acting *na nibadhyate* : is not bound.

22. Satisfied with whatever comes without calculations, rising above the contrasting conditions of life, without any competitive spirit, and alike in success and in failure, a man, though working, incurs no sin.

गतसङ्गस्य मुक्तस्य ज्ञानावस्थितचेतसः ।
यज्ञायाचरतः कर्म समग्रं प्रविलीयते ॥ 23 ॥

Gata-saṅgasya muktasya jñān'āvasthita-cetasaḥ /
yajñāy'ācarataḥ karma samagraṁ pravilīyate //23//

Gatasaṅgasya : Of one without attachment *muktasya* : of one who is free (from the sense of agency) *jñānāvasthitacetasaḥ* : of one whose mind is well established in the knowledge of God *Yajñāya* : by way of dedication to the Lord *karma* : work *ācarataḥ* : performing *samagram* : in entirety i.e. along with the tendencies responsible for it *pravilīyate* : melt away.

23. In the case of one who is without attachments and the sense of agency, and whose mind is fully established in the knowledge of God,—his actions, being done in dedication to the Lord, melt away with their very tendencies.

ब्रह्मार्पणं ब्रह्म हविर्ब्रह्माग्नौ ब्रह्मणा हुतम् ।
ब्रह्मैव तेन गन्तव्यं ब्रह्मकर्मसमाधिना ॥ 24 ॥

Brahm'ārpaṇaṁ brahma havir brahm'āgnau brahmaṇā hutam /
brahm'āiva tena gantavyaṁ brahma-karma-samādhinā //24//

Arpaṇam : Offering *Brahma* : is Brahman, *haviḥ* : oblations *Brahman* : is Brahman; *Brahmāgnau* : in the fire that is Brahman *Brahmaṇā* : by the sacrificer who is Brahman *hutam* : sacrificial rite performed (*Brahma* : is Brahman); *Brahmakarmasamādhinā* : by one who has this absorpition in work as Brahman *tena* : by him *gantavyam* : should be reached *Brahma eva* : Brahman alone.

24. To one of the above description, the ladle with which the offering is made and the oblations are Brahman; and the sacrificial rite (which is Brahman) is performed by the sacrificer who is Brahman, in the fire which too is Brahman. He who is thus absorbed in work as Brahman, attains to Brahman alone.[9]

दैवमेवापरे यज्ञं योगिनः पर्युपासते ।
ब्रह्माग्नावपरे यज्ञं यज्ञेनैवोपजुह्वति ॥ 25 ॥

Daivam ev'āpare yajñaṁ yoginaḥ paryupāsate /
brahm'āgnau apare yajñaṁ yajñen' aiv'opajuhvati //25//

Apare : Other *yoginaḥ* : Yogins *daivam eva* : relating to Devas alone *Yajñam* : sacrifice *paryupāsate* : perform. *Apare* : Still others *yajñena eva* : by sacrifice itself (by Ātman) *yajñam* : sacrifice (oblation) *brahmāgnau* : in the fire of Brahman *upajuhvati* : make oblations.

25. Some Yogis perform sacrifices especially wanting to propitiate deities. Still others offer sacrifice (the Ātman) itself as oblation (Yajña) in the fire of Brahman.[10]

श्रोत्रादीनीन्द्रियाण्यन्ये संयमाग्निषु जुह्वति ।
शब्दादीन्विषयानन्य इन्द्रियाग्निषु जुह्वति ॥ 26 ॥

Śrotrādīnī'ndriyāṇy anye saṁyam'āgniṣu juhvati /
śabdādīn viṣayān anya indriy'āgniṣu juhvati //26//

Anye : Other Yogins *śrotrādīni* : hearing and other *indriyāṇi* : organs of knowledge *samyamāgniṣu* : in the fire of restraint *juhvati* : offer as sacrifice. *Anye* : Some *sabdadīn* : sound and other *viṣayān* : sense objects *indriyāgniṣu* : in the fire of senses *juhvati* : offer as sacrifice.

26. Some offer their organs of knowledge like hearing as sacrifice in the fire of restraint, while others take in all their sense perceptions as oblations made in the fire of their respective senses.

सर्वाणीन्द्रियकर्माणि प्राणकर्माणि चापरे ।
आत्मसंयमयोगाग्नौ जुह्वति ज्ञानदीपिते ॥ 27 ॥

Sarvāṇī'ndriya-karmāṇi prāṇakarmāṇi cā'pare /
ātma-samyama yogāgnau juhvati jñāna-dīpite //27//

Apare : Others *sarvāṇi* : all *indriyakarmāṇi* : functions of the sense organs *prāṇakarmāṇi ca* : and the functionings of Prāṇa (vital energy) *jñānadīpite* : enkindled by knowledge *ātmasamyama-yogāgnau* : in the fire of the discipline of self-restraint *juhvati* : offer as sacrifice.

27. Others offer all the functions of their senses and vital energy as sacrificial offerings in the fire of self-restraint kindled by knowledge.

द्रव्ययज्ञास्तपोयज्ञा योगयज्ञास्तथापरे ।
स्वाध्यायज्ञानयज्ञाश्च यतयः संशितव्रताः ॥ 28 ॥

Dravya-yajñās tapo-yajñā yoga-yajñās tathā'pare /
svādhyāya-jñāna-yajñāś ca yatayaḥ saṁśita-vratāḥ //28//

Tathā : Likewise *apare* : some ***saṁśitavratāḥ*** *yatayaḥ* : being of rigid vows and hard practice *dravyayajñāḥ* : offerers of their wealth as sacrifice, *tapoyajñāḥ* : offerers of austerity as sacrifice, *yogayajñāḥ* : offerers of their Yogic practice as sacrifice, *svādhyāya-jñānayajñāḥ ca* : and offerers of daily study of the Vedas as knowledge sacrifice.

28. Likewise others, being of rigid vows and hard practice, offer their wealth, their austerities, their Yogic practices, and their daily study of the Vedas as sacrifice.

अपाने जुह्वति प्राणं प्राणेऽपानं तथापरे ।
प्राणापानगती रुद्ध्वा प्राणायामपरायणाः ॥ 29 ॥

Apāne juhvati prāṇaṁ prāṇe'pānaṁ tathā'pare /
prāṇ'āpāna-gatī ruddhvā prāṇāyāma-parāyaṇāḥ //29//

Prāṇāyāma-parāyaṇāḥ : Devoted to the practice of Prāṇāyāma *apare* : some others *prāṇāpāna-gatī ruddhvā* : regulating the movement of Prāṇa and Apāna, *apāne* : in Apāna *prāṇam* : Prāṇa, *tathā* : in the same way *prāṇe* : in Prāṇa *apānam* : Apāna *juhvati* : offer oblations.

29. Others devoted to the practice of Prāṇāyāma, regulate the movement of Prāṇa and Apāna, and offer as oblation Prāṇa in Apāna, and likewise Apāna in Prāṇa.

अपरे नियताहाराः प्राणान्प्राणेषु जुह्वति ।
सर्वेऽप्येते यज्ञविदो यज्ञक्षपितकल्मषाः ॥ 30 ॥

Apare niyat'āhārāḥ prāṇān prāṇeṣu juhvati /
sarve'py ete yajña-vido yajña-kṣapita-kalmaṣāḥ //30//

Apare : Some others *niyatāhārāḥ* : regulating their food *prāṇān* : Prāṇas (vital energy acquired from food) *prāṇeṣu* : in Prāṇas (vital energy in the body) *juhvati* : offer as a sacrificial offering; *ete sarve api* : all these *yajñavidaḥ* : knowers of Yajña, *yajñakṣapitakalmaṣāḥ* : men having their impurities washed away by Yajña.

30. Some others, who observe regulation of food, make a sacrificial offering of the Prāṇa as the vital energy present in food stuffs, into the Prāṇa as the vital energy enlivening the body. All these know the true nature of sacrifice and have all evil in them washed away by Yajña (sacrifice).

यज्ञशिष्टामृतभुजो यान्ति ब्रह्म सनातनम् ।
नायं लोकोऽस्त्ययज्ञस्य कुतोऽन्यः कुरुसत्तम ॥ 31 ॥

Yajña-śiṣṭāmṛta-bhujo yānti brahma sanātanam /
n'āyaṁ loko'sty ayajñasya kuto'nyaḥ Kuru-sattama //31//

Yajña-śiṣṭāmṛta-bhujaḥ : Those who partake of nectar, the sacred remnants of a sacrifice *sanātanam* : eternal *brahma* : Brahman *yānti* : attain to *Kurusattma* : O Thou the best among the Kurus! *ayajñasya* : for one who does not follow the discipline of Yajña *ayam* : this *lokaḥ* : world *na asti* : is not, *anyaḥ* : the other *kutaḥ*: where?

31. Those who partake of nectar, the sacramental remnants of sacrifice, attain to the eternal Brahman. O Thou the best of the Kurus! For one who sacrifices not, this world is lost, not to speak then of the hereafter.[11]

एवं बहुविधा यज्ञा वितता ब्रह्मणो मुखे ।
कर्मजान्विद्धि तान्सर्वानेवं ज्ञात्वा विमोक्ष्यसे ॥ 32 ॥

Evaṁ bahuvidhā yajñā vitatā brahmaṇo mukhe |
karmajān viddhi tān sarvān evaṁ jñātvā vimokṣyase //32//

Evam : In this way *bahuvidhāḥ* : many kinds of *yajñāḥ* : sacrifices *brahmaṇaḥ mukhe* : in the face of Brahman i.e. in the Vedas as their prominent teaching. *vitatāḥ* : are set forth. *Sarvān tān* : All of them *karmajān viddhi* : know as springing from work. *Evam* : Thus *jñātvā* : knowing *vimokṣyase* : you will be free.

32. Thus many forms of sacrifice are set forth prominently in the Vedas (as paths to Brahman). All of them spring from work (done by body, mind, and speech). Knowing this, you will attain liberation.

श्रेयान्द्रव्यमयाद्यज्ञाज्ज्ञानयज्ञः परंतप ।
सर्वं कर्माखिलं पार्थ ज्ञाने परिसमाप्यते ॥ 33 ॥

Śreyān dravyamayād yajñāt jñāna-yajñaḥ Paraṁtapa |
sarvaṁ karmā'khilaṁ Pārtha jñāne parisamāpyate //33//

Paraṁtapa : O Scorcher of enemies *dravyamayāt* : than material *yajñāt* : sacrifice *Jñānayajñaḥ* : knowledge sacrifice *śreyān*: is superior. *Pārtha* : O son of Pṛthā. *sarvam* : all *karma* : work *akhilam* : without exception *jñāne* : in knowledge *parisamāpyate*: culminates.

33. O scorcher of enemies! Sacrifice involving knowledge is superior to sacrifice with material objects; for, O son of Pṛthā, all works without exception culminate in knowledge.[12]

तद्विद्धि प्रणिपातेन परिप्रश्नेन सेवया ।
उपदेक्ष्यन्ति ते ज्ञानं ज्ञानिनस्तत्त्वदर्शिनः ॥ 34 ॥

Tad viddhi praṇipātena paripraśnena sevayā |
upadekṣyanti te jñānaṁ jñāninas tattva-darśinaḥ //34//

Praṇipātena : With prostrations *paripraśnena* : with repeated questionings *sevayā* : with service *tat* : that *viddhi* : learn. *Tattvadarśinaḥ* : The knowers of the Truth *jñāninaḥ* : wise men *jñānam* : knowledge of the Truth *te* : to you *upadekṣyanti* : will teach.

34. With reverential salutations do you approach them—the wise men who have known the Truth. Serve them, and question them repeatedly (with due respect until your doubts are clarified). These wise men will impart the knowledge of this divine Truth unto you.

यज्ज्ञात्वा न पुनर्मोहमेवं यास्यसि पाण्डव ।
येन भूतान्यशेषेण द्रक्ष्यस्यात्मन्यथो मयि ॥ 35 ॥

Yaj jñātvā na punar mohaṁ evaṁ yāsyasi Pāṇḍava /
yena bhūtāny aśeṣeṇa drakṣyasy ātmany atho mayi //35//

Pāṇḍava : O son of Pāṇḍu *yat jñātvā* : knowing which *punaḥ* : again *evam* : in this way *moham* : delusion *na yāsyasi* : will not get; *yena* : by which *bhūtāni* : beings *aśeṣeṇa* : in their entirety *ātmani* : in the Ātman *atha* : also *mayi* : in Me *ca* : and *drakṣyasi* : will see.

35. They will impart to you that divine knowledge by knowing which you will not again fall into such delusion, for you will then see all beings in their entirety in the Self and also in Me.[13]

अपि चेदसि पापेभ्यः सर्वेभ्यः पापकृत्तमः ।
सर्वं ज्ञानप्लवेनैव वृजिनं संतरिष्यसि ॥ 36 ॥

Api ced asi pāpebhyaḥ sarvebhyaḥ pāpa-kṛttamaḥ /
sarvaṁ jñāna-plaven'aiva vṛjinaṁ saṁtariṣyasi //36/

Tvam : You *sarvebhyaḥ* : of all *papebhyaḥ* : of sinful beings *papakṛttamaḥ* : the worst sinner *api chet asi* : even if you be, *sarvam* : all *vṛjinam* : sin *jñānaplavena eva* : by the raft of divine knowledge alone *samtariṣyasi* : will cross over.

36. Even if you happen to be the worst of sinners, you will surely go across all sin by the raft of divine knowledge.

यथैधांसि समिद्धोऽग्निर्भस्मसात्कुरुतेऽर्जुन ।
ज्ञानाग्निः सर्वकर्माणि भस्मसात्कुरुते तथा ॥ 37 ॥

Yath'aidhāṁsi samiddho'gnir bhasmasāt kurute'rjuna /
jñān'āgniḥ sarva-karmāṇi bhasmasāt kurute tathā //37//

Arjuna : O Arjuna *samiddhaḥ* : well kindled *agniḥ* : fire *edhāṁsi*, fuel *yathā* : in which way *bhasmasāt kurute* : reduces to ashes *tathā* : in that way *jñānāgniḥ* : the fire of knowledge *sarvakarmāṇi* all works *bhasmasāt kurute* : reduces to ashes.

37. Just as a well-kindled fire reduces a heap of fire-wood to ashes, so does the fire of divine knowledge reduce all sins to ashes.

न हि ज्ञानेन सदृशं पवित्रमिह विद्यते ।
तत्स्वयं योगसंसिद्धः कालेनात्मनि विन्दति ॥ 38 ॥

Na hi jñānena sadṛśaṁ pavitram iha vidyate /
tat svayaṁ yoga-saṁsiddhaḥ kālen'ātmani vindati //38//

Iha : In this world *jñānena sadṛśam*: equal to divine knowledge *pavitram* : purifier *na vidyate* : does not exist *hi* : verily; *Yoga saṁsiddhaḥ* : one who has attained perfection in Yoga *kālena* : in course of time *tat* : that knowledge *ātmani* : in oneself *svayam* : by oneself *vindati* : finds.

38. Verily there is nothing so purifying as knowledge in this world. One who is perfect in Yoga discovers it in oneself in course of time.

श्रद्धावाँल्लभते ज्ञानं तत्परः संयतेन्द्रियः ।
ज्ञानं लब्ध्वा परां शान्तिमचिरेणाधिगच्छति ॥ 39 ॥

Śraddhāvāṁl labhate jñānaṁ tat-paraḥ saṁyat'endriyaḥ /
jñānaṁ labdhvā parāṁ śāntim aciren'ādhigacchati //39//

Sraddhāvān : One with deep faith *tatparaḥ* : one having zeal and devotion for it *samyatendriyaḥ* : one with subdued senses *jñānaṁ labhate* : gains the divine knowledge ; *jñānaṁ labdhvā* : having obtained knowledge, *acirena* : quickly *parām* : supreme *śāntim* : peace, *adhigacchati* : gets.

39. A man of deep Faith (Śraddhā) obtains this divine knowledge, being full of zeal and devotion for it and endowed with mastery of the senses. Having obtained that knowledge, he is established in supreme peace very soon.[14]

अज्ञश्चाश्रद्दधानश्च संशयात्मा विनश्यति ।
नायं लोकोऽस्ति न परो न सुखं संशयात्मनः ॥ 40 ॥

Ajñaś c'āśraddadhānaś ca saṁśay'ātmā vinaśyati /
n'āyaṁ loko'sti na paro na sukhaṁ saṁśay'ātmanaḥ //40//

Ajñaḥ : An ignorant man *ca*: and *aśraddhadhānaḥ* : a man without faith *ca* : and *samśayātmā* : a man whose nature is to doubt *vinaśyati* : is ruined; *samśayātmanaḥ* : for the doubting man *ayam lokaḥ* : this world *na asti* : is not, *na paraḥ* : nor the world beyond, *na sukham* : nor happiness.

40. An ignorant man without any positive faith, who knows only to doubt, goes to ruin. To such a doubting soul there is neither this world nor the world beyond. There is no happiness for him.[15]

योगसंन्यस्तकर्माणं ज्ञानसंछिन्नसंशयम् ।
आत्मवन्तं न कर्माणि निबध्नन्ति धनंजय ॥ 41 ॥

Yoga-saṁnyasta-karmāṇaṁ jñāna-saṁchinna-saṁśayam /
ātmavantaṁ na karmāṇi nibadhnanti Dhanañjaya //41//

Dhanañjaya : O Dhanañjaya! *yoga-saṁnyasta-karmāṇam* : him who has abandoned work through Yoga of dedication and detachment *jñāna-saṁchinna-saṁśayam* : him whose doubts have been dispelled by divine knowledge *ātmavantam* : him who is poised in the Self *karmāṇi* : works *na nibadhnanti* : do not bind.

41. O Arjuna! Works do not bind one who has abandoned them through Yoga consisting in dedication and detachment,

whose doubts have been dispelled by divine knowledge, and who is poised in the Self.

तस्मादज्ञानसंभूतं हृत्स्थं ज्ञानासिनात्मनः ।
छित्त्वैनं संशयं योगमातिष्ठोत्तिष्ठ भारत ॥ 42 ॥

Tasmād ajñāna-saṁbhūtaṁ hṛt-sthaṁ jñān'āsinā'tmanaḥ /
chittv'ainaṁ saṁśayaṁ yogam ātiṣṭh'ottiṣṭha Bhārata //42//

Tasmāt : Therefore *ātmanaḥ* : of the Ātman *hṛtstham* : abiding in the heart *ajñānasambhūtam* : born of ignorance *enam* : this *saṁśayam* : doubt *jñānāsinā* : by the sword of knowledge *chittvā* : cutting asunder *yogam* : Yoga *ātiṣṭha* : follow *Bhārata* : O scion of Bharata race! *uttiṣṭha* : arise.

42. Therefore cutting asunder the sceptical tendency of the heart by the sword of divine knowledge, betake yourself to Yoga (communion through sacrificial action) and arise, O scion of the Bharata race!

ॐ तत्सदिति श्रीमद्भगवद्गीतासूपनिषत्सु ब्रह्मविद्यायां
योगशास्त्रे श्रीकृष्णार्जुनसंवादे ज्ञानकर्मसंन्यासयोगो
नाम चतुर्थोऽध्यायः ॥ 4 ॥

NOTES

1. *Vrs.*5-7: The deep mystery of Divine Incarnation is stated here. It is a mystery, because the infinite and the omnipotent being is, according to this doctrine, born as a man, a limited being. This is unaccountable and mysterious, yet a little thought will make it clear that the mystery in it is not more than what is involved in the Supreme Being manifesting Himself as the universe. So according to the *Bhāgavata* the first and the primeval Incarnation is the Puruṣa, the Cosmic Whole ensouled by Him, and out of this Puruṣa all the Līlāvatāras (sportive Descents) have come.

How the Incarnation takes place is indicated by two expressions *Ātma-māyayā* and *Prakṛtim svām adhiṣṭhāya.* Ātma-māyā is His 'inherent Power or Will.' No limited being can set any limitation to that Power. It is 'what makes the impossible possible'. It implies that manifestation in any limited or imperfect form does not affect His infinitude and perfection. In the Incarnation this infinitude and perfection are present, in spite of the human form through which these manifest. The worship of the Incarnation is therefore equal to the worship of the Supreme Being Himself.

Prakṛti is His material Nature, constituted of the three Guṇas of Sattva, Rajas and Tamas. The body and mind of all beings are the combinations of their evolutes. But in their case these combinations are formed subject to Karma. But the body of the Incarnation is not subject to Karma, but is formed by the Divine will for the purpose of world-redemption. He is born not as a slave but as the master of Nature out of His free will, and His body is formed of pure Sattva. The individual, on the other hand, is born as the slave of Karma for attaining the individual ends of Dharma, Artha, Kāma and Mokṣa. His body is formed mostly of Tamas and Rajas, and as he advances spiritually, a little of Sattva also enters into its make-up. Thus the embodiment of the Incarnation is vastly different from that of the individual. The individualisation of the Absolute Being, which is called an Incarnation, is an expression of self-mastery and is meant to serve a cosmic and not an individual purpose.

2. *V*.8: Here the purpose of a Divine Incarnation is given as the establishment of Dharma (righteousness), the destruction of the wicked, and the protection of the good. This description of the purpose of an Incarnation has to be widened, if we are to bring the lives of all recognised by the Puranas as Incarnations, within its ambit. Many of them like Kapila, Nara-Narāyaṇa, Vyāsa, Buddha, etc., were great teachers only and did not take any part in wars to destroy the wicked and protect the good. But their personalities, activities and teachings have had far-reaching effects on the life of man. In that way, they may be said to have established Dharma—a scheme of life which has man's spiritual elevation as its ultimate aim. The *Bhāgavata* adds one more purpose to those stated above. It is said that the life of a Divine Incarnation and his relation with His various associates and devotees leave behind a very rich tradi-

tion of holy acts and ways of living which form the subject-matter for devotional texts, and these become themes for pious contemplation by generations of their followers and devotees. Thus we have the *Rāmāyaṇa* and the *Bhāgavata*, which set forth the spiritual glory of Rāma and Kṛṣṇa, and have formed the centre of the devotional life of countless generations. The teachings set forth in such texts have these wide-ranging effects on the life of man. The *Bhagavad-Gītā* itself is an example of it. So it is better to take the establishment of Dharma in a wider sense and interpret it as bringing a greater and greater awareness of man's spiritual goal, with which his worldly welfare also is closely associated.

A criticism is made of the Hindu theory of Incarnations that the great Incarnations like Rāma and Kṛṣṇa only kill evil ones who oppose them. Unlike Jesus Christ, Hindu Incarnations are not found to die for the salvation of man. In answer to this it may be said that the relation between Christ's death on the cross and man's salvation is a pure assumption which finds no justification except among those who share the Christian faith. The followers of Rāma and Kṛṣṇa also believe that by dying at the hands of these Divinities or even in their presence, their opponents gained salvation. So slaughter is one of the ways by which certain Incarnations, with particular world missions, bestowed their grace and gave salvation to those who cultivated the attitude of antagonism to them.

3. *Vrs.*9-10: The trans-physical importance of the divine Incarnation, already stated in the earlier note, is referred to in this passage. It is more often after his life-time than when he is alive, that an Incarnation receives wide recognition. After the Incarnation disappears, He is worshipped as the Deity by His followers, and his personality, deeds and teachings become the centre of a cult. A person may not understand philosophies and theologies, but through faith and devoted worship of the Incarnation, even a man of little learning can attain salvation. An Incarnation is always hypostatic with Brahman, and even after his physical body passes away, he is available for worship to those with faith. That faith consists in the capacity to grasp the identity of the Incarnation with the Deity Himself. Just as a backwater is linked with the sea and is one with it always, the Divine Incarnate also is always linked with the Infinite and Absolute Brahman. He is an expression

of the Anugraha-śakti or Grace of Brahman, and not a mere individual centre of power. So he is one with the eternal Godhead. The worship of any personalised conception becomes object for practising Bhakti and Jñāna, and a means for salvation, only if this faith is dominantly present in the mind of the worshipper. Bhakti, Jñāna and Mukti can be given only by the Supreme Being, and the Incarnation is essentially this Supreme Being—His Redeeming Power or His *Anugraha-śakti.*

4. *V.*11: This verse is the fundametal tenet of universal religion. Wherever worship is done, only the one Supreme Being is worshipped. No one, except the perfected sage, can worship Him in His fullness, since the human mind can grasp only limited aspects of Him. The more an individual or a community is evolved, the more noble and comprehensive will be their conception of the Deity. But the less evolved man too is adoring the same Deity, grasping such aspects of His as his undeveloped mind would allow. It is just like various forms being chipped from a huge block of marble. The more skilled the workman, the more artistic will be the form he chips out of the block. Even if it is crude, it is of the same block. Such are the various conceptions of the Deity; none can claim that his conception embraces the whole of Him, because He cannot be contained within the limitation of a mind, as a bottle cannot contain the whole of the sea. He reveals only what one is fit to receive. So according to the stages of human evolution, there will be different conceptions of the Deity, and the followers of one, even if they think that theirs is more refined, need not look down upon others as heathens or Kaffirs worshipping false deities, and consider themselves alone as the followers of the true Deity. For whatever the path, God approaches man through that path, and if the faith of the votary is genuine, he will be led to higher and higher forms of worship. So the followers of every religion must have respect for, and acceptance of, the faith and form of worship of other religions in spite of the differences that are sure to prevail in their ideologies and practices. For, it is the same God that is worshipped by them all. Just as all rivers, in spite of their divergent courses, lead to the same ocean, so do all faiths lead to Him i.e., take one to the same God who inspires them all. This Gitā teaching has been proclaimed to the modern world by Sri Ramakrishna in his saying: "As many faiths, so many paths."

5. *V*.12: Deities are the power aspects of the Divine worshipped in separation from Him, the Infinite and the Absolute Being. They are expressions of His power, but manifesting under limitations. Devotees who want boons, or divine favours, worship them according to the ritualistic code with offerings and Mantras and prayer for the fulfilment of their particular wants. But it is only He, the one God, who fulfils even these wants. It is only the Supreme Lord who fulfils such prayers to the Deities. These Deities are like the vassals and high officers of an emperor, and their powers are only the reflection of the Power of the Supreme Being. So even the fulfilments that come through the worship of the Deities come from Him, the Supreme Being only, as He alone is the Sat-chid-ānanda, the Absolute Existence-Knowledge-Bliss. But the ordinary votaries do not know this metaphysical truth and worship Deities as separate centres of high power. They may get their favours, but they do not gain any spiritual elevation by such adoration. Spiritual elevation means the attainment of Bhakti, Jñāna and Mukti. Only the Supreme Being, the Parabrahman, can grant these; no Deity as such can. But if any Deity is recognised by the worshipper as an expression of Sat-chid-ananda Parabrahman, the Supreme Being, the worship becomes theadoration of the Supreme Being Himself. But then the devotee's outlook has to change from a seeker after petty worldly fulfilments to a seeker after Bhakti, Jñāna and Mukti. In the devotional tradition it is said that seeking boons relating to worldly fulfilments from the Sat-chid-ānanda Parabrahman is like praying to an emperor for a cucumber or a few brinjals. Spiritual excellences like Bhakti, Jñāna and Mukti are the only gifts to be sought of Him, and He is the only one that can grant these. The Incarnation too is one with the Supreme Being, and can bestow the highest spiritual blessings. Thus to seek one's daily bread of Parabrahman is too silly for words according to the devotional system of thought.

The *Bhāgavata Purāṇa* seems to think that all the manifestations etc., as Deities are according to the attitude of the devotee. Tāmasika devotees are interested in such achievements as killing one's enemies, wreaking vengeance etc. They adore evil deities or psychic forces like spirits and goblins. The Rājasika devotees who seek worldly prosperity, success etc. adore Deities according to the Agamas with elaborate rituals and offering. The Mokṣa-seekers who are Sāttvika in nature, do their duties as offerings to Him without claiming the fruits for themselves and adore Him in a philosophical spirit. Superior to them are Nirguṇabhaktas, who have transcended the three Guṇas, as they abjure even liberation or Mukti as a desire, and seek the Lord for the sake of pure and unalloyed love, merely to serve Him with their whole being without the expectation of any return. Such devotees are above Guṇas, and they apprehend the Sat-chid-ānanda Parabrahman as such, without the colouring or association of the Guṇas. To all the others the Sat-chid-ānanda Parabrahman presents as Deities i.e., associated with the Guṇas of Prakṛti—Tamas, Rajas and Sattva or their combinations.

It must be clearly understood that this doctrine of the Deities is not polytheism. God is only one and the Deities are only His power manifestations in subtle dimensions, just as there are many power manifestations in Nature. When there is the recognition of this truth, their worship becomes the worship of the Supreme Being Himself.

6. *Vrs.*13-15: *Cāturvarṇya* or the social order of fourfold division is not the caste system, which is a system of social grouping solely bassed on birth. Brāhmaṇa, Kṣatriya, Vaiśya and Śūdra, as conceived in the Vedas, is a division based on the natural constitution of man arising from the dominance of Sattva, Rajas, and Tamas, the constituents of Nature (Guṇas), as also on the duties they are fit to perform according to the aptitudes arising from their constitution. They are mere character types. In this context, the reference to *Cāturvarṇya* is meant not to single out any particular society, but to generalise about the institution of society among men. Just as He is the author of the Order of Nature, so is He the author of the Order of Society among men also. This can be inferred from the next line stating that though He is the creator of all these, the Order of Nature and the Order of Society, out of Himself and by Himself, He is really a non-creator, because He is not in the least affected by creation. This is reiterated in the next verse. He is the unchanging and all-comprehending Spirit both with creation and without creation. Those who contemplate on Him as unaffected by creation, will be unaffected by Karma.

7. *Vrs.* 16-17: There are two questions here at issue—one ethical and the other metaphysical. What is the distinction between

the right or the moral act, and the wrong or the immoral act—is the ethical question. What distinguishes action from inaction is a metaphysical question. In that great branch of philosophy called ethics, distinguished thinkers have attempted to find out a universally acceptable criterion of ethics without success. Pursuit of the via media, pleasure, the greatest good of the greatest number, the example of great men, doing to others what is good for oneself, the categorical imperative, conscience, etc., are among the rational criteria of moral action put forward. But the claim of every one of them is open to scathing criticism.

As against these rational theories, all the great religions of the world have put forward the theory that the right conduct is what the scripture has sanctioned. It is laid down in the Gitā too: "Therefore let Śāstra (Scripture) be your measuring rod for what ought and ought not to be done" (16.24). The idea of a scriptural sanction has got a great advantage in that it gives a definite objective criterion. But in application it has its own difficulties. When there are several scriptural texts in the same religion, especially in those having a very long evolution, there can be contradictions. Next, between the scriptures of several religions there may be no uniformity of view in many matters. There is also the danger of fundamentalism and impracticality and inapplicability due to change of time and circumstances, if scriptures are taken literally and as given once for all. Thus the difficulty in determining what is right action, and what is wrong action (Karma and Vikarma) is very real.

Another difficulty in evaluating Karma as stated in the passage, is metaphysical. What is real action and what is true inaction is difficult to determine, as shown in the next verse.

8. *Vrs.*18-23: The really wise man is one who identifies himself with the Ātman, who is only the uninvolved Witness, in the midst of the non-stop activities of the body-mind. So also a wise man perceives that when an ignorant man wilfully keeps idle and says he has abandoned work and is restful, he is so only identifying himself with the body-mind without any perception of the Ātman-consciousness. In Atman-consciousness alone is true *Naiṣkarmya* or worklessness. Besides, physical worklessness, whether forcefully adopted or born of idleness, is an effect of the will like all actions.

A person who has attained to this state of Atman-consciousness may be engaged in all kinds of action, but he is ever in Yoga or a state of unruffled non-attachment. This idea is elaborated in the succeeding verses upto verse 23.

9. *V.*24: This is the unitary spiritual consciousness arrived at through the practice of Karma Yoga But whether this is attained through Karma Yoga where work is continued even after illumination, or it is attained through pure Jñāna Yōga where there is complete abandonment of all works even externally at a certain stage—is immaterial. What is important in understanding this passage is not any idea of super-imposing Brahman on various ingredients of a sacrifice like offerings, fire, sacrifice etc., as one would do in invoking the presence of a Deity in an image. For a man of illumination, unitary consciousness is an experience, and does not require any assertion of the will to invoke divinity in Yajña and its parts. Even the Yajña ritual is used here only as a symbol standing for the outlook of an illumined man on all work, not necessarily Yajña alone. Yajña is the holiest act known to man and it is therefore appropriate to use it for illustrating the outlook towards Karma of one who has reached the summit of wisdom through Karma Yoga. The actor, instruments of action, the object of action and action itself, he realises as grounded in the Supreme Spirit. So he is described as one having *Brahma-karma-samādhi*—one having Samādhi or absorption in Brahman even when performing action. A child seeing many interesting forms of animals and birds made of gold would be caught up with the forms that interest it, irrespective of the value of the substance it is made of. But a dealer in gold will only look at the weight of the gold and not at its form in evaluating it. The form is relevant to him only in so far as it reveals the substance which is his sole concern. Through all forms he sees only the substance. So through all actions and objects, the enlightened one sees their ground, the Sat-chid-ānanda Parabrahman.

10. *Vrs.*25-30: The meaning especially of the latter half of the verse is obscure. The meaning of the expression *Yajñena eva* is puzzling. Following Śrī Śankara we have taken it to mean the Ātman. The first Yajña is worship of Divine manifestations conceived as separate from oneself. It is Dravya Yajña, the offering of material objects.

The second is Jñāna Yajña, the sacrifice of the individual self in the universal self through enlightened understanding.

From this up to verse 30 various phases of man's physical, moral and mental life are taken and interpreted in terms of Yajña, the holiest and universally accepted rite of the followers of the Veda. They are roughly grouped as *Dravya-yajña* (sacrifice of material goods), *Tapo-yajña* (sacrifice through austerity), *Yoga-yajña* (sacrifice in the form of spiritual communion), *Svādhyāya-yajña* (sacrifice through religious study), and *Jñāna-Yajña* (sacrifice constituted of knowledge).

11. *V.*31: This is a very obscure verse. One can easily understand the idea of 'remnants' in material sacrifice, but it is puzzling to be told of 'remnants' in the other forms of mental, ethical and intellectual sacrifices alluded to in the foregoing verses. Commentaries are silent on this. Either we have to say that 'partaking of remnants' does not apply to them, but only to material sacrifices, in which 'remnant' means what is left of one's resources after giving their due shares to others—the Devas, Pitṛs (Manes), Ṛṣis, men and brute creations. Such sharing is called the *Panca-mahàyajña*—the five great sacrifices which all householders are asked to perform. We may add to this list of recipients the State also. People who do these sacrifices live a moral life, which is the basis of all spiritual development. For it involves the offering of things that are precious to oneself for the good of others, and thus it helps to eradicate self-centredness from the mind of man. Elimination of self-centredness is the prime requirement for all spiritual development. What is left afterwards for one's consumption is considered pure.

All the other non-material sacrifices referred to are directly related to the ethical and spiritual development of man. The difficulty is to know how the concept of 'remnant' is to be applied to them. Or the 'remnant' may be the time left after devoting oneself to these noble endeavours, which can be utilised for one's worldly affairs. Time is as precious as, or more so than, material wealth. Or the idea may be that in the practice of all these disciplines, the aspirant, besides achieving the specific purposes of the practice, has to develop the highly subtle and observant attitude of the pure subject without letting the mind get mixed up with its form-taking tendency. This may be considered the sacrificial residue.

In short, whatever is left after offering to God and to one's fellow beings, whether it be food, wealth or time, is sanctifying and is comparable to the immortality-giving Amṛta or divine nectar. Its use by oneself is free from any stain and is conducive to one's spiritual progress.

12. *V.*33: If that is not so, man will be working like a machine, animal, or slave. In works for the fruits, the material gains may be more important for the worker, but in desireless action self-improvement is the result. It is not fruits but knowledge or spiritual enhancement that forms the rationale of the actions undertaken by a true spiritual aspirant.

13. *Vrs.*35-38: These verses are highly suggestive in their meaning and give the answer to any doubt as to whether the so-called spiritual awakening might be a purely subjective feeling without any reality value. This unitive experience swallows up the distinction between the subject and the object in one all-comprehensive understanding, resulting in a permanent transformation of consciousness in its sweep and depth. An analogy can be found in the relation between the dream and waking consciousness. In a dream, the dream ego has a real apprehension of several centres of consciousness and of objects external, common to himself and all the dream participants. If that dream ego gets a sense of awakening in the dream itself, he will perceive how all the dream entities are resting on him (the dream ego), and how, through himself, they are resting in the waking ego or the real man. The real man is ultimately the support of all—of the dream ego as also of the egos of all the participants in the dream. The real waking consciousness is only the Parabrahman, the Supreme Being. All other centres of consciousness like the Jivas and all insentient entities are supported by His unitive consciousness. The new vision that the awakening of Jñāna gives may be analogous to this.

The other consequences that result from this awakening, effecting the enrichment of the knower's consciousness, are: (1) The effect of the transformation is permanent and one will never again fall into delusion leading to fear and suffering. (2) Just as an awakened man is absolutely free from the effects of the actions of the dream ego, so the knowing one gets an enlightened and purified ego that is free from the imperfections, obsessions and sinfulness of the ego of ignorance; the erstwhile fool becomes wise, and the sinner a saint. As stated in the next verse, Jñāna is like a fire which burns up all rubbish and purifies everything. It would be seen that psychic powers, which popular imagination associates with saintly personages, are not according to the Gītā a sign of enlightenment or a necessary accompaniment.

14. *V.*39: The three qualities absolutely necessary for progress in spiritual life are mentioned here. These are: (1) Sraddha or Faith, (2) Ardent practice (3) Control of the senses. Of these, the first alone needs some explanation. Sraddha or Faith with a capital is not credulity and superstitious acceptance of unknown and unverifiable entities and claims of individuals. It is a positive attitude towards the ultimate verities that do not fall within the ken of the senses and reason, but on which indirect information can be had through authentic scriptures and genuine teachers. Faith is as much a unique quality of the human mind as reason. Animals have no capacity for faith even as they do not have for reasoning. Faith is sometimes condemned as blind and superstitious. But it is forgotten that parallel to this, reasoning too is bound to lead one to wrong conclusions unless those powers are refined by training. In the same way faith develops in the right direction as the man's heart becomes purer and purer by sense control and aspiration to know the meaning of life. Impure minds full of hankerings of a lower nature will open themselves only to superstitious and degrading practices. So, for a pure and sincere mind, faith is the greatest support in spiritual life. It is the first and foremost quality of a pure mind, that it is automatically receptive to the true and the good even with a partial understanding. Sraddha also means Bhakti.

Anything that has become a matter of faith in a man, unlike what is a mere belief, works as an operative force, enthusing him to put the content of his faith to practice, and to struggle towards the realisation of the ideal it presents. Ardour and sincerity are of the very stuff of faith. Faith in what, is a question unanswered in the text. The general answer of all authorities is—in the teaching of the scripture and of the Guru. Faith is a firm and active acceptance unlike belief or a conventional conformity which has no power to move a person to action.

15. *V*.40: While putting questions to gain a full understanding is a healthy habit, the tendency of doubting without any positive attitude to anything, is a disease comparable to hydromania—the tendency to unending washing with water on account of an incurable sense of impurity. A man's life will be paralysed, if some positive verities of a credible nature are not accepted after due enquiry and investigation.

———

Chapter V

कर्मसंन्यासयोगः

COMMUNION THROUGH RENUNCIATION

SUMMARY

The harmony of the paths of knowledge and work: (1-7) Feeling confused, Arjuna asks the Lord again: You seem to advocate the abandonment of all Karma in one breath and in the next praise the discharge of all actions in a disinterested manner. Which of these two should I follow for my good?

To this Sri Krishna replies: A contemplative life, characterised by the abandonment of all actions externally too, as also the discharge of all actions with detachment—are both valid spiritual paths leading to an identical spiritual goal. As paths they may look different, but in the end they are the same. There is, however, this important link between them. Without undergoing the discipline of detached action, it is vain to abandon all external action; for it will result only in idleness and hypocrisy. To an average aspirant it is a mere pitfall, while discriminative wisdom combined with detached action will take him forward gradually. So it comes to this, that the attainment of detachment in action is the very essence of spiritual life, and once this is acquired, it is immaterial whether one abandons actions externally or continues to perform them. For, one who is truly detached becomes, through that detachment, fit to be united with the Self of all—the Supreme Being who is the goal of all spiritual striving. He is no longer affected by action.

The way of illumined ones: (8-29) A truth-knower with such detachment feels: "I do nothing in all the movements of the body, even in the very winking of the eyes." Having abandoned all actions, mentally, he rests in the nine-gated citadel of the body, undisturbed by the hurry and bustle of the activities of its members. In all his bodily and mental activities, his detachment is so complete that he feels that it is Prakṛti (Nature), of which the body-mind is a part, that works and reaps the fruits, not he, the Spirit, who is only the unconcerned witness of all these movemnts of Prakṛti. Remaining in that Spirit-consciousness, he is unperturbed by all experiences of life, pleasant or unpleasant. And in his dealings with all fellow beings—high and low, holy and unholy, men and animals—he has a sense of equality, knowing, as he does, that they are all the unaffected Spirit, and not the bodies to which alone the distinction of purity and impurity applies. Even in this embodied state, he is able to contain the pull of the passions and the senses. Knowing that contactual joys only bring on sufferings in the end, he turns for satisfaction inward to the Bliss of the Supreme Spirit, of whom he is a part. He becomes an adept in the practice of Samādhi, and at any time he can withdraw himself from the surface life of the body and be merged in the Bliss of the Spirit within.

Knowing Me, as the friend of all, and at the same time the maker and master of everything—to whom all worship and austerities have to be offered—man attains Supreme Peace.

अर्जुन उवाच

संन्यासं कर्मणां कृष्ण पुनर्योगं च शंससि ।
यच्छ्रेय एतयोरेकं तन्मे ब्रूहि सुनिश्चितम् ॥ 1 ॥

Arjuna uvāca:

Saṁnyāsaṁ karmaṇāṁ Kṛṣṇa punar yogaṁ ca śaṁsasi /
yac chreya etayor ekaṁ tan me brūhi suniścitam //1//

Kṛṣṇa : O Krishna : *karmaṇām* : of works *saṁnyāsam*: abandonment *punaḥ* : afterwards *yogam* : communion through work *ca* : and *śaṁsasi* : Thou praisest, *etayoḥ* : of these *yat*: which *śreyaḥ*: the better in leading to one's good *tat* : that *ekam*: one *suniścitam*: with certainty *me* : to me *brūhi* : tell.

Arjuna said:

1. O Kṛṣṇa! Thou praisest in one breath both abandonment of works and communion through their preformance. Now tell me with certainity which of them leads to one's good.[1]

श्रीभगवानुवाच

संन्यासः कर्मयोगश्च निःश्रेयसकरावुभौ ।
तयोस्तु कर्मसंन्यासात्कर्मयोगो विशिष्यते ॥ 2 ॥

Śri Bhagavān uvāca:

Saṁnyāsaḥ karma-yogaś ca niḥśreyasa-karāv ubhau /
tayos tu karma-saṁnyāsāt karma-yogo viśiṣyate //2//

Saṁnyāsaḥ : Abandonment of works *karmayogaḥ*: communion through work *ca* : and *ubhau*: both *niḥśreyasa-karau* : bestowing liberation; *tayoḥ* : of these *tu* : but *karmasaṁnyāsāt* : than abandonment of action *karmayogaḥ* : communion through work *viśiṣyate*: excels.

The Blessed Lord said:

2. Both abandonment of works and communion through works lead to liberation. But of them, communion through work excels over abandonment of work.[2]

ज्ञेयः स नित्यसंन्यासी यो न द्वेष्टि न काङ्क्षति ।
निर्द्वन्द्वो हि महाबाहो सुखं बन्धात्प्रमुच्यते ॥ 3 ॥

Jñeyaḥ sa nitya-saṁnyāsī yo na dveṣṭi na kāṅkṣati !
nirdvandvo hi mahā-bāho sukhaṁ bandhāt pramucyate //3//

Mahābāho: : O mighty-armed one! *yaḥ* : who *na dveṣṭi* : hates not, *na kāṅkṣati* : desires not *saḥ* : he *nityasaṁnyāsī* : as one ever-established in renunciation *jñeyaḥ* : should be known. *Hi* : Indeed *nirdvandvaḥ* : one above such contraries *bandhāt* : from bondage *sukham* : easily *pramucyate* : is liberated.

3. O mighty-armed one! Whoever hates not, nor desires, should be known as one established in renunciation. Indeed,

one who is above such contraries is easily liberated from bondage.

सांख्ययोगौ पृथग्बालाः प्रवदन्ति न पण्डिताः ।
एकमप्यास्थितः सम्यगुभयोर्विन्दते फलम् ॥ 4 ॥

Sāṁkhya-yogau pṛthag bālāḥ pravadanti na paṇḍitāḥ /
ekam apy āsthitaḥ saṁyag ubhayor vindate phalam //4//

Sāṁkhya-yogau : Sāṁkhya and Yoga *pṛthak* : as different *bālāḥ* : children *pravadanti* : speak of, *na paṇḍitāḥ* : not the wise. *Ekam* : One of these *api* : even *samyak āsthitaḥ* : well set on *ubhayoḥ* : of both *phalam* : the end *vindate* : obtains.

4. It is only the childish and not the wise that speak of Sāṁkhya (or knowledge accompanied by abandonment of work) and Yoga (or communion through detached and dedicated work) as different. A person well-established in even one of these, attains the end that is the common goal of both (That is, in the means they employ, they look different, but their end or ultimate purpose is identical.)

यत्सांख्यैः प्राप्यते स्थानं तद्योगैरपि गम्यते ।
एकं सांख्यं च योगं च यः पश्यति स पश्यति ॥ 5 ॥

Yat sāṁkhyaiḥ prāpyate sthānaṁ tad yogair api gamyate /
ekaṁ sāṁkhyaṁ ca yogaṁ ca yaḥ paśyati sa paśyati //5//

Sāṁkhyaiḥ : By Sāṁkhya *yat sthānam* : what state *prāpyate* : is reached, *tat* : that *yogaiḥ* : by Yoga *api* : also *gamyate* : is reached. *Sāṁkhyam* : Sāṁkhya *ca* : and *yogam ca* : and Yoga *ekam* : one *yaḥ* : who *paśyati* : sees, *saḥ* : he *paśyati* : sees.

5. The state which one attains by Sāṁkhya, that same state is attained by Yoga too. He who sees both Sāṁkhya and Yoga as one, sees indeed.

संन्यासस्तु महाबाहो दुःखमाप्तुमयोगतः ।
योगयुक्तो मुनिर्ब्रह्म नचिरेणाधिगच्छति ॥ 6 ॥

Saṁnyāsas tu mahā-bāho duḥkham āptum ayogataḥ /
yoga-yukto munir brahma nacireṇ'ādhigacchati //6//

Mahābāho : O mighty-armed! *Saṁnyāsaḥ* : abandonment of work (which accompanies the Sāṁkhya discipline) *ayogataḥ* : for one without Yoga *āptum* : to attain to *duḥkham* : difficult; *tu* : but *yogayuktaḥ* : one established in Yoga *muniḥ* : sage *na cireṇa* : in no long time *Brahma* : Brahman *adhigacchati* : attains.

6. O mighty-armed Arjuna! True abandonment of work (which the discipline of Sāṁkhya implies) is difficult to practise for one who is not accomplished in the Yoga discipline of detached work. But the sage accomplished in Yoga attains to *Brahman (renunciation?) in no long time.*

योगयुक्तो विशुद्धात्मा विजितात्मा जितेन्द्रियः ।
सर्वभूतात्मभूतात्मा कुर्वन्नपि न लिप्यते ॥ 7 ॥

Yoga-yukto viśuddh'ātmā vijit'ātmā jit'endriyaḥ /
sarva-bhūtātma-bhūtātmā kurvann api na lipyate //7//

Yogayuktaḥ : Established in selfless and detached action *viśuddhātmā* purified soul *vijitātmā* : one of controlled mind *jitendriyaḥ* : one having the senses under control *sarvabūtātmabūtātmā* : one who has identified one's self with the self of all, *kurvan api* : though working *na lipyate* : is not bound.

7. One who is established in selfless and detached action, who is pure, whose mind and senses are under control, and whose self is identified with the self of all—he is never bound, though he be engaged in work.[3]

नैव किंचित्करोमीति युक्तो मन्येत तत्त्ववित् ।
पश्यञ्शृण्वन्स्पृशञ्जिघ्रन्नश्नन्गच्छन्स्वपञ्श्वसन् ॥ 8 ॥

प्रलपन्विसृजन्गृह्णन्नुन्मिषन्निमिषन्नपि ।
इन्द्रियाणीन्द्रियार्थेषु वर्तन्त इति धारयन् ॥ 9 ॥

N'aiva kiñcit karomi'ti yukto manyeta tattva-vit /
paśyan śṛṇvan spṛśan jighr'ann aśnan gacchan svapan śvasan //8//

Pralapan visṛjan gṛhṇann unmiṣan nimiṣann api /
indriyāṇī'ndriy'ārtheṣu vartanta iti dhārayan //9//

Yuktaḥ : A man of selfless and detached action *tattvavit* : knower of the Truth *paśyan* : seeing *śṛṇvan* : hearing *spṛśan* : touching *jighran*: smelling *aśnan*: eating *pralapan*: conversing *gṛhṇan* : holding *gacchan*: walking *visṛjan* : giving up *śvasan* : breathing *unmiṣan nimiṣan* : opening and closing the eyes *svapan api* : even sleeping, *indriyāṇi* : senses *indriyārtheṣu* : in objects of the senses *vartante* : are occupied with *iti dhārayan* : convinced thus, *kiñcit* : anything *na eva karomi* : I do not do, *iti manyeta* : should think thus.

8-9. I (the Self) do naught; only the senses are occupied with their objects—this should be the conviction of one who is detached in action and established in the truth (that he is the Ātman), even while seeing, hearing, touching, smelling, eating, conversing, holding, walking, giving up, winking and even sleeping.

ब्रह्मण्याधाय कर्माणि सङ्गं त्यक्त्वा करोति यः।
लिप्यते न स पापेन पद्मपत्रमिवाम्भसा ॥ 10 ॥

Brahmaṇy ādhāya karmāṇi saṅgaṁ tyaktvā karoti yaḥ /
lipyate na sa pāpena padma-patram iv'āmbhasā //10//

Yaḥ : Who *karmāṇi* : works *Brahmaṇi* : in Brahman *ādhāya* : resigning *saṅgam* : attachment *tyaktvā* : abandoning *karoti* : does *saḥ* : he *ambhasā* : in water *padmapatram iva* : like the lotus leaf *pāpena* : by sin *na lipyate* : not affected.

10. One who resigns all his actions to Brahma and works without any personal attachments, is not soiled by sin, as a lotus leaf is not wetted by water.

कायेन मनसा बुद्ध्या केवलैरिन्द्रियैरपि।
योगिनः कर्म कुर्वन्ति सङ्गं त्यक्त्वाऽऽत्मशुद्धये ॥ 11 ॥

Kāyena manasā buddhyā kevalair indriyair api /
yoginaḥ karma kurvanti saṅgaṁ tyaktvā'tma-śuddhaye //11//

Yoginaḥ : Yogins (spiritual aspiants) *saṅgam* : attachment *tyaktvā* : abandoning *ātmaśuddhaye* : for purification of mind *kāyena* : with body *manasā* : by mind *buddhyā* : by intellect *kevalaiḥ indriyaiḥ api* : even merely with the senses *karma* : works *kurvanti* : perform.

11. For the attainment of mental purity, spiritual aspirants (Yogins) perform action devoid of attachment, with their body, mind, intellect or even merely with the senses.

युक्तः कर्मफलं त्यक्त्वा शान्तिमाप्नोति नैष्ठिकीम् ।
अयुक्तः कामकारेण फले सक्तो निबध्यते ॥ 12 ॥

Yuktaḥ karma-phalaṁ tyaktvā śāntim āpnoti naiṣṭhikīm /
ayuktaḥ kāma-kāreṇa phale sakto nibadhyate //12//

Yuktaḥ : A man of restrained mind *karmaphalam* : the fruits of action *tyaktvā* : giving up *naiṣṭhikīm* : abiding *śāntim* : peace *āpnoti* : attains. *Ayuktaḥ* : One with unrestrained mind *kāma-kāreṇa* : prompted by desire *phale* : in the fruits *saktaḥ* : attached *nibadhyate* : gets bound.

12. By abandoning the fruits of action a man of restrained mind attains to abiding peace. But the one with unrestrained mind, being prompted by desire for the fruits of action, gets bound.

सर्वकर्माणि मनसा संन्यस्यास्ते सुखं वशी ।
नवद्वारे पुरे देही नैव कुर्वन्न कारयन् ॥ 13 ॥

Sarva-karmāṇi manasā saṁnyasy'āste sukhaṁ vaśī /
nava-dvāre pure dehī n'aiva kurvan na kārayan //13//

Vaśī dehī : A person who has controlled the senses *sarvakarmāṇi*: all actions *manasā* : with the mind *saṁnyasya* : abandoning *navadvāre pure* : in the corporeal mansion with nine gates *na eva kurvan* : neither working *na kārayan* : nor causing work to be done *sukham* : at ease *āste* : resides.

13. A self-controlled soul, having abandoned all work mentally (in the way described above), resides at ease (as a witness) in this corporeal mansion with nine gates, neither working nor causing work to be done.

न कर्तृत्वं न कर्माणि लोकस्य सृजति प्रभुः ।
न कर्मफलसंयोगं स्वभावस्तु प्रवर्तते ॥ 14 ॥

Na kartṛtvaṁ na karmāṇi lokasya sṛjati prabhuḥ /
na karma-phala-saṁyogaṁ svabhāvas tu pravartate //14//

Prabhuḥ : The sovereign soul *lokasya* : for the world *kartṛtvam* : agency *na sṛjati*: does not cause, *karmāṇi na* : nor actions, *karma-phala-saṁyogam na* : nor union with the results of action, *svabhāvaḥ tu* : Nature only *pravartate* : does this.

14. In regard to all beings in this world, the sovereign soul is not the cause of the sense of agency, nor of actions, nor of the fruition of actions. It is Nature that does all this.[4]

नादत्ते कस्यचित्पापं न चैव सुकृतं विभुः ।
अज्ञानेनावृतं ज्ञानं तेन मुह्यन्ति जन्तवः ॥ 15 ॥

N'ādatte kasyacit pāpaṁ na c'aiva sukṛtaṁ vibhuḥ /
ajñānen'āvṛtaṁ jñānaṁ tena muhyanti jantavaḥ //15//

Vibhuḥ : The all-pervading one *kasyacit* : of any *pāpam* : sin *na ādatte* : accepts, *sukṛtam*: merits *ca na eva*: also not; *ajñānena* : by ignorance *āvṛtam* : is covered *jñānam* : knowledge, *tena* by that *jantavaḥ* : creatures *muhyanti* : are deluded.

15. The all-pervading Being does not accept the sins or merits of any one. Knowledge of the Divine Spirit is veiled in ignorance, and therefore beings are deluded.

ज्ञानेन तु तदज्ञानं येषां नाशितमात्मनः ।
तेषामादित्यवज्ज्ञानं प्रकाशयति तत्परम् ॥ 16 ॥

Jñānena tu tad ajñānaṁ yeṣāṁ nāśitam ātmanaḥ /
teṣām adityavaj jñānaṁ prakāśayati tat param //16//

Ātmanaḥ : Of the Ātman *jñānena* : by knowlege *tu*: but *yeṣām* : whose *tat*: that *ajñānam* : ignorance *nāśitam* : is destroyed, *teṣām*: of them *jñānam* : knowledge *ādityavat* : like the sun *tat param* : that supreme truth *prakāśayati* : reveals.

16. But in the case of those whose ignorance has been destroyed by the knowledge of the Ātman, to them that knowledge reveals the supreme Truth, as the sun does the objects of the world.

तद्बुद्धयस्तदात्मानस्तन्निष्ठास्तत्परायणाः ।
गच्छन्त्यपुनरावृत्तिं ज्ञाननिर्धूतकल्मषाः ॥ 17 ॥

Tad-buddhayas tad-ātmānas tan-niṣṭhās tat-parāyaṇāḥ /
gacchanty apunar-āvṛttiṁ jñāna-nirdhūta-kalmaṣāḥ //17//

Tadbuddhayaḥ : Thinking always of Him, *tadātmānaḥ* : ever at one with Him, *tanniṣṭhāḥ* : deeply devoted to Him, *tatparāyaṇāḥ* : looking upon Him as one's goal, *jñānanirdhūtakalmaṣāḥ* : becoming purified of their sin by divine knowledge *apunarāvṛttim* : the state from which there is no return *gacchanti* : go.

17. Those who think of Him always, who are ever at one with Him, who are deeply devoted to Him, and who look upon Him as their goal, get purified of their sins by divine knowledge and go to the state from which there is no return to worldly life.

विद्याविनयसंपन्ने ब्राह्मणे गवि हस्तिनि ।
शुनि चैव श्वपाके च पण्डिताः समदर्शिनः ॥ 18 ॥

Vidyā-vinaya-sampanne brāhmaṇe gavi hastini /
śuni c'aiva śvapāke ca paṇḍitāḥ sama-darśinaḥ //18//

Vidyāvinayasampanne : Endowed with learning and humility, *brāhmaṇe* : in a Brāhmaṇa *gavi* : in a cow *hastini* : in an elephant *śuni ca eva* : and even in a dog *śvapāke ca* : and in an eater of dog's meat *paṇḍitāḥ* : enlightened men *samadarśinaḥ* : are seers of the same.

18. Enlightened men are those who see the same (i.e. the Ātman) in a Brāhmaṇa with learning and humility, in a cow, in an elephant, and even in a dog or in an eater of dog-meat (outcaste).

इहैव तैर्जितः सर्गो येषां साम्ये स्थितं मनः ।
निर्दोषं हि समं ब्रह्म तस्माद्ब्रह्मणि ते स्थिताः ॥ 19 ॥

Ih'aiva tair jitaḥ sargo yeṣāṁ sāmye sthitaṁ manaḥ /
nirdoṣaṁ hi samaṁ brahma tasmād brahmaṇi te sthitāḥ //19//

Yeṣām : Whose *manaḥ* : mind *sāmye sthitam* : remain in this vision of sameness in all *taiḥ* : by them *iha eva* : here in this world itself, in the embodied state itself *sargaḥ* : cycle of births and deaths *jitaḥ* : has been overcome. *Brahma* : Brahman *nirdoṣam* : the unsullied *samam* : the same *hi* : verily, *tasmāt* : therefore *te* : they *Brahmaṇi* : in Brahman *sthitāḥ* : are established.

19. Even here in this embodied state, the cycle of births and deaths has been overcome by those who have this vision of sameness in all. Verily, Brahman is the Unsullied and the Pure. Therefore are those seers of sameness said to be established in Brahman.

न प्रहृष्येत्प्रियं प्राप्य नोद्विजेत्प्राप्य चाप्रियम् ।
स्थिरबुद्धिरसंमूढो ब्रह्मविद् ब्रह्मणि स्थितः ॥ 20 ॥

Na prahṛṣyet priyaṁ prāpya n'odivijet prāpya c'ā priyam /
sthira-buddhir asaṁmūḍho brahma-vid brahmaṇi sthitaḥ //20/

Sthirabuddhiḥ : Unperturbed *asaṁmūḍhaḥ* : undeluded *brahmaṇi* : in Brahman *sthitaḥ* : established *brahmavit* : the knower of Brahman *priyam* : pleasing *prāpya* : attaining *na prahṛṣyet* : does not rejoice, *apriyam* : unpleasant *prāpya* : attaining *na udvijet* : is not agitated.

20. Unperturbed and undeluded, a knower of Brahman, who is established in Him, neither rejoices at pleasant experiences nor gets agitated at unpleasant ones.

बाह्यस्पर्शेष्वसक्तात्मा विन्दत्यात्मनि यत्सुखम् ।
स ब्रह्मयोगयुक्तात्मा सुखमक्षयमश्नुते ॥ 21 ॥

Bāhya-sparśeṣv asakt'ātmā vindatyātmani yat sukham /
sa brahma-yoga-yuktātmā sukham akṣayam aśnute //21//

Bāhyasparśeṣu : In contactual experiences of the external world *asaktātmā* : one unattached *ātmani* : in the Self *yat*: what *sukham*: happiness *vindati* : obtains, *saḥ* : he *brahmayogayuktātmā* : with mind absorbed in communion with Brahman *akṣayam* : unending *sukham* : bliss *aśnute* : experiences.

21. An aspirant who is unattached to the contactual experiences of the external world, gains the joy that is in the Self within. He thereby enjoys unending bliss with his mind absorbed in communion with Brahman (who is both within and without).[5]

ये हि संस्पर्शजा भोगा दुःखयोनय एव ते ।
आद्यन्तवन्तः कौन्तेय न तेषु रमते बुधः ॥ 22 ॥

Ye hi saṁsparśa-jā bhogā duḥkha-yonaya eva te /
ādy-antavantaḥ Kaunteya na teṣu ramate budhaḥ //22//

Kaunteya : O son of Kuntī! *ye* : which *saṁsparśajāḥ* : born of contacts *bhogāḥ* : enjoyments *te* : they *duḥkhayonayaḥ* ; cause of sorrow *eva*: only. *Hi*: For, *ādyantavantaḥ*: they are with a beginning and an end. *Budhaḥ* : The wise man *teṣu* : in them *na* : not *ramate*: delights.

22. Whatever enjoyments are there born of sense contact, they are sources of suffering only. For, they are with a beginning and an end. A wise man finds no delight in them.

शक्नोतीहैव यः सोढुं प्राक्शरीरविमोक्षणात् ।
कामक्रोधोद्भवं वेगं स युक्तः स सुखी नरः ॥ 23 ॥

Śaknotī'h'aiva yaḥ soḍhuṁ prāk śarīra-vimokṣaṇāt /
kāma-krodh'odbhavaṁ vegam sa yuktaḥ sa sukhī naraḥ //23//

Yaḥ : Which *naraḥ* : man *śarīravimokṣaṇāt prāk* : before release from the body *iha eva* : here itself *kāmakrodhodbhavam* : born of lust and anger *vegam* : agitation *soḍhum* : withstand *śaknoti* : is able, *saḥ* : he *yuktaḥ* : is the self-controlled, *saḥ* : he *sukhī* : is the happy man.

23. Here, even while in the body, whoever is able to withstand the agitation caused by lust and anger, he is the self-controlled one, he is the happy man.

योऽन्तःसुखोऽन्तरारामस्तथान्तर्ज्योतिरेव यः ।
स योगी ब्रह्मनिर्वाणं ब्रह्मभूतोऽधिगच्छति ॥ 24 ॥

Yo'ntaḥ-sukho'nytar-ārāmas tathāntar-jyotir eva yaḥ /
sa yogī brahma-nirvāṇaṁ brahma-bhūto'dhigacchati //24//

Yaḥ : Who *antaḥsukhaḥ* : is with happiness within, *antarārāmaḥ*: is with joy within, *tathā* : in the same way *yaḥ* : who *antharjyotiḥ* : experiences the light within *eva* : likewise, *saḥ* : that *yogī* : Yogin *brahmabhūtaḥ* : having become Brahman i.e., having realised his spiritual plenitude *brahmanirvāṇam* : beatitude in Brahman *adhigacchati* : attains.

24. The Yogin whose happiness is within, whose resting place is within, who likewise experiences the light within—he realises himself to be the Spirit and attains to beatitude in Brahman.[6]

लभन्ते ब्रह्मनिर्वाणमृषयः क्षीणकल्मषाः ।
छिन्नद्वैधा यतात्मानः सर्वभूतहिते रताः ॥ 25 ॥

Labhante brahma-nirvāṇaṁ ṛṣayaḥ kṣīṇa-kalmaṣāḥ /
chinna-dvaidhā yat'ātmānaḥ sarva-bhūta-hite ratāḥ //25//

Kṣīṇakalmaṣāḥ : Those who are sinless, *chinnadvaidhāḥ* : whose doubts have been destroyed, *yatātmānaḥ* : who are self-controlled, *sarvabhūtahite ratāḥ* : who rejoice in the good of all beings, *ṛṣayaḥ*: holy men *brahmanirvāṇam labhante* : attain to beatitude in Brahman.

25. Verily, they attain to beatitude in Brahman who are sinless, whose doubts have been destroyed, whose self is under their control and who rejoice in the good of all.

कामक्रोधवियुक्तानां यतीनां यतचेतसाम् ।
अभितो ब्रह्मनिर्वाणं वर्तते विदितात्मनाम् ॥ 26 ॥

Kāma-krodha-viyuktānāṁ yatīnāṁ yata-cetasām /
abhito brahma-nirvāṇaṁ vartate vidit'ātmanām //26//

Kāmakrodhaviyuktānām : Men who are devoid of lust and anger, *yatacetasām* : whose minds are controlled, *viditātmanām* : who have known their real nature as the spirit, *yatīnām* : of the self-controlled ones *brahmanirvāṇam* : attainment of beatitude in Brahman *abhitaḥ vartate* : abides near at hand.

26. To those self-controlled ones (ascetics) who are free from lust and anger, who have controlled their minds and who have known their real nature as the spirit—the attainment of beatitude in Brahman is near at hand.

स्पर्शान्कृत्वा बहिर्बाह्यांश्चक्षुश्चैवान्तरे भ्रुवोः ।
प्राणापानौ समौ कृत्वा नासाभ्यन्तरचारिणौ ॥ 27 ॥
यतेन्द्रियमनोबुद्धिर्मुनिर्मोक्षपरायणः ।
विगतेच्छाभयक्रोधो यः सदा मुक्त एव सः ॥ 28 ॥

Sparśān kṛtvā bahir bāhyāṁś cakṣuś c'aiv'āntare bhruvoḥ /
prāṇ'āpanau samau kṛtvā nās'ābhyantara-cāriṇau //27//

Yat'endriya-mano-buddhir munir mokṣa-parāyaṇaḥ
vigat'ecchā-bhaya-krodho yaḥ sadā mukta eva saḥ //28//

Bāhyān: External *sparśān*: contacts *bahiḥ kṛtvā*: excluding *cakṣuḥ*: the look *bhruvoḥ*: of the brows *antare eva*: between (*kṛtvā* : fixing), *nāsābhyantaracāriṇau* : moving in the nostrils *prāṇāpānau* : Prāṇa (out-going breath) and Apāna (incoming breath). *samau ca kṛtvā* : equalising or making even *yatendriyamano-buddhiḥ* : with senses, mind and intellect under control, *vigatecchā-bhayakrodhaḥ* : devoid of desire, fear and anger *mokṣaparāyaṇaḥ* : aspiring for liberation alone *muniḥ* : meditative man *yaḥ* : who *saḥ* : he *sadā* : ever *muktaḥ* : liberated *eva* : indeed.

27-28. Excluding all sense perceptions; fixing the look between the eye brows; steadying the flow of Prāṇa (out-going breath) and Apāna (incoming breath) through the nostrils; controlling the senses, mind and intellect; devoid of desires, fear and anger; and aspiring for liberation alone—a meditative sage so established, is liberated for ever.

भोक्तारं यज्ञतपसां सर्वलोकमहेश्वरम् ।
सुहृदं सर्वभूतानां ज्ञात्वा मां शान्तिमृच्छति ॥ 29 ॥

Bhoktāraṁ yajña-tapasāṁ sarva-loka-maheśvaram |
suhṛdaṁ sarva-bhūtānāṁ jñātvā māṁ śāntiṁ ṛcchati ||29||

Yajñatapasām : Of sacrifice and austerity *bhoktāram* : recipient, *sarvaloka-maheśvaram* : the supreme Lord of all the worlds, *sarvabhūtānām* : of all the worlds *suhṛdam* : friend *mām* : Me *jñātvā* : knowing, *śāntim* : peace *ṛcchati* : attains.

29. Knowing Me, the recipient of all worship and austere practices, the Supreme Lord of all the worlds, and the friend of all beings, man attains to eternal peace.

ओं तत्सदिति श्रीमद्भगवद्गीतासूपनिषत्सु ब्रह्मविद्यायां
योगशास्त्रे श्रीकृष्णार्जुनसंवादे कर्मसंन्यासयोगो
नाम पञ्चमोऽध्यायः ॥ 5 ॥

NOTES

1. *V.*1: This question of Arjuna expresses more or less the same doubt which he had at the beginning of the third chapter. In spite of all the disquisitions of Kṛṣṇa in Chapters II and IV, Arjuna fails to understand the relevance of work. The question here is put in a slightly different form. The praise that is bestowed on both work and the workless state simultaneously has only added to his confusion. He wants a clear and unambiguous answer, as to what he should follow.

2. *Vrs.*2-6: The contradiction in the situation is evident in Kṛṣṇa's answer. It is a clear question, and the answer too is supposed to be clear. In Ch. III, Kṛṣṇa has clearly stated that there are two ways proclaimed by him—the path of the Sāṁkhyas or pure contemplatives, and the path of the Yogins or active communionists. Here he says that Sāṁkhya and Yoga are one and the same and to say they are different is only children's prattle and not the words of mature thinkers. Is not Kṛṣṇa contradicting himself here, is a doubt that will come to any one's mind. The clarification that Kṛṣṇa himself gives occurs immediately in verse 4: "A person well established in even one of these, attains the end that is the common goal of both." It is clear from this that Kṛṣṇa would prefer to say that as paths they are distinct, but the spiritual realisation they confer on the aspirant is the same.

The distinctiveness of both these paths is thus clearly given as far as the Gita is concerned. But the confusion comes in considering: (1) Are these two paths open to one according to one's unrestricted choice? (2) Do they impinge upon each other at any stage of man's spiritual development to form a combined discipline or are they absolute antipodes as disciplines? These two alternatives look as possibilities even when the autonomy of the two paths is granted.

The answer of traditional Kevalādvaita to this is as follows: There is absolute contradiction between contemplativeness of the Sāṁkhya and communion through action of the Yoga discipline. One who is fit for it, can practise the contemplative discipline without going in for work at all. By work or Karma, the ancients mainly meant the *Śrauta-karma,* the works enjoined by the Vedas, which were purely ritualistic, and *Smārta-karma* or duties imposed by the Smṛties (Law Codes), which were partly ritualistic and partly the duties accruing to one according to one's state in life. It was held that by performing these works one will get that purity of mind and intellect, which alone will give that competence needed for the contemplative discipline called here Sāṁkhya. When one has attained to that competence, one should abandon all Karma. To continue the practice of Karma Yoga afterwards will be like husking the already husked paddy. So it is said, for the Yogi who is ascending along the path of Yoga, Karma is the means, and for him who has attained to perfection, tranquillity or workless contemplation is the means (Ch. VI-3). Besides, Karma strengthens the ego and takes the multiplicity for granted. It makes the mind outward-going while the Vedantic reflection consists in asserting the mere phenomenality of the ego and of the world of multiplicity. There is therefore a contradiction between Karma and this type of contemplation, and Karma has therefore to be completely abandoned at a certain stage.

In the earlier stages of the aspirant's life, Karma and devotional meditation of the Upasana type may be combined, but the pure contemplative discipline of practising unitary Consciousness (*Jñāna-niṣṭhā*) involves a type of contemplation where meditation of the Upāsana type has no place, and Karma of any kind, much less. Hence their abandonment is advocated.

The advocates of total *Karma-sanyāsa* maintain that such aspirants are required to abandon Karma of every kind, ritualistic and social, except that of collecting holy alms for the bare maintenance of the body (cf. IV. 21.)

No one can deny that the Gītā speaks in several places of such an absolutely pacific and contemplative perfection. Such a life was associated with the Sannyāsin. In the Vedic society, if a Brāhmaṇa or Kṣatriya lived without performing his ritualistic duties of the *Smārta* and *Śrauta* type, it was considered degrading. Those who had gone beyond the need of it were therefore expected to take to the Āśrama of the Sannyāsins, who were free from the obligation to do the *Śrauta* and *Smārta Karmas*. In much of the criticism of Karma by Vedantic Ācāryas, they seem to have ritualism in view chiefly. Though they were aware of social duties for the good of society, they seem to get overlooked in their criticism, although in the Gita the social duties of man alone are taken into consideration. Beyond a criticism of Vedic ritualism in verses 42-44 of the second chapter and a favourable reference in verses 10 to 16 of the third chapter, there is little reference to them in the Gītā, whereas the social duties of man are elaborately described and advocated. For a modern student of the Gītā, too, ritualistic work is not of much significance. He is only concerned with works for the improvement of the quality of man's life on earth, and he will be interested only to know what the Gītā has to say on this question—whether he has to abandon the pursuit of all altruistic values also at some stage in the pursuit of the highest spiritual ideal.

While the Gītā maintains that there is such a path, which is calls Sāṁkhya, it points to the existence of an alternative path, which it calls Yoga or Karma Yoga, which is self-sufficient in itself. It is said in verses 1 to 4 of Ch. IV that this tradition was known among *Rajarṣis,* but was forgotten in course of time and that Kṛṣṇa was reviving it through the instruction he was giving to Arjuna.

That this path is in itself self-sufficient, that man need not necessarily abandon the pursuit of social welfare through dedicated and non-attached action and adopt the discipline of pure Sāṁkhya of worklessness both internal and external, is borne out by the following passage (*V*.6): "The sage accomplished in Yoga attains to Brahman in no long time." The meaning of this obviously is that he need not necessarily take to any new discipline. By continuing the practice of Karma Yoga, the highest *summum bonum* will certainly be his. This was the view of Swami Vivekananda also, as expressed in his Karma Yoga lectures.

But pure Advaita interpreters will not concede the above interpretation of Verse 6, as according to them the discipline of Yoga is only for mental purification. So they interpret the word Brahman as 'renunciation', the justification for it being that renunciation is the proximate condition for attaining the spiritual *summum bonum.* This only shows how even orthodox commentators have to go out of the way to interpret the word Brhaman occurring in the Gītā. This makes the modern interpreter's view that words like Brahman, Brahma-bhuta etc., are often used in the Buddhistic sense, look credible. If Brahman is interpreted here as that 'unruffled state of peace and poise' identical with the state of Sthitaprajña of the 2nd chapter, which precedes the supreme spiritual illumination as described in chapter 18, the expression becomes understandable. *See* notes 6 of 14th and 9 of 18th chapters for more information on the use of the word Brahman.

3. *Vrs.*7-13: The state of equipoise and detachment that is gained in course of time through Karma Yoga, or unselfish and dedicated action is described in these verses.

The expression *sarva-bhūtātma-bhū tātmā* in *V.*7 need not necessarily mean the unitary consciousness of pure Advaita. For the state described here is that intermediary spirtual awareness, which has been described by epithets like Brahma-bhūta, Brahma-bhūyam etc. It is the enlarged and unperturbed state of consciousness which is the prelude to higher realisations. A person who has attained to that stage is said to attain to a state described in the 18th chapter of the Gita as *samaḥ sarveṣu bhūteṣu*—of being alike to all beings. The shell of self-centredness is broken in him, giving way to a feeling of identity of interest and experience with all. The present phrase also means the same –a sense of intense kinship and sharing with all.

The expression *brahmaṇyādhāya* in Verse 10 does not seem to indicate the Supreme Parabrahman but only Prakṛti. Many of the actions of the body and mind are enumerated in this context in verses 8 and 9 and they are spoken of as 'deposited in Brahman' in Verse 10. Body and mind are the products of Prakṛti or Nature. and to recognise this, and consequently feel unegoistic, is 'depositing one's actions in Brahman' in this context. For more information on the use of the word Brahman, see notes 6 of 14th and 9 of 18th chapters. One of the greatest difficulties in understanding the meaning of the Gītā is the widely varying senses in which it is used in different contexts. The supreme Being, Nature, Jīvā, Vēda, Omkāra, renunciation, an unruffled state of mind, etc., are some of the meanings it is made to convey in diffierent contexts.

4. *Vrs.*14-15: The Ātman is only the uninvolved witness in whose presence Nature and its evolutes function, giving a false sense of involvement to the Spirit. The Ātman is not actually

involved, and his pristine purity is not affected. Knowledge is the recognition of this truth and the consequent fading of ignorance resulting from identification with the movements of Nature. The words *Prabhu* and *Vibhu* in these two verses can mean only the 'Lord of the body' or Jīva, and not God, the Lord of the universe. The context warrants this only. For, immediately before, in verse 13, reference is made to the Jiva as sitting in the 'nine-gated city of the body' as the witness, neither acting nor making one act. Hence the merit and demerit of the actions of the body-mind cannot really stain and change the nature of the Jīva. The experience of such stain is due to identification with the body-mind, which does not effect any permanent change in the nature of the Ātman.

5. *V*.21: In this and in many of the preceding verses (see verses 6, 10, 19, 25, 26 etc.,) expressions like 'Brahman', 'Brahma-bhūta' and 'Brahma-nirvāṇa' are used. The use of the word Brahma in the Gītā is often ambiguous and problematic. The word has been used to mean the Supreme Being, Prakṛti or Nature, the Jīva or the Ātman, and the Veda. Here in this and the earlier verses the word can mean the Self or the Ātman. In this verse 21, the joy that is in the Self within, is identified with the bliss of Brahman. For those systems that accept the identity of the Ātman with Brahman, this poses no difficulty. But for philosophies which make a distinction between Ātman and Brahman, Ātmajñāna (or knowledge that one is the immaterial Self or Ātman) is the stepping stone to *Brahma Jñāna* (or the Knowledge of one's right relationship with Brahman). On the basis of this difference in their metaphysical position, there can be difference in the interpretation given to this and other similar verses by different schools of Vedānta.

6. *Vrs*.24-25: Literally the translation would be 'the *brahma-bhūta* (one who has become Brahman) attains to *brahma-nirvāṇa* (cessation in Brahman). We have given a simple non-technical translation. The expressions bristle with difficulties in interpreting. Some Western scholars find Buddhistic influence in this introduction of the concept of Nirvāṇa (blowing out of self-conscious individuality and desires as a light is put out). In this connection, note 6 of 14th chapter and note 9 of 18th chapter may be read for more details.

That the meaning of these words is not something negative

but a positive experience of the Divine in fullness is made plain in 18. 54-56. "Brahman-become, with self serene. free from sorrow and desire, and the same to all beings, he gains supreme devotion to Me. By devotion he comes to know Me, as I really am—how great I am and who I am. Having known Me thus in truth, he enters into Me. Even though he may be engaged in all kinds of works, such a person, being completely given over to Me, attains to the eternal and undecaying state due to My grace." Whether this **consummation** offered to the human spirit here is purely Advaitic i.e.,the result of the sublation of all diversity, or whether it is qualified Advaitism i.e.,the result of the subordination of all diversity to a Supreme Unity, is for the student to judge. One thing seems certain if we take these verses together. There is no contradiction here between the attainment of such a state and work.

It also looks that a distinction is made between a '*Brahma-bhūta*' (the Brahma-become) and one who has attained *Brahma-nirvāṇa.* It looks that the former is the stepping stone to the latter, and not in itself the terminal state. The *Brahma-bhūta* becomes fit to get supreme devotion, which helps him to have a full understanding of the Divine and enter into the Divine Consciousness. In terms of the terminology used by Sri Ramakrishna in his teachings, the former is Jñāna and the latter Vijñāna. The Jñāni looks upon the world as a mere appearance, but the Vijñāni sees it as a Divine Play, and action in it for him is being a participant in that Divine play.

———

Chapter VI

ध्यानयोगः

COMMUNION THROUGH MEDITATION

SUMMARY

Detached work leads to Enlightenment: (1-9) Sri Kṛṣṇa said: The real Sannyāsin and Yogin is the man who works with detachment in mind, not the one who puts on the symbols of renunciation and avoids works. Real Sannyāsa and real Karma Yoga are not so different as people think. Both have the common point that the mind should have the capacity to abandon all hankerings and attachments, hopes and expectations. The only difference is that to one who is in the early stages of the discipline, struggling to gain this non-attached condition, work in a literal sense is essential, because he would otherwise lapse into idleness and hypocrisy. Along with work he should practise introspection and meditation also; for without that he cannot keep up the sense of detachment, dedication and desirelessness while working. Work or Karma becomes Yoga (Karma Yoga), only under this condition of supplementing work with meditation. But for one who has become established in this detachment, Śama or introspection becomes the main means for further progress. The test of having reached this state is that there is no expectation of fruits and no sense of agency. One with such attainment can abandon actions without any fear of degeneration, but need not necessarily do so. While practising the introspective discipline intensively, he can engage himself also in actions that are contributive to the welfare of the world. Whereas action is a 'must' for the former, it is only a 'may' for the latter. But the cultivation of a detached mind free from hopes and expectations, is common and essential to both.

Practice of Meditation: (10-32) The practice of meditation is as follows: The mind of one who has succeeded in it is compared to a steady flame undisturbed by winds. He becomes established in the experience that he is the Spirit and not the body, and consequently he is steeped in the non-contactual, intellectually intuited Bliss that is of the nature of the Spirit. It is a state, on being established in which nothing else is felt as attractive or valuable, and one is not in the least distracted even by great worldly sorrows. An adept in it also attains to a new vision of the totality of existence, the experience of the Divine as residing in all entities and all entities as residing in the Divine.

The Difficulty of Inward Concentration: (33-47) Arjuna now raises two questions: As the mind is very unsteady the work of making it steady is as difficult as stilling the air. How could this then be accomplished? Also what is the fate of one who attempts this very difficult discipline and fails to achieve much success even by the end of his life? Is he to be a lost soul, his whole life's effort having ended in failure?

To these doubts Sri Krishna answers: Though the mind is difficult to control, this can be done by steady practice and cultivation of dispassion for worldly enjoyments, coupled with strong aspiration for the higher life. If the latter is not present, practice alone will not be of much use. Failure in Yoga is largely due to the absence of the latter quality. But there is no absolute failure in Yoga. If a person dies before attaining to success in it, he carries the legacy of his present life into his next embodiment. He will be born under conditions that are very favourable to spiritual development. With the power of his earlier practice as his background, he will strive forward, life after life, until success is attained. Thus nothing is lost by one striving in the spiritual path.

One practising the discipline of concentration is immensely greater than one engaging himself entirely in scripture-ordained works, or in intellectual studies of Vedanta. But the practice of concentration should be accompanied with intense faith and devotion to the Lord. Then Yoga becomes the most potent spiritual discipline.

श्रीभगवानुवाच

अनाश्रितः कर्मफलं कार्यं कर्म करोति यः ।
स संन्यासी च योगी च न निरग्निर्न चाक्रियः ॥ 1 ॥

Śri Bhagavān uvāca:
Anāśritaḥ karma-phalaṁ kāryaṁ karma karoti yaḥ /
sa saṁnyāsī ca yogī ca na niragnir na c'ākriyaḥ //1//

Karmaphalam : The fruits of action *anāśritaḥ* : without dependence on *kāryaṁ karma* : work that ought to be done or duty *yaḥ* : who *karoti* : performs, *saḥ* : he *saṁnyāsī ca, yogī ca* : both Sannyāsī and Yogī, *na niragniḥ* : not one without fire; *akriyaḥ* : one who avoids work *na ca* : not.

The Blessed Lord said:

1. It is the man who performs his duties without dependence on the fruits that deserves to be called a Sannyāsin (renouncer) and a Yogin, not the one who keeps no fire or avoids works.

यं संन्यासमिति प्राहुर्योगं तं विद्धि पाण्डव ।
न ह्यसंन्यस्तसंकल्पो योगी भवति कश्चन ॥ 2 ॥

Yaṁ saṁnyāsam iti prāhur yogaṁ taṁ viddhi Pāṇḍava /
na hy asaṁnyasta-saṅkalpo yogī bhavati kaścana //2//

Yam : What *saṁnyāsam* : renunciation *iti prāhuḥ* : is called as *tam* : that *yogam* : communion through action *viddhi* : know *Pāṇḍava* : son of Pāṇḍu. *Hi* : For *asaṁnyastasaṅkalpaḥ* : one who has not abandoned subtle hankerings *kaścana* : any one *yogī* : a practitioner of spiritual communion through work *na bhavati* : cannot become.

2. O son of Pāṇḍu! What is called Sannyāsa or renunciation, know that to be identical with Yoga or discipline of selfless action. For, whoever has not abandoned subtle hankerings and self-centred objectives, can never become a Yogī, or a practitioner of spiritual communion through works.[1]

आरुरुक्षोर्मुनेर्योगं कर्म कारणमुच्यते ।
योगारूढस्य तस्यैव शमः कारणमुच्यते ॥ 3 ॥

Ārurukṣor muner yogaṁ karma kāraṇaṁ ucyate /
yog'ārūḍhasya tasy'aiva śamaḥ kāraṇam ucyate //3//

Yogam : Spiritual communion *āruruksoḥ* : of one wishing to ascend *muneḥ* : for the sage *karma* : work *kāraṇam* : means *ucyate* : is said to be. *Yogārūḍhasya* : Of one who has ascended to Yoga *tasya* : his *śamaḥ* : quiescence *eva* : verily *kāraṇam* : cause *ucyate* : is said.

3. For one who desires to ascend the path leading to the heights of spiritual communion (Yoga), detached work is the means. For one who has ascended it, quiescence is verily the means.[2]

यदा हि नेन्द्रियार्थेषु न कर्मस्वनुषज्जते ।
सर्वसंकल्पसंन्यासी योगारूढस्तदोच्यते ॥ 4 ॥

Yadā hi n'endriy'ārtheṣu na karmasv anuṣajjate /
sarva-saṁkalpa-saṁnyāsī yog'ārūḍhas tad'ocyate //4//

Yadā : When *indriyārtheṣu*: in the objects of the senses *na anuṣajjate*: is not attached, *karmasu na* : nor to works, *tadā* : then *sarva-saṅkalpasaṁnyāsī* : that one who has abandoned all subtle hankerings and objectives *yogārūḍhaḥ* : ascended the heights of Yoga *ucyate* : is said to be.

4. When one ceases to be attached to sense objects and to one's actions, then that one, who has thus abandoned all subtle hankerings and self-centred objectives, is said to have ascended the heights of spiritual communion (Yoga).

उद्धरेदात्मनात्मानं नात्मानमवसादयेत् ।
आत्मैव ह्यात्मनो बन्धुरात्मैव रिपुरात्मनः ॥ 5 ॥

Uddhared ātmanā'tmānaṁ n'ātmānam avasādayet /
ātm'aiva hy ātmano bandhur ātm'aiva ripur ātmanaḥ //5//

Ātmanā : By one's higher self *ātmānam* : the lower self *uddharet* : should raise, *ātmānam* : the higher self *na avasādayet* : not depress. *Hi* : For *ātmanaḥ* : of the lower self *bandhuḥ* : friend *ātmā eva* : is verily the higher self; *ātmanaḥ* : of the higher self *ātmā eva* the lower self alone *ripuḥ* (is) the enemy.

5. One should uplift one's lower self by the higher self. One should not depress or downgrade one's self. For the self verily is both the friend and the foe of the self.[3]

बन्धुरात्मात्मनस्तस्य येनात्मैवात्मना जितः।
अनात्मनस्तु शत्रुत्वे वर्तेतात्मैव शत्रुवत् ॥ 6 ॥

Bandhur ātmā'tmanas tasya yen'ātm'aiv'ātmanā jitaḥ /
anātmanas tu śatrutve vartet'ātm'aiva śatruvat //6//

Yena : By whom *atmanā eva* : by the higher self *atmā jitaḥ* : the lower self is subdued *tasya* : of him *bandhuḥ* : friend *atmā eva* : is verily the self himself. *Anātmanaḥ tu* : For the man with the lower self unconquered *atmā eva* : he himself *śatruvat* : like a foe *śatrutve*: in the role of an enemy *varteta*: remains.

6. To him who has subdued the lower self by the higher self, the self acts like a friend. But to him who has lost his higher self by the dominance of the lower one, the self functions as the enemy, always hostile to him.

जितात्मनः प्रशान्तस्य परमात्मा समाहितः।
शीतोष्णसुखदुःखेषु तथा मानापमानयोः ॥ 7 ॥

Jit'ātmanaḥ praśāntasya param'ātmā samāhitaḥ /
śīt'oṣṇa-sukha-duḥkheṣu tathā mān'āpamānayoḥ //7//

Jitātmanaḥ: For one who has conquered the mind *praśāntasya* : of the serene *paramātmā* : the Self *samāhitaḥ* : remains steady and unperturbed *śītoṣṇasukhaduḥkheṣu* : in heat and cold, as also in pleasure and pain *tathā* : in the same way *mānāpamānayoḥ* : in honour and dishonour.

7. In one who has conquered his mind, the Self remains steady and unperturbed in the experience of the pairs of opposites like heat and cold, pleasure and pain, honour and dishonour.

ज्ञानविज्ञानतृप्तात्मा कूटस्थो विजितेन्द्रियः ।
युक्त इत्युच्यते योगी समलोष्टाश्मकाञ्चनः ॥ 8 ॥

Jñāna-vijñāna-tṛptātmā kūṭa-stho vijit' endriyaḥ
yukta ity ucyate yogī sama-loṣṭ'āśma-kāñcanaḥ //8//

Jñānavijñānatṛptātmā : One whose spirit has attained contentment through wisdom and experience *kūṭasthaḥ* : unperturbed *vijitendriyaḥ* : one who has conquered the senses *samaloṣṭāśmakāñcanaḥ*: to whom a lump of earth and a bar of gold are alike *yogī* : the Yogī *yuktaḥ iti* : as steadfast in spiritual communion *ucyate* : is said to be.

8. A Yogin whose spirit has attained contentment through knowledge and experience, who is unperturbed, who has subdued his senses, to whom a lump of earth and a bar of gold are alike—such a Yogī is said to have attained steadfastness in spiritual communion.

सुहृन्मित्रार्युदासीनमध्यस्थद्वेष्यबन्धुषु ।
साधुष्वपि च पापेषु समबुद्धिर्विशिष्यते ॥ 9 ॥

Suhṛn-mitr'āry-udāsīna-madhyastha-dveṣya-bandhuṣu /
sādhuṣv api ca pāpeṣu sama-buddhir viśiṣyate //9//

Suhṛn-mitrāryudāsīna-madhyastha-dveṣya-bandhuṣu: Towards friend, comrades, the indifferent, the neutral, the inimical, and the ally *sādhuṣu* : towards the good *api pāpeṣu ca* : and even towards the wicked *samabuddhiḥ* : one who is equal-minded *viśiṣyate* : is noted for his excellence.

9. Specially noteworthy in excellence is he who is even-minded in his outlook on friend and foe, on comrade and

stranger, on the neutral, on the ally, on the good, and even on the evil ones.

योगी युञ्जीत सततमात्मानं रहसि स्थितः ।
एकाकी यतचित्तात्मा निराशीरपरिग्रहः ॥ 10 ॥

Yogī yuñjīta satatam ātmānaṁ rahasi sthitaḥ /
ekākī yata-citt'ātmā nirāśīr aparigrahaḥ //10//

Yogī : Yogī, an aspirant after Yoga *yatacittātmā* : with the mind and body under control *nirāśīḥ* : without hopes and expectations *aparigrahaḥ* : without possessions *ekākī* : alone *rahasi sthitaḥ* : remaining in solitude *ātmānam* : the self (the mind) *satatam* : always *yuñjīta* : let him practise spiritual communion.

10. Let a Yogin constantly practise spiritual communion, residing alone in a solitary spot, desireless, possessionless, and disciplined in body and mind.

शुचौ देशे प्रतिष्ठाप्य स्थिरमासनमात्मनः ।
नात्युच्छ्रितं नातिनीचं चैलाजिनकुशोत्तरम् ॥ 11 ॥

तत्रैकाग्रं मनः कृत्वा यतचित्तेन्द्रियक्रियः ।
उपविश्यासने युञ्ज्याद्योगमात्मविशुद्धये ॥ 12 ॥

Śucau deśe pratiṣṭhāpya sthiram āsanam ātmanaḥ /
n'ātyucchritaṁ n'ātinīcaṁ cail'ājina-kuśottaram //11//

Tatr'aikāgraṁ manaḥ kṛtvā yata-citt'endriya-kriyaḥ /
upaviśy'āsane yuñjyād yogam ātma-viśuddhaye //12//

Śucau deśe: In a clean place *nātyucchritam*: not very high *nātinīcam*: not very low *cailājina-kuśottaram* : with cloth, skin and grass in the reverse order *sthiram* : steady *ātmanaḥ* : for onself *āsanam* : seat *pratiṣṭhāpya* : having established, *tatra āsane* : on that seat *upaviśya*: sitting *manaḥ* : mind *ekāgram kṛtvā* : making onepointed *yata-chittendriya-kriyaḥ* : with the functions of the mind and the senses under control *ātmaviśuddhaye* : for the purification of the self *yogam yuñjyād* : let him practise spiritual communion.

11-12. At a clean spot, which is neither too high nor too low, a seat should be made with Kuśa grass, spread over with a skin and a cloth. Firmly seated on it, the Yogī should practise spiritual communion, with mind concentrated and with the working of the imaginative faculty and the senses under control, for self-purification.

समं कायशिरोग्रीवं धारयन्नचलं स्थिरः ।
संप्रेक्ष्य नासिकाग्रं स्वं दिशश्चानवलोकयन् ॥ 13 ॥

प्रशान्तात्मा विगतभीर्ब्रह्मचारिव्रते स्थितः ।
मनः संयम्य मच्चित्तो युक्त आसीत मत्परः ॥ 14 ॥

Samaṁ kāya-śiro-grīvaṁ dhārayann acalaṁ sthiraḥ /
saṁprekṣya nāsik'āgraṁ svaṁ diśaś c'ānavalokayan //13//

Praśānt'ātmā vigata-bhīr brahmacārivrate sthitaḥ /
manaḥ saṁyamya maccitto yukta āsita matparaḥ //14//

Kāyaśirogrīvam : Body, head and neck *samam* : erect *acalam* : firm *dhārayan* : holding, *svam* : one's own *nāsikāgram* : tip of the nose *samprekṣya* : gazing *diśaḥ ca na avalokayan*: without looking round, *vigatabhīḥ* : fearless *praśāntātmā* : serene *brahmacārivrate sthitaḥ* : established in the vow of continence, *manaḥ* : mind *samyamya* : restrained, *maccittaḥ* : meditating on Me *matparaḥ* : with Me as the highest end *yuktaḥ āsīta* : let him sit in spiritual communion.

13-14. Holding the body, head and neck erect, motionless and firm, gazing at the tip of the nose and not round about, fearless, serene, restrained in mind, and established in the vow of continence, he should sit in spiritual communion with Me, looking upon Me as his highest and most precious end.

युञ्जन्नेवं सदात्मानं योगी नियतमानसः ।
शान्ति निर्वाणपरमां मत्संस्थामधिगच्छति ॥ 15 ॥

Yuñjann evaṁ sadā'tmānaṁ yogī niyata-mānasaḥ /
śāntiṁ nirvāṇa-paramāṁ mat-saṁsthām adhigacchati //15//

Niyatamānasaḥ : With mind restrained from going towards objects *Yogī* : Yogī *sadā eva* : always *atmānam yuñjan* : uniting himself with the Supreme Spirit in spiritual communion *matsaṁsthām* : enduring establishment in Me *nirvāṇa paramām*: supreme salvation of bliss *śāntim* : peace *adhigacchati* : attains to.

15. With the mind restrained from going outward to objects and always uniting with the Supreme in spiritual communion, the Yogi attains to Peace, which is supreme salvation and enduring establishment in My state.

नात्यश्नतस्तु योगोऽस्ति न चैकान्तमनश्नतः ।
न चातिस्वप्नशीलस्य जाग्रतो नैव चार्जुन ॥ 16 ॥

N'ātyaśnatas tu yogo'sti na c'aikāntam anaśnataḥ /
na c'ātisvapna-śīlasya jāgrato n'aiva c'ārjuna //16//

Arjuna : O Arjuna *atyaśnataḥ* : to one who eats too much *yogaḥ na asti* : Yoga is not possible, *ekāntam anaśnataḥ ca* : also for one who eats too little, *atisvapna-śīlasya na* : nor for one who sleeps too much, *jāgrataḥ ca na eva* : nor for one who keeps awake too much.

16. O Arjuna! Success in Yoga is not for those who eat too much, nor for those who eat too little. It is not also for those given to too much sleeping, nor to those who keep vigil too long.

युक्ताहारविहारस्य युक्तचेष्टस्य कर्मसु ।
युक्तस्वप्नावबोधस्य योगो भवति दुःखहा ॥ 17 ॥

Yukt'āhāra-vihārasya yukta-ceṣṭasya karmasu /
yukta-svapn'āvabodhasya yogo bhavati duḥkha-hā //17//

Yuktāhāra-vihārasya : For one temperate in food and recreation *karmasu* : in work *yuktaceṣtasya* : detached and self-restrained *yukta-svapnāvabodhasya* : regulated in sleep and in vigils *yogaḥ* : Yoga *duḥkhahā* : destructive of the travail of Samsāra *bhavati* : becomes.

17. For one who is temperate in food and recreation, who is detached and self-restrained in work, who is regulated in sleep and in vigil—Yoga brings about the cessation of the travail of Samsāra.

यदा विनियतं चित्तमात्मन्येवावतिष्ठते ।
निःस्पृहः सर्वकामेभ्यो युक्त इत्युच्यते तदा ॥ 18 ॥

Yadā viniyatam cittam atmany ev'āvatiṣṭhate
niḥspṛhaḥ sarva-kāmebhyo yukta ity ucyate tadā //18//

Yadā : When *viniyatam* : disciplined *cittam* : mind *ātmani eva* : in the Ātman alone *avatiṣṭhate* : remains established, (*yadā* : when) *sarvakāmebhyaḥ* : from all desires *niḥspṛhaḥ* : free from longing, *tadā* : then *yuktaḥ* : attained to spiritual communion *iti* : thus *ucyate* : is said.

18. When the disciplined mind is able to remain established in the Ātman alone, when it is free from longing for all objects of desire—then is it spoken of as having attained to spiritual communion.

यथा दीपो निवातस्थो नेङ्गते सोपमा स्मृता ।
योगिनो यतचित्तस्य युञ्जतो योगमात्मनः ॥ 19 ॥

Yathā dīpo nivāta-stho n'eṅgate s'opamā smṛtā
yogino yata-cittasya yuñjato yogam ātmanaḥ //19//

Ātmanaḥ : With the Ātman *yogam* : communion *yuñjataḥ* : of the one practising *yatacittasya* : with controlled mind *yoginaḥ* : of the Yogi : *nivātasthaḥ* : in a place sheltered from wind *dīpaḥ yathā* : like the flame of lamp *na iṅgate* : does not flicker, *sā* : that *upamā* : comparison *smṛtā* : is recalled.

19. The flame of a lamp sheltered from wind does not flicker. This is the comparison used to describe a Yogi's mind that is well under control and united with the Ātman.

यत्रोपरमते चित्तं निरुद्धं योगसेवया ।
यत्र चैवात्मनात्मानं पश्यन्नात्मनि तुष्यति ॥ 20 ॥

Yatr'oparamate cittaṁ niruddhaṁ yoga-sevayā /
yatra c'aiv'ātmanā'tmānaṁ paśyann ātmani tuṣyati //20//

Yatra : In which *yogasevayā niruddham* : restrained by the practice of Yoga *cittam* : the movements of the Chitta *uparamate* : finds rest; *yatra ca* : wherein *ātmanā* : by the higher mind *ātmānam*: the Spirit *paśyan* : having intuited, *ātmani eva* : in the Spirit itself *tuṣyati* : rejoices.

20. That state in which the Chitta (mind stuff), with its movements restrained by the practice of Yoga, finds rest; in which is experienced the joy of the Spirit born of the higher mind intuiting the Spirit;

सुखमात्यन्तिकं यत्तद्बुद्धिग्राह्यमतीन्द्रियम् ।
वेत्ति यत्र न चैवायं स्थितश्चलति तत्त्वतः ॥ 21 ॥

Sukham ātyantikaṁ yat tad buddhi-grāhyam atīndriyam /
vetti yatra na c'aiv'āyaṁ sthitaś calati tattvataḥ //21//

Yatra ca : Wherein *ayam* : he *yat* : what *atīndriyam* : beyond the ken of the senses *buddhigrāhyam* : capable of being grasped by the purified intellect *tat* : that *ātyantikam* : endless *sukham* : bliss *vetti* : experiences, (*yatra* : wherein) *sthitaḥ* : established *tattvataḥ* from the Truth *na eva chalati* : does not waver at all.

21. In which he (the Yogin) experiences that endless bliss which is beyond the ken of the senses but is intuited by the purified intellect; wherein established, one does not waver from the Truth;

यं लब्ध्वा चापरं लाभं मन्यते नाधिकं ततः ।
यस्मिन्स्थितो न दुःखेन गुरुणापि विचाल्यते ॥ 22 ॥

Yaṁ labdhvā c'āparaṁ lābhaṁ manyate n'ādhikaṁ tataḥ /
yasmin sthito na duḥkhena guruṇā'pi vicālyate //22//

Yaṁ labdhvā : Having obtained which *tataḥ* : from it *aparam* : another *adhikam lābham* : as greater gain *na manyate* : does not think, *yasmin ca* : in which *sthitaḥ* : established *guruṇā* : heavy *duḥkhena* : by afflictions *api* : even *na vicālyate* : is not shaken;

22. Having obtained which no other gain is considered as greater; remaining in which one is not shaken even by the heaviest of afflictions,—

तं विद्याद् दुःखसंयोगवियोगं योगसंज्ञितम् ।
स निश्चयेन योक्तव्यो योगोऽनिर्विण्णचेतसा ॥ 23

Taṁ vidyād duḥkha-saṁyoga-viyogaṁ yoga-saṁjñitam |
sa niścayena yoktavyo yogo'nirviṇṇa-cetasā ||23||

Duḥkha-saṁyoga-viyogam : severance of connection with pain *tam* : that *yogasaṁjñitam* : what is described as Yoga *vidyāt* : let one know. *Saḥ yogaḥ* : That Yoga *niścayena* : with determination *anirviṇṇacetasā* : with untiring mind *yoktavyam* : should be practised.

23. Know that severance of connection with pain as what is designated as Yoga. It has to be practised tirelessly with determination.

संकल्पप्रभवान्कामांस्त्यक्त्वा सर्वानशेषतः ।
मनसैवेन्द्रियग्रामं विनियम्य समन्ततः ॥ 24 ॥

शनैः शनैरुपरमेद् बुद्ध्या धृतिगृहीतया ।
आत्मसंस्थं मनः कृत्वा न किंचिदपि चिन्तयेत् ॥ 25 ।

Saṁkalpa-prabhavān kāmāṁs tyaktvā sarvān aśeṣataḥ |
manas'aiv'endriya-grāmaṁ viniyamya samantataḥ ||24||

Śanaiḥ śanair uparamed buddhyā dhṛti-gṛhītayā |
ātma-saṁsthaṁ manaḥ kṛtvā na kiñcid api cintayet ||25||

Saṁkalpaprabhavān : Imagination-born *sarvān* : all *kāmān* : desires *aśeṣataḥ* in completeness *tyaktvā* : abandoning, *manasā eva* :

with the mind itself *indriyagrāmam* : the group of senses *samantataḥ* : on every side *viniyamya* : controlling, *dhṛtigṛhītayā* : held with firmness *buddhyā* : by the intellect *manaḥ* : mind *ātmasaṁstham kṛtvā* : held firm in the Self *śanaiḥ śanaiḥ* : little by little *uparamet* : let one withdraw (become tranquil); *kiñcit api* : anything at all *na cintayet* : let one not think of.

24-25. Abandoning imagination-born longings in their entirety, restraining all the senses with the mind on every side, and setting that mind firmly on the Self under the direction of a steadfast intellect, one should practise tranquillity little by little, and abstain from every kind of thought.

यतो यतो निश्चरति मनश्चञ्चलमस्थिरम्
ततस्ततो नियम्यैतदात्मन्येव वशं नयेत् ॥ 26 ॥

Yato-yato niścarati manaś c'añcalam asthiram /
tatas tato niyamy'aitad ātmany eva vaśaṁ nayet //26//

Cancalam : Wavering *asthiram* : fickle *manaḥ* : mind *yataḥ yataḥ* : from whatsoever reason *niścarati* : wanders away, *tataḥ tataḥ* : from that *etat* : this mind *niyamya* : curbing *ātmani eva* : in the Ātman alone *vaśam* : subordinate *nayet* : should bring.

26. From whatsoever reason this wavering and fickle mind wanders away, it should be curbed and brought to abide in the Self alone.

प्रशान्तमनसं ह्येनं योगिनं सुखमुत्तमम् ।
उपैति शान्तरजसं ब्रह्मभूतमकल्मषम् ॥ 27 ॥

Praśānta-manasaṁ hy enaṁ yoginaṁ sukham uttamam /
upaiti śānta-rajasaṁ brahma-bhūtam akalmaṣam //27//

Praśāntamanasam : Tranquil in mind *śāntarajasam* : with passions subsided *akalmaṣam* : free from impurities *Brahmabhūtam* : Brahman-become *enam yoginam* : to this Yogin *uttamaṁ sukham* : supreme Bliss *upaiti hi* : wells up.

27. Supreme Bliss wells up in a Yogī, who is tranquil in mind, whose passions are subdued, who is free from impurities and who is in the Brahmic state[4].

युञ्जन्नेवं सदात्मानं योगी विगतकल्मषः
सुखेन ब्रह्मसंस्पर्शमत्यन्तं सुखमश्नुते ॥ 28 ॥

Yuñjann evaṁ sadā'tmānaṁ yogī vigata-kalmaṣaḥ /
sukhena brahma-saṁsparśam atyantaṁ sukham aśnute //28//

Evam : Thus *sadā* : always *ātmānam* : mind *yuñjan* : steadfast in communion *vigatakalmaṣaḥ* : with the impurities of the mind effaced *yogī* : Yogin *sukhena* : with ease *Brahmasaṁsparśam* : contact with Brahman *atyantam* : intense *sukham* : bliss *aśnute* : experiences.

28. Thus, ever engaged in making the mind steadfast in spiritual communion and having all the impurities of the mind effaced thereby, the Yogin easily experiences the intense Bliss of contact with Brahman.

सर्वभूतस्थमात्मानं सर्वभूतानि चात्मनि
ईक्षते योगयुक्तात्मा सर्वत्र समदर्शनः ॥ 29 ॥

Sarva-bhūta-stham ātmānaṁ sarva-bhūtāni c'ātmani /
īkṣate yoga-yukt'ātmā sarvatra sama-darśanaḥ //29//

Sarvatra : In all beings *samadarśanaḥ* : one who sees the same *yogayuktātmā* : the man established in spiritual communion *ātmānam* : the Self *sarvabhūtastham* : residing in all things, *ātmani* : in the Self *sarvabhūtani* : all beings *ca* : and *īkṣate* : sees.

29. The man of spiritual insight, established in same-sightedness, sees the Self as residing in all beings and all beings as resting in the Self.[5]

यो मां पश्यति सर्वत्र सर्वं च मयि पश्यति ।
तस्याहं न प्रणश्यामि स च मे न प्रणश्यति ॥ 30 ॥

Yo māṁ paśyati sarvatra sarvaṁ ca mayi paśyati /
tasy'āhaṁ na praṇaśyāmi sa ca me na praṇaśyati //30//

Yaḥ : who *sarvatra* : in all beings *mām* : Me *paśyati* : sees, *sarvaṁ ca* : and all *mayi* : in Me *paśyati* : sees, *tasya* : for him *aham* : I *na praṇaśyāmi* : am never lost, *saḥ ca* : and he *na me* : to me *na praṇaśyati* : is never lost.

30. He who sees Me in all beings, and all beings in Me—to him I am never lost, nor he to Me.

सर्वभूतस्थितं यो मां भजत्येकत्वमास्थितः ।
सर्वथा वर्तमानोऽपि स योगी मयि वर्तते ॥ 31 ॥

Sarva-bhūta-sthitaṁ yo māṁ bhajaty ekatvam āsthitaḥ /
sarvathā vartamāno'pi sa yogī mayi vartate //31//

Yaḥ : Who *ekatvam āsthitaḥ* : established in the unity of existence *sarvabhūtasthitam* : present in all beings *mām* : Me *bhajati* : serves *saḥ yogī* : that Yogin *sarvathā* : in any condition *vartamānaḥ* : remaining *api* : even *mayi* : in Me *vartate* : abides.

31. Established in the unity of all existence, a Yogin who serves Me present in all beings. verily abides in Me, whatever be his mode of life.

आत्मौपम्येन सर्वत्र समं पश्यति योऽर्जुन ।
सुखं वा यदि वा दुःखं स योगी परमो मतः ॥ 32 ॥

Ātm'aupamyena sarvatra samaṁ paśyati yo'rjuna /
sukhaṁ vā yadi vā duḥkhaṁ sa yogī paramo mataḥ //32//

Arjuna : O Arjuna! *sarvatra* : in all beings *sukham vā yadi vā duḥkham* : whether pleasure or pain (is experienced) *ātmaupamyena*: by comparison with oneself *samam* : as same *yaḥ* : who *paśyati* : sees, *saḥ* : that *yogī* : Yogin *paramaḥ* : highest *mataḥ* : in my view.

32. O Arjuna! In My view that Yogi is the best who, out of a sense of identity with others on account of the perception of the same Atman in all, feels their joy and suffering as his own.

अर्जुन उवाच

योऽयं योगस्त्वया प्रोक्तः साम्येन मधुसूदन ।
एतस्याहं न पश्यामि चञ्चलत्वात् स्थितिं स्थिराम् ॥ 33 ॥

Arjuna uvāca:

Yo'yaṁ yogas tvayā proktaḥ sāmyena Madhusūdana |
etasy'āhaṁ na paśyāmi cañcalatvāt sthitiṁ sthirām ||33||

Madhusūdana : O Slayer of Madhu! *sāmyena* : by cultivation of evenness *yaḥ* : which *ayam* : this *yogaḥ* : Yoga *tvayā* : by you *proktaḥ* : instructed, *etasya* : of this Yoga *sthirāṁ sthitim* : firm establishment *cañcalatvāt* : due to fickleness of mind *aham* : I *na paśyāmi* : do not see.

Arjuna said:

33. O Slayer of Madhu! Owing to the fickleness of the mind, I find no way of firm establishment in spiritual communion through equanimity as instructed by you.

चञ्चलं हि मनः कृष्ण प्रमाथि बलवद् दृढम् ।
तस्याहं निग्रहं मन्ये वायोरिव सुदुष्करम् ॥ 34 ॥

Cañcalaṁ hi manaḥ Kṛṣṇa pramāthi balavad dṛḍham |
tasy'āhaṁ nigrahaṁ manye vāyor iva suduṣkaram ||34||

Kṛṣṇa : O Kṛṣṇa! *hi* : verily *manaḥ* : mind *cañcalam* : restless, *pramāthi* : liable to violent agitation, *balavat* : powerful, *dṛḍham* : unyielding. *Tasya* : Of it *nigraham* : control *vāyoḥ* : of wind *iva* : like *suduṣkaram* : difficult *aham* : I *manye* : think.

34. O Kṛṣṇa! Verily, the mind is fickle, turbulent, powerful and unyielding. To control it, I think, is as difficult as controlling the wind itself.

श्रीभगवानुवाच

असंशयं महाबाहो मनो दुर्निग्रहं चलम् ।
अभ्यासेन तु कौन्तेय वैराग्येण च गृह्यते ॥ 35 ॥

Śrī Bhagavān uvāca:

Asaṁśayaṁ mahā-bāho, mano durnigrahaṁ calam
abhyāsena tu Kaunteya vairāgyeṇa ca gṛhyate //35//

Mahābāho : O mighty armed one! *manaḥ* : mind *durnigraham* : difficult to control *calam* : fickle *iti* : this *asaṁśayam* : is doubtless. *Tu* : Still *Kaunteya* : O son of Kuntī! *abhyāsena* : by spiritual practice *vairāgyeṇa* : by dispassion *ca* : and *gṛhyate* : is controlled.

The Blessed Lord said:

35. O mighty armed one! Undoubtedly the mind is fickle and difficult to be checked. Yet, O son of Kunti, it can be brought under control by dispassion and spiritual practice.

असंयतात्मना योगो दुष्प्राप इति मे मतिः ।
वश्यात्मना तु यतता शक्योऽवाप्तुमुपायतः ॥ 36 ॥

Asaṁyat'ātmanā yogo duṣprāpa iti me matiḥ /
vaśy'ātmanā tu yatatā śakyo'vāptum upāyataḥ //36//

Asaṁyatātmanā : By one of uncontrolled mind *yogaḥ* : spiritual communion *duṣprāpaḥ* : difficult of attainment, *iti* : this *me* : My *matiḥ* : view. *Vaśyātmanā tu* : But by a man of controlled mind *upāyataḥ* : by the proper means *yatatā* : by those striving *avāptum* : to obtain *śakyaḥ* : possible.

36. My view is that Yoga is difficult of attainment by men of uncontrolled mind. But for those who have their minds under control, it is possible to attain, if they strive with the proper means.

अर्जुन उवाच
अयतिः श्रद्धयोपेतो योगाच्चलितमानसः ।
अप्राप्य योगसंसिद्धिं कां गतिं कृष्ण गच्छति ॥ 37 ॥

Arjuna uvāca:
Ayatiḥ śraddhay'opeto yogāc calita-mānasaḥ /
aprāpya yoga-saṁsiddhiṁ kāṁ gatiṁ Kṛṣṇa gacchati? //37//

Kṛṣṇa : O Kṛṣṇa! *śraddhayā* : with **Sraddha** or faith *upetaḥ* : endowed *ayatiḥ* : not steadfast in striving. *yogāt* : from the spiritual path *calitamānasaḥ* : having the mind distracted, *yogasaṁsiddhim* : spiritual perfection *aprāpya* : without attaining, *kām* : what *gatim* : way *gacchati* : does he attain?

Arjuna said:
37. What, O Kṛṣṇa, is the fate of a man who, though endowed with firm faith, is not steadfast in his practices owing to distractions, and therefore fails to reach spiritual perfection?

कच्चिन्नोभयविभ्रष्टश्छिन्नाभ्रमिव नश्यति ।
अप्रतिष्ठो महाबाहो विमूढो ब्रह्मणः पथि ॥ 38 ॥

Kaccin n'obhaya-vibhraṣṭas chinn'ābhram iva naśyati /
apratiṣṭho mahā-bāho vimūḍho brahmaṇaḥ pathi //38//

Mahābāho : O mighty-armed Lord! *vimūḍhaḥ* : bewildered, *brahmaṇaḥ pathi* : in the path to **Brahman** *apratiṣṭaḥ* : not firmly established, *ubhaya-vibhraṣṭah* : deprived of both *chinnābhram iva* : like a rent cloud *na naśyati kaccit* : is it not that he is destroyed?

38. O mighty-armed Lord! Bewildered in the path of Brahman, supportless, does he not lose both this world and the next? Does he not perish like a rain-cloud rent asunder?

एतन्मे संशयं कृष्ण छेत्तुमर्हस्यशेषतः ।
त्वदन्यः संशयस्यास्य छेत्ता न ह्युपपद्यते ॥ 39 ॥

Etan me saṁśayaṁ Kṛṣṇa chettum arhasy aśeṣataḥ /
tvad-anyaḥ saṁśayasy'āsya chettā na hy upapadyate //39//

Kṛṣṇa : O Kṛṣṇa! *me* : my *etat* : this *samśayam*: doubt *aśeṣataḥ*: entirely *chettum* : to destroy *arhasi* : deserve. *Hi* : Indeed *asya* : of this *samśayasya* : doubt *chettā* : destroyer *tvadanyaḥ* : other than Thee *na upapadyate* : is fit.

39. O Kṛṣṇa! My doubt in this respect has yet to be cleared completely. Indeed! I find none better than Thee to be that doubt-dispeller.

श्रीभगवानुवाच

पार्थ नैवेह नामुत्र विनाशस्तस्य विद्यते ।
न हि कल्याणकृत्कश्चिद् दुर्गतिं तात गच्छति ॥ 40 ॥

Śrī *Bhagavān uvāca:*

Pārtha n'aiveha n'āmutra vināśas tasya vidyate /
na hi kalyāṇa-kṛt kaścid durgatim tāta gacchati //40//

Pārtha : O son of Prithā! *asya* : of him *iha* : here *vināśaḥ* : destruction *na vidyate* : is not, *na amutra eva* : not in the hereafter too. *Tāta* : O dear one. *kalyāṇakṛt* : a doer of good *kaścit* : never *durgatim* : path of ruin *na gacchati* : does not go *hi* : indeed!

The Blessed Lord said:

40. O son of Prithā! He does not meet with downfall either here in this world or in the hereafter. Know for certain, O dear one, that one who treads the path of virtue never goes to ruin (i.e., gets an inferior birth).

प्राप्य पुण्यकृतां लोकानुषित्वा शाश्वतीः समाः ।
शुचीनां श्रीमतां गेहे योगभ्रष्टोऽभिजायते ॥ 41 ॥

Prāpya puṇya-kṛtām lokān uṣitvā śāśvatīḥ samāḥ /
śucīnām śrīmatām gehe yoga-bhraṣṭo'bhijāyate //41//

Yogabhraṣṭaḥ : One fallen from the path of Yoga *puṇyakṛtām* : of doers of good works *lokān* : the worlds *prāpya* : having attained, *śāśvatīḥ samāḥ* : unnumbered years *uṣitvā* : staying, *śucīnām* : of the pure *śrīmatām* : of the prosperous *gehe* : in the house *abhijāyate* : is born.

46. A Yogī (one practising meditation) is superior to a man of austerity; he is superior to a scholar; he is superior to a ritualist too. Therefore, O Arjuna, be you a Yogī.[6]

योगिनामपि सर्वेषां मद्गतेनान्तरात्मना ।
श्रद्धावान्भजते यो मां स मे युक्ततमो मतः ॥ 47 ॥

Yogīnām api sarveṣāṁ mad-gaten' āntar'ātmanā /
śraddhāvān bhajate yo māṁ sa me yuktatamo mataḥ //47//

Yaḥ : who *madgatena* : entered into My being *antarātmanā* : with the inner self, *śraddhāvan* : endowed with faith *mām* : Me *bhajate* : worships, *saḥ*: he *sarveṣām api*: of all *yoginām* : Yogins *yuktatamaḥ*: most well established in spiritual communion *me* : My *mataḥ* : view.

47. Of all the Yogins, he is the most attuned in spiritual communion, who worships Me with abiding faith and with his innermost self fused with Me.[7]

ओं तत्सदिति श्रीमद्भगवद्गीतासूपनिषत्सु ब्रह्मविद्यायां
योगशास्त्रे श्रीकृष्णार्जुनसंवादे आत्मसंयमयोगो
नाम षष्ठोऽध्यायः ॥ 6 ॥

NOTES

1. *V*.2: The point is that abandonment of self-centred values is the common discipline to be observed by both the Sannyasin and the Yogī. Mere abandonment of all actions externally will take one nowhere; for self-centredness remains unless it is eliminated by some means. It is true too that much involvement in unnecessary works, done without any discrimination or reflection, will only increase desires and further strengthen self-centredness. But discharge of one's Svadharma as an offering to God, and eliminating self-centredness in so discharging it through practice of discrimina-

tion and devotion, will gradually make one rise above self-centredness.

2. *V.*3: The two stages of spiritual life are pointed out here—that of the Ā*rurukṣu* (one desiring to ascend) and that of the Ā*rūḍha* (one who has ascended to Yoga). In the first stage dedicated works or discharge of **Svadharma** as an offering to the Divine is the means of higher evolution, whereas in the second stage introspective quiescence (Śama) becomes the means of perfection. This does not mean that every one of that type need withdraw from all action and become a recluse. For, as given in verse 56 of the previous chapter, it is said of such persons: "Even though he may be engaged in all kinds of work, such a person, being completely given over to Me, attains to the eternal and undecaying state." It shows that though work is no longer a discipline for further progress for such an '*ārūḍha*', he can engage himself in God-centred action. This way of life was preached by Śrī Kṛṣṇa, and it is known as the *Bhāgavata Dharma.* It is amplified in the *Bhāgavata Purāṇa* under nine heads—*śravaṇam* (hearing) *kīrtanam* (hymning), *smaraṇam* (remembering), *pādasevanam* (service), *arcanam* (worship), *vandanam* (salutation), *dāsyam* (servitude), *sakhyam* (comradeship), *ātmanivedanam* (total surrender). Here under *pādasevanam,* works of service are included; because the manifested world is a '*pāda*' or part of the Lord. Its service implies a God-centred life. Thus Sāṁkhya and Yoga are self-contained paths. They may look separate at a certain stage, but they end in the same state of spiritual integration. One need not be merely considered as a feeder to the other.

3. *Vrs.* 5-6: These verses seem to imply that there are two aspects to the Self of man—one higher and the other lower. The higher self is the Buddhi turned towards the Ātman, the spiritual essence. The lower self is the mind dominated by the senses. It is said the sense-dominated mind should not be allowed to overpower the Buddhi, the higher self. If this is to be avoided, the Buddhi should draw strength from the Ātman by communion with it. Such a Buddhi, fortified by the Ātman consciousness, can easily uplift the sense-bound mind and integrate it with itself.

4. *Vrs.* 27-28: The word *Brahmabhūta* cannot have been used here in the sense of 'one having become one with the Supreme

Being (Brahman); for immediately following in the Verse 28 is mentioned *Brahma-saṁsparśa*—contact with Brahman, where the Yogi's distinction from Brahman should necessarily be still retained. It is one who is *Brahma-bhūta* that gains *Brahma-saṁsparśa*. *Brahma-bhūta* must therefore mean that state of unruffled inward consciousness which precedes the dawn of supreme devotion and enlightenment (cf.ch.18-54) and which is described at the end of the second chapter as *Brāhmīsthiti*. The word Brahman is used in different meanings in different contexts in the Gita, as has been shown in these notes from place to place. For a detailed discussion see note 6 in Chapter 14 and 9 in 18. Here that state is described as *śānta-rajasam*, as one free from passions, and *akalmaṣam*, free from impurities.

5. *Vrs*. 29-32: These verses are of considerable metaphysical, ethical and psychological importance. These are: (1) Metaphysically it asserts the unity of all existence in a spiritual Self, which is both impersonal and personal, and emphasises the intimate relation between that Spiritual Self and the individual self. For in Verse 29 the Yogī is said to see the Self in all and all in this Self. In the very next verse, 'I, the Supreme Lord,' is substituted in place of Self, thus indicating the basic unity of both. (2) Ethically it teaches the most universal principle of ethics. To do towards, and feel for, others' selves as for one's own self, is the highest principle of ethics. This is the implication of seeing the Self in all and all in the Self. (3) Psychologically it shows that spiritual intuition which Yoga gives has a distinct content of a unique nature and is not a mere fantasy without any life-enhancing value. The new contents of consciousness are: (*a*) establishment in an unabating state of bliss from which even the greatest sorrow cannot shake one (cf V. 21-23 and V. 28 of this chapter). (*b*) Self-centredness goes away when one finds the same Self in all. It thus leads to an all-comprehending extension of the subjective side of consciousness, which now dominates the objective side just as the substantiality of a tree subordinates that of its shadow. A Universal Self becomes a matter of experience.

6. *V*.46: This verse at first appears a little enigmatic, especially so when one takes the words denoting the different disciplines in their usual sense. For example the Yogı is said to be superior to a

Jñāni, a knowing one, while the Advaita commentators uncompromisingly state that Jñāna is the last word in spiritual life and all the other Yogas are only stepping stones to it. To save Jñāna from this eclipse by Yoga, Jñāna here has to be arbitrarily interpreted as scholarship, intellectual understanding, as against Yoga which is intuitive realization. Or Jñāna may be the discriminative knowledge enabling the Spirit to be distinguished from matter and not the unitary consciousness of Advaita. Even then this one verse is enough to disprove the Advaitic contention of exalting Jñāna Yoga to a position of supremacy and hegemony, and the other Yogas of Bhakti, Karma and Yoga to the position of mere vassal disciplines. The Gīta text however does not do so. All Yogas are equally valid and are independent paths to the Supreme. Independence does not mean the exclusion of other disciplines. Man is an integrated whole, his mind being a complex of feeling (emotion), will and intellection. In the four spiritual disciplines, one of these dominates, while the others, though subordinate, complete the discipline. This is the integrated Yoga of the Gīta. Swami Vivekananda too has interpreted Vedanta in this way, giving equal place to all the four Yogas.

7. *V*.47: This verse, immediately following the praise of Yoga, tells us that devotion to God, which makes one cling to the Lord in utter faith and self-surrender, makes Yoga all the more exalted. The word Yoga, like Brahman, is used in many senses in the Gīta. Here in this chapter the word is used mainly in the sense of *Aṣṭāṅga-yoga*—the eight-limbed Yoga of Patanjali. It is the science of concentration and stilling of the modes of the mind. The philosophy with which it supports its practices is the *Sāṁkhya,* which teaches the discrimination between the Puruṣa and Prakṛti, and establishment in the knowledge that the Puruṣa, the Spirit, is entirely different from Prakṛti or Material Nature. There is not much of a place for God and devotion in it. But the Gītā everywhere stresses the supreme importance of Iśvara and devotion to Him in making all spiritual disciplines complete. So it is pointed out here that the Yoga discipline of concentration will be more perfect if the object of concentration is the Lord.

Just as the Lord exalts Aṣṭānga-Yoga here, he exalts Karma Yoga in verses 8-12 of Chapter 12, and says that total surrender of the fruits of action leads to peace at once. But here also Karma is coupled with devotion to Iśvara. But, just as concentration is the form that Yoga should take in Aṣṭānga-yoga, in Karma Yoga, work for the Lord is the form that spiritual discipline takes. Thus the Gītā does not downgrade any of these disciplines as the handmaid of Jñāna, or for the matter of that, even of Bhakti. It wants that in each Yoga, its specific discipline must have the dominant place, but that it should also integrate into itself the essential contributions of the others also. If it tilts towards any of the Yogas, it is towards Bhakti, with the other Yogas integrated into it.

Chapter VII

ज्ञानविज्ञानयोगः

COMMUNION THROUGH KNOWLEDGE AND REALIZATION

SUMMARY

The Lower and Higher Prakṛtis: (1-6) The Lord speaks to Arjuna about Divine knowledge thus: Among men there are only a few who aspire and strive to know Me, and even from among them, only a few succeed after many births. I have two powers of manifestation (Prakṛtis), the lower and the higher. The lower Prakṛti is material Nature consisting of earth, water, fire, air, sky, mind, intellect and egoity. The higher Prakṛti is My manifestation as Jīvas or centres of consciousness. The former is My Unconscious Nature and the latter Conscious Nature. It is my Conscious Nature that supports and sustains the world made of the latter Unconscious Nature, because the evolution of into various spheres and numerous species of beings is for Jīvas to reap the fruits of their Karma and gradually evolve into perfection.

The All-embracing Divine: (7-11) There is none higher than Me, or outside My being, limiting Me. As a string supports all the beads in a necklace, so are all things sustained by Me. My immanent Self is the Essence in all entities, manifesting as their characteristic nature and function—in water as taste, in earth as smell, in fire as heat, in all beings as life, in the thoughtful as intellect, in the strong as their strength, in embodied beings as desire conducive to growth and so on.

Who transcends Māyā: The four types of Devotees: (12-19) All beings high and low have originated from Me and are contained in Me, but they do not limit me. No being subject to My Māyā constituted of the three Guṇas, can know Me, the immanent yet transcendent Being. For, this Māyā that obstructs their vision is My power, and only by surrendering to Me with one's whole being can one get across its obstruction and know Me. But so long as man is dominated by evil tendencies and is a slave of demoniac nature, he does not devote himself to Me. Four types of persons become devoted to Me—the sufferer, the enquirer, the boon-seeker and the knowing one. Though they are all to be considered noble and virtuous, the knowing one is to Me like My very self. His love stems from his sense of innate unity with Me, and is therefore unmotivated and constant. To him I am dearer than anything else, and so is he to Me. It is only after many births of spiritual striving that man is established in this form of love based on the knowledge that it is Vāsudeva alone who is seen as this world of multiplicity.

The One God forms the object of all worship: (20-30) In whatever aspect devotees adore Me, I strengthen their faith in that aspect and approach them in that form. To those who worship Me in the form of various deities for attaining worldly fulfilments, I, who indwell these deities, strengthen their faith in their objects of worship and grant them their prayer; but they only attain to those deities, and the fruit they get is of short duration. Not understanding Me as the Universal Being, indwelling even the deities, they adore particularised and limited deities. Due to the obstruction of My Yoga-māyā, men do not understand Me as the unborn and the undecaying. I know all beings, past, present and future, but none knows Me. For their body-consciousness and passions based on it, obstruct men's understanding from the very start. It is only those whose sinful tendencies have been counteracted by good works, that worship Me with steadfastness of mind. Those who thus worship Me for liberation from the cycle of births and deaths, come to know that I am the sole existence, as also the sole doer and the sole enjoyer.

श्रीभगवानुवाच

मय्यासक्तमनाः पार्थ योगं युञ्जन्मदाश्रयः ।
असंशयं समग्रं मां यथा ज्ञास्यसि तच्छृणु ॥ 1 ॥

Śrī Bhagavān uvāca:

Mayy āsakta-manāḥ Pārtha yogaṁ yuñjan mad-āśrayaḥ |
asaṁśayaṁ samagraṁ māṁ yathā jñāsyasi tac chṛṇu //1//

Pārtha : O son of Pṛthā! *mayi* : in Me *āsaktamanāḥ* : mind absorbed in love *madāśrayaḥ* : resigned to Me *yogam* communion *yuñjan* : practising, *yathā* : how *mām* : Me *samagram* : in fullness *asaṁśayam* : without doubt *jñāsyasi* : know, *tat* : that *śṛṇu* : hear.

The Blessed Lord said:

1. Hear now, O son of Pṛthā, how one resigned to Me and absorbed in love of Me, attains to full knowledge of Me through the practice of spiritual communion.[1]

ज्ञानं तेऽहं सविज्ञानमिदं वक्ष्याम्यशेषतः ।
यज्ज्ञात्वा नेह भूयोऽन्यज्ज्ञातव्यमवशिष्यते ॥ 2 ॥

Jñānaṁ te'haṁ savijñānam idaṁ vakṣyāmy aśeṣataḥ |
yaj jñātvā n'eha bhūyo'nyaj jñātavyam avaśiṣyate //2//

Yat : What *jñātvā* : having known *iha* : here *bhūyaḥ* : more *anyat* : other things *jñātavyam* : that which has to be understood *na avaśiṣyate* : remains not, *idam* : this *jñānam* : Knowledge *savijñānam* : along with special Knowledge of it *aśeṣataḥ* : in fullness *aham* : I *te* : to you *vakṣyāmi* : shall tell.

2. I shall now declare to you in fullness that Knowledge along with Special Knowledge (its higher development), by means of which there will remain nothing more for you to understand.

मनुष्याणां सहस्रेषु कश्चिद्यतति सिद्धये ।
यततामपि सिद्धानां कश्चिन्मां वेत्ति तत्त्वतः ॥ 3 ॥

Manuṣyāṇāṁ sahasreṣu kaścid yatati siddhaye |
yatatām api siddhānāṁ kaścin māṁ vetti tattvataḥ //3//

Manuṣyāṇāṁ sahasreṣu : Among thousands of men *kaścit* : some one *siddhaye* : for spiritual perfection *yatati* : strives; *yatatām siddhānām* : of the striving aspirants *api* : even *kaścit* : some one *mām* : Me *tattvataḥ* : in truth *vetti* : knows.

3. Among thousands of men, there will just be one here or there striving for spiritual perfection. From among the aspirants so striving, one perchance knows Me in truth.

भूमिरापोऽनलो वायुः खं मनो बुद्धिरेव च ।
अहंकार इतीयं मे भिन्ना प्रकृतिरष्टधा ॥ 4 ॥

Bhūmir āpo'nalo vāyuḥ khaṁ mano buddhir eva ca /
ahaṁkāra itī'yaṁ me bhinnā prakṛtir aṣṭadhā //4//

Bhūmiḥ : Earth, *āpaḥ* : water, *analaḥ* : fire, *vāyuḥ* : air, *kham* : sky, *manaḥ* : mind, *buddhiḥ* : understanding, *ahaṁkāraḥ* : I-sense or egoism *ca* : and *iti* : thus *aṣṭadhā* : into eight *bhinnāḥ eva* : divided *me* : My *iyam* : this *prakṛtiḥ* : Nature.

4. My Nature is divided into eight categories—earth, water, fire, air, sky, mind, understanding, and I-sense.

अपरेयमितस्त्वन्यां प्रकृतिं विद्धि मे पराम् ।
जीवभूतां महाबाहो ययेदं धार्यते जगत् ॥ 5 ॥

Apar'eyam itas tv anyāṁ prakṛtiṁ viddhi me parām /
jīva-bhūtāṁ mahā-bāho yay'edaṁ dhāryate jagat //5//

Mahābāho : O mighty-armed! *iyam* : this *aparā* : lower; *itaḥ tu* : from this *anyām* : different *jīvabhūtām* : that which has manifested as the Jīva (the self-conscious individual centre) *yayā* : by which *idam* : this *jagat* : universe *dhāryate* : is sustained, *tām*: that *me* : My *parām* : higher *prakṛtim* : nature *viddhi* : know.

5. This, O mighty armed, is My lower nature. Know that, as different from it, is My higher nature forming the source of all Jivas and the support of the whole universe.

एतद्योनीनि भूतानि सर्वाणीत्युपधारय ।
अहं कृत्स्नस्य जगतः प्रभवः प्रलयस्तथा ॥ 6 ॥

Etad-yonīni bhūtāni sarvāṇī'ty upadhāraya |
ahaṁ kṛtsnasya jagataḥ prabhavaḥ pralayas tathā //6//

Sarvāṇi : All *bhūtāni* : beings *etad yonīni* : as entities having these two as their source, *iti* : thus *upadhāraya* : know. *Aham* : I *kṛtsnasya* : of the entire *jagataḥ* : universe *prabhavaḥ* : the origin, *tathā* : likewise *pralayah* : the dissolution.

6. Know that all beings have these two natures of Mine as their source. I am the origin and the dissolution of this entire universe.

मत्तः परतरं नान्यत्किञ्चिदस्ति धनंजय ।
मयि सर्वमिदं प्रोतं सूत्रे मणिगणा इव ॥ 7 ॥

Mattaḥ parataraṁ n'ānyat kiṁcid asti Dhanaṁjaya |
mayi sarvam idaṁ protaṁ sūtre maṇi-gaṇā iva //7//

Dhanaṁjaya : O Arjuna! *mattaḥ* : than Me *parataram* : higher *anyat* : other *kiṁcit* : any one *na asti* : does not exist. *Sūtre* : in a thread *maṇigaṇāḥ* : gems *iva* : like *mayi* : in Me *idam* : this *sarvam* : all *protam* : strung.

7. O Arjuna! There is no being higher than Me. As a row of pearls threaded on a string, all the worlds are held on Me.

रसोऽहमप्सु कौन्तेय प्रभास्मि शशिसूर्ययोः ।
प्रणवः सर्ववेदेषु शब्दः खे पौरुषं नृषु ॥ 8 ॥

Raso'ham apsu Kaunteya paabhā'smi śaśi-sūryayoḥ |
praṇavaḥ sarva-vedeṣu śabdaḥ khe pauruṣaṁ nṛṣu //8//

Kaunteya : O son of Kuntī! *apsu* : in water *rasaḥ* : taste *aham* : I, *śaśisūryayoḥ* : of the moon and the sun *prabhā* : brilliance *asmi* : I am, *sarvavedeṣu* : in all Vedas *praṇavaḥ* : Praṇava (the sound symbol Om), *khe* : in sky *śabdaḥ* : sound, *nṛṣu* : in men *pauruṣam* : manliness.

8. O son of Kuntī! In water I am taste; in sun and moon, their brilliance; in all the Vedas, the sound symbol Om; in the sky-element, sound; and in men, their manliness.

पुण्यो गन्धः पृथिव्यां च तेजश्चास्मि विभावसौ ।
जीवनं सर्वभूतेषु तपश्चास्मि तपस्विषु ॥ 9 ॥

Puṇyo gandhah pṛthivyāṁ ca tejaś c'āsmi vibhāvasau /
jīvanaṁ sarva-bhūteṣu tapaś c'āsmi tapasviṣu //9//

Pṛthivyām : In the earth element *puṇyaḥ gandhah* sweet fragrance *ca* : and, *vibhāvasau* : in fire *tejaḥ* : light *ca* : and *asmi* : I am, *sarvabhūteṣu* : in all beings *jīvanam* life-principle, *tapasviṣu* : in austere men *tapaḥ* : austerity *ca* : too *asmi* : am.

9. In the earth element I am sweet fragrance; in fire I am brilliance; in living beings I am the life-principle; and in austere men, I am austerity.

बीजं मां सर्वभूतानां विद्धि पार्थ सनातनम् ।
बुद्धिर्बुद्धिमतामस्मि तेजस्तेजस्विनामहम् ॥ 10 ॥

Bījaṁ māṁ sarva-bhūtānāṁ viddhi Pārtha sanātanam /
buddhir buddhimatām asmi tejas tejasvinām aham //10//

Pārtha : O son of Pṛthā! *mām* : Me *sarvabhūtānām* : of all beings *sanātanam* : eternal *bījam* : seed *viddhi* : know. *Buddhimatām* : Of the intelligent *buddhiḥ* : intelligence, *tejasvinām* : of puissant men *tejaḥ* : puissance *aham* : I *asmi* : am.

10. Know me, O Pārtha! to be the eternal seed of all beings. In the wise I am their wisdom, and in puissant men their prowess.

बलं बलवतां चाहं कामरागविवर्जितम् ।
धर्माविरुद्धो भूतेषु कामोऽस्मि भरतर्षभ ॥ 11 ॥

Balaṁ balavatām asmi kāma-rāga-vivarjitam /
dharmị'āviruddho bhūteṣu kāmo'smi Bharata' rṣabha //11//

Balavatām : In the strong *kāma-ràgavivarjitam* : free from lust and attachment *balam* : strength *asmi* : I am, *bhūteṣu* : in living beings *dharmāviruddhaḥ* : not opposed to virtue *kāmaḥ* : desire *asmi* : I am.

11. In the strong I am strength uncorrupted by desire and attachment, and in living beings I am desire not contrary to virtue.

ये चैव सात्त्विका भावा राजसास्तामसाश्च ये ।
मत्त एवेति तान्विद्धि न त्वहं तेषु ते मयि ॥ 12 ॥

Ye c'aiva sāttvikā bhāvā rājasās tāmasāś ca ye /
matta ev'eti tān viddhi na tv ahaṁ teṣu te mayi //12//

Ye ca : And whatever *sāttvikāḥ* : characterised by Sattva *rājasāḥ* : characterised by Rajas *ye* : whatever *tāmasāḥ* : characterised by Tamas *ca* : and *bhāvāḥ* : manifestations, *tān* : them *mattaḥ* : from Me *eva* : verily *viddhi* : know. *Aham* : I *tu* : but *teṣu* : in them *na* : not, *te* : they *mayi* : in Me.

12. Whatever manifestations there are of Sattva, Rajas and Tamas, they have all come from Me. They are in Me, not I in them.[2]

त्रिभिर्गुणमयैर्भावैरेभिः सर्वमिदं जगत् ।
मोहितं नाभिजानाति मामेभ्यः परमव्ययम् ॥ 13 ॥

Tribhir guṇamayair bhāvair ebhiḥ sarvam idaṁ jagat /
mohitaṁ n'ābhijānāti mām ebhyaḥ param avyayam //13//

Ebhiḥ : By these *tribhiḥ* : by three *guṇamayaiḥ* : formed of Guṇas *bhāvaiḥ* : mental states *sarvam* : all *idam* : this *jagat* : world *mohitam* : deluded, *ebhyaḥ param* : superior to them *avyayam* imperishable *mām* : Me *na* : not *abhijānāti* : knows.

13. Deluded by the mental states accruing from the three Guṇas of Prakṛti, this world knows not Me, the Imperishable, transcending these Guṇas.

दैवी ह्येषा गुणमयी मम माया दुरत्यया ।
मामेव ये प्रपद्यन्ते मायामेतां तरन्ति ते ॥ 14 ॥

Daivī hy eṣā guṇamayī mama māyā duratyayā |
mām eva ye prapadyante māyām etāṁ taranti te //14//

Guṇamayī: Constituted of Guṇas *daivī* : divine *mama* : My *eṣā* : this *māyā* : Māyā *duratyayā hi* : difficult to overcome. *Ye* : Who *mām* : Me *eva* : only *prapadyante* : take refuge in *te* : they *etām* : this *māyām* : Māyā *taranti* : overcome.

14. My divine Māyā (power) constituted of the three Guṇas is difficult to overcome. Whoever takes refuge in Me alone, in utter devotion, overcomes it.

न मां दुष्कृतिनो मूढाः प्रपद्यन्ते नराधमाः ।
माययापहृतज्ञाना आसुरं भावमाश्रिताः ॥ 15 ॥

Na māṁ duṣkṛtino mūḍhāḥ prapadyante nar'ādhamāḥ |
māyayā'pahṛta-jñānā āsuraṁ bhāvam āśritāḥ //15//

Āsuram : Demoniac *bhāvam* : disposition, nature *āśritāḥ* : partaking of, *māyayā* : by Māyā *apahṛtajñānāḥ* : deprived of right understanding *duṣkṛtinaḥ* : the evil doers *mūḍhāḥ* : the foolish *narādhamāḥ* : lowest of men *mām* : Me *na prapadyante* : never seek refuge in.

15. The lowest type of men, evil, foolish and demoniac in nature, being deprived of right understanding by Māyā, never take refuge in Me with devotion.[3]

चतुर्विधा भजन्ते मां जनाः सुकृतिनोऽर्जुन ।
आर्तो जिज्ञासुरर्थार्थी ज्ञानी च भरतर्षभ ॥ 16 ॥

Catur-vidhā bhajante māṁ janāḥ sukṛtino'rjuna /
ārto jijñāsur arth'ārthī jñānī ca bharata'rṣabha //16//

Bharatarṣabha : O greatest of the Bharatas! *Arjuna* : O Arjuna! *caturvidhāḥ* : four types *sukṛtinaḥ janāḥ* : pious men *mām* : Me *bhajante* : worship, *ārtaḥ* : the distressed *jijñāsuḥ* : the enquirer *arthārthī* : wealth-seeker *jñānī* : knower *ca* : and.

16. O Arjuna, the greatest of the Bharata race! Four kinds of pious men adore Me. They are the distressed one, the Knowledge-seeker, the wealth-seeker, and the knower.

तेषां ज्ञानी नित्ययुक्त एकभक्तिर्विशिष्यते ।
प्रियो हि ज्ञानिनोऽत्यर्थमहं स च मम प्रियः ॥ 17 ॥

Teṣāṁ jñānī nitya-yukta eka-bhaktir viśiṣyate /
priyo hi jñānino'tyartham ahaṁ sa ca mama priyaḥ //17//

Teṣam : Among them *nityayuktaḥ* : ever communing *ekabhaktiḥ* : single-minded in devotion *jñānī* : knower *viśiṣyate* : is the best. *Aham* : I *jñāninaḥ* : of the knower *atyartham priyaḥ* : extremely dear *hi* : verily *saḥ* : he *ca* : and *mama* : My *priyaḥ* : dear.

17. Among them, the knower (or the man of wisdom), ever-communing and single-minded in devotion, is the best. I am indeed supremely dear to such a knower, and he in turn is dear to Me.

उदाराः सर्व एवैते ज्ञानी त्वात्मैव मे मतम् ।
आस्थितः स हि युक्तात्मा मामेवानुत्तमां गतिम् ॥ 18 ॥

Udārāḥ sarva ev'aite jñānī tv ātm'aiva me matam /
āsthitaḥ sa hi yukt'ātmā mām ev'ānuttamāṁ gatim //18//

Ete sarve : All these *udārāḥ eva* : are noble certainly, *jñānī* : knower *tu* : but *atmā eva* : self itself *me* : My *matam* : view *hi* :

indeed. *Saḥ* : He *yuktātmā* : ever in union with Me *mām eva* : Me alone *anuttamām* : the highest *gatim* : goal *āsthitaḥ*: established (in the conviction).

18. While all of them are certainly noble, the knower I cherish as My very self—such is My view. For, ever in union with Me, he is established in the conviction that I am his highest goal.[4]

बहूनां जन्मनामन्ते ज्ञानवान्मां प्रपद्यते ।
वासुदेवः सर्वमिति स महात्मा सुदुर्लभः ॥ 19 ॥

Bahūnāṁ janmanām ante jñānavān māṁ prapadyate /
vāsudevaḥ sarvam iti sa mah'ātmā sudurlabhaḥ //19//

Bahūnām : Of many *janmanām* : births *ante* : at the end of *jñānavān* : the knowing one *vāsudevaḥ* : Vāsudeva *sarvam* : everything *iti* : thus *mām* : Me *prapadyate* : seeks refuge in. *Saḥ* : That *mahātmā* : great soul *sudurlabhaḥ* : very rare.

19. At the end of many births (of striving), the knowing one makes Me his refuge, realising that Vāsudeva is All. A great soul of that type is rare to find.

कामैस्तैस्तैर्हृतज्ञानाः प्रपद्यन्तेऽन्यदेवताः ।
तं तं नियममास्थाय प्रकृत्या नियताः स्वया ॥ 20 ॥

Kāmais tais-tair hṛta-jñānāḥ prapadyante' nya-devatāḥ /
taṁ-taṁ niyamam āsthāya prakṛtyā niyatāḥ svayā //20//

Svayā : By one's own *prakṛtyā* : by nature *niyatāḥ* : directed, *taiḥ taiḥ kāmaiḥ* : by this and that desire *hṛtajñānāḥ* : deprived of judgement *tam tam niyamam* : ways of worship pertaining to each *āsthāya* : adopting *anyadevatāḥ* : other deities *prapadyante* : worship.

20. Influenced by their inherent nature and deprived of correct judgement by numerous desires, people adore other deities with various forms of worship pertaining to them.[5]

यो यो यां यां तनुं भक्तः श्रद्धयार्चितुमिच्छति ।
तस्य तस्याचलां श्रद्धां तामेव विदधाम्यहम् ॥ 21 ॥

Yo yo yāṁ yāṁ tanuṁ bhaktaḥ śraddhayā'rcitum icchati /
tasya-tasy'ācalāṁ śraddhāṁ tām eva vidadhāmy aham //21//

Yaḥ Yaḥ bhaktaḥ : Whichever devotee *yām yām tanum* : whatever form or aspect *śraddhayā* : with faith *arcitum* : to worship *icchati* : desires, *tasya tasya* : of each of these votaries *tām* : that *śraddhām* : faith *eva* : verily *aham* : I *acalām* : unshakable *vidadhāmi* : render.

21. Whichever devotee desires to adore whatever such aspect with faith, in all such votaries I make that particular faith unshakable.

स तया श्रद्धया युक्तस्तस्याराधनमीहते ।
लभते च ततः कामान्मयैव विहितान्हि तान् ॥ 22 ॥

Sa tayā śraddhayā yuktas tasy'ārādhanam īhate /
labhate ca tataḥ kāmān may'aiva vihitān hi tān //22//

Saḥ: He *tayā:* with that *śraddhayā* faith *yuktaḥ*: endowed with, *tasya* : of that deity *arādhanam* : worship *īhate* : performs. *Tataḥ* : Consequently *mayā* : by Me *vihitān* : granted *eva* : alone *tān* : those *kāmān* : objects of desire *labhate ca hi* : obtains verily.

22. Endowed with that faith, a votary performs the worship of that particular deity and obtains the fruits thereof, these being granted by Me alone.

अन्तवत्तु फलं तेषां तद्भवत्यल्पमेधसाम् ।
देवान्देवयजो यान्ति मद्भक्ता यान्ति मामपि ॥ 23 ॥

Antavat tu phalaṁ teṣaṁ tad bhavaty alpa-medhasām /
devān deva-yajo yānti mad-bhaktā yānti mām api //23//

Alpamedhasām : Of little minds *teṣam* : of them *tat* : that *phalam* : result *antavat tu* : finite only *bhavati* : is. *Devayajāḥ* : Those who worship the Devas *devān* : Devas *yānti* : attain, *mad-bhaktāḥ api* : but My devotees *mām* : Me *yānti* : attain.

23. The results accruing to such small-minded people are finite only. Those who worship the Devas go to the Devas, but My devotees attain to Me.

अव्यक्तं व्यक्तिमापन्नं मन्यन्ते मामबुद्धयः ।
परं भावमजानन्तो ममाव्ययमनुत्तमम् ॥ 24 ॥

Avyaktaṁ vyaktim āpannaṁ manyante mām abuddhayaḥ /
paraṁ bhāvam ajānanto mamā'vyayam anuttamam //24//

Avyayam : Immutable *anuttamam* : unique *mama* : My *paraṁ-bhāvam* : transcendental being *ajānantāḥ* : without knowing *abuddhayaḥ* : men of little intelligence *avyaktam* : unclear or unmanifested state *vyaktim* : individuality *āpannam* : come to possess *manyante* : think.

24. Without any insight into My transcendental nature, unique and immutable, men of little understanding look upon Me as a mere human individual, having come into manifestation from an unmanifested state.[6]

नाहं प्रकाशः सर्वस्य योगमायासमावृतः ।
मूढोऽयं नाभिजानाति लोको मामजमव्ययम् ॥ 25 ॥

N'āhaṁ prakāśaḥ sarvasya yoga-māyā samāvṛtaḥ /
mūḍho' yaṁ n'ābhijānāti loko mām ajam avyayam //25//

Yogamāyāsamāvṛtaḥ: Veiled by My divine power *aham* : I *sarvasya* : to all *na prakāśaḥ* : not revealed. *Mūḍhaḥ* : deluded *ayam lokaḥ* : this world *mām* : Me *ajam* : the unoriginated *avyayam* : the indestructible *na abhijānāti* : does not know.

25. Veiled as I am in My Yogamāyā (Divine Power), I am not revealed to all. This deluded world does not know Me, the unoriginated and the indestructible.[7]

वेदाहं समतीतानि वर्तमानानि चार्जुन ।
भविष्याणि च भूतानि मां तु वेद न कश्चन ॥ 26 ॥

Ved'āhaṁ samatītāni vartamānāni c'ārjuna
bhaviṣyāṇi ca bhūtāni māṁ tu veda na kaścana //26//

Arjuna : O Arjuna! *samatītāni* : the past *vartamānāni* : the present *ca* : and *bhaviṣyāṇi* : future *ca* : and *bhūtāni* : beings *aham veda* : I know, *mām tu* : but Me *kaścana*: any one *na veda* : does not know.

26. O Arjuna! I know all beings—past, present and future. But none knows me.

इच्छाद्वेषसमुत्थेन द्वन्द्वमोहेन भारत ।
सर्वभूतानि संमोहं सर्गे यान्ति परंतप ॥ 27 ॥

Icchā-dveṣa-samutthena dvandva-mohena Bhārata /
sarva-bhutāni saṁmohaṁ sarge yānti paraṁtapa //27//

Bhārata : O scion of Bhārata's house *paraṁtapa* : O destroyer of enemies *sarge* : from birth *icchādveṣa samutthena* : springing from instinctive attractions and aversions *dvandva mohena* : by the bewitchment of opposites *sarvabhūtāni* : all beings *saṁmoham* : state of delusion *yānti* : attain.

27. O scion of Bharata's house! From their very birth all beings are deluded by the bewitchment of the pairs of opposites like pleasure and pain, sprung from the instinctive feelings of attraction and aversion for them.

येषां त्वन्तगतं पापं जनानां पुण्यकर्मणाम् ।
ते द्वन्द्वमोहनिर्मुक्ता भजन्ते मां दृढव्रताः ॥ 28 ॥

Yeṣāṁ tv anta-gataṁ pāpaṁ janānāṁ puṇya-karmaṇām /
te dvandva-moha-nirmuktā bhajante māṁ dṛḍha-vratāḥ //28//

Puṇyakarmaṇām : Doers of virtuous deeds *yeṣām* : whose *janānām* : of persons *pāpam* : sin *antagatam* : come to an end *tu* : but, *te* : they *dvandvamohanirmuktāḥ* : freed from the bewilderment of the pairs of opposites *dṛḍhavratāḥ* : steadfast in their vows *mām*: Me *bhajante* : adore.

28. But those men of virtuous deeds, in whom sinfulness has been effaced—they, freed from the bewilderment of sense life, worship Me with great steadfastness in their vows.

जरामरणमोक्षाय मामाश्रित्य यतन्ति ये ।
ते ब्रह्म तद्विदुः कृत्स्नमध्यात्मं कर्म चाखिलम् ॥ 29 ॥

Jarā-maraṇa-mokṣāya mām āśritva yatanti ye /
te brahma tad viduḥ kṛtsnam adhyātmaṁ karma c'ākhilam //29//

Jarāmaraṇa-mokṣāya : For freedom from old age and death *ye* : whoever *mām* : Me *āśritya* : depending *yatanti* : strive, *te* : they *tat* : that *Brahma* : Brahman or the Absolute *Kṛtsnam* : entire *adhyātmam* : spirit in manifestation *akhilam* : whole of *karma* : work *ca* : and *viduḥ* : know.

29. Those that strive for liberation from the travails of old age and death in complete trust and dependence on Me, shall know all about the Absolute, His spiritual manifestation and His works of spiritual import.[8]

साधिभूताधिदैवं मां साधियज्ञं च ये विदुः ।
प्रयाणकालेऽपि च मां ते विदुर्युक्तचेतसः ॥ 30 ॥

Sādhibhūt'ādhidaivaṁ māṁ sādhiyajñaṁ ca ye viduḥ /
prayāṇa-kāle'pi ca māṁ te vidur yukta-cetasaḥ //30//

Mām : Me *sādhibhūtādhidaivam*: as underlying all material manifestations and all divinites *sādhiyajñam* : as underlying all sacrifices *ca*: and *ye*: who *viduḥ*: know, *te*: they *yuktacetasaḥ*: with the mind absorbed in Me *prayāṇakāle* : at the time of death *api ca*; even *mām* : Me *viduḥ* : know.

30. Those who have grasped that I am the spiritual power that sustains all material manifestations, all divine expressions

and all spiritual endeavours—they continue to know Me as such even at the time of death, their mind being ever absorbed in Me.

ॐ तत्सदिति श्रीमद्भगवद्गीतासूपनिषत्सु ब्रह्मविद्यायां
योगशास्त्रे श्रीकृष्णार्जुनसंवादे ज्ञानविज्ञानयोगो
नाम सप्तमोऽध्यायः ॥ 7 ॥

NOTES

1. *Vrs*.1-6: These verses set forth that in the creative process the Lord's power of manifestation functions as His two Natures—the material i.e. unconscious Nature or Prakṛti, and His spiritual Nature or the Jīvas. Strangely enough the Jīva, which should be called Puruṣa, is classified with Prakṛti here, thereby obliterating the dichotomy between the two terms familiar in the Sāṁkhya.

The material Nature is here treated in its cosmic aspect and is spoken of as eightfold. But that is done by counting only the effect categories and leaving the causal categories as implied. Fully stated, according to the analysis of the Sankhya philosophy, the categories of Prakṛti and its evolutes are twenty four. These are: Prakṛti (with its three Guṇas of Sattva, Rajas and Tamas); **Mahattattva;Ahamkara;** Manas; the five organs of knowledge; the five organs of action; the five Tanmatras; and the five gross elements of Sky, Air, Fire, Water, and Earth. From these categories the material universe is evolved. Also the psycho-physical organism of the Jīva, consisting of his subtle and gross bodies, evolves out of these. The subtle body persists through all embodiments, until the Jīva gains liberation, attaining to his natural state as Puruṣa. This material Nature or Prakṛti is infinite with countless dimensions in which different world systems (Lokas) of different subtlety co-exist without mutual intrusion and the Jīva finds embodiment in these different Lokas according to his Karma.

The material Nature is called by the Lord here as his Aparā Prakṛti or Lower Nature. In contrast to this He speaks of his Parā Prakṛti or higher Nature as 'what has become the Jīva' (*Jīva-bhūtam*). Both Natures have their origin and dissolution in Him. Origin and dissolution here means the relative beginning and dissolution at the beginning and end of the Kalpa or cycle of time. As creation and dissolution constitute a cyclic process, there is no absolute beginning for both these manifestations of His Powers. As His Prakṛti or Nature, they are one with Him just as light and heat are one with fire, though they are attributively distinguishable from fire. Ontologically they are distinct from, and dependent on, Him but not different at the same time. For absolute dependence pre-supposes a basic unity.

Creation as taught in Chapter 8.17-20 is an eternal process. So the Parā and Aparā Prakṛtis of the Lord are eternally expressing as the cyclic process of time consisting in Kalpa or a period of manifestation. and Pralaya or a period of dissolution. They come into being through a process of evolution, and dissolve into the original state through a process of involution. This alternation goes on eternally.

The Parā Prakṛti or Jīva in its collectivity is thus involved in this eternal process. but with a difference. A Jīva. a unit of this Prakṛti. undergoes evolution in this creative process and ultimately manifests the fullness of his divine nature. For a Jīva is described in 15.7 by the Lord thus: "An *Aṁsa* (a fraction or particle of His) has become the Jīva in the universe" Elsewhere in the Upaniṣads he is described as a spark of the Divine Fire. So he has got all the potentialities of **Iśvara,** as Sat, Chit and Ānanda. But this Divine nature is hidden or contracted in the state of ignorance. The process of creation and dissolution is sometimes described as a Play or *līla* of the Lord as there is no purpose for the Lord to gain through it. But from the point of view of the Jīva it has a purpose, and that purpose is to help the Jīva regain his full divine nature, overcoming the domination of material Nature in the state of ignorance. Karmas, good and bad, accrue to the Jīva in the course of the creative process, giving him different embodiments, until he attains illumination through Divine grace. Then the Jīva, the individual unit of Parā Prakṛti, is freed from the thraldom of matter and involvement in the cycle of births and deaths. According to pure monistic doctrine the Jīva is then dissolved in Brahman and becomes one with Him as a drop of water in the ocean. According to theistic Vedanta, or qualified monism, the Jīva continues to have his identity even in Mukti, but participates in the spiritual excellences of the Lord and continues in deathless and blissful service of Him.

Though individual Jīvas attain salvation and go out of Samsāra, the Jīva-Sakti (higher Nature) in its collectivity functions eternally like the Aparā-Śakti (lower Nature). For, the number of Jīvas are infinite, and those in a state of contraction and abeyance are always evolving into greater and greater perfection. Now the Parā or Jīva-Śakti is here spoken of as that which sustains the universe (*dhāryate jagat*). Generally we say that the Lord supports the universe, but here this is said to be done by the collectivity of Jīvas. The idea here is that it is the presence of countless **Jīvas** that necessitates the eternal cyclic process of Time to revolve, initiating Kalpas and Pralayas. For the Karmas of the Jīvas come to fruition in the process of Time, and they have to reap their rewards, which requires embodiment. Embodiment of Jīvas requires the evolution of the various world systems. Thus the Jīva is, in this sense, the cause of the creative process and is therefore spoken of as the sustaining force of the universe. In terms of the Paurāṇika **ideology,** the Jīva is therefore described as the *hetu*, the cause of the creative process. Thus in this sense the creative process has a purpose, as far as the Jīva is concerned. That purpose is the **Jīva**'s evolution—evolution leading to perfection. But the Lord Himself has no extraneous purpose in creation, and so it is said to be His Līla or play.

This perception of the whole creative process as a divine play in which the Lord Himself becomes the Jīva, the Jagat (world) and their master--(the playmates, the play things and the player)—is the Vijñāna or the special knowledge spoken of here in verse two. This is in agreement with Sri Ramakrishna's teaching on the Vijñāni.

As contrasted with Vijñāna, Jñāna is simple knowledge. It is not mere knowledge of scriptures, but **illumination** in a general sense which gives the understanding that God is the reality and the multiplicity is a mere appearance, a false presentation to be rejected.

One having mere Jñāna does not understand that it is a manifestation of His Śakti, which is one with Him but through which He can project multiplicity without Himself being affected by it. The Vijñāni is one who has this higher illumination and therefore knows the creative process and the evolution of multiplicity as the Play of the Lord—a play in the sense that it has no ulterior purpose and is only an expression of His inherent Bliss. Sri Ramakrishna has expounded this doctrine of the Vijñāni in his teachings. The distinction that the Gītā draws here between Jñāna and Vijñāna can be understood only in the light of this teaching. The interpretation that the former, i.e., Jñāna, means knowledge of scriptures, and the latter, namely Vijñāna, is experience, is inadequate.

2. *Vrs.*12-14: Sattva, Rajas and Tamas, the three constituents or Guṇas of Prakṛti, are clearly enumerated here for the first time, although reference to them is made earlier collectively in 2.45, 3.5 and 3.27. The whole world of multiplicity is evolved by the permutation and combination of these three Guṇās or constituents of Prakṛti, the material Nature and their evolutes. Detailed description of these with reference to their part in producing multiplicity in creation and various character types is given in later chapters, especially in 14.5-19, 17. 2-22, 18. 7-9, 18.40 etc. In the Sāṁkhya system Prakṛti with its constituents is an independent existence, moved by its own inherent dynamism for the fulfilment of the purpose of the Puruṣas or centres of consciousness. with which it is associated. In classical Sāṁkhya, there is no place for an Iśvara, a Supreme Spirit in whom Prakṛti and Puruṣa are unified and who controls them in their evolution.

Now the Vedanta rejects this position and accepts the Prakṛti and the Puruṣas of the Sāṁkhya only as the Śaktis or potencies of **Iśvara**, the Supreme Being. The former, as has already been taught, is His Lower Nature, (*Aparā-prakṛti*) and the latter Higher Nature (*parā-prakṛti*). So the three Guṇas, the constituents of Prakṛti, are spoken of as being in Him, because He is their support. But they do not affect Him in any way, as they do the individual centres of consciousness or the Jīvas forming His Higher **Prakṛti.** Sri Ramakrishna explains this by an analogy: the snake has within itself poison, but that poison has no effect on it, although it is deadly to others.

Prakṛti with its three Guṇas deludes the Jīva with body-consciousness and hides the Divine from him. This is the state of ignorance which leads to the Jīva's involvement in the transmigratory cycle. This ignorance can be overcome only by Divine grace, which He bestows on a Jīva that takes absolute shelter in Him.

3. *Vr.*15: The Gītā in the 16th Chapter elaborates these two types of characters—the *Daivī* or the divine, and *Āsurī,* or the demoniac. The latter type is dominated by lust and greed, and has a sense of value, and therefore of reality, only for objects that satisfy these cravings and for their off-shoots like pride, jealously, cruelty etc. Their nature makes them think of spiritual verities and values as purely illusory, a pursuit reserved for fools. They wallow in worldliness without attaining to salvation in any near future, until suffering mellows their pride or the grace of God or of any divine personage lifts them up. Sri Ramakrishna illustrates this type in his parable of the fisherman and the three kinds of fish. Some fish escape before the net falls. They are the Nitya Siddhas, the ever free. Some break open the net after it has fallen; they are the aspirants who strive and get liberation. The third type are the fish that burrow into the mud as the net falls, thinking that security lies there. These are the *Baddhas,* the bound ones, who wallow in worldliness and never seek to get out of it. These correspond to the persons with Āsuric nature mentioned here.

This division of the Jīvas into Daivic and Āsuric is the basis of the doctrine of Tāratamya or comparative qualitative difference between Jīvas, forming an important teaching in the systems of Mādhva and Vallabhācārya.

4. *V.*18: This can be translated also as 'Jñāni is my own self', and interpreted as asserting the unity of the individual self with Iśvara. While monistic thinkers interpret it that way, others take it to mean that God is so fond of the devotee of this type that He is almost dependent on him. In the *Bhāgavata* (S.K. IX. 63) it is stated: "I am a slave of My devotees. I am as it were without freedom. For My heart is in the grip of the devotee; for, such is my love of the devotee." Such devotees feel 'God as their own' and God too loves them as His own; in this sense they are one with Him. The Bhakta of this type, is called here a Jñāni. He is distinguished from the three other types of Bhaktas in that he

seeks nothing from the Lord, not even Mokṣa. Such a state of mind is described in the *Bhāgavata* as '*Nairapekṣya*'. To such a one the Lord gives Himself. This doctrine is embodied in the *Bhāgavata* Verse V. 6.18: "I give Mukti to some, but Bhakti seldom." The Bhakta referred to here as Jñāni, is a devotee of this unique type, before whom God even humbles Himself, as in the case of Yudhiṣṭhira, Ambarīṣa etc. For, such exalted souls reject liberation, the supreme gift of the Lord and choose eternal service of Him without any ultimate motive and irrespective of what comes to them, be it enjoyment or suffering.

5. *Vrs.*20-23: The Vedic religion maintains that the Supreme Being has manifested Himself as several Deities, who represent His particular powers. It is not that Vedic religion teaches a primitive polytheism, as its detractors hold. Unity of Godhead is a well-known doctrine, but it is also accepted that just as the one God has manifested Himself as the world of multiplicity, so also He has manifested Himself as Deities. They are the expressions of His power. There are various texts inculcating the worship of Deities for the attainment of boons or material welfare. The devotion of most persons is mainly motivated by worldly needs like cure of diseases, success in one's effort, securing wealth etc., and when the worship of a particular Deity is found efficacious, many become votaries of that Deity. It is here pointed out that these ignorant votaries do not understand that the powers of the Deities are derived from the Supreme Being and that it is the Supreme Being Himself that gives them the desired fulfilment.

It appears from this that Kṛṣṇa is hereby exhorting people to worship the Supreme Being Himself for their material wants too or to look upon the Deities only as the symbols of the Supreme Being and thereby convert their worship into the worship of the Most High. There is an idea among devotional circles that devotees should approach the Supreme Being only for enlightenment and liberation and that praying to Him for small fulfilments will be like seeking a fruit or a cucumber from an emperor. But here Sri Kṛṣṇa seems to hold a different view, as he considers both the distressed (*ārta*) and the success-seeker (*arthārthī*) as devotees, and calls them also as noble (*udārāḥ*). Purāṇas have many examples of high-souled devotees seeking these smaller helps from the Supreme Being. Dhruva, Gajendra, Pāṇḍavas etc. are examples of this.

In recent times there is the conspicuous example of Nārāyaṇa Bhaṭṭatiri, the author of *Nārāyaṇīyam* who approached the Lord for relief from ailment, but he adds, while praying for health, that a modicum of health is needed for the practice of devotion, and that it is why he is approaching Him for it.

Or perhaps Sri Kṛṣṇa is referring here to the tradition of propitiating Deities by some and thereby showing the difference between such worship and the adoration of Divine Incarnations. This becomes clear in the very next verse where he criticises the blindness of people in not recognising the Divine Incarnations and not taking to their adoration.

6. *V*.24: The materialistic or the common sense point of view of man is expressed in Gītā 2.28 where it is said of man: "Living beings came from where we do not know (*avyaktādīni*). They are seen as distinct individuals in the middle (*vyaktamadhyāni*). And they pass away into where we do not know (*avyakta-nidhanāni*)." Ordinary men, especially most of His contemporaries, take the Lord Incarnate only as an ordinary man, may be with great powers, with a background and future as described in the verses quoted above. It will be seen that this was true of Rāma of whom even many of the Ṛṣis of Danḍakāraṇya declared that they knew him to be the 'son of Daśaratha' and not as the Divinity Incarnate. Even Kṛṣṇa was not recognised by many of his contemporaries as anything more than a great Yādava, though according to the *Bhāgavata* account many great men and those who came into intimate contact with him recognised his divinity. Here in the verse under comment, it is said that this is the case with the average men who are characterised as *abuddhayaḥ*, ignorant. It is probably worldly attachments that stand in the way of their recognising Him. The recognition and worship of the Incarnation stands on a different footing from that of deities. The Lord Incarnate is hypostatic with the Supreme Being, and His worship is the worship of the Supreme Being Himself. Devotion to the Lord Incarnate leads directly to Bhakti, Jñāna and Mukti.

But the background of the Divine Incarnate, making him specially significant, is his being rooted in the Supreme Divinity. He is the Anugraha-Śakti, the redeeming power of God, manifesting as an embodied being for a cosmic purpose. Men at large are not able to plumb the depths of the personality of the Incarnate and grasp his transcendental significance.

7. *V*.25: The reason for all not recognising Him when he incarnates is given. He appears veiled by the Yogamāyā or His Divine Power. This obscuration is caused by His assuming the nature of a human being. A Divine Incarnation is the expression of Divinity through humanity. Unless He lives the life of man with many of his limitations, the Incarnation defeats the purpose of His manifestation to a great extent. The disciples and followers of Incarnations of the past, especially in the case of the Paurāṇika Incarnations, have depicted the miraculous side of Incarnations to such an extent as to obliterate their humanity and convert them into Deities to be worshipped and not followed. Swami Saradananda has discussed this point elaborately in his *Sri Ramakrishna the Great Master*, wherein he has attributed this tendency on the part of the followers of Incarnations to the fear that if their human side is too much revealed, people's faith in their divinity may be affected.

A desperate effort to hide the human side of an Incarnation is seen among the interpreters of the *Bhāgavata* in regard to Kṛṣṇa. In the Text it is clearly stated that he was struck by the arrow of a hunter and shortly after, he passed away, burning his body in the fire of Yoga. But the *Bhāgavata* interpreters do not want to admit that his body was destroyed like that of a mortal, and so by clever devices of interpretation, they seek to construe this passage to mean that his very physical body disappeared into Vaikuntha, more or less like what is believed about Jesus. These interpreters in their vain effort to hide everything human about Kṛṣṇa, forget that a few verses later, the Text itself states again that he allowed his physical body, though it was a perfect one, to be destroyed, so that his followers might not attach too much importance to their own physical bodies.

This intermingling of the human and the divine is most clearly seen in a perfectly historical Incarnation as Sri Ramakrishna. The disciples of the Master never tried to hide his human side and the weaknesses incidental to it. The human side of his character is most candidly disclosed in his biography, and the fact of his having passed away due to cancer of the throat is also openly discussed and described. But none the less the disciples were also witnesses to the manifestation of Divinity in him side by side. This consisted chiefly in his capacity to rouse the spiritual consciousness of ignorant people. How the impetuous free thinker Narendra Nāth was converted into Swami Vivekananda, how the Bohemian Girish Chandra was made into an ideal devotee, and how on occasions like the Kalpataru day the Master roused the spiritual consciousness of large numbers of people at once, are well-known to the readers of his biography. Less widely known instances are those of how a rowdy named Manmatha was converted into a saint, and how a scavanger who approached him for liberation was blessed by him to become a man of illumination.

In fact the real divinity of Incarnations does not consist in the miracles that poets and mythologists have described with avidity in their language of exaggeration, but in their capacity to help man overcome the effect of Karma and gain spiritual enlightenment. Ordinary men do not see this side of Divine Incarnations clearly, because they are moved by gross worldly desires and are able to see divinity only when something extraordinary in a physical sense like the lifting of the Govardhana or the destruction of Pūtana or the building of a bridge across the sea are brought to their notice. It is long after the Incarnation passes away that his personality and teachings gain momentum and wide acceptance and He is recognised by large numbers of men.

8. *Vrs.*29-30: The technical terms contained in these verses are explained in the early verses of the next chapter.

———

Chapter VIII

अक्षरब्रह्मयोगः

THE WAY TO IMPERISHABLE BRAHMAN

SUMMARY

Divine Immanence and Transcendence: (1-4) Explaining the Divine mystery, Sri Krishna says: I am the Supreme Imperishable Brahman. My Inherent Nature is what manifests as the Indwelling Spirit and as the Creative Act which brings forth all beings into existence. There is also My perishable manifestation as the great elements; there is My presence in them as the Puruṣa (Immanent Self) guiding their evolution. And in all individual beings I am present as the Lord of Sacrifice, the generator and enjoyer of all actions.

Remembrance of the Lord at Death: (5-14) Whoever leaves the body thinking of Me alone, attains to My state undoubtedly. It is only those who think of Me intently during their life-time that will have this good fortune of remembering Me at death. Therefore remember Me always and do your duty in life. Practise the discipline of concentration on Me, the omniscient, the eternal, the Foundational Being, whose spiritual radiance dispels all darkness of ignorance. The syllable Om is My sound symbol. With that as the support, draw the mind into your innermost being and then concentrate on Me, the subtlest of entities and the seed of all forms.

Creative Cycles: (15-22) For those who attain to Me through the practice of this all-absorbing devotion, there is no return to this mortal sphere in the course of this endless cosmic cycles. For a thousand divine years, which is the day-time of Brahmā, the creator, the universe is manifest, and during the succeeding thousand divine years, the night of Brahmā, it lies latent in Me. Thus all beings up to Brahmā dissolve in Me and come out into manifestation. Only the devotee whose mind is ever fixed on Me, is able to come out of this eternally recurring cyclic process, fraught with impermanence and suffering. The manifested universe is My gross form, and the subtle state into which it relapses in dissolution is the causal state of that form of Mine. Transcending this universe in its gross and subtle conditions but at the same time containing and indwelling them, is My supreme aspect, attainable by single-minded and whole-hearted devotion.

The Life Hereafter: (23-28) There are two paths by which embodied beings depart after death—the dark path and the radiant path. Those who are attached to worldly values go along the dark path and come back to this world again at the exhaustion of the effects of their Karma. Those who are unattached and practise whole-hearted devotion to the Supreme Being, go along the bright path and never return.

अर्जुन उवाच

किं तद्ब्रह्म किमध्यात्मं किं कर्म पुरुषोत्तम ।
अधिभूतं च किं प्रोक्तमधिदैवं किमुच्यते ॥ 1 ॥

Arjuna uvāca:

Kiṁ tad brahma kim adhyātmaṁ kiṁ karma puruṣ'ottama /
adhibhūtaṁ ca kiṁ proktam adhidaivaṁ kiṁ ucyate? //1//

Puruṣottama : O Supreme Lord! *proktam* : spoken of *tat* : that *Brahma* : Brahman *kim* : what? *adhyātmam* : spirit in manifestation *kim* : what? *karma* : work *kim* : what? *adhibhūtam* : underlying material manifestation *kim* : what? *adhidaivam* : underlying manifestation as divinities *ca* : and *kim* : what *ucyate* : is spoken of?

Arjuna said:

1. O Supreme Lord! What is Brahman (the Absolute)? What is the Spirit (the Adhyātma)? What is work (Karma)? And what is that which underlies the material manifestations (Adhibhūta), and what, the divinities (Adhidaiva)?

अधियज्ञः कथं कोऽत्र देहेऽस्मिन्मधुसूदन ।
प्रयाणकाले च कथं ज्ञेयोऽसि नियतात्मभिः ॥ 2 ॥

Adhiyajñaḥ kathaṁ ko'tra dehe'smin Madhusūdana /
prayāṇa-kāle ca kathaṁ jñeyo'si niyat'ātmabhiḥ //2//

Madhūsūdana : O slayer of Madhu! *atra* : here *asmin* : in this *dehe* : body *adhiyajñaḥ* : one underlying all sacrifices *kaḥ* : who? *katham* : how? *Prayāṇakāle ca* : And at the time of death *niyatātmabhiḥ* : by self-restrained ones *katham* : how *jñeyaḥ asi* : ought to be known?

2. O slayer of Madhu! Who is the Adhiyajña (the spirit underlying sacrifices) that resides in this body, and how does he do so? How should a man of self-restraint meditate on the Supreme Being at the time of death?

श्रीभगवानुवाच

अक्षरं ब्रह्म परमं स्वभावोऽध्यात्ममुच्यते ।
भूतभावोद्भवकरो विसर्गः कर्मसंज्ञितः ॥ 3 ॥

Sri Bhagavān uvāca:

Akṣaraṁ brahma paramaṁ svabhāvo'dhyātmam ucyate /
bhūta-bhāvodbhava-karo visargaḥ karma-samjñitaḥ //3//

Paramam : Supreme *akṣaram* : the immutable Being *brahma* : Brahman *svabhāvaḥ* : Brahman's manifestation as spirit (Jīva) indwelling the body *adhyatma* : pertaining to the body *ucyate* : is spoken of; *bhūtabhāvotbhavakaraḥ* : what brings all objects into being *visargaḥ*: creative act *karma-samjñitaḥ* : what is called work.

The Blessed Lord said:

3. Brahman is Akṣara, the Immutable Being than whom there is none higher. Brahman's power manifested in every body as the transmigrating self (the Jīva) is the *Adhyātma*. The creative act (identified with sacrificial offering) which brings all beings into existence is *Karma* (work).

अधिभूतं क्षरो भावः पुरुषश्चाधिदैवतम् ।
अधियज्ञोऽहमेवात्र देहे देहभृतां वर ॥ 4 ॥

Adhibhūtaṁ kṣaro bhāvaḥ puruṣaś' c'ādhidaivatam /
adhiyajño'ham ev'ātra dehe deha-bhṛtāṁ vara //4//

Dehabhṛtānivara : O noblest among men! *adhibhūtam* : material nature *kṣaraḥ* : perishable, changeful *bhāvaḥ* : aspect; *puruṣah* : indwelling spirit or cosmic soul *ca* : and *adhidaivatam* : that which underlies all the divinities; *atra dehe* : in this body *aham eva* : I myself am : *adhiyajñaḥ* : that which underlies all worship.

4. O noble One! The perishable Nature is the material aspect (Adhibhūta). The cosmic soul is the basis of all divine manifestations (Adhidaivata); and I verily form the Adhiyajña, the one object of all worship which men perform with their body and mind.

अन्तकाले च मामेव स्मरन्मुक्त्वा कलेवरम् ।
यः प्रयाति स मद्भावं याति नास्त्यत्र संशयः ॥ 5 ॥

Anta-kāle ca mām eva smaran muktvā kalevaram /
yaḥ prayāti sa mad-bhāvaṁ yāti n'āstyatra saṁśayaḥ //5//

Yaḥ : Who *antakāle* : at the time of death *ca* : even *mām* : Me *eva* : alone *smaran* : thinking of *kalevaram* : body *muktvā* : abandoning *prayāti* : goes, *saḥ* : he *madbhāvam*: my state *yāti*: attains; *atra* : in this *na* : no *samśayaḥ* : doubt.

5. Whoever thinks of Me alone even at the time of death, attains to My state on abandoning the body. There is no doubt about this.[2]

यं यं वापि स्मरन्भावं त्यजत्यन्ते कलेवरम् ।
तं तमेवैति कौन्तेय सदा तद्भावभावितः ॥ 6 ॥

Yaṁ-yaṁ v'āpi smaran bhāvaṁ tyajaty ante kalevaram /
taṁ-tam ev'aiti Kaunteya sadā tad-bhāva-bhāvitaḥ //6//

Kaunteya : O son of Kuntī! *ante* : at the time of death *yam yam vā api bhāvam* : whatever object *smaran* : thinking of *kalevaram* : body *tyajati* : leaves, *sadā* : always *tad-bhāva-bhāvitaḥ* : having been ever absorbed in the thought thereof *tam tam eva* : that alone *eti* : attains.

6. O son of Kuntī! Whatever object a person thinks of at the time of death, having been absorbed in its thought all through,—he attains to that object alone.

तस्मात्सर्वेषु कालेषु मामनुस्मर युध्य च ।
मय्यर्पितमनोबुद्धिर्मामेवैष्यस्यसंशयः ॥ 7 ॥

Tasmāt sarveṣu kāleṣu mām anusmara yudhya ca /
mayy arpita-mano-buddhir mām ev'aiṣyasy asaṁśayaḥ //7//

Tasmāt : Therefore *sarveṣu-kāleṣu* : at all times *mām* : Me *anusmara* remember *yudhya ca* : and fight. *Mayyarpita-manobuddhiḥ*: One whose mind and understanding are dedicated to Me, *mām eva* : Me alone *eṣyasi* : shall come *asaṁśayaḥ* : undoubtedly.

7. Therefore fight, remembering Me always. One who has dedicated his mind and understanding to Me, shall come to Me alone, undoubtedly.

अभ्यासयोगयुक्तेन चेतसा नान्यगामिना ।
परमं पुरुषं दिव्यं याति पार्थानुचिन्तयन् ॥ 8 ॥

Abhyāsa-yoga-yuktena cetasā n'ānya-gāminā /
paramaṁ puruṣaṁ divyaṁ yāti Pārth'ānucintayan //8//

Abhyāsayogayuktena : Established in spiritual communion through practice *nānyagāminā* : not straying to anything else *cetasā* : with a mind *anucintayan* : continuously thinking *divyam* : divine *paramam puruṣam* : Supreme Being *Yāti* : goes.

8. Thinking of Me continuously, with a mind trained in the practice of spiritual communion and freed from the ten-

dency to stray away to other objects, one attains to the Divine Spirit Supreme.

कविं पुराणमनुशासितारमणोरणीयांसमनुस्मरेद्यः ।
सर्वस्य धातारमचिन्त्यरूपमादित्यवर्णं तमसः परस्तात् ॥ 9 ॥

प्रयाणकाले मनसाचलेन भक्त्यायुक्तो योगबलेन चैव ।
भ्रुवोर्मध्ये प्राणमावेश्य सम्यक् स तं परं पुरुषमुपैति दिव्यम् ॥

Kaviṁ purāṇam anuśāsitāram aṇor aṇīyāṁsam anusmared yaḥ /
sarvasya dhātāram acintya-rūpam āditya-varṇaṁ tamasaḥ parastāt //9//

prayāṇa-kāle manasā'calena bhaktyā yukto yoga-balena c'aiva /
bhruvor madhye prāṇam āveśya saṁyak sa taṁ paraṁ puruṣam upaiti divyam //10//

Acalena manasā : with a steady mind *bhaktyā* : with devotion *yogabalena ca* : and with the strength born of Yoga *eva* : verily *yuktaḥ* : endowed *yaḥ* : who *prāṇam* : vital energy *bhruvoḥ* : of the brows *madhye* : middle *saṁyak* : properly *āveśya* : having fixed, *kavim* : all-knowing *purāṇam* : primeval *aṇoraṇīyāṁsam* : subtler than an atom *sarvasya* : of all *dhātāram* : sustainer *anuśāsitāram* : director *acintyarūpam* : of incomprehensible form *ādityavarṇam* : glorious as the sun *tamasaḥ parastāt* : beyond darkness *puruṣam* : Indwelling Spirit *prayāṇakāle* : at the time of death *anusmaret* : remembers, *saḥ* : he *divyam* : divine *tam* : that *param* : Supreme Being *upaiti* : attains.

9-10. He who, with a mind steady and endued with devotion and strength born of spiritual practice, fixes his entire life-force between the eye-brows at the time of death, and contemplates on Him who is all-knowing, primeval, subtler than even an atom, sustainer and director of all, glorious like the sun, and beyond all darkness of inertia and ignorance—he verily attains to that Supreme Being.

यदक्षरं वेदविदो वदन्ति विशन्ति यद्यतयो वीतरागाः ।
यदिच्छन्तो ब्रह्मचर्यं चरन्ति तत्ते पदं संग्रहेण प्रवक्ष्ये ॥ 11 ॥

Yad akṣaraṁ veda-vido vadanti viśanti yad yatayo vīta-rāgāḥ |
yad icchanto brahma-caryaṁ caranti tat te padaṁ saṁgraheṇa pravakṣye //11//

Yat : What *vedavidaḥ* : Vedic scholars *akṣaram* : the imperishable *vadanti* : call, *vītarāgāḥ* : devoid of all worldly attachments *yatayaḥ* : Sannyasins *viśanti* : enter, *yat* : what *icchantaḥ* : desiring to know *brahmacaryam* : life of continence and asceticism *caranti* : follow, *tat* : that *padam* : state *saṁgraheṇa* : in brief *te* : to you *pravakṣye* : I shall tell.

11. That which Vedic scholars call the Imperishable (Akṣara), which Sannyasins devoid of worldly attachments enter, desiring which men follow the life of continence and asceticism,— that state I shall declare to you in brief.

सर्वद्वाराणि संयम्य मनो हृदि निरुध्य च ।
मूर्ध्न्याधायात्मनः प्राणमास्थितो योगधारणम् ॥ 12 ॥

ओमित्येकाक्षरं ब्रह्म व्याहरन्मामनुस्मरन् ।
यः प्रयाति त्यजन्देहं स याति परमां गतिम् ॥ 13 ॥

Sarva-dvārāṇi saṁyamya mano hṛdi nirudhya ca |
mūrdhny ādhāy' ātmanaḥ prāṇam āsthito yoga-dhāraṇam //12//

Om ity ek'ākṣaraṁ brahma vyāharan mām anusmaran |
yaḥ prayāti tyajan dehaṁ sa yāti paramāṁ gatim //13//

Yaḥ : Who *sarvadvārāṇi* : all the portals of the body *saṁyamya* : closing *manaḥ* : the mind *hṛdi* : in the heart *nirudhya* : confining *ātmanaḥ* : one's own *prāṇam* : vital energy *mūrdhni* : into the head *ādhāya* : depositing *yogadhāraṇam* : concentration *āsthitaḥ* : established in '*om*' *iti ekākṣaram brahma* : the single syllabled Mantra 'Om' denoting Brahman *vyāharan* : uttering *mām* : Me *ca* : and *anusmaran* : remembering *deham* : body *tyajan* : abandoning *prayāti* : departs, *saḥ* : he *paramām gatim* : to the highest state, liberation *yāti* ; goes.

12-13. Established in spiritual communion by inhibiting all sensations, concentrating on the heart centre, and drawing up the vital energies to the head, one should meditate on Me along with the utterance of the single-syllabled mantra Om denoting Brahman. Departing from the body in this state, one attains liberation.

अनन्यचेताः सततं यो मां स्मरति नित्यशः ।
तस्याहं सुलभः पार्थ नित्ययुक्तस्य योगिनः ॥ 14 ॥

Ananya-cetāḥ satataṁ yo māṁ smarati nityaśaḥ /
tasy'āhaṁ sulabhaḥ Pārtha nitya-yuktasya yoginaḥ //14//

Pārtha : O son of Pṛthā! *yaḥ* : who *ananyacetāḥ* : having no thought on other matters *satatam* : constantly *nityaśaḥ* : daily *mām* : Me *smarati* : remembers, *tasya* : of that *nityayuktasya* : of ever-attuned *yoginaḥ* : of the Yogin *aham* : I *sulabhaḥ* : one easily attained.

14. He who, with a mind undistracted by other things, thinks of Me constantly every day—to the Yogi thus ever-attuned, I am easy of attainment, O son of Pṛthā!

मामुपेत्य पुनर्जन्म दुःखालयमशाश्वतम् ।
नाप्नुवन्ति महात्मानः संसिद्धिं परमां गताः ॥ 15 ॥

Mām upetya punar-janma duḥkh'ālayam aśāśvatam /
n'āpnuvanti mah'ātmānaḥ saṁsiddhiṁ paramāṁ gatāḥ //15//

Mām: Me *upetya* : having realised *paramām* : supreme *samsiddhim* : perfection *gatāḥ* : reaching *mahātmānaḥ* : great ones *punaḥ* : again *duḥkhālayam* : the abode of sorrows *aśāśvatam* : transient *janma* : birth *na*: not *āpnuvanti* : attain.

15. No more is re-birth, no more this home of transience and misery, for those great-souled ones who have attained to supreme perfection by realising Me.

आब्रह्मभुवनाल्लोकाः पुनरावर्तिनोऽर्जुन ।
मामुपेत्य तु कौन्तेय पुनर्जन्म न विद्यते ॥ 16 ॥

Ābrahma-bhuvanāl lokāḥ punar-āvartino'rjuna /
mām upetya tu Kaunteya punarjanma na vidyate //16//

Arjuna: O Arjuna! *ābrahmabhuvanāt* : from the world of Brahmā to the earth *lokāḥ* : all spheres *punarāvartinaḥ* : are subject to re-birth. *Kaunteya* : O son of Kunti! *mām* : Me *upetya* : having attained *tu* : but *punarjanma* : re-birth *na vidyate* : does not occur.

16. All the worlds from the realm of Brahmā down to the earth, are subject to re-birth. But, O Arjuna, one who has attained to Me is never reborn.[3]

सहस्रयुगपर्यन्तमहर्यद्ब्रह्मणो विदुः ।
रात्रिं युगसहस्रान्तां तेऽहोरात्रविदो जनाः ॥ 17 ॥

Sahasra-yuga-paryantam ahar yad brahmano viduḥ /
rātriṁ yuga-sahasr'āntāṁ te'ho-rātra-vido janāḥ //17//

Sahasra-yuga-paryantam : Lasting for a thousand Yugas (ages) *yat* : which *Brahmaṇah* : of Brahmā *ahaḥ* : day time, *yugasahasrāntam* : ending in thousand years *rātrim* : night, (*ye* : who) *janāḥ* : people *viduḥ* : know, *te* : they *ahorātravidaḥ* : knowers of night and day.

17. Those who have an understanding of Brahmā's day time, which lasts for a thousand ages, and of his night time, which too is of equal length,—they indeed understand what a day is and what a night.

अव्यक्ताद्व्यक्तयः सर्वाः प्रभवन्त्यहरागमे ।
रात्र्यागमे प्रलीयन्ते तत्रैवाव्यक्तसंज्ञके ॥ 18 ॥

Avyaktād vyaktayaḥ sarvāḥ prabhavanty aharāgame /
Ratry-āgame pralīyante tatr'aiv'āvyakta saṁjñake //18//

Aharāgame : At the dawn of the day (of Brahmā) *avyaktāt* : from the unmanifest (Prakṛti) *sarvāḥ* : all *vyaktayaḥ* : manifestations *prabhavanti* : come to have. *Rātry-āgame* : At the beginning of the night (of Brahmā) *avyvakta-samjñake* : in what is called unmanifest *eva ca* : in that itself *pralīyante* : dissolve.

18. At the dawn of the day of Brahmā this whole universe comes into manifestation from the Unmanifest (Prakṛti). When the night begins, it dissolves in that Unmanifest itself.

भूतग्रामः स एवायं भूत्वा भूत्वा प्रलीयते ।
रात्र्यागमेऽवशः पार्थ प्रभवत्यहरागमे ॥ 19 ॥

Bhūta-grāmaḥ sa ev'āyaṁ bhūtvā bhūtvā pralīyate /
rātry-āgame'vaśaḥ Pārtha prabhavaty ahar-āgame //19//

Pārtha : O son of Pṛthā! *saḥ eva* : that *bhūtagrāmaḥ* : collectivity of beings *avaśaḥ* : inexorably *bhūtvā bhūtvā* : coming into being again and again *rātryāgame* : at the coming of night *pralīyate* : dissolves, *aharāgame* : at the dawn of day *prabhavati* : comes forth.

19. O son of Pṛthā! This vast collectivity of beings comes inexorably into manifestation again and again, dissolving at the commencement of night, and again coming forth at the dawn of day.

परस्तस्मात्तु भावोऽन्योऽव्यक्तोव्यक्तात्सनातनः ।
यः स सर्वेषु भूतेषु नश्यत्सु न विनश्यति ॥ 20 ॥

Paras tasmāt tu bhāvo'nyo'vyakto'vyaktāt sanātanaḥ /
yaḥ sa sarveṣu bhuteṣu naśyatsu na vinaśyati //20//

Yaḥ : Which *tasmāt avyaktāt* : from the unmanifested state *tu*: but *anyaḥ* : different *paraḥ* : supreme *sanātanaḥ* : eternal *avyaktaḥ* : Unmanifested, *saḥ bhāvaḥ* : that being *sarveṣu* : all *bhūteṣu* : entities *naśyatsu* : when destroyed *na vinaśyati* : is not destroyed.

20. Different from this unmanifested state is the supreme and eternal Unmanifested whose Being remains unaffected even when everything is destroyed.[4]

अव्यक्तोऽक्षर इत्युक्तस्तमाहुः परमां गतिम् ।
यं प्राप्य न निवर्तन्ते तद्धाम परमं मम ॥ 21 ॥

Avyakto'kṣara ity uktas tam āhuḥ paramām gatim /
yaṁ prāpya na nivartante tad dhāma paramaṁ mama //21//

Avyaktaḥ : The Unmanifested *akṣaraḥ* : the Imperishable *iti* : thus *uktaḥ* : called *tam* : that (state) *paramām* : ultimate *gatim* : goal *āhuḥ* : describe; *yam* : which *prāpya* : attaining *na nivartante* : do not return; *tat* : that *mama* : My *paramam* : supreme *dhāma* : abode.

21. Know that state, which is called the Unmanifested and the Imperishable, to be the ultimate goal of all. That is My supreme abode. Attaining to that man is not reborn.

पुरुषः स परः पार्थ भक्त्या लभ्यस्त्वनन्यया ।
यस्यान्तःस्थानि भूतानि येन सर्वमिदं ततम् ॥ 22 ॥

Puruṣaḥ sa paraḥ Pārtha bhaktyā labhyas tv ananyayā /
yasy'āntaḥsthāni bhūtāni yena sarvam idaṁ tatam //22//

Pārtha : O son of Pṛthā! *bhūtāni* : beings *yasya* : whose *antaḥsthāni* : residing within, *yena* : by whom *sarvam idam* : all this *tatam* : is pervaded, *saḥ* : that *paraḥ* : supreme *Puruṣaḥ* : Being *ananyayā* : unswerving and exclusive *bhaktyā* : by devotion *labhyaḥ tu* : attainable.

22. That Supreme Puruṣa, the abode of all beings and the indweller of them all, can be attained by unswerving and exclusive devotion to Him.

यत्र काले त्वनावृत्तिमावृत्तिं चैव योगिनः ।
प्रयाता यान्ति तं कालं वक्ष्यामि भरतर्षभ ॥ 23 ॥

Yatra kāle tv anāvṛttim āvṛttiṁ c'aiva yoginaḥ /
prayātā yānti taṁ kālaṁ vakṣyāmi Bharatarṣabha //23//

Bharatarṣabha : O the noblest of the Bharata race! *Yatra kāle tu* : during what time (under the guidance of which deities) *prayātāḥ* : dying *yoginaḥ*: Yogis *anāvṛttim tu*: the path of non-return *yānti* : go, *āvṛttim ca eva* : the path of return also, *tam* ; that *kālam* : time *vakṣyāmi* : I shall declare.

23. I shall now tell you, O noblest of Bharatas, of the circumstances, dying under which a Yogi never returns to this world and also of the time, dying when, he is sure to return.[5]

अग्निर्ज्योतिरहः शुक्लःषण्मासा उत्तरायणम् ।
तत्र प्रयाता गच्छन्ति ब्रह्म ब्रह्मविदो जनाः ॥ 24 ॥

Agnir jyotir ahaḥ śuklaḥ ṣaṇmāsā uttar-āyaṇam /
tatra prayātā gacchanti brahma brahma-vido janāḥ //24//

Agniḥ : Fire *jyotiḥ* : light *ahaḥ* : day-time *śuklaḥ* : the bright fortnight *ṣaṇmāsāḥ* : six months *uttarāyaṇam* : northern course of the sun, *tatra prayātāḥ* : departing by this path *Brahmavidaḥ janāḥ* : knowers of Brahman *Brahma* : Brahman *gacchanti* : go.

24. Fire, light, day-time, bright fortnight, six months of the northern course of the sun—the knowers of Brahman who depart along this path, attain to Brahman.

धूमो रात्रिस्तथा कृष्णः षण्मासा दक्षिणायनम् ।
तत्र चान्द्रमसं ज्योतिर्योगी प्राप्य निवर्तते ॥ 25 ॥

Dhūmo rātris tathā kṛṣṇaḥ ṣaṇmāsā dakṣiṇ'āyanam /
tatra cāndramasaṁ jyotir yogī prāpya nivartate //25//

Dhūmaḥ : Smoke *rātriḥ* : night *tathā* : likewise *kṛṣṇaḥ* : black fortnight *ṣaṇmāsāḥ dakṣiṇāyanam* : the six months of the southern course of the sun *tatra* (*prayātāḥ*) : taking this path *yogī* : the Yogi *cāndramasaṁ jyotiḥ* : the lunar light *prāpya* : attaining *nivartate* : returns.

25. Smoke, night and likewise the black fortnight and the six months of the southern course of the sun—the Yogi

departing by this path attains to the lunar sphere and thence returns.

शुक्लकृष्णे गती ह्येते जगतः शाश्वते मते ।
एकया यात्यनावृत्तिमन्ययावर्तते पुनः ॥ 26 ॥

Śukla-kṛṣṇe gatī hy ete jagataḥ śāśvate mate
ekayā yāty anāvṛttim anyayā'vartate punaḥ //26//

Hi : Verily *śuklakṛṣṇe* : bright and the dark *ete gatī* : these two ways *jagataḥ* : for the world *śāśvate* : eternal *mate* : considered. *Ekayā* : By one *anāvṛttim* : non-return (mokṣa) *yāti* : attains, *anyayā* : by the other *punaḥ āvartate* : takes birth again.

26. Verily, these two paths—the bright and the dark—are accepted as everlasting verities. By the one, the aspirant gains Mokṣa, the state of non-return, while the other leads him to rebirth.

नैते सृती पार्थ जानन्योगी मुह्यति कश्चन ।
तस्मात्सर्वेषु कालेषु योगयुक्तो भवार्जुन ॥ 27 ॥

N'aite sṛtī Pārtha jānan yogī muhyati kaścana /
tasmāt sarveṣu kāleṣu yogayukto bhav'ārjuna //27//

Pārtha : O son of Pṛthā'. *ete* : these two *sṛtī* : paths *jānan* : knowing *kaścana yogī* : whichever Yogi *na muhyati* : is not deluded. *Tasmāt* : Therefore *Arjuna* : O Arjuna! *sarveṣu* : at all *kāleṣu* : times *yoga yuktaḥ* : steadfast in Yoga *bhava* : be.

27. O son of Pṛthā! Whoever among Yogis know these two paths, they are never deluded. Therefore, O Arjuna, be steadfast in Yoga at all times.

वेदेषु यज्ञेषु तपःसु चैव दानेषु यत्पुण्यफलं प्रदिष्टम् ।
अत्येति तत्सर्वमिदं विदित्वा योगी परं स्थानमुपैति चाद्यम् ॥ 28 ॥

Vedeṣu yajñeṣu tapaḥsu c'aiva dāneṣu yat puṇya-phalaṁ
pradiṣṭam /
atyeti tat sarvam idaṁ viditvā yogī paraṁ sthānam upaiti
c'ādyam //28//

Vedeṣu : In the Vedas *yajñeṣu*: in the sacrifices *tapaḥsu* : in austerities *dāneṣu* : in charities *ca* : and *eva* : also *yat* : whatever *puṇya-phalam* : meritorious rewards *pradiṣṭam* : prescribed, *tat sarvam* : all that *yogī* : Yogi *idam* : this *viditvā* : knowing *atyeti* : transcends; *ādyam* : primeval *param* : supreme *padam* : state *upaiti ca* : and attains.

28. Knowing this, a Yogi transcends all the meritorious rewards that are prescribed for the study of the Vedas, for the performance of austerities, and for charities too, and attains to that primeval state which is the Supreme Being.

ओं तत्सदिति श्रीमद्भगवद्गीतासूपनिषत्सु ब्रह्मविद्यायां
योगशास्त्रे श्रीकृष्णार्जुनसंवादे अक्षरब्रह्मयोगो
नामाष्टमोऽध्यायः ॥ 8 ॥

NOTES

1. *Vrs.*1-4: There are six sets of words of technical significance—the Supreme *Brahman* equated with *Akṣara* ; the *Adhyātma* with *Svabhāva* ; *Visarga* with creative *Karma* ; the *Adhibūta* with *Kṣara* nature; the *Adhidaiva* with *Puruṣa;* and *Adhiyajña* with *Iśvara.*

In this very obscure passage, the Divine in His various aspects and functions seems to be described. Akṣara is undoubtedly the Supreme as the Impersonal Being.

The word *Svabhāva* is generally used for material Nature, known also as Aparā-prakṛti of the Lord. But here by equating the expression with *Adhyātma*, what is generally described as His Para-prakṛti or higher Spiritual Nature i.e. the Jīva, is referred to by the expression. It is called *Adhyātma,* because it pertains to Self in relation to the body. It is the spirit manifest in every body, who is described in the Upaniṣads as the Jīva, a spark of the Fire.

The term Visarga, which is equated with Karma, literally means 'excretion, emission', which according to some interpreters means sexual intercourse. In a cosmic sense it is the creative will of God which is metaphorically referred to in terms of the same idiom as in the passage: "Great Nature is a womb to Me. I impregnate it with my seed (14.3)". It has also been interpreted in relation to the Vedic rite of sacrifice, and is referred to as such in Gita in 3.14 '*karma brahmodbhavam*', sacrificial work arises from the Veda. It is the sacrificial offering, according to the Vedic ideology, that procures rain which helps the growth of vegetation, eating which men derive their fecundity. Thus Vedic Karma is connected with procreation.

That which pertains to the bodies of all beings is *Adhibhūta*. It is the changeful Nature, described as the *Aparā Prakṛti* of the Lord. All material combinations, including the bodies of beings, come out of it and undergo six kinds of modifications. When they perish, the substances constituting their bodies go back to their constituents. Thus material Nature as the substance subject to constant change is also imperishable *as a whole*. For the combinations coming out of it like the bodies of beings, change means in the end complete dissolution into the constituent elements.

Puruṣa is He who 'infills' everything. He is *Hiraṇyagarbha,* the first born in the creative process, who endows the senses with their powers and directs them in their functions. Another interpretation of the word is the 'collectivity of all individual spirits'. This will suit philosophies that admit ultimacy to the Jīvas as distinct entities. According to some the *Puruṣa* is the *Puruṣa* of the *Puruṣa sūkta*, the Cosmic Person, the dismemberment of whose body in sacrifice is the origin of the universe.

Adhiyajña means He who is the very practice of worship and who gives the fruits of all worship, whatever may be the Deity that is invoked. So the Vedas declare *Yajño vai viṣṇuḥ—Yajña* is verily Viṣṇu. Man's tendency to worship arises from the sense of some power higher than himself presiding over his destiny. The Supreme Being is that power, and in whatever conception of Him or in the name of whatever deity worship and prayers are offered, it is only He who gives the rewards. The word '*dehe*', in the body, is used because all worship is done with the body and the mind depending on it.

2. *V*.5: The force of the word *ca*, translated here as 'even', is that it is only if the thought of God is the dominant idea of one's life, and has been occupying one's mind all through one's life, that the thought of Him will come to one's mind at the last moment. Man should not think hypocritically that he can live an unholy life all through, and achieve his spiritual welfare by thinking of Him at the last moment. One will find it impossible to do so.

3. *Vrs*.16-19: In these verses the Hindu doctrine of Samsāra and the cyclic process of time are stated. Creation is coterminous with time. Time has no beginning or end. It is endless, being cyclic. It is cyclic in its movement just as the individual's day and night are. The creative period, when all the worlds are in manifestation, is called Kalpa. It is followed by dissolution of the manifested world into the elemental condition. The period of dissolution is called *Pralaya*. *Pralaya* and *Kalpa*, which are of equal duration, alternate in a cyclic process. All the Jīvas are involved in this cyclic process, undergoing birth and death continuously according to their Karma, enjoying and suffering, subject to a temporary abeyance of the process when the whole of Prakṛti is in dissolution. But they come back to the old condition when a new Kalpa begins just as plants spring from seeds and man emerges from sleep. This entanglement in the cycle of births and deaths is *Saṁsāra*. The Hindu scriptures hold forth the delinking of the Jīva from this cyclic process of Time as the ultimate aim of evolution. The attainment of the delinking is called Mokṣa, liberation, to which reference is made in verse 16. Attaining the Lord is the way to Mokṣa.

The 17th verse also refers to the length of the periods of cosmic manifestation and dissolution. These periods are spoken of as the day-time and night of Brahmā, who is the Lord of creation.

Only a brief description of time scale is given. A fuller description is as follows: 1 human year makes a day and night of the celestials i.e. a full celestial day. 1200 such celestial years make one *catur-yuga* (i.e., 4,32,000 human years make one *Chaturyuga* or a cycle of four Yugas). 1000 *chatur-yugas* make one day-time of Brahmā (*Kalpa*). An equally long period is his night (*pralaya*). 365 such days and nights make 1 year of Brahmā. A hundred such years constitute his life span. The end of his life is marked by a major Pralaya (*Mahā-pralaya*) of duration equal to his life time. After that the creative cycle (*Mahā-kalpa*) starts again under a new Brahmā. The infinitude of time is thus depicted.

4. *Vrs*.20-22: In this and the succeeding verses, two *avyaktas* or undifferentiated entities are mentioned. One of them is Prakṛti in its rudimentary condition. This is called *Avyakta,* because all the effects dissolve in it without being destroyed. They remain latent in it as potentialities, under an unseen and unperceivable condition just as a tree exists in its seed. This *Avyakta* is the same as what is called *Aparā-Prakṛti*, the lower or material Power of the Lord, referred to in verses 7. 1-6.

As distinguished from this *Avyakta* is another *Avyakta* which is described in verse 21 as *Akṣara* or 'unchanging' also. Besides, it is described in verse 22 as *Puruṣa* or the 'All-pervading' attained through devotion of the highest order'. *Akṣara* means 'unchanging' or 'undecaying', this being its principal difference from the first *Avyakta*. The first *Avyakta,* though eternal as a collectivity, is pure change, under the influence of Time, involved in the cyclic and repetitive process of manifestation into effects and dissolution into seminal condition. But the second *Avyakta* is *Puruṣa,* the all-pervading Spirit, who is beyond the influence of Time, and whose power Time is. It is through devotion and surrender to Him that the Jīva, involved in *Saṁsāra,* the cyclic and continuing process of birth and deaths, can get release, as stated in verse 22. So the two *Avyaktas* are entirely different—the first called so because it is the unmanifest or *Avyakta* condition of effects, and the second because it is beyond the grasp of the senses and the mind.

5. *Vrs*.23-26: The teachings on eschatology contained in these verses are rather obscure, though the general meaning of it, being the description of the two ways of the progress of the Jīva

after death, is quite clear. *Deva-yāna* and *pitṛ-yāna* or *arcirādi-mārga* and *dhūmādi-mārga* are the technical terms for these two paths. The former means the Path of the Devas and the latter the Path of the Manes, as also the Path of Light and the Path of Smoke. The most confusing part of it is that it appears to give too much importance to the time of death, which is very difficult to associate with man's merits and demerits and his progress after death. For, many meritorious men can be seen to be dying at an inauspicious time and vice versa. Commentators therefore maintain that these references to time really denote the deities presiding over the entities,times and realms mentioned.

So we have to understand the passage as meaning thus: The Jīvas of persons who have practised devotion to God and performed all their duties and works as offering to Him and without any desire for their fruits, will have a gradual spiritual progress, passing through the various realms, Fire, Light, etc., presided over by deities known by those names. The Jīva gradually attains to higher spiritual evolution in realms that foster spiritual growth and finally attains liberation. He does not come back to the earth sphere. This way of gradual spiritual progress is called *devayāna* or *archirādi-mārga* (the Path of Light).

The other way known as *Pitṛyāna* (the Way of the Manes) or *dhumādi mārga* (the non-luminous path) is through realms known as *dhūma*, *rātri* etc.. presided over by deities of those names. They attain to the Lunar Sphere. There they enjoy the fruits of the ritualistic and philanthropic actions of a meritorious nature, which they have performed with an eye on their fruits, and when the merits are exhausted they take rebirth on earth.

Notorious sinners go to the purgatory (*naraka*) where they suffer for their sinful acts, after which they are born in animal bodies or as humans under very miserable conditions. There is a fourth category of persons who have neither great merits nor great sins to their credit. They are the ineffective persons who live a humdrum life of a self-centred nature without being virtuous or vicious. They die and are again re-born without going to any other sphere, and go on continuously drifting in the cycle of birth and death with its petty enjoyments and great sorrows until they become spiritually awakened, and begin to cultivate devotion and dedicated action.

Chapter IX

राजविद्याराजगुह्ययोगः

THE SOVEREIGN SCIENCE AND SOVEREIGN SECRET

SUMMARY

Devotion as the highest value: (1-3) Sri Kṛṣṇa said: The doctrine of devotion is the noblest and the profoundest of all sciences. Experience is its proof. It is easy to practise and it is contributive to human welfare. Those who neglect it will be subject to the cycle of births and deaths, and will not attain to Me.

Devotion and understanding of the divine mystery: (4-10) Devotion is generated by the contemplation of My mystery and My transcendent glory. See how I am the Indwelling Spirit in all; but they do not contain Me; it is I that contain them. Yet in another sense it is not true that they rest in Me, because I, the pure and incorruptible Spirit, remain absolutely unaffected by their presence. Contemplate on this divine mystery—to be the creator and sustainer of this mighty universe and yet be not affected by it, as space is not by the fast and powerful winds that blow through it. My Power projects and withdraws into itself this extensive universe in Time's endless cyclic process. I remain the unaffected Overseer and Witness of this eternal process which my Prakṛti executes.

The Divine in all his aspects: (11-19) When I incarnate Myself as man, foolish people disdain Me, not recognising My transcendent nature, even as they do not recognise it behind this mighty manifested Nature. This is due to the dominance of demoniacal tendencies in them. But great men endowed with godly tendencies, get an understanding of My divine mystery as the creator and as the incarnate, and thrilled by that knowledge, devote themselves to Me with an undivided mind. They sing My praise always, they prostrate to Me in loving adoration. Others worship Me with wisdom-sacrifice, communing with Me as the non-dual Self or as the distinct Divine Person or as the Immanent Spirit manifesting through all. I am the father, friend, witness, support and resting place of everything. All the universe is My manifestation, and I direct its evolution and its destiny. I am both immortality and total destruction, both Being (manifested effect state) and Non-being (unmanifested causal state).

The true worship of the Divine: (20-28) Those who adore Me with sacrifices desiring heavenly regions attain to them, but they have to return when the sacrificial merits are exhausted. But those who have no desire and think of Me alone always, are ever under My protection, and their welfare here and hereafter will be looked after by Me. Even persons who worship various Deities, are in fact worshipping Me alone, as I am their soul and they, My bodies; only their worship is crude and uninformed. My worship, however, is very simple. Very little of rituals and ingredients are required for it. A few flowers, water and leaves will do. If these offerings are sweetened with whole-hearted devotion, I consume them, as it were, eagerly. But all external worship is only a symbol of the total sacrifice and dedication one should practise. Whatever you do, eat, or give, whatever austerities you perform and charities you make,—all should be done as an offering unto Me. You should feel that the agency in respect of them as also their fruits are Mine and not yours. This is real Sannyasa, renunciation, and no action will then bind you with their good or bad effects.

Redemption open to all: (29-34) All are alike to Me, and to none am I hostile. If you find a difference in My relationship with devotees, it is only because the devotees cling to Me, and so I to them also. However degenerate a man may be, he is free to devote himself to My worship. One who is firmly resolved to do so, is on the path of moral and spiritual fulfilment, which will be his without much delay. Thus in the past, countless men, though low-born and sinful, have attained to Me through whole-hearted self-surrender. How much more easily will well-born and righteous persons like you do so! Therefore love Me and surrender yourself to Me, body, mind and soul, and you will surely attain to Me.

श्रीभगवानुवाच

इदं तु ते गुह्यतमं प्रवक्ष्याम्यनसूयवे ।
ज्ञानं विज्ञानसहितं यज्ज्ञात्वा मोक्ष्यसेऽशुभात् ॥ 1 ॥

Sri Bhagavān uvāca:
Idaṁ tu te guhyatamaṁ pravakṣyāmy anasūyave /
jñānaṁ vijñāna-sahitaṁ yaj jñātva mokṣyase'śubhāt //1//

Yat jñātva : Knowing which *aśubhāt* : from evil or Saṁsāra *mokṣyase* : shall be free, *idam* : this *guhyatamam* : profoundly secret *jñānam* : knowledge *vijñānasahitam* : along with its realisation *anasūyave* : to one who does not cavil *te* : to you *pravakṣyāmi* : shall declare.

The Blessed Lord said:

1. I shall now declare to you, who are endowed with reverence, that profoundest of all mystic doctrines and the way to its experience, by which you will be free from the baneful life of Samsāra.

राजविद्या राजगुह्यं पवित्रमिदमुत्तमम् ।
प्रत्यक्षावगमं धर्म्यं सुसुखं कर्तुमव्ययम् ॥ 2 ॥

Rāja-vidyā rāja-guhyaṁ pavitraṁ idam uttamam /
pratyakṣ'āvagamaṁ dharmyaṁ susukhaṁ kartum avyayam //2//

Idam : This *rājavidyā* : sovereign science *rājaguhyam* : sovereign mystery *uttamam* : supreme *pavitram* : sanctifying *pratyakṣāvagamam* : capable of direct experience *dharmyam* : in accordance with Dharma or moral law *kartum* : to accomplish *susukham* : easy *avyayam* : eternal.

2. It is a soverign science, and a profound mystery. Supremely sanctifying, demonstrable by experience, and yielding imperishable results, it is also easy to perform and is in agreement with the moral law.[1]

अश्रद्दधानाः पुरुषा धर्मस्यास्य परंतप ।
अप्राप्य मां निवर्तन्ते मृत्युसंसारवर्त्मनि ॥ 3 ॥

Aśraddadhānāḥ puruṣā dharmasy'āsya paraṁtapa /
aprāpya māṁ nivartante mṛtyu-samsāra-vartmani //3//

Paraṁtapa : O the dread of opponents! *asya* : of this *dharmasya* : sacred doctrine *aśraddadhānāḥ* : having no faith *puruṣāḥ* : persons *mām* : Me *aprāpya* : not attaining *mṛtyu saṁsāra vartmani* : in the path of repetitive births and deaths *nivartante* : remain caught up.

3. Men without faith in this sacred doctrine (who continue to look upon the body as the self) fail to attain Me. They remain caught up in Samsāra, the eternally recurring cycle of births and deaths.

मया ततमिदं सर्वं जगदव्यक्तमूर्तिना ।
मत्स्थानि सर्वभूतानि न चाहं तेष्ववस्थितः ॥ 4 ॥

Mayā tatam idaṁ sarvaṁ jagad avyakta-mūrtinā /
mat-sthāni sarva-bhūtāni na c'āhaṁ teṣv avasthitaḥ //4//

Avyaktamūrtinā mayā : By Me the Unmanifested Being *idam* : this *sarvam jagat* : whole universe *tatam* : is pervaded; *sarvabhūtani* : all objects *matsthāni* : subsist in Me, *aham* : I *teṣu* : in them *na* : not *ca* : and *avasthitaḥ* : abiding.

4. All this world is pervaded by Me, the Unmanifested Being. All objects subsist in Me, but not I in them.[2]

न च मत्स्थानि भूतानि पश्य मे योगमैश्वरम् ।
भूतभृन्न च भूतस्थो ममात्मा भूतभावनः ॥ 5 ॥

Na ca mat-sthāni bhūtāni paśya me yogam aiśvaram /
bhūta-bhṛn na ca bhūta-stho mam'ātmā bhūta-bhāvanaḥ //5//

Bhūtāni : Objects *matsthāni na* : do not subsist in Me *ca* : and yet, *paśya* : behold *me* : My *aiśvaram* : divine *yogam* : mysterious power; *bhūtabṛt* : support of all objects *bhūtabhāvanaḥ* : source of all objects *bhūtasthaḥ na ca* : and yet not abiding in them i.e. limited by them *mama* : My *atmā* : being.

5. And yet objects do not abide in Me! Behold My mysterious Divine Power! Source and support of all objects, and yet not abiding in (i.e. limited by) them![3]

यथाकाशस्थितो नित्यं वायुः सर्वत्रगो महान् ।
तथा सर्वाणि भूतानि मत्स्थानीत्युपधारय ॥ 6 ॥

Yath'ākāśa-sthito nityaṁ vāyuḥ sarvatra-go mahān /
tathā sarvāṇi bhūtāni mat-sthānī'ty upadhāraya //6//

Sarvatragaḥ: Pervading everything *mahān* : mighty *vāyuḥ* : atmosphere *yathā* : in what way *nityam* : always *akāśasthitaḥ* : abides in space, *tathā* : in that way *sarvāṇi bhūtāni* : all objects *matsthāni*: abide in Me, *iti* thus *upadhāraya* : know.

6. Know that, as the mighty atmosphere ever abides in space, so do all objects abide in Me (without restricting or limiting Me in the least).[4]

सर्वभूतानि कौन्तेय प्रकृतिं यान्ति मामिकाम् ।
कल्पक्षये पुनस्तानि कल्पादौ विसृजाम्यहम् ॥ 7 ॥

Sarva-bhūtāni Kaunteya prakṛtim yānti māmikām /
kalpa-kṣaye punas tāni kalp'ādau visṛjāmy aham //7//

Kaunteya : O son of Kunti! *kalpakṣaye* : at the end of a cosmic cycle (Kalpa) *sarva bhūtāni* : all beings *māmikām* : my own *Prakṛtim*: Prakṛti or Nature *yānti* : pass into, *kalpādau*: at the beginning of a cycle *punaḥ* : again *aham* : I *tāni* : them *visṛjāmi* : bring out again.

7. At the end of a cosmic cycle, O son of Kunti! all beings resolve into Nature (Prakṛti), which is My own, and at the the beginning of a new one (after the period of dissolution or Pralaya is over), I bring them out again.[5]

प्रकृतिं स्वामवष्टभ्य विसृजामि पुनः पुनः ।
भूतग्राममिमं कृत्स्नमवशं प्रकृतेर्वशात् ॥ 8 ॥

Prakṛtiṁ svām avaṣṭabhya visṛjāmi punaḥ-punaḥ /
bhūta-grāmam imaṁ kṛtsnam avaśaṁ prakṛter vaśāt //8//

Svām: My *prakṛtim* : Nature *avaṣṭabhya* : resorting to *prakṛteḥ* : of Nature *vaśāt* : under the sway *avaśam* : without freedom *imam* : this *kṛtsnam* : all *bhūta grāmam* : multitude of beings *punaḥ-punaḥ* : again and again *visṛjāmi* : send forth.

8. Resorting to Prakṛti, Nature, which is My own Power, I send forth again and again this multitude of beings that are without any freedom, owing to Nature's sway over them.

न च मां तानि कर्माणि निबध्नन्ति धनंजय ।
उदासीनवदासीनमसक्तं तेषु कर्मसु ॥ 9 ॥

Na ca mām tāni karmāṇi nibadhnanti dhanaṁjaya /
udāsīnavad āsīnam asaktaṁ teṣu karmasu //9//

Dhanaṁjaya : O Arjuna! *teṣu* : in those *karmasu* : activities *asaktam* unattached *udāsīnavad āsīnam* : remaining like one unconcerned *ca* : and *mām* : Me *tāni* : those *karmāṇi* : activities *na nibadhnanti* : not bind.

9. These activities do not in any way bind me, because I remain detached like one unconcerned in their midst.[6]

मयाध्यक्षेण प्रकृतिः सूयते सचराचरम् ।
हेतुनानेन कौन्तेय जगद्विपरिवर्तते ॥ 10 ॥

Mayā'dhyakṣeṇa prakṛtiḥ sūyate sacar' ācaram /
hetunā'nena Kaunteya jagad viparivartate //10//

Kaunteya : O son of Kuntī! *mayā adhyakṣena* : with Me as the witnessing director *prakṛtiḥ* : Nature *sacarācaram* : this mighty universe of moving and non-moving beings *sūyate* : gives birth to; *anena* : by this *hetunā* : means *jagat* : the world *viparivartate* : revolves.

10. Under My direction and control, Nature brings out this mighty universe of living and non-living beings. Thus does the wheel of this world revolve.

अवजानन्ति मां मूढा मानुषीं तनुमाश्रितम् ।
परं भावमजानन्तो मम भूतमहेश्वरम् ॥ 11 ॥

Avajānanti māṁ mūḍhā mānuṣīṁ tanum āśritam /
paraṁ bhāvam ajānanto mama bhūta-mah'eśvaram //11//

Mama : My *bhūtamaheśvaram* : as the supreme Lord of all that exists *param bhāvam* : higher nature *ajānantaḥ* : not knowing *mūḍhāḥ* : foolish men *mām* : Me *mānuṣīm tanum* : human form *āśritam* : assumed *avajananti* : disregard.

11. Foolish men, without an understanding of My higher nature as the Supreme Lord of all that exists, disregard Me manifest in the human body.[7]

मोघाशा मोघकर्माणो मोघज्ञाना विचेतसः ।
राक्षसीमासुरीं चैव प्रकृतिं मोहिनीं श्रिताः ॥ 12 ॥

Mogh'āśā mogha-karmāṇo mogha-jñānā vicetasaḥ /
rākṣasīm āsurīṁ c'aiva prakṛtiṁ mohinīṁ śritāḥ //12//

Pārtha : O son of Pṛthā! *mohinīm* : deluding *rakṣasīm* : of the Rakshasas or beings of cruel nature *āsurīm* : of the Asuras or beings of proud and passionate nature *ca* : and *prakṛtim eva* : nature *śritāḥ* : possessed of, *moghāśāḥ* : futile in their hopes *moghakarmāṇaḥ* : futile in their work *moghajñānāḥ* : futile in their knowledge *vicetasaḥ* : of perverted understanding.

12. Futile are the hopes, futile the works, and futile the knowledge of these men of perverted understanding who are deluded by their cruel, proud and passionate nature, characteristic of Rākṣasas and Asuras.

महात्मानस्तु मां पार्थ दैवीं प्रकृतिमाश्रिताः ।
भजन्त्यनन्यमनसो ज्ञात्वा भूतादिमव्ययम् ॥ 13 ॥

Mah'ātmānas tu māṁ Pārtha daivīṁ prakṛtim āśritāḥ
bhajanty ananya-manaso jñātvā bhūt'ādim avyayam //13//

Pārtha : O son of Pṛthā! *mahātmānaḥ* : high-souled ones *tu* : but *daivīm prakṛtim* : virtues characteristic of Devas *āśritāḥ* : partake of *mām* : Me *bhūtādim* : the source of all beings *avyayam* : the immutable *jñātvā* : understanding *ananyamanasaḥ* : with undistracted mind *bhajanti* : adore.

13. But the high souled ones, endowed with virtues characteristic of Devas, understand Me to be the Immutable and the source of all beings, and adore Me with a mind undistracted by anything else.[8]

सततं कीर्तयन्तो मां यतन्तश्च दृढव्रताः ।
नमस्यन्तश्च मां भक्त्या नित्ययुक्ता उपासते ॥ 14 ॥

Satataṁ kīrtayanto māṁ yatantaś ca dṛḍha-vratāḥ /
namasyantaś ca māṁ bhaktyā nitya-yuktā upāsate //14//

Dṛḍhavratāḥ: Steadfast in their vows *yatantaḥ* : strenuous *ca* : and *satatam* : ever *mām* : Me *kīrtayantaḥ* : glorifying *nitya yuktāḥ* : ever integrated *mām* : Me *namasyantaḥ* : bowing to *ca* : and *bhaktyā* : with devotion *mām* : Me *upāsate* : worship.

14. Strenuous and steadfast in their vows, these ever-integrated devotees worship Me with devotion, always singing My glories and prostrating before Me.[9]

ज्ञानयज्ञेन चाप्यन्ये यजन्तो मामुपासते ।
एकत्वेन पृथक्त्वेन बहुधा विश्वतोमुखम् ॥ 15 ॥

Jñāna-yajñena c'āpy anye yajanto māṁ upāsate /
ekatvena pṛthaktvena bahudhā viśvato-mukham //15//

Anye : Others *api ca* : again *jñānayajñena* : by knowledge sacrifice *yajantaḥ* : making offering *viśvatomukham mām* : Me the All-inclusive whole *ekatvena* : as the One *pṛthaktvena*: as the Distinct *bahudhā* : as the immanent in the many *upāsate* : adore.

15. Others, again, who offer wisdom sacrifice to Me, worship Me the All-inclusive whole (All-formed)—as the One, as the Distinct, and as the Immanent in all.[10]

अहं क्रतुरहं यज्ञः स्वधाहमहमौषधम् ।
मन्त्रोऽहमहमेवाज्यमहमग्निरहं हुतम् ॥ 16 ॥

Aham kratur ahaṁ yajñaḥ svadhā'ham aham auṣadham |
mantro'ham aham ev'ājyam aham agnir aham hutam //16//

Aham kratuḥ : I am the sacrifice, *aham yajñaḥ* : I am the worship, *aham svadhā* : I am the ancestral offerings, *aham auṣadham* : I am the medicinal herb. *aham mantraḥ*: I am the Vedic hymn, *aham ājyam* : I am the sacrificial ingredients, *aham agniḥ* : I am the sacrificial fire, *aham hutam* : I am the sacificial oblation also.

16. I am the sacrifice (*kratu*), I am the worship(*yajña*), I am the ancestral offering (*svadhā*), I am the medicinal herb. Again I am the Vedic hymn, I am the sacrificial ingredients. I am the sacrificial fire, and I am the sacrificial "oblation too".[11]

पिताहमस्य जगतो माता धाता पितामहः ।
वेद्यं पवित्रमोंकार ऋक्साम यजुरेव च ॥ 17 ॥

Pitā'ham asya jagato mātā dhātā pitāmahaḥ |
vedyaṁ pavitram oṁ-kāra ṛk sāma yajur eva ca //17//

Asya : Of this *jagataḥ* : universe *pitā* : father, *mātā* : mother, *pitāmahaḥ* : grandsire, *dhāta* : sustainer, *vedyam pavitram* : the Holy One to be known *Omkāraḥ* : the syllable Om, *ṛk yajuḥ sāma ca* : also Ṛk, Yajus and Sāma.

17. To this world I am the father, the mother, the grandsire and the sustainer. I am the Holy One to be known, as also the syllable Om, the Ṛk, Sāma and Yajus.

गतिर्भर्ता प्रभुः साक्षी निवासः शरणं सुहृत् ।
प्रभवः प्रलयः स्थानं निधानं बीजमव्ययम् ॥ 18 ॥

Gatir bhartā prabhuḥ sākṣī nivāsaḥ śaraṇaṁ suhṛt /
prabhavaḥ pralayaḥ sthānaṁ nidhānaṁ bījam avyayam //18//

Gatiḥ : The goal *bhartā* : the supporter, *prabhuḥ* : the Lord, *sākṣī* : the witnessing consciousness, *nivāsaḥ* : the abode, *śaraṇam* : the refuge, *suhṛt* : the friend, *prabhavaḥ* : the origin, *pralayaḥ* : the dissolution, *sthānam* : the ground, *nidhānam* : treasure-house, *avyayam bījam* : imperishable seed.

18. The goal, the support, the Lord, and the consciousness witnessing—all this I am. I am again the abode, the refuge, and the friend of all, as also their origin, their dissolution, their ground, their treasure-house and their seed imperishable.

तपाम्यहमहं वर्षं निगृह्णाम्युत्सृजामि च ।
अमृतं चैव मृत्युश्च सदसच्चाहमर्जुन ॥ 19 ॥

Tapāmy aham, ahaṁ varṣaṁ nigṛhṇāmy utsṛjāmi ca /
amṛtaṁ c'aiva mṛtyuś ca sad asac c'āham Arjuna //19//

Arjuna : O Arjuna! *aham* : I *tapāmi* : give heat, *aham* : I *varṣam*: rain *utsṛjāmi* : send forth, *nigṛhṇāmi* : hold forth *ca*: and, *amṛtam ca* : immortality, *mṛtyuh* : death *ca* : and, *sat* : being *asat* : non-being *ca* : and *aham* : I *eva* : alone am.

19. I give heat, and I send forth as well as withhold rain. I am, O Arjuna! both immortality and death, both being and non-being.[12]

त्रैविद्या मां सोमपाः पूतपापा यज्ञैरिष्ट्वा स्वर्गतिं प्रार्थयन्ते ।
ते पुण्यमासाद्य सुरेन्द्रलोकमश्नन्ति दिव्यान्दिवि देवभोगान् ॥20॥

Traividyā māṁ soma-pāḥ pūta-pāpā
yajñair iṣṭvā svar-gatiṁ prārthayante /
te puṇyam āsādya sur'endra-lokam
aśnanti divyān divi deva-bhogān //20//

Traividyāḥ : Those who are versed in the three Vedas *somapāḥ* : those who drink the consecrated Soma juice in sacrificial rites *pūtapāpāḥ* : cleansed of their sins *yajñaiḥ* : with sacrifices *mām* : Me *iṣṭvā* : worshipping *svargatim* : attainment of heaven *prārthayante* : pray for. *te* : They *puṇyam* : attainable by meritorious deeds *surendralokam* : the heaven of Indra *āsādya*: having attained, *divi* : in the heaven *divyān* : heavenly *devabhogān* : celestial enjoyments *aśnanti* : enjoy.

20. Men versed in the Vedas, cleansed of their sins by the performance of sacrifices attended with the drinking of consecrated Soma juice, pray for heavenly regions (as the reward for adoring Me with those rites). They go to the heaven of Indra, attainable by meritorious deeds, and enjoy heavenly felicities there.[13]

ते तं भुक्त्वा स्वर्गलोकं विशालं क्षीणे पुण्ये मर्त्यलोकं विशन्ति
एवं त्रयीधर्ममनुप्रपन्ना गतागतं कामकामा लभन्ते ॥ 21 ॥

Te tam bhuktvā svarga-lokaṁ viśālaṁ
kṣīṇe puṇye martya-lokaṁ viśanti /

evaṁ trayī-dharmam anuprapannā
'gatāgataṁ kāma-kāmā labhante //21//

Te : They *viśālam* : the vast or having varied felicities *svargalokam* : heavenly regions *bhuktvā* : having enjoyed, *puṇye kṣīṇe* : when the merits accruing from their deeds are exhausted *martyalokam*: the world of men *viśanti* : enter. *Evam* : In this way *trayīdharmam* : the Vedic sacrificial duties *anuprapannāḥ* : following *kāma kāmāḥ* : desire-ridden people *gatāgatam* : Samsāra or the repetitive state of going and returning *labhante* : obtain.

21. Having enjoyed the varied felicities of heaven for long, they come back to the world of human beings when their asset of meritorious deeds is exhausted. Thus, being desire-ridden, the followers of the Vedic sacrificial rites stagnate in Samsāra, the repetitive state of going and returning.

अनन्याश्चिन्तयन्तो मां ये जनाः पर्युपासते ।
तेषां नित्याभियुक्तानां योगक्षेमं वहाम्यहम् ॥ 22 ॥

Ananyāś cintayanto māṁ ye janāḥ paryupāsate /
teṣāṁ nity'ābhiyuktānāṁ yoga-kṣemaṁ vahāmy aham //22//

Ye janāḥ : Whoever *ananyāḥ* : devoted to Me solely *cintayantaḥ* : thinking of *mām* : Me *paryupāsate* : continuously worship *nityābhiyuktānām teṣām* : of those ever-steadfast devotees *yogakṣemam* : supplying their wants and preserving their assets *aham* : I *vahāmi* : ensure.

22. Whoever, being devoted to me solely, engage themselves always in contemplation and worship of Me—to such ever-steadfast devotees I ensure the procurement of all their wants (salvation) and the preservation of their assets (worldly interests).[14]

येऽप्यन्यदेवताभक्ता यजन्ते श्रद्धयान्विताः ।
तेऽपि मामेव कौन्तेय यजन्त्यविधिपूर्वकम् ॥ 23 ॥

Ye'py anya-devatā-bhaktā yajante śraddhayā'nvitāḥ /
te'pi mām eva Kaunteya yajanty avidhi-pūrvakam //23//

Kaunteya : O son of Kuntī! *ye* : who *bhaktāḥ* : devotees *śraddhayānvitāḥ* : endowed with faith *anyadevatāḥ* : other deities *api* : even *yajante* : worship, *te* : they *api* : also *avidhipūrvakam* : contrary to injunctions *mām* : Me *eva* : alone *yajante* : worship.

23. O son of Kuntī! Those devotees who worship even other deities with deep faith, they also are worshipping Me alone, though contrary to injunctions.[15]

अहं हि सर्वयज्ञानां भोक्ता च प्रभुरेव च ।
न तु मामभिजानन्ति तत्त्वेनातश्च्यवन्ति ते 24 ॥

Aham hi sarva-yajñānāṁ bhoktā ca prabhur eva ca /
na tu mām abhijānanti tattven'ātaś cyavanti te //24//

Sarvayajñānām : Of all sacrifices *bhoktā* : enjoyer *ca* : and *prabhuḥ* : lord *ca* : and *aham* : I *eva* : only *hi* : indeed; *mām* : Me *tu* : but *tattvena* : in true nature *na abhijānanti* : do not know, *ataḥ* : therefore *te* : they *cyavanti* : fall.

24. I am indeed the only enjoyer and the Lord of all sacrifices. But they (the worshippers of other deities) do not understand Me in My true nature (as the object of all worship). So they fall.

यान्ति देवव्रता देवान्पितॄन्यान्ति पितृव्रताः ।
भूतानि यान्ति भूतेज्या यान्ति मद्याजिनोऽपि माम् ॥ 25 ॥

Yānti deva-vratā devān pitṛn yānti pitṛ-vratāḥ /
bhūtāni yānti bhūt'ejyā yānti mad-yājino'pi mām //25//

Devavratāḥ : Those devoted to the deities *devān* : the deities *yānti* : go to, *pitṛvratāḥ* : those devoted to the manes *pitṛn* : the manes *yānti* : go to, *bhutejyāḥ* : those who worship the spirits *bhūtani* : spirits *yānti* : attain to, *madyājinaḥ* : My worshippers *api* : but *mām* : Me *yānti* : come to.

25. The votaries of the deities go to the deities; of the manes, to the manes; and of the spirits, to the spirits, while My worshippers come to Me.

पत्रं पुष्पं फलं तोयं यो मे भक्त्याप्रयच्छति ।
तदहं भक्त्युपहृतमश्नामि प्रयतात्मनः ॥ 26 ॥

Patraṁ puṣpaṁ phalaṁ toyaṁ yo me bhaktyā prayacchati
tad ahaṁ bhakty-upahṛtam aśnāmi prayat'ātmanaḥ //26//

Yaḥ : Who *patram* : leaf *puṣpam* : flower *phalam* : fruit *toyam* : water *bhaktyā* : with devotion *me* : to Me *prayacchati* : offer, *prayatātmanaḥ* : of that pure-hearted man *bhaktyupahṛtam tat* : that devout offering *aham* : I *aśnāmi* : joyously accept.

26. Whoever makes an offering to Me with devotion, be it of leaf, flower, fruit or water—that devout offering made by a pure-hearted man, I accept with joy.[16]

यत्करोषियदश्नासि यज्जुहोषि ददासि यत् ।
यत्तपस्यसि कौन्तेय तत्कुरुष्व मदर्पणम् ॥ 27 ॥

Yat karoṣi yad aśnāsi yaj juhoṣi dadāsi yat |
yat tapasyasi Kaunteya tat kuruṣva mad-arpaṇam ||27|

Kaunteya : O son of Kuntī! *yat* : whatever *karoṣi* : you do, *yat* : whatever *aśnāsi* : you eat, *yat* : whatever *juhoṣi* : you offer in sacrifice , *yat* : whatever *dadāsi* : you give in charity, *yat* : whatever *tapasyasi* : austerity you perform, *tat* : that *madarpaṇam* : as offering to Me *Kuru* : do.

27. O son of Kuntī! Whatever you do, whatever you eat, whatever you offer in sacrifice, whatever you give as charity, whatever austerity you perform—do that as offering unto Me.[17]

शुभाशुभफलैरेवं मोक्ष्यसे कर्मबन्धनैः ।
संन्यासयोगयुक्तात्मा विमुक्तो मामुपैष्यसि ॥ 28 ॥

Śubhāśubha-phalair evaṁ mokṣyase karma-bandhanaiḥ |
sannyāsa-yoga yuktātmā vimukto mām upaiṣyasi ||28||

Evam : Thus *śubhāśubhaphalaiḥ* : bearing good or evil fruits *karmabandhanaiḥ* : from bonds of Karma *mokṣyase* : shall be freed, *sannyāsayoga-yuktātmā* : with the heart firmly set on renunciation *vimuktaḥ* : liberated *mām* : Me *upaiṣyasi* : will come to.

28. Thus shall you be freed from the bonds of Karma bearing good and evil fruits. With the heart firmly set on renunciation, you will attain liberation and thereby come to Me.

समोऽहं सर्वभूतेषु न मे द्वेष्योऽस्ति न प्रियः ।
ये भजन्ति तु मां भक्त्या मयि ते तेषु चाप्यहम् ॥ 29 ॥

Samo'ham sarvabhūteṣu na me dveṣyo'sti na priyaḥ |
ye bhajanti tu māṁ bhaktyā mayi te teṣu c'āpy aham ||29||

Aham : I *sarvabhūteṣu* : towards all beings *samaḥ* : the same; *Me* : to Me *dveṣyaḥ na* : none is hateful, *priyaḥ na asti* : none is dear. *Ye* : Who *tu* : but *mām* : Me *bhaktyā* : with devotion *bhajanti* : worship, *te* : they *mayi* : in Me, *aham* : I *api* : too *teṣu* : in them *ca* : and.

29. I am the same towards all beings. None is hateful, and none, dear to Me. But those who worship Me with devotion dwell in Me, and I too dwell in them.[18]

अपि चेत्सुदुराचारो भजते मामनन्यभाक् ।
साधुरेव स मन्तव्यः सम्यग्व्यवसितो हि सः ॥ 30 ॥

Api cet sudurācāro bhajate mām ananya-bhāk /
sādhur eva sa mantavyaḥ samyag vyavasito hi saḥ //30//

Sudurācāraḥ : Confirmed sinner *api* : even *ananyabhāk* : with unwavering faith and devotion *mām* : Me *bhajate* : worships *cet* : if, *saḥ* : he *sādhuḥ* : righteous *eva* : verily *mantavyaḥ* : must be considered. *Hi* : indeed, *saḥ* : he *samyak* : rightly *vyavasitaḥ* : resolved.

30. Even a confirmed sinner, if he worships Me with unwavering faith and devotion, must verily be considered as righteous; for he has indeed taken the right resolve.[19]

क्षिप्रं भवति धर्मात्मा शश्वच्छान्तिं निगच्छति ।
कौन्तेय प्रतिजानीहि न मे भक्तः प्रणश्यति ॥ 31 ॥

Kṣipraṁ bhavati dharm'ātmā śaśvac-chāntiṁ nigacchati /
Kaunteya pratijānīhi na me bhaktaḥ praṇaśyati //31//

Saḥ : He *kṣipram* : soon *dharmātmā* : righteous *bhavati* : becomes, *śaśvat* : lasting *śāntim* : peace *nigacchati* : attains. *Kaunteya* : O son of Kuntī! *Me* : My *bhaktaḥ* : devotee *na praṇaśyati* : never perishes *pratijānīhi* : may swear to this effect.

31. Soon will he become righteous and attain to lasting peace. No devotee of Mine will ever perish; you may swear to this effect, O Arjuna!

मां हि पार्थ व्यपाश्रित्य येऽपि स्युः पापयोनयः ।
स्त्रियो वैश्यास्तथा शूद्रास्तेऽपि यान्ति परां गतिम् ॥ 32 ॥

Mām hi Pārtha vyapāśritya ye'pi syuḥ papa-yonayaḥ /
striyo vaiśyās tathā śūdrās te'pi yānti parāṁ gatim //32//

Pārtha : O son of Pṛthā! *striyaḥ* : women *vaiśyāḥ* : Vaiśyas *śūdrāḥ* : Sūdras *ye* : who *syuḥ* : exist, *tathā* : in the same way *pāpayonayaḥ* : persons of inferior origin (*ye syuḥ* : whoever exist), *te* : they *api* : even *mām* : Me *vyapāśritya* : taking refuge in *parām gatim* : the highest spiritual goal *yānti* : attain to.

32. O son of Prithā! Taking refuge in Me, women, Vaisyas, Sudras, and likewise even men of inferior birth, attain to the highest spiritual goal.

किं पुनर्ब्राह्मणाः पुण्या भक्ता राजर्षयस्तथा ।
अनित्यमसुखं लोकमिमं प्राप्य भजस्व माम् ॥ 33 ॥

Kiṁ punar brāhmaṇāḥ puṇyā bhaktā rāja-ṛṣayas tathā /
anityam asukhaṁ lokam imaṁ prāpya bhajasva mām //33//

Puṇyāḥ : Holy *brāhmaṇāḥ* : Brāhmaṇas *tathā* : also *bhaktāḥ* : devoted *rajarṣayaḥ* : royal sages *kiṁ punaḥ* : how much more! *Anityam* : Impermanent *asukham* : unhappy *imam* : this *lokam* : world *prāpya* : having come into *mām* : Me *bhajasva* : worship.

33. Then how much more so in the case of holy Brāhmaṇas and also of devoted royal sages! Having come into this impermanent and unhappy world, engage yourself in My worship.

मन्मना भव मद्भक्तो मद्याजी मां नमस्कुरु ।
मामेवैष्यसि युक्त्वैवमात्मानं मत्परायणः ॥ 34 ॥

Man-manā bhava mad-bhakto madyājī māṁ namas-kuru /
mām ev'aiṣyasi yuktv'aivam ātmānaṁ mat-parāyaṇaḥ //34//

Manmanāḥ : One with mind absorbed in Me *madbhaktaḥ* : My devotee *madyājī* : one sacrificing to Me *bhava* : become, *mām* : to Me *namskuru* : bow down. *Evam* : In this way *matparāyaṇaḥ* : having Me as the highest goal *ātmānam* : the mind *mayi* : in Me *yuktvā* : united *mām* : Me *eva* : alone *eşyasi* : shall come to.

34. Let your mind be absorbed in Me. Be devoted to Me, sacrifice unto Me, and bow down to Me. Thus, having Me as your highest goal, and united with Me in mind, you shall come to Me alone.

ओं तत्सदिति श्रीमद्भगवद्गीतासूपनिषत्सु ब्रह्मविद्यायां योगशास्त्रे श्रीकृष्णार्जुनसंवादे राजविद्याराजगुह्य-

योगो नाम नवमोऽध्यायः ॥ 9 ॥

NOTES

1. *Vr.*2: There are two words *Rājavidyā* and *Rājaguhyam*, translated here as sovereign knowledge and sovereign mystery. The prefix *Rāja* in these words is taken as showing the importance of the subject, and this it may very well be. But if we connect this passage with the two verses in an earlier chapter (Ch. 4. 1 & 2), where Kṛṣṇa speaks of the Yoga, which was known to *Rājarşis* and forgotten in course of time, and which he was going to revive by imparting it now to Arjuna, we have to understand these teachings in a different way. He describes that teaching also as *rahasyam*, esoteric knowledge or a mystery. This word is used here too. There is then every possibility that the words *Rājavidyā* and *Rājaguhyam* are not merely meant to show the importance of the topic by describing it as 'a king among Vidyas and mysteries', but also to show that it is that forgotten Yoga of *Rājarşis,* which was now being revived by Kṛṣṇa. This brings us to the distinction between the Vedic sacrificial cult and the *Bhāgavata Dharma* which Kṛṣṇa proclaimed. Kṛṣṇa directs a shattering criticism on the sacrificial cult in Gīta 2.42-44. It occurs also in a mild form in Verses 20

and 21 of this chapter also. Vedic ritualism was elaborate, requiring meticulous performance with diverse ingredients. Its object was heavenly felicities. It was open only to Kṣatriyas and Brāhmanas. Both women and members of non-Brāhmanical classes were excluded from it.

Now the *Bhāgavata Dharma,* which Kṛṣṇa proclaimed, though it did not rebel against Vedic ritualism, has characteristics of a very different nature. Its important features are: (1) Faith in the One Supreme Spirit, called Vāsudeva, Nārāyaṇa, Mahāviṣṇu, Kṛṣṇa etc., and adoration of Him with devotion.

(2) In this adoration rituals and ingredients are very subordinate. In this very chapter Kṛṣṇa says: "Leaves, flowers, water etc. given to Me with love and dedication, I consume with supreme satisfaction" (Gīta IX. 28). In the *Bhāgavata Purāṇa,* another great text of the *Bhāgavata Dharma,* it is said, "If a man disregards and persecutes fellow beings, but worships Me in images with numerous rituals and rich offerings, I am not at all pleased with him for proffering such worship." (Bh. III 29.24). Thus worship is effective not by the complexity of its rituals and the elaborateness of ingredients and offerings, but by devotion and by service of fellow beings done as part of worship.

(3) Highest worship, according to the *Bhāgavata Dharma,* consists in the total surrender of all the fruits of actions and finally even the sense of agency to Him. So says the *Bhāgavata,* "Whatever man does by the body, by mind, by Buddhi, and by the senses according to his nature (i.e. due to the prompting of the tendencies acquired by his Karma), let all that be dedicated to the Supreme Being" (Bh. XI. 2.36).

Here, in this very chapter, the Gīta too says: "Whatever you do, whatever you eat, whatever you give away in charity, whatever austerity you perform—do all that as offering unto Me" (9-27). In the *Bhāgavata Dharma,* unlike in Vedic ritualism, Karma is not so much performance of rituals as performance of one's duties in a spirit of dedication. Thus the Gīta says: "By making all one's actions constituting one's duty, an offering to Him, from whom the world has come and by whom it is pervaded, man attains perfection" (Gīta 18.46).

In the full-fledged description of the *Bhāgavata Dharma*, as we get it in the *Bhāgavata Purāṇa*, a spiritual discipline of a very wide scope is presented. It has nine steps: *Śravaṇa* (hearing), Kīrtana (hymning), *Smaraṇa* (remembering), *Pādaseva* (service) *Arcana* (worship), *Vandana* (saluting all as the tabernacles of God), *Dāsya* (cultivating the attitude of the servant of God), Sakhya (comradeship with Him), Ātmanivedana (complete self-surrender). The Gītā takes into account mainly Padaseva (*Pāda* being taken as manifestation of the Supreme Being as the world), and *Ātmanivedana*. We have to take the others as included in these two.

(4) The *Bhāgavata Dharma* is open to all, including women and the outcastes, unlike the Vedic sacrificial rites, which are open only to men of the twice born Varnas (Dvijas). The Gītā openly declares: "Even a confirmed sinner, if he worships Me with unwavering faith and devotion, must verily be considered as righteous; for he has taken the right resolve....O son of Prithā! Taking refuge in Me, women, Vaiśyas, Śūdras, and likewise even men of inferior birth attain to the highest spiritual goal." (9.30 & 33).

(5) In the Vedic way of life those who lost faith in the enjoyments offered by the sacrificial cults took to *Karma-sannyāsa* or abandonment of all ritualistic works, and became ascetics practising the meditative life prescribed by the Upaniṣads. It is what is described in the Gītā as Sāṁkhya and is more popularly known as Jñāna Yoga, the way of knowledge. In the *Bhāgavata Dharma*, there is no abandonment of works. Work discharged as offering to the Divine is sanctifying and is always to be done. Says the Gīta: "Worship, charity, austerity etc. should not be abandoned. They should be performed. They purify the wise. They have to be done without attachment and desire for their merits. This is My firm and final word on the question." (18.5 & 6). This applies to those who follow the *Bhāgavata Dharma*.

By showing this contrast between the Vedic sacrificial religion and the *Bhāgavata Dharma*, it is not meant that the Gīta decries the one and accepts only the other. While it criticises desire-prompted ritualism, it accepts its abandonment at a mature stage and the adoption of the contemplative and workless way of Jñāna Yoga or the Sāṁkhya, as it is called here. (Gītā 6.3). But it accepts equally the validity of the *Bhāgavata Dharma* as a self-sufficient discipline taking the aspirant to the highest goal, which is the goal also of one following the discipline of Jñāna.

According to the Gīta, Jñāna as well as Bhakti discipline is each in itself self-sufficient, and can take an aspirant to the highest. Karma has however no place in the Jñāna discipline, except in the early stages of a man's spiritual life; but in Bhakti, dedicated Karma is a part of its practice, and there is no opposition between the two. Dedicated Karma can also become the main discipline with Bhakti as an aid and directive force. Great men of action with a spiritual background are examples of this. Yoga, as a scientific system of concentration, can be an aid in both Bhakti and Jñāna. But just as Karma can be the main discipline, so Yoga too can be the main form of discipline, with Bhakti and Jñāna as the directive forces. Chapter 6 of the Gīta is devoted to Yoga in this sense as the main discipline.

In fact it is unpsychological to make a water-tight compartmentalization of these four Yogas. These Yogas are based upon the three aspects of the human mind—the intellectual, the emotional and the voilitional. Jñāna Yoga is essentially intellectual, Bhakti Yoga emotional, and Karma and Yoga volitional. The last requires some explanation. In Yoga, or to be more accurate, in Rāja Yoga, which is the science of concentration, what is done is to use the will power to make the mind one-pointed. Will is here used for an inward purpose. In Karma Yoga also the application of will is the main feature of the discipline, but it takes an external direction.

Now thinking, feeling and willing, which are the faculties of the human mind on which these Yogas are based, do not exist in the human mind in isolation from one another. The human mind is a whole, constituted of these faculties, and so all these faculties have in some way or other to enter into all these Yogas. The *Vicāra* or the discriminative process has to be supported by the whole of the chastened emotional and volitional powers of the mind, if the mind were to keep awake and dynamic instead of lapsing into dullness and sleep. In the Bhakti discipline, if emotion is not supported by thought and volition, an understanding of one's true relationship with the Divine activised by will power, it will degenerate into vapid sentimentalism or into a dull routine of procedures. So also Karma Yoga, if it degenerates into mere Karma, will become the restless activity of a busy-body, without raising the moral and spiritual stature of the man concerned. Yoga as practice of concentration will become mere psychism and pursuit of occult powers, unless it has a spiritual objective. Thus it will be seen that none of these four disciplines can stand as water-tight compartments. What is meant by differentiating them into four is to put the stress on one or the other of the mental faculties on which these disciplines rest. The Gīta accepts all these disciplines, and gives equal importance to all, though Jñāna and Bhakti are shown as the two main and dominant disciplines.

2. *Vr.* 4: The Supreme Being is called the Unmanifested Being, because He is invisible or unknown to man in ignorance, though in truth everything is included in Him and there is nothing beside Him. He is described as pervading everything; but pervading does not mean that some parts of Him are contained and imprisoned within objects. To ward off such misconception, it is said that though He is pervading all objects, they are in Him and are supported by Him and not vice versa. All things exist in His Sankalpa or will. So they all depend on Him but not He on them. He sustains them all from within and without but He is not contained by them or limited by them. This is so because He is Spirit and not a material substance. The impossible is possible for His mysterious power to accomplish, as is stated in the next verse—"See My Yoga or mysterious Power."

3. *Vr.*5: What is accomplished by His Yoga or Yoga-Māyā (mysterious power) is further explained here as follows: He is the source and support of all existence, but He has no contact with them i.e. they do not limit or affect Him in anyway, nor is He dependent on them. But all objects are given their status as existent entities because of His will. But for Him they would have had no existence, but He is self-existent. Nor does their existence affect His infinity in any way. The Lord uses the word *Mamātmā*—My Ātma—only for purpose of human understanding. He is really 'egoless' unlike Jīvas, but still all this is accomplished by His Power.

4. *Vr.*6: An illustration, however inadequate, is given to

explain this Divine mystery. The atmosphere is existing in Ākāsa, without limiting or in any way affecting the Ākāsa. Ākāsa, being a much more subtle medium, is able to sustain a grosser entity, namely, atmosphere, without itself being affected by the gross entity. The subtlest of all entities is the Lord, and He is therefore not in the least affected by the manifestation. But this example is meant only to give an approximate idea by showing how a subtle entity can contain and pervade something more gross. But the true explanation is only in the Lord's mysterious Power, Māyā or Yoga-Māyā, which makes Him transcend laws applicable to material entities, rendering it possible for him to be both the material and the efficient cause of the world-manifestation outside, His Infinity and Lordship being not affected in the least thereby.

5. *Vr.*7: The *Kalpa* (manifestation) and *Pralaya* (dissolution) have been explained at length in Note 3 of the previous chapter. The Lord's creative activity is an eternal cyclic process of *Kalpas* and *Pralayas*, one alternating with the other just like day and night.

6. *Vr.*9: The use of *udāsīnavad*—like or as if unconcerned—is significant. 'Unconcernedness' is only in being non-attached, but it does not preclude Him from loving those who are truly devoted to Him. The Lord's love for the devotee is neither partiality nor attachment, as in the case of worldly love. For there is in Him no self-centredness, and His love goes to all who seek Him with devotion. He is open to all who choose to seek Him.

7. *Vrs.*11-12: The reference here may be to God as the Divine Incarnate and to the reason for men's failure to recognise Him. But this topic has been discussed in chapter four 7 to 9 (cf. Note 1) and in chapter seven 24 to 25 (cf. Notes 7 and 8). So this may be a reference to men not recognising that the Divine is immanent in all beings, and for this reason living a self-centred life without any real heartfelt faith in the Divine at all, but professing such faith only hypocritically. The worship of such people who oppress God in man but worship Him in images with elaborate rituals is condemned in the *Bhāgavata Purāṇa*. This may as well be a general condemnation of the atheistic attitude towards life. A man who does not accept God, a spiritual background for the world, will not accept an eternal spiritual principle in man too. He will look upon man as a mere body-mind, and his attitude

towards life will be formed on that belief. He can be only a pure self-centred materialist. The attitude and ways of life of such persons are described as *Rākṣasi* and *Āsurī* or demoniac in verse 12, i.e., the next verse.

8. *Vr.*13: The Gītā seems to recognise some kind of a basic divergence in the nature of people as *Daivī-prakṛti* and *Āsurī-prakṛti,* the divine and the demoniac. The characteristics and the ways of life of these two types are more elaborately described in chapter 16.

According to some philosophers, who accept the doctrine of *Tāratamya,* or basic contrast in the nature of Jīvas and the course their life takes, the Daivī type evolves spiritually till they obtain liberation, while the Āsurī type goes down deeper and deeper into worldly entanglement. They become *Nityasamsārīs*—permanent worldlings.

But it is pointed out that the spirit in man is essentially Divine The Gīta says: "A particle of mine has become a Jīva in the world of beings" (Ch. 15. 7). The Jīva cannot lose that basic nature. So the two character types must have developed in the course of evolution due to their Karma. Repeated performance of good and evil acts must have produced what appears to be the basic tendencies.

Included in the Lord's Power or Māyā, are two tendencies working in opposite directions. These tendencies are Vidyā (enlightenment), which works towards the liberation of the soul, and Avidyā (ignorance) which leads to more and more of worldly bondage of the Jīva. Moral and pious actions bring one more and more under the influence of Vidyā, and immoral and sensous indulgences bring him more and more into the sphere of Avidyā. Spiritual growth and spiritual degeneration accrue to the Jīva from his own actions under the influence of the one or the other of these aspects of Māyā. See also Note 3 on verse 15 of the 7th chapter.

9. *Vr.*14: In this verse Kīrtana hymning and Vandanam (saluting), two of the nine-pronged Bhakti discipline, are added to worship. See for details Note 1 on verse 2 of this Chapter.

10. *Vr.*15: Jñāna-Yajña is not mere study of scriptures or lecturing on spiritual themes. Coming as it does immediately after reference to Kīrtana and Vandana i.e. hymning and saluting all as the temple of the Lord—the Jñāna described here must be the attitudes of devotion born of knowledge or Jñāna of one's relationship with the Divine. For, an attitude towards God can be maintained only on an understanding of one's relationship with Him. These attitudes are given in Bhakti disciplines as Dāsya (servitude), Sakhya (intimacy of comradeship) and Ātmanivedana (whole-hearted self-surrender). Unless one knows, or has an awareness of, how one is related to the Supreme Being, love of Him cannot become firm and constant. An awareness of one's closeness to Him alone can produce that intimacy contemplated in Sakhya and Ātmanivedana. Thus Jñāna supports Bhakti, and Bhakti deepens Jñāna. The Gīta therefore says: "By Bhakti one comes to know Me —who I am and how great I am" Ch. 18.55). To separate them and make them independent disciplines or one subservient to the other may be correct in the lower stages of spiritual development. But finally they are mutual supports and form the obverse and reverse of the same coin. So it is appropriate to term the attitudes of Bhakti as Jñāna-Yajña.

The forms of Jñāna-Yajña here referred to are three—those based on unity (*ekatva*), separateness (*pṛthaktva*), , and multiplicity (*bahudhā*). Bhakti of the *ekatva* type is based on the realisation of the Jīva's oneness with Him, and such Bhakti is described as ***svasvarūpānusandhānam***—uniting with what is one's own pristine nature. Bhakti of the *Pṛthaktva* type is to know Him as the Father and Master of all. Adoring Him as Friend or Husband too will come under this. To adore Him in multiplicity (*bahudhā*) can mean, to know that He is immanent in all beings, and do service to all beings with that attitude in mind. It is the Sevādharma as adumbrated by Swami Vivekananda, in which Bhakti takes the form of Karma Yoga. This part of the passage is also interpreted as the worship of many deities like Śiva, Viṣṇu, the Incarnations, the Divine Mother in various aspects etc., where worship is done with the understanding that it is the one Supreme Being who has manifested as all these Deities and that it is He who is worshipped through them all. Worship with such understanding is a part of Bhakti. Thus Jñāna-Yajña includes all forms of adoration with understanding.

11. *Vrs.*16-18 These verses seem to explain what is meant by calling the Lord as *Viśvatomukham*—All-inclusive Whole. As there is nothing outside Him, all entities included in the Universe are adjuncts or instruments or forms of His, through which He functions in the Cosmic Play. So also all functions which are being fulfilled by different powers and beings are really the stirrings of His will. His many-sided relationship with the world is set forth in these verses.

12. *Vr.*19: *Sat* and *Asat*, apart from the usual meaning, 'being' and 'non-being', are used in many other senses in the Hindu scriptures. In the well-known Vedic prayer '*Asato ma sad gamaya . . . mrityor ma amṛtam gamaya*", *Asat* (Non-being) is put in apposition with Death and *Sat* (Being) with Immortality. Here we may exclude this meaning, as *Amṛta* and *Mṛtyu* are mentioned separately just earlier in this very Verse 19. Besides, the words are connected by the conjunction ' and ', and are not in apposition. So the words can be interpreted as done in other places: *Sat* is the manifested or gross condition, and *Asat*, the unmanifested and subtle causal condition. In this context also the same may be the meaning of the two words.

It is interesting to note that in 11.87 Arjuna describes the Lord as *tvam akṣaram sad asad tat-param yat*—Thou art that Imperishable which is both *sat* and *asat* (being and non-being) and what is beyond both these. In 13.12 Brahman is described as *na sat tan n'āsat*--neither Being nor Non-being.

13. *Vrs.*20-21: In these verses is brought out the clear-cut distinction between attaining heaven and attaining salvation in the eschatology based on Hindu scriptures. In other religions heaven or paradise is the final destiny of all pious believers. But in Vedic religion heaven is just a state like our life on earth, only providing enjoyments of greater refinement as a reward for Vedic rituals performed and charities done with their fruits in view. Just like money put in the bank, these merits are exhausted by enjoyment, and when their credit of merits is exhausted, those Jīvas have to come back to the earth to acquire new merits and have more enjoyments after the end of their earthly life. This *Samsāra* or repetitive process of birth and death offering enjoyments and sufferings, is the lot of people who live with bodily fulfilments as their aim

in life. In contrast to these pseudo-religionists, who are only worldlings in the garb of orthodoxy, are the real lovers of God who live a holy life of surrender to God and service of His creatures without praying for any reward. They attain liberation (Mukti) or freedom from Samsāra. For further information on these two kinds of attainments, reference may be made to Note 5 in chapter 8.

14. *Vr.*22: In contrast to the pseudo-religionists, who are really mere worldlings, the Lord speaks of true devotees termed here as *ananyāḥ*, a very highly suggestive term. In a pure Advaitic sense it can mean—those who do not think of Him as different from their real Self. In a purely devotional sense it can mean—those who love Him, looking upon Him, the Supreme Being, as their 'own', and not as a strange Power to be propitiated for favours. There is greater appropriateness in the latter, because what is being expounded is the pure devotional Gospel of the *Bhāgavatas*. This will look justified also, if it is seen that in the very next verse the Lord speaks of *anya devatā bhaktāḥ* — devotees of other Deities whom they invoke for favours. *Anya* means a 'stranger', and *Ananyaḥ*, its opposite, is therefore "one's own". It indicates intimacy and unselfish love.

These are the words of assurance that the Lord gives to true devotees. In the midst of their devotional pre-occupations, they may neglect to preserve what they have (*Kṣemam*) or worldly interests. Absorbed in His service they may not care for their future interests (*Yoga*), consisting in liberation or *Mokṣa*. But the Lord of Love assures that He Himself will see to it that their interests in these respects are secured. These devotees never pray to the Lord for anything, even for liberation. They only love Him and serve Him and forget everything about themselves. They look upon the Lord as their 'own', and they have no selfish and extraneous interests in adoring Him, including salvation. Love is the only motive power.

15. *Vrs.*23—25: 'Contrary to injunctions' means contrary to the principles of the devotional scriptures. Devotional scriptures inculcate the worship of the Supreme Being who may be looked upon as a Person, but not as an individual. The Deities are His manifestations for cosmic purposes. If people worship them for particular purposes, without an understanding that only

He, the Supreme Being, is worshipped through them, it becomes a kind of idolatry—worshipping something to whom worship is not due. They may be propitiated with offerings, but not adored and worshipped. These deities are His Kalas or powers conceived in separation from Him. People who are worldly-minded and who go to religion only for worldly fulfilments, think that propitiating deities is an easy way of gaining their ends. But the Lord has said in Chapter 7.18 that His pure devotees also—the suffering, the enquirers, the boon-seekers, and the knowing ones—can all approach Him directly. He considers them too as noble (*udārāḥ*). There is however this great difference. The propitiation of deities is bound by rituals and requires elaborate offerings. If the propitiating is not done according to the ritualistic codes, it may be even counter-productive. But the worship of the Lord is simple. As stated in 9.26 the ingredients offered may even be such common things as leaf, water, fruit, etc. But the offering must be done with pure love and submission to His will. This is a commodity that the devotees of deities lack. They are commercial in their outlook. In spite of all the difficulties and expenses undergone, the result got by their worship is temporary. The devotees of deities fall from their attainments in course of time, but the devotees of the God of Love are liberated. Note 6 in Chapter 7 may also be read in this connection.

16. *Vr.*26: The simplicity of devotional worship should not be understood as encouragement of miserliness. It is only to point out the dominance of devotion, unlike in ritualistic worship of deities where punctiliousness and wealth of offerings count. A true devotee will offer the best he can procure and not stint in the matter. Liberal gifts to holy men and the poor also form an important part of devotional worship. External worship of this kind is very important in the early stages of devotional life. Meditation is too abstract for beginners. Prayer without an object before one is also vague. But if there is an image or symbol before one to pray to and to worship, it gives a sense of realism to the ordinary man. He feels that some concrete communion is done. Without realising this, there are intellectuals who scorn external worship without themselves being fit for anything better.

17. *Vrs.*27-28: External worship is symbolic. The true and the highest worship that the *Bhāgavata Dharma* inculcates is

total offering of oneself, one's possessions, and one's actions and even the sense of agency to Him. Such total offering to God is the real renunciation, and a person who does so is a real Sannyāsin, as declared in the next verse. It is also declared in this and the next verse that in the discipline of Bhakti, abandonment of work means this kind of renunciation and not of all external actions. Such renunciation leads one to the highest. He need not give up his adherence to the nine disciplines of Bhakti as something inferior and take to the so-called *jñāna-niṣṭa* for enlightenment. The Lord of Love bestows it on Him by His grace.

18. *Vr.*29: This is the answer to the question: Is God then partial towards His devotees as against those who do not adore Him? Among worldly men of high position such an invidious attitude is common. Those who flatter them are rewarded and those who do not do so are excluded from favour. Is God also like that? This criticism is answered here. Those who adore Him approach close to Him and dwell in Him, and therefore participate in His blissful nature, whereas the others ignorantly or deliberately exclude themselves from Him and become exclusively interested in worldly life with its inevitable consequences. The *Bhāgavata Purāṇa* illustrates this point by describing God as *Kalpataru-svabhāvaḥ*—comparable to the wish-yielding tree of heaven. Those who go under the tree and pray are rewarded. Those who exclude themselves from it fail to get those blessings due to their own fault. A question may now arise: "Is God then simply a passive element, just like beauties of Nature? Is He not responsive to the devotee's attitude? Does not the devotee get any active help from Him?" Sri Ramakrishna answers this declaring that if the devotee takes two steps towards Him, He takes ten steps to the devotee. A devotee will find from experience that God's grace works on him in a hundred ways without his actually knowing it.

19. *Vrs.*30-32: These verses breathe the extreme liberalism of the *Bhāgavata Dharma* in contrast to the Vedic ritualism and philosophy, to which only the twice born classes were considered eligible according to the orthodox traditions of the Mīmāmsakas or Vedic savants. Bhakti discipline, however, is for all without any consideration of birth, sex or social status, and the Gīta holds that through that discipline, one can reach the highest.

The *Bhāgavata Purāṇa* goes a step still further. A sinner even, is not without hope. The way is open even for him to receive the grace of the Lord, be purified and saved. That way consists in worshipping the Lord with unwavering faith and devotion (*ananya-bhakti*). Sometimes a sectarian interpretation is given to this expression as worshipping no other deity than Kṛṣṇa. Such a meaning is not consistent with the spirit of the Gīta and is to be rejected. If that interpretaion is accepted, it will be a doctrine akin to the Christian doctrine of 'No salvation except through Christ'.

Chapter X

विभूतियोगः

MANIFESTATIONS OF DIVINE GLORIES

Summary

Contemplation on Divine Excellences: (1-11) As an aid to devotion and self-surrender, the Lord expounds the Divine majesties and excellences, by contemplating on which the devotional mood is reinforced. The Lord says to Arjuna: No person, however great, knows Me; for I pre-exist all. Knowing Me as the unoriginated and eternal Lord of all, man becomes sinless and free from delusions. All the higher faculties of man are but a faint reflection of My excellences. All great men, saints and saviours, are indeed projections of My thought. To contemplate on Me as the source of all this world-manifestation, to recognise My essence in all that is glorious and impressive, is the way to get thrilled with the devotional experience and attain perpetual communion with Me. To those whose very vital energy is drawn to Me through devotion, I bring the illumination of spiritual insight: I light within them the lamp of wisdom, revealing Myself as the Soul of their soul.

The Vibhutis: (12-42) Moved by utter reverence springing from an apprehension of the divine mystery, Arjuna now wants to know about the Bhagavān's glorious manifestations in life and in Nature, and the Lord lists some of them for the edification of Arjuna. He says: I am what manifests as the Self in all beings. Among Adityas, I am Viṣṇu; among luminaries, the Sun; among the Maruts, Marīci; among the stars, the moon; among the Vedas, Sāma; among the Devas, Indra; among the senses, the mind; in living creatures, consciousness; among mountains, Meru;

among the priests, Bṛhaspati; among the commanders, Skanda; among water reservoirs, the ocean; among Maharṣis, Bhṛgu; among sounds, Oṁkāra; among Yajñas, Japa Yajña; among immobile entities, the Himālaya; among trees, the Asvattha (fig-tree); among Devarṣis, Nārada; among Gandharvas, Citraratha; among perfected beings, Kapila; among horses, Ucchaiśravas; among elephants, Airāvata; among men, the king; among weapons, the thunderbolt; among cows, the Kāmadhenu; among progenitors, Cupid; among serpents, Vāsuki; among Nāgas, Ananta; among aquatic residents, Varuṇa; among Pitṛs, Aryamā; among enforcers, Yama: among Daityas, Prahlāda; among measuring agents, Time; among animals, the lion; among birds, Garuḍa; among the fish, Makara; among rivers, the Gaṅga; among forms of knowledge, the knowledge of the Self; among letters, the letter A; among compound word-formations, the Dvandva form; among destroyers, death; among months, the Mārgaśīrṣa; among seasons, spring; among deceitful ways, the game of dice; of the powerful, their power; of the meritorious, their virtues; among the Vṛṣṇis, Kṛṣṇa; among the Pāṇḍavas, Arjuna; among sages, Vyāsa; among poets, Śukra; in the disciplinarians, the sense of discipline; among the factors for success, justice; in the knowing ones, knowledge—in short I am the seed of everything, and without Me nothing can exist. There is no end to My manifestations. Wherever you see anything powerful, good and glorious, know that to be a manifestation of an atom of My Power. But why all these details! Suffice for you to understand that with an atom of My being. I pervade and sustain everything.

श्रीभगवानुवाच

भूय एव महाबाहो श्रृणु मे परमं वचः ।
यत्तेऽहं प्रीयमाणाय वक्ष्यामि हितकाम्यया ॥ 1 ॥

Sri Bhagavān uvāca:

Bhūya eva mahā-bāho śṛṇu me paramaṁ vacaḥ /
yat te'haṁ prīyamāṇāya vakṣyāmi hita-kāmyayā //1//

Mahābāho : O mighty armed! *prīyamāṇāya te* : to you who are beloved *hitakāmyayā* : desirous of your good *yat* : what *me* :

my *paramam vacaḥ* : words on the Supreme Truth, *aham* : I *vakṣyāmi* : shall declare, *bhūyah eva* : again *śṛṇu* : hear.

The Blessed Lord said:

1. Hear again, O mighty armed one, My words on the Supreme Truth. Desirous of your good, I want to declare it to you, who are so beloved of Me.

न मे विदुः सुरगणाः प्रभवं न महर्षयः ।
अहमादिर्हि देवानां महर्षीणां च सर्वशः ॥ 2 ॥

Na me viduḥ sura-gaṇāḥ prabhavaṁ na maharṣayaḥ
aham ādir hi devānāṁ maharṣiṇāṁ ca sarvaśaḥ //2//

Me : My *prabhavam* : origin *suragaṇāḥ* : hosts of gods *na viduḥ* : do not know; *maharṣayaḥ* : Maharṣis *na* : nor; *hi* : for *aham* : I *devānām* : of the Devas *maharṣiṇām:* of the Maharṣis (great sages) *ca* : and *sarvaśaḥ* : to all *ādiḥ* : origin.

2. Neither the hosts of gods nor Maharṣis (great sages) know my origin, for I am Myself the origin of all those gods and great sages.

यो मामजमनादिं च वेत्ति लोकमहेश्वरम् ।
असंमूढः स मर्त्येषु सर्वपापैः प्रमुच्यते ॥ 3 ॥

Yo mām ajam anādiṁ ca vetti loka-mah'eśvaram /
asaṁmūḍhaḥ sa martyeṣu sarva-pāpaiḥ pramucyate //3//

Yaḥ : Who *mām* : Me *anādiṁ* : without beginning *ajam* : unborn *lokamaheśvaram* : the Master of all the worlds *ca* : and *vetti* : knows; *martyeṣu* : among mortals *asammūḍhaḥ* : undeluded, *saḥ* : he *sarva pāpaiḥ* : from all sins *pramucyate* : is released.

3. He who knows Me as the beginningless, the unborn and the Master of the worlds—he among mortals becomes undeluded, and he is freed from all sins.

बुद्धिर्ज्ञानमसंमोहः क्षमा सत्यं दमः शमः ।
सुखं दुःखं भवोऽभावो भयं चाभयमेव च ॥ 4 ॥

अहिंसा समता तुष्टिस्तपो दानं यशोऽयशः ।
भवन्ति भावा भूतानां मत्त एव पृथग्विधाः ॥ 5 ॥

Buddhir jñānam asammohaḥ kṣamā satyam damaḥ śamaḥ /
sukhaṁ duḥkhaṁ bhavo'bhāvo bhayaṁ c'ābhayam eva ca //4//

Ahimsā samatā tuṣṭis tapo dānaṁ yaśo'yaśaḥ /
bhavanti bhāvā bhūtānāṁ matta eva pṛthag-vidhāḥ //5//

Buddhiḥ : Intelligence *jñānam* : knowledge *asammohaḥ* : sanity *kṣamā* : patience *satyam* : truth *damaḥ* : sense control *śamaḥ* : mind control *sukham* : pleasure *duḥkham* : pain *bhavaḥ* : birth *abhāvaḥ* : death *bhayam* : fear *abhayam* : fearlessness *eva* : also *ca* : and *ahimsā* : non-injury *samatā* : same-sightedness *tuṣṭih* : contentment *tapaḥ*: austerity *dānam*: benevolent disposition *yaśaḥ*: fame *ayaśaḥ* : obloquy *bhūtānām*: of beings *pṛthak-vidhāḥ* : diverse *bhāvāḥ* : expressions *matta eva* : from Me alone *bhavanti* : arise.

4-5. Intelligence, knowledge, sanity, patience, truth, sense-control, mind-control, pleasure, pain, birth, death, fear and also fearlessness; non-injury, same-sightedness, contentment, austerity, benevolence, fame and obloquy—all these diverse modes of the mind seen in all beings proceed from Me alone, their ultimate sanctioner.

महर्षयः सप्त पूर्वे चत्वारो मनवस्तथा ।
मद्भावा मानसा जाता येषां लोक इमाः प्रजाः ॥ 6 ॥

Maharṣayaḥ sapta pūrve catvāro manavas tathā /
mad-bhāvā mānasā jātā yeṣāṁ loka imāḥ prajāḥ //6//

Sapta: Seven *maharṣayaḥ*: great sages *pūrve* : more ancient *catvāro*: the four sages *tathā* : in the same way *Manavaḥ* : Manus *matbhāvāḥ*: are my emanations, *mānasāḥ jātāḥ* : born of my mind. *Loke* : In the world *imāḥ* : all these *prajāḥ* : beings *yeṣāṁ jātāḥ* : from whom were born.

6. The seven great sages (beginning with Marīci) as also the four earlier ones like Sanaka and the rest and the Manus likewise are My emanations, being projections of my thought. All this race of men is their progeny.

एतां विभूतिं योगं च मम यो वेत्ति तत्त्वतः ।
सोऽविकम्पेन योगेन युज्यते नात्र संशयः ॥ 7 ॥

Etāṁ vibhūtiṁ yogaṁ ca mama yo vetti tattvataḥ /
so'vikampena yogena yujyate n'ātra saṁśayaḥ //7//

Mama : My *etam* : above-mentioned *vibhūtim* : manifestation of Divine majesties *yogam* : powers *ca* : and *yaḥ* : who *tattvataḥ* : in their true nature *vetti* : understands, *saḥ* : he *avikampena yogena* : in steady and unfaltering communion *yujyate* : unites with; *atra* : about this *na saṁśyaḥ* : there is no doubt.

7. He who knows the truth about this manifestation of My Divine majesties and about My power, gets united with Me in steady and unfaltering communion. There is no doubt about this.

अहं सर्वस्य प्रभवो मत्तः सर्वं प्रवर्तते ।
इति मत्वा भजन्ते मां बुधा भावसमन्विताः ॥ 8 ॥

Ahaṁ sarvasya prabhavo mattaḥ sarvaṁ pravartate /
iti matvā bhajante māṁ budhā bhāva-samanvitāḥ //8//

Aham : I *sarvasya* : of all *prabhavaḥ* : source, *mattaḥ* : from me *sarvam* : all *pravartate* : go forth, *iti* : thus *matvā* : knowing *budhāḥ*: the wise *bhāvasamanvitāḥ* : becoming ecstatic with devotion *mām* : Me *bhajante* : worship.

8. I am the source of all things, from Me all these go forth—knowing thus the wise ones worship Me, being filled with ecstatic devotional fervour .

मच्चित्ता मद्गतप्राणा बोधयन्तः परस्परम् ।
कथयन्तश्च मां नित्यं तुष्यन्ति च रमन्ति च ॥ 9 ॥

Mac-cittā mad-gata-prāṇā bodhayantaḥ parasparam /
kathayantaś ca māṁ nityaṁ tuṣyanti ca ramanti ca //9//

Maccittāḥ : With minds engrossed in Me *madgataprāṇāḥ* : with their vital energies deeply involved in Me *parasparam* : mutually *bodhayantaḥ*: enlightening *kathayantaḥ*: conversing *ca*: and *nityam*: ever *tuṣyanti* : feel contented *ramanti* : feel delighted *ca* : and.

9. With their minds engrossed and their vital energies deeply involved in Me, they are ever contented and delighted by mutually conversing about Me and enlightening each other thereby.

तेषां सततयुक्तानां भजतां प्रीतिपूर्वकम् ।
ददामि बुद्धियोगं तं येन मामुपयान्ति ते ॥ 10 ॥

Teṣāṁ satata-yuktānāṁ bhajatāṁ prīti-pūrvakam /
dadāmi buddhi-yogaṁ taṁ yena mām upayānti te //10//

Yena : By which *te* : they *mām* : Me *upayānti* : attain to *tam* : that *buddhiyogam* : intellectual intuition or intuitive understanding *satatayuktānām* : ever-steadfast in spiritual communion *prītipūrvakam* : with delight *bhajatām* : serving *teṣam* : to them *dadāmi* : give.

10. To those who serve Me with delight and are ever steadfast in spiritual communion, I bestow intuitive understanding by means of which they come to Me.[1]

तेषामेवानुकम्पार्थमहमज्ञानजं तमः ।
नाशयाम्यात्मभावस्थो ज्ञानदीपेन भास्वता ॥ 11 ॥

Teṣām ev'ānukamp'ārtham aham ajñāna-jam tamaḥ /
nāśayāmy ātma-bhāva-stho jñāna-dīpena bhāsvatā //11//

Teṣām : For them *anukampārtham* : out of compassion *eva* : sheer *aham* : I *ātmabhāvasthaḥ* : residing as the innermost self *ajñānajam tamaḥ* : darkness born of ignorance *bhāsvatā*: brilliant *jñānadīpena:* by the lamp of wisdom *nāśayāmi* : destroy.

11. Out of sheer compassion for them, residing within as their innermost self, I destroy the darkness born of ignorance in them by the brilliant lamp of wisdom.[2]

अर्जुन उवाच

परं ब्रह्म परं धाम पवित्रं परमं भवान् ।
पुरुषं शाश्वतं दिव्यमादिदेवमजं विभुम् ॥ 12 ॥

आहुस्त्वामृषयः सर्वे देवर्षिर्नारदस्तथा ।
असितो देवलो व्यासः स्वयं चैव ब्रवीषि मे ॥ 13 ॥

Arjuna uvāca:

Paraṁ brahma paraṁ dhāma pavitraṁ paramaṁ bhavān /
puruṣaṁ śāśvataṁ divyam ādi-devam ajaṁ vibhum //12//

Āhus tvām ṛṣayaḥ sarve deva'rṣir Nāradas tathā /
Asito Devalo Vyāsaḥ svayaṁ c'aiva bravīṣi me //13//

Param brahma : Supreme Brahman *param dhāma* : supreme Abode *paramam* : supreme *pavitram* : purifier (the Holy) *bhavān* : Thou art. *Tvam* : Thou *śāśvatam* : eternal *divyam*: divine *ādidevam*: first among the Devas *ajam* : unborn *vibhum* : all-pervading *puruṣam* : Person *sarve* : all *ṛṣayaḥ* : Rishis *āhuḥ* : proclaim. *Tathā* : Similarly *devarṣiḥ* : Rishi among the Devas *Nāradaḥ* : Nārada *Asitaḥ* : Asita *Devalaḥ* : Devala *Vyāsaḥ* : Vyāsa (āhuḥ : proclaim); *svayam ca* : and Thyself *eva* : too *me* : to me *bravīṣi* : sayest.

Arjuna said:

12-13. Thou art the Supreme Brahman, the Supreme Abode, the utterly Holy. Thou art the eternal divine Person—the birthless and all-pervading Divinity supreme. All the Rishis proclaim this—the divine sage Nārada as also Asita, Devala and Vyāsa; Thou Thyself too dost tell Me the same.

सर्वमेतदृतं मन्ये यन्मां वदसि केशव ।
न हि ते भगवन्व्यक्तिं विदुर्देवा न दानवाः ॥ 14 ॥

Sarvam etad ṛtaṁ manye yan māṁ vadasi Keśava /
nahi te bhagavan vyaktiṁ vidur devā na dānavāḥ //14//

Keśava : O Keśava! *mām* : to me *yat* : what *vadasi* : Thou sayest, *etat* : that *sarvam* : all *ṛtam* : as true *manye* : I deem. *Bhagavan* : O Lord *te vyaktim* : Thy manifestation *devāḥ* : The Devas *na viduh* : do not know *hi* : indeed, *dānavāḥ* : Dānavas *na* : not.

14. O Keśava! Whatever Thou hast told me, I deem as true. Verily, O Lord, neither the Devas nor the Dānavas know what Thy manifestations are.

स्वयमेवात्मनात्मानं वेत्थ त्वं पुरुषोत्तम ।
भूतभावन भूतेश देवदेव जगत्पते ॥ 15 ॥

Svyam ev' ātman' ātmānaṁ vettha tvaṁ Puruṣottama /
bhūta-bhāvana bhūt'eśa deva-deva jagat-pate //15//

Puruṣottama : O Thou the highest of all beings! *bhūtabhāvana* : O Creator of all! *bhūteśa* : O Lord of all! *deva deva* : O God of gods! *jagatpate* : O ruler of the worlds! *tvam* : Thou *eva* : alone *svayam* : Thyself *ātmānam* : Thyself *ātmanā* : by Thyself *vettha* : knowest.

15. O Thou the highest of all beings! O Creator of all! O Lord of all! O God of gods! O Ruler of the world! Thou art known only to Thyself through self-intuition.

वक्तुमर्हस्यशेषेण दिव्या ह्यात्मविभूतयः ।
याभिर्विभूतिभिर्लोकानिमांस्त्वं व्याप्य तिष्ठसि ॥ 16 ॥

Vaktum arhasy aśeṣeṇa divyā hy ātma-vibhūtayaḥ /
yābhir vibhūtibhir lokān imāṁs tvam vyāpya tiṣṭhasi //16//

Yābhiḥ : By which *vibhūtibhiḥ* : manifestations of glory *imān* : these *lokān* : worlds *vyāpya* : pervading *tiṣṭhasi* : abidest (in them), *divyam* : divine *ātmavibhūtayaḥ* : manifestations of the glory of Thyself *aśeṣena* : in entirety *tvam* : Thou *vaktum arhasi* : shouldst tell *hi* : verily.

16. Deign to speak to me in entirety of those divine manifestations of Thy glory, whereby, pervading all these worlds, Thou abidest in them and beyond.

कथं विद्यामहं योगिंस्त्वां सदा परिचिन्तयन् ।
केषु केषु च भावेषु चिन्त्योऽसि भगवन्मया ॥ 17 ॥

Kathaṁ vidyām ahaṁ yogiṁs tvāṁ sadā paricintayan /
keṣu-keṣu ca bhāveṣu cintyo'si bhagavan mayā //17//

Yogin: O Yogin! *aham* : I *katham* : how *sadā* : always *paricintayan*: meditating *tvām* : Thee *vidyām* : may know. *Bhagavan* : O Lord! *keṣu keṣu* : in what all *bhāveṣu* : aspects *ca* : and *mayā* : by me *cintyaḥ* : to be contemplated *tvam* : Thou *asi* : art.

17. How am I to know Thee, O Yogin, through constant meditation? In what all aspects shouldst Thou be contemplated upon by me, O Lord?

विस्तरेणात्मनो योगं विभूतिं च जनार्दन ।
भूयः कथय तृप्तिर्हि श्रृण्वतो नास्ति मेऽमृतम् ॥ 18 ॥

Vistareṇ'ātmano yogaṁ vibhūtiṁ ca Janārdana /
bhūyaḥ kathaya tṛptir hi śṛṇvato n'āsti me'mṛtam //18//

Janārdana : O Janārdana! *ātmanaḥ* : Thy own *yogam* : Yogic power *vibhūtim* : majesty *ca* : and *vistareṇa* : in detail *bhūyaḥ* : again *kathaya* : speak of. *Hi* : For *amṛtam* : nectarine words *śṛṇvataḥ me* : to me who am hearing *tṛptiḥ* : satiation *na asti* : does not exist.

18. O Janārdana! Tell me again and again of Thy divine powers and majesties; for I am ever eager to hear more and more of Thy nectarine words.

श्रीभगवानुवाच
हन्त ते कथयिष्यामि दिव्या ह्यात्मविभूतयः ।
प्राधान्यतः कुरुश्रेष्ठ नास्त्यन्तो विस्तरस्य मे ॥ 19 ॥

Śri Bhagavān uvāca:
Hanta te kathayiṣyāmi divyā hy ātma-vibhūtayaḥ /
prādhānyataḥ Kuru-śreṣṭha n'āstyanto vistarasya me //19//

Hanta : Behold *Kuruśreṣṭha* : O the best of the Kurus! *divyāḥ* : divine *ātmavibhūtayaḥ* :self-manifestations *prādhānyataḥ* : according to their importance *te* : to you *kathayiṣyāmi* : I shall tell; *hi* : for *vistarasya* : of the details *antaḥ* : end *na asti* : is not.

The Blessed Lord said:
19. Behold, O best of the Kurus! I shall declare unto you what My divine self-manifestations are; but I shall mention only the chief of them. For, there is no end to their details.[3]

अहमात्मा गुडाकेश सर्वभूताशयस्थितः ।
अहमादिश्च मध्यं च भूतानामन्त एव च ॥ 20 ॥

Aham ātmā Guḍākeśa sarva-bhūt'āśaya-sthitaḥ /
aham ādiś ca madhyaṁ ca bhūtānām anta eva ca //20//

Guḍākeśa : O conqueror of sleep *sarvabhūtāśayasthitaḥ* : residing in the heart of every being *ātmā* : the self *aham* : I am, *bhūtānām* : of all beings *ādiḥ* : beginning *ca* : and *madhyam* : middle (of life-span) *ca* : and *antaḥ* : end *ca* : and *aham* : I *eva* : also.

20. O Arjuna! I am the Self residing in the heart of every being. I am their beginning, their life-span, and their end.

आदित्यानामहं विष्णुर्ज्योतिषां रविरंशुमान् ।
मरीचिर्मरुतामस्मि नक्षत्राणामहं शशी ॥ 21 ॥

Ādityānām ahaṁ Visnur jyotiṣāṁ ravir aṁśumān /
Marīcir Marutām asmi nakṣatrāṇām aham śaśī //21//

Ādityānām : Of Ādityas *Viṣṇuḥ* : Viṣṇu *aham* : I am, *jyotiṣām* among luminaries *aṁśumān* : radiant *raviḥ* : sun, *marutām* : among the Maruts (winds) *Marīciḥ* : Marīci *asmi* : I am, *nakṣatrāṇām* : among the asterisms *śaśī*: moon *aham* : I am.

21. Of the twelve Ādityas (suns), I am Viṣṇu; among the luminaries I am the radiant sun; among the seven Maruts (winds) I am Marīci; and of the Nakṣatras (asterisms), I am the moon.

वेदानां सामवेदोऽस्मि देवानामस्मि वासवः ।
इन्द्रियाणां मनश्चास्मि भूतानामस्मि चेतना ॥ 22 ॥

Vedānāṁ sāma-vedo'smi devānām asmi Vāsavaḥ /
indriyāṇāṁ manaś c'āsmi bhūtānām asmi cetanā //22//

Vedānām : Of the Vedas *sāmavedaḥ* : the Sama Veda *asmi* : I am, *devānām* : of the Devas *vāsavaḥ* : Indra *asmi* : I am, *indriyāṇām*: among Indriyas *manaḥ* : mind *ca* : and *asmi* : I am, *bhūtānām* : in beings *cetanā* : intelligence *asmi* : I am.

22. Of the Vedas, I am the Sāma Veda; among the Devas, I am Indra; of the senses, I am the mind; and of living beings, I am intelligence.

रुद्राणां शंकरश्चास्मि वित्तेशो यक्षरक्षसाम् ।
वसूनां पावकश्चास्मि मेरुः शिखरिणामहम् ॥ 23 ॥

Rudrāṇāṁ Śaṅkaraś c'āsmi vitt'eśo yakṣa-rakṣasām /
Vasūnāṁ pāvakaś c'āsmi Meruḥ śikhariṇām aham //23//

Rudrāṇām : Of the Rudras *Śaṅkaraḥ* : Śaṅkara *ca* : and *asmi* : I am, *yakṣarakṣasām* : among Yakṣās and Rākṣasas (Demigods and Titans), *Vitteśaḥ* : I am the Lord of wealth (Kubera), *Vasūnāṁ pāvakaḥ* : of the Vasus I am Agni *ca* : and *asmi* : I am, *śikhariṇām* : of mountains *Meruḥ* : Mount Meru *aham* : I am.

23. Of the eleven Rudras, I am Śaṅkara; among the Demigods and Titans, I am Kubera; of the eight Vasus, I am Agni; among mountains, I am the Meru.

पुरोधसां च मुख्यं मां विद्धि पार्थ बृहस्पतिम् ।
सेनानीनामहं स्कन्दः सरसामस्मि सागरः ॥ 24 ॥

Purodhasāṁ ca mukhyaṁ māṁ viddhi Pārtha Bṛhaspatim /
senānīnām aham skandaḥ sarasāṁ asmi sāgaraḥ //24//

Pārtha : O son of Pṛthā! *Māṁ* : Me *Purodhasām* : among priests *mukhyam* : the chief *Bṛhaspatiṁ* : Bṛhaspati, the priest of the Devas *viddhi* : know, *senānīnām* : among war-lords *skandaḥ* : Skanda or Subrahmaṇya *aham* : I am, *sarasām* : of lakes *sāgaraḥ* : ocean *asmi* : I am.

24. Among the priests, know me to be the chief of them—Bṛhaspati, the priest of the Devas, O Arjuna. Among the war-lords I am Skanda; among the water reservoirs, I am the ocean.

महर्षीणां भृगुरहं गिरामस्म्येकमक्षरम् ।
यज्ञानां जपयज्ञोऽस्मि स्थावराणां हिमालयः ॥ 25 ॥

Maharṣīṇāṁ Bhṛgur ahaṁ girām asmy ekam akṣaram /
yajñānāṁ japa-yajño'smi sthāvarāṇām Himālayaḥ //25//

Maharṣīṇām : Among the great sages *Bhṛguḥ* : the sage Bhṛgu *aham* : I am, *girām* : among utterances *ekamakṣaram* : the mono-syllable 'Om', *yajñānām* : among forms of worship *japayajñaḥ* : silent repetition of Divine names *asmi* : I am, *sthāvarāṇām* : among immovable objects *Himālayaḥ* : I am Mount Himālaya.

25. Among the great sages, I am Bhṛgu; among utterances I am the mono-syllabled 'Om'; among holy offerings, I am the offering of Japa (silent repetition of Divine names); among immovable objects, I am the mount Himālaya.

अश्वत्थः सर्ववृक्षाणां देवर्षीणां च नारदः ।
गन्धर्वाणां चित्ररथः सिद्धानां कपिलो मुनिः ॥ 26 ॥

Aśvatthaḥ sarva-vṛkṣāṇāṁ devarṣīṇāṁ ca Nāradaḥ /
gandharvāṇāṁ Citrarathaḥ siddhānāṁ Kapilo muniḥ //26//

Sarvavṛkṣāṇām: Among all trees *aśvatthaḥ* : I am the holy fig tree, *devarṣiṇām* : among the divine sages *Nāradaḥ* : I am Nārada, *ca* : and *gandharvāṇām* : among the celestial artistes *Citrarathaḥ* : I am Citraratha, *siddhānām* : among perfected ones *Kapilaḥ muniḥ* : I am Kapila the sage.

26. Among all trees, I am the holy fig-tree; among the divine sages, I am Nārada; among celestial artistes, I am Citraratha; among perfected souls, I am Kapila the sage.

उच्चैःश्रवसमश्वानां विद्धि माममृतोद्भवम् ।
ऐरावतं गजेन्द्राणां नराणां च नराधिपम् ॥ 27 ॥

Uccaiḥśrvasam aśvānāṁ viddhi māṁ amṛt'odbhavam /
Airāvataṁ gaj'endrāṇāṁ narāṇāṁ ca nar'ādhipam //27//

Aśvānām: Among horses *amṛtodbhavam*: emerged at the time of the churning of the milk-ocean for ambrosia *Uccaiśravasam* : the horse Uccaiśravas, *gajendrāṇām* : of lordly elephants *Airāvatam* : the white elephant Airāvata, *narāṇāṁ* : among men *narādhipam* : king (leader of men) *ca* : and *mām* : Me *viddhi* : know.

27. Among horses know Me to be the nectar-born Uccaiśravas, among the lordly elephants, the white celestial elephant Airāvata; and among men, persons endowed with leadership.

आयुधानामहं वज्रं धेनूनामस्मि कामधुक् ।
प्रजनश्चास्मि कन्दर्पः सर्पाणामस्मि वासुकिः ॥ 28 ॥

Āyudhānām ahaṁ vajraṁ dhenūnām asmi kāma-dhuk /
prajanaś c'āsmi Kandarpaḥ sarpāṇām asmi Vāsukiḥ //28//

Ayudhānām : Among weapons *vajram* : thunderbolt *aham* : I am, *dhenūnam* : among cows *Kāmadhuk* : Kamadhenu *asmi* : I am, *prajanaḥ* : of progenitors *Kandarpaḥ* : god of love *asmi* : I am, *sarpāṇām* : among serpents *Vāsukiḥ* : Vāsuki *asmi* : I am *ca* : and.

28. Among weapons I am the thunderbolt; among cows, Kāmadhenu the celestial cow of plenty; among progeni-

tors, Kāma the god of love; and among serpents, Vāsuki.

अनन्तश्चास्मि नागानां वरुणो यादसामहम् ।
पितॄणामर्यमा चास्मि यमः संयमतामहम् ॥ 29 ॥

Anantaś c'āsmi nāgānāṁ Varuṇo yādasām aham /
pitṛṇām Aryamā c'āsmi Yamaḥ saṁyamatām aham //29//

Nāgānām : Among Nāgas *Anantaḥ* : Ananta *ca* : and *asmi* : I am, *yādasām* : among water-dwellers *varuṇaḥ* : Varuṇa *aham* : I am, *pitṛṇām* : among the Pitṛs (manes) *Aryamā* : their leader Aryamā *ca* : and *asmi* : I am, *śamyamatām* : among the enforcers of law *Yamaḥ* : Yama *aham* : I am.

29. Among serpents I am Ananta; among water dwellers I am Varuṇa; among the manes I am Aryamā; and among the enforcers of law I am Yama.

प्रह्लादश्चास्मि दैत्यानां कालः कलयतामहम् ।
मृगाणां च मृगेन्द्रोऽहं वैनतेयश्च पक्षिणाम् ॥ 30 ॥

Prahlādaś c'āsmi daityānāṁ kālaḥ kalayatām aham /
mṛgāṇāṁ ca mṛg'endro'haṁ Vainateyaś ca pakṣiṇām //30//

Daityānām : Among Daityas *Prahlādaḥ* : Prahlāda *ca* : and *asmi* : I am, *kalayatām* : among measurers *kālaḥ* : Time *aham* : I am, *mṛgāṇām* : among animals *mṛgendraḥ* : the lion *ca*: and, *pakṣiṇām*: among birds *vainateyaḥ* : Garuḍa *ca* : and *aham* : I am.

30. Among Daityas I am Prahlāda; among calculators I am time; among animals I am the lion; and among birds I am Garuḍa.

पवनः पवतामस्मि रामः शस्त्रभृतामहम् ।
झषाणां मकरश्चास्मि स्रोतसामस्मि जाह्नवी ॥ 31 ॥

Pavanaḥ pavatām asmi Rāmaḥ saśtra-bhṛtām aham /
jhaṣāṇāṁ makaraś c'āsmi srotasām asmi Jāhnavī //31//

Pavatām : Among purifying agents *pavanaḥ* : wind *asmi* : I am, ***sastrabhṛtām:*** among warriors ***rāmaḥ***: Rāma *aham* : I am, *jhaṣāṇām*: among the fish *makaraḥ* : the shark *asmi* : I am, *srotasām* : among rivers *jāhnavī* : the Ganga *asmi* : I am.

31. Among purifying agents I am the wind; among warriors I am Rāma; among the fish I am the shark; and among rivers I am the Ganga.

सर्गाणामादिरन्तश्च मध्यं चैवाहमर्जुन ।
अध्यात्मविद्या विद्यानां वादः प्रवदतामहम् ॥ 32 ॥

Sargāṇām ādir antaś ca madhyaṁ c'aiv'āham Arjuna /
adhyātma-vidyā vidyānāṁ vādaḥ pravadatām aham //32//

Arjuna : O Arjuna! *sargāṇām* : of the created objects *ādiḥ* : beginning *madhyam* : middle *ca* : and *antaḥ* : end *ca* : and *aham* : I am, *vidyānām* : of sciences *adhyātmavidyā* : I am the science of the spirit, *pravadatām* : among the debators *vādaḥ* : I am the correct reasoning power.

32. O Arjuna! Of the created objects I am the beginning, middle and end; among the sciences, I am the science of the spirit; and of debators I am the power of correct reasoning.

अक्षराणामकारोऽस्मि द्वन्द्वः सामासिकस्य च ।
अहमेवाक्षयः कालो धाताहं विश्वतोमुखः ॥ 33 ॥

Akṣarāṇām akāro'smi dvandvaḥ sāmāsikasya ca /
aham ev'ākṣayaḥ kālo dhātā'haṁ viśvato-mukhaḥ //33//

Akṣarāṇām : Among letters ***akāraḥ*** : letter A ***asmi*** : I am, *sāmāsikasya* : of compound word formations ***dvandvaḥ***: I am the Dvandva compound (the copulative), *aham*: I am *akṣayaḥ*: the never ending *kālaḥ* : time *ca* : and, *viśvatomukhaḥ* : with face on all sides, all-seeing *dhātā* : Brahmā the dispenser of Karma *aham*: I am.

33. Among letters I am the letter 'A', among compound word formations I am the copulative (***dvandva***). I am also the never-ending Time and the all-seeing Brahmā (the dispenser of the Karmas of all beings).

मृत्युः सर्वहरश्चाहमुद्भवश्च भविष्यताम् ।
कीर्तिः श्रीर्वाक्च नारीणां स्मृतिर्मेधा धृतिः क्षमा ॥ 34 ॥

Mṛtyuḥ sarva-haraś c'āham udbhavaś ca bhaviṣyatām /
kīrtiḥ śrīr vāk ca nārīṇāṁ smṛtir medhā dhṛtiḥ kṣamā //34//

Sarvaharaḥ : All-destroying *mṛtyuḥ* : Death *ca* : and, *bhaviṣyatām* : of things yet to come *udbhavaḥ* : origin *ca* : and, *nārīṇām* : of powers considered female *kīrtiḥ* : fame *śrīḥ* : fortune *vāk* : speech *smṛtiḥ* : memory *medhā* : intelligence *dhṛtiḥ* : constancy *kṣamā* : patience *aham* : I am.

34. I am the all-destroying Death, and I am the origin of all that are to come too. Among virtues considered as female I am fame, fortune, speech, memory, intelligence, constancy and patience.

बृहत्साम तथा साम्नां गायत्री छन्दसामहम् ।
मासानां मार्गशीर्षोऽहमृतूनां कुसुमाकरः ॥ 35 ॥

Bṛhat-sāma tathā sāmnāṁ gāyatrī chandasām aham /
māsānāṁ mārgaśīrṣo'ham ṛtūnām kusum'ākaraḥ //35//

Sāmnām : Among Sāma hymns *bṛhatsāmā* : I am the Bṛhatsāman (the Great Chant), *tathā* : so also *chandasām* : among the Vedic metres *gāyatrī* : I am Gāyatrī, *māsānām* : among months *mārgaśīrṣaḥ* : the month Mārgaśīrṣa (Nov-Dec), *ṛtūnām* : of seasons *kusumākaraḥ* : I am the flower-bearing spring.

35. Among the Sāma hymns I am the Bṛhatsāman (the Great Chant); among the Vedic metres, I am the Gāyatrī; among months, I am Mārgaśīrṣa (Nov-Dec.); and among seasons, I am the flower-bearing spring.

द्यूतं छलयतामस्मि तेजस्तेजस्विनामहम् ।
जयोऽस्मि व्यवसायोऽस्मि सत्त्वं सत्त्ववतामहम् ॥ 36 ॥

Dyūtaṁ chalayatām asmi tejas tejasvinām aham /
jayo'smi vyavasāyo'smi sattvaṁ sattvavatām aham //36//

Chalayatām: Of the deceitful *dyūtaḥ* : dicing *asmi* : I am, *tejasvinām*: of the powerful *tejaḥ* : power *aham* : I am, *jayaḥ* : victory *aham asmi* : I am, *vyavasāyaḥ* : determination *asmi* : I am, *sattvavatām*: of the good *sattvam* : goodness *aham* : I am.

36. I am the dicing of the deceitful, the power of the powerful and the goodness of the good. I am victory, determination and constancy too.[4]

वृष्णीनां वासुदेवोऽस्मि पाण्डवानां धनंजयः ।
मुनीनामप्यहं व्यासः कवीनामुशना कविः ॥ 37 ॥

Vṛṣṇīnāṁ Vāsudevósmi Pāṇḍavānāṁ Dhanaṁjayaḥ /
munīnam apy ahaṁ Vyāsah kavīnām Uśanā kaviḥ //37//

Vṛṣṇīnām : Among the Vṛṣṇis *Vāsudevaḥ*; Vāsudeva, *pāṇḍavānām* : among Pāṇḍavas *Dhanamjayaḥ* : Arjuna *asmi* : I am, *api* : also *munīnām* : among sages *Vyāsaḥ* : Vyāsa, *kavīnām* : among poets *Uśanā* : Uśanas *kaviḥ* : the poet *asi* : I am.

37. I am Vāsudeva among the Vṛṣnis and Arjuna among the Pāndavas. I am Vyāsa among sages, and Uśanas (Ācārya Sukra) among the far-sighted.

दण्डो दमयतामस्मि नीतिरस्मि जिगीषताम् ।
मौनं चैवास्मि गुह्यानां ज्ञानं ज्ञानवतामहम् ॥ 38 ॥

Daṇḍo damayatām asmi nītirasmi jigīṣatām /
maunaṁ c'aiv'āsmi guhyānāṁ jñānaṁ jñānavatām aham //38//

Damayatām : Of the disciplinarians *daṇḍaḥ* : rod of chastisement *asmi* : I am, *jigīṣatām* : of those who seek success *nītiḥ* : wise policy *asmi* : I am, *guhyānām* : in the art of secrecy *maunam* : silence *asmi* : I am, *jñānavatām* : of the wise *jñānam* : wisdom *aham* : I am.

38. I am the rod of chastisement in the disciplinarians; I am the wise policy in those seeking success; I am silence in the art of secrecy; and I am wisdom in the wise.

यच्चापि सर्वभूतानां बीजं तदहमर्जुन ।
न तदस्ति विना यत्स्यान्मया भूतं चराचरम् ॥ 39 ॥

Yac c'āpi sarva-bhūtānāṁ bījaṁ tad aham Arjuna /
na tad asti vinā yat syān mayā bhūtaṁ car'ācaram //39//

Arjuna : O Arjuna *sarvabhūtānām* : of all beings *bījam* : seed *yat* : what *ca* : and *tat* : that *aham* : I am, *carācaram* : fleeting and lasting (living and non-living) *yat* : what *bhūtam* : entities *asti* : exist *tat* : that *api* : also, *mayā vinā* : without Me, *na syāt* : cannot exist.

39. Of all beings I am the seed, O Arjuna. Whatever exists in this world, living or non-living, none of them can be, if I were not.

नान्तोऽस्ति मम दिव्यानां विभूतीनां परंतप ।
एष तूद्देशतः प्रोक्तो विभूतेर्विस्तरो मया ॥ 40 ॥

Nā'nto'sti mama divyānāṁ vibhūtīnāṁ paraṁtapa /
eṣa tū'ddeśataḥ prokto vibhūter vistaro mayā //40//

Paraṁtapa : O scorcher of enemies, *mama* : My *divyānām* : divine *vibhūtīnām* : manifestations *antaḥ* : end *na asti* : there is not. *Vibhūteh* : Of the manifestations *eṣaḥ* : this *vistaraḥ* : description *tu* : only *uddeśataḥ* : by way of examples *mayā* : by Me, *proktaḥ* : expounded.

40. O great warrior! There is no end to my divine manifestations. What I have expounded forms only a few of them by way of examples.

यद्यद्विभूतिमत्सत्त्वं श्रीमदूर्जितमेव वा ।
तत्तदेवावगच्छ त्वं मम तेजोंऽशसंभवम् ॥ 41 ॥

Yad-yad vibhūtimat sattvaṁ śrīmad ūrjitam eva vā /
tat-tad evā'vagaccha tvaṁ mama tejo'mśa-sambhavam //41//

Vibūtimat : Endowed with glory *śrīmat* : with attractiveness *ūrjitam*: with vigour *eva vā* : also *yat yat* : whatever *sattvam* : entities (exist) *tat tat* : all that *mama* : My *tejomśasambhavam* : born of a fragment of my splendour avagaecha : understand.

41. Whatever there is endowed with extraordinary glory, attractiveness and vigour, know all that to be born of a fragment of my power.

अथवा बहुनैतेन किं ज्ञातेन तवार्जुन ।
विष्टभ्याहमिदं कृत्स्नमेकांशेन स्थितो जगत् ॥ 42 ॥

Athavā bahun'aitena kiṁ jñātena tavā'rjuna /
viṣṭabhy'āham idaṁ kṛtsnaṁ ek'āmśena sthito jagat //42//

Arjuna : O Arjuna! *athavā* : but then *bahunā* : by detailed *jñānena* : knowledge *etena* : by this *tava* : to you *kim* : what avails? *Kṛtsnam*: whole *idam* : this *jagat* : world *ekāmśena* : by one single fragment *viṣṭabhya* : supporting *aham sthitaḥ* : I remain.

42. But then, of what avail is this detailed understanding of my manifestations to you, O Arjuna! Supporting this migthty universe with but one single fragment of My self, I remain unchanged and transcendent.

ओं तत्सदिति श्रीमद्भगवद्गीतासूपनिषत्सु ब्रह्मविद्यायां
योगशास्त्रे श्रीकृष्णार्जुनसंवादे विभूति
योगो नाम दशमोऽध्यायः ॥ 10 ॥

NOTES

1. *Vr.*10: The exact meaning of *Buddhi Yoga* is difficult to arrive at. It must mean the rousing of a new power of understanding, which may be described as intuitive power. The word 'intuition' is a very treacherous and deceptive word. Many people

use it for irrational and arbitrary conclusions of theirs, which are the mere projections of their desire-nature. A true intuition can come only in the mind of one who is pure and free from desires and passions. He must be a *satata yuktaḥ*, one whose inner life is fully integrated by the practice of self-control and mental discipline. The so-called intuitions of others are only projections of their desires by way of wish-fulfilment. The mind must be free from all desires born of sensate life. The mind should become free from modes based on such desires. It must become moulded into a single mode of aspiration for Truth—*bhajatām prītipūrvakam* or yearning for Him with whole-hearted love. To such persons the Lord gives *Buddhi-yoga* or intuitive power. It is a new capacity of understanding. Just as sense powers and rationality give us capacity to know certain vistas of Reality, intuition gives a new view of things dominated by the Divine Presence. It is entirely different from the so-called intuitions of desire-bound people.

2. *Vr.*11: It is stated here that the enlightenment thus given is a gift of God out of His grace—*anukampārtham*. It is a purely Bhakti idea, and will suit only a Bhedābheda metaphysics or identity in difference, in which God, though not different, is distinct from the Jīva in ignorance. But He is not something extraneous to the Jīva. This is shown by the expression *ātmabhāvasthaḥ*—by revealing His presence in the innermost core of the Jīva. That this intuition is not any kind of wish-fulfilment, but a revelation of the nature of things is shown by its comparison to what happens when a light is introduced where darkness was reigning. A new vista opens itself to the spirit so illumined. Thus the Gītā clearly accepts the doctrines of Divine grace and the self-sufficiency of Bhakti to give enlightenment through the bestowal of Divine grace. The place of self-effort is to aspire for Him with all one's heart and soul, but its fulfilment in spiritual realization depends entirely on His grace..

3. *Vr.*19: Vibhūti means special manifestations of Divine majesty, power and glory. The word arises from *Vi* + *bhū*, meaning 'arise, expand, appear'. The whole of Nature, including the mighty universe and what is experienced in it, is a declaration of the power and majesty of the Creator. Three attitudes are possible in regard to things experienced in Nature. Sri Ramakrishna expounds these attitudes in a simple analogy of a well-designed

garden. A common sight-seer goes there and sees the fine flowers. His interest is only to pluck some flowers for his buttonholes and to carry home a handful of them. A botanist goes there. He is interested in the scientific side of it, and studies the plants and their flowers from that point of view. A man of a devotional and philosophic mind goes there. The design of the whole garden and the beauty of flowers charm him, but in place of being merely taken up with them, he looks for the designer of the garden whose wisdom is reflected in it. These three approaches are possible towards Nature as a whole. For the practical man it is only some thing to be exploited for his enjoyment. For a scientist, who is actuated by curiosity to know, it is something to be investigated and studied for the sake of understanding it. For a spiritual man, the wisdom and power revealed in Nature is a pointer to Nature's God—to Him whose mere shadow Nature is. This last is the view that the Hindu scriptures take. Creation, sustentation and dissolution form an overflow of Divine Bliss. These are no doubt an expression, but only an infinitely small expression, of His majesty and power. So the Gītā, in concluding the section on Vibhūtis, gives out as the Bhagavān's declaration, "Supporting this whole universe with a fragment of My self, I remain unchanging and transcendent."

Man's mind is generally outward-going. So if he is educated into the faith that all that he sees outside is an expression of His glory, that will be a way to teach him remembrance of God through all perceptions, and thus it will add to the width and depth of his devotion. So it is in order to help man with a means for generating and strengthening devotion to God, that the Vibhūtis are enumerated. In this enumeration only some very striking items are mentioned. It must be taken as covering all other aspects also.

It is perhaps to convey this very idea of Nature as a pointer to the Divine that the **Iśopaniṣad** declares: "All this is fit to be covered with the Lord—all these that are moving in this moving world."

4. *Vr.*36: It is rather puzzling to note that dicing, which is a form of gambling, and which is recognised here itself as a field for the deceitful, is called a Vibhūti of the Lord. It is definitely a disvalue and a source of evil. All the other manifestations

mentioned here are values noble and desirable. Can it be that dicing is introduced here in a symbolic way, to indicate that even what man considers the opposite of virtue, has also got its ultimate source in Him? Both Vidya and Avidya are aspects of His Māya, and must be considered as having their support in Him. Otherwise we shall have to posit a Devil, an anti-God, as some other religions do, for explaining evil. If we accept that, this anti-God or Devil also comes within the will of God; then it ceases to be different from the Avidya theory. The other alternative of accepting the Devil as outside God's will, is to accept another existence and power equal to God Himself. This is repugnant to the teachings of Hindu scriptures.

The mention of dicing in the *Bhagavad Gītā*, which is a part of *Mahābhārata,* seems to be meaningful in another way. It is a deceitful game of dice, by which the Pāṇḍava brothers are deprived of their kingdom, leading to the great Mahābhārata war fought for the recovery of the lost kingdom. It is through this war that Kṛṣṇa fulfils the purpose of his Incarnation in two ways — one, by effecting the destruction of all the evil and oppressive rulers, and two, by using the occasion for delivering His great message to mankind through the Gītā, with Arjuna as the medium for it. Can it therefore be a suggestion that what is considered evil also will appear meaningful, when the full perspective of the Divine plan is gained in the long run!

5. *Vr.*42: This verse gives the general purpose of the enumeration of Divine manifestations given above. They are just to draw man's attention to a few of the very striking manifestations of divine power, glory and wisdom. Through them it is taught that the whole of the manifested universe, which is so vast that human thought can contemplate it only very partially, is but a faint reflection of the Divine. In this way the outward-going mind is trained to contemplate the Divine. Through this, devotion to Him is generated, and augmented in those who have already the germs of it in them.

Chapter XI

विश्वरूपदर्शनयोगः

THE VISION OF THE COSMIC FORM

Summary

The Vision Described: (1-55) Arjuna now wants to have a direct experience of the Divine majesty, the source and support of all that exists. The Lord gives him a new power of insight with which Arjuna becomes capable of having a direct experience of the Divine. The Lord reveals to him His cosmic form in which he finds in an instant all that exists, past, present and future, spread out as it were as part and parcel of an all-comprehending Whole, a Divine Person, whose awful majesty and stupefying splendour are too much for him to bear. He finds that all beings are helplessly drawn and absorbed into His being—by inexorable Time, with which He declares His identity. Arjuna experiences that there is only one Will, namely the Divine will, and that the will of all the centres of consciousness included in His being are but instruments for serving Him and accomplishing His purposes. He finds that all the armies mobilised and arrayed for battle have already been destroyed by the Lord's will, and that he himself is just an occasion for this.

Transformation of Arjuna: The experience shakes Arjuna to the very core of his being and he loses himself in utter self-abnegation and devotional absorption. At the end of it, Arjuna is informed by the Lord that such an experience as he has had is very rare, and only through unswerving devotion can man achieve this. So he is exhorted to be a devotee of the Lord, carrying out His will, looking upon Him as the highest, and having attachment for nothing but the Lord.

अर्जुन उवाच

मदनुग्रहाय परमं गुह्यमध्यात्मसंज्ञितम् ।
यत्त्वयोक्तं वचस्तेन मोहोऽयं विगतो मम ॥ 1 ॥

Arjuna uvāca:

Madanugrahāya paramaṁ guhyam adhyātma saṁjñitam /
yat tvay'oktaṁ vacas tena moho'yaṁ vigato mama //1//

Madanugrahāya: For blessing me *paramam* : the highest *guhyam* : known only in select circles *adhyātmasaṁjñitam* : what concerns the spirit *yat* : what *vacaḥ* : instruction *tvayā* : by Thee *uktam* : spoken, *tena* : by that *mama* : my *ayam* : this *mohaḥ* : delusion *vigataḥ* : is gone.

Arjuna said:

1. Thy instructions on the grand Mystery, the highest spiritual Truth, imparted to me out of Thy abounding grace, have dispelled my delusion.

भवाप्ययौ हि भूतानां श्रुतौ विस्तरशो मया ।
त्वत्तः कमलपत्राक्ष माहात्म्यमपि चाव्ययम् ॥ 2 ॥

Bhav'āpyayau hi bhūtānāṁ śrutau vistaraśo mayā
tvattaḥ kamala-patr'ākṣa māhātmyam api c'āvyayam //2//

Kamalapatrākṣa : O lotus eyed one! *tvattaḥ* : from Thee *bhūtānām* : of creatures *bhavāpyayau* : origin and dissolution *mayā* : by me *vistaraśaḥ* : at length *śrutau* : have been heard *hi* : indeed; *avyayam*: undecaying *māhātmyam* : greatness *api ca* : also.

2. O lotus-eyed One! From Thee I have heard at length about the origin and dissolution of creatures as also about Thy greatness that knows no decay.[1]

एवमेतद्यथात्थ त्वमात्मानं परमेश्वर ।
द्रष्टुमिच्छामि ते रूपमैश्वरं पुरुषोत्तम ॥ 3 ॥

Evam etad yath'āttha tvam ātmānaṁ param'eśvara /
draṣṭum icchāmi te rūpam aiśvaraṁ puruṣ'ottama //3//

Parameśvara : O Supreme Being! *tvam* : Thou *ātmānaṁ* : Thyself *yathā* : in what way *āttha* : describe *evam* : in that way *etat* : it is *Puruṣottama* : O greatest among men! *te* : Thy *aiśvaram* : as the God of all *rūpam* : form *draṣṭum* : to see *icchāmi* : I desire.

3. Thou art, O Lord Supreme, even as what Thou hast declared Thyself to be. (I understand and accept it.) Yet I now desire to see that form of Thine as the Lord of all.

मन्यसे यदि तच्छक्यं मया द्रष्टुमिति प्रभो ।
योगेश्वर ततो मे त्वं दर्शयात्मानमव्ययम् ॥ 4 ॥

Manyase yadi tac chakyaṁ mayā draṣṭum iti prabho /
yog'eśvara tato me tvaṁ darśay'ātmānam avyayam //4//

Prabho : O Lord *tat* : that *draṣṭum* : to experience *mayā* : by me *śakyam* : possible *iti* : thus *yadi* : if *manyase* : Thou thinkest, *tataḥ* : then *yogeśvara* : O Lord of Yoga! *tvam* : Thou *avyayam* : immutable *ātmānam* : form *me* : to me *darśaya* : reveal.

4. If, O Lord, Thou thinkest me worthy of experiencing that immutable form of Thine, then deign to reveal the same to me, O Thou Master of all Yoga!

श्रीभगवानुवाच
पश्य मे पार्थ रूपाणि शतशोऽथ सहस्रशः ।
नानाविधानि दिव्यानि नानावर्णाकृतीनि च ॥ 5 ॥

Srī bhagavān uvāca:
Paśya me Pārtha rūpāṇi śataśo'tha sahasraśaḥ /
nānā-vidhāni divyāni nānā-varṇ'ākṛtīni ca //5//

Pārtha : O son of Pṛthā! *nānāvidhāni* : manifold *nānāvarṇākṛtīni*: of varied hues and shapes *ca* : and *me* : My *śataśaḥ* : in hundreds *atha* : and *sahsraśaḥ* : in thousands *divyāni* : divine *rūpāṇi* : forms *paśya* : see.

The Blessed Lord said:

5. Behold, O Pārtha, My manifold forms in their hundreds and thousands—all divine and all of varied hues and shapes.

पश्यादित्यान्वसून् रुद्रानश्विनौ मरुतस्तथा ।
बहून्यदृष्टपूर्वाणि पश्याश्चर्याणि भारत ॥ 6 ॥

Paśy'ādityān Vasūn Rudrān Aśvinau Marutas tathā /
bahūny adṛṣṭa-pūrvāṇi paśy'āścaryāṇi Bhārata //6//

Bhārata : O scion of Bharata's clan! *ādityān* : suns *vasūn* : Vasus *rudrān* : Rudras *aśvinau* : the pair of Aśvins *marutaḥ* : winds *atha* : likewise *paśya* : behold; *tathā* : in the same way *adṛṣṭapūrvāṇi* : of forms unseen before *bahūni* : many *āścaryāṇi* : marvels *paśya* : behold.

6. Behold the Adityas and the Vasus, the Rudras and the Aśvins, and the Maruts likewise — behold these marvels unseen by any before, O scion of Bharata's clan!

इहैकस्थं जगत्कृत्स्नं पश्याद्य सचराचरम् ।
मम देहे गुडाकेश यच्चान्यद्द्रष्टुमिच्छसि ॥ 7 ॥

Ih'aika-sthaṁ jagat kṛtsnaṁ paśy'ādya sacar'ācaram /
mama dehe Guḍākeśa yac c'ānyad draṣṭum icchasi //7//

Guḍākeśa : O conqueror of sleep! *sacarācaram* : with objects moving and not moving *kṛtsnam* : entire *jagat* : world *anyat yat* : whatever else *ca* : and *draṣṭum* : to see *icchasi* : desire, *tat* : that *mama* : My *dehe* : in body *iha* : here *ekastham* : abiding as a unity *adya* : now *paśya* : see.

7. O conqueror of sleep! Behold here and now the whole of this universe of conscious and unconscious entities as also

anything else you desire to experience—all abiding as a unity in My body.

न तु मां शक्यसे द्रष्टुमनेनैव स्वचक्षुषा ।
दिव्यं ददामि ते चक्षुः पश्य मे योगमैश्वरम् ॥ 8 ॥

Na tu māṁ śakyase draṣṭum anen'aiva sva-cakṣuṣā /
divyaṁ dadāmi te cakṣuḥ paśya me yogam aiśvaram //8//

Anena : By this *svacakṣuṣā eva* : merely with your physical eye *mām* : Me *draṣṭum* : to see *na śakyase* : is not possible; *tu* : at all *divyam* : divine *cakṣuḥ* : eyes *te* : to you *dadāmi* : I give; *me* : My *aiśvaraṁ yogam* : power as the Lord of all might *paśya* : behold.

8. You cannot have an experience of Me merely with your physical eye. I therefore give you the power of divine vision. Behold with that My power as the Lord of all.

संजय उवाच

एवमुक्त्वा ततो राजन्महायोगेश्वरो हरिः ।
दर्शयामास पार्थाय परमं रूपमैश्वरम् ॥ 9 ॥

Sañjaya uvāca
Evam uktvā tato rājan mahā-yog'eśvaro hariḥ /
darśayāmāsa Pārthāya paramaṁ rūpam aiśvaram //9//

Rājan : O King! *mahāyogeśvaraḥ* : master of spiritual powers *Hariḥ* : Hari *evam* : in this way *uktvā* : saying *tataḥ* : afterwards *paramam* : transcendent *aiśvaram* : Divine *rūpam* : form *pārthāya* : to Arjuna *darśayāmāsa* : revealed.

Sanjaya said:

9. So saying, Hari, the Master of all spiritual powers, now revealed to Arjuna His transcendent form as the Lord of the universe.

अनेकवक्त्रनयनमनेकाद्भुतदर्शनम् ।
अनेकदिव्याभरणं दिव्यानेकोद्यतायुधम् ॥ 10 ॥

Aneka-vaktra-nayanam anek' ādbhuta-darśanam /
aneka-divy' ābharaṇaṁ divy' ānek' odyat' āyudham /10//

Anekavaktranayanam : Having countless faces and eyes *anekādbhuta darśanam* : exhibiting countless features provoking wonder *anekadivyābharaṇam* : bedecked with countless celestial ornaments *divyānekodyatāyudham* : equipped with countless divine weapons held aloft.

10. Having countless faces and eyes; exhibiting countless features; provoking wonder; bedecked with countless celestial ornaments; equipped with countless divine weapons held aloft;

दिव्यमाल्याम्बरधरं दिव्यगन्धानुलेपनम् ।
सर्वाश्चर्यमयं देवमनन्तं विश्वतोमुखम् ॥ 11 ॥

Divya-maly' āmbara-dharaṁ divya-gandh' ānulepanam /
sarv' āścaryamayaṁ devam anantaṁ viśvato-mukham //11//

Divyamālyāmbaradharam : Wearing celestial garlands and vestments *divyagandhānulepanam* : anointed with celestial unguents and perfumes *sarvāścaryamayam* : replete with expressions of most surprising marvel *devam* : the divinity *anantam* : boundless *viśvatomukham* : with face everywhere.

11. Wearing heavenly garlands and vestments; anointed with celestial unguents and perfumes; replete with incredible, marvellous features—a divinity boundless and all-seeing.

दिवि सूर्यसहस्रस्य भवेद्युगपदुत्थिता ।
यदि भाः सदृशी सा स्याद्भासस्तस्य महात्मनः ॥ 12 ॥

Divi sūrya-sahasrasya bhaved yugapad utthitā /
yadi bhāḥ sadṛśī sā syād bhāsas tasya mah' ātmanaḥ //12//

Divi : In the sky *sūryasahasrasya* : of innumerable suns *bhāḥ* : brilliance *yugapat* : all at once *utthitā bhavet* : were to blaze forth *yadi* : if, *sā* : that *tasya* : of that *mahātmanaḥ* : of the great Being *bhāsaḥ* : splendour *sadṛśī syāt* : would be like.

12. What brilliance there would have been if a thousand suns were to blaze forth all of a sudden in the sky—to that was comparable the splendour of that great Being.

तत्रैकस्थं जगत्कृत्स्नं प्रविभक्तमनेकधा ।
अपश्यद्देवदेवस्य शरीरे पाण्डवस्तदा ॥ 13 ॥

Tatr'aika-sthaṁ jagat kṛtsnaṁ pravibhaktam anekadhā /
apaśyad deva-devasya śarīre Pāṇḍavas tadā //13//

Anekadhā pravibhaktam : Divided into the manifold *kṛtsnam* : the entire *jagat* : the world *devadevasya* : of the God of all divinities *tatra* : there *śarīre* : in the body *ekastham* : as abiding in the unity of His being *tadā* : then *Pāṇḍavaḥ* : the son of Pāṇḍu *apaśyat* : saw.

13. There in the body of that God of all divinities, the son of Pāṇḍu then saw the whole universe — a multiplicity abiding unified in His being.[2]

ततः स विस्मयाविष्टो हृष्टरोमा धनंजयः ।
प्रणम्य शिरसा देवं कृताञ्जलिरभाषत ॥ 14 ॥

Tataḥ sa vismay'āviṣṭo hṛṣṭa-romā dhanaṁjayaḥ /
praṇamya śirasā devaṁ kṛt'āñjalir abhāṣata //14//

Tataḥ : Thereupon *vismayāviṣṭaḥ* : overwhelmed with amazement *hṛṣṭaromāḥ* : with hair standing on end *saḥ* : that *dhanamjayaḥ*: Arjuna *devam* : to the Lord *śirasā praṇamya* : bowing with his head *kṛtāñjaliḥ* : with hands folded in salutation *abhāṣata* : said.

14. Thereupon Arjuna, struck with amazement and his hairs standing on end, bowed down before the Lord and said with hands folded in salutation.

अर्जुन उवाच

पश्यामि देवांस्तव देव देहे सर्वांस्तथा भूतविशेषसङ्घान् ।
ब्रह्माणमीशं कमलासनस्थमृषींश्च सर्वानुरगांश्च दिव्यान् ॥ 15 ॥

Arjuna uvāca
Paśyāmi devāṁs tava deva dehe, sarvāṁs tathā
bhūta-viśeṣa-saṁghān /
brahmāṇam īśaṁ kamal'āsana-sthaṁ, ṛṣīṁś ca
sarvān uragāṁś ca divyān //15//

Deva : O Lord *tava* : Thy *dehe* : in the body *devān* : Devas *tathā* : likewise *sarvān* : all *bhūtaviśeṣasaṅghān* : varied hosts of beings *divyān* : divine *sarvān* : all *ṛṣīn* : Ṛṣhis *uragān* : serpents *ca* : and *tathā* : likewise *kamalāsanastham* : seated on a lotus *īśam* : Lord *brahmāṇam* : Brahmā *ca* : and *paśyāmi* : I see.

Arjuna said:

15. In Thy form I see, O Lord, all the Devas and all the varied hosts of other beings—the divine Ṛṣis, the celestial serpents and likewise Brahmā the Lord of creation, seated on his lotus throne.

अनेकबाहूदरवक्त्रनेत्रं पश्यामि त्वां सर्वतोऽनन्तरूपम् ।
नान्तं न मध्यं न पुनस्तवादिं पश्यामि विश्वेश्वर विश्वरूप ॥16॥

Aneka-bāhū'dara-vaktra-netraṁ, paśyāmi tvām
sarvato'nantarūpam /
n'āntaṁ na madhyaṁ na punas tav'ādiṁ, paśyāmi
viśveśvara viśva-rūpa //16//

Anekabahūdaravaktranetram : With a myriad arms, trunks, faces, eyes, *anantarūpam* : with all-encompassing form *tvām* : Thee *sarvataḥ* : everywhere *paśyāmi* : I see *Viśveśvara* : O Lord of all! *viśvarūpa* : O All-formed Being! *Tava* : Thy *antam* : end *na* : not, *madhyam* : middle *na* : not, *punaḥ* : again *ādim* : beginning *na* : not *paśyāmi* : see.

16. I see Thee in Thy all-encompassing form everywhere—with myriad arms, myriad trunks, myriad mouths, myriad eyes. O Lord of all! O the All-formed! I see not Thy beginning, Thy middle, or Thy end.

किरीटिनं गदिनं चक्रिणं च तेजोराशिं सर्वतो दीप्तिमन्तम् ।
पश्यामि त्वां दुर्निरीक्ष्यं समन्ताद्दीप्तानलार्कद्युतिमप्रमेयम् ॥ 17 ॥

Kirīṭinaṁ gadinaṁ cakriṇaṁ ca, tejo-rāśiṁ sarvato dīptimantam /
paśyāmi tvāṁ durnirīkṣyaṁ samantād, dīpt' ānalārka-dyutim aprameyam //17//

Kirīṭinam : With diadem *gadinam* : with mace *cakriṇam* : with discus *ca* : and *tejorāśim* : mass of brilliance *sarvataḥ* : on all sides *dīptimantam* : shining *durnirīkṣyam* : hard to look at *dīptānalārkadyutim* : having the brilliance of burning fire or the blazing sun *aprameyam* : passing all bounds *tvām* : Thee *samantāt* : everywhere *paśyāmi* : I see.

17. Diademed and armed with mace and discus, I see Thee, boundless Being, shining everywhere as a mass of light difficult to look at, like the blazing fire or the incandescent sun.

त्वमक्षरं परमं वेदितव्यं त्वमस्य विश्वस्य परं निधानम् ।
त्वमव्ययः शाश्वतधर्मगोप्ता सनातनस्त्वं पुरुषो मतो मे ॥ 18 ॥

Tvam akṣaraṁ paramaṁ veditavyaṁ, tvam asya viśvasya paraṁ nidhānam /
tvam avyayaḥ śāśvata-dharma-goptā, sanātanas tvaṁ puruṣo mato me //18//

Tvam : Thou *veditavyam* : to be realised *paramam* : the supreme *akṣaram* : the Imperishable; *tvam* : Thou *asya* : of this *viśvasya* : world *param* : ultimate *nidhānam* : abode; *tvam* : Thou *avyayaḥ* : perennial *śāśvata dharma goptā* : Guardian of the eternal law; *tvam* : Thou *sanātanaḥ puruṣaḥ* : ancient being *me* : my *mataḥ* : view.

18. In my view Thou art the Supreme, Imperishable Being to be realised—the world's ultimate refuge and the guardian of eternal law, most ancient and perennial.

अनादिमध्यान्तमनन्तवीर्यमनन्तबाहुं शशिसूर्यनेत्रम् ।
पश्यामि त्वां दीप्तहुताशवक्त्रं स्वतेजसा विश्वमिदं तपन्तम् ॥19॥

Anādi-madhy'āntam ananta-vīryam, ananta-bāhuṁ
śaśi-sūrya-netram /
paśyāmi tvāṁ dīpta-hutāśa-vaktraṁ, sva-tejasā
viśvam idaṁ tapantam //19//

Anādimadhyāntam : Without beginning, middle and end *ananta-vīryam* : infinite in puissance *ananta bāhum* : with countless arms i.e., boundless energy functioning everywhere *śaśisūryanetram* : with the sun and moon as eyes *dīptahutāśavaktram* : with a face which shines like flaming fire *svatejasā* : with one's own spiritual radiance *idaṁ viśvam* : this universe *tapantam* : heating, energising *tvām* : Thee *paśyāmi* : I see.

19. I see Thee—beginningless, middleless and endless; infinite in puissance; of boundless energy active everywhere; having the sun and the moon for eyes; with a face luminous like a flaming fire, and with spiritual radiance energising everything.

द्यावापृथिव्योरिदमन्तरं हि व्याप्तं त्वयैकेन दिशश्च सर्वाः ।
दृष्ट्वाऽद्भुतं रूपमुग्रं तवेदं लोकत्रयं प्रव्यथितं महात्मन् ॥20॥

Dyāvā-pṛthivyor idam antaraṁ hi, vyāptaṁ tvay'aikena
diśaś ca sarvāḥ /
dṛṣṭvā' dbhutaṁ rūpam ugraṁ tav'edaṁ loka-trayaṁ
pravyathitaṁ mah'ātman //20//

Mahātman : O High-souled One! *dyāvāpṛthivyoḥ* : between heaven and earth *idam antaram*: this inter-space i.e., all space *tvayā ekena* : by Thee, the One existence *vyāptam* : permeated *hi* : indeed, *sarvāḥ* : all *diśaḥ* : quarters *ca* : and. *Adbhutam* : Wondrous *ugram* : awe-inspiring *tava* : Thy *idam*: this *rūpam* : form *dṛṣṭvā* : seeing *lokatra-*

yam : all the three worlds *pravyathitam* : are trembling with fear.

20. O High-souled One! All the three worlds tremble with fear at the sight of this wondrous, awe-inspiring form of Thine -- the one existence that fills all space betwixt heaven and earth and all the quarters as well.

अमी हि त्वां सुरसङ्घा विशन्ति केचिद्भीताः प्राञ्जलयो गृणन्ति ।
स्वस्तीत्युक्त्वा महर्षिसिद्धसङ्घाः स्तुवन्ति त्वां स्तुतिभिः
पुष्कलाभिः ॥ 21 ॥

Amī hi tvāṁ sura-saṅghā viśanti, kecid bhītāḥ
prāñjalayo gṛṇanti /
svastī'ty uktvā maharṣi-siddha-saṅghāḥ stuvanti
tvāṁ stutibhiḥ puṣkalābhiḥ //21/

Amī : These *surasaṅghāḥ* : the host of Devas *tvām* : Thee *viśanti* : enter *hi* : verily; *kecit* : some *bhītāḥ* : struck with fear *prāñjalayaḥ* : with hands joined in salutation *gṛṇanti* : praise; *svasti* : hail *iti* : thus *uktvā* : saying; *maharṣisiddhasaṅghāḥ* : bands of sages and celestial singers *puṣkalābhiḥ stutibhiḥ* : with hymns of abounding praise *tvām* : Thee *stuvanti* : extol.

21. Verily, these bands of Devas enter into Thee, while others, awe-struck, stand with hands joined in salutation. Hosts of sages and celestial singers cry 'Hail' unto Thee, and extol Thee with hymns of abounding praise.

रुद्रादित्या वसवो ये च साध्या विश्वेऽश्विनौ मरुतश्चोष्मपाश्च ।
गन्धर्वयक्षासुरसिद्धसङ्घा वीक्षन्ते त्वां विस्मिताश्चैव सर्वे ॥ 22 ॥

Rudrādityā Vasavo ye ca Sādhyā, Viśve'śvinau
Marutaś c'oṣmapāś ca /
Gandharva-yakṣ'āsura-siddha-saṁghā, vīkṣante
tvāṁ vismitāś c'aiva sarve //22//

Rudrādityāḥ : Rudras and Ādityas *vasavaḥ* : Vasus *ye* : who *ca* : and *sādhyāḥ* : Sādhyas *visve* : Viśve-devas *Aśvinau* : Aśvins

Marutaḥ : Maruts *ca* : and *uṣmapāḥ* : Manes *ca* : and *gandharva-yakṣāsurasiddhasaṅghāḥ* : the hosts of Gandharvas, Yakshas, Asuras and Siddhas *sarve eva* : all of them *ca* : and *vismitāḥ* : amazed *tvām* : Thee *vīkṣante* : see.

22. And the Rudras, Ādityas, Vasus and Sādhyas; Viśvas, Aśvins, Maruts and Manes; and the hosts of Gandharvas, Yakṣas, Asuras and Siddhas—all view Thee in utter amazement.

रूपं महत्ते बहुवक्त्रनेत्रं महाबाहो बहुबाहूरुपादम् ।
बहूदरं बहुदंष्ट्राकरालं दृष्ट्वा लोकाः प्रव्यथितास्तथाहम् ॥ 23 ॥

Rūpaṁ mahat te bahu-vaktra-netraṁ, mahā-bāho
bahu-bāhūrupādam /
bah'ūdaraṁ bahu-damṣṭrā-karālaṁ, dṛṣṭvā lokāḥ
pravyathitās tathā'ham //23//

Mahābāho : O mighty one! *bahuvaktranetram* : having many faces and eyes *bahubāhūrupādam* : with many arms, thighs and legs *bahūdaram* : with many trunks *bahudamṣṭrākarālam* : with many terrific fangs *te* : Thy *mahat* : stupendous *rūpam* : form *dṛṣṭvā* : seeing, *lokāḥ* : the worlds *pravyathitāḥ* : immensely awe-struck *aham* : I too *tathā* : am so.

23. At the sight of Thy stupendous form, with faces, eyes, arms, trunks, thighs and legs in myriads, and Thy numerous fangs of forbidding appearance—the whole world, O mighty one, is trembling in awe, even as I.

नभःस्पृशं दीप्तमनेकवर्णं व्यात्ताननं दीप्तविशालनेत्रम् ।
दृष्ट्वा हि त्वां प्रव्यथितान्तरात्मा धृतिं न विन्दामि शमं
च विष्णो ॥ 24 ॥

Nabhaḥ-spṛśaṁ dīptam aneka-varṇaṁ, vyātt'ānanaṁ
dīpta-viśāla-netram /
dṛṣṭvā hi tvāṁ pravyathit'āntarātmā dhṛtiṁ na
vindāmi śamaṁ ca Viṣṇo //24//

Nabhaspṛśam : Reaching to the skies *dīptam* : brilliant *anekavarṇam*: varied in colours *vyāttānanam* : with mouth wide open *dīptaviśāla-netram* : with large eyes glowing bright *tvām* : Thee *dṛṣṭvā* : seeing *pravyathitāntarātmā* : one shaken with awe to the core of one's being *Viṣṇo* : O All pervading Being! *dhṛtim* : strength of mind *śamam* : mental equanimity *ca* : and *na vindāmi* : I do not find.

24. When I see Thy form reaching up to the skies and shining in varied hues, when I see Thy face with mouth wide open and eyes large and glowing bright, I feel shaken to the core of my being with awe. O All-pervading One! My strength is exhausted and my mind is without peace.

दंष्ट्राकरालानि च ते मुखानि दृष्ट्वैव कालानलसन्निभानि ।
दिशो न जाने न लभे च शर्म प्रसीद देवेश जगन्निवास ॥ 25 ॥

Daṁṣṭrā-karālāni ca te mukhāni, dṛṣṭv'aiva
kāl'ānala-sannibhāni /
diśo na jāne na labhe ca śarma, prasīda dev'eśa
jagan-nivāsa //25//

Daṁṣṭrākarālāni : With fangs striking terror *ca* : and *kālānala-sannibhāni* : resembling the fire of cosmic destruction *te* : Thy *mukhāni* : faces *dṛṣṭvā eva* : by seeing itself *diśaḥ* : quarters *na jāne* : do not know, *śarma* : peace *ca* : and *na labhe* : I do not find; *deveśa* : O Lord of Lords! *jagannivāsa* : O the home of the worlds! *prasīda* : be propitious.

25. Even by beholding Thy faces, resembling the fire of cosmic destruction and striking terror with the fangs, I lose all sense of direction as also my presence of mind. O Thou the Lord of all and the home of the worlds! be propitious unto me!

अमी च त्वां धृतराष्ट्रस्य पुत्राः सर्वे सहैवावनिपालसङ्घैः ।
भीष्मो द्रोणः सूतपुत्रस्तथासौ सहास्मदीयैरपि योधमुख्यैः ॥ 26 ॥

वक्त्राणि ते त्वरमाणा विशन्ति दंष्ट्राकरालानि भयानकानि ।
केचिद्विलग्ना दशनान्तरेषु संदृश्यन्ते चूर्णितैरुत्तमाङ्गैः ॥ 27 ॥

Amī ca tvāṁ Dhṛtarāṣṭrasya putrāḥ
sarve sah' aiv' āvani-pālasaṅghaiḥ /
Bhīṣmo Droṇaḥ sūta-putras tathā'sau
sahā'smadīyair api yodha-mukhyaiḥ //26//

Vaktrāṇi te tvaramāṇā viśanti
daṁṣṭrā-karālāni bhay'ānakāni /
kecid vilagnā daśan'āntareṣu
saṁdṛśyante cūrṇitair uttamāṅgaiḥ //27//

Avanipālasaṅghaiḥ saha eva : Along with the hosts of kings *amī* : these *Dhṛtarāṣṭrasya putrāḥ* : the sons of Dhṛtarāṣṭra *Bhīṣmaḥ* : Bhīṣma *Droṇaḥ* : Droṇa *asau* : this *sūtaputraḥ* : Karṇa *ca* : and *tathā* : in the same way *asmadīyaiḥ* : with our *yodhamukhyaiḥ* : principal warriors *api* : also *saha* : with *sarve* : all *daṁṣṭrākarālāni* : with fangs striking terror *te* : Thy *vaktrāṇi* : mouths *tvaramāṇāḥ* : rushing *viśanti* : enter; *kecit* : some *cūrṇitaiḥ* : crushed *uttamāṅgaiḥ*: with heads *daśanāntareṣu* : in the gaps between teeth *vilagnāḥ* : sticking *saṁdṛśyante* : are seen.

26-27. All these hosts of kings, along with the sons of Dhṛtarāṣṭra, Bhīṣma, Droṇa and yonder Karṇa, as also the principal warriors on our side—all are rushing headlong into Thy fearful mouth set with terrible fangs. Some are seen with their heads crushed and caught in the gaps of Thy teeth.

यथा नदीनां बहवोऽम्बुवेगाः समुद्रमेवाभिमुखा द्रवन्ति ।
तथा तवामी नरलोकवीरा विशन्ति वक्त्राण्यभिविज्वलन्ति ॥28॥

Yathā nadīnāṁ bahavo'mbu-vegāḥ
samudram ev'ābhimukhā dravanti /
tathā tav'āmī nara-loka-vīrā
viśanti vaktrāṇy abhivijvalanti //28//

Nadīnām : Of the rivers *bahavaḥ* : numerous *ambuvegāḥ* : swift-flowing waters *yathā* : as *samudram* : sea *eva* : verily *abhimukhāḥ* : towards *dravanti* : rush, *tathā* : in the same way *amī* : these *naralokavīrāḥ* : heroes among men *abhivijvalanti* : flaming *tava* : Thy *vaktrāṇi* : mouths *viśanti* : enter.

28. As the swift-flowing waters of numerous rivers rush verily towards the sea, so these heroes among men are rushing into Thy flaming mouth.

यथा प्रदीप्तं ज्वलनं पतङ्गा विशन्ति नाशाय समृद्धवेगाः ।
तथैव नाशाय विशन्ति लोकास्तवापि वक्त्राणि समृद्धवेगाः ॥29॥

Yathā pradīptaṁ jvalanaṁ pataṅgā
viśanti nāśāya samṛddhavegāḥ /
tath'aiva nāśāya viśanti lokās
tav'āpi vaktrāṇi samṛddha-vegāḥ //29//

Pataṅgāḥ : Moths *nāśāya* : for their destruction *samṛddhavegāḥ* : swiftly *pradīptam* : blazing *jvalanam* : fire *yathā* : how *viśanti* : enter, *tathā eva* : in the same way *lokāḥ* : men *api* : also *nāśāya* : for their destruction *samṛddhavegāḥ* : with great speed *tava* : Thy *vaktrāṇi* : mouths *viśanti* : enter.

29. As moths swarm swiftly into a flaming fire and perish, so do these men rush headlong into Thy mouth to meet with sure destruction.

लेलिह्यसे ग्रसमानः समन्ताल्लोकान्समग्रान्वदनैर्ज्वलद्भिः ।
तेजोभिरापूर्य जगत्समग्रं भासस्तवोग्राः प्रतपन्ति विष्णो ॥ 30 ॥

Lelihyase grasamānaḥ samantāt
lokān samagrān vadanair jvaladbhiḥ /
tejobhir āpūrya jagat samagraṁ
bhāsas tav'ogrāḥ pratapanti Viṣṇo //30//

Jvaladbhiḥ : Flaming *vadanaiḥ* : mouths *samantāt* : from all sides *samagrān lokān* : all the worlds *grasamānaḥ* : swallowing *lelihyase* : Thou lappest *Viṣṇo* : O all pervading Being! *Tava* : Thy *ugrāḥ* : awful *bhāsaḥ* : brilliance *samagraṁ jagat* : the whole universe *tejobhiḥ* : with radiance *āpūrya* : filling *pratapanti* : scorches.

30. Thou lappest up all these worlds around, devouring them with Thy flaming mouth. Thy lustre, striking awe into the

minds of all, fills this entire universe with its radiance and scorches it, O Viṣṇu!

आख्याहि मे को भवानुग्ररूपो नमोऽस्तु ते देववर प्रसीद ।
विज्ञातुमिच्छामि भवन्तमाद्यं न हि प्रजानामि तव प्रवृत्तिम् ॥31॥

Ākhyāhi me ko bhavān ugra-rūpo
namo'stu te deva-vara prasīda /
vijñātum icchāmi bhavantam ādyaṁ
na hi prajānāmi tava pravṛttim //31//

Ugrarūpaḥ : Of awe-inspiring form *bhavān* : Thou *kaḥ* : who art, *me* : to me *ākhyāhi* : tell. *Devavara* : O Supreme Lord! *te* : to Thee *namaḥ* : salutation *astu* : be; *prasīda* : be propitious. *Ādyam* : Primal Being *bhavantam* : Thee *vijñātuṁ* : to know *icchāmi* : I desire; *tava* : Thy *pravṛttim* : working or purpose *na prajānāmi* : I do not understand *hi* : indeed.

31. Deign to tell me who Thou art with this awe-inspiring form. To Thee, O Supreme Lord, my salutation, and also my prayers for Thy grace. I wish to know more about Thee, the Primal Being, as also of Thy purpose here, of which I am in ignorance.

श्रीभगवानुवाच
कालोऽस्मि लोकक्षयकृत्प्रवृद्धो लोकान्समाहर्तुमिह प्रवृत्तः ।
ऋतेऽपि त्वां न भविष्यन्ति सर्वे येऽवस्थिताः प्रत्यनीकेषु योधाः ॥

Sri Bhagavān uvāca:
Kālo'smi loka-kṣaya-kṛt pravṛddho
lokān samāhartum iha pravṛttaḥ /
ṛte'pi tvāṁ na bhaviṣyanti sarve
ye'vasthitāḥ pratyanīkeṣu yodhāḥ //32//

Lokakṣayakṛt : World-consuming *pravṛddhaḥ* : vast, mighty *kālaḥ* : Time *asmi* : I am; *lokān* : all beings *samāhartum* : to annihilate *iha* : here *pravṛttaḥ* : engaged; *pratyanīkeṣu* : in rival armies *ye* :

whichever *yodhāḥ* : warriors *avasthitāḥ* : stand arrayed *te sarve* : all of them *tvām* : you *ṛte* : without *api* : even *na bhaviṣyanti* : shall not survive.

The Blessed Lord said:

32. I am the mighty world-destroying Time, engaged here in annihilating all beings. Even without you, not one of all the warriors arrayed in these rival armies shall survive.

तस्मात्त्वमुत्तिष्ठ यशो लभस्व जित्वा शत्रून् भुङ्क्ष्व राज्यं समृद्धम् ।
मयैवैते निहताः पूर्वमेव निमित्तमात्रं भव सव्यसाचिन् ॥ 33 ॥

Tasmāt tvam uttiṣṭha yaśo labhasva
jitvā śatrūn bhuṅkṣva rājyaṁ samṛddham /
may'aiv'aite nihatāḥ pūrvam eva
nimitta-mātraṁ bhava savyasācin //33//

Tasmāt : Therefore *tvam* : you *uttiṣṭha* : arise, *yaśaḥ*: fame *labhasva*: win, *śatrūn* : enemies *jitvā* : subduing *samṛddham* : prosperous *rājyam* : kingdom *bhuṅkṣva* : enjoy. *Mayā eva* : By myself *pūrvam eva* : even before *ete* : they *nihatāḥ* : slain. *Savyasācin* : O Master-bowman, Arjuna *nimittamātram* : an instrument alone *bhava* : be you.

33. Therefore arise! Win renown! And destroying your enemies, enjoy the prosperous kingdom. For these warriors have already been slain by Me. Be you but an instrument thereof, O thou master-bowman, Arjuna.[3]

द्रोणं च भीष्मं च जयद्रथं च कर्णं तथान्यानपि योधवीरान् ।
मया हतांस्त्वं जहि मा व्यथिष्ठा युध्यस्व जेतासि रणे सपत्नान् ॥

Droṇaṁ ca bhīṣmaṁ ca Jayadrathaṁ ca
Karṇaṁ tathā'nyān api yodha-vīrān /
mayā hatāṁs tvaṁ jahi mā vyathiṣṭhā
yudhyasva jetāsi raṇe sapatnān //34//

Mayā : By me *hatān* : doomed *Droṇam* : Droṇa *ca* : and *Bhīṣmam ca* : and Bhīṣma *Jayadratham ca* : as also Jayadratha *tathā* :

likewise *anyān* : other *yodhavīrān* : brave warriors *api* : too *tvam* : you *jahi* : kill; *mā* : do not *vyathiṣṭhāḥ* : grieve, *yudhyasva* : fight on, *raṇe*: in battle *sapatnān* : enemies *jetāsi* : you shall conquer.

34. Kill Droṇa and Bhīṣma, Jayadratha and Karṇa, as also these other heroic warriors, who are already doomed by Me. Fight on, and you shall conquer the enemies in battle.

संजय उवाच

एतच्छ्रुत्वा वचनं केशवस्य कृताञ्जलिर्वेपमानः किरीटी ।

नमस्कृत्वा भूय एवाह कृष्णं सगद्गदं भीतभीतः प्रणम्य ॥ 35 ॥

Sañjaya uvāca:

Etac chrutvā vacanaṁ Keśavasya
kṛtāñjalir vepamānaḥ Kirīṭī /
namas-kṛtvā bhūya ev'āha Kṛṣṇaṁ
sagadgadaṁ bhīta-bhītaḥ praṇamya //35//

Keśavasya : Of Keśava *etat* : that *vacanam* : word, declaration, *śrūtvā* : having heard, *vepamānaḥ* : trembling *Kirīṭī* : Arjuna *kṛtāñjaliḥ* : with palms joined in salutation *Kṛṣṇam* : Kṛṣṇa *bhūyaḥ eva* : again and again *namskṛtvā* : saluting *bhītabhītaḥ* : overwhelmed with awe *praṇamya* : prostrating *sagadgadam* : in a faltering voice *āha* : said.

Sañjaya said:

35. Hearing this declaration of Kṛṣṇa, Arjuna, with his frame trembling, saluted Him again and again with joined palms. Prostrating himself before Him in utter awe, Arjuna addressed Him in faltering voice.

अर्जुन उवाच

स्थाने हृषीकेश तव प्रकीर्त्या जगत्प्रहृष्यत्यनुरज्यते च ।

रक्षांसि भीतानि दिशो द्रवन्ति सर्वे नमस्यन्ति च सिद्धसङ्घाः ॥

Arjuna uvāca:

Sthāne Hṛṣīkeśa tava prakīrtyā
jagat prahṛṣyaty anurajyate ca /
rakṣāṁsi bhītāni diśo dravanti
sarve namasyanti ca siddhasaṅghāḥ //36//

Hṛṣīkeśa: O conqueror of the senses (Kṛṣṇa)! *tava*: Thy *prakīrtyā*: by glorification *jagat* : the world *prahṛṣyati* : rejoices, *anurajyate* : delights *ca* : and; *sthāne* : rightly *rakṣāṁsi* : Rākṣasas *bhītāni* : frightened *diśaḥ* : in all directions *dravanti* : flee, *sarve* : all *siddha-saṅghāḥ* : hosts of Siddhas *namasyanti* : bow *ca* : and.

Arjuna said:

36. Rightly do the worlds rejoice and delight in glorifying Thee. In Thy presence the Rākṣasas melt away in fear in all directions, while the hosts of Siddhas bow in adoration.

कस्माच्च ते न नमेरन्महात्मन् गरीयसे ब्रह्मणोऽप्यादिकर्त्रे ।
अनन्त देवेश जगन्निवास त्वमक्षरं सदसत्तत्परं यत् ॥ 37 ॥

Kasmāc ca te na nameran mahātman
garīyase brahmaṇo'py ādi-kartre /
ananta dev'eśa jagan-nivāsa
tvam akṣaraṁ sad asat tat-paraṁ yat //37//

Mahātman : O Great One! *garīyase* : greater than all *brahmaṇaḥ api* : even of Brahmā *ādikartre* : primal cause *ca* : and *te* : to Thee *kasmāt* : why *na nameran* : should they not bow down? *Ananta* : O Infinite Being *deveśa* : O Lord of Gods *jagannivāsa* : O abode of the worlds *sat* : being *asat* : non-being *yat* : which *tat param* : beyond that *akṣaram* : Imperishable Being *tvam* : Thou art.

37. O High-souled one! Why should they not bow down to Thee who art the highest of all beings and the primal cause of even Brahmā the creator! O Infinite One! O Lord of all Gods and the Abode of all the worlds! Thou art that Imperishable Being who is both existence (effect condition) and non-existence (causal state) as also that which is beyond them both.[4]

त्वमादिदेवः पुरुषः पुराणस्त्वमस्य विश्वस्य परं निधानम् ।
वेत्तासि वेद्यं च परं च धाम त्वया ततं विश्वमनन्तरूप ॥ 38 ॥

Tvam ādi-devaḥ puruṣaḥ purāṇas
tvam asya viśvasya paraṁ nidhānam /
vettā'si vedyaṁ ca paraṁ ca dhāma
tvayā tataṁ viśvam anantarūpa //38//

Tvam : Thou *ādidevaḥ* : the first of divinities *purāṇaḥ* : ancient *puruṣaḥ* : Being ; *tvam* : Thou *asya viśvasya* : of this world *param* : ultimate *nidhānam* : haven of rest; *vettā* : the knower *vedyam* : the known *ca* : and *param* : supreme *dhāma* : Abode *ca* : and *asi* : art; *anantarūpa* : O Thou of countless forms *tvayā* : by Thee *viśwam* : the universe *tatam* : pervaded.

38. Thou art the first of all divinities and the most ancient of all beings. Thou art the ultimate haven of rest and safety for the worlds. Thou art both the knower and the known as also the supreme Abode. O Thou of countless forms! By Thee the whole universe is pervaded.

वायुर्यमोऽग्निर्वरुणः शशाङ्कः प्रजापतिस्त्वं प्रपितामहश्च ।
नमो नमस्तेऽस्तु सहस्रकृत्वः पुनश्च भूयोऽपि नमो नमस्ते ॥39॥

Vāyur Yamo'gnir Varuṇaḥ śaśāṅkaḥ
Prajāpatis tvaṁ prapitāmahaś ca /
namo namas te'stu sahasra-kṛtvaḥ
punaś ca bhūyo'pi namo namas te //39//

Vāyuḥ : Vayu *Yamaḥ* : Yama *Agniḥ* : Agni *Varuṇaḥ* : Varuṇa *Śaśāṅkaḥ* : moon *Prajāpatiḥ* : Prajāpati *prapitāmahaḥ* : Brahmā's progenitor *te* : to Thee *sahasrakṛtvaḥ* : a thousand times, *namaḥ* : salutation *namaḥ* : salutation; *bhūyaḥ api* : again *punaḥ ca* : and again *te* : to Thee *namaḥ namaḥ* : salutation, salutation.

39. Manifested as Vāyu the god of winds, as Yama the god of death, as Varuna the god of the seas, and as the moon with the hare-mark on the face—Thou art the Progenitor of all and the source of him as well. Hail, hail unto Thee a thousand times! Hail, and hail again and yet again.

नमः पुरस्तादथ पृष्ठतस्ते नमोऽस्तु ते सर्वत एव सर्व ।
अनन्तवीर्यामितविक्रमस्त्वं सर्वं समाप्नोषि ततोऽसि सर्वः ॥40॥

Namaḥ purastād atha pṛṣṭhatas te
namo'stu te sarvata eva sarva /
ananta-vīry'āmita-vikramas tvaṁ
sarvaṁ samāpnoṣi tato'si sarvaḥ //40//

Sarva : O All! *purastāt* : in front *pṛṣṭhataḥ* : behind *te* : to Thee *namaḥ* : salutations *astu* : be! *Atha* : in the same way *sarvataḥ eva* : on every side *te* : to Thee *astu* : be! *Anantavīryaḥ* : Infinite in puissance *amita vikramaḥ* : limitless in might *tvam* : Thou *sarvam* : all *samāpnoṣi* : pervadest, *tataḥ* : therefore *sarvaḥ* : the All *asi*: Thou art.

40. Salutations unto Thee, the All-formed, from before, from behind and from all directions! Infinite in puissance and limitless in might, Thou pervadest everything and Thou art verily the All.

सखेति मत्वा प्रसभं यदुक्तं हे कृष्ण हे यादव हे सखेति ।
अजानता महिमानं तवेदं मया प्रमादात्प्रणयेन वाऽपि ॥ 41 ॥

यच्चावहासार्थमसत्कृतोऽसि विहारशय्यासनभोजनेषु ।
एकोऽथवाप्यच्युत तत्समक्षं तत्क्षामये त्वामहमप्रमेयम् ॥ 42 ॥

Sakh'eti matvā prasabhaṁ yad uktaṁ
he Kṛṣṇa he Yādava he sakh'eti |
ajānatā mahimānaṁ tav'edaṁ
mayā pramādāt praṇayena vāpi //41//

Yac c'āvahās'ārtham asatkṛto'si
vihāra-śayyāsana-bhojaneṣu /
eko'thavā'py acyuta tat-samakṣaṁ
tat kṣāmaye tvām aham aprameyam //42//

Acyuta : O Thou the undecaying one! *tava* : Thy *idam* : this *mahimānam* : greatness *ajānatā* : not knowing *mayā* : by me *sakhā*: friend *iti*: as *matvā* : thinking *pramādāt* : out of ignorance *praṇayena* out of love *vā* : or *api* : merely *prasabham* : carelessly *vihāra-śayyāsana-bhojaneṣu* while at play or on bed or on the seat or while feasting *ekaḥ* : alone *athavā* : or *tatsamakṣam* : in the company of others *api* : even *he Kṛṣṇa* : O Kṛṣṇa *he Yādava* : O one of Yādava clan! *he sakhe* : O friend! *iti* : in this way *yat* : what *uktam* : was said *avahāsārtham* : for fun *asatkṛtaḥ* : disrespectfully *asi* : there is, *tat* : that *aprameyam* : immeasurable *tvām* : to Thee *aham* : I *kṣāmaye* : implore for forgiveness.

41-42. O undecaying One! If, without knowing Thy greatness and taking Thee only to be a friend, I have, out of ignorance or love, alone or even in company, addressed Thee discourteously in fun, while playing, relaxing, sitting or feasting, with words such as, "O Krishna! O Yadava!"—I beseech Thee, O Boundless One, do pardon me for the same.

पितासि लोकस्य चराचरस्य त्वमस्य पूज्यश्च गुरुर्गरीयान् ।
न त्वत्समोऽस्त्यभ्यधिकः कुतोऽन्यो लोकत्रयेऽप्यप्रतिमप्रभाव ॥43

Pitā'si lokasya car'ācarasya
tvam asya pūjyaś ca gurur garīyān /
na tvat-samo'sty abhyadhikaḥ kuto'nyo
loka-traye'py apratima prabhāva //43//

Apratimaprabhāva : O Thou of incomparable puissance! *tvam* : Thou *carācarasya* : of all that is moving and unmoving *asya lokasya* : of this world *pitā* : father *asi* : art; *pūjyaḥ* : worthy object of worship *guruḥ* : teacher *garīyān* : weightier (than others) *ca* : and (*asi* : art); *lokatraye* : in all the three worlds *tvatsamaḥ* : equal to Thee *api* : even *na asti* : does not exist; *abhyadhikaḥ* : greater *anyaḥ* : another *kutaḥ* : where?

43. Thou art the father of the world—of all that is moving and unmoving. Thou art the object of its worship, the most venerable of its Teachers. In all the worlds there is not another equal to Thee, much less one greater, O Thou of incomparable puissance!

तस्मात्प्रणम्य प्रणिधाय कायं प्रसादये त्वामहमीशमीड्यम् ।
पितेव पुत्रस्य सखेव सख्युः प्रियः प्रियायार्हसि देव सोढुम् ॥ 44

Tasmāt praṇamya praṇidhāya kāyaṁ
prasādaye tvām aham īśam īḍyam /
pit'eva putrasya sakh'eva sakhyuḥ
priyaḥ priyāy'ārhasi deva soḍhum //44//

Tasmāt : Therefore *aham* : I *īśam* : Lord *īḍhyam* : adorable *tvām* : Thee *kāyam* : body *praṇidhāya* : bending in prostration *praṇamya*: greeting, *prasādaye* : propitiate; *putrasya* : of the son *pitā* : father, *sakhyuḥ* : of the friend *sakhā* : friend *iva* : as, *priyāyāḥ* : of the beloved *priyaḥ* : lover *iva* : as, *deva* : O Lord! *soḍhum* : to bear *arhasi* : deservest.

44. Therefore greeting Thee with my body stretched in prostration, I beseech Thee, O worshipful Lord, to be gracious unto me. Bear with me as a father with a son, as a friend with a friend, and as a lover with his beloved.

अदृष्टपूर्वं हृषितोऽस्मि दृष्ट्वा भयेन च प्रव्यथितं मनो मे ।
तदेव मे दर्शय देव रूपं प्रसीद देवेश जगन्निवास ॥ 45 ॥

Adṛṣṭa-pūrvaṁ hṛṣito'smi dṛṣṭvā
bhayena ca pravyathitaṁ mano me /
tad eva me darśaya deva rūpaṁ
prasīda dev'eśa jagan-nivāsa //45//

Adṛṣṭapūrvam (*rūpam*) : A form that has never been seen before *dṛṣṭvā* : seeing *hṛṣitaḥ asmi* : I am overjoyed; *bhayena* : by fear *ca* : also *me* : my *manaḥ* : mind *pravyathitam* : perturbed; *deva* : O Lord! *tat* : that other *eva* : only *rūpam* : form *me* : to me *darśaya* : reveal, *deveśa* : O God of gods, *jagannivāsa* : O Indwelling spirit of the world! *prasīda* : be propitious.

45. Seeing this form unseen before, I am overjoyed but my mind is also perturbed with fear. Reveal to me that other familiar form of Thine and be gracious unto me, O Thou God of all gods, and Indwelling Spirit of the worlds.[5]

किरीटिनं गदिनं चक्रहस्तमिच्छामि त्वां द्रष्टुमहं तथैव ।
तेनैव रूपेण चतुर्भुजेन सहस्रबाहो भव विश्वमूर्ते ॥ 46 ॥

Kirīṭinaṁ gadinaṁ cakra-hastam
icchāmi tvāṁ draṣṭum ahaṁ tath'aiva /
ten'aiva rūpeṇa catur-bhujena
sahasra-bāho bhava viśva-mūrte //46//

Tathā eva : In the same way *Kirīṭinam* : with a diadem *gadinam*: with mace *cakrahastam* : with discus in hand *tvām* : Thee *draṣṭum*: to see *aham* : I *icchāmi* : desire, *sahasra bāho* : O Thou the thousand armed! *viśvamūrte* : O Thou of universal form! *tenaiva* : in that *caturbhujena* : four-armed *rūpeṇa* : form *bhava* : become.

46. I desire to see Thee as before crowned with a diadem, and holding a mace and discus in hand. Deign to assume that four-armed shape, O Thou of a thousand arms and of universal form!

श्रीभगवानुवाच

मया प्रसन्नेन तवार्जुनेदं रूपं परं दर्शितमात्मयोगात् ।
तेजोमयं विश्वमनन्तमाद्यं यन्मे त्वदन्येन न दृष्टपूर्वम् ॥ 47 ॥

Śri Bhagavān uvāca:

Mayā prasannena tav' ārjun' edaṁ
rūpaṁ paraṁ darśitam ātmayogāt /
tejomayaṁ viśvam anantam ādyaṁ
yan me tvad-anyena na dṛṣṭa-pūrvam //47//

Tejomayam : Of pure brilliance *viśvam* : all-inclusive *anantam* : infinite *ādyam* : primeval *tvadanyena* : any one other than you *na dṛṣṭa-pūrvam* : unseen before *me* : My *idaṁ paraṁ rūpam* : this transcendent form, *yat* : which, *Arjuna* : O Arjuna! (*tat rupam* : that form) *prasannena* : graciously inclined *mayā* : by Me *ātmayogāt* : by divine power *tava* : for you *darśitam* : shown.

The Blessed Lord said:

47. Out of My grace, I have, by My divine power, revealed to you this transcendent form of Mine—infinite, primeval, radiant and all-inclusive. Never has it been seen by any one before except by you.

न वेदयज्ञाध्ययनैर्न दानैर्न च क्रियाभिर्न तपोभिरुग्रैः ।
एवंरूपः शक्य अहं नृलोके द्रष्टुं त्वदन्येन कुरुप्रवीर ॥ 48 ॥

Na veda-yajñ' ādhyayanair na dānair
na ca kriyābhir na tapobhir ugraiḥ /
evaṁ-rūpaḥ śakya ahaṁ nṛ-loke
draṣṭuṁ tvad-anyena Kurupravīra //48//

Kurupravīra : O Thou the most heroic among the Kurus! *Vedayajñādhyayanaiḥ* : by the study and practice of the Vedas and sacrifices *evaṁ rūpaḥ* : in such form *aham* : I *nṛloke* : in the world of men *tvadanyena* : by any one other than you *na draṣṭum śakyaḥ* : not possible to be seen; *na dānaiḥ* : nor by charity *na kriyābhiḥ* : nor by rituals *na ugraiḥ tapobhiḥ* : nor by severe austerities *ca* : and.

48. Except by you (on whom My grace has been bestowed), none in this world could see Me in this Cosmic Form—be it by Vedic study, by sacrifice, by good works, by rituals, or by severe austerities.

मा ते व्यथा मा च विमूढभावो दृष्ट्वा रूपं घोरमीदृङ्ममेदम् ।
व्यपेतभीः प्रीतमनाः पुनस्त्वं तदेव मे रूपमिदं प्रपश्य ॥ 49 ॥

Mā te vyathā mā ca vimūḍha-bhāvo
dṛṣṭvā rūpaṁ ghoram īdṛṅ mam'edam /
vyapeta-bhīḥ prīta-manāḥ punas tvaṁ
tad eva me rūpam idaṁ prapaśya //49//

Īdṛk : In this way *ghoram* : awe-inspiring *mama* : My *idam* : this *rūpam* : form *dṛṣṭvā* : seeing *te* : for you *vyathā* : fear *mā* : not, *vimūḍhabhāvaḥ* : bewilderment *ca* : and *mā* : not; *tvam* : you *vyapetabhīḥ* : with fear assuaged *prītamanāḥ* : with a joyful heart *me* : My *tat* : that *idaṁ rūpam eva* : this form (the ordinary form) *punaḥ* : again *paśya* : see.

49. Fear not; nor be bewildered at seeing this awe-inspiring form of Mine. With fear assuaged and a heart full of joy, behold now this, my familiar form, again!

संजय उवाच

इत्यर्जुनं वासुदेवस्तथोक्त्वा स्वकं रूपं दर्शयामास भूयः ।
आश्वासयामास च भीतमेनं भूत्वा पुनः सौम्यवपुर्महात्मा ॥50॥

Sañjaya uvāca:

Ity Arjunaṁ Vāsudevas tath'oktvā
svakaṁ rūpaṁ darśayāmāsa bhūyaḥ /
āśvāsayāmāsa ca bhītam enaṁ
bhūtvā punaḥ saumya-vapur mah'ātmā //50//

Vāsudevaḥ : Vāsudeva *Arjunam* : to Arjuna *iti* : thus *uktvā* : saying *tathā* : accordingly *svakaṁ rūpam* : own usual form *bhūyaḥ* : again *darśayāmāsa* : revealed; *mahātmā* : the exalted one; *saumyavapuḥ* : serene form *bhūtvā* : becoming *bhītam* : awestruck *enam* : him *punaḥ* : again *āśvāsayāmāsa* : comforted.

Sañjaya said:

50. Saying thus to Arjuna, Krishna revealed again his own familiar form. Having thus assumed that gentle form, the Exalted One comforted the awe-struck Arjuna over again.

अर्जुन उवाच

दृष्ट्वेदं मानुषं रूपं तव सौम्यं जनार्दन ।
इदानीमस्मि संवृत्तः सचेताः प्रकृतिं गतः ॥ 51 ॥

Arjuna uvāca:

Dṛṣṭv'edaṁ mānuṣaṁ rūpaṁ tava saumyaṁ janārdana /
idānīm asmi samvṛttaḥ sacetāḥ prakṛtiṁ gataḥ //51//

Janārdana : O Janārdana! *Tava* : Thy *idam* : this *saumyam* : serene *mānuṣam* : human *rūpam* : form *dṛṣṭvā* : seeing *idānīm* : now *sacetāḥ* : one with balance of mind recovered *prakṛtiṁ gataḥ* : one attained to one's natural state *samvṛttaḥ asmi* : become.

Arjuna said:

51. Seeing this gentle human form of Thine, O Janārdana, I am now composed and restored to my natural state of mind.

श्रीभगवानुवाच

सुदुर्दर्शमिदं रूपं दृष्टवानसि यन्मम ।
देवा अप्यस्य रूपस्य नित्यं दर्शनकाङ्क्षिणः ॥ 52 ॥

Śri Bhagavān uvāca:

Sudurdarśam idaṁ rūpaṁ dṛṣṭavān asi yan mama /
devā apy asya rūpasya nityaṁ darśana-kāṅkṣiṇaḥ //52//

Mama : My *yat* : which *rūpam* : form *dṛṣṭavān asi* : you have seen (*tat* : that) *idam* : this *sudurdarśam* : is extremely difficult to see; *devāḥ* : the Devas *api* : even *nityam* : always *asya rūpasya* : of this form *darśanakāṅkṣiṇaḥ* : are desirous of seeing.

The Blessed Lord said:

52. This form of Mine which you have seen is extremely difficult to behold. Even Devas themselves are ever eager to see it.

नाहं वेदैर्न तपसा न दानेन न चेज्यया ।
शक्य एवंविधो द्रष्टुं दृष्टवानसि मां यथा ॥ 53 ॥

N'āhaṁ vedair na tapasā na dānena na c'ejyayā /
śakya evaṁ-vidho draṣṭuṁ dṛṣṭavān asi māṁ yathā //53//

Mām : Me *yathā* : in which way *dṛṣṭavān asi* : you have seen, *evaṁ vidhaḥ* : in that way *aham* : I *vedaiḥ* : by Vedas *na* : nor *tapasa* : by austerities *na* : nor *dānena* : by charities *ijyayā* : by sacrifices *ca* : and *na* : not *draṣṭum* : to be seen *śakyaḥ* : possible.

53. Neither by Vedic study, nor by austerities, nor by charities, nor by sacrifices could one behold Me in the way you have done.[6]

भक्त्या त्वनन्यया शक्य अहमेवंविधोऽर्जुन ।
ज्ञातुं द्रष्टुं च तत्त्वेन प्रवेष्टुं च परंतप ॥ 54 ॥

Bhaktyā tv'ananyayā śakya aham evaṁ-vidho'rjuna /
jñātuṁ draṣṭuṁ ca tattvena praveṣṭuṁ ca paraṁtapa //54//

Arjuna : O Arjuna! *Paraṁtapa* : O scorcher of enemies! *evaṁ vidhaḥ* : in this way *aham* : I *tattvena jñātum* : to be known in my true nature *draṣṭum* : to be seen *praveṣṭum* : to be entered into *ca* : and *ananyayā* : by unswerving *bhaktyā* : devotion *tu* : but *śakyaḥ* : possible.

54. But, O Arjuna, Thou great warrior! Through unswerving devotion this form of Mine may be known in truth and in reality, may be experienced and entered into.

मत्कर्मकृन्मत्परमो मद्भक्तः सङ्गवर्जितः ।
निर्वैरः सर्वभूतेषु यः स मामेति पाण्डव ॥ 55 ॥

Mat-karma-kṛn mat-paramo mad-bhaktaḥ saṅga-varjitaḥ /
nirvairaḥ sarva-bhūteṣu yaḥ sa mām eti Pāṇḍava //55//

Pāṇḍava : O Son of Pāṇḍu! *matkarmakṛt* : one doing My work *matparamaḥ* : one looking upon Me as the goal *madbhaktaḥ* : My devotee *sangavarjitaḥ* : one without attachments *sarvabhūteṣu* : towards all creatures *nirvairaḥ* : one without antagonism *yaḥ* : whoever *saḥ* : he *mām* : Me *eti* : goes to.

55. Whoever works for Me, looking upon Me as the goal; whoever is My devotee, free from attachments and from antagonism to any being—such a man, O son of Pāṇḍu, shall enter into Me.[7]

ओं तत्सदिति श्रीमद्भगवद्गीतासूपनिषत्सु ब्रह्मविद्यायां
योगशास्त्रे श्रीकृष्णार्जुनसंवादे विश्वरूपदर्शनयोगो
नामैकादशोऽध्यायः ॥ 11 ॥

NOTES

1. *Vr*.2: That greatness specially consists in the fact that it knows no decay i.e., the Lord is not in any way affected by creating, preserving and dissolving this unimaginably vast and mysterious universe by Himself and out of Himself. Any material substance, when something is made out of it, suffers decay to that extent. So also any agent gets affected and exhausted through endless effort. But the Lord is not. That is His unique greatness.

2. *Vr*.13: In this idea, that the whole of the manifested universe is the body of God, the metaphysical support of devotional philosophy is clearly stated. The relation between the Lord and the universe is the crux of the Vedantic metaphysics. Pure non-dualism

holds that the universe is not actually there but only seems to be so like the snake in a rope seen in a visual illusion. Qualified monism holds that the world is real, and that, though separate from Him, it still forms a unity with Him as His body. In some systems, in place of body, it is called manifestation of His Sakti or Power, which is intimately related to Him and is one with Him as light and heat are with the sun. This comes under the doctrine of identity-in-difference. Pure dualism would have the universe as completely separate from Him, but having only the status of an existence dependent on Him. Devotion requires an object to love and to adore, which is at the same time very close to one, and is responsive to prayer and love. So a devotional philosophy requires to posit a distinction without a difference between God and the manifested universe, which includes the Jivas or centres of consciousness also. Therefore, the Gītā, being essentially a devotional text of the Bhāgavata tradition, highlights this relation of body-soul between the universe and God in this chapter, which marks the climax of its teachings.

3.*Vr.*33: This idea "Be Thou but an instrument" marks the acme of the Gītā teachings. It states the changed outlook of a mind that has had the illumination that the Cosmic Vision brings. An unillumined mind is ego-centred, and works with the sense of agency and with an eye on the fruits of actions. The *Gītā*, to start with, teaches that a spiritual aspirant should work, offering all the merits of his works to God. And as far as the material fruits of work are concerned, he should not make that the motive power of his action. He should be moved by a sense of duty, and the material reward he gets must be only a secondary consideration, not affecting the quality of his work. One must feel that the Lord is the Master and oneself is His servant, and that the work one does is for His sake and His satisfaction. This is what the *Gītā* describes as "being devoted to My work" (11.55) and "abandonment of all the fruits of one's actions" (18.2).

But here the aspirant still has the feeling that he is the doer. In other words, he retains the sense of agency. The illumination of the type that Arjuna gets, establishes the aspirant in the truth that the Lord's will is the only working force in the universe and that all the individual wills, which in ignorance appropriate for themselves the agency of the work done apparently by themselves, are really accomplished by that Supreme Will. The individual concerned is only an occasion. To illustrate it, consider an old building that has lost all strength and is on the point of dilapidation. A strong wind comes and brings down the building. Here the wind is only an occasion, whereas the natural processes that have worked all through the ages are the real cause. Another illustration is of a factory. The main shaft is moved by the power of steam coming from the boiler. Moved by that power, the various cogs in the big workshop are functioning, but to an onlooker they seem to work independently. Such a view is wrong, the fact being that the power from the source is the real agency and all the cogs are but its instruments.

To have a view of the Total is illumination and liberation To be restricted to the ego-centred view, is ignorance and bondage. Surrender to the Divine means the abandonment of this false view and surrendering the agentship also to Him, besides the fruits. Strictly speaking, the agentship has also been with Him always, but it is falsely appropriated to oneself by the ignorant man. Surrender strictly means only this recognition. And it is this recognition that comes to Arjuna on his experiencing the cosmic form of the Lord.

The all-comprehensive dominance of the Divine will can be illustrated also by the example of a living body. The living body of a man has several millions of cells. Each cell has an individuality and a function. The cells of the heart, the cells of the digestive system, the cells of the brain, the cells of the muscles etc., all carry on different activities individually and collectively. But in spite of the distinctiveness in entity and function of the cells, they are all sharers of the total energy of the organism, and they are functioning for the ego tenanting that organism. They live and function by, and for, that ego, and separated from it they have no meaning and they perish. If any of those cells considers its individuality as independence and seeks to function independently, it become a cancerous cell and perishes. The individuality of the Jiva and its freedom are only like this. The Divine will alone functions in the whole universe, which is His body, as it were, and all individuals derive their power from His will, and exist and function for His purpose. The recognition of this is to become a mere instrument or occasion—*nimitta-mātram*—for His functioning.

This is perfect self-surrender wherein not only the fruits of works are surrendered, but even the agentship. In Bhakti therefore the Jiva becomes one with the Lord in point of will, just as in Jñāna, he becomes one with Him in being. And since 'will' and 'being' cannot be separated in God, both these disciplines carry one to the same end. They can both be self-sufficient disciplines.

4. *Vr.*37: In the Verse 19 of the 9th Chapter (see note 12 of that Chapter) the Lord described Himself as *Sadasaccāhamarjuna*—I am both being and non-being, O Arjuna. Here He is spoken of as *Sat* (being) and *Asat* (non-being) and what is beyond them both. By *Sat* and *Asat* here are meant what is manifest and unmanifest. What is unmanifest need not be non-existent, but can be latent and unperceived. A tree is invisible in a seed, but it is latent as the seminal or causal condition. Here in Arjuna's vision the whole universe is seen as spread out in the body of God. This is the manifest condition, which lasts till the Kalpa is over. When the Kalpa ends and the Pralaya sets in, the manifest universe dissolves into the latent condition as the tree does into the seeds. This unmanifest latent condition is here called *Asat* or non-existence, in the sense that none can perceive it, being latent.

When God is spoken of as both Sat and Asat, what is meant is that these two conditions are his adjuncts, and that His existence is ordinarily understood by man in His relation to these adjuncts. For, man understands God as the creator and the cause of the universe. He cannot form any notion of Him, except in this relative sense, just as the word father cannot be understood except in relation to a son. But he has an identity apart from the one related to the universe in its latent and patent conditions and that is indicated by the expression "What is beyond"—*tat param*. If this is not granted, God can as well turn out to be an existence dependent on the manifested world. It is the universe that is dependent on God and not vice versa. The idea of *tat param* is necessary to secure this.

5. *Vr.*45: Three types of feelings overcome Arjuna's mind on seeing the Cosmic Form of the Lord, as Time the destroyer. These are joy, fear and perturbation. It is difficult to understand why a divine vision causes fear in the mind of even a hero like Arjuna,

making him pray for its withdrawal. It can be understood only if we accept that Arjuna's mind is not fully prepared as yet for it. Before the life of ego-centred consciousness is transcended, one has to pass through the experience of Kāla or Kālī, the all-consuming Time, which is Death. So long as the ego clings to itself, it is afraid to face Death in all her stark nakedness. A parallel to Arjuna's experience one finds in the life of the modern Incarnation Sri Ramakrishna, in his relation to his disciple Naren, who became Swami Vivekananda afterwards. Just as Sri Kṛṣṇa gave the divine eye to Arjuna to perceive the Cosmic Whole, Sri Ramakrishna by the exercise of his will wanted to give that climateric experience to Narendra. When Naren began to experience the whole universe dissolving into its elements and his own ego too being blasted, he felt terribly frightened like Arjuna and cried out. "What is happening to me! I have a father and a mother." Then the Master, finding Naren not yet ready for the experience, withdrew it from his consciousness. Similar experiences are recorded of other saints too.

Spiritual experience may be compared to an electric current of very high voltage. Suppose it is passed through a machine that can stand only 250 volts. Then the machine, unable to stand it, will break. Man's gross and subtle bodies must be prepared to stand it. To use a technical terminology, they must become highly Sāttvika. Until this condition is fulfilled wise Providence keeps human consciousness insulated from these experiences.

6. *Vrs.*53-54: In these verses is given an uncompromising statement of the self-sufficiency of Bhakti for the highest spiritual attainment. It is not a mere subordinate discipline for gaining what some call *cittaśuddhi* (purification of the mind), to be abandoned in preference to a more advanced discipline which is called *jñāna-niṣṭhā,* considered the direct establishment in non-dual understnding, and thus the immediate means of spiritual enlightenment. To a devotee with unswerving devotion, it is stated that the Lord bestows the awakening from the life of ignorance. He is then said to enter into Him i.e., his ego is dissipated and he becomes an unobstructed part and parcel of the Divine Life.

7. *Vr.*55: The way for the achievement of this is stated very briefly, but pointedly and exhaustively, in this verse. A devotee

is asked to serve Him alone as the Master and work whole-heartedly for Him. The servant may work faithfully for the master, but he does not look upon the latter as the highest. But a devotee sees in God the highest and the most precious of all beings. Such a person alone deserves the name of a Bhakta or devotee. He will have no attachments in work, and he will have no enmity to anyone, as he sees all as the children of God. This is an introduction to the next chapter, where the ideals of Bhakti are highlighted.

Chapter XII

भक्तियोगः

BHAKTI-YOGA

COMMUNION THROUGH LOVING DEVOTION

SUMMARY

The Impersonal and the Personal: (1-7) Arjuna now wants to know who is a better Yogi—the one who follows the path of devotion, looking upon God as the Supreme Person, or the one who looks upon Him as the Impersonal Absolute. Sri Krishna answers: All who worship Me with intense faith and adore Me, are praiseworthy. Of the two paths, that of the Impersonal Absolute is too difficult for men who are entrenched in body-consciousness. Besides, in this path one has to depend on one's effort alone. The devotee has the advantage that, as he depends on Me and not on his effort alone, I am always at his back to lift him out of the ocean of Samsāra.

The Practice of Devotion: (8-12) Therefore let men practise whole-hearted devotion to Me. If their mind does not automatically flow towards Me, they can try Yoga practices and gain concentration. If they cannot do that, they can engage themselves in works that are devoted to Me and are pleasing to Me. If even that is not possible, let them abandon the fruits of all works to Me. Such abandonment in truth and in reality is very potent; for it can bring peace instantaneously.

Who is a Bhakta?: (13-20) The qualities of an ideal Bhakta are then described. It can be studied in comparison with the ideal of the *Sthitaprajña* described in Ch. II. 55. He is a friend of all, free from self-centredness, unaffected by vanity and pride, ever cheerful, patient in all circumstances and situations, firm in his resolves, absolutely self-surrendered to the Lord, attracting the love and affection of all, unperturbed, pure, indifferent to worldly values, devoid of the feeling that he is the doer of anything, alike to friend and foe, alike in praise and insult, and looking on the whole world as his home.

अर्जुन उवाच

एवं सततयुक्ता ये भक्तास्त्वां पर्युपासते ।
ये चाप्यक्षरमव्यक्तं तेषां के योगवित्तमाः ॥ 1 ॥

Arjuna uvāca:

Evaṁ satata-yuktā ye bhaktās tvāṁ paryupāsate /
ye c' āpy akṣaram avyaktaṁ teṣāṁ ke yoga-vittamāḥ //1//

Evam : In this way *satatayuktāḥ* : ever-steadfast *ye* : who *bhaktāḥ* : devotees *tvām* : Thee *upāsate* : worship, *ye* : who *ca* : and *api* : again *akṣaraṁ avyaktam* : the Imperishable Unmanifest (*upāsate* : worship), *teṣām* : of them *ke* : who *yogavittamāḥ* : greater knowers of Yoga.

Arjuna said:

1. There are Thy ever-steadfast devotees who love and worship Thee in the above way (as the Divine Person); there are again others who contemplate on Thee as the Imperishable Unmanifest (Impersonal Absolute)—which of these has a greater understanding of Yoga.[1]

श्रीभगवानुवाच

मय्यावेश्य मनो ये मां नित्ययुक्ता उपासते ।
श्रद्धया परयोपेतास्ते मे युक्ततमा मताः ॥ 2 ॥

Srī bhagavān uvāca:

Mayy āveśya mano ye māṁ nitya-yuktā upāsate /
śraddhayā paray' opetās te me yuktatamā matāḥ //2//

Mayi : In Me *manaḥ* : mind *āveśya* : fixing *nityayuktāḥ* : ever steadfast *parayā śraddhayā* : with absolute faith *upetāḥ* : endowed with *ye* : who *mām* : Me *upāsate* : worship, *te* : they *yuktatamāḥ* : most perfect in Yoga, *me* : My *mataḥ* : I consider.

The Blessed Lord said:

2. Those I consider as the most perfect in Yoga, who, with their minds fixed intently on Me in steadfast love, worship Me with absolute faith.[2]

ये त्वक्षरमनिर्देश्यमव्यक्तं पर्युपासते ।
सर्वत्रगमचिन्त्यं च कूटस्थमचलं ध्रुवम् ॥ 3 ॥
संनियम्येन्द्रियग्रामं सर्वत्र समबुद्धयः ।
ते प्राप्नुवन्ति मामेव सर्वभूतहिते रताः ॥ 4 ॥

Ye tv akṣaram anirdeśyam avyaktaṁ paryupāsate /
sarvatragam acintyaṁ ca kūṭa-stham acalaṁ dhruvam //3//

Saṁniyamy'endriya-grāmaṁ sarvatra sama-buddhayaḥ /
te prāpnuvanti mām eva sarva-bhūta-hite ratāḥ //4//

Indriya-grāmam : The aggregate of the senses *saṁniyamya* : controlling, *sarvatra* : in all conditions *samabuddhayaḥ* : even-minded, *sarvabhūtahite* : in the welfare of all beings *ratāḥ* : mindful *ye* : who *tu* : but *anirdeśyam* : the undefinable *avyaktam* : the unmanifested *acintyam*: the unthinkable or transcendent *kūṭastham* : the firm support of the world *acalam* : the motionless *dhruvam* : the eternal *sarvatragam* : the all-pervading *ca* : and *akṣaram* : the imperishable (i.e., the Impersonal Absolute) *paryupāsate* : worship, *te* : they *mām* : Me *eva* : alone *prāpnuvanti* : attain.

3-4. Those who are devoted to the Imperishable (the Impersonal Absolute),—who is the firm support of the world and is also undefinable, unmanifested, transcendent, motionless, eternal and all-pervading—even they reach Me alone, striving with their senses controlled, and with mind tranquillised and set on the welfare of all.[3]

क्लेशोऽधिकतरस्तेषामव्यक्तासक्तचेतसाम् ।
अव्यक्ता हि गतिर्दुःखं देहवद्भिरवाप्यते ॥ 5 ॥

Kleśo'dhikataras teṣāṁ avyakt'āsakta-cetasām |
avyaktā hi gatir duḥkhaṁ dehavadbhir avāpyate //5//

Avyaktāsakta-cetasāṁ teṣām : Of those whose mind clings to the Unmanifested (i.e., the Impersonal Absolute) *kleśaḥ* : difficulty *adhikataraḥ* : is greater; *hi* : for *avyaktā gatiḥ* : the way of an unclear ideal i.e., the Absolute *dehavadbhiḥ*: for the embodied i.e., the body-centred *duḥkham* : with difficulty *avāpyate* : is attained.

5. The obstacles facing those devoted to the Impersonal Absolute are far greater; for the way of an unclear ideal is difficult for an embodied being (the body-centred man) to understand or follow.[4]

ये तु सर्वाणि कर्माणि मयि संन्यस्य मत्पराः ।
अनन्येनैव योगेन मां ध्यायन्त उपासते ॥ 6 ॥

तेषामहं समुद्धर्ता मृत्युसंसारसागरात् ।
भवामि न चिरात्पार्थ मय्यावेशितचेतसाम् ॥ 7 ॥

Ye tu sarvāṇi karmāṇi mayi saṁnyasya mat-parāḥ |
ananyen'aiva yogena māṁ dhyāyanta upāsate— //6//

Teṣāṁ ahaṁ samuddhartā mṛtyu-saṁsāra-sāgarāt |
bhavāmi nacirāt Pārtha mayy āveśita-cetasām //7//

Pārtha: O son of Pṛthā *ye* : whoever *tu*: but *sarvāṇi*: *all karmāṇi*: actions (along with sense of agency) *mayi* : in Me *samnyasya* : abandoning,resigning *matparāḥ* : taking refuge in Me as the Supreme *ananyena yogena eva*: by communion through love that knows not other objects to love *mām* : Me *dyayantaḥ* : meditating *upāsate:* worship, *mayi: in* Me *āveśitacetasām* : whose minds are firmly set *teṣām* : of those *aham*: I *nacirāt* soon *mṛtyu-samsārasāgarāt* : from the ocean of worldly existence characterised by death *samuddhartā*; saviour *bhavāmi*: I become.

6-7. But, O son of Pṛthā, soon will I lift from this ocean of death-bound worldly existence, those whose minds are ever set on Me—those who abandon to Me the fruits of all their actions together with the sense of agency thereof, and who worship Me, meditating on Me as their sole refuge and their only love.[5]

मय्येव मन आधत्स्व मयि बुद्धिं निवेशय ।
निवसिष्यसि मय्येव अत ऊर्ध्वं न संशयः ॥ 8 ॥

Mayy eva mana ādhatsva mayi buddhiṁ niveśaya /
nivasiṣyasi mayy eva ata ūrdhvaṁ na saṁśayaḥ //8//

Mayi eva : In Me alone *manaḥ* : mind *ādhatsva* : fix, *mayi* : in Me *buddhim* : reason, or understanding *niveśaya* : let penetrate; *ataḥ ūrdhvam* : thereafter *mayi* : in Me *eva* : alone *nivasiṣyasi* : you will live; *na saṁśayaḥ* : there is no doubt about it.

8. Fix your mind on Me alone; let your reason penetrate into Me; without doubt you will then abide in Me alone for ever more.[6]

अथ चित्तं समाधातुं न शक्नोषि मयि स्थिरम् ।
अभ्यासयोगेन ततो मामिच्छाप्तुं धनंजय ॥ 9 ॥

Atha cittaṁ samādhātuṁ na śaknoṣi mayi sthiram /
abhyāsa-yogena tato māṁ icch' āptuṁ Dhanañjaya //9//

Dhanañjaya : O Arjuna! *atha* : if *cittam* : mind *mayi* : in Me *sthiram* : steadily *samādhātum* : to fix *na śaknoṣi* : unable, *tataḥ* : then *abhyāsa-yogena* : by practice of concentration *mām* : Me *āptum* : to reach *iccha* : seek.

9. If you are unable to fix your mind steadily on Me (even at the start) then try to reach Me through the systematic practice of concentration.

21

अभ्यासेऽप्यसमर्थोऽसि मत्कर्मपरमो भव ।
मदर्थमपि कर्माणि कुर्वन्सिद्धिमवाप्स्यसि ॥ 10 ॥

Abhyāse'py asamartho'si mat-karma-paramo bhava /
mad-artham api karmāṇi kurvan siddhim avāpsyasi //10//

Abhyāse : In the systematic practice of concentration *api* : even *asamarthaḥ* : incapable *asi* : are, *matkarmaparamaḥ* : one having My work as one's highest aim *bhava* : you be; *madartham* : for My sake *karmāṇi* : works *kurvan* : doing *siddhim* : perfection *avāpsyasi*: will attain.

10. If you are not capable of practising systematic concentration, then devote yourself wholeheartedly to works of service to Me (consisting in external worship and discharge of duties for My sake). Thus working for Me, man can attain to perfection.

अथैतदप्यशक्तोऽसि कर्तुं मद्योगमाश्रितः ।
सर्वकर्मफलत्यागं ततः कुरु यतात्मवान् ॥ 11 ॥

Ath'aitad apy aśakto'si kartuṁ mad-yogam āśritaḥ /
sarva-karma-phala tyāgaṁ tataḥ kuru yat'ātmavān //11//

Atha : If then *etat api* : even that *kartum* : to perform *aśaktaḥ asi* : you are incapable, *tataḥ* : then *madyogamāśritaḥ* : one taking refuge in Me *yatātmavān* : one become self-controlled *sarvakarmaphalatyāgam* : surrender of the fruits of all action to Me *kuru* : perform.

11. If even this is too difficult for you to perform, then taking refuge in Me and thus controlling the mind, give up the fruits of all your actions (recognising Me as their agent and enjoyer).

श्रेयो हि ज्ञानमभ्यासाज्ज्ञानाद्ध्यानं विशिष्यते ।
ध्यानात्कर्मफलत्यागस्त्यागाच्छान्तिरनन्तरम् ॥ 12 ॥

Śreyo hi jñānam abhyāsāt jñānād dhyānaṁ viśiṣyate /
dhyānāt karma-phala-tyāgas tyāgāc chāntir anantaram //12//

Abhyāsāt : Than (mechanical) practice of disciplines *jñānam* : knowledge, philosophic understanding *śreyaḥ* : superior *hi* : indeed; *jñānāt* : than intellectual knowledge *dhyānaṁ* : meditation *viśiṣyate*: excels; *dhyānāt* : than meditation *karmaphala-tyāgam* : abandoning the fruits of all actions *śreyaḥ* : superior; *tyāgāt* : from renunciation *anantaram* : after *śāntiḥ* : peace.

12. Than (a mere formal) practice of disciplines, a clear intellectual understanding (of the doctrine) is better. Than such understanding, meditation is better. Even better than meditation is the abandonment of the fruits of action. For, such abandonment (of the fruits of works and sense of their agency) is immediately followed by peace.[7]

अद्वेष्टा सर्वभूतानां मैत्रः करुण एव च ।
निर्ममो निरहंकारः समदुःखसुखः क्षमी ॥ 13 ॥

संतुष्टः सततं योगी यतात्मा दृढनिश्चयः ।
मय्यर्पितमनोबुद्धिर्यो मद्भक्तः स मे प्रियः ॥ 14 ॥

Adveṣṭā sarva-bhūtānāṁ maitraḥ karuṇa eva ca /
nirmamo nirahaṁkāraḥ sama-duḥkha-sukhaḥ kṣamī //13//

santuṣṭaḥ satataṁ yogī yat'ātmā dṛḍha-niścayaḥ /
mayy arpita-mano-buddhir yo mad-bhaktaḥ sa me priyaḥ //14/

Sarvabhūtānām : Towards all beings *adveṣṭā* : without enmity; *maitraḥ* : friendly *karuṇaḥ* : compassionate *eva* : also *ca* : and *nirmamaḥ* : without the sense of mine *nirahaṅkāraḥ* : without the sense of 'I', *samaduḥkha-sukhaḥ* : alike in happiness and misery, *kṣamī* : having forbearance, *satatam* : always *santuṣṭaḥ* : content *yogī* : contemplative *yatātmā* : self-controlled *dṛḍhaniścayaḥ* : firm in conviction, *mayi* : in Me *arpitamanobuddhiḥ* : with mind and understanding dedicated *madbhaktaḥ* : My devotee *yaḥ* : who, *saḥ* : he *ca* : and *me priyaḥ* : dear to Me.

13-14. Friendly and compassionate to all and without any touch of hatred; devoid of possessiveness and arrogance; ever content and contemplative; alike in happiness and misery;

self-controlled and firm in conviction; dedicated to Me with all his heart and all his soul—dear to Me is a man who is thus devoted.[8]

यस्मान्नोद्विजते लोको लोकान्नोद्विजते च यः ।
हर्षामर्षभयोद्वेगैर्मुक्तो यः स च मे प्रियः ॥ 15 ॥

Yasmān n'odvijate loko lokān n'odvijate ca yaḥ /
harṣ'āmarṣa-bhay'odvegair mukto yaḥ sa ca me priyaḥ //15//

Yasmāt : From (due to) whom *lokaḥ* : the world *na udvijate* : is not agitated by fear, *yaḥ* : who *lokāt* : by the world *na udvijate* : is not agitated *ca* : and *harṣāmarṣa-bhayodvegaiḥ* : mental agitation caused by euphoria or anger or fear or excitement *yaḥ* : who *muktaḥ* : is free, *saḥ* : he *ca* : too *me priyaḥ* : dear to Me.

15. Who causes fear to none and whom none can frighten, who is thus free from the agitation of the moods caused by euphoria, anger, and excitement—such a person too is dear to Me.

अनपेक्षः शुचिर्दक्ष उदासीनो गतव्यथः ।
सर्वारम्भपरित्यागी यो मद्भक्तः स मे प्रियः ॥ 16 ॥

Anapekṣaḥ śucir dakṣa udāsīno gata-vyathaḥ /
sarvārambha-parityāgī yo mad-bhaktaḥ sa me priyaḥ //16//

Anapekṣaḥ : Desireless, *śuciḥ* : pure, *dakṣaḥ* : resourceful, *udāsīnaḥ* : unattached, *gatavyathaḥ* : free from all worries, *sarvārambha-parityāgī* : one who has abandoned all efforts i.e., without any sense of self-centred agency, *madbhaktaḥ* : My devotee *yaḥ* : who, *saḥ* : he *me* : to Me *priyaḥ* : is dear.

16. Desireless, pure, resourceful, unattached, unworried and without any sense of self-centred agency—a devotee thus endowed is dear to Me.

यो न हृष्यति न द्वेष्टि न शोचति न काङ्क्षति ।
शुभाशुभपरित्यागी भक्तिमान् यः स मे प्रियः ॥ 17 ॥

Yo na hṛṣyati na dveṣṭi na śocati na kāṅkṣati /
śubh'āśubha-parityāgī bhaktimān yaḥ sa me priyaḥ //17//

Yaḥ : Who *na hṛṣyati* : exults not, *na dveṣṭi* : is free from anger, *na śocati* : is free from sorrow, *na kāṅkṣati* : is free from desire, *yaḥ* : who *śubhāśubhaparityāgī* : abandons the pleasant and the unpleasant alike *bhaktimān* : one endowed with devotion, *saḥ* : he *me* : to Me *priyaḥ* : dear.

17. He who is free from elation, anger, sorrow, and craving, who neither seeks the pleasant nor shuns the unpleasant—dear to Me is the man who is thus devoted.

समः शत्रौ च मित्रे च तथा मानापमानयोः ।
शीतोष्णसुखदुःखेषु समः सङ्गविवर्जितः ॥ 18 ॥

तुल्यनिन्दास्तुतिर्मौनी संतुष्टो येन केनचित् ।
अनिकेतः स्थिरमतिर्भक्तिमान् मे प्रियो नरः ॥ 19 ॥

Samaḥ śatrau ca mitre ca tathā mān'āpamānayoḥ /
śītoṣṇa-sukha-duḥkheṣu samaḥ saṅga-vivarjitaḥ //18//

Tulya-nindā-stutir maunī saṁtuṣṭo yena kenacit /
aniketaḥ sthira-matir bhaktimān me priyo naraḥ //19//

Śatrau : Towards the enemy *ca* : and *mitre* : towards friend *ca* : and, *tathā* : in the same way *mānāpamānayoḥ* : in honour and in insult *samaḥ* : alike, *śītoṣṇa sukha-duḥkheṣu* : in sufferings caused by heat and cold *samaḥ* : alike, *saṅgavivarjitaḥ* : without attachment *tulyanindāstutiḥ* : alike in praise and blame, *maunī* : silent, *yena-kenacit* : with anything *saṁtuṣṭaḥ* : satisfied, *aniketaḥ* : without a permanent home, *sthiramatiḥ* : with a strong mind *bhaktimān* : a devotee *naraḥ* : man *me* : to Me *priyaḥ* : dear.

18-19. Alike to friend and foe, alike in honour and insult, alike in heat and cold, alike in praise and blame—unattached, contented, homeless, and steady in mind—dear to Me is a man who is thus devoted.

ये तु धर्म्यामृतमिदं यथोक्तं पर्युपासते ।
श्रद्दधाना मत्परमा भक्तास्तेऽतीव मे प्रियाः ॥ 20 ॥

Ye tu dharmyāmṛtam idaṁ yathoktaṁ paryupāsate /
śraddadhānā mat-paramā bhaktās te'tīva me priyāḥ //20//

Yathoktam : Thus set forth ***idam*** : this ***dharmyāmṛtam*** virtuous path to immortality ***śraddadhānāḥ*** : endowed with faith ***matparamāḥ*** : regarding Me as the Supreme Goal ***ye tu*** : even whoever ***paryupāsate*** : seek to practise, ***te bhaktāḥ*** : such devotees ***me*** : to Me ***atīva priyāḥ*** : are exceedingly dear.

20. Whosoever even seek to follow the virtuous path to Immortality thus set forth, with a mind full of faith and acceptance of Me as their supreme goal—exceedingly dear to Me are men who are thus devoted.

ओं तत्सदिति श्रीमद्भगवद्गीतासूपनिषत्सु ब्रह्मविद्यायां
योगशास्त्रे श्रीकृष्णार्जुनसंवादे भक्तियोगो
नाम द्वादशोऽध्यायः ॥ 12 ॥

NOTES

1. *Vr.*1: Pointed comparison and contrast between the paths of Bhakti and of Jñāna are here made in these words of Arjuna. An estimate of their comparative relevance in the life of ordinary man is also given. As for the ideals of Bhakti, reference is made to them in the concluding verses of the last chapter (eleven). It was also discussed in chapter X 9-11. Reference to that which is eternal and unmanifest (*sanātanaḥ* and *avyaktaḥ*), different

from 'the other unmanifest', i.e., the changeful unmanifest, or Prakṛti in the state of dissolution, is made in VIII. 20. The 'eternal and unmanifest' of the first kind is also described as *Akṣaram* or the Imperishable in the very next verse of the same chapter. These two terms Akṣara and Avyakta are used here to denote the Impersonal Absolute, the pursuit of which is contrasted with that of loving devotion to the Supreme Being as Person, and a pointed question is asked as to which is better, taking both these paths as distinct. Here Bhakti is not treated as a feeder to Jñāna, but as in itself self-sufficient. All attempts at trying to prove the contrary by quoting from different contexts, are frustrated by this one chapter which is unequivocal in its meaning. Kṛṣṇa also gives a clear answer to the questions in the next verse.

2. *Vr.*2: The clear and unequivocal answer given by the Lord is that He considers a true lover of God (Bhakta) as more perfect in spiritual communion. As against this, it is only interpretative high-handedness to say that the Bhakti discipline forms only a handmaid of the Jñāna discipline. At least the doctrine of the Gītā is that both these are self-sufficient spiritual disciplines, that neither need be subordinated to the other, and that in the end they take the spiritual pilgrim to the same Supreme Being. Thus though in the end they are the same, Bhakti has got its special excellences. What they are, will be stated in the next few verses.

3. *Vrs.*3-4: The ideal pursued (the Impersonal Absolute) and the means adopted in the path of Jñāna are described by various expressions of a very abstract nature. Some of these expressions have already been used to convey the idea of the Impersonal Absolute. They are: *Akṣaram* or the Imperishable and *Avyaktam* or the Unmanifest. In VIII. 3 it is said: *Akṣaraṁ brahma paramam*—the Supreme Brahman is meant by *Akṣara*. In VIII. 21 it is identified with *Avyakta*, the Unmanifest—*Avyakto'kṣara ityuktaḥ*. In XI. 18 Krishna is praised by Arjuna as *Akṣaram*. Later in XV. 16 the expressions *Kṣara, Akṣara* and *Kūṭastha* are used to indicate the Supreme Being and His manifestations.

The epithet *Kūṭastha* is a very intriguing word, as it is used in many places in the Gītā with different meanings. In VI.8 it is used to describe the unperturbed state of mind of a Yogi whereas here it is used to describe the Impersonal Absolute. The literal meaning of the word is 'one standing on a peak'—which means aloof and unaffected by all surroundings—on a firm foundation. So it gives the combined sense of firmness, aloofness and stablity. A totally different meaning also is given for it as follows: *Kūṭam* means 'crooked' or something that appears good and attractive but is really defective. It can therefore be applied to *Māyā*, the false world of appearances which ultimately causes suffering and death. So the word is interpreted to mean that which is the support of this world of falsity (*Māyā*). cf. Gītā Verses 6, 7; 15, 16.

It is stated in these verses that the man of knowledge who contemplates on the Impersonal Absolute attains to the same goal as the devotee who has deep and unswerving love of God and devotes himself to work for His sake and adores Him. So from the point of view of the end, Arjuna's question as to which is preferable has no meaning. It becomes relevant from the point of view of practicality, as explained in the next verse.

4. *Vr.5*: The difficulty in the path of the Impersonal Absolute is described as the state of 'embodiedness'. It is impossible to conceive of any spiritual aspirant who is not an 'embodied being'. So the expression means only 'one on whom body-consciousness is very strong'. There may be Jīvan-muktas (those liberated in life) who are not body-conscious, but few aspirants can really be so. So the demand for this qualification excludes ninety nine percent of aspirants from this path. In addition to the handicap of body-consciousness, there is another great disadvantage in this path, which will be clearly stated by the Lord in the next verses. The disadvantge consists in that, that such aspirants will have to stand on their own strength and cannot hope for a helping hand from the Ideal they pursue.

Some may point out that the path of the Impersonal Absolute is the superior, because it is difficult and because only a few are qualified for it. But merely because something is difficult, it cannot be called superior. Superiority consists in a thing being easy and at the same time most effective. So the *Bhāgavata Purāṇa* compares Bhakti to a morsel of food eaten. By itself it appeases hunger, gives good taste, and strengthens the body at the same time. All these constitute one process. The function of Bhakti is similar. It confers renunciation, bliss and knowledge, all at one stroke.

How the path of devotion fulfils these is made clear in the next verse.

5. *Vrs.*6-7: These two verses set forth the special advantage of the path of devotion. It consists in the fact that the God of love is an active factor in the devotee's life. What is said here is that He lifts up the sincere and whole-hearted devotee from the ocean of Saṁsāra. In Chaps. 10 and 11 the Lord says He illumines his intellect, and remaining within the devotee's innermost being, shatters the darkness of ignorance by the shining lamp of wisdom. Is He then cold to the one on the path of the Impersonal Absolute? No, He is not cold but the aspirant is cold. The aspirant's understanding of the Divine is that He is Impersonal and therefore without responsiveness. An Impersonal Being cannot be prayed to nor does He respond. By one's discriminative effort one can rise up to His level and be He. In the path of pure Yoga also it is the same. By the power of concentration one reaches His being. As a person's faith is, so the Lord is to him. The aspirant on the path of Love understands Him as a loving Person—a Being whom one can adore and pray to, and who responds to the devotees' earnest call by bestowing His grace on him and uplifting Him from Saṁsāra.

These verses are a conclusive proof of the fact that the Gītā accepts both the paths of Bhakti (the adoration of God as the Personal) and the path of Jñāna (the pursuit of the Impersonal) as self-sufficient disciplines to attain the spiritual *summum bonum*. In the path of Bhakti, the aspirant may work at all stages, as mentioned in the previous chapter (XI. 55), '*Matkarmakṛt*, (engaged in My work), and as said later in XVIII. 54, '*Sarva-karmāṇyapi sadā kurvāṇo-mad-vyapāśrayaḥ*' (one doing all kinds of works always, fully resigned to Me). In the path of devotion there is no contradiction between work and spiritual pursuit, if the work is of the nature of service of the Lord, either at the preparatory stage or at the stage of perfection. And it is the Gītā doctrine that by itself, the path of devotion can give the highest illumination.

Sri Ramakrishna makes plain the meaning of the Gītā in a homely parable. A master has a garden supervisor who is very faithful and hardworking and serves the master to his perfect satisfaction. Highly pleased with him, the Master puts the servant on his own seat, telling him, 'You are as good as myself.' This is the meaning of the Verse 7.18, '*Jñānī tu ātmaiva me matam*' (The man of knowledge is My very self), although from the pure Advaita point of view it is interpreted as meaning that the Jñāni and Myself are one.

It has to be noted that Jñāna or knowledge need not necessarily mean the knowledge of the oneness of the Jīva with the Supreme Being. All understanding of one's relationship with the Supreme can be called Jñāna. So in the Bhakti context, the above passage can very well mean the understanding of the extreme closeness and intimacy between the devotee and the Lord, as implied in Sri Ramakrishna's parable. Even if it is taken otherwise, it can be said that, according to the Gītā, knowledge of unity is a gift of God on a devotee. To attempt to gain that by a direct recourse to the philosophy of the Impersonal is fraught with very great difficulties for man, who is entrenched in the feeling that his self is the body. And a man who is not dominated by that sense is only a hypothetical entity, to be found nowhere in actual life. (Also see No. 5 on Gītā VII. 18 elsewhere.)

It is perhaps relevant to quote here what Sri Kṛṣṇa himself says to his disciple Uddhava on the self-sufficiency of Bhakti discipline in *Bhāgavata* XI. 20.29-35. It is said there: "When a man thus continues to follow the disciplines of Bhakti without break, I begin to dwell in his heart, and thereupon, all the desires of the heart are destroyed owing to My presence. When an aspirant realises Me, the soul of all, his ego-sense, which constitutes the knot of the heart, is cut asunder; all his doubts about God, the Atman etc., are dispelled; and the hold of past Karma on him gets attenuated. For one who is thus endowed with devotion that constantly makes the mind centred in Me, there is no need of knowledge and renunciation, as disciplines separate from the practice of devotion, for the attainment of the highest spiritual *summum bonum*. Whatever can be attained by Vedic rituals, austerities, knowledge, dispassion, Yoga, charities and other spiritual disciplines—be that the abode of the celestials, liberation, or Vaikuntha—all these can be attained by a votary of the path of devotion without any difficulty, if he so desires. But holy men of firm mind, who are endowed with unwavering devotion to Me, do not desire or accept even Mokṣa, which gives the freedom from birth and death, even if I Myself offer it to them. The state of mind in which a man is free from wants of every kind is declared to be the Supreme Blessedness (Niḥśreyas), infinite in its scope. Pure devotion for Me dawns only on such a person who wants nothing from Me—worldly fulfilments or even salvation."

6. *Vrs.*8-11: The Path of Devotion is, according to the Gītā, the easy and the royal road to the attainment of the Divine. Even in that path there are disciplines that are varying in their practicality for aspirants at different stages of development. They are mentioned one after another in these verses. First come those who have inborn hankering for God and whose mind always tends towards Him. Next, if one is incapable of it, systematic practices to draw the mind to God are advocated. These can include the early disciplines of Bhakti like *śravaṇa* (hearing), *kīrtaṇa* (hymning) and *smaraṇa* (remembering). In *smaraṇa* can be included such practices as Japa (repetition of a holy name) and attempt at meditation. Through these the mind can be constantly fixed on the Divine. For people who cannot do these even because of temperamental reasons, and because of the extreme difficulty felt by many to concentrate in meditation, is given the discipline of God's work. It has got the virtue of complete objectivity, and objective concentration is much easier than subjective concentration.

But what is God's work? In a very wide sense, the whole universe is the Lord's and all the works that one devotes oneself to as a member of the social order are works of God. To discharge all one's duties with the feeling that one is His servant, that one's capacity for work is His gift, and that the fruits of the work are also His, may be called doing God's work. So the Gītā in 18.46 says that "by adoring Him, from whom all this creation has originated, with the discharge of the duties that devolve on one, an aspirant attains Siddhi (perfection)."

This is also the significance of the discipline of Pādaseva included in the nine-limbed Sādhana of Bhakti. Pādaseva is not shampooing the feet of some one. Pāda means a part of God. The scriptures say that a small part of Him is the seen universe, while the rest is transcendent. Now the service of God as manifested in the society of men and other living beings with the feeling that

God indwells them all, is the real Pādaseva, and one devoted to it in this spirit, is doing God's work.

Apart from this very wide sense, God's work can have a restricted meaning also. Work for a holy cause or for the cause of a Divine incarnation is God's work in a special sense. Such a cause was given to mankind by Swami Vivekananda when he founded the Ramakrishna Math and Ramakrishna Mission as a vehicle for the spread of the teachings of the Great Master, Sri Ramakrishna, and the service of Him through works consecrated to Him.

External worship of God through images installed in temples is also doing 'God's work'. Worship can be done at the individual level, forming the external counterpart of adoration of Him through meditation and Japa. So 'Archanam', worship through images, forms a part of the nine disciplines of Bhakti. It can take the shape of maintenance of great temples and the organising of religious festivals. But it has to be remembered that such organised ritualism must be accompanied by service of society, of the poor and the holy ones. It is said in the *Bhāgavata* that ritualism without the service of fellow beings as a part of it is like offerings made in ashes in place of fire. It is infructuous and ceases to be 'a work of God'. But organised ritualism together with service of living beings as a part of it, provides an excellent means of doing 'God's work'.

If a devotee feels too weak to do it even, he is asked to abandon the fruits of all works he does, and he is told that renunciation of this kind is highly effective.

But a question will arise in the mind of an enquirer, whether this is easier and more feasible than 'doing God's work'. For a man of exceedingly strong faith, it may be so, but for devotees in general it is not less difficult than the earlier discipline. For, what man is asked to do is to surrender his sense of agency and the results of action, realising that the Lord is the sole agent and oneself is only a small instrument.

This advice of the Gītā is reminiscent of Sri Ramakrishna's advice to his Bohemian disciple, Girish Chandra Ghosh. When Girish asked Sri Ramakrishna for instruction in spiritual practice, the Great Master instructed him in the usual way to repeat the name of God at particular times, meditate on Him, etc. Girish replied that he could not undertake to do anything regularly, because there was no certainty or punctuality about anything in life as far as he was concerned. He did not even know at what time he would take his meal the next day. His life being so irregular, he wanted to be told something that was possible for him to do in the midst of his pre-occupations. Then the Master asked him to give him his (Girish's) 'power of attorney', meaning that he should completely give up his sense of agency in all actions, and put his trust in the Master at all times. Girish, who was a man of great faith, thought that this was quite easy, and agreed to do so. But as he tried to practise it and as he began to think over its implications, he found that it required him to constantly remember the Master and be resigned to him.

Such is also the implication of resigning the fruits of all works to God. The *Bhāgavata Purāṇa* XI. 2.36 explains this central discipline of the Bhāgavata Dharma thus: "Whatever work I do by body, word, mind, senses, Buddhi, and ego-sense, prompted by my nature, all that I offer to Nārāyaṇa."

7. *Vr.*12: In the previous verses it was suggested to those whose minds do not get absorbed in God naturally, to practise concentration, to do God's work, and to surrender all the fruits of actions to Him. These are given as relevant to less competent persons in the succeeding order. But here in this verse the last discipline prescribed to the least competent, namely, the surrender of the fruits of all actions, is given the highest place as leading to immediate attainment of spiritual realisation. That looks very puzzling. But the puzzle will be solved to a considerable extent if we remember the instruction of Sri Ramakrishna to Girish mentioned in the previous note. Its superiority consists in that any man placed in any situation can begin to practise it, provided he has a strong faith in God and the spiritual Gospel. But as one practises and reflects on it, one will find that the other disciplines are all involved in it, and that constant remembrance of God and practice of meditation automatically follow the successful performance of surrendering the sense of agency and the fruits of work to God.

There is also a suggestion in it that the practice of concentration, knowledge of scriptures, and doing God's work are to be considered successful to the extent that they enable one to surrender the agency and the fruits of works to God. It is the touchstone of the sincere and successful practice of the other disciplines.

The verse also means that at least as far as Bhakti is concerned there is no opposition between its disciplines and works at any stage.

8. *Vrs.*13-20: Just like the description of the *Sthitaprajña*, the man of steady wisdom, in Chapter 2, this is stated to be a description of a Bhakta, a devotee. A question may arise here. Two types of aspirants are described in this chapter—the Bhaktas who devote themselves heart and soul to the God of love (the Supreme Being as Person) and those who devote themselves to Him as Avyakta and Akṣara, the Impersonal Absolute referred to in the verses 3 and 4 of this chapter. The ideal of which of these two paths is portrayed by this description of the Bhakta given here? There is a view that this refers to the ideal of a follower of the Impersonal Absolute, who is usually referred to as Jñāni. But right through the description, the ideal man is referred to as *Bhakta* and *Bhaktimān*. It will not therefore be appropriate to consider this as an exclusive description of the Jñāni. In fact in this chapter as also in earlier ones, it is expressly stated that the goal of the paths of Bhakti and of Jñāna is the same in the final state. The difference is only at the stage of disciplines. As has been stated in many places, each discipline is self-sufficient in itself and one need not be subordinated to the others. Detachment, universal love, resignation, self-control, absence of egoism etc., are the common characteristics of perfect men, whatever might be the discipline they adopt. They are also virtues to be cultivated by aspirants of all types. So it is better to take this passage as referring to both the types of aspirants mentioned in this chapter.

Chapter XIII

क्षेत्रक्षेत्रज्ञविभागयोगः

DIFFERENTIATION OF THE KNOWER FROM THE KNOWN

SUMMARY

The field and its knower: (1-6) The Bhagavan said: There are two categories in the consciousness of man—the object and the subject, the 'seen' and the 'seer'. The 'seen' is in the field, the body: the 'seer' is the Spirit, the Jīva. The body-mind is the 'field', because it is the environment in association with which the 'seer' the Jīva, enjoys the fruits of his actions and also undergoes spiritual evolution. Thus the body-mind is its adjunct, the instrument through which the Spirit contacts objects. Still, it is only the 'seen', the 'object', because the 'seer', the Jīva, is not part of it but distinct from it and master of it.

In a broader sense the field is not merely the individual body, but Universal Nature, of which the individual body is a part. This Universal Nature, the Field, is constituted of the following: The great elements, Egoity, Intellect, the Unmanifested State, the eleven organs, the five objects of perception, will, aversion, joy, sorrow, combination, life and vitality. All the individual fields are made of the combination of these, and in all of them the Seer is Myself (My part or reflection in them).

Knowledge and its means: (7-11) The Seen and the Seer, the body and the Spirit, are inextricably mixed up in man in the state of ignorance. To know them in their distinctiveness is Knowledge, and this knowledge grows by the cultivation of the following disciplines: Absence of pride and vanity, non-injury, patience, perseverance, service of the teacher, self-control, revulsion to tempting objects of senses, reflection on the ephemerality of life, non-attachment, non-entanglement with family, imperturbability, intense devotion to Me, frequenting solitude, steady pursuit of spiritual enquiry, and strong aspiration for the Truth. These constitute knowledge or spirituality, and the opposite is ignorance or unspirituality.

The object to be known: (12-15) The object to be known is the Supreme Being, who cannot be described by words like 'existent' and 'non-existent'. He enfolds everything in Himself and also indwells everything. Though devoid of senses He enlivens all sense powers; though unattached and unrelated, He supports everything; and though beyond the Gunas of Prakṛti, He is the enjoyer of all the Guṇas. He is both far and near, and because of his subtlety, He appears to be not. He is the originator and the consumer of everything. He is the Lord of all and remains undivided in the apparently diversified phenomena. He is the ultimate consciousness that reveals everything. The source of all light and life and the centre to which all spiritual quest is directed, He verily resides in the heart of all.

Knowledge as discovery of one's spiritual identity: (16-34) Thus there are two aspects in man—the body-mind which is a part and parcel of Universal Nature, and the Spirit which is ultimately one with Me, the supreme Subject. Not aware of his real nature, the Spirit identifies himself with the properties of material nature, and becomes subject to repeated embodiments in Samsāra. Identification makes him the enjoyer of what is really of the body-mind. But there is present in the embodied being another Puruṣa, the witness of all, the sanctioner of all, the Lord and Support of all, the Master of soul and matter. It is the Paramātman. Let the aspirant, overcoming the identification of the Spirit with material Nature, find his identity in Me, the Supreme Lord, who is always the nearest and the closest to him—who is, as it were, his matrix, who is the One spiritual Sun reflecting as all the individual Spirits in the reflector of the body-mind—, and then he shall instantly be redeemed. Real Knowledge consists in the understanding of this distinction between Nature and Spirit, and the Spirit's absolute freedom from Nature.

श्रीभगवानुवाच

इदं शरीरं कौन्तेय क्षेत्रमित्यभिधीयते ।
एतद्यो वेत्ति तं प्राहुः क्षेत्रज्ञ इति तद्विदः ॥ १ ॥

Śrī Bhagavān uvāca:

Idaṁ śarīraṁ Kaunteya kṣetram ity abhidhīyate /
etad yo vetti taṁ prāhuḥ kṣetra-jña iti tad-vidaḥ //1//

Kaunteya : O Son of Kuntī *idam* : this *śarīram* : body *kṣetram* : Kṣetra i.e., field (for reaping the fruits of action) *iti abhidhīyate* : is spoken of as. *Etat* : This body *yaḥ* : who *vetti* : knows it (as one's property) *tam* : him *kṣetrajñaḥ* : as Kṣetrajña (knower of the field) *iti* : as *tadvidaḥ* : men versed in this subject *prāhuḥ* : say.

The Blessed Lord said:

1. This body, O son of Kunti, is called the Kṣetra, the field (because the fruits of action are reaped in it). He who knows it (as his property) is the Kṣetrajña or the Spirit who knows the field. So say those versed in this subject.[1]

क्षेत्रज्ञं चापि मां विद्धि सर्वक्षेत्रेषु भारत ।
क्षेत्रक्षेत्रज्ञयोर्ज्ञानं यत्तज्ज्ञानं मतं मम ॥ २ ॥

Kṣetra-jñaṁ c'āpi māṁ viddhi sarva-kṣetreṣu Bhārata /
kṣetra-kṣetrajñayor jñānaṁ yat taj jñānaṁ mataṁ mama //2//

Bhārata : O scion of the Bharata race! *sarvakṣetreṣu* : in all the kṣetras *ca* : and *mām* : Me *api* : alone *kṣetrjñam* : as Kṣetrajña *viddhi* : know. *Kṣetra-kṣetrajñayoḥ* : regarding Kṣetra and Kṣetrajña *yat* : which *jñānam* : knowledge *tat* : that *jñānam* : knowledge (*iti* : this) *mama* : My *matam* : view.

2. Know Me, O scion of the Bharata race, to be the Kṣetrajña (the Spirit) in all Kṣetras (bodies). The knowledge of the distinction between Kṣetra and Kṣetrajña alone is real knowledge according to Me.

तत्क्षेत्रं यच्च यादृक्च यद्विकारि यतश्च यत् ।
स च यो यत्प्रभावश्च तत्समासेन मे शृणु ॥ 3 ॥

Tat kṣetraṁ yac ca yādṛk ca yad-vikāri yataś ca yat /
sa ca yo yat prabhāvaś ca tat samāsena me śṛṇu //3//

Tat : That *kṣetra* :Kṣetram *yat* : which *ca* : and, *yādṛk* : of what nature *ca* : and, *yadvikāri* : what its modifications, *yataḥ* : from what *yat* : which *ca* : and, *saḥ* : he (the Kṣetrajña) *yaḥ* : who *ca* : and, *yat prabhāvaḥ* : what his powers are *ca* : and, *tat* : that *samāsena* : in brief *me* : from Me *sṛṇu* : hear.

3. Hear from Me in brief what the Kṣetra is, of what nature it is, what its modifications are, and from what causes what effects have sprung. Also know who the Kṣetrajña is and what his powers consist in.

ऋषिभिर्बहुधा गीतं छन्दोभिर्विविधैः पृथक् ।
ब्रह्मसूत्रपदैश्चैव हेतुमद्भिर्विनिश्चितैः ॥ 4 ॥

Ṛṣibhir bahudhā gītaṁ chandobhir vividhaiḥ pṛthak /
brahma-sūtra-padaiś c'aiva hetumadbhir viniścitaiḥ //4//

Ṛṣibhiḥ : By Ṛṣis *bahudhā* : in many ways *vividhaiḥ* : in varying *chandobhiḥ* : in metres *pṛthak gītam* : sung in various hymns, *hetumatbhiḥ* : well-reasoned *viniścitaiḥ* : conclusive *brahma-sūtra padaiḥ* : in the aphorisms of the Brahma-sūtras *ca* : and *eva* : also.

4. In many and different ways have the Rishis sung about this subject in metres of varying description. The well-reasoned and definitive aphorisms of the Brahma-sūtras too have discussed it.

महाभूतान्यहंकारो बुद्धिरव्यक्तमेव च ।
इन्द्रियाणि दशैकं च पञ्च चेन्द्रियगोचराः ॥ 5 ॥

इच्छा द्वेषः सुखं दुःखं संघातश्चेतना धृतिः ।
एतत्क्षेत्रं समासेन सविकारमुदाहृतम् ॥ 6 ॥

Mahā-bhūtāny ahaṁkāro buddhir avyaktam eva ca /
indriyāṇi daś'aikaṁ ca pañca c'endriya-gocarāḥ //5//

Icchā dveṣaḥ sukhaṁ duḥkhaṁ saṁghātaś cetanā dhṛtiḥ
etat kṣetraṁ samāsena savikāram udāhṛtam //6//

Mahābhūtani : The five great elements beginning with the sky *ahaṁkāraḥ* : the I-sense *buddhiḥ* : intellect *avyaktạm* : the Unmanifested Root Matter *ca* : and *daśa indriyāṇi* : the ten organs *ekam ca* : and one more (i.e., the mind as the eleventh organ) *pañca* : five *indriya-gocarāḥ* : objects of senses *icchā* : desire *dveṣaḥ* : hatred *sukham* : pleasure *duḥkham* : pain *saṅghātaḥ* : the aggregate i.e., the body *cetanā* : consciousness *dhṛtiḥ* : will *savikāram* : along with its modifications *etat kṣetram* : this Kṣetra *samāsena* : briefly *udāhṛtam* : has been described.

5-6. The five great elements, the I-sense, the intellect, and the Unmanifested (Root Matter); the ten organs along with the mind as the eleventh, and the five objects of the senses; desire, hatred, pleasure and pain; the body, consciousness, and will—such is a brief description of the Kṣetra with all its modifications.[2]

अमानित्वमदम्भित्वमहिंसा क्षान्तिरार्जवम् ।
आचार्योपासनं शौचं स्थैर्यमात्मविनिग्रहः ॥ 7 ॥

Amānitvam adambhitvam ahiṁsā kṣāntir ārjavam /
ācāry'opāsanaṁ śaucaṁ sthairyam ātma-vinigrahaḥ //7//

Amānitvam : Absence of self-importance *adambhitvam* : unpretentiousness *ahimsā* : non-violence *kṣāntiḥ* : patience *ārjavam* : straight-forwardness; *ācāryopāsanam* : service of the teacher *śaucam* : cleanliness *sthairyam* : steadfastness *ātmavinigrahaḥ* : self-control.

7. Freedom from self-importance, unpretentiousness, non-violence, patience, straight-forwardness, service of the teacher, cleanliness, steadfastness, and self-control;[3]

इन्द्रियार्थेषु वैराग्यमनहंकार एव च ।
जन्ममृत्युजराव्याधिदुःखदोषानुदर्शनम् ॥ 8 ॥

Indriy'ārtheṣu vairāgyam anahaṁkāra eva ca /
janma-mṛtyu-jarā-vyādhi-duḥkha-doṣ'ānudarśanam //8//

Indriyārtheṣu : Towards sense objects *vairāgyam* : abhorrence *anahaṁkāraḥ* : self-effacement *eva* : also *ca* : and *janma-mṛtyu-jarā-vyādhi-duḥkha-doṣ'ānudarśanam* : perception of evil and misery in birth, death, old age and sickness.

8. Abhorrence of sensuality, self-effacement and perception of evil and misery in birth, death, old age and sickness;

असक्तिरनभिष्वङ्गः पुत्रदारगृहादिषु ।
नित्यं च समचित्तत्वमिष्टानिष्टोपपत्तिषु ॥ 9 ॥

Asaktir anabhiṣvaṅgaḥ putra-dāra-gṛhādiṣu /
nityaṁ ca sama-cittatvam iṣṭ'āniṣṭ'opapattiṣu //9//

Putra-dāra-gṛhādiṣu : In respect of son, wife, house etc., *asaktiḥ* : detachment *anabhiṣvaṅgaḥ* : non-identification with, *iṣṭāniṣto-papattiṣu* in the attainment of the favourable and the unfavourable *nityam* : always *samacittatvam* : evenness of mind.

9. Detachment from property and family members, non-identification with them and their fortunes, and constant evenness of mind in favourable and unfavourable situations;

मयि चानन्ययोगेन भक्तिरव्यभिचारिणी ।
विविक्तदेशसेवित्वमरतिर्जनसंसदि ॥ 10 ॥

Mayi c'ānanya-yogena bhaktir avyabhicāriṇī /
vivikta-deśa-sevitvam aratir jana-samsadi //10//

Mayi : To Me *ananya-yogena* : through communion with a sense of intimacy (non-separateness) *avyabhicāriṇī* : unswerving *bhaktiḥ* :

devotion, *viviktadeśa sevitvam* : resort to solitude, *janasaṁsadi* : for vulgar company *aratiḥ* : abhorrence.

10. Practice of unswerving devotion through contemplation on Me as one's 'own' (or on Me in non-separation), resort to solitude, and abhorrence of vulgar company;

अध्यात्मज्ञाननित्यत्वं तत्त्वज्ञानार्थदर्शनम् ।
एतज्ज्ञानमिति प्रोक्तमज्ञानं यदतोऽन्यथा ॥ 11 ॥

Adhyātma-jñāna-nityatvaṁ tattva jñānārtha-darśanam /
etat jñānam iti proktam ajñānaṁ yad ato'nyathā //11//

Adhyātma-jñāna-nityatvam : Constant application to spiritual studies and practices, *tattva-jñānārtha-darśanam* : a comprehension of the goal of spiritual enlightenment (and the destiny of man), *etat* : this *jñānam* : knowledge *iti* : as *proktam* : is spoken of, *yat* : what *ataḥ* : to it *anyathā* : opposed *ajñānam* : ignorance.

11. Constant application to the study of spiritual texts and practice of spiritual disciplines, and a clear comprehension of the goal of spiritual enlightenment and the destiny of man—all these described before constitute knowledge; what is opposed to it is all ignorance.

ज्ञेयं यत्तत्प्रवक्ष्यामि यज्ज्ञात्वामृतमश्नुते ।
अनादिमत्परं ब्रह्म न सत्तन्नासदुच्यते ॥ 12 ॥

Jñeyaṁ yat tat pravakṣyāmi yat jñātvā'mṛtam aśnute /
anādimat paraṁ brahma na sat tan n'āsad ucyate //12//

Yat : Which *jñeyam* : ought to be known, *yat* : which *jñātvā* : knowing *amṛtam* : immortality *aśnute* : is attained, *tat* : that *pravakṣyāmi* : I shall declare; *anādimat* : without beginning *param* : supreme *Brahma* : Brahman *na* : neither *sat* : being *na* : nor *asat* : non-being *ucyate* : is described as.

12. I shall now declare the Object which ought to be known, by knowing which one attains to immortality. It is the Supreme

Brahman, the eternal Being who cannot be described either as existent or non-existent (in the way sense-bound material objects are described)[4]

सर्वतः पाणिपादं तत्सर्वतोऽक्षिशिरोमुखम् ।
सर्वतः श्रुतिमल्लोके सर्वमावृत्य तिष्ठति ॥ 13 ॥

Sarvatah pāṇi-pādaṁ tat sarvato'kṣi-śiro-mukham /
sarvataḥ śrutimal loke sarvam āvṛtya tiṣṭhati //13//

Sarvataḥ : Everywhere *pāṇipādam* : hands and feet, *sarvataḥ* : everywhere *akṣiśiromukham* : eyes, head and face, *sarvataḥ* : everywhere *śrutimat* : with ears, *tat* : that *loke*: in the world *sarvam* : everything *āvṛtya* : enveloping and transcending *tiṣṭhati* :

13. His hands and feet are everywhere. His eyes, ears and mouth grasp everything. His face is in all directions. He is the transcendent Spirit, enveloping all that exists in the world.

सर्वेन्द्रियगुणाभासं सर्वेन्द्रियविवर्जितम् ।
असक्तं सर्वभृच्चैव निर्गुणं गुणभोक्तृ च ॥ 14 ॥

Sarv'endriya-guṇ'ābhāsaṁ sarv'endriya-vivarjitam /
asaktaṁ sarva-bhṛc c'aiva nirguṇaṁ guṇa-bhoktṛ ca //14//

Sarvendriya-guṇābhāsam : Revealing all senses i.e., enabling all the senses to function, *sarvendriya-vivarjitam* : devoid of all senses, *asaktam* : unattached *sarvabhṛt* : support of all *ca eva* : and yet, *nirguṇam* : beyond the Guṇas of Prakṛti *guṇabhoktā* : the enjoyer of the Guṇas *ca* : and yet.

14. By His power the faculties of the senses function, but sense organs He has none. He is the support of all things, but they do not affect Him. He transcends Nature and its functions, but these constitute the objects for His enjoyment.

बहिरन्तश्च भूतानामचरं चरमेव च ।
सूक्ष्मत्वात्तदविज्ञेयं दूरस्थं चान्तिके च तत् ॥ 15 ॥

Bahir antaś ca bhūtānām acaraṁ caram eva ca /
sūkṣmatvāt tad avijñeyaṁ dūrasthaṁ c'āntike ca tat //15//

Tat : That *bhūtānām* : of beings *bahiḥ* : without *antaḥ* : within *ca* : and, *acaram* : not moving *caram* : moving *eva* : also *ca* : and; *sūkṣmatvāt* : because of subtlety *tat* : that *avijñeyam* : cannot be an object of knowledge, *dūrastham* : it is far off *antike* : near by *ca* : also.

15. He is within and without all beings. Though unmoving, He looks like one moving (because He is everywhere). He is both far and near—far to the ignorant and near to the knowing ones. Owing to subtlety, He cannot be known like gross objects.

अविभक्तं च भूतेषु विभक्तमिव च स्थितम् ।
भूतभर्तृ च तज्ज्ञेयं ग्रसिष्णु प्रभविष्णु च ॥ 16 ॥

Avibhaktaṁ ca bhūteṣu vibhaktam iva ca sthitam /
bhūta-bhartṛ ca tat jñeyaṁ grasiṣṇu prabhaviṣṇu ca //16//

Jñeyam : What is to be known *tat* : that *avibhaktam* : impartible whole *ca* : yet *bhūteṣu* : among all beings *vibhaktam* : divided *iva ca* : as if *sthitam* : remains, **bhutabhartṛ** : the support of all beings *ca* : and, also, *grasiṣṇu* : devourer *prabhaviṣṇu* : originator *ca* : and also.

16. He, (the Brahman) whom aspirants seek to know, is the impartible Whole, yet does He seem to dwell in all beings as if divided into many. He is the generator and supporter of all beings, and their devourer too.

ज्योतिषामपि तज्ज्योतिस्तमसः परमुच्यते ।
ज्ञानं ज्ञेयं ज्ञानगम्यं हृदि सर्वस्य धिष्ठितम् ॥ 17 ॥

Jyotiṣām api taj jyotis tamasaḥ param ucyate /
jñānaṁ jñeyaṁ jñāna-gamyaṁ hṛdi sarvasya dhiṣṭhitam //17//

Tat : That *jyotiṣām* : of things having light *api* : even *jyotiḥ* : the revealing light *tamasaḥ* : of darkness *param* : beyond *ucyate* : is said to be; *jñānam* : knowledge *jñeyam* : the object of knowledge *jñānagamyam* : the one to whom knowledge is the way of approach *sarvasya* : of all things *hṛdi* : in the heart *dhiṣṭhitam* : is established.

17. The self-luminuous light of consciousness revealing even all that is luminous, He is beyond obscuration by the darkness of ignorance. He, the light of knowledge, He, the quest of knowledge, He, the way to whom is knowledge—in the innermost recess of all beings is He established.

इति क्षेत्रं तथा ज्ञानं ज्ञेयं चोक्तं समासतः ।
मद्भक्त एतद्विज्ञाय मद्भावायोपपद्यते ॥ 18 ॥

Iti kṣetraṁ tathā jñānaṁ jñeyaṁ c'oktaṁ samāsataḥ /
mad-bhakta etad vijñāya mad-bhāvāy'opapadyate //18//

Iti : Thus *kṣetram* : field (material nature, body) *tathā* : as also *jñānam* : knowledge *jñeyam* : the object of knowledge ca : and *samāsataḥ* : in brief *uktam* : has been expounded; *madbhaktaḥ* : My devotee *etat* : this *vijñāya* : having known *madbhāvāya* : for My state *upapadyate* : becomes fit.

18. Thus has been briefly expounded what the Kṣetra (material Nature) is, as also what constitutes knowledge and the object of knowledge. My devotee who understands these verities becomes worthy of My state.

प्रकृतिं पुरुषं चैव विद्ध्यनादी उभावपि ।
विकारांश्च गुणांश्चैव विद्धि प्रकृतिसंभवान् ॥ 19 ॥

Prakṛtiṁ puruṣaṁ c'aiva viddhy anādī ubhāvapi /
vikārāṁś ca guṇāṁś c'aiva viddhi prakṛti-sambhavān //19//

Prakṛtim : Prakṛti (material Nature) *puruṣam* : Puruṣa (Spirit) *ca* : and *eva* : indeed *ubhau* : both *api* : also *anādī* : without beginning *viddhi* : know; *vikārān ca* : changeful objects *guṇān* :

qualities *ca* : and *eva* : also *prakṛtisambhavān* : as sprung from Prakṛti *viddhi* : know.

19. Know both Prakṛti (Nature) and Puruṣa (Spirit) to be beginningless, eternal verities. Know also that all changeful objects and attributes (that constitute the world of daily experience) are sprung from Prakṛti.[5]

कार्यकरणकर्तृत्वे हेतुः प्रकृतिरुच्यते ।
पुरुषः सुखदुःखानां भोक्तृत्वे हेतुरुच्यते ॥ 20 ॥

Kārya-karaṇa-kartṛtve hetuḥ prakṛtir ucyate /
puruṣaḥ sukha-duḥkhānāṁ bhoktṛtve hetur ucyate //20//

Kārya-karaṇa-kartṛtve : In the formation (and functioning) of the body and its sense organs *prakṛtiḥ* : Prakṛti *hetuḥ* : cause *ucyate* : is said to be; *sukhaduḥkhānām* : of pleasure and pain *bhoktṛtve* : in the enjoyment of *puruṣaḥ* : Puruṣa *hetuḥ* : cause *ucyate* : is spoken of.

20. Prakṛti is the cause of the formation and functioning of the body and the senses, while it is the Puruṣa that experiences pleasure and pain, joy and sorrow.

पुरुषः प्रकृतिस्थो हि भुङ्क्ते प्रकृतिजान्गुणान् ।
कारणं गुणसङ्गोऽस्य सदसद्योनिजन्मसु ॥ 21 ॥

Puruṣaḥ prakṛti-stho hi bhuṅkte prakṛti-jān guṇān /
kāraṇaṁ guṇa-saṅgo'sya sad-asad-yoni-janmasu //21//

Puruṣaḥ : Puruṣa *Prakṛtisthaḥ* : remaining in Prakṛti *Prakṛtijān* : born of Prakṛti *guṇān* : objects and their qualities *bhuṅkte* : experiences *hi* : indeed; *asya* : of the individual spirit *guṇasaṅgaḥ* : attachment to these objects *sadasad-yoni-janmasu* : for the birth in good and evil wombs *kāraṇam* : cause.

21. Seated in bodies, which are the products of Prakṛti, the Puruṣa enjoys the objects and qualities born of Prakṛti. Attachment to these objects is the cause of the Spirit getting embodiments in evil or exalted wombs.

उपद्रष्टानुमन्ता च भर्ता भोक्ता महेश्वरः ।
परमात्मेति चाप्युक्तो देहेऽस्मिन्पुरुषः परः ॥ 22 ॥

Upadraṣṭā'numantā ca bhartā bhoktā mah'eśvaraḥ /
param' ātm' eti c'āpy ukto dehe' smin puruṣaḥ paraḥ //22//

Asmin dehe : In this body *upadraṣṭā* : witness *anumantā* : sanctioner *ca* : and *bhartā* : supporter *bhoktā* : enjoyer *maheśvaraḥ* : sovereign Lord *paramātmā* : the Supreme Self *iti* : thus *ca* : and *uktaḥ* : spoken of *paraḥ* : supreme, transcendent (or another) *puruṣaḥ* : Spirit *api* (*asti*) : also exists.

22. In this body there is also the Transcendent and the Supreme Spirit, who is described as the Supreme Self and Sovereign Lord, the unconcerned Witness, the Sanctioner, the Supporter and the Enjoyer.

य एवं वेत्ति पुरुषं प्रकृतिं च गुणैः सह ।
सर्वथा वर्तमानोऽपि न स भूयोऽभिजायते ॥ 23 ॥

Ya evaṁ vetti puruṣaṁ prakṛtiṁ ca guṇaih saha /
sarvathā vartamano'pi na sa bhūyo'bhijāyate //23//

Evam : In this way *puruṣam* : Puruṣa (Spirit) *guṇaiḥ saha* : along with Guṇas *prakṛtim* : Nature *ca* : and *yaḥ* : who *vetti* : knows, *saḥ* : he *sarvathā* : in whatever way *vartamānaḥ api* : might be living *bhūyaḥ* : again *na abhijāyate* : is not born.

23. Whoever thus knows the Puruṣa (Spirit) and Prakṛti (Nature) along with its effects, will never be born again, whatever be his mode of living.

ध्यानेनात्मनि पश्यन्ति केचिदात्मानमात्मना ।
अन्ये सांख्येन योगेन कर्मयोगेन चापरे ॥ 24 ॥

Dhyānen' ātmani paśyanti kecid ātmānam ātmanā /
anye sāṁkhyena yogena karma-yogena c'āpare //24//

Kecit : Some *ātmānam* : the Ātman *dhyānena* : by means of meditation *ātmani* : within oneself *ātmanā* : by the purified mind *paśyanti* : perceive; *anye* : others *sāṁkhyena yogena* : by the path of knowledge; *apare* : others *ca* : again *karma yogena* : by the path of action.

24. There are some who perceive the Ātman within themselves by the practice of meditation with a purified mind. There are also others who approach Him through the discipline of knowledge or of work.[6]

अन्ये त्वेवमजानन्तः श्रुत्वान्येभ्य उपासते ।
तेऽपि चातितरन्त्येव मृत्युं श्रुतिपरायणाः ॥ 25 ॥

Anye tvevam ajānantaḥ śrutvā'nyebhya upāsate /
te'pi c'ātitaranty eva mṛtyuṁ śruti-parāyaṇāḥ //25//

Evam : In the manner described *ajānantaḥ* : not knowing *anye* : some others *tu* : as for, *anyebhyaḥ* : from others (teachers or elders) *śrutvā* : hearing *upāsate* : worship; *śruti-parāyaṇāḥ te* : those who are full of faith in what they have heard from the teacher *api ca* : also *mṛtyum* : death *atitaranti* : overcome *eva* : certainly.

25. There are still others, who, being unfit to follow the disciplines described before—for they lack the knowledge of the Yoga Sāstra and the Vedas—, adopt forms of worship (devotional disciplines) under instruction from teachers or elders. Full of faith in these instructions heard, and following them sincerely as their only refuge, they too certainly overcome the cycle of births and deaths.

यावत्संजायते किंचित्सत्त्वं स्थावरजङ्गमम् ।
क्षेत्रक्षेत्रज्ञसंयोगात्तद्विद्धि भरतर्षभ ॥ 26 ॥

Yāvat saṁjāyate kiñcit sattvaṁ sthāvara-jaṅgamam /
kṣetra-kṣetrajña-samyogāt tad viddhi Bharata'rṣabha //26//

Bharatarṣabha : O the best of the Bharata clan! *sthāvara-jaṅgamam* : the moving and the unmoving *yāvat kiñcit* : whatever *sattvam* :

object *saṁjāyate* : is born *tat* : that *kṣetra-kṣetrajña-saṁyogāt* : due to the union of Kṣetra and Kṣetrajña *viddhi* : know to be.

26. O thou the best of the Bharata clan! Whatever there is born—whether moving or unmoving—it has come into being due to the union of Kṣetra (body) and Kṣetrajña (Spirit).[7]

समं सर्वेषु भूतेषु तिष्ठन्तं परमेश्वरम् ।
विनश्यत्स्वविनश्यन्तं यः पश्यति स पश्यति ॥ 27 ॥

Samaṁ sarveṣu bhūteṣu tiṣṭhantaṁ param'eśvaram /
vinaśyatsv avinaśyantaṁ yaḥ paśyati sa paśyati //27//

Sarveṣu bhūteṣu : In all beings *samam* : alike *tiṣṭhantam* : abiding *paramesvaram* : the Supreme Lord *vinaśyatsu* : when everything perishes *avinaśyantam*: as imperishable substance *yaḥ*: who *paśyati*: sees, *saḥ* : he *paśyati* : sees.

27. He really sees who perceives the Supreme Lord alike in everything—as the Imperishable Substance abiding amidst perishing phenomena.[8]

समं पश्यन्हि सर्वत्र समवस्थितमीश्वरम् ।
न हिनस्त्यात्मनात्मानं ततो याति परां गतिम् ॥ 28 ॥

Samaṁ paśyan hi sarvatra samavasthitam īśvaram /
na hinasty ātmanā'tmānaṁ tato yāti parāṁ gatim //28//

Hi : For *sarvatra* : everywhere *samam* : alike *samavasthitam* : abiding *īśvaram* : the Lord *paśyan* : seeing, *ātmanā* : by the self (the ego) *ātmānam* : the Self (the true spiritual self) *na hinasti* : does not destroy; *tataḥ* : therefore *parāṁ gatim* : the supreme goal *yāti* : attains.

28. For, he who perceives the Lord's presence alike everywhere no longer works against his own spiritual well-being (by mistaking the ego for the true spiritual Self as men in ignorance do). He therefore attains to the Supreme Goal.

प्रकृत्यैव च कर्माणि क्रियमाणानि सर्वशः ।
यः पश्यति तथात्मानमकर्तारं स पश्यति ॥ 29 ॥

Prakṛty'aiva ca karmāṇi kriyamāṇāni sarvaśaḥ /
yaḥ paśyati tathā'tmānam akartāraṁ sa paśyati //29//

Sarvaśaḥ : In all ways *karmāṇi* : actions *prakṛtyā eva* : by Prakṛti (Nature) alone *kriyamāṇāni* : as being done, *tathā* : in the same way *ātmānam* : the Ātman *akartāram* : actionless *ca* : and *yaḥ* : who *paśyati* : sees, *saḥ* : he *paśyati* : sees.

29. He is the real seer who perceives that Prakṛti (i.e., one's body-mind born of Prakṛti) alone is doing all works and that the Ātman, the true spiritual self, is the actionless witness.[9]

यदा भूतपृथग्भावमेकस्थमनुपश्यति ।
तत एव च विस्तारं ब्रह्म संपद्यते तदा ॥ 30 ॥

Yadā bhūta-pṛthag-bhāvam eka-stham anupaśyati /
tata eva ca vistāraṁ brahma saṁpadyate tadā //30//

Bhūta-pṛthag-bhāvam : The manifoldness of beings *ekastham* : as centred in the One *tataḥ* : from that alone *vistāraṁ ca* : their evolution as well *yadā* : when *anupaśyati* : perceives, *tadā* : then *brahma* : Brahman *saṁpadyate* : he attains.

30. When one perceives the manifold objects as centred in the One and as evolved from It as well—then he attains Brahman.[10]

अनादित्वान्निर्गुणत्वात्परमात्मायमव्ययः ।
शरीरस्थोऽपि कौन्तेय न करोति न लिप्यते ॥ 31 ॥

Anāditvān nirguṇatvāt paramātmā'yam avyayaḥ /
śarīra-stho'pi Kaunteya na karoti na lipyate //31//

Kaunteya : O son of Kuntī! *anāditvāt* : being beginningless *nirguṇatvāt* : not being a product of the Guṇas of Prakṛti or Nature *avyayaḥ* : immutable *ayam* : this *paramātmā* : the highest Self *śarīrasthaḥ api* : though dwelling in the body *na karoti* : is actionless, *na lipyate* : is untainted.

31. That highest Self, being the immutable and unoriginated Spirit beyond Nature, is free from all action and stain, though dwelling in the body.

यथा सर्वगतं सौक्ष्म्यादाकाशं नोपलिप्यते ।
सर्वत्रावस्थितो देहे तथात्मा नोपलिप्यते ॥ 32 ॥

Yathā sarva-gataṁ saukṣmyād ākāśaṁ n'opalipyate /
sarvatr'āvasthito dehe tathā'tmā n'opalipyate //32//

Sarvagatam : All-pervading *ākāśam* : Ākāśa (space, sky, ether) *saukṣmyāt* : because of subtlety *yathā* : as *na upalipyate* : is not stained, *tathā* : in the same way *sarvatra dehe* : in all bodies *avasthitaḥ* : though existing *ātmā* : Ātman *na upalipyate* : is not stained by anything.

32. Just as the all-pervading Ākāśa, because of its subtlety, is not stained by anything, so this Ātman, though abiding in all bodies, is never affected by any impurity.

यथा प्रकाशयत्येकः कृत्स्नं लोकमिमं रविः ।
क्षेत्रं क्षेत्री तथा कृत्स्नं प्रकाशयति भारत ॥ 33 ॥

Yathā prakāśayaty ekaḥ kṛtsnaṁ lokam imaṁ raviḥ /
kṣetraṁ kṣetrī tathā kṛtsnaṁ prakāśayati Bhārata //33//

Bhārata : O scion of the Bharata clan! *ekaḥ raviḥ* : the one sun *kṛtsnam imam* : this entire *lokam* : world *yathā* : as *prakāśayati* : illumines *tathā* : in that way *kṣetrī* : the Indwelling Spirit *kṛtsnam kṣetram* : all bodies *prakāśayati* : illumines.

33. Just as the single sun illumines the whole universe, so the (one) Indwelling Spirit enlivens all bodies (with self-consciousness).[11]

क्षेत्रक्षेत्रज्ञयोरेवमन्तरं ज्ञानचक्षुषा ।
भूतप्रकृतिमोक्षं च ये विदुर्यान्ति ते परम् ॥ 34 ॥

Kṣetra-kṣetrajñayor evam antaraṁ jñāna-cakṣuṣā /
bhūta-prakṛti-mokṣaṁ ca ye vidur yānti te param //34//

Evam : In this way *kṣetra-kṣetrajñayoḥ* : between Kṣetra and Kṣetrajña *antaram* : distinction, *bhūta-prakṛti-mokṣam ca* : and freedom of the Spirit from the bondage of Prakṛti *jñānacakṣuṣā* : by spiritual insight *ye* : who *viduḥ* : know, *te* : they *param* : the Supreme *yānti* : reach.

34. Whoever perceives by spiritual insight the distinction between Kṣetra (Nature) and Kṣetrajña (Spirit) as also the freedom of the Spirit from the hold of Nature, they reach the Supreme.

ओं तत्सदिति श्रीमद्भगवद्गीतासूपनिषत्सु ब्रह्मविद्यायां
योगशास्त्रे श्रीकृष्णार्जुनसंवादे क्षेत्रक्षेत्रज्ञविभागयोगो
नाम त्रयोदशोऽध्यायः ॥ 13 ॥

NOTES

1. *Vrs.*1-2: In contrast to the devotional doctrine taught in the last chapter, here the knowledge discipline or Jñāna Yoga is described. The ideal of the Impersonal Absolute (the Akṣara) was described in the previous chapter in order to draw a contrast between the two paths. But the steps of the discipline of Jñāna are not stated there. Here it is given as consisting in the discrimination between the body (Kṣetra) and the Spirit (Kṣetrajña), to whom the body in reality is only an adjunct but which (body) is taken as one with the Spirit through identification arising from ignorance (Ajñāna). Jñāna or knowledge consists in the dissipation of this ignorance through discrimination and the recognition of the unity of the substratum of the Jīva with Brahman. In pure Advaita the

unity is one of absolute identity, while the Advaitins upholding identity-in-difference call it a unity between a part and the whole, and the dualists, an absolutely dependent existence on its principal and creator.

The spirit (Ātman) is called here as Kṣetrajña, the knower of the field, and the body-mind combination, Kṣetra or the Field. As the fruits of Karma are realised through the body-mind combination it is appropriate to call it a field. Strictly speaking, the body-mind combination is the instrument through which enjoyments and sufferings are had by the Jīva. It is spoken of here as something known, and the Kṣetrajña as the knower. In fact the external objects contacted through the body-mind are the 'objects known'. But the instrument, the body-mind, through which their knowledge is gained, is also an object known. It forms both the instrument and the object known. Though only an instrument or Upadhi of the Jīva, the Jīva is in identification with it, until spiritual enlightenment reveals its objectivity.

Usually in the Vedantic texts, what is called here as the Kṣetra in order to distinguish it from the *Dṛśyas* or objects seen as separate entities, is known as the Kośa, vestment or sheath of the Ātman. They are classified as five—Annamaya-Kośa (the sheath of physical body) Prāṇamaya-Kośa (the vitalistic sheath), Manomaya-Kośa (mental sheath), Vijñānamaya-Kośa (knowledge-sheath), and Ānanda-maya-Kośa (sheath of bliss).

2. *Vrs.*5-6: What are mentioned in the fifth verse are the twentyfour categories of the Sāmkhyas. By the expression Mahābhūtas is meant the Tanmatras (or the subtle aspect) of the Bhūtas. For, their gross aspects are referred to in the expression the five 'objects of the senses' (*indriya-gocarāḥ*). What follows in the sixth verse (*icchā-dveṣaḥ* etc.) are what the Vaiṣeṣikas consider as the attributes of the Spirit. But really they are psychic and mental, and are functions of the Kṣetra. So they are added to the twenty-four Sāmkhya categories.

While in the first two verses the analysis appears to be at the individual level, it receives a cosmic significance in the enumeration contained in verses five and six. It is sensible to take this passage as implying both the body-mind of the individual and the Cosmos as a whole constituting the body of the Divine—a vision of which Arjuna had a little while ago. It has already been said that both the material Prakṛti and the Jīvas are his two Saktis and that He holds together all entities interpenetrating them as a thread interpenetrates the beads of a necklace. According to some schools of Vedanta like the Qualified Monistic, the Lord ensouls every atom and every Jīva individually and in their totality. The Jīvas and the Jagat constitute His body and He ensouls them. The true understanding of this can also be called enlightenment, which the Lord imparted to Arjuna when he exhorted him to be a mere instrument (*nimittamātraṁ bhava savya-sācin*) in the 11th chapter.

3. *Vrs.*7-11: In verse 3 Kṛṣṇa had offered to describe both the Kṣetra and the Kṣetrajña. But having described the Kṣetra, he is describing what is meant by Jñāna or enlightenment, instead of describing the Kṣetrajña. Jñāna or enlightenment was described in verse 2 as consisting in the understanding of the difference between the Kṣetrajña and the Kṣetra. In place of elucidating this conception of Jñāna, he gives here a list of virtues to be practised, and calls these virtues Jñāna. The justification for this must be that Jñāna dawns in one only by cultivating the virtues enlisted.

4. *Vrs.*12-18: After the description of the Kṣetra in Verses 5-6, what one expects is a description of the Kṣetrajña, as implied in verse 2. But in the teaching set forth thereafter, in verses 7-11, is given a number of qualities constituting Jñāna. Next we are getting in these verses 12-17, a description of what is called Jñeya, or the object to be known. The description given is of the Supreme Spirit as immanent in and upholding all the manifested universe, termed here as Brahman, the beginningless and the all-pervading. This description can very well suit what Arjuna experienced in the theophany of the Cosmic Form, minus its pictorial details. So the Jñeyam here is the Supreme Being not as the Impersonal Absolute described in Chapter 12, but as the Spirit ensouling all that exists. And he who knows it is called 'My Bhakta' (*Mad-bhakta etad vijñāya* Ch. 13.18). So it looks that this chapter is also dealing with the Bhakti doctrine, revealing God as the Universal Spirit ensouling all existence and not the Avyakta and the Akṣara spoken of in Chapter 12. He is also described as He who consumes everything and also projects everything.

The description of the Jñeyam, the object to be known, as

neither 'being' nor 'non-being' is somewhat puzzling. It can mean that it is the Absolute Subject. The subject cannot be seen as the 'this', an object of cognition, just as the eye cannot be seen by itself. Not being an object of cognition, it cannot be described as 'being'. At the same time, it is not 'non-being', since the subject is what guarantees the existence of the object. Though the eye is not perceived by the eye, it still 'is', in its own unique sense. It is what guarantees the existence of all other things. This is one meaning for this puzzling characterisation of the Jñeyam.

But the use of the word 'Jneyam', the object to be *known,* for the Absolute Subject, which can never be an object, seems to contradict that conception itself. The description too answers more to the idea of the immanent Spirit than that of the Absolute Subject as shown earlier. It is therefore more appropriate to understand 'non-being' as meaning the causal unmanifest condition, and the effect condition or the manifest state as 'being'. All gross entities are subject to the states of cause and effect. But the Supreme Spirit is not so, as He is uncaused and changeless.

5. *Vrs.*19-23: The distinction between the Kṣetra and the Kṣetrajña is what was taken for discussion. After describing the Kṣetra, no description of Kṣetrajña, beyond the statement that it is He Himself, was given. In place of it, what is called Jñāna and Jñeya (knowledge and object of knowledge) were described. Even the term Kṣetrajña does not occur till verse 26.

Instead, the concepts of Puruṣa and Prakṛti are now taken for discussion. The justification probably is that the ideas are the same, though these technical terms are different. Puruṣa and Prakṛti are the terms used in the Sāṁkhya philosophy for Spirit and Nature respectively. They correspond to Kṣetrajña and Kṣetra, though the Sāṁkhyan term Puruṣa conveys only the idea of the individual soul and not of the Supreme Being as is suggested when it is stated that Kṣetrajña is Myself.

Now the Sāṁkhya philosophy has no place for a Supreme Spirit. There are only Puruṣas or spiritual monads which are centres of pure consciousness without any activity. Prakṛti on the other hand has no consciousness, but is a stuff purely dynamic and ever changeful. A Puruṣa or a spiritual monad gets associated with an aspect of Prakṛti through super-imposition and thus becomes the Jīva, the living spirit, entangled in the transmigratory cycle. As stated in verse 20 and 21, the Puruṣa involved in Prakṛti or the body, becomes the enjoyer of the transformations of Prakṛti, through superimposition.

But the Gītā, though it accepts the Sāṁkhyan terminology and the doctrine of the Puruṣa's involvement in Prakṛti, reduces both Prakṛti and Puruṣa into the two powers of Iśvara, the Supreme Lord (cf. 10.4-5). Here also it is stated in verse 22, that there is the *puruṣaḥ paraḥ*—, "another transcendent Puruṣa who is described as the Supreme Self, sovereign Lord, the unconcerned Witness, the Sanctioner, the Supporter, the Enjoyer." So the Puruṣa and Prakṛti of the Sāṁkhya are unified in a Supreme Lord whose powers Prakṛti and Puruṣa are.

6. *Vrs.*24-25: The Yogas referred to in the 24th verse are the paths of concentration (Rāja Yoga), the path of knowledge (Jñāna Yoga), and the path of work (Karma Yoga). What exactly is the Yoga referred to in verse 25 is not clear. It must be a reference to the path of devotion to which every one is eligible, irrespective of the knowledge of the scriptures and the philosophies. It is also based upon faith, as is implied in the expression *śrutvānyebhya upāsate*—worships hearing from others. Faith is involved in all the other Yogas also. But as they are open only to learned men, they have the advantage of the Śāstra, the scriptural and philosophical texts. But Bhakti Yoga is open even to people who have no learning, but have firm faith in a teacher, or in a family tradition of devotion, or have an inherent longing for God. By faith and longing alone, unaccompanied by learning, man can attain the spiritual *summum bonum.* The example of Sri Ramakrishna is the most noted and the most unquestionable example of this. Aspiration alone, unaided by any outside help, brought realisation to him. In the Sādhanas of the various spiritual traditions that he practised afterwards, he sought no help from any texts. Faith in the words of the teachers who instructed him was his sole guide and help. In the past spiritual traditions of India also there are examples like Kaṇṇappa-naiṉār, who were low-born and ignorant, but attained to spiritual heights through faith.

This does not of course preclude learning from the followers of the path of devotion, nor does it necessarily mean that they should be unlearned.

This is another passage wherein the Gītā gives equal status and importance to all the four recognised paths of spiritual discipline, without downgrading any one of them. In practice each is generally also combined with one or the other of them. Especially Karma and Yoga can be combined with Bhakti, and Yoga with Jñāna.

7. *Vr.*26: The Chapter started with the offer to describe Kṣetra and Kṣetrajña. Kṣetra was analysed and described in verses 5 and 6. But nothing was said about Kṣetrajña till now, except what was said in verse 2—'know that I am the knower of the field'. Even the word Kṣetrajña comes only now in Verse 26, wherein it is taught that in all living beings, there is the union of Kṣetrajña and Kṣetra, (spirit and body). The word is left out again till the verses 33 and 34, where it is shown in what sense the Kṣetrajña in all bodies is the same. It is declared that just as the one sun illumines all bodies, evidently by his rays of light, so the Kṣetrajña in all bodies is a reflection, a part, of the one Kṣetrajña, the Supreme Being. The idea is made more clear in the analogy of the image of the one sun reflected in innumerable pots of water.

8. *Vrs.*27-28: The immanence of the Lord in everything is taught. Those who realise this, will never be entrenched in their small ego.

9. *Vr.*29: The Lord is ultimately the source of everything including actions. But He is not affected by them, because He functions through Prakṛti, His Power, which can be distinguished from Him, but which, being His Power, cannot be treated as different from Him. For this reason He is unattached to, and unaffectd by, all the world transformations. The aspirant who realises his spiritual identity with Him, as a spark or ray or reflection of His, also participates in that Divine aloofness and unaffectedness. The same is more or less repeated in verse 31 also.

10. *Vr.*30: An important content of spiritual realisation is here described. It is the perception of the origin of the many from the One. The same was stated and elaborately pictured in the theophany vouschsafed to Arjuna in Chapter 11. It is stated there

tatr'aika-sthaṁ jagat kṛtsnaṁ pravibhaktam anekadhā—the whole universe abiding in the One, yet divided as the multiplicity.

11. *Vr.*33: Kṣetrī (Field-dweller) and Kṣetrajña (Field-knower) mean the same thing. It is the In-dwelling Spirit. It is stated here that basically that Indwelling Spirit is only the One in all and it is illustrated by the idea of the one sun illuminating numberless media without losing his universality and oneness. It has been discussed in note 5 also.

A complication arises when this is read with verse 22 where, after analysing the individual personality as a union of Prakṛti (body) and Puruṣa (spirit), it is stated that there is in the body also *Puruṣaḥ paraḥ*—a Puruṣa other than the one stated, a transcendent Puruṣa. This transcendent Puruṣa is what stands for the one universal sun brought as an analogy here. Though the individualised Puruṣa and the Universal Puruṣa may be one, we have to understand the former as distinct, just as a ray of the sun illumining a surface of water gets an identity of its own, which is distinct, though not totally different, from the universal sun. The distinction is made by viewing the ray as a particle of the sun in association with a medium, a surface of water. It is this distinction without a difference that exists between the Individual Spirit and the Universal Spirit that is conveyed by the doctrine of His two Prakṛtis or Saktis (Powers) spoken of in Ch. 7.4-5—the Aparā Prakṛti being Nature and the Parā Prakṛti being the Jīva, the living spirit of man. Without accepting this 'distinction without a difference' (bheda-abheda or identity-cum-difference) no spiritual doctrine, dualistic or non-dualistic, could be formulated and stated in understandable concepts. If the distinctiveness of the Jīva is not granted, there is no one involved in Saṁsāra or transmigratory cycle, and the whole of the Gītā and other scriptures dealing with liberation become redundant. The Gītā therefore very clearly states in Ch. 15.5—a particle or part of Mine of untraceable origination has become the Jīva, and is involved in Prakṛti, having attracted to itself the mind and the senses. If this distinction is not granted, we shall logically have got to take shelter in a philosophy of acosmism, which is an ungraspable theoretical position.

Chapter XIV

गुणत्रयविभागयोगः

DIVISION ACCORDING TO THE THREE GUNAS

SUMMARY

The Lord as the Universal Father: (1-5) Sri Kṛṣṇa said: I shall declare to you that knowledge by which you can attain unity in nature with Me. My Nature is the universal womb in which I place the seed. From this all beings are born, and therefore know that beings born of all wombs, are born of my universal womb, and I am their originating father.

The Three Guṇas of Nature and their functions: (6-20) This Nature of mine has three aspects known as Guṇas—Constituents or Dispositions–, Sattva, Rajas and Tamas, characterised by expressions like purity, passion and dullness i.e., happiness, energy and delusion, respectively. Everything in life is bound and dominated by these Guṇas, and man's life and action, and his progress hereafter, are determined by the ramifying influence of these on him. He is the wise man who is able to perceive that all the movements of his body-mind are really the movements of these Guṇas of which it is constituted, and that he, the real he, transcends them. When this illumination dawns, the Jīva is fit for the Immortal State. One who has thus risen above the Guṇas is called Triguṇātīta.

Who is a Triguṇātīta: /(21-27) Arjuna now asks what are the signs of a Triguṇātīta, and the account given in the reply is not much different from that of Sthitaprajña (II. 55-72) and the Bhakta (XII. 13-20). The Triguṇātīta is thus described: He never identifies himself with the passing moods of elation, excitement and depression, which are the characteristics of the body-mind. In all disturbances of the mental and physical environment, he remains unperturbed, seeing in them only movements of Prakṛti and not of himself. He is alike in pleasure and pain, to friend and foe, and he never feels he is the doer of anything. It is only one who serves Me with unswerving and exclusive devotion that can thus hope to overcome the dominance of the Guṇas; for I, the Lord of all, is the one on whom the Brahman-state has its foundation.

श्रीभगवानुवाच

परं भूयः प्रवक्ष्यामि ज्ञानानां ज्ञानमुत्तमम् ।
यज्ज्ञात्वा मुनयः सर्वे परां सिद्धिमितो गताः ॥ 1 ॥

Śrī Bhagavān uvāca:

Paraṁ bhūyaḥ pravakṣyāmi jñānānāṁ jñānam uttamam /
yaj jñātvā munayaḥ sarve parāṁ siddhim ito gatāḥ //1//

Yat : Which *jñātvā* : knowing *sarve* : all *munayaḥ* : sages *itaḥ* : from the state of bondage *parāṁ siddhim* : highest perfection *gatāḥ* : attained, *param* : relating to the Supreme Being *jñānānām* : of knowledge *uttamam* : the most exalted *jñānam* : knowledge *bhūyaḥ* : again *pravakṣyāmi* : I shall expound.

The Blessed Lord said:

1. I shall now expound to you again that knowledge relating to the Supreme Being, the most exalted of all forms of knowledge, by gaining which all sages passed from this state of bondage into the highest perfection.[1]

इदं ज्ञानमुपाश्रित्य मम साधर्म्यमागताः ।
सर्गेऽपि नोपजायन्ते प्रलये न व्यथन्ति च ॥ 2 ॥

Idaṁ jñānam upāśritya mama sādharmyam āgatāḥ /
sarge'pi n'opajāyante pralaye na vyathanti ca //2//

Idam : This *jñānam* : knowledge *upāśritya* : depending on *mama sādharmyam* : unity with My nature *āgatāḥ* : those who have attained, *sarge* : at the start of a new creative cycle *api* : even *na upajāyante* : are not born, *pralaye* : in dissolution *na vyathanti* : not distressed *ca* : and.

2. Those who have attained unity with My nature through this knowledge are not born again even at the beginning of a new creative cycle, nor are they subjected to the distress of dissolution.

मम योनिर्महद्ब्रह्म तस्मिन्गर्भं दधाम्यहम् ।
संभवः सर्वभूतानां ततो भवति भारत ॥ 3 ॥

Mama yonir mahad brahma tasmin garbhaṁ dadhāmy aham /
saṁbhavaḥ sarva-bhūtānāṁ tato bhavati Bhārata //3//

Bhārata : O scion of the Bharata race! *mahat* : the great *Brahma* : Prakṛti, Nature *mama* : My *yoniḥ* : womb; *tasmin* : in that *aham* : I *garbham* : the germ (the impulse) of creation *dadhāmi* : impart; *tataḥ* : out of that *sarvabhūtānām* : of all beings *saṁbhavaḥ* : birth *bhavati* : takes place.

3. The Great Nature Prakṛti is like a womb to Me. I deposit therein the germ of creation, the creative impulse, out of which everything comes into being.[2]

सर्वयोनिषु कौन्तेय मूर्तयः संभवन्ति याः ।
तासां ब्रह्म महद्योनिरहं बीजप्रदः पिता ॥ 4 ॥

Sarva-yoniṣu Kaunteya mūrtayaḥ saṁbhavanti yāḥ /
tāsāṁ brahma mahad yonir ahaṁ bīja-pradaḥ pitā //4//

Kaunteya : O son of Kuntī *sarva yoniṣu* : in all wombs *yāḥ* : whatever *mūrtayaḥ* : forms *saṁbhavanti* : are born, *tāsām* : of them all *mahat brahma* : great Nature *yoniḥ* : is the womb ; *aham* : I *pitā* : the father *bījapradaḥ* : the seed imparter.

4. O son of Kuntī! All creatures, whatever might be the womb from which they are born, have really the Great Nature as the womb—the source of their origin. And I am their father, the bestower of the seed.

सत्त्वं रजस्तम इति गुणाः प्रकृतिसंभवाः ।
निबध्नन्ति महाबाहो देहे देहिनमव्ययम् ॥ 5 ॥

Sattvaṁ rajas tama iti guṇāḥ prakṛti-saṁbhavāḥ /
nibadhnanti mahā-bāho dehe dehinam avyayam //5/

Mahābāho : O great warrior! *sattvam* : Sattva (the balanced, the peaceful, the bright) *rajaḥ* : Rajas (passion, agitation) *tamaḥ* : Tamas (dullness, inertia) *iti* : these *prakṛtisaṁbhavāḥ* : born of Prakṛti *guṇāḥ* : Guṇas (qualities or dispositions) *avyayam*: immortal *dehinam* : the soul *dehe* : in the body *nibadhnanti* : bind.

5. The three Guṇas of Sattva, Rajas and Tamas born of Prakṛti, bind down the immortal soul to the body in its embodied state.[3]

तत्र सत्त्वं निर्मलत्वात्प्रकाशकमनामयम् ।
सुखसङ्गेन बध्नाति ज्ञानसङ्गेन चानघ ॥ 6 ॥

Tatra sattvaṁ nirmalatvāt prakāśakam anāmayam /
sukha-saṅgena badhnāti jñāna-saṅgena c'ānagha //6//

Anagha : O sinless one! *tatra* : among these *nirmalatvāt* : owing to its essential purity *prakāśakam* : luminous (like a mirror capable of reflecting and revealing things) *anāmayam* : free from ill-health, harmonious *sattvam* : the Guṇa called Sattva *sukhasaṅgena* : by identification with happiness *jñānasaṅgena* : by identification with knowledge *badhnāti* : binds.

6. Among these, Sattva is luminous and harmonious due to its essential purity. It binds the soul, O sinless one, with the feeling 'I am happy, I am full of knowledge.'[4]

रजो रागात्मकं विद्धि तृष्णासङ्गसमुद्भवम् ।
तन्निबध्नाति कौन्तेय कर्मसङ्गेन देहिनम् ॥ 7 ॥

Rajo rāg'ātmakaṁ viddhi tṛṣṇā-saṅga-samudbhavam /
tan nibadhnāti Kaunteya karma-saṅgena dehinam //7//

Kaunteya : O son of Kuntī! *rajaḥ* : the Guṇa known as Rajas *rāgātmakam* : passion-based *tṛṣṇā-saṅga-samudbhavam* : productive of longings and attachments, *viddhi* : know; *tat* : that *karma-saṅgena* : by attachment to work *dehinam* : the soul *nibadhnāti* : binds fast.

7. Know Rajas to be passion-based, and productive of longings for unattained objects and attachment for those in one's possession. It binds the (actionless) soul, O son of Kuntī, by entangling it in action (through the feeling 'I am the doer').

तमस्त्वज्ञानजं विद्धि मोहनं सर्वदेहिनाम् ।
प्रमादालस्यनिद्राभिस्तन्निबध्नाति भारत ॥ 8 ॥

Tamas tu ajñāna-jaṁ viddhi mohanaṁ sarva-dehinām /
pramād'ālasya-nidrābhis tan nibadhnāti Bhārata //8//

Bhārata : O scion of the Bhārata clan! *tamaḥ* : the Guṇa known as Tamas *tu* : as for *ajñānajam* : ignorance-born *sarvadehinām* : to all embodied beings *mohanam* : delusion-producing *viddhi* : know; *tat* : that *pramādālasya-nidrābhiḥ* : by negligence, indolence, and sleep.

8. As for the Guṇa known as Tamas, it is ignorance-born and is productive of delusion in all beings. It binds the soul, O scion of the Bhārata clan! with the obsession of a disposition characterised by negligence, indolence and sleepiness.

सत्त्वं सुखे संजयति रजः कर्मणि भारत ।
ज्ञानमावृत्य तु तमः प्रमादे संजयत्युत ॥ 9 ॥

Sattvaṁ sukhe sañjayati rajaḥ karmaṇi Bhārata /
jñānam āvṛtya tu tamaḥ pramāde sañjayaty uta //9//

Bhārata : O scion of the Bharata race! *sattvam* : the Guṇa called Sattva *sukhe* : in happiness *sañjayati* : binds, *rajas* : Rajas *karmaṇi* : to action, *tamaḥ* : Tamas *tu* : indeed *jñānam* : knowledge *āvṛtya* : covering *pramāde* : to negligence *sañjayati* : binds.

9. Sattva enslaves one to a mood of joy and happiness, and Rajas to one of activity, while Tamas, which veils up knowledge, fills one with negligence and laziness.

रजस्तमश्चाभिभूय सत्त्वं भवति भारत ।
रजः सत्त्वं तमश्चैव तमः सत्त्वं रजस्तथा ॥ 10 ॥

Rajas tamaś c'ābhibhūya sattvaṁ bhavati Bhārata /
rajaḥ sattvaṁ tamaś c'aiva tamaḥ sattvaṁ rajas tathā //10//

Rajas : Rajas *tamaḥ* : Tamas *ca* : and *abhibhūya* : overpowering *sattvam* : Sattva *bhavati* : prevails, *rajaḥ* : Rajas (prevails) *sattvam*: (over-powering) Sattva *tamaḥ ca* : and Tamas; *tathā* : in the same way *tamaḥ* : Tamas (prevails) *sattvam* : (overpowering) Sattva *Rajas ca* : and Rajas.

10. Overpowering Rajas and Tamas, Sattva prevails (sometimes); suppressing Sattva and Tamas, Rajas becomes dominant; and likewise dominating over Sattva and Rajas, Tamas holds the field.

सर्वद्वारेषु देहेऽस्मिन्प्रकाश उपजायते ।
ज्ञानं यदा तदा विद्याद्विवृद्धं सत्त्वमित्युत ॥ 11 ॥

Sarva-dvāreṣu dehe'smin prakāśa upajāyate /
jñānaṁ yadā tadā vidyād vivṛddhaṁ sattvam ity uta //11//

Asmin dehe : In this body *sarvadvāreṣu* : in all gateways *jñānaṁ prakāśaḥ* : light of knowledge *yadā* : when *upajāyate* : is born, *tadā* : then *sattvam*: Sattva *vivṛddham* : is dominant, *uta* : indeed *iti vidyāt* : should be known thus.

11. When through all the senses, which are the portals of the body, knowledge, happiness and similar characteristics manifest, then indeed it should be understood that Sattva is dominant.

लोभः प्रवृत्तिरारम्भः कर्मणामशमः स्पृहा ।
रजस्येतानि जायन्ते विवृद्धे भरतर्षभ ॥ 12 ॥

Lobhaḥ pravṛttir-ārambhaḥ karmaṇāṁ aśamaḥ spṛhā /
rajasy etāni jāyante vivṛddhe Bharatarṣabha //i2//

Rajasi vivṛddhe : When Rajas prevails *lobhaḥ* : avarice *pravṛttiḥ* : extroversion *karmaṇām ārambhaḥ* : ceaseless planning and execution of works *aśamaḥ* : restlessness *spṛhā* : desire for enjoyments *etāni* : these *jāyante* : arise.

12. Avarice, extroversion, ceaseless planning and execution of works, restlessness, desire for enjoyments—these arise when Rajas prevails.

अप्रकाशोऽप्रवृत्तिश्च प्रमादो मोह एव च ।
तमस्येतानि जायन्ते विवृद्धे कुरुनन्दन ॥ 13 ॥

Aprakāśo' pravṛttiś ca pramādo moha eva ca /
tamasy etāni jāyante vivṛddhe Kuru-nandana //13//

Kurunandana : O Joy of the Kurus! *tamasi vivṛddhe* : when Tamas dominates *aprakāśaḥ* : lack of intelligence *apravṛttiḥ* : lack of effort *ca* : and *pramādaḥ* : heedlessness, negligence *mohaḥ* : delusion *eva* : also *ca* : and *etāni* : these *jāyante* : arise.

13. When Tamas dominates, there is lack of intelligence, lack of effort, negligence and delusion.

यदा सत्त्वे प्रवृद्धे तु प्रलयं याति देहभृत् ।
तदोत्तमविदां लोकानमलान्प्रतिपद्यते ॥ 14 ॥

Yadā sattve pravṛddhe tu pralayaṁ yāti deha-bhṛt /
tadottama-vidāṁ lokān amalān pratipadyate //14//

Yadā tu : If *sattve pravṛddhe* : when Sattva is prevailing predominantly *dehabhṛt* : an embodied being *pralayaṁ yāti* : dies, *tadā* : then *uttamavidām* : of the knowers of the highest *amalān* : pure *lokān* : regions *pratipadyate* : attains.

14. If one dies when Sattva is prevailing predominantly, then one attains to the pure regions of the knowers of the Highest.

रजसि प्रलयं गत्वा कर्मसङ्गिषु जायते ।
तथा प्रलीनस्तमसि मूढयोनिषु जायते ॥ 15 ॥

Rajasi pralayaṁ gatvā karma-saṅgiṣu jāyate /
tathā pralīnas tamasi mūḍha-yoniṣu jāyate //15//

Rajasi : During the dominance of Rajas *pralayaṁ gatvā* : dying *karmasaṅgiṣu* : among beings attached to works *jāyate* : is born; *tathā* : likewise *tamasi* : in Tamas *pralīnaḥ* : dying *mūḍha-yoniṣu* : in the wombs of creatures without reason *jāyate* : is born.

15. Those who die when Rajas dominates are born among those attached to action (men); and likewise those dying in Tamas are born in the wombs of creatures without reason.

कर्मणः सुकृतस्याहुः सात्त्विकं निर्मलं फलम् ।
रजसस्तु फलं दुःखमज्ञानं तमसः फलम् ॥ 16 ॥

Karmaṇaḥ sukṛtasy'āhuḥ sāttvikaṁ nirmalaṁ phalam /
rajasas tu phalaṁ duḥkham ajñānaṁ tamasaḥ phalam //16//

Sukṛtasya karmaṇaḥ : Of virtuous action *phalam* : result *sāttvikaṁ nirmalam* : conducive to spirituality and purity *āhuḥ* : is said to be; *rajasaḥ tu* : of works dominated by Rajas *phalam* : result *duḥkham* : pain; *tamasaḥ* : of Tamas-dominated work *phalam* : result *ajñānam* : is ignorance.

16. Virtuous actions promote spirituality and purity (Sattva), while the Rajas-dominated ones result in pain, and the Tamas-dominated ones in ignorance.

सत्त्वात्संजायते ज्ञानं रजसो लोभ एव च ।
प्रमादमोहौ तमसो भवतोऽज्ञानमेव च ॥ 17 ॥

Sattvāt saṁjāyate jñānaṁ rajaso lobha eva ca /
pramāda-mohau tamaso bhavato'jñānam eva ca //17//

Sattvāt : From Sattva *jñānam* : knowledge, *rajasaḥ* : from Rajas *lobhaḥ eva* : avarice *ca* : and *saṁjāyate* : arise; *tamasaḥ* : of Tamas *pramādamohau* : negligence and delusion *ajñānam eva ca* : and also ignorance.

17. From Sattva arises knowledge, and from Rajas, avarice. Negligence, delusion and also ignorance are the products of Tamas.

ऊर्ध्वं गच्छन्ति सत्त्वस्था मध्ये तिष्ठन्ति राजसाः ।
जघन्यगुणवृत्तिस्था अधो गच्छन्ति तामसाः ॥ 18 ॥

Ūrdhvaṁ gacchanti sattva-sthā madhye tiṣṭhanti rājasāḥ /
jaghanya-guṇa-vṛtti-sthā adho gacchanti tāmasāḥ //18//

Sattvasthāḥ : Those established in Sattva *ūrdhvam* : upwards *gacchanti* : go, *rājasāḥ* : those established in Rajas *madhye* : in the middle *tiṣṭhanti* : remain, *jaghanya-guṇa-vṛtti-sthāḥ* : steeped in evil tendencies *tāmasāḥ* : those endowed with Tamas *adhaḥ gacchanti* : go downwards.

18. Those established in Sattva evolve to higher goals, while those abiding in Rajas remain in the mid-course. Steeped in evil tendencies, the Tamas-dominated ones degenerate.

नान्यं गुणेभ्यः कर्तारं यदा द्रष्टानुपश्यति ।
गुणेभ्यश्च परं वेत्ति मद्भावं सोऽधिगच्छति ॥ 19 ॥

N'ānyaṁ guṇebhyaḥ kartāraṁ yadā draṣṭā'nupaśyati /
guṇebhyaś ca paraṁ vetti mad-bhāvaṁ so'dhigacchati //19//

Yadā : When *draṣṭā* : the seer, the subject *guṇebhyaḥ anyam* : different from Guṇas *kartāram* : doer, agent *na anupaśyati* : does not see, *guṇebhayaḥ ca param* : that which is beyond the Guṇas *vetti* : knows, *saḥ*: he *madbhāvam* : My state *adhigacchati* : attains.

19. When the subject (Jīva) recognises the Guṇas alone as the agent in all actions, and himself as transcending the Guṇas—then he attains to My state.[5]

गुणानेतानतीत्य त्रीन्देही देहसमुद्भवान् ।
जन्ममृत्युजरादुःखैर्विमुक्तोऽमृतमश्नुते ॥ 20 ॥

Guṇān etān atītya trīn dehī deha-samudbhavān /
janma-mṛtyu-jarā-duḥkhair vimukto'mṛtam aśnute //20//

Dehī : The embodied being *dehasamudbhavān* : the source of this body *etān trīn* : these three *guṇān* : Guṇas *atītya* : transcending, *janma-mṛtyu-jarāduḥkhaiḥ* : from the misery of birth, death, and old age *vimuktaḥ* : liberated, *amṛtam* : state of immortality *aśnute* : attains to.

20. The embodied spirit (Jīva), having transcended the Guṇas from which the body has sprung, gains deliverance from the miseries of birth, death and old age, and attains to Immortality.

अर्जुन उवाच

कैर्लिङ्गैस्त्रीन्गुणानेतानतीतो भवति प्रभो ।
किमाचारः कथं चैतांस्त्रीन्गुणानतिवर्तते ॥ 21 ॥

Arjuna uvāca:

Kair liṅgais trīn guṇān etān atīto bhavati prabho /
kim-ācāraḥ kathaṁ c'aitāṁs trīn guṇān ativartate //21//

Prabho : Lord! *etān* : these *trīn guṇān* : three Guṇas *atītaḥ* : one who has transcended *kaiḥ* : by what *liṅgaiḥ* : marks *bhavati* : is characterised, *kimācāraḥ* : how does he behave? *kathaṁ ca* : and how *etān trīn guṇān* : these three Guṇas *ativartate* : one rises above.

Arjuna said:

21. Lord! What are the marks of one who has transcended these three Guṇas? How does he behave? And how does he rise above them?

श्रीभगवानुवाच

प्रकाशं च प्रवृत्तिं च मोहमेव च पाण्डव ।
न द्वेष्टि संप्रवृत्तानि न निवृत्तानि काङ्क्षति ॥ 22 ॥

Śrī *Bhagavān uvāca:*

Prakāśaṁ ca pravṛttiṁ ca moham eva ca Pāṇḍava /
na dveṣṭi sampravṛttāni na nivṛttāni kāṅkṣati //22//

Pāṇḍava : O son of Pāṇḍu! (*yaḥ* : who) *prakāśam* : knowledge *pravṛttim* : activity *moham* : delusion *eva* : also *ca* : and *sampravṛttāni* : on becoming dominant *na dveṣṭi* : shows no aversion *nivṛttāni* : in their absence *na kāṅkṣati* : does not long for.

The Blessed Lord said:

22. O son of Pāṇḍu! He who shows no aversion to knowledge, activity, or delusion when any of them is dominant, nor longs for them when absent;

उदासीनवदासीनो गुणैर्यो न विचाल्यते ।
गुणा वर्तन्त इत्येव योऽवतिष्ठति नेङ्गते ॥ 23 ॥

Udāsīnavad āsīno guṇair yo na vicālyate /
guṇā vartanta ity eva yo'vatiṣṭhati n'eṅgate //23//

Yaḥ : Who *udāsīnavat* : like an unconcerned witness *āsīnaḥ* : remaining *guṇaiḥ* : by the experience of sense objects, which are the products of the Guṇas *na vicālyate* : is not perturbed, *yaḥ* : who *guṇāḥ* : Guṇas (as instruments) *eva* : alone *vartante* : act (on Guṇas as objects, and not oneself). *iti* : thus *avatiṣṭhati* : remains firm *yaḥ* : who *na iṅgate* : does not waver.

23. Who remains like an unconcerned witness and is unperturbed by the Guṇa-born sense objects; who knows that it is only the Guṇa-born senses and mind that act and enjoy (and not his real self); who remains unwavering in all situations;

समदुःखसुखः स्वस्थः समलोष्टाश्मकाञ्चनः ।
तुल्यप्रियाप्रियो धीरस्तुल्यनिन्दात्मसंस्तुतिः ॥ 24 ॥

Sama-duḥkha-sukhaḥ svasthaḥ sama-loṣṭāśma-kāñcanaḥ /
tulya-priy'āpriyo dhīras tulya-nind'ātma-saṁstutiḥ //24//

(*Yaḥ* : who) *sama-duḥkha-sukhaḥ* : alike in pleasure and in pain *svasthaḥ* : self-poised *sama-loṣṭāśma-kāñcanaḥ* : viewing alike stone, iron and gold *tulya-priyāpriyaḥ* : alike towards men and things, dear or repugnant *yaḥ* : who *dhīraḥ* : firm, unmoved *tulya-nindātma-saṁstutiḥ* : alike in praise and in blame:

24. Who is self-poised alike in pleasure and in pain; who makes no difference between stone, iron, and gold; who is the same towards the loving and the hating; who is unmoved by praise and blame alike;

मानापमानयोस्तुल्यस्तुल्यो मित्रारिपक्षयोः ।
सर्वारम्भपरित्यागी गुणातीतः स उच्यते ॥ 25 ॥

mān'āpamānayos tulyas tulyo mitr'āripakṣayoḥ /
sarv'ārambha-parityāgī guṇ'ātītaḥ sa ucyate //25//

Mānāpamānayoḥ : in honour and in insult *tulyaḥ* : alike, *mitrāri pakṣayoḥ* : towards friend and foe *tulyaḥ* : alike, *sarvārambha-parityāgī* : who has totally abandoned the sense of agency *saḥ* : such a person *guṇātītaḥ* : one who has transcended the Guṇas *iti*: thus *ucyate* : is spoken of.

25. Who is alike in honour and in humiliation; who views a friend and a foe alike; who has abandoned all sense of agency—such a person is said to have transcended the Guṇas.

मां च योऽव्यभिचारेण भक्तियोगेन सेवते ।
स गुणान्समतीत्यैतान् ब्रह्मभूयाय कल्पते ॥ 26 ॥

Māṁ ca yo'vyabhicāreṇa bhakti-yogena sevate /
sa guṇān samatīty'aitān brahma-bhūyāya kalpate //26//

Yaḥ : Who *mām* : Me *ca* : and *avyabhicāreṇa* : unwavering and exclusive *bhakti yogena* : communion through love *sevate* : serves *saḥ* : he, *etān* : these *guṇān* : Guṇas *samatītya* : transcending, *brahmabhūyāya* : to become Brahman *kalpate* : attains fitness.

26. He who serves Me through the communion of unswerving and exclusive devotion, transcends the Guṇas and attains fitness to become Brahman.

ब्रह्मणो हि प्रतिष्ठाहममृतस्याव्ययस्य च ।
शाश्वतस्य च धर्मस्य सुखस्यैकान्तिकस्य च ॥ 27 ॥

Brahmaṇo hi pratiṣṭhā'ham amṛtasy' āvyayasya ca /
śāśvatasya ca dharmasya sukhasy'aikāntikasya ca //27//

Hi : Indeed *aham* : I am *Brahmaṇaḥ* : of Brahman *pratiṣṭhā* : basic support, *avyayasya* : unending, incorruptible *amṛtasya* : of immortality, Mokṣa, *śāśvatasya* : of eternal *dharmasya* : law *ca* : and, *ekāntikasya sukhasya* : of absolute bliss *ca* : and *pratiṣṭhā*: seat.

27. Indeed, I (Kṛṣṇa, the God of love and grace ,or Pratyagātman, the true Inner Self), am the basic support of Brahman—of the incorruptible state of Mokṣa ,of the Eternal Law and of undending Bliss. 7

ओं तत्सदिति श्रीमद्भगवद्गीतासूपनिषत्सु ब्रह्मविद्यायां योगशास्त्रे श्रीकृष्णार्जुनसंवादे गुणत्रयविभागयोगो नाम चतुर्दशोऽध्यायः ॥ 14 ॥

NOTES

1. *Vrs.*1-2: This chapter deals with the description of the nature and functions of the three Guṇas, the constituents of Prakṛti, which cause bondage to the Puruṣa. How a knowledge of the Guṇas and their functions is praised here as leading to liberation may look a bit puzzling at first. But its relevancy can

be easily perceived on the analogy of a patient undergoing treatment. It is important for him to know what are contra-indicated in the matter of diet and habits of life while the treatment is going on. For an intelligent patient it is also advantageous to know something about the nature of his disease. In the same way an aspirant must understand what bondage consists in and what he has to guard against in the pursuit of the spiritual ideal. Hence the importance of this and the succeeding chapters in which all aspects of the doctrine of Prakṛti and its three Guṇas are treated.

2. *Vrs.*3-4: Here the Gītā registers its divergence from the *Sāṅ*khyan conception of Prakṛti and Puruṣa as independent entities. They are only the powers of God as already stated in Chaps. 10 and 13 (Cf. Note 5 of Ch. 13).

It is sometimes said that the doctrine of the Fatherhood of God and the Brotherhood of man are special doctrines of Christianity. But nowhere has this doctrine been stated so plainly and powerfully as here in the Gītā.

3. *Vr.*5: The doctrine of Guṇas of Prakṛti—Sattva, Rajas and Tamas—was mentioned here and there in the Gītā in many places, but in this and subsequent chapters to the last we get an elaborate consideration of their effect on the character and personality of man. Therefore, as a background understanding of one of the fundamental ideas behind the theory of Prakṛti and its three Guṇas will be helpful, the same is given below in a nutshell.

Prakṛti is the Sanskrit expression for Nature. It does not mean matter as we understand it today, because the matter of the scientist is a late evolute of Prakṛti. It is an expression and a theory introduced by the the *Sāṅ*khya philosophy, and this *Sāṅ*khya conception of it and its analysis have entered into all systems of Indian philosophy and even the sciences as they were developed in ancient India.

Prakṛti has three constituents, Sattva, Rajas and Tamas called Guṇas. These three are in a state of equilibrium. It is on the disturbance of this equilibrium that evolution and involution of the creative cycle depends. A Guṇa in ordinary language means a quality or attribute, but the Guṇas of Prakṛti are its constituents. Even the word 'constituent' is misleading. Perhaps 'dispositions' may be more appropriate. They cannot be isolated as substances or as quantities but are known only through their effects in the form of various qualities and substances that constitute the world of experience and are classifiable into these three groups. In this and succeeding chapters the teaching on the Guṇas is elaborated through a consideration of their manifestations. As far as this threefold analysis of Prakṛti into Sattva, Rajas and Tamas is concerned, Sattva has effects like luminosity, peace, knowledge and pleasure and objects with such properties; Rajas expresses as dynamism, passion, attachment and the like; and Tamas, as inertia, darkness, dullness, ignorance and the like. Objects partaking of such characteristics are the products of Sattva, Rajas and Tamas respectively.

While the Gītā is mainly concerned with the psychological and spiritual aspects of the Guṇas, the Śāṁkhya philosophy, which originally propounded this doctrine of Prakṛti with its three constituents called Guṇas, derived all the cosmic categories as their evolutes, and the whole universe in its subtle and gross aspects, as the permutations and combinations of these categories. We give below a table showing Prakṛti and all its evolutes in full:

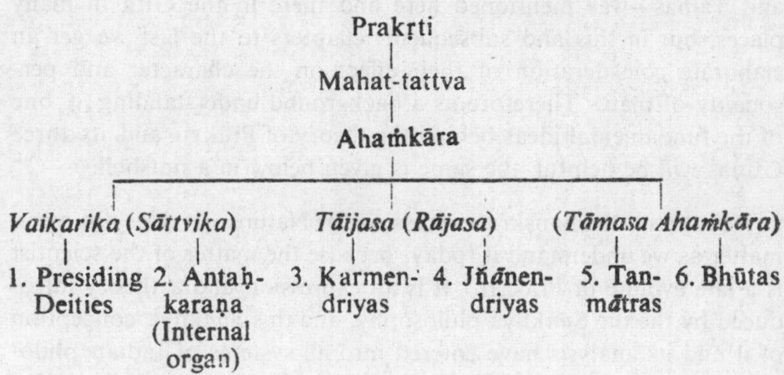

1. *Presiding Deities*: These are fourteen—Dik, Vāyu, Āditya, Varuṇa and Aswins, controlling the five Jñānendriyas, (organs of knowledge); Agni, Indra, Viṣṇu, Mitra, and Prajāpati controlling the five Karmendriyas (organs of action); and Candra, Brahma, Rudra and Kṣetrajña presiding over the four aspects of Antaḥkaraṇa. These are however excluded in the sāṁkhyan analysis.

2. *Antaḥkaraṇa* : This is what is ordinarily called the mind,

but is termed 'inner organ' to show that it includes several aspects and stands in contrast to the outer organs to be described separately. Its four aspects are: mind, intellect, egoity, and mind-stuff (Chitta). Each of the last mentioned four deities presides over each of these aspects. The above two items (1 & 2) are the products of Sattvika-ahaṁkāra.

3. *Karmendriyas*: These are the organs of action and are five in number—speech, hands, feet, excretory organs and the generative organ. The five deities controlling these are mentioned under item 1 above.

4. *Jñānendriyas*: These are the five organs of knowledge. They are: ear, skin, eye, tongue and nose. The deities controlling these are mentioned above in item 1.

The above two items (3 & 4) are the products of Rājasa-ahaṁkāra.

5&6. *Tanmātras & Bhūtas*: The Tanmātras are the subtle essences of elements and the Bhūtas, their gross expressions. They are causally related. The details under these two items are stated below in the order of their origination. Out of Tāmasa-ahaṁkāra emerges Tanmātra Sound; and from it Bhūta Sky; from Bhūta Sky, Tanmātra Touch; from Tanmātra Touch, Bhūta Air; from Bhūta Air, Tanmātra Rūpa; from Tanmātra Rūpa, Bhūta Tejas; from Bhūta Tejas, Tanmātra Taste; from Tanmātra Taste, Bhūta Water; and from Bhūta Water, Tanmātra Smell; and from Tanmātra Smell, Bhūta Earth. Each Tanmātra, which is also a form of sensation, transmits that particular form of sensation to the Bhūta coming out of it, and each Bhūta to the Tanmātra springing from it, the succeeding category thereby inheriting all the properties of the earlier one. In saṁkya proper there are only24categories(cf.p.206)

These are the psychological and physical evolutes of Prakṛti, out of whose permutations and combinations the whole world of mind and matter has evolved. How the Guṇas bind the spirit is described in the subsequent verses.

4. *Vr*.6: The Jñāna or knowledge referred to here is not the intuitive illumination of non-duality, nor the knowledge of the right relationship of the Jīvā with God. It means mere intellectualism.

5. *Vrs.* 19-26: Spiritual maturity consists in a split in consciousness, by which the conscious centre (Puruṣa or Jīva) ceases to identify himself with the movements of Prakṛti and its evolutes consisting in body-mind, and instead of feeling 'I act', stands poised in the witnesshood of Divine Consciousness, in whose presence Prakṛti functions without in the least affecting Him. Just as God is unaffected by the world, of which He is the creator, sustentator and destroyer, the Jīvā, by becoming a participant in His Consciousness, also shares that unaffectedness. In bondage the Puruṣa identifies himself with the movements of Prakṛti, and thus feels himself to be the actor and enjoyer. When identification with Prakṛti and its Guṇas is snapped by identification with the Divine Consciousness, the Puruṣa too, like God, becomes neither the actor nor the enjoyer, but the unaffected witness. The state of mind of one who has transcended the Guṇas—the *triguṇātīta*—is described in the succeeding verses.

According to the Gītā this transcendence of the Guṇas and the unity with Divine Consciousness are attained by one who serves the Lord through the communion of unswerving and exclusive devotion *avyabhicāriṇā bhakti-yogena*. (14.26). The Yoga recommended here is the same as what has been recommended in the 12th chapter in reply to Arjuna's question–who is the better of the two, Bhaktas who worship Him in ever-steadfast devotion as the Divine Person, or those who contemplate on the Akṣara and the Avyakta (the Imperishable and the Transcendent).

It is however to be noted that the Gītā often uses Jñāna or knowledge of God, and Bhakti or the love of Him, almost as identical. For example, the Lord opens this chapter with the declaration that He is going to give out the highest of all forms of knowledge—*jñānānāṁ jñānamuttamam.* And yet He says in this verse of that very chapter that it is one who serves Him in utter devotion that attains to this transcendence of the Guṇas (which is also said to be the state of one with Jñāna).

6. *Vr.* 27: The meanings of the expressions 'to become Brahma' (*Brahmabhūyāya*) and 'I am the support of Brahman' (*Brahmaṇohi pratiṣṭhā'ham*) are difficult to derive. The first verse and the expression 'fitness to attain Brahman', contained in it would have been very easy to understand, had it not been for the

next verse where it is stated, 'I am the support of Brahman'. Understood in the ordinary sense of Brahman as the Supreme Absolute Being, the first verse would only mean that when a man attains to mature devotion, he becomes fit to intuit the Absolute also. But when immediately after, it is said in verse 27, "I, the Lord, am the support of Brahman", it becomes a riddle. For, in the usual Advaidic ideology the Impersonal Absolute is the support of Iswara, the Personal Being, and of the whole manifested universe. But here it is turned the other way, saying that the Personal is the support of the Impersonal Absolute. Some schools of Vedantins, who are not pure Non-dualists, actually understand it in this way and maintain that Kṛṣṇa, the God of love, is the support of the all-pervading Impersonal Caitanya, Consciousness, just as the disk of the sun is of the spreading formless light.

To get over the obvious difficulty, pure non-dualists maintain that here 'I', Kṛṣṇa," stands for the Nirguṇa Brahman (the Impersonal Absolute), and that Brahman means here Saguṇa-Brahman (the Personal Brahman or Īsvara). How arbitrary this interpretation is, is obvious.

The difficulty seems to arise from the fact that the word Brahman is used here in a peculiar sense. In Sanskrit literature the word Brahma occurs both in its neuter and masculine forms as Brahman and Brahmā, to indicate the Supreme Being and the creator Brahma respectively: When various case endings are added and compound words are formed, it will be difficult to distinguish it except from the context. This gives scope for different schools to interpret it in their own way. Besides, the word is used in different meanings in different contexts, by all commentators. Brahma means Veda in 3.14—*brahmākṣarasamudbhavam.* It means Nature in 14.3—*mama yonir mahadbrahma.* It is identified with Om-kāra in 8.13—*Om ityekākṣaraṁ brahma.* In 8.3 it is equated with the transcendent Absolute—*akṣaraṁ brahma paramam.* According to some commentators Brahma in the present context means Jīva.

Those varying meanings of the word Brahma in the *Gītā* are recognised by all the traditional intrepretors of the Text, but there is another sense for the word, especially when it is combined with suffixes like Brahma-bhūta, Brahma-bhūyam etc. It is the view of modern interpreters of the Gītā like Zaehner, who have made a comparative study of the Gītā and Buddhist scriptures in Pāli, that through such words formed by adding suffixes to Brahman like *Brahma-bhūta, Brāhmī-sthiti, Brahma-nirvāṇa, Brahma-bhūyam* etc, the Gīta is trying to absorb certain current Buddhist ideologies into its thought. Every one accepts that Sāṁkhyan thought has been absorbed by the Gītā through the acceptance of the Sāṁkhya analysis of reality into Puruṣa and Prakṛti, and of the latter into the twentyfour categories. But the Gīta annexes the Saṁkhya's Puruṣa and Prakṛti into its own ideology by positing a Puruṣottama, in whom the Prakṛti and Puruṣa find their unity. It is therefore nothing unusual or strange, if certain Buddhist ideas have entered into the Gītā and got amalgamated with its ideology.

Now in Buddhist Pāli literature *Brahma-bhūta* is a common expression to describe one who has attained Nirvāṇa. The usual phrase is: *nicehāto nibbūto siti-bhūto sukha-patisaṁvedi brahma-bhūtena āttana*—without craving, appeased, cooled, experiencing joy, with his self Brahman (*Digha Nikāya* III.233). This is the description of those who have attained Nirvāṇa like the Buddha and the Arhats. It is a state in which 'becoming' and individuality are transcended into a boundless peace, free from passions and cravings, which is thus described in *Udāna* 55. "Just as, whatever streams flow into the mighty ocean and whatever floods pour from the sky, there is no shrinkage or overflow seen thereby in the mighty ocean, even so though many mendicants pass finally away into that condition of Nirvāṇa, which has no remainder, yet there is no shrinkage nor over-flow in that condition of Nirvāṇa seen thereby" (quoted and translated by Zaehner). Many of these descriptions of *Brahma-bhūta-āttana*—with self become Brahman—is very much reminiscent of the description of the sage—the *sthitaprajña*—in the 2nd chapter of the Gīta, whose state is called *Brāhmī-sthiti* which ends in *Brahma-nirvāṇa.*

What is important here is that *Brāhmī-sthiti, Brahma-bhūyam* etc., do not seem to be the intuition of the Supreme Being, but a state mid-way, through which alone true intuition is attained. It is stated here in Gīta 14.26, that this state of *Brahmī-sthiti* or *Brahma-bhūyam* is attained through steady devotion to the Lord. For the Lord, it is declared here, is the support of Brahman, *the state of a steady mind free from cravings and passions and established in a sense of unruffled stillness.* On such a mental state only can true intuition arise. The intuitions of persons who have not struck this dimension of their being, are the projections of the impressions and desires with which their minds are full. That dimension of boundless peace, free from passions and cravings, which the Buddhist accepted as the final state, is, according to the declaration of the Gītā here, only the state nearest to the Lord, having its support in Him.

This idea is made very clear in the last or the 18th chapter of the Gītā. There from verse 49 to 53 are given the disciplines to attain to the state of *Brahma-bhūyam*—the state of being Brahman. If this were the culmination of spiritual attainment, the Gītā must have stopped with it. But it definitely puts it as an intermediary state of attainment, and then proceeds to present the still higher steps in verses 54 to 56. The *Brahma-bhūta,* it is said, becomes peaceful, without sorrows and fears, and is established in an attitude of equality towards all beings. He then gains supreme devotion to the Lord and through devotion, comes to have an intimate understanding of Him and his majesty. Knowing Him thus in truth and in reality he enters into Him. (Cf. Notes 6 and 7 of the 18th Chapter).

It is plainly stated here in the passage referred to above that *Brahma-bhūta* has not yet attained to the highest enlightenment. He has come to have that moral perfection to attain to the highest form of devotion—*mad-bhaktiṁ parām,* which is a higher form or development of Bhakti than what is indicated in 14.26. It is not the Bhakti of the early stages of spiritual development when it is motivated by individual fulfilments. Even the desire for Mokṣa is an individual fulfilment. This supreme Bhakti is spontaneous, motiveless, and unswerving. It is accompanied with illumination, and the devotee enters into Divine life. This consummation, it must be noted, is the spiritual fulfilment, of which the earlier stage is called *Brahma-bhūyam* i.e., of being established in the unbounded state of bliss free from individuality, craving and passion.

Chapter XV

पुरुषोत्तमयोगः

THE MYSTERY OF THE ALL-PERVADING PERSON

SUMMARY

The Mystic Aśvattha tree: (1-3) Sri Kṛṣṇa said: The created world is like a mighty Pīpal Tree, rooted above in the unseen, with branches spreading everywhere in the world of the seen. Entangled in its branches, no one understands its source, nor does one grasp the utterly flimsy and momentary nature of the values it yields. With the powerful weapon of non-attachment, cut, O man, the taproots that bind you to it, and go into the empyrean heights to seek Me, its source—the Supreme Puruṣottama.

Transcendence and immanence of the Divine: (4-15) I am transcendent, beyond time and space, but yet immanent in Nature and in all beings—as light in the sun and other luminaries, as gravitation that keeps the galaxies in position, as fertility in soil, as the digestive powers in all living beings, and above all in the hearts of all as the living spirit from whom life, memory, knowledge and everything else proceed.

The Puruṣottama: (16-20) My being has a threefold aspect. As the changeful Matter I constitute the bodies of all (*Kṣara Puruṣa*) As the unchanging Witness Consciousness, the Jīva, I dwell in all these bodies (*Akṣara Puruṣa*). But I am, above all, the Puruṣottama, (the Supreme Puruṣa), who manifests all these, supports all these, indwells them all, and yet remains the Transcendent Spirit, an iota even of whom is not affected by all these manifestations. He who contemplates on this mystery that I am, the Supreme Puruṣottama, he understands all and offers himself to Me with his whole being.

श्रीभगवानुवाच

ऊर्ध्वमूलमधःशाखमश्वत्थं प्राहुरव्ययम् ।
छन्दांसि यस्य पर्णानि यस्तं वेद स वेदवित् ॥ 1 ॥

Śri Bhagavān uvāca:

Ūrdhva-mūlam adhaḥ-śākham aśvatthaṁ prāhur avyayam /
chandāṁsi yasya parṇāni yas taṁ veda sa veda-vit //1//

Ūrdhva-mūlam : Rooted in the most High *adhaḥśākham* : with branches below *avyayam* : imperishable, eternal *aśvattham* : Aśvattha, the Tree of this transitory world *prāhuḥ* : they (scriptures) speak of; *yasya* : of which *chandāṁsi* : Vedic hymns *parṇāni* : are the leaves; *yaḥ* : who *tam* : it *veda* : knows, *saḥ* : he *vedavit* : is a knower of the Veda.

The Blessed Lord said:

1. The scriptures speak of the eternal Aśvattha, the World Tree, whose roots are in the Most High, branches in the lower regions, and leaves in Vedic hymns. He who knows it, understands the Veda really.[1]

अधश्चोर्ध्वं प्रसृतास्तस्य शाखा गुणप्रवृद्धा विषयप्रवालाः ।
अधश्च मूलान्यनुसंततानि कर्मानुबन्धीनि मनुष्यलोके ॥ 2 ॥

Adhaś c'ordhvaṁ prasṛtās tasya śākhā
guṇa-pravṛddhā viṣaya-pravālāḥ /
adhaś ca mūlāny anusaṁtatāni
karm'ānubandhīni manuṣya-loke //2//

Guṇa-pravṛddhāḥ : Nourished by the Guṇas *viṣayapravālāḥ* : having the sense objects as sprouts *tasya* : of it *śākhāḥ* : branches *adhaḥ* : below *ūrdhvam* : above *ca* : and *prasṛtāḥ* : are spreading; *karmānubandhīni* : generating the bondage of action *mūlāni* : secondary roots *adhaḥ* : below *ca* : and *manuṣya loke* : in the world of men *anusaṁtatāni* : are stretching.

2. Nourished by the Guṇas and covered with the budding foliage of sense objects, its branches spread into regions high

and low. Stretching forth on the ground below in the world of men, are its secondary roots, entangling man in the bondage of action.

न रूपमस्येह तथोपलभ्यते नान्तो न चादिर्न च संप्रतिष्ठा ।
अश्वत्थमेनं सुविरूढमूलमसङ्गशस्त्रेण दृढेन छित्त्वा ॥ 3 ॥

ततः पदं तत्परिमार्गितव्यं यस्मिन्गता न निवर्तन्ति भूयः ।
तमेव चाद्यं पुरुषं प्रपद्ये यतः प्रवृत्तिः प्रसृता पुराणी ॥ 4 ॥

Na rūpam asy'eha tath'opalabhyate
n'ānto na c'ādir na ca sampratiṣṭhā /
aśvattham enam suvirūḍha-mūlam
asaṅga-śastreṇa dṛḍhena chittvā //3//

Tataḥ padaṁ tat parimārgitavyaṁ
yasmin gatā na nivartanti bhūyaḥ /
tam eva c'ādyaṁ puruṣaṁ prapadye
yataḥ pravṛttiḥ prasṛtā purāṇī //4//

Iha : Here i.e., while involved in worldly life *asya* : of it *rūpam* : form *na upalabhyate* : is not understood; *tathā* : in the same way *ādiḥ* : its beginning *na* : not *ca* : and; *antaḥ* : end *na* : not *ca* : and; *sampratiṣṭhā* : its foundation *na* : not; *suvirūḍhamūlam* : firmly rooted *enam* : this *aśvattham* : Aśvattha (the World Tree) *dṛḍhena* : powerful *asaṅgaśastreṇa* : weapon of non-attachment *chittvā* : cutting asunder, *tataḥ* : after that *yataḥ* : from where *purāṇī pravṛttiḥ* : the eternal process *prasṛtā* : streamed forth, *tam* : Him *eva ca* : alone *ādyaṁ puruṣam* : Primeval Person *prapadye* : seek as refuge, *iti* : resolving thus *yasmin gatāḥ* : attaining to which state *bhūyaḥ* : again *na nivartanti* : do not come back, *tat* : that *padam* : state *parimārgitavyam* : is to be sought.

3-4. For one involved in worldly life, the form of this World-Tree is not visible, nor its origin, nor its end, nor its foundation. Cutting asunder the firmly rooted Aśvattha (World-Tree) with the powerful axe of non-attachment, and saying, "I seek refuge in that Primeval Person from whom this eternal cosmic activity has streamed forth", man should seek that Status, attaining to which there is no more return to this life of Saṁsāra.

निर्मानमोहा जितसङ्गदोषा अध्यात्मनित्या विनिवृत्तकामाः ।
द्वन्द्वैर्विमुक्ताः सुखदुःखसंज्ञैर्गच्छन्त्यमूढाः पदमव्ययं तत् ॥ 5 ॥

Nirmāna-mohā-jita-saṅga-doṣā
adhyātma-nityā vinivṛtta-kāmāḥ /
dvandvair vimuktāḥ sukha-duḥkha-saṁjñair
gacchanty amūḍhāḥ padam avyayaṁ tat //5//

Nirmānamohāḥ : Free from pride and delusion, *jitasaṅgadoṣāḥ:* having overcome the evil of attachment, *adhyātmanityāḥ* : ever-absorbed in spiritual pursuit, *vinivṛtta kāmāḥ* : free from desires, *sukha-duḥkha-saṁjñaiḥ* : called pleasure and pain *dvandaiḥ* : from the pair of opposites *vimuktāḥ* : freed from, *amūḍhāḥ* : delivered from ignorance, *tat* : that *avyayam* : eternal *padam* : state *gacchanti*: go to.

5. They who are free from pride and delusion, who have no attachments, who are ever absorbed in spiritual pursuits, who are free from all worldly desires, who are unaffected by the varying situations of pleasurable and painful nature—such persons, freed from ignorance, attain to the Eternal State.

न तद्भासयते सूर्यो न शशाङ्को न पावकः ।
यद्गत्वा न निवर्तन्ते तद्धाम परमं मम ॥ 6 ॥

Na tad bhāsayate sūryo na śaśāṅko na pāvakaḥ /
yad gatvā na nivartarte tad dhāma paramaṁ mama //6//

Tat : That *sūryaḥ* : the sun *na bhāsayate* : does not illumine, *śaśāṅkaḥ na* : nor the moon, *na pāvakaḥ* : nor fire, *yat gatvā* : having reached which *na nivartante* : one does not return, *tat* : that *mama* : My *paramaṁ dhāma* : Supreme Abode.

6. That the sun does not illumine, nor the moon, nor the fire; (for it is the Light of Pure Consciousness). Having attained It, the Spirit does not return again to the life of Saṁsāra. Such is My Supreme Abode.

ममैवांशो जीवलोके जीवभूतः सनातनः ।
मनःषष्ठानीन्द्रियाणि प्रकृतिस्थानि कर्षति ॥ 7 ॥

Mam'aivāṁśo jīva-loke jīva-bhūtaḥ sanātanaḥ /
manaḥ-ṣaṣṭhānī'ndriyāṇi prakṛti-sthāni karṣati //7//

Mama eva : My own *sanātanaḥ* : immortal *amśaḥ* : portion *jīva-bhūtaḥ* : having become an embodied soul *jīvaloke* : in the world of living beings *prakṛtisthāni* : abiding in Prakṛti *manaḥ-ṣaṣṭhāni* : with mind as the sixth *indriyāṇi* : senses *karṣati* : attracts.

7. A fragment of Myself, immortal in nature, having become the embodied spirit in the world of the living, attracts to Himself the mind and the five senses born of Prakṛti.[2]

शरीरं यदवाप्नोति यच्चाप्युत्क्रामतीश्वरः ।
गृहीत्वैतानि संयाति वायुर्गन्धानिवाशयात् ॥ 8 ॥

Śarīraṁ yad avāpnoti yac c'āpy utkrāmatī śvaraḥ /
gṛhītv'aitāni saṁyāti vāyur gandhān iv'āśayāt //8//

Īśvaraḥ : Jiva or the lord of the body *śarīram* : body *yat* : when *avāpnoti* : acquires, *yat* : when *ca* : and *api* : also *utkrāmati* : leaves, *vāyuḥ* : air *āśayāt gandhān iva* : as smell from their seats *etāni* : these *gṛhītvā* : taking with, *saṁyāti* : goes.

8. When he gets a new body or abandons an old one, the Jīva, the lord of the body, moves, carrying them (the mind and the senses) with him, as the wind carries smells from their seats (in flowers and the like)[3].

श्रोत्रं चक्षुः स्पर्शनं च रसनं घ्राणमेव च ।
अधिष्ठाय मनश्चायं विषयानुपसेवते ॥ 9 ॥

Śrotraṁ cakṣuḥ sparśanaṁ ca rasanaṁ ghrāṇam eva ca /
adhiṣṭhāya manaś c'āyaṁ viṣayān upasevate //9//

Ayam : This Jiva *śrotraṁ* : hearing *cakṣuḥ* : sight *sparśam* : touch *ca* : and *rasanam* : taste *ghrāṇam* : smell *eva ca* : as also *manaḥ* : mind *ca* : and *adhiṣṭhāya* : presiding over; in identification with *viṣayān* : sense objects *upasevate* : experiences.

9. In identification with the senses like hearing, sight, touch, taste and smell, this Jīva experiences their respective objects.

उत्क्रामन्तं स्थितं वापि भुञ्जानं वा गुणान्वितम् ।
विमूढा नानुपश्यन्ति पश्यन्ति ज्ञानचक्षुषः ॥ 10 ॥

Utkrāmantaṁ sthitaṁ vā'pi bhuñjānaṁ vā guṇ'ānvitam /
vimūḍhā n'ānupaśyanti paśyanti jñāna-cakṣuṣaḥ //10//

Utkrāmantam : On departing, *sthitam* : while staying, *bhuñjānaṁ* : experiencing *vā* : or, *guṇānvitaṁ vā api* : or when remaining identified with the Guṇas, *vimūḍhāḥ* : the deluded *na anupaśyanti* : do not perceive him; *jñānacakṣuṣaḥ* : those with the eye of wisdom *paśyanti* : see.

10. The deluded do not recognise the Spirit (Jīva) when, in identification with the Guṇas, he tenants or leaves a body, or when he experiences objects through it; but those endowed with the eye of wisdom do.

यतन्तो योगिनश्चैनं पश्यन्त्यात्मन्यवस्थितम् ।
यतन्तोऽप्यकृतात्मानो नैनं पश्यन्त्यचेतसः ॥ 11 ॥

Yatanto yoginaś c'ainaṁ paśyanty ātmany avasthitam /
yatanto'py akṛt'ātmāno n'ainaṁ paśyanty acetasaḥ //11//

Yatantaḥ : Striving *yoginaḥ ca* : Yogis *ātmani* : within themselves *avasthitam* : dwelling *enam* : this Atman *paśyanti* : perceive; *yatantaḥ api* : though striving *akṛtātmānaḥ* : the impure and devotionless *acetasaḥ* : the unregenerate men *enam* : them *na paśyanti* : do not perceive.

11. The striving contemplatives perceive the Atman within themselves, but not the impure and the unregenerate, though they be striving.

यदादित्यगतं तेजो जगद्भासयतेऽखिलम् ।
यच्चन्द्रमसि यच्चाग्नौ तत्तेजो विद्धि मामकम् ॥ 12 ॥

Yad āditya-gataṁ tejo jagad bhāsayate'khilam /
yac candramasi yac c'āgnau tat tejo viddhi māmakam //12//

Ādityagatam : Residing in the sun *yat* : which *tejaḥ* : light *akhilaṁ jagat* : the whole universe *bhāsayate* : illumines, *candramasi* : in the moon *yat* : which *agnau ca* : and in Agni *yat* : which, *tat* : that *tejaḥ* : splendour *māmakam* : mine *viddhi* : know.

12. That light of the sun which illumines the whole universe, which is present in the moon and in fire likewise—know that splendour to be Mine.[4]

गामाविश्य च भूतानि धारयाम्यहमोजसा ।
पुष्णामि चौषधीः सर्वाः सोमो भूत्वा रसात्मकः ॥ 13 ॥

Gām āviśya ca bhūtāni dhārayāmy aham ojasā /
puṣṇāmi c'auṣadhīḥ sarvāḥ somo bhūtvā ras'ātmakaḥ //13//

Aham : I *ojasā* : by spiritual energy *gām* : the earth *āviśya* : entering *ca* : and *bhūtāni* : all beings *dhārayāmi* : sustain; *rasātmakaḥ* : watery *somaḥ* : moon *bhūtvā* : becoming *sarvāḥ* : all *oṣadhīḥ* : herbs *puṣṇāmi* : nourish *ca* : and.

13. Entering the earth by My spiritual energy, I sustain all beings residing in it. As the watery moon, I nourish all herbs.

अहं वैश्वानरो भूत्वा प्राणिनां देहमाश्रितः ।
प्राणापानसमायुक्तः पचाम्यन्नं चतुर्विधम् ॥ 14 ॥

Ahaṁ vaiśvānaro bhūtvā prāṇināṁ deham āśritaḥ /
prāṇ' āpāna-samāyuktaḥ pacāmy annaṁ catur-vidham //14//

Aham : I *prāṇinām* : of living beings *deham* : body *āśritaḥ* : based in *vaiśvānaraḥ* : the digestive Fire *bhūtvā* : manifesting as *prāṇāpānasamāyuktaḥ* : in combination with Prāṇa and Apāna *catur-vidham annam* : four kinds of food *pacāmi* : digest.

14. Based in the body of living beings, I manifest as the digestive Fire, Vaiśvānara, and in combination with the vital energies known as Prāṇa and Apāna, digest the four kinds of food taken by them.

सर्वस्य चाहं हृदि संनिविष्टो मत्तः स्मृतिर्ज्ञानमपोहनं च ।
वेदैश्च सर्वैरहमेव वेद्यो वेदान्तकृद्वेदविदेव चाहम् ॥ 15 ॥

Sarvasya c' āhaṁ hṛdi saṁniviṣṭo
mattaḥ smṛtir jñānam apohanaṁ ca /
vedaiś ca sarvair aham eva vedyo
vedānta-kṛd-veda-vid eva c' āham //15//

Sarvasya : Of all *ca* : and *hṛdi* : in the heart *aham* : I *saṁniviṣṭaḥ* : reside; *mattaḥ* : from Me *smṛtiḥ* : memory *jñānam* : knowledge *apohanaṁ*: their loss *ca*: and; *sarvaiḥ vedaiḥ* : through all the Vedas *ca* : and *vedyaḥ* : the one to be known *aham* : I *eva* : verily; *vedāntakṛt* : the originator of the Vedānta *vedavid* : knower of the Veda *ca* : and *aham* : I *eva* : also.

15. I abide in the hearts of all. From Me arise the remembrance and knowledge of the spiritual Verity as also their effacement. The original teacher of the Vedānta I am, as also the knower of the Veda.

द्वाविमौ पुरुषौ लोके क्षरश्चाक्षर एव च ।
क्षरः सर्वाणि भूतानि कूटस्थोऽक्षर उच्यते ॥ 16 ॥

***Dvāv imau puruṣau** loke kṣaraś c' ākṣara eva ca /*
kṣaraḥ sarvāṇi bhūtāni kūṭa-stho'kṣara ucyate //16//

Loke : In the world *kṣaraḥ* : the perishable *ca* : and *akṣaraḥ* : the imperishable *eva* : indeed *ca* : and *imau* : these *dvau* : two *puruṣau* : Puruṣas there are; *kṣaraḥ* : the perishable *sarvāṇi* : all *bhūtāni* : manifested beings; *akṣaraḥ* : the imperishable *kūṭasthaḥ* : aloof and unchanging or in the alternative, the Creative power Māyā Śakti the source of falsity *ucyate* : is called.

16. It is well known that there are two types of Puruṣas (spirits or categories)—the Kṣara or the Perishable and Akṣara, the Imperishable. The Kṣara consists of all the Jīvas in embodiment who are subject to change, while the Akṣara, consists of the collectivity of liberated Jīvas who remain aloof from changeful matter and are unaffected by it; (Or in the alternative, the Creative Power Māyā-śakti, which is the source of all falsity and the cause of endless Saṁsāra).[5]

उत्तमः पुरुषस्त्वन्यः परमात्मेत्युदाहृतः ।
यो लोकत्रयमाविश्य बिभर्त्यव्यय ईश्वरः ॥ 17 ॥

Uttamaḥ puruṣas tu anyaḥ param'ātm'ety udāhṛtaḥ /
yo loka-trayam āviśya bibharty avyaya īśvaraḥ //17//

Paramātmā : The highest of Spirits *iti* : thus *udāhṛtaḥ* : called *yaḥ* : who *avyayaḥ* : eternal *īśvaraḥ* : Lord *lokatrayam* : the three worlds *āviśya* : pervading *bibharti* : sustains, *saḥ uttamaḥ puruṣaḥ* : that Supreme Being *tu* : but *anyaḥ* : is yet another.

17. But there is yet another Puruṣa, known as the Supreme Being or the Puruṣottama, who is the highest of spirits, and who pervades all the three worlds and sustains them.

यस्मात्क्षरमतीतोऽहमक्षरादपि चोत्तमः ।
अतोऽस्मि लोके वेदे च प्रथितः पुरुषोत्तमः ॥ 18 ॥

Yasmāt kṣaram atīto'ham akṣarād api c'ottamaḥ /
ato'smi loke vede ca prathitaḥ puruṣottamaḥ //18//

Yasmāt : For the reason that *aham* : I *kṣaram* : the Perishable *atītaḥ* : transcends *akṣarāt api* : than the Imperishable *uttamaḥ* : superior *ca* : and; *ataḥ* : for this reason *loke* : in the world *vede* : in the Vedas *ca* : and *puruṣottamaḥ* : as Puruṣottama, as the Supreme Puruṣa *prathitaḥ* : celebrated *asmi* : I am.

18. As I transcend the Perishable and am also superior to the Imperishable, I am well-known as the Puruṣottama (the Supreme Being) in both the Vedic and secular literature.

यो मामेवमसंमूढो जानाति पुरुषोत्तमम् ।
स सर्वविद्भजति मां सर्वभावेन भारत ॥ 19 ॥

Yo mām evam asammūḍho jānāti puruṣ'ottamam /
sa sarvavid bhajati māṁ sarva bhāvena bhārata //19//

Bhārata : O scion of Bharata's clan! *yaḥ* : who *asammūḍhaḥ* : undeluded *evam* : in this way *puruṣottamam* : as Purusottama *jānāti* : knows, *saḥ* : he *sarvavid* : one having a true knowledge of the Totality *sarvabhāvena* : with all his heart *mām* : Me *bhajati* : worships.

19. He who knows Me in this way as the Puruṣottama, he understands the true nature of this Totality, and he loves and adores Me with his whole being.

इति गुह्यतमं शास्त्रमिदमुक्तं मयानघ ।
एतद्बुद्ध्वा बुद्धिमान्स्यात्कृतकृत्यश्च भारत ॥ 20 ॥

Iti guhyatamaṁ śāstram idam uktaṁ mayā'nagha /
etad buddhvā buddhimān syāt kṛta-kṛtyaś ca Bhārata //20//

Anagha : O sinless one! *iti* : thus *guhyatamam* : the most profound in all spiritual lore *idam* : this *śāstram* : spiritual doctrine *mayā* : by Me *uktam* : revealed; *etat* : this *buddhvā* : understanding *buddhimān* : one having attained wisdom *kṛtakṛtyaḥ* : one with the satisfaction of having done one's duties *ca* : and *syāt* : shall become.

20. O sinless one! This spiritual doctrine, the most profound of all in the sacred lore, has now been revealed by Me. A true understanding of it makes a man really wise and estabished in a sense of total fulfilment.[6]

ओं तत्सदिति श्रीमद्भगवद्गीतासूपनिषत्सु ब्रह्मविद्यायां योगशास्त्रे श्रीकृष्णार्जुनसंवादे पुरुषोत्तमयोगो नाम पञ्चदशोऽध्यायः ॥ 15 ॥

NOTES

1. *Vrs.*1-4: By a figure of speech the transmigratory cycle or Saṁsāra is compared to an Aśvattha tree (Pipal tree) with the roots in 'the Above' i.e., the Supreme Being. He is called 'the Above', not in a physical sense, but because He is the Highest Being. Aśvattha is interpreted to mean that which does not last even for tomorrow—*śva api na sthāsyate.* It is the realm of change, of becoming. The categories from Mahattattva down are evolved from Prakṛti, the Power of Brahman. Being later in evolution and grosser in nature they are called the trunk and the branches spreading downwards. From the evolutes of Prakṛti or the categories, are formed the various worlds, and these are compared to subsidiary branches that extend below i.e., below the human level as subhuman, animal and vegetable creations, and above i.e., as the realm of the Devas up to that of Satyaloka. They are augmented by the constituents of Prakṛti—Sattva, Rajas and Tamas, of which everything in the creative scheme is formed. Besides the primary root in 'the Above', there are the subsidiary roots which subsist in the human world where beings acquire Karma for enjoyment in spheres above and below. It is the Karma thus generated that determines the evolution and degradation of the Jīvas involved in the scheme of Saṁsāra.

Now looking from the point of view of man, with the aid of his senses and intelligence, he is not able to discover the real nature of Saṁsāra in two respects: (1) One fails to find the Supreme Being who is the support of it. For, we see Nature, and the scientific intelligence, which marks the highwater mark of man's intellectual growth, interprets Nature as a self-contained entity, without any transcendent divine background. (2) Next the human mind is not able to really grasp the extremely temporary nature of life and its concerns. Though the intellect can see it, the heart assumes it to be permanent, and man seeks to order his life accordingly.

But those who want to free themselves from this involvement in the cycle of births and deaths, are asked in the first place to cultivate detachment by reflection on the temporary nature of life and on the evils of births and deaths arising from involvement in the cyclic process of Saṁsāra. Cultivating detachment from the world, the Jīva is asked to develop attachment to the Supreme Being from whom this Saṁsāra has sprung. That attachment or Bhakti is to end in total self-surrender to Him. It is the conviction of the Gospel of devotion that God alone can lift the Jīva from the whirlpool of Saṁsāra. It is not by his choice that man finds himself in it. It must be only due to the will of the Supreme Being. And so His will alone can lift one up. The grace of the Supreme Divine comes on those who surrender themselves whole-heartedly to Him, and that grace accomplishes what one cannot do by one's own effort.

2. *Vr.*7: These verses set forth the Gītā conception of the personality of man or in fact of all Jīvas. The Jīva is basically a spirit, an *Aṁśa* or part of the Supreme Being. Immediately the logician raises the question: "How can God, who is also the Infinite Being, have parts? The Absolute must be without parts." Now in terms of Christian thought an answer may be given that He creates it out of nothing. This is only to say that He manifests the Jīva and the world by His will. But if differentiating parts from the whole with reference to the Absolute is illegitimate, it is equally so to differentiate between the Absolute and His will. It is only to say, in a different language, that a part of Him manifests as the Jīva.

Some Advaitic thinkers would say a part means a reflection of Him in an adjunct (*upādhi*) of body-mind, just like the reflection of the sun in pots of water. Not much is gained by this, because the question will arise wherefrom the *upādhi,* in which He reflects, has come. One has to say that He has manifested Himself as the Upādhi, and in that He reflects Himself as the Jīva. Now if He can manifest as the Upādhi and yet remain unaffected, He can as well manifest as the Jīva directly and remain unaffected.

So all these logical ways of putting the relation are self-defeating, because the Infinite and the Absolute Being cannot be put into the strait-jacket of logic without converting Spirit into matter. It is therefore better to take the Gīta statement as it is without going in for the logician's interpretations of it. The Jiva is a part of the Infinite Spirit, just as a spark from a huge conflagration is a part of that fire. It may be a small particle, but it retains in itself all the potentialities of the mighty Divine fire. Thus it forms the basis of Swami Vivekananda's dictum, 'Every soul is potentially divine.'

The question whether the Infinite is not reduced to the finite if it has parts, is mere sophistry. The Supreme Being is not only infinite, but He is also omnipotent. The Omnipotent Spirit can manifest as the many without being affected by such manifestation. To say that this manifestation into the many is only apparent is another sophistry, because the question arises, to whom it appears so. In answer, we have to assume another entity than the Infinite and the Absolute Being, who is the basis of this illusory perception. This will again involve dualism. So to take it exactly as the Gītā states it and accept it as a Divine mystery incapable of being put in logical terms, will be a more straightforward and simple course. We have above all got to remember the Upanishadic dictum, ***pūrṇamadaḥ pūrṇamidam*** etc.,—That is Infinite, this is Infinite. From the Infinite, the Infinite has come forth. When the Infinite is subtracted from the Infinite, the Infinite remains.

3. *Vrs.*8-11: Here is a clear statement of the doctrine of transmigration of the Jīva,—of how the Divine Spark in man on account of identification with parts of the evolutes of Prakṛti gets embodiments. Besides the physical side of personality, the psychic part of it, consisting of the 'Manas or mind and the five Indriyas or senses', is also formed of Prakṛti. This psycho-physical combination is a complex with which the Divine Spark identifies Himself, and thus he gets involved in the transmigratory cycle. But there is no beginning for this involvement. The body-mind is a part of Time's cyclic process of births and deaths, and there is no ultimate beginning for it. But there can be an end to it, a way of liberation

from this beginningless process when. through repeated embodiments the Jīva or embodied being evolves into greater stages of perfection. Through Bhakti and Jñāna, the Ātman realises his spiritual identity apart from the body-mind, and attains liberation. In all these repeated embodiments the Jīva leaves only the old body at death, but carries the mind and the senses, which form the psychic body that conserves and conveys the impressions of the good and the bad Karma potential acquired by the Jīva through actions and contacts. The Jīva's departure from the body, endowed with the Karma-potential, and his enjoyment of it through a new body-mind maintaining his distinctiveness throughout, are matters of experience to the enlightened ones, but the ignorant are so identified with the body-mind that they take the body-mind as their entire personality.

4. *Vrs.*12-15: The immanence of the Divine in oneself and in all Nature is stated in these verses.

5. *Vrs.*16-17: This passage is very obscure because of the different meanings that have been given to the word Kūṭastha in different interpretations. The meaning given to the word in the Advaitic commentary on the Gītā verse 6.7 is 'unshakable', and 'changeless'. That is the common meaning of the word. But the same commentary interprets it also in a totally different way in Gītā 12.3. Thus Kūṭa is interpreted as 'the false and the evil'. It is identified with the Prakṛti or the Māyā Śakti, which is the cause of falsity, bondage and the evil of involvement in Saṁsāra. The Absolute is what presides over or underlies this principle of evil and falsity. This same derivation is more or less applied in the present context also, and the Akṣara Puruṣa referred to here is interpreted as the Prakṛti or Māyā Śakti. This principle of falsity and evil causes Saṁsāra or the transmigratory cycle. Through other derivations also, the meaning of the word is established as Prakṛti or Māyā Śakti.

In contrast to Māyā Śakti, the cause of multiplicity, there is multiplicity itself as the effect of that Power. This multiplicity, which consists of changeful beings, is the other Puruṣa known as the Kṣara or the collectivity of changeful beings.

The obvious difficulty in accepting this interpretation is the use of the word Puruṣa for both the Kṣara and the Akṣara. The word Puruṣa has been variously interpreted, but it is used only in the sense 'Spirit' as in the Sāṁkhya philosophy, the terminologies of which have been accepted in the Gīta with more or less the same meanings, only amplifying them from its theistic point of view. In the Advaitic interpretations referred to above, what are spoken of in the text as the two Puruṣas (Spirits) become Prakṛti in its two aspects of cause and effect—Māyā Śakti, the cause, and multiplicity, the effect. This complete transformation of the meaning of the word Puruṣa, which means 'the Spirit', and never Prakṛti and its effects, makes this interpretation unconvincing.

So we have to look also for an alternative interpretation, which retains the meaning of the word Puruṣa as Spirit. Of the two Spirits, one, the Kṣara or the changeful, consists of all the Spirits or Jīvas in bondage who are in varying states of identification with matter. They are undergoing the changes involved in births and deaths in the transmigratory cycle. So they are the Kṣara or the changeful. The Akṣara or the changeless denotes the Jīvas who are liberated from the hold of Prakṛti and are therefore established in aloofness and unaffectedness (Kūṭastha). Thus this interpretation has the special advantage that it does not resort to any interpretative distortion by converting Puruṣa into its opposite Prakṛti or Māyā-Śakti. Superior to these two categories of Puruṣas is 'another', the Puruṣottama, the Supreme Spirit, who pervades all the worlds and supports everything.

An obvious difficulty in both these interpretations, whether we take the second Puruṣa as Maya-śakti or liberated souls, is that they are said to be in 'the world'—*loke*. Now the word can mean 'the transmigratory cycle and the Jīvas involved in it', which the second of the category of Puruṣas referred to, namely liberated ones, is not. But the term *loke* has also a wider meaning—'the world of Divine manifestation'. Māyā-śakti then will be the cause of that Divine manifestation, and the liberated Jīvas will be Spirits who prefer to be in the manifested condition as the servants of the Lord. Thus both are in the *loka* in this sense.

Now this interpretation has the advantage of preserving the original meaning of the word Puruṣa, the Spirit, by which these three categories are denoted. The question, however, will arise whether this will not involve contradiction of Non-dualism. No doubt it will not be justifiable from the point of view of pure non-dualism, but non-dualism understood as unity in diversity is quite consistent with it. It may, however, be asked how liberated Jīvas can exist as separate entities in Advaitism, as liberation means becoming one with the Supreme Spirit, even as rivers become one with the ocean. But the Advaita as expounded in the Bhakti tradition of the *Bhāgavata Purāṇa* maintains that those Jīvas who aspire for salvation as 'obliteration of individuality' attain to oneness in being with the Supreme Lord, but there are many blessed Jīvas that prefer to keep up their individuality so that they may serve the Lord and attain to that Bhajanananda (bliss of service) which is higher than Brahmananda (the bliss of oneness with Him). Such Spirits are free from the bondage of Nature even as the Lord Himself. They remain as the servants of God in His creative and redemptive activity. This is a theory developed in the *Bhāgavata Purāṇa.*

A third meaning is given overlooking the Saṁkhyan dichotmy of Purusa and Prakṛti in the light of a sanction from the Gīta itself. In Gīta 7.4-5, the Lord speaks of his two Prakṛtis—the *Aparā* (lower) and the *Parā* (higher), the changing world of matter being the lower, and the changeless Jīva, the higher. Here we get a sanction for calling Jīva itself as Prakṛti, thus breaking the Saṁkhyan dichotomy between Purusa and Prakṛti. In the light of this clarification, the *Kṣara Puruṣa* and *Akṣara* (*Kūṭastha*) *Puruṣa* are the two Prakṛtis of the Lord taught in Gīta 7.4-5. The *Kṣara-puruṣa* is the embodied Jīva in identification with the body or the conventional superficial man as the body-mind. The Puruṣa who is Akṣara (imperishable) and Kūṭastha (firm and aloof), is the Jīva in his real or non-phenomenal nature. This identification will make the two terms Kṣara and Kūṭastha-Akṣara synonymous with the Aparā-prakṛti or the material power, and with the Jīva or the spiritual emanation of the Lord, respectively. A meaning like this is plausible, but not perhaps in any way more satisfactory than the other two.

6. *Vr.*20: The special importance of this Chapter, even in a scripture profound throughout like the Gītā, is emphasised by calling it *iti guhyatamaṁ idaṁ śāstram*—this spiritual doctrine, the most profound, *guhyatamaṁ*, of all in the sacred lore. The Gīta is called a Śāstra—a book on spiritual truth. In the eighteen chapters of the Gīta-śāstra this particular chapter is specially called the *Śāstra*, because it epitomises the teachings of the whole Gītā,—nay,

of the whole Vedanta. A careful study of it will show that it expounds all the fundamental doctrines of the Vedanta—the doctrine of Saṁsara and man's involvement in it, the doctrine of Karma and transmigration, the way to overcome Saṁsara, the nature of the Jīva and how it transmigrates, the doctrine of Iśvara, the transcendence of the Divine, the doctrine of renunciation of worldly values, and the ways of Bhakti and Jñāna as an integrated spiritual discipline. It is therefore the most important chapter of the Gīta, and a careful study of it will put one in touch with the whole theme of the Vedanta.

Chapter XVI

दैवासुरसंपद्विभागयोगः

THE DIVINE AND THE DEMONIAC TYPES

SUMMARY

The Divine and the Diabolic types: (1-18) *The Lord said*: In creation there are two character types—the Āsuric and the Daivic. The former is hostile to all spiritual values , while the latter is fully receptive to them. The Āsuric type makes no distinction between the righteous and the unrighteous, the pure and the impure, truth and untruth. In their world view there is no place for God, the abiding spiritual background for this world of change. Pursuit of lust and lucre is their supreme quest in life, and success in this, the only criterion of respectability. "Who is there equal to Me?" is their watch-word; and to amass wealth, to destroy their enemies, to satisfy their lusts, to acquire name and fame by any means, fair or foul, are their sole objects in life. With such an outlook they exploit and oppress all their fellow beings, as also the Lord who is immanent in all. Such persons go down in the spiritual scale.

As distinguished from this is the divine or the spiritual type. They are pure, fearless, full of spiritual aspiration, self-controlled, generous, loving, truthful, patient, benevolent and free from pride and vanity.

The Gateway to Hell: (19-24) Those who want to rise spiritually should follow these divine ideals, and shun the Āsuric traits. **Sexuality, anger and greed are** the factors that make man more and more Āsuric. They are the three gate-ways to hell. Let all **right-thinking men avoid them. Sexuality, anger and greed are** natural to the unregenerate man. Regulating and overcoming them is morality, the gate-way to spirituality. For this, man has to depend on the guidance of a Śāstra, a scripture. For, left to his own unguided intelligence, his tendency will be only to yield to the evil in him and not to master it. So man requires an external authority, prescribing what to do and what not to do. That authority is called a scripture, a text believed to have the sanction of God. Unless guided by an objective authority to whom sanctity is attached, man in his natural state will degenerate into a slave of passions.

While many other chapters of the Gītā are of great metaphysical and devotional significance and deserve close study, this particular chapter specially calls for the attention of every man. The Āsuric tendency analysed and criticised in it, has a home in the hearts of most people, and to be aware of this fact is the first step to master it and lay the foundation for the edifice of spiritual life. The reader will therefore do well to memorize this chapter and reflect on its implications.

श्रीभगवानुवाच

अभयं सत्त्वसंशुद्धिर्ज्ञानयोगव्यवस्थितिः ।
दानं दमश्च यज्ञश्च स्वाध्यायस्तप आर्जवम् ॥ 1 ॥

Śrī Bhagavān uvāca:

Abhayaṁ sattva-saṁśuddhir jñāna-yoga-vyavasthitiḥ /
dānaṁ damaś ca yajñaś ca svādhyāyas tapa ārjavam //1//

Abhayam : Fearlessness *sattva-saṁśuddhiḥ* : purity of the heart *jñānayoga-vyavasthitiḥ* : steadfastness in knowledge and devotion *dānam* : charity, benevolence *damaḥ* : control of the senses : *ca* and *yajñaḥ* : worship *ca* : and *svādhyāyaḥ* : study of scriptures *tapaḥ* : austerity *ārjavam* : uprightness.

The Blessed Lord said:

1. Fearlessness, purity of heart, steadfastness in knowledge and devotion, benevolence, control of the senses, worship, study of scriptures, austerity, uprightness;

अहिंसा सत्यमक्रोधस्त्यागः शान्तिरपैशुनम् ।
दया भूतेष्वलोलुप्त्वं मार्दवं ह्रीरचापलम् ॥ 2 ॥

Ahiṁsā satyaṁ akrodhas tyāgaḥ śāntir apaiśunam /
dayā bhūteṣu aloluptvaṁ mārdavaṁ hrīr acāpalam //2//

Ahiṁsā : Non-violence *satyam* : truthfulness *akrodhaḥ* : freedom from anger *tyāgaḥ* : renunciation *śāntih* : tranquillity *apaiśunam* : aversion to slander *bhūteṣu dayā* : compassion to living beings *aloluptvam* : freedom from sensuality *mārdavam* : gentleness *hrīḥ* : modesty *acāpalam* : steadiness.

2. Non-violence, truthfulness, freedom from anger, renunciation, tranquillity, aversion to slander, compassion to living beings, freedom from sensuality, gentleness, modesty, steadfastness;

तेजः क्षमा धृतिः शौचमद्रोहो नातिमानिता ।
भवन्ति संम्पदं दैवीमभिजातस्य भारत ॥ 3 ॥

Tejaḥ kṣamā dhṛtiḥ śaucam adroho n'ātimānitā /
bhavanti saṁpadaṁ daivīm abhijātasya Bhārata //3//

Bhārata : O scion of the Bharata clan! *Tejaḥ* : vigour *kṣamā* : patience *dritiḥ* : fortitude *śaucam* : purity *adrohaḥ* : harmlessness *nātimānitā* : freedom from vanity *daivīm* : divine *sampadam* : heritage *abhijātasya* : born to *bhavanti* : belong.

3. Vigour, patience, fortitude, purity, harmlessness, freedom from vanity—all these, O scion of the Bharatas, are present in those born to a divine heritage.

दम्भो दर्पोऽभिमानश्च क्रोधः पारुष्यमेव च ।
अज्ञानं चाभिजातस्य पार्थ संम्पदमासुरीम् ॥ 4 ॥

Daṁbho darpo'bhimānaś ca krodhaḥ pāruṣyam eva ca /
ajñānaṁ c'ābhijātasya Pārtha saṁpadam āsurīṁ //4//

Pārtha : O son of Pṛthā! *dambhaḥ* : pretentiousness *darpaḥ* : arrogance *abhimānaḥ* : overweening pride *ca* : and *krodhaḥ* : wrath *pāruṣyam* : rudeness *eva ca* : as also *ajñānam* : insensitiveness to spiritual values *āsurīṁ saṁpadam* : demoniac heritage *abhijātasya* : of one born to.

4. O son of Pṛthā! Pretentiousness, arrogance, overweening pride, wrath, rudeness, as also insensitiveness to spiritual values—all these are found in those born to a demoniac heritage.

दैवी संम्पद्विमोक्षाय निबन्धायासुरी मता ।
मा शुचः सम्पदं दैवीमभिजातोऽसि पाण्डव ॥ 5 ॥

Daivī saṁpad vimokṣāya nibandhāy'āsurī matā /
mā śucaḥ saṁpadaṁ daivīm abhijāto'si Pāṇḍava //5//

Daivī saṁpat : The divine heritage *vimokṣāya*: for liberation, *āsurī*: demoniac heritage *nibandhāya* : for bondage *matā* : deemed. *Pāṇḍava* : O son of Pāṇḍu! *daivīṁ saṁpadam* : to a divine heritage *abhijātaḥ asi* : you are born to, *mā śucaḥ* : do not grieve.

5. It is deemed that the divine heritage leads to liberation and the demoniac to bondage. Grieve not, O son of Pāṇḍu! You are born to a divine heritage.

द्वौ भूतसर्गौ लोकेऽस्मिन्दैव आसुर एव च ।
दैवो विस्तरशः प्रोक्त आसुरं पार्थ मे शृणु ॥ 6 ॥

Dvau bhūta-sargau loke'smin daiva āsura eva ca /
daivo vistaraśaḥ prokta āsuraṁ Pārtha me śṛṇu //6//

Asmin loke : In this world *daivaḥ* : Divine *āsuraḥ* : demoniac *eva* : thiswise *ca* : and *bhūtasargau* : types of creation *dvau* : are two; *daivaḥ* : the divine *vistaraśaḥ* : in detail *proktaḥ* : has been enumerated. *āsuram* : the demoniac *me* : from Me *śṛṇu* : hear.

6. In this world there are two types of creation, the divine and the demoniac. The divine heritage has already been described. Now hear from Me what constitutes the demoniac heritage, O son of Pṛthā.

प्रवृत्तिं च निवृत्तिं च जना न विदुरासुराः ।
न शौचं नापि चाचारो न सत्यं तेषु विद्यते ॥ 7 ॥

Pravṛttiṁ ca nivṛttiṁ ca janā na vidur āsurāḥ /
na śaucaṁ nā'pi c'ācāro na satyaṁ teṣu vidyate //7//

Āsurāḥ janāḥ : The demoniac type *pravṛttim* : what should be done *nivṛttiṁ ca* : and what should not be done *na viduḥ* : do not know; *teṣu* : in them *śaucaṁ na vidyate* : there is no purity, *ācāraṁ ca na* : no good conduct too, *satyam api na* : truth also has no place.

7. Men of demoniac nature know not what should be done and what should be avoided. Neither purity, nor good conduct, nor truthfulness is found in them.

असत्यमप्रतिष्ठं ते जगदाहुरनीश्वरम् ।
अपरस्परसम्भूतं किमन्यत्कामहैतुकम् ॥ 8 ॥

Asatyam apratiṣṭhaṁ te jagad āhur anīśvaram /
aparaspara-sambhūtaṁ kim anyat kāma-haitukam //8//

Te : They (say) *jagat* : the universe *asatyam* : is without truth, *apratiṣṭham* : is without a support, *anīśvaram* : is without a God, *aparaspara-sambhūtam* : is born of sexual union, *kāmahaitukam* : is having lust as its cause; *kim anyat āhuḥ* : what else can be said.

8. According to them nothing is ultimately real in this world. It is Godless and without any moral basis. Being born of sex union, what else but lust can be said to be its cause?

एतां दृष्टिमवष्टभ्य नष्टात्मानोऽल्पबुद्धयः।
प्रभवन्त्युग्रकर्माणः क्षयाय जगतोऽहिताः ॥ 9 ॥

Etāṁ dṛṣṭim avaṣṭabhya naṣṭ'ātmāno' lpa-buddhayaḥ /
prabhavanty ugra-karmāṇaḥ kṣayāya jagato'hitāḥ //9//

Etām : This *dṛṣṭim* : outlook *avaṣṭabhya* : adopting, *naṣṭātmānaḥ* : these lost souls *alpabuddhayaḥ* : men of little understanding *ugrakarmāṇaḥ* : given to cruel deeds *ahitāḥ* : opposed to general well-being *jagataḥ* : of the world *kṣayāya* : for destruction *prabhavanti* are born.

9. Holding such views, these lost souls—these men of little understanding—given, as they are, to cruel deeds opposed to general well-being, appear as agents for the destruction of the world.

काममाश्रित्य दुष्पूरं दम्भमानमदान्विताः।
मोहाद्गृहीत्वाऽसद्ग्राहान्प्रवर्तन्तेऽशुचिव्रताः ॥ 10 ॥

Kāmam āśritya duṣpūraṁ dambha-māna-mad'ānvitāḥ /
mohād gṛhītvā'sad-grāhān pravartante'śuci-vratāḥ //10//

Duṣpūram : Insatiable *kāmam* : lust *āśritya* : steeped in *dambha-māna-madānvitāḥ* : full of hypocrisy, pride and arrogance *aśucivratāḥ* : given to corrupt and impure ways of life *mohāt* : due to delusion *asad-grāhān* : false values *gṛhītvā* : entertaining *pravartante* : they work.

10. Steeped in insatiable lust, motivated by hypocrisy, vanity, arrogance and avarice, given to corrupt and impure ways of life, they work in pursuit of false values entertained through delusion.

चिन्तामपरिमेयां च प्रलयान्तामुपाश्रिताः।
कामोपभोगपरमा एतावदिति निश्चिताः ॥ 11 ॥

Cintām aparimeyāṁ ca pralay'āntām upāśritāḥ /
kām'opabhoga-paramā etāvad iti niścitāḥ //11//

Aparimeyām : Without end, numerous *pralayāntām* : ending only with death, life-long *cintām* : cares *upāśritya* : obsessed with, *kāmopabhoga-paramāḥ* : who have indulgence in sex as their highest end in life, *etāvad* : this is all *iti* : thus *niścitāḥ* : convinced.

11. Obsessed with numerous cares all through life, looking on sex indulgence as the highest aim, convinced that there is no higher purpose in life than this,

आशापाशशतैर्बद्धाः कामक्रोधपरायणाः ।
ईहन्ते कामभोगार्थमन्यायेनार्थसञ्चयान् ॥ 12 ॥

Īśā-pāśa-śatair baddhāḥ kāma-krodha-parāyaṇāḥ /
īhante kāma-bhog'ārtham anyāyen'ārtha-sañcayān //12//

Āśā-pāśa-śatair-baddhāḥ : Bound with a hundred cords of hopes and expectations *kāma-krodha-parāyaṇāḥ* : enslaved by lust and anger *kāma-bhogārtham* : for the fulfilment of their sensuous desires *anyāyena* : in improper ways *artha-sañcayān* : accumulation of wealth *īhante* : they strive for.

12. Bound with a hundred cords of hopes and expectations, and enslaved by lust and anger, they strive to accumulate wealth in improper ways for the fulfilment of their sensuous desires.

इदमद्य मया लब्धमिमं प्राप्स्ये मनोरथम् ।
इदमस्तीदमपि मे भविष्यति पुनर्धनम् ॥ 13 ॥

Idam adya mayā labdham imaṁ prāpsye manoratham /
idam ast'īdam api me bhaviṣyati punar dhanam //13//

Idam : This *adya* : today *mayā* : by me *labdham* : has been gained, *imam* : that *manoratham* : desire *prāpsye* : I shall attain, *idam asti* : I have this much wealth now, *idam* : this *dhanam api* : wealth too *me* : mine *punaḥ* : again, hereafter *bhaviṣyati* : will become.

13. "Today I have gained this object, tomorrow I shall gain that object of desire too; I have this much wealth now, much more will be mine hereafter;

असौ मया हतः शत्रुर्हनिष्ये चापरानपि ।
ईश्वरोऽहमहं भोगी सिद्धोऽहं बलवान्सुखी ॥ 14 ॥

Asau mayā hataḥ śatrur haniṣye ca'parān api /
īśvaro'ham ahaṁ bhogī siddho'haṁ balavān sukhī //14//

Asau : This *śatruḥ* : enemy *mayā* : by Me *hataḥ* : has been slain, *aparān* : others *api* : also *haniṣye ca* : I will destroy; *aham īśvaraḥ*: I am the master; *aham* : I am *bhogī* : the enjoyer (of everything); *ahaṁ siddhaḥ* : I am the successful man, *balavān* : the powerful man, *sukhī* : the happy man.

14. "This enemy has been slain, the others too I will soon destroy; I am the master; everything is for my enjoyment; I am the successful man, the powerful man, the happy man;

आढ्योऽभिजनवानस्मि कोऽन्योऽस्ति सदृशो मया ।
यक्ष्ये दास्यामि मोदिष्य इत्यज्ञानविमोहिताः ॥ 15 ॥

Āḍhyo'bhijanavān asmi ko'nyo'sti sadṛśo mayā /
yakṣye dāsyāmi modiṣya ity ajñāna-vimohitāḥ //15//

Āḍhyaḥ : Wealthy *abhijanavān* : high-born *asmi* : I am; *mayā sadṛśaḥ* : equal to me *anyaḥ* : another *kaḥ* : who *asti* : is there; *yakṣye* : I shall sacrifice, *dāsyāmi* : will do charity, *modiṣye* : will rejoice, *iti* : thus *ajñānavimohitāḥ* : deluded by ignorance.

15. "I am wealthy and high-born; who is there like unto me? I will perform sacrifices, I will make charity, and I will rejoice"—deluded thus by ignorance;

अनेकचित्तविभ्रान्ता मोहजालसमावृताः ।
प्रसक्ताः कामभोगेषु पतन्ति नरकेऽशुचौ ॥ 16 ॥

Aneka-citta-vibhrāntā moha-jāla-samāvṛtāḥ /
prasaktāḥ kāma-bhogeṣu patanti narake'śucau //16//

Aneka-citta-vibhrāntāḥ : Gripped by numerous bewildering thoughts *mohajāla samāvṛtāḥ* : entangled in the meshes of delusion *kāmabhogeṣu prasaktāḥ* : ever given to sex-indulgences *aśucau narake* : into loathsome hell *patanti* : fall.

16. Gripped by numerous bewildering thoughts, entangled in the meshes of delusion, and ever given to sex indulgences, they are degraded into states that are loathsome and full of suffering.

आत्मसंभाविताः स्तब्धा धनमानमदान्विताः ।
यजन्ते नामयज्ञैस्ते दम्भेनाविधिपूर्वकम् ॥ 17 ॥

Ātma-saṁbhāvitāḥ stabdhā dhana-māna-mad'ānvitāḥ /
yajante nāma-yajñais te daṁbhen'āvidhipūrvakam //17//

Ātmasaṁbhāvitāḥ : Vain-glorious *stabdhāḥ* : obstinate *dhana-māna-madānvitāḥ* : intoxicated with the pride of wealth *daṁbhena* : for mere show *avidhi-pūrvakam* : in disregard of all commandments *nāma-yajñaiḥ* : by nominal Yajñas *yajante* : worship.

17. Vain-glorious, stubborn and intoxicated with the pride of wealth, they perform for mere show Yajñas that are so in name only, being done without the observance of the commandments of the scriptures.

अहंकारं बलं दर्पं कामं क्रोधं च संश्रिताः ।
मामात्मपरदेहेषु प्रद्विषन्तोऽभ्यसूयकाः ॥ 18 ॥

Ahaṁkāraṁ balaṁ darpaṁ kāmaṁ krodhaṁ ca saṁśritāḥ /
māṁ ātma-para-deheṣu pradviṣanto'bhyasūyakāḥ //18//

Ahaṁkāram : Self-conceit *balam* : proneness to physical violence *darpam* : arrogance *kāmam* : lust *krodham* : anger *ca* : and *saṁśritāḥ* : possessed of, *abhyasūyakāḥ* : traducers of virtue *ātmaparadeheṣu* : residing in themselves and in others *mām* : Me *pradviṣantaḥ (bhavanti)* : violate.

18. Dominated by self-conceit, prone to the use of force, arrogant, lustful and choleric, these traducers of virtue violate Me, dwelling in them and also in others.

तानहं द्विषतः क्रूरान्संसारेषु नराधमान् ।
क्षिपाम्यजस्रमशुभानासुरीष्वेव योनिषु ॥ 19 ॥

Tān ahaṁ dviṣataḥ krūrān saṁsāreṣu nar'ādhamān /
kṣipāmy ajasram aśubhān āsurīṣveva yoniṣu //19//

Dviṣataḥ : Oppressive *krūrān* : cruel *aśubhān* : sinful *narādhamān* : vicious men *tān* : these *saṁsāreṣu* : in the transmigratory cycle *āsurīṣu yoniṣu* : in demoniac wombs *eva* : only *aham* : I *ajasram* : always *kṣipāmi* : hurl.

19. These vicious men, oppressive, cruel and sinful as they are,--are always hurled down by Me into demoniac wombs in life after life, in the transmigratory cycle.

आसुरीं योनिमापन्ना मूढा जन्मनि जन्मनि ।
मामप्राप्यैव कौन्तेय ततो यान्त्यधमां गतिम् ॥ 20 ॥

Āsurīṁ yonim āpannā mūḍhā janmani janmani /
mām aprāpy'aiva Kaunteya tato yānty adhamāṁ gatim //20//

Kaunteya : O son of Kuntī *mūḍhāh* : these senseless men *janmani janmani* : in life after life *āsurīṁ yonim* : demoniac wombs *āpannāḥ* : falling into *mām* : Me *aprāpya eva* : not attaining *tataḥ*: than that *adhamām* : lower *gatim* : state *yānti* : attain.

20. O son of Kuntī! Falling into demoniac wombs, in life after life, they go to still lower states of degradation, without attaining Me.

त्रिविधं नरकस्येदं द्वारं नाशनमात्मनः ।
कामः क्रोधस्तथा लोभस्तस्मादेतत्त्रयं त्यजेत् ॥ 21 ॥

Tri-vidhaṁ narakasy'edaṁ dvāraṁ nāśanam ātmanaḥ /
kāmaḥ krodhas tathā lobhas-tasmād etat trayaṁ tyajet //21//

Kāmaḥ: **Sexuality** *krodhaḥ:* **anger** *tathā:* **and** *lobhaḥ* : greed *idam* : this *trividham* : triad *ātmanaḥ* : of the spiritual self in man *nāśanam* destructive; *narakasya* : of the hell *dvāram* : gateway; *tasmād* : therefore *etat* : this *trayam* : triad *tyajet* : should give up.

21. Lust, anger and greed— this triad leads to the destruction of man's spiritual nature. They form the gateway to hell; they should be abandoned.[2]

एतैर्विमुक्तः कौन्तेय तमोद्वारैस्त्रिभिर्नरः ।
आचरत्यात्मनः श्रेयस्ततो याति परां गतिम् ॥ 22 ॥

Etair vimuktaḥ Kaunteya tamo-dvārais-tribhir naraḥ /
ācaraty ātmanaḥ śreyas-tato yāti parāṁ gatim //22//

Kaunteya : O Arjuna! *tamodvāraiḥ* : by the gateway to hell *etaiḥ tribhiḥ* : from these three *vimuktaḥ* : free, *naraḥ* : man *ātmanaḥ* : his own *śreyaḥ* : good *ācarati* : works out; *tataḥ* : then *parāṁ gatim* : the highest goal *yāti* : reaches.

22. If a man is free from these three, the gateways to hell, he can work out his own good and reach the highest goal.

यः शास्त्रविधिमुत्सृज्य वर्तते कामकारतः ।
न स सिद्धिमवाप्नोति न सुखं न परां गतिम् ॥ 23 ॥

Yaḥ śāstra-vidhim utsṛjya vartate kāma-kārataḥ /
na sa siddhim avāpnoti na sukhaṁ na parāṁ gatim //23//

Yaḥ : Who *śāstravidhim* : commandment of scriptures *utsṛjya* : abandoning *kāmakārataḥ vartate* : lives as his desires prompt him *saḥ* : he *siddhim* : spiritual perfection *na avāpnoti* : does not attain, *na sukham* : nor worldly happiness *na parāṁ gatim* : nor liberation.

23. He who abandons the commandments of the scriptures and lives as his desires prompt him, he attains neither spiritual perfection, nor worldly happiness, nor liberation.[3]

तस्माच्छास्त्रं प्रमाणं ते कार्याकार्यव्यवस्थितौ ।
ज्ञात्वा शास्त्रविधानोक्तं कर्म कर्तुमिहार्हसि ॥ 24 ॥

Tasmāc chāstraṁ pramāṇaṁ te kāry'ākārya-vyavasthitau /
jñātvā śāstra-vidhān'oktaṁ karma **kartum ih' ārhasi** *//24//*

Tasmāt : Therefore *kāryākārya-vyavasthitau* : in determining what should be done and what not *te* : to you *śāstraṁ pramāṇam* : let the scriptures be the norm; *śāstra-vidhānoktam* : the injunction of the scriptures *jñātvā* : knowing *karma kartum arhasi* : you should perform work.

24. Therefore let the scriptures be your norm in determining what should be done and what not. Understand the injunction of the scriptures first and then set yourself to work.

ओं तत्सदिति श्रीमद्भगवद्गीतासूपनिषत्सु ब्रह्मविद्यायां
योगशास्त्रे श्रीकृष्णार्जुनसंवादे दैवासुरसंपद्विभागयोगो
नाम षोडशोऽध्यायः ॥ 16 ॥

NOTES

1. *Vrs.*6-20: In these verses and those preceeding them, a theory of two types of souls with inherently opposite tendencies seems to be propounded. Vivid description of both these types is given in verses 1 to 5 and 7 to 20. One type called *Daivī* or divine, is Godward-looking and is receptive to ideas leading to liberation from the clutches of Prakṛti. The other type called

Āsurī is just the opposite. Those who are included in it are steeped in worldliness, and are anti-God and anti-spiritual. According to the theory propounded here, the former gradually evolve their higher faculties and attain liberation from Prakṛti, while the latter become eternally involved in Saṁsāra. It is also said in verse 20 that they are repeatedly born in 'devilish wombs' (*āsurīṁ yonim*) and without taking the Godward path, attain to *adhamāṁ gatim*—'the most heinous destiny'.

On the basis of such texts, some schools of Vedānta like those of Sri Madhva and Sri Vallabha have propounded the theory of *tāratamya* or inherent qualitative differences in Jīvas, some being made for salvation and others for degradation. There is no eternal damnation in Hinduism, but this confinement to '*adhamāṁ gatim*' or continued embodiments among the lowest creatures like insects, fish, snakes etc., corresponds to it as the wages for confirmed evil doers.

There is a theoretical possibility of salvation even for such degraded souls when Divine grace descends on them through Incarnations and through very holy saints. Since Saṁsāra or the transmigratory cycle is a never-ending process, perpetual involvement in it is the attaining to that most heinous destiny—*yānt-yadhamāṁ gatim*.

2. *Vrs.*21-22: The cause of all degeneration in the individual and society is here traced to the three factors, sexuality, anger and greed, which are described as factors leading to the destruction of man's spiritual nature—*dvāraṁ nāśanam ātmanaḥ*. Animals have lust, but it is limited by Nature's call. They have also greed in the sense of urge to eat out of hunger, but when their hunger is satisfied, they are not concerned with accumulation like man, and they have therefore nothing like human greed. Animals have anger, but it is limited in its scope, and is roused only when they are hungry or face to face with danger. It is not that all-consuming and vindictive passion as in man.

The nature of man is such that he is given unrestricted scope to indulge in these urges until ruin seizes him. He is, however, given also an in-built capacity to control, regulate, and ultimately overcome these passions. If he does not exercise this capacity and fails to control the lower nature in him, he will lose his humanity, and will be consigned to birth in low orders like animals, insects, snakes etc., (*āsurīṁ-yonim*), as warned in the earlier passages.

The one point to be understood from this is that at the human level, growth or evolution is through control of instincts and not by submission to them. The latter is the path to degradation and spiritual death through the growth of *Āsurīsampat* (demoniac nature), while the former is the way to rise in the spiritual scale through the acquisition of *Daivīsampat* (godly nature).

It has to be pointed out, that though there is not much of metaphysical and theological doctrines in this chapter, it is however of great importance in the study of the Gītā from a spiritual point of view. A daily study of it will remind one of the importance of self-control for avoiding absolute degradation.

3. *Vrs.*23-24: Scripture is held forth before man as the most important help in providing the criteria by which one could determine what should be done and what should not be done. With its help, the growth of demoniac qualities is arrested, and the development of divine qualities helped.

How are we to determine a moral act? The branch of philosophy called ethics has attempted to find out a purely rational basis for morality. The rational criteria offered are often subjective. It is said that conscience must be the criterion. But the conscience of people is often pliable by self-interest and self-love, and may become very unreliable in judging moral worth. If a person has a pure and refined mind, conscience may be reliable to a great extent, as an improper act will be instinctively repugnant to such minds. But such persons are very few, and the majority of men have only a time-serving conscience.

Another criterion given is the dictum to do unto others what you like to be done unto yourself. It means to have a sense of 'sameness' between oneself and others, and regulate one's behaviour towards others by this sense. In simple language it means to be unselfish.

Most men are not inward looking enough to be benefited by such considerations. They want an objective criterion which will be precise and fit to be practised without much subjective reflection. The Śāstra or the scripture is one of them. Another is the conduct of wise men.

Even these are not without drawbacks. The conduct of great men has varied. Some of the greatest personages classed as incarnations like Sri Krishna have behaved in a way contrary to accepted codes, and so men are warned that as their behaviour was regulated by considerations of their world-saving mission, men should follow not their actions, but their instructions, and their actions only to the extent they tally with their teachings. Still the conduct of leading men can, in a way, be a guidance to the common man.

The next and the most important criterion is the Śāstra, or the scripture. Any text in Sanskrit will not be a scripture. There are many texts which are accepted by some as scriptures, but the texts vary in their teachings and prescribe practices which are not compatible with the needs of varying times. Such is the case with many of the Smṛtis of the Hindus. Even practices like untouchability and unapproachability have been advocated by several Smṛtis. The observance of caste rules, which many Smṛtis prescribe, will not be compatible with the non-feudal and democratic ideologies of modern times. In them there are of course many great moral teachings of universal interst. If it is said that the Vedas are to be followed, there also there are many difficulties. Few can understand them today and interpretations, which are conflicting, have to be depended upon. They are often too complex and remote for ordinary man to understand and follow.

There are many great moral dicta in these varied scriptures; these can be selected and followed. Besides, the Mahabharata has laid down fourteen virtues as Samānya Dharma—duties common to all*. These are: Forbearance, truthfulness, self-restraint, cleanliness, charity, control of the senses, non-violence, service of the elders, pilgrimages, compassion, keeping vows, freedom from avarice, worship of the deities, and absence of jealousy. These are sufficiently broad in scope, and one following them, will certainly rise very high in the moral scale.

There are other religions like Christianity and Islam which too have their scriptures. Since Christianity is a highly organised

***Kṣamā satyaṁ damaḥ śaucaṁ dānam indriyasaṁyamaḥ*
ahiṁsā guruśuśrūṣā tīrthānusaraṇaṁ dayā;
ātmavratam alobhitvaṁ devatānāṁ ca pūjanaṁ
anabhyasūyā ca tathā dharmaḥ sāmānya ucyate.

religion, there is some sort of uniformity of conduct laid down by the Churches. Even such rules of conduct are becoming incompatible with changing times and their needs, and are therefore obeyed more in their breach than in their observance. Islam swears by the book, and Islamic fundamentalism turns men into two groups, the believers and the non-believers, and makes invidious distinction in the behaviour of one towards his fellow religionists and non-believers. Besides, many of the practices sanctioned by Islamic fundamentalism will go counter to modern trends.

So from a practical point of view, a scripture can lay down only the main moral principles and leave the details to be worked out according to time and place. In this respect the Gītā is a perfect scripture and its universal moral doctrine laid down in the verses 21-22 of this chapter, is unexceptionable. **It states: "Sexuality,** anger and greed lead to the destruction of man's spiritual nature. They form the gateways to hell. They should be abandoned. If a man is free from these three, the gateways to hell, he can work out his own good and reach the highest goal." Gītā prescribes self-control as the means to achieve this. It is thus the perfect universal Śāstra for all mankind, whatever **might be the religion one follows.**

In the application of these principles to life, one can form a code of conduct for oneself in their light, and keep that as a norm, an objective criterion for regulating one's life. Thus pure subjectiveness involved in the acceptance of conscience can be avoided. An objective criterion of some kind is very necessary for man. That is the simple meaning of the dictum, 'Let the Śāstra be your guidance.'

The whole of the Gītā itself is a proof of the need for an objective criterion for regulating one's conduct. Arjuna was in confusion as to what his duty was—to fight or not to fight in that war with momentous consequences. He could not come to a decision. Even the ordinarily accepted code of conduct for Kṣatriyas of those days, did not satisfy him. It required a Kṛṣṇa, the greatest of Gurus, to convince him. A real Guru is thus the best objective authority for giving a code of conduct. But in life such Gurus are seldom to be had. So we have to turn to a scripture like the Gītā and to the Lord for enlightening us on what is good and what is bad in a complex situation.

———

Chapter XVII

श्रद्धात्रयविभागयोगः

THE THREE DIVISIONS OF FAITH

SUMMARY

Faith as rooted in the Guṇas : (1-22) The Lord now speaks of Śraddhā (Faith), the inner intuition and natural receptivity of the mind to ideals, which ultimately settles man's preference for the scripture. 'Man is verily constituted of his Faith, and he is what his Faith is.' Man's faith is determined by the dominance of one or the other of the three qualities of Nature—Sattva, Rajas, and Tamas. His preference in respect of objects of worship food, activities etc., will depend upon his Śraddhā. Whatever is done without vanity, but is motivated by the good of others and has the grace of God in mind, is Sāttvika. Whatever is sought or done with desire, vanity, and for self-glorification, is Rājasa. And whatever is done indifferently, with evil motives, thoughtlessly, and in a grumbling spirit is Tāmasa. Such conduct is futile in respect of man's higher evolution.

Om, Tat, Sat (23-28): Om, Tat, Sat are the holy syllables indicating the sacrificial mentality. Whatever man does as an offering unto God with the utterance of these syallables, promotes his spiritual evolution. All sacrificial rites, all austerity practised, all charity done are of no spiritual efficacy if they are not supported by Faith.

अर्जुन उवाच

ये शास्त्रविधिमुत्सृज्य यजन्ते श्रद्धयान्विताः ।
तेषां निष्ठा तु का कृष्ण सत्त्वमाहो रजस्तमः ॥ 1 ॥

Arjuna uvāca:
Ye śāstra-vidhim utsṛjya yajante śraddhayā'nvitāḥ /
teṣāṁ niṣṭhā tu kā Kṛṣṇa sattvam āho rajas tamaḥ //1//

Kṛṣṇa : O Kṛṣṇa! ***ye*** : who ***śāstravidhim*** : injunction of the scriptures ***utsṛjya***: without observing ***śraddhayā anvitāḥ***: with Faith ***yajante*** : offer sacrifices, perform worship, ***teṣām*** : of these ***niṣṭhā*** : faith ***tu*** : indeed ***kā*** : what (***kim***) ***sattvam aho*** : is it to be considered as a product of Sattva, ***rajaḥ*** : Rajas, ***tamaḥ*** : or of Tamas.

Arjuna said:

1. There are persons who offer worship full of Faith, but without observing scriptural injunctions while doing so—of what nature is their Faith? Is it born of Sattva, Rajas or Tamas?[1]

श्रीभगवानुवाच
त्रिविधा भवति श्रद्धा देहिनां सा स्वभावजा ।
सात्विकी राजसी चैव तामसी चेति तां शृणु ॥ 2 ॥

Sri Bhagavānuvāca:
Tri-vidhā bhavati śraddhā dehināṁ sā svabhāva-jā /
sāttvikī rājasī c'aiva tāmasī c'eti tāṁ śṛṇu //2//

Dehinām : Of embodied souls ***svabhāvajā*** : rooted in their nature ***sā śraddhā*** : that Faith ***sāttvikī*** : of Sattva, ***Rājasī*** : of Rajas, ***ca*** : and ***tāmasī*** : of Tamas ***iti*** : thus ***trividhā eva bhavati*** : occurs in these three ways ***tām:*** It ***śṛṇu:*** do listen.

The Blessed Lord said:

2. The Faith of embodied beings, which is rooted in their natural disposition (derived from the impressions of past births), is of three kinds—those of the nature of Sattva, of Rajas and of Tamas.[2] Please listen.

सत्त्वानुरूपा सर्वस्य श्रद्धा भवति भारत ।
श्रद्धामयोऽयं पुरुषो यो यच्छ्रद्धः स एव सः ॥ 3 ॥

Sattv'ānurūpā sarvasya śraddhā bhavati Bhārata /
śraddhāmayo'yaṁ puruṣo yo yac-chraddhaḥ sa eva saḥ //3//

Bhārata : O scion of the Bharata race! *sarvasya* : of all *śraddhā* : Faith *sattvānurūpā* : is in accordance with the natural disposition; *ayam* : this *puruṣaḥ* : man *śraddhāmayaḥ* : is made of his Faith; *yaḥ* : he *yac-chraddhaḥ*: what happens to be his Faith *saḥ* : he *eva* : indeed *saḥ* : is that.

3. O scion of the Bharata race! The Faith of everyone is according to his natural disposition (derived from past impressions). Man is constituted of his Faith. What his Faith is, that verily he is.

यजन्ते सात्त्विका देवान्यक्षरक्षांसि राजसाः ।
प्रेतान्भूतगणांश्चान्ये यजन्ते तामसा जनाः ॥ 4 ॥

Yajante sāttvikā devān yakṣa-rakṣāṁsi rājasāḥ /
pretān bhūta-gaṇāṁś c'ānye yajante tāmasā janāḥ //4//

Sāttvikāḥ : Those endowed with Sattva *devān* : Devas *yajante* : worship *rājasāḥ* : those endowed with Rajas *Yakṣarakṣāṁsi* : Yakṣas (demi-gods) and Rākṣasas (demons); *anye* : others *tāmasāḥ janāḥ* : who are possessed of Tamas *pretān* : spirits of the dead *bhūtagaṇān* : elementals *ca* : and *yajante* : worship.

4. Those endowed with the quality of Sattva worship the Devas; those with Rajas, the Yaksas and the Rākṣasas; and those with Tamas, the spirits of the dead and the elementals.[3]

अशास्त्रविहितं घोरं तप्यन्ते ये तपो जनाः ।
दम्भाहंकारसंयुक्ताः कामरागबलान्विताः ॥ 5 ॥
कर्षयन्तः शरीरस्थं भूतग्राममचेतसः ।
मां चैवान्तःशरीरस्थं तान्विद्ध्यासुरनिश्चयान् ॥ 6 ॥

Aśāstra-vihitaṁ ghoraṁ tapyante ye tapo janāḥ /
daṁbh'āhaṁkāra- saṁyuktāḥ kāma-rāga-balānvitāḥ //5//
karṣayantaḥ śarīra-sthaṁ bhūta-grāmam acetasaḥ /
māṁ c'aivā'ntaḥ-śarīra-sthaṁ tān viddhy āsura-niścayān //6//

Ye janāḥ : Those men who *daṁbhā-haṁkāra-saṁyuktāḥ* : who are vain and conceited *kāma-rāga-balānvitāḥ* : impelled by the force of their inordinate desires and attachments *acetasaḥ* : who are senseless *śarīra-sthaṁ bhūtagrāmaṁ* : the assemblage of elements that constitute the body *antaḥ-śarīra-sthaṁ māṁ* : Me residing in the body *ca* : and *eva* : also *karṣayantaḥ* : torture, *aśāstra-vihitam* : contrary to scriptural injunction *ghoram* : terrible *tapaḥ* : mortification *tapyante* : perform, *tān* : them *āsuraniścayān* : demoniac in their resolve *viddhi* : know.

5-6. Vain, conceited and moved by powerful passions and attachments, they perform various terrible mortifications contrary to scriptural injunctions. Thus do these senseless men torture their own bodies and Me dwelling in them. Know such persons to be of demoniac resolve.

आहारस्त्वपि सर्वस्य त्रिविधो भवति प्रियः ।
यज्ञस्तपस्तथा दानं तेषां भेदमिमं शृणु ॥ 7 ॥

Āhārastv api sarvasya tri-vidho bhavati priyaḥ /
yajñas tapas tathā dānaṁ teṣāṁ bhedam imaṁ śṛṇu //7//

Sarvasya tu : Of all the three types *priyaḥ* : dear *āhāraḥ* : food *api* : even *trividhaḥ bhavati* : is of three kinds; *tathā* : in the same way *yajñaḥ* : worship *tapaḥ* : austerity *dānam* : charity *teṣām* : of them; *imaṁ bhedam* : this distinction *śṛṇu* : hear.

7. Even the food dear to these three types is of three different kinds. The same is the case with worship, austerity and charity. Hear from Me about this distinction regarding them.[4]

आयुःसत्त्वबलारोग्यसुखप्रीतिविवर्धनाः ।
रस्याः स्निग्धाः स्थिरा हृद्या आहाराः सात्त्विकप्रियाः ॥ 8 ॥

Āyuḥ-sattva-bal'ārogya-sukha-prīti-vivardhanāḥ /
rasyāḥ snigdhāḥ sthirā hṛdyā āhārāḥ sāttvika-priyāḥ //8//

Āyuḥ-sattva-bal'ārogya-sukha-prīti-vivardhanāḥ : Those that promote longevity, vitality, energy, health, happiness and cheerfulness *rasyāḥ* : juicy *snigdhāḥ* : soft *sthirāḥ* : nourishing *hṛdyāḥ* : agreeable *āhārāḥ* : foods *sāttvikapriyāḥ* : are liked by people who are Sāttvika by nature.

8. Persons who are Śāttvika by nature like foods that promote longevity, vitality, energy, health, happiness and cheerfulness, as also those that are juicy, soft, nourishing and agreeable.

कट्वम्ललवणात्युष्णतीक्ष्णरूक्षविदाहिनः ।
आहारा राजसस्येष्टा दुःखशोकामयप्रदाः ॥ 9 ॥

Kaṭv-amla-lavaṇ'ātyuṣṇa-tīkṣṇa-rūkṣa-vidāhinaḥ /
āhārā rājasasy'eṣṭā duḥkha-śok'āmaya-pradāḥ //9//

Kaṭv-aṁla-lavaṇ'ātyuṣṇa-tīkṣṇa-rūkṣa-vidāhinaḥ : Foods that are bitter, sour, salty, excessively heating, pungent, burning and thirst-producing *duḥkha-śokā'mayapradāḥ* : causing uneasiness, depression and disease *āhārāḥ* : foods *rājasasya* : of persons who are Rājasa by nature *iṣṭāḥ* : are liked.

9. Persons who are Rājasa by nature like foods that are bitter, sour, salty, excessively heating, pungent, burning and thirst-producing as also what bring on uneasiness, depression and disease.

यातयामं गतरसं पूति पर्युषितं च यत् ।
उच्छिष्टमपि चामेध्यं भोजनं तामसप्रियम् ॥ 10 ॥

Yātayāmaṁ gatarasaṁ pūti paryuṣitaṁ ca yat /
ucchiṣṭam api cā'medhyaṁ bhojanaṁ tāmasa-priyam //10//

Yātayāmam: Prepared before a Yāma (three hours), stale *gatarasam*: tasteless *pūti* : putrid *paryuṣitam* : decayed *ca* : and *ucchiṣṭam* : leavings of what others have eaten *api* : also *amedhyam* : unclean *ca* : and *yat* : which *bhojanam* : food *tāmasa-priyam* : dear to men of Tamas.

10. Persons who are Tāmasa by nature like foods that are stale, tasteless, putrid, decayed and unclean, and constitute the leavings of others.

अफलाकाङ्क्षिभिर्यज्ञो विधिदृष्टो य इज्यते ।
यष्टव्यमेवेति मनः समाधाय स सात्त्विकः ॥ 11 ॥

Aphal'ākāṅkṣibhir yajño vidhi-dṛṣṭo ya ijyate /
yaṣṭavyam ev'eti manaḥ samādhāya sa sāttvikaḥ //11//

Yaṣṭavyam eva : What ought to be done as duty *iti* : thus *manaḥ*: mind *samādhāya* : having fixed *vidhi-dṛṣṭaḥ* : as ordained by the scriptures *yaḥ*: which *yajñaḥ*: sacrifice, worship *aphal'ākāṅkṣibhiḥ*: by those who have no desire for fruits *ijyate* : is offered, *saḥ* : that *sāttvikaḥ* : is of the nature of Sattva.

11. That worship is of the nature of Sattva which is in accordance with scriptural injunctions, and which is performed by one not with an eye for its fruits but merely out of the feeling that it is one's duty to perform it.

अभिसंधाय तु फलं दम्भार्थमपि चैव यत् ।
इज्यते भरतश्रेष्ठ तं यज्ञं विद्धि राजसम् ॥ 12 ॥

Abhisaṁdhāya tu phalaṁ dambh'ārtham api c'aiva yat /
ijyate bharata-śreṣṭha taṁ yajñaṁ viddhi rājasam //12//

Bharata-śreṣṭha : O scion of the Bharata race! *phalam* : result *abhisaṁdhāya* : having in mind *tu* : indeed *daṁbhārtham* : for vain display *api* : also *ca* : and *eva* : even *yat* : what *ijyate* : is offered (as worship), *tam* : that *yajñam* : sacrifice, worship *rājasam* : of the nature of Rajas *viddhi* : know it to be.

12. O scion of the Bharata race! Know that worship to be of the nature of Rajas, which is performed with its fruits in mind and for vain display.

विधिहीनमसृष्टान्नं मन्त्रहीनमदक्षिणम् ।
श्रद्धाविरहितं यज्ञं तामसं परिचक्षते ॥ 13 ॥

Vidhihīnam asṛṣṭ'ānnaṁ mantra-hīnam adakṣiṇam /
śraddhā-virahitaṁ yajñaṁ tāmasaṁ paricakṣate //13//

Vidhihīnam : Without scriptural sanction *asṛṣṭānnam* : without distribution of food *mantrahīnam* : without the chanting of Mantras *adakṣiṇam* : without gifts *śraddhāvirahitam* : without faith *yajñam* : sacrifice *tāmasam* : of the nature of Tamas *paricakṣate* : is said to be.

13. That worship is of the nature of Tamas which is not sanctioned by scriptures, which is without gift of food, without the chanting of holy Mantras, without sacramental presents and without sincere faith.

देवद्विजगुरुप्राज्ञपूजनं शौचमार्जवम् ।
ब्रह्मचर्यमहिंसा च शारीरं तप उच्यते ॥ 14 ॥

Deva-dvija-guru-prājña-pūjanaṁ śaucam ārjavam /
brahmacaryam ahiṁsā ca śārīraṁ tapa ucyate //14//

Deva-dvija-guru-prājña-pūjanam : Honouring of Devas, holy men, teachers and wise men *śaucam* : cleanliness *ārjavam* : uprightness *brahmacaryam* : celibacy *ahimsā* : non-injury *ca* : and *śārīram* : of the body *tapaḥ* : Tapas *ucyate* : is said to be.

14. Service of the Devas, holy men, teachers, parents and wise persons, as also observance of cleanliness, uprightness, continence and non-injury—these constitute austerities pertaining to the body.

अनुद्वेगकरं वाक्यं सत्यं प्रियहितं च यत् ।
स्वाध्यायाभ्यसनं चैव वाङ्मयं तप उच्यते ॥ 15 ।

Anudvega-karaṁ vākyaṁ satyaṁ priya-hitaṁ ca yat /
svādhyāy'ābhyasanaṁ c'aiva vāṅmayaṁ tapa ucyate //15//

Anudvega-karam : Not painful *satyam* : true *priya-hitam* : pleasant and beneficial *vākyam* : words *ca* : and *svādhyāy' ābhyasanam* : regular recitation of scriptures *ca* : and *eva* : also *yat* : which *tat* : that *vāṅmayam* : of speech *tapaḥ* : austerity *ucyate* : is said to be.

15. Speaking only words that are inoffensive, true, pleasant and beneficial as also regular recitation of scriptures constitute austerity pertaining to speech.

मनःप्रसादः सौम्यत्वं मौनमात्मविनिग्रहः ।
भावसंशुद्धिरित्येतत्तपो मानसमुच्यते ॥ 16 ॥

Manaḥ-prasādaḥ saumyatvaṁ maunam ātma-vinigrahaḥ /
bhāva-saṁśuddhir ity-etat tapo mānasam ucyate //16//

Manaḥ-prasādaḥ : Serenity of mind *saumyatvam* : gentleness *maunam* : moderation in speech *ātma-vinigrahaḥ* : self-control *bhāva-saṁsuddhiḥ* : purity of heart *iti etat* : this *mānasam* : mental *tapaḥ* : austerity *ucyate* : is said to be.

16. Serenity of mind, gentleness, moderation in speech, self-control, and purity of heart—these are called austerity of the mind.

श्रद्धया परया तप्तं तपस्तत्त्रिविधं नरैः ।
अफलाकाङ्क्षिभिर्युक्तैः सात्त्विकं परिचक्षते ॥ 17 ॥

Śraddhayā parayā taptaṁ tapas tat trividhaṁ naraiḥ /
aphal'ākāṅkṣibhir-yuktaiḥ sāttvikaṁ paricakṣate //17//

Aphal'ākāṅkṣibhiḥ: Without desire for the fruits of action *yuktaiḥ* : established in mental equipoise *naraiḥ* : by men *parayā śraddhayā* : with the highest faith *taptam* : practised, *tat* : that *trividham* : threefold *tapaḥ* : austerity *sāttvikam* : of the nature of Sattva *paricakṣate* : they declare.

17. This threefold austerity, performed with the highest faith, by men who are not motivated by expectations of reward and who are established in mental equipoise, is declared to be of the nature of Sattva.

सत्कारमानपूजार्थं तपो दम्भेन चैव यत् ।
क्रियते तदिह प्रोक्तं राजसं चलमध्रुवम् ॥ 18 ॥

Satkāra-māna-puj'ārthaṁ tapo daṁbhena c'aiva yat /
kriyate tad iha proktaṁ rājasaṁ calam adhruvam //18//

Satkāra-māna-pujārthaṁ : For gaining recognition, praise and adoration *daṁbhena* : with show and ostentation *ca* : and *eva* : even *yat* : which *tapaḥ* : austerity *kriyate* : is performed, *calam* : unsteady *adhruvam* : leading to no permanent result *tat* : that *iha* : here *rājasam* : of the nature of Rajas *proktam* : is said to be.

18. The austerity that is performed with much show and ostentation, and having in view recognition, praise and adoration as a pious man by others, is said to be of the nature of Rajas. It is unstable and leads to no permanent good.

मूढग्राहेणात्मनो यत्पीडया क्रियते तपः ।
परस्योत्सादनार्थं वा तत्तामसमुदाहृतम् ॥ 19 ॥

Mūḍha-grāheṇ'ātmano yat pīḍayā kriyate tapaḥ |
parasy'otsādanārthaṁ vā tat tāmasam udāhṛtam //19//

Mūḍha-grāheṇa : Prompted by perverse desires *ātmanaḥ pīḍayā* : by means of self-torture, *parasya* : of another *utsādanārtham*: destruction *vā* : or *yat* : which *tapaḥ* : austerity *kriyate* : is performed, *tat* : that *tāmasam*: of the nature of Tamas *udāhṛtam*: is spoken of as.

19. The austerity performed through the practice of self-torture under the influence of perverse theories or done for the destruction of another, is spoken of as Tāmasa by nature.

दातव्यमिति यद्दानं दीयतेऽनुपकारिणे ।
देशे काले च पात्रे च तद्दानं सात्त्विकं स्मृतम् ॥ 20 ॥

Dātavyam iti yad dānaṁ dīyate'nupakāriṇe |
deśe kāle ca pātre ca tad dānaṁ sāttvikaṁ smṛtam //20//

Dātavyam : This gift should be given *iti* : thus *deśe* : in proper place *kāle* : at proper time *pātre* : to the proper recipients *ca* : and *anupakāriṇe* : to one who does not do anything in return *yat* : whicn *dānam* : gift *dīyate* : is done, *tat* : that *dānam* : gift *sāttvikam*: of the nature of Sattva *smṛtam* : is considered.

20. That gift which is made out of a sheer sense of duty, without expectation of any kind of return, at the proper time and place, to a fit recipient, is said to be of the nature of Sattva.

यत्तु प्रत्युपकारार्थं फलमुद्दिश्य वा पुनः ।
दीयते च परिक्लिष्टं तद्दानं राजसं स्मृतम् ॥ 21 ॥

Yat tu pratyupakā'rārthaṁ phalam uddiśya vā punaḥ
dīyate ca parikliṣṭaṁ tad dānaṁ rājasaṁ smṛtam //21//

Pratyupakārārtham : From considerations of some benefit in return *phalam* : fruit, gain *uddiśya* : in view *vā* : or *parikliṣṭam* : grudgingly *yat* : which *tu* : indeed *punaḥ* : again *dīyate* : is given *ca* : and, *tat* : that *dānam* : gift *rājasam* : of the nature of Rajas *smṛtam* : is considered.

21. The gift which is given in consideration of some gift in return, or with some fruit to be reaped in future, or in a grudging mood—that is considered to be of the nature of Rajas.

अदेशकाले यद्दानमपात्रेभ्यश्च दीयते ।
असत्कृतमवज्ञातं तत्तामसमुदाहृतम् ॥ 22 ॥

Adeśa-kāle yad dānam apātrebhyaś ca dīyate /
asatkṛtam avajñātaṁ tat tāmasam udāhṛtam //22//

Adeśakāle : At an improper place and time *apātrebhyaḥ* : to unworthy recipients *ca* : and *asatkṛtam* : unceremoniously *avajñātam* : slightingly *yaḥ* : which *dānam* : gift *dīyate* : is given, *tat* : that *tāmasam* : of the nature of Tamas *udāhṛtam* : is called.

22. The gift that is made at an improper time and place, to an unworthy recipient, unceremoniously and in a slighting manner —that is said to be of the nature of Tamas.

ओं तत्सदिति निर्देशो ब्रह्मणस्त्रिविधः स्मृतः ।
ब्राह्मणास्तेन वेदाश्च यज्ञाश्च विहिताः पुरा ॥ 23 ॥

Om tat sad iti nirdeśo brahmaṇas tri-vidhaḥ smṛtaḥ /
brāhmaṇās tena vedāś ca yajñāś ca vihitāḥ purā //23//

Om tat sat : Om Tat Sat *iti* : thus *brahmaṇaḥ* : of Brahman *trividhaḥ* : threefold *nirdeśaḥ* : symbolic designation *smṛtaḥ* : is spoken of; *tena* : by that *brāhmaṇāḥ* : Brāhmaṇas *vedāḥ* : Vedas *ca* : and *yajñāḥ* : sacrifices *ca* : and *purā* : in ancient times *vihitāḥ* : were ordained.

23. Om Tat Sat—these are the three symbolic designations of Brahman. By thesc were ordained the Brāḥmaṇas, the Vedas and the Yajñas in ancient times.[5]

तस्मादोमित्युदाहृत्य यज्ञदानतपःक्रियाः ।
प्रवर्तन्ते विधानोक्ताः सततं ब्रह्मवादिनाम् ॥ 24 ॥

Tasmād om ity udāhṛtya yajña-dāna-tapaḥ-kriyāḥ /
pravartante vidhān'oktāḥ satataṁ brahma-vādinām //24//

Tasmāt : Therefore *Brahma-vādinām* : of the followers of the Vedas *vidhānoktāḥ* : the ordained *yajña-dāna-tapaḥ-kriyāḥ* : works of the nature of sacrifice, gift and austerities *Om iti udāhṛtya* : with the utterance of Om *satatam* : always *pravartante* are worked out.

24. Therefore the followers of the Vedas always start their ordained works like sacrifice, gift, and austerities with the utterance of Om.

तदित्यनभिसंधाय फलं यज्ञतपःक्रियाः ।
दानक्रियाश्च विविधाः क्रियन्ते मोक्षकाङ्क्षिभिः ॥ 25 ॥

Tad ity anabhisaṁdhāya phalaṁ yajña-tapaḥ-kriyāḥ /
dāna-kriyāś ca vividhāḥ kriyante mokṣa-kāṅkṣibhiḥ //25//

Phalam : Fruits *anabhisandhāya* : without desiring for *vividhāḥ* : various *yajña-tapaḥ kriyāḥ* : acts of sacrifice and austerity *dānakriyāḥ ca*: also works of a charitable nature *mokṣa-kāṅkṣibhiḥ*: by those who seek liberation *tat* : Tat (That) *iti* : thus *udāhṛtya* : uttering *kriyante* : are performed.

25. Various forms of sacrifices, austerities and charities are performed without any desire for the fruits by seekers after liberation, along with the utterance of the syllable Tat (That).

सद्भावे साधुभावे च सदित्येतत्प्रयुज्यते ।
प्रशस्ते कर्मणि तथा सच्छब्दः पार्थ युज्यते ॥ 26 ॥

Sad-bhāve sādhu-bhāve ca sad ity etat prayujyate /
praśaste karmaṇi tathā sac-chabdaḥ Pārtha yujyate //26//

Pārtha : O son of Pṛthā! *sadbhāve* : in the sense of reality *sādhu-bhāve ca* : in the sense of goodness also *sat iti etat* : the syllable known as Sat *prayujyate* : is used; *tathā* : in the same way *praśaste karmaṇi* : in auspicious rites *sac-chabdaḥ* : the syllable Sat *yujyate* : is used.

26. O son of Pṛthā! The syllable Sat is used in the sense of reality and goodness. It is also used to indicate an auspicious rite or act.

यज्ञे तपसि दाने च स्थितिः सदिति चोच्यते ।
कर्म चैव तदर्थीयं सदित्येवाभिधीयते ॥ 27 ॥

Yajñe tapasi dāne ca sthitiḥ sad-iti-c'ocyate /
karma c'aiva tad-arthīyaṁ sad ity ev'ābhidhīyate //27//

Yajñe : In Yajña or sacrifice *ca* : and *tapasi* : in austerity *dāne ca* and in charity *sthitiḥ* : steadfastness *sat* : Sat (good) *iti ucyate* is called; *tad-arthīyam karma* : any action connected with these *ca* and *eva* : also *sat iti* : as Sat *abhidhīyate* : is called.

27. Steadfastness in sacrifice (or worship), in austerity and in charity is called Sat (good). Any action connected with these is also called Sat.

अश्रद्धया हुतं दत्तं तपस्तप्तं कृतं च यत् ।
असदित्युच्यते पार्थ न च तत्प्रेत्य नो इह ॥ 28 ॥

Aśraddhayā hutaṁ dattaṁ tapas-taptaṁ kṛtaṁ ca yat /
asad-ity-ucyate Pārtha na ca tat pretya no iha //28//

Pārtha : O son of Pṛthā! *aśraddhayā* : without faith *hutam* : offered in sacrifice *dattam* : offered in charity *taptaṁ tapaḥ* : performed as austerity *yat ca kṛtam* : whatever else is done too, *tat* : that *asat* : Asat, not good *ucyate* : is called; *pretya* : in the hereafter *na ca*: it is not, *na iha* : here also it is not.

28. O son of Pṛthā! Whatever is performed as a sacrifice, charity, or austerity without Faith—in fact anything done without Faith—is declared to be Asat (not good). It is of no significance here or in the hereafter.

ओं तत्सदिति श्रीमद्भगवद्गीतासूपनिषत्सु ब्रह्मविद्यायां
योगशास्त्रे श्रीकृष्णार्जुनसंवादे श्रद्धात्रयविभागयोगो
नाम सप्तदशोऽध्यायः ॥ 17 ॥

NOTES

1. *Vr*.1: The topic of *Śraddhā* is discussed. It is translated as Faith with a capital. In its ideal form it is the whole-hearted and sincere acceptance of a supreme Spiritual Principle giving a meaning and direction to life, combined with a readiness to put into practice what one has accepted with conviction. It is much more than mere belief (*Viśvāsa*), which is a mere conventional acceptance of an idea without any conscious intention to put it into practice.

It is from the teaching of a scripture and of a teacher that one develops Faith. Now even without these authentic sources of Faith, there are people who develop faith in God and worship Him seeing others doing so. In their practice they may not follow all scriptural injunctions, not with intention to flout them, but because of their unawareness of them or lack of facilities to observe them. Enquiry is made as to whether this kind of *Śraddhā* is ***Sāttvika***, ***Rājasa***, or ***Tāmasa***.

2. *Vrs*.2-3: Śraddhā is said to be born of *Svabhāva*—the character potential that one brings down from all one's past lives and attainments. So the firm and sincere acceptance of a spiritual principle depends not so much on reasoning or sense perception, but on an inner compulsion born of purity of character, which makes one feel that life is meaningless, and therefore useless, unless it has a spiritual source and purpose. As the verse 3 states, it is the Sāttvika element in man that generates Śraddhā in him. It is only diluted and diverted into different channels by Rajas or desire nature, and by Tamas or animal nature. All this depends on the *Svabhāva,* the character potential which one brings from one's evolution in past births. According to that, the nature of Śraddhā will vary as shown in subsequent verses.

Now the one point made clear is that the capacity found in man to have *Śraddhā*, Faith in a higher spiritual principle, is the result of *Sattva-guṇa*. In this respect man is entirely different from animals which are predominently *Tāmasika* and have no Sattva at all. So Faith is a rare gift of God at the human level, just like reason and other higher faculties. So the tendency of some, who consider themselves super-rationalists, to look down upon Faith, reveals only their thoughtless ignorance. Only this rare faculty has to be purified by the elimination of Rajas and Tamas, and the enhancement of Sattva in which it is rooted.

Faith and reason are the two unique powers that come up at the human level of evolution. Animals do not have them. Both these powers function properly under favourable conditions alone—reason when well-cultivated under proper training and Faith when supported by a pure nature without much influence of passion and inertia. Purity of being is the nourishment that the latter requires. It is without understanding this uniqueness of Faith that ignorant critics speak of it as 'blind faith'. It is blind only when not nourished by purity.

The importance of Śraddhā is further emphasised by equating man's 'humanity' with the Śraddhā he entertains. It means that the stature of a man consists in the loftiness of the ideals and aspirations he sincerely cherishes and tries to practise.

3. *Vrs.*4-6: The aspirations and the types of ideals that attract the men dominated by each of the three Guṇas, are shown here. Those who are *Sāttvika* desire salvation and cultivate renunciation, divine love without motive, actions dedicated to God etc., and they will be drawn to Divine manifestations that bestow these excellences. These deities or ideals that attract the Sattva-bound souls can be called the Devas. The Rājasa worshippers are prompted by desires and ambitions, by greed of wealth and power. The attributes of the Divine that cater to such prayers and which attract such Rājasic minds is called here *Yakṣas* and *Rākṣasas.* The very unevolved and animal-like men, called here *Tāmasas,* can think of only ancestral spirits and elementals as objects of worship. But the most important point here is that all these types of men have Faith in some power higher than human and feel the need of prayer to, and worship of, that higher being. They have some Śraddhā, and this is so because in all beings that have evolved up to the human level there is an element of Sattva, which is the source of Faith. At the animal level it is not present. Atheism at the human level is a perversion arising from misapplied reasoning power. So too low forms of faith are perversions arising from an impure animal-like nature.

4. *Vr.*7-10: Purity of food has been very much insisted upon by the scriptures of Hinduism, as the body and the mind, being formed out of the food eaten, are very much influenced by it. In other religions there are only certain dogmatic prohibitions regarding the eating of some types of meat. While the influence of food on character has to be conceded in principle, whether all the theoretical ideas associated with this question are practicable in the present day conditions of life by aspirants in general, is open to question.

What the Gītā gives here is the enumeration of the qualities of food which people dominated by the three constituents of Nature prefer. Conversely it may also be taken that the consumption of foods belonging to the types mentioned, enhances the particular elements in one—be it Sattva, Rajas or Tamas. An impartial consideration of the characterisation of food given here in the Gītā will make one seriously doubt the soundness of some of the conventional ideas on food held in Hindu society. What would be the classification of meat in the light of the Gīta description of food?

It agrees with most of the qualities mentioned for *Sāttvika* food. Perhaps one may say it is *amedhya,* unclean, and therefore not *Sāttvika.* But one forgets that in Vedic society many kinds of meat were considered *medhya*—offerable in sacrifice—and therefore fit to be eaten. What will be the place given for cheese, which is foul smelling to non-eaters, but has all the qualities of a *Sāttvika* food, excepting the smell? What will be the place of all refrigerated foods, as also of those prepared long hours before but preserved in hot air compartments? So while these characteristics cited may be taken as helpful in a general assessment of the purity and impurity of food, it will be unreasonable to be too dogmatic. Dogmatic views about food held by many pious Hindus deserve rethinking in the modern conditions of life, giving place to a less fanatical and narrow out-look on the whole question.

5. *Vrs.*23-26: *Om, Tat, Sat* are very holy words. They represent Brahman, and are Brahman Himself in sound form. *Om* is called *Śabda-brahma,* Sound-Brahman, as it is said to be the essence of the Veda, and the sound-symbol of Brahman and the seed of all Mantras. *Tat* or That is equally indicative of Brahman, as borne out by the great Vedic dictum *Tat tvam asi*—That Thou art. Here the That is Brahman. So also Sat, meaning Truth or Reality, is equally representative of Brahman. The Upanishad says *Sad evedam agra āsīt*—in the beginning Sat alone existed. Thus these three words indicate Brahman, and are very holy—so holy that they can never be polluted. but on the other hand remedy all pollutions and shortcomings. In the performance of all Vedic rites, there are likely to be shortcomings of the nature of omissions and commissions in respect of the Mantras and forms used, or in the persons performing, or in the time and place of their performance. So the utterance of these words are offered as the remedy against all such actual, suspected or possible shortcomings. The utterance of these holy words are therefore an unavoidable part of all Yajñas and holy work. *Brāhmaṇa* is one who knows the Veda or Brahma. Veda is the basis of all Yajñas. So all these three go together.

Chapter XVIII

मोक्षसंन्यासयोगः

LIBERATION THROUGH RENUNCIATION

SUMMARY

True Abandonment: (1-12) As in the previous chapter, the early sections of this the last chapter also emphasize the part played by the three Guṇas of Prakṛti in all human affairs. It opens with a question by Arjuna about the distinction between *Sannyāsa* and *Tyāga*. The Lord replies: Abandonment of ritualistic works with promises of specific rewards is called by sages as *Sannyāsa,* while performance of all action without an eye on their fruits is *Tyāga*. Some say that all actions are to be abandoned because there is some element of evil in every action, but others are of the opinion that actions like Yajña, charity, austerity etc., are never to be abandoned. My view is that actions like Yajña, charity and austerity are never to be abandoned, because they purify man when performed without attachment and desire for fruits. To abandon a duty because of fear of difficulties involved, is positively bad. It is impossible for any embodied being to abandon all work. So true abandonment has to be taken to mean work without attachment to fruits and without the sense of ego. Actions done in that spirit never bind.

How the Bondage of Actions is overcome: (13-18) In all actions there are five factors involved—the body, the I-sense of the performer, senses, expression of energy through them, and as the fifth, the unknown and incalculable factor. All these are factors belonging to Prakṛti. Behind it is the pure light of consciousness, the Atman, who is the unaffected witness. In ignorance, this pure witness identifies himself with these factors external to him and their performances, and creates bondage for himself. So if the actor has no feeling like 'I am doing', and no attachment to the fruits accruing, it can be said that he does not act, even if all the world sees him acting in the physical sense.

The Three Guṇas as the determinative factors: (18-39) *Sattva:* Dispositions of Prakṛti—Sattva, Rajas and Tamas—determine the nature of knowledge, action and agent. Knowledge dominated by Sattva leads to the understanding of unity in diversity; actions dominated by it tend to detachment and freedom from passionate affiliations; a doer dominated by it is comparatively free from ego-sense and attachment but yet does not lack enthusiasm and interest in the work; the intelligence dominated by it is always accompanied by moral sensibility and an eye to the spiritual side of things; strength of mind dominated by it is expressed as control of the senses and the mind, and as strict adherence to principles; and experience dominated by it is painful in the beginning due to difficulties of discipline, but ends in great bliss.

Rajas: Knowledge dominated by Rajas directs attention to the diversity of things and not their unity; work dominated by it results in actions done with great attachment, egotism and expenditure of energy; an agent dominated by it is greedy, cruel, attached and subject to elation and depression; intelligence dominated by it is riddled with confusion about right and wrong and has little sense of duty; strength dominated by it is under the sway of ambitions, desires and worldly status; and happiness dominated by it is extremely attractive in the beginning due to sensual excitement but in its final result brings about suffering.

Tamas: Knowledge dominated by Tamas sees mere side-issues as the whole truth and doggedly holds on to them without due thought, under the prompting of passions; action dominated by Tamas is undertaken thoughtlessly without any estimate of one's capacity or resources, and is prompted by delusions and cruel motives; the agent dominated by Tamas is fickleminded, insolent, exploiting, procrastinating and slipshod in his methods; intelligence dominated by Tamas sees unrighteousness as righteousness and takes the wrong side of everything; strength or determination dominated by Tamas is always subject to depression, vacillation, and overbearing insolence; and pleasure dominated by Tamas is from the beginning to the end riddled with delusion, lethargy and heedlessness.

Guṇas and character types: (40-44) Everything in Nature being thus dominated by the Guṇas, the character types—Brāhmaṇa, Kṣatriya, Vaiśya and Śūdra—and the duties pertaining to them are also no exception to this domination. Intellectualism and introspectiveness; dynamism and leadership; industry and productiveness; discipline and service at all levels—these are the duties of the four character types based on their natural constitutions.

Work as worship: (45-49) Knowing that all one's endowments are derived from universal Nature, which is the Lord's power of manifestation, man must worship that Supreme Being with the faithful and non-attached discharge of the duties that devolve on him. That is real worship, and by that man evolves spiritually. By the mere fact that there are some defective elements in a work, one's duty cannot be abandoned. For, defects are natural to all works as smoke is to fire. If discharged in a dedicated and detached spirit, as an offering to the Lord who manifests as society, all blemishes are overcome.

Spiritual fulfilment through total abandonment: (50-56) For men who have grown mature through devotion and dedicated work and attained to detachment and dispassion, there are two courses open. Those who are favourably situated for it may take to a pure ascetic life in solitude, and devote themselves to the practice of pure introspection. Such practice endows him with motiveless love of the Lord—a love not influenced by any of the forces of Nature (*Nirguṇa-bhakti*). By such love he attains to a comprehensive and intuitive understanding of the Divine and realises himself as a part and parcel of the Divine Life.

Spiritual fulfilment through resignation: (56-66) Those who have not that facility for complete withdrawal from social life, can continue to do their Svadharma with complete dependence on Me, the Lord of all. Such a one should mentally renounce all sense of agency for the works that flow through him, and externally he should have no longing or attachment for the fruits of his actions. One who thus infills his mind with Me, overcomes all difficulties and attains to the highest spiritual fulfilment. For the truth is that all beings are like objects placed on a wheel, and I (the Lord of all) alone turn the wheel. Those on the wheel, if they think they are turning it, are in utter ignorance. Seek shelter in Me with your whole being, and you shall attain peace. This profoundest spiritual Gospel I reveal to you now. Be filled with Me; worship Me; make prostrations to Me. Abandoning dependence on every kind of ego-centred support, seek Me alone as your refuge. I shall save you from the life of ignorance and sin.

To whom the Gītā is relevant: (67-68): This great spiritual doctrine is to be taught only to those who are spiritually inclined. Such teaching is highly pleasing to Me, as they are thereby worshipping Me with *Jñāna-yajña.*

Conclusion: Wherever Kṛṣṇa the Lord of Yoga, and Arjuna the enforcer of Dharma, function unitedly, there will reign both prosperity and spirituality.

अर्जुन उवाच

संन्यासस्य महाबाहो तत्त्वमिच्छामि वेदितुम् ।
त्यागस्य च हृषीकेश पृथक्केशिनिषूदन ॥ 1 ॥

Arjuna uvāca:

Saṁnyāsasya mahā-bāho tattvam icchāmi veditum
tyāgasya ca Hṛṣīkeśa pṛthak Keśi-niṣūdana //1//

Hṛṣīkeśa: O conqurer of the senses! *Keśiniṣūdana*: O destroyer of Keśin! *Mahabāho* : O mighty armed one! *saṁnyāsasya* : of Samnyāsa (renunciation) *tyāgasya* : of Tyāga (abandonment, resignation) *ca* : and *tattvam* : the true nature *pṛthak* : in their distinctive meanings *veditum* : to know *icchāmi* : I desire.

Arjuna said:

1. O mighty-armed One, famed as the destroyer of Keśin and the conqueror of the senses! I desire to know the true nature of Saṁnyāsa, and as distinguished from it, of Tyāga **too.**[1]

श्रीभगवानुवाच

काम्यानां कर्मणां न्यासं संन्यासं कवयो विदुः ।
सर्वकर्मफलत्यागं प्राहुस्त्यागं विचक्षणाः ॥ 2 ॥

Śri Bhagavān uvāca:

Kāmyānāṁ karmaṇāṁ nyāsaṁ saṁnyāsaṁ kavayo viduḥ /
sarva-karma-phala-tyāgaṁ prāhus tyāgaṁ vicakṣaṇāḥ //2//

Kāmyānām : of desire-prompted *karmaṇām* : actions *nyāsam* : abandonment *saṁnyāsam* : Saṁnyāsa *kavayaḥ* : sages *viduḥ* : speak of;***sarva-karma-phala-tyāgam*** : giving up the fruits of all actions *tyāgam* : Tyāga *vicakṣaṇāḥ* : men with insight *prāhuḥ* : declare.

2. Abandonment of all desire-prompted actions is Saṁnyāsa (renunciation) according to the wise. Men of discernment speak of the abandonment of the fruits of all actions as Tyāga (relinquishment).

त्याज्यं दोषवदित्येके कर्म प्राहुर्मनीषिणः ।
यज्ञदानतपःकर्म न त्याज्यमिति चापरे ॥ 3 ॥

Tyājyaṁ doṣavad ity eke karma prāhur manīṣiṇaḥ /
yajña-dāna-tapaḥ-karma na tyājyam iti c'āpare //3//

Karma : Action *doṣavat* : as being evil *tyājyam* : is to be abandoned, *iti* : thus *eke* : some *manīṣiṇaḥ* : wise men *prāhuḥ* : say, *yajña-dāna-tapaḥ-karma* : actions like sacrifice (worship), charity and practice of austerity *na tyājyam* : are not to be abandoned *iti* : thus *ca* : and *apare* : others.

3. Some wise men say that all action is to be abandoned as evil. Others maintain that good works like worship, charity and practice of austerity are not to be abandoned.

निश्चयं शृणु मे तत्र त्यागे भरतसत्तम ।
त्यागो हि पुरुषव्याघ्र त्रिविधः संप्रकीर्तितः ॥ 4 ॥

Niścayaṁ sṛṇu me tatra tyāge Bharata-sattama /
tyago hi puruṣa-vyāghra tri-vidhaḥ saṁprakīrtitaḥ //4//

Bharatasattama : The best among the Bhārata clan! *tatra* : in the matter *tyāge* : regarding abandonment *me* : My *niścayam* : conclusive view *sṛṇu* : hear; *puruṣavyāghra* : O best of men! *tyāgaḥ* : abandonment *trividhaḥ* : three kinds *samprakīrtitaḥ* : is declared to be *hi* : indeed.

4. O the best of the Bhārata race! Hear my conclusive view on this subject of Tyāga (relinquishment). It is said that there are three types of Tyāga.

यज्ञदानतपःकर्म न त्याज्यं कार्यमेव तत् ।
यज्ञो दानं तपश्चैव पावनानि मनीषिणाम् ॥ 5 ॥

Yajña-dāna-tapaḥ-karma na tyājyaṁ kāryam eva tat /
yajño dānaṁ tapaś-c'aiva pāvanāni manīṣiṇām //5//

Yajña-dāna-tapaḥ-karma: works like sacrifice, charity and austerity *na tyājyam*:are not to be given up,*tat*:they *kāryam eva*:are to be performed; *yajñaḥ* : sacrifice *dānaḥ* : charity *tapaḥ* : austerity *ca eva* : and also *manīṣiṇām* : for the wise men *pāvanāni* : purifying *eva* : indeed.

5. Works like sacrifice, charity and austerity should not be abandoned. They should be performed; for sacrifice, charity and austerity are indeed purifying for the wise.

एतान्यपि तु कर्माणि सङ्गं त्यक्त्वा फलानि च ।
कर्तव्यानीति मे पार्थ निश्चितं मतमुत्तमम् ॥ 6 ॥

Etāny api tu karmāṇi saṅgaṁ tyaktvā phalāni ca /
kartavyānī'ti me Pārtha niścitaṁ matam uttamam //6//

Pārtha : O son of Pṛthā! *etāni* : these *Karmāṇi* : actions *api tu* : even *saṅgam* : attachment *phalāni* : fruits *ca* : and *tyaktvā* : abandoning *kartavyāni* : are to be performed, *iti* : this *me* : My *niścitam* : settled *uttamam* : final *matam* : view.

6. O Son of Pṛthā! Even these works are to be performed without attachment and desire for their fruits. This is My settled and decisive view.

नियतस्य तु संन्यासः कर्मणो नोपपद्यते ।
मोहात्तस्य परित्यागस्तामसः परिकीर्तितः ॥ 7 ॥

Niyatasya tu saṁnyāsaḥ karmaṇo n'opapadyate |
mohāt tasya parityāgas tāmasaḥ parikīrtitaḥ //7//

Niyatasya: What should necessarily be performed as duty *karmaṇaḥ*: of works *saṁnyāsaḥ* : renouncing *tu*: indeed *na upapadyate*: is not proper; *mohāt* : through delusion *tasya* : its *parityāgaḥ* : abandonment *tāmasaḥ* : of the nature of Tamas *parikīrtitaḥ* : is spoken of.

7. It is not at all proper to renounce works that ought to be done as duty. Their abandonment out of delusion is considered to be of the nature of Tamas.

दुःखमित्येव यत्कर्म कायक्लेशभयात्त्यजेत् ।
स कृत्वा राजसं त्यागं नैव त्यागफलं लभेत् ॥ 8 ॥

Duḥkham ity eva yat karma kāya-kleśa-bhayāt tyajet |
sa kṛtvā rājasaṁ tyāgaṁ n'aiva tyāga-phalaṁ labhet //8//

Kāyakleśabhayāt : Out of fear of physical suffering *duḥkham* : painful *iti eva* : this is indeed (*yaḥ* : who) *yat* : which *karma* : action *tyajet* : abandons, *saḥ* : he *rājasam* : of the nature of Rajas *tyāgam* : relinquishment *kṛtvā* : doing, *tyāgaphalam* : the result of relinqishment *na labhet eva* : does not at all get.

8. Those who give up work out of a dread of physical suffering, out of a feeling that it is painful, they, performing relinquishment of a Rājasa nature, do not obtain the results of true relinquishment.

कार्यमित्येव यत्कर्म नियतं क्रियतेऽर्जुन ।
सङ्गं त्यक्त्वा फलं चैव स त्यागः सात्त्विको मतः ॥ 9 ॥

Kāryam ity eva yat karma niyataṁ kriyate'rjuna |
Saṅgaṁ tyaktvā phalaṁ c'aiva sa tyāgaḥ sāttviko mataḥ //9//

Arjuna : O Arjuna! *niyataṁ karma* : ordained work, duty *kāryam eva* : ought to be done, *iti* : feeling thus *saṅgam* : attachment *phalam* : results *ca* : and *eva* : also *tyaktvā* : relinquishing *kriyate* : is performed *yat* : which, *saḥ* : that *tyāgaḥ* : relinquishment *sāttvikaḥ* : born of Sattva *mataḥ* : is considered.

9. But, O Arjuna! That relinquishment is considered as Sāttvika, which consists in giving up attachment and thoughts of returns in respect of works, and which is done with the feeling that it is an obligatory duty that must necessarily be performed.

न द्वेष्ट्यकुशलं कर्म कुशले नानुषज्जते ।
त्यागी सत्त्वसमाविष्टो मेधावी छिन्नसंशयः ॥ 10 ॥

Na dveṣṭy akuśalaṁ karma kuśale n'ānuṣajjate /
tyāgī sattva-samāviṣṭo medhāvī chinna-saṁśayaḥ //10//

Sattva-samāviṣṭaḥ : One imbued with the Sattva quality *medhāvī* : wise man *chinna-saṁśayaḥ* : one whose doubts have been dispelled *tyāgī* : relinquisher *akuśalam karma* : unpleasant duty *na dveṣṭi* : never hates *kuśale* : in pleasant duties *na anuṣajjate* : is not attached.

10. The relinquisher (Tyāgī), if he is endowed with the qualities of Sattva, wisdom and conviction in regard to the spiritual ideal, never avoids duties merely because they are unpleasant, nor does he get attached to works that seem pleasant to him.

न हि देहभृता शक्यं त्यक्तुं कर्माण्यशेषतः ।
यस्तु कर्मफलत्यागी स त्यागीत्यभिधीयते ॥ 11 ॥

Na hi deha-bhṛtā śakyaṁ tyaktuṁ karmāṇy aśeṣataḥ /
yas tu karma-phala-tyāgī sa tyagī'ty abhidhīyate //11//

Dehabhṛtā : By one having a body *karmāṇi* : actions *aśeṣataḥ* : in their entirety *tyaktum* : to abandon *na śakyam* : not possible *hi* : indeed; *yaḥ* : who *tu* : but *karma-phala-tyāgī* : gives up the fruits of actions *saḥ* : he tyāgī : relinquisher *iti* : thus *abhidhīyate* : is called.

11. It is not indeed possible for any embodied being (i.e., one with body consciousness) to abandon works in entirety. So all that one can do is to abandon the fruits of action. One doing so is called a Tyāgī (a relinquisher).[2]

अनिष्टमिष्टं मिश्रं च त्रिविधं कर्मणः फलम् ।
भवत्यत्यागिनां प्रेत्य न तु संन्यासिनां क्वचित् ॥ 12 ॥

Aniṣṭam iṣṭaṁ miśraṁ ca tri-vidhaṁ karmaṇaḥ phalam /
bhavaty-atyāgināṁ pretya na tu saṁnyāsināṁ kvacit //12//

Karmaṇaḥ : Of Karma *aniṣṭam* : unpleasant *iṣṭam* : pleasant *miśram* : mixed *ca* : and *trividham* : threefold *phalam* : fruits *atyāginām* : for those who do not relinquish the fruits of actions *pretya* : after death *bhavati* : accrues; *saṁnyāsinām* : to those who renounce *tu* : but *kvacit na* : never.

12. Regarding those who have not relinquished their desires (*a-tyāginām*), they reap after death the fruits of their actions performed with desire. They are of three sorts—'unpleasant' like degradation into animal life or stay in purgatory for the very wicked; 'pleasant' like attainment of heavenly felicities for the virtuous; and 'mixed' as in human birth, for those who have Karmas of both these types to their credit. But Saṁnyāsins (true renouncers) will have none of these.[3]

पञ्चैतानि महाबाहो कारणानि निबोध मे ।
सांख्ये कृतान्ते प्रोक्तानि सिद्धये सर्वकर्मणाम् ॥ 13 ॥

Pañc'aitāni mahā-bāho kāraṇāni nibodha me /
sāṁkhye kṛtānte proktāni siddhaye sarva-karmaṇām //13//

Mahābāho : O mighty armed! *sarvakarmaṇām* : of all actions *siddhaye* : required for the accomplishment *kṛtānte* : which is the end of all actions *sāṁkhye* : in the philosophy of spiritual illumination *proktāni* : described *imāni* : these *pañca* : five *kāraṇāni* : causal factors *me* : from Me *nibodha* : understand.

13. Learn from me, O mighty armed! about the five causal factors required for all actions as described in the Sāṁkhya, the philosophy of spiritual illumination, which is the ultimate purpose of all actions.[4]

अधिष्ठानं तथा कर्ता करणं च पृथग्विधम् ।
विविधाश्च पृथक्चेष्टा दैवं चैवात्र पञ्चमम् ॥ 14 ॥

Adhiṣṭhānaṁ tathā kartā karaṇaṁ ca pṛthag-vidham /
vividhāś ca pṛthak ceṣṭā daivaṁ c'aiv'ātra pañcamam //14//

Adhiṣṭhānam : the seat of action i.e. the body *tathā* : also *kartā* : the ego that claims to be the actor *pṛthagvidham* : various kinds of *karaṇam* : instruments of action *ca* : and *vividhāḥ* : varied *pṛthak* : distinct *ceṣṭāḥ* : movements *ca* : and *atra* : in this *pañcamam* : the fifth *daivam* : the unknown factor or the deities presiding over the senses *ca eva* : and also.

14. One's body which is the seat of action, the ego claiming to be the actor, the several instruments of actions (like the senses, the mind etc.), the varied and the distinct types of movements involved, and finally the unknown factor (or the deities presiding over the senses) as the fifth—these are the five causal factors.

शरीरवाङ्मनोभिर्यत्कर्म प्रारभते नरः ।
न्याय्यं वा विपरीतं वा पञ्चैते तस्य हेतवः ॥ 15 ॥

Śarīra-vāṅ-manobhir yat karma prārabhate naraḥ /
nyāyyaṁ va viparītaṁ vā pañc'aite tasya hetavaḥ //15//

Naraḥ : Man *śarīra-vāṅ-manobhiḥ* : with the body, word and mind *nyāyyam* : right *vā* : or *viparītam* : opposite i.e. wrong *yat* : which *karma* : Karma *prārabhate* : performs, *tasya* : of that *ete* : these *pañcahetavaḥ* : are the five causal factors.

15. These are the five causal factors involved in all actions, good as also bad, which men undertake with this body, speech and mind.

तत्रैवं सति कर्तारमात्मानं केवलं तु यः ।
पश्यत्यकृतबुद्धित्वान्न स पश्यति दुर्मतिः ॥ 16 ॥

Tatr'aivaṁ sati kartāram atmānaṁ kevalaṁ tu yaḥ /
paśyaty akṛta-buddhitvān na sa paśyati durmatiḥ //16//

Tatra evam sati : That being so, *ātmānam* : the Self *kevalam* : alone (or the unlimited and unrelated Being) *tu* : verily *kartāram* : as actor *yaḥ* : who *paśyati* : sees, *durmatiḥ* : of perverted outlook, *saḥ* : he *akṛta-buddhitvāt* : on account of the impurity of his intellect *na paśyati* : does not perceive the truth.

16. That being so, he whose imperfect understanding makes him think that the self alone (or the unlimited and unrelated Ātman) is the agent involved in work—he verily sees not, being perverted in outlook.

यस्य नाहंकृतो भावो बुद्धिर्यस्य न लिप्यते ।
हत्वापि स इमाँल्लोकान्न हन्ति न निबध्यते ॥ 17 ॥

Yasya n'āhaṁkṛto bhāvo buddhir yasya na lipyate /
hattvā'pi sa imāṁl lokān na hanti na nibadhyate //17//

Yasya : For whom *ahaṁkṛtaḥ bhāvaḥ* : the feeling 'I am the agent' *na asti* : there is not, *yasya* : whose *buddhiḥ* : intellect *na lipyate* : is unsullied, *saḥ* : he *imān lokān* : these beings *hattvā* : killing *api* : even *na hanti* : does not kill, *na nibadhyate* : is not bound by the action.

17. He who is ever established in the feeling 'I am not the agent' and whose mind is consequently unsullied by attachments—he kills not really, nor is he bound, even though he annihilates all these beings.

ज्ञानं ज्ञेयं परिज्ञाता त्रिविधा कर्मचोदना ।
करणं कर्म कर्तेति त्रिविधः कर्मसंग्रहः ॥ 18 ॥

Jñānaṁ jñeyaṁ parijñātā tri-vidhā karma-codanā /
karaṇaṁ karma kart'eti tri-vidhaḥ karma-saṁgrahaḥ //18//

Jñānam : Knowledge *jñeyam* : object of knowledge *parijñātā* : the knower *trividhā* : threefold *karma codanā* : incitement to action; *karaṇam* : instruments of action (senses) *karma* : the purpose of action *kartā:* the agent *iti trividhaḥ*: these three *karmasaṁgrahaḥ:* form the **constituents** of action.

18. Knowledge, object of knowledge, and knower—these constitute the threefold incitement to action. And the three constituents of action are the instruments of action, the purpose of action, and the agent.

ज्ञानं कर्म च कर्ता च त्रिधैव गुणभेदतः ।
प्रोच्यते गुणसंख्याने यथावच्छृणु तान्यपि ॥ 19 ॥

Jñānaṁ karma ca kartā ca tridh'aiva guṇa-bhedataḥ /
procyate guṇa-saṁkhyāne yathāvacchṛṇu tāny-api //19//

Guṇa-saṁkhyāne : In the philosophy of Guṇas and their evolutes i.e. in the Sāṁkhya philosophy *jñānam* : knowledge *karma* : action *ca* : and *kartā* : agent *ca* : and *guṇabhedataḥ* : according to the different Guṇas *tridhā* : of three kinds *eva* : as *procyate* : is spoken of; *tāni api* : of them also *yathāvat* : as they are *śṛṇu* : hear.

19. In the Sāṁkhya philosophy dealing with the Guṇas and their evolutes, knowledge, action and agent are each divided into three according to the preponderance of each Guṇa in them. Hear of them also as they are.

सर्वभूतेषु येनैकं भावमव्ययमीक्षते ।
अविभक्तं विभक्तेषु तज्ज्ञानं विद्धि सात्त्विकम् ॥ 20 ॥

Sarva-bhūteṣu yen'aikaṁ bhāvam avyayam īkṣate /
avibhaktaṁ vibhakteṣu taj jñānaṁ viddhi sāttvikam //20//

Vibhakteṣu : Divided *sarvabhūteṣu* : in all beings *avibhaktam* : undivided *ekam* : unitary *avyayam* : unmodifiable *bhāvam* : Essence *yena* : by whom *īkṣate* : sees, *tat* : that *jñānam* : knowledge *sāttvikam* : of Sattva *viddhi* : know.

20. That knowledge by which one is able to see a unitary unmodifiable Essence, undivided among the divided,—know that knowledge to be of the nature of Sattva.

पृथक्त्वेन तु यज्ज्ञानं नानाभावान्पृथग्विधान् ।
वेत्ति सर्वेषु भूतेषु तज्ज्ञानं विद्धि राजसम् ॥ 21 ॥

Pṛthaktvena tu yaj jñānaṁ nānā-bhāvān pṛthag-vidhān /
vetti sarveṣu bhūteṣu taj jñānaṁ viddhi rājasam //21//

Sarveṣu bhūteṣu : In all beings *nānābhāvān* : multiplicity *pṛthag-vidhān* : mutually distinct *pṛthaktvena tu* : in their separateness only without perception of an underlying unity *yat* : which *jñānam* : knowledge *vetti* : knows, *tat* : that *jñānam* : knowledge *rājasam* : of the nature of Rajas *viddhi* : know.

21. That knowledge which apprehends all beings as a multiplicity with mutual distinction and in their separateness only, without any apprehension of an underlying unity--know that knowledge to be born of Rajas.

यत्तु कृत्स्नवदेकस्मिन्कार्ये सक्तमहैतुकम् ।
अतत्त्वार्थवदल्पं च तत्तामसमुदाहृतम् ॥ 22 ॥

Yat tu kṛtsnavad ekasmin kārye saktam ahaitukam /
atattv'ārthavad alpaṁ ca tat tāmasam udāhṛtam //22//

Ekasmin : In one single *kārye* : effect, part *kṛtsnavat* : as if it were the whole *saktam* : is attached i.e. dogmatically holds on *ahaitukam* irrational *atattvārthavat* : untrue *alpam* : silly *ca* : and *yat tu* : which, *tat* : that knowledge *tāmasam* : born of Tamas *udāhṛtam* is spoken of as.

22. That by which one dogmatically holds on to a part as if it were the whole (or looks on the body, an effect, as the whole man)—a view which is irrational, untrue and silly—that knowledge is said to be born of Tamas.

नियतं सङ्गरहितमरागद्वेषतः कृतम् ।
अफलप्रेप्सुना कर्म यत्तत्सात्त्विकमुच्यते ॥ 23 ॥

Niyataṁ saṅga-rahitam arāga-dveṣataḥ kṛtam /
aphala-prepsunā karma yat tat sāttvikam ucyate //23//

Yat : Which *niyataṁ karma* : obligatory work, duty *aphala-prepsunā* : by one without hankering for the fruits *saṅga-rahitam* : without attachment *arāga-dveṣataḥ* : without passion or hate *kṛtam* : done, *tat* : that work *sāttvikam* : as born of Sattva *ucyate* : is spoken of.

23. Work of the nature of duty done by one without hankering for fruits, and without attachment, or passion or hate—such work is spoken of as born of Sattva.

यत्तु कामेप्सुना कर्म साहंकारेण वा पुनः ।
क्रियते बहुलायासं तद्राजसमुदाहृतम् ॥ 24 ॥

Yat tu kām'epsunā karma s'āhaṁkāreṇa vā punaḥ
kriyate bahul'āyāsaṁ tad rājasam udāhṛtam //24//

Yat : which *tu* : but *karma* : action *kāmepsunā* : by one wanting to gratify one's desires *sāhaṁkāreṇa* : with the feeling of self-importance *vā* : or *punaḥ* : again *bahulāyāsam* : with great strain *kriyate* : is performed, *tat* : that *rājasam* : born of Rajas *udāhṛtam* : is said to be.

24. But work that is done by a person merely for the gratification of his desire, and with great strain and a feeling of self-importance is said to be born of Rajas.

अनुबन्धं क्षयं हिंसामनपेक्ष्य च पौरुषम् ।
मोहादारभ्यते कर्म यत्तत्तामसमुच्यते ॥ 25 ॥

Anubandhaṁ kṣayaṁ hiṁsām anapekṣya ca pauruṣam /
mohād ārabhyate karma yat tat tāmasam ucyate //25//

Anubandham : Consequences *kṣayam* : loss *hiṁsām* : injury to others *pauruṣam* : one's own capacity *ca* : and *anapekṣya* : without regard to *mohāt* : due to delusion *yat* : which *karma* : action *ārabhyate* : is begun, *tat* : that *tāmasam* : born of Tamas *ucyate* : is spoken of as.

25. And that work which is performed under delusion, without any regard to consequences, loss, injury to others, and to one's own capacity—is said to be born of Tamas.

मुक्तसङ्गोऽनहंवादी धृत्युत्साहसमन्वितः ।
सिद्ध्यसिद्ध्योर्निर्विकारः कर्ता सात्त्विक उच्यते ॥ 26 ॥

Mukta-saṅgo'nahaṁ-vādī dhṛty-utsāha-samanvitaḥ /
siddhy-asiddhyor nirvikāraḥ kartā sāttvika ucyate //26//

Muktasaṅgaḥ : Free from attachment *anahaṁvādī* : without pride and self-importance *dhṛty-utsāha-samanvitaḥ:* endowed with steadiness and zeal *siddhy-asiddhyoḥ* : in success and failure *nirvikāraḥ* : unruffled *kartā* : doer *sāttvikaḥ* : possessed of Sattva *ucyate* : is spoken of as.

26. A 'doer' (an agent of an action) who is without any attachment and sense of pride and self-importance, who is endowed with steadiness and zeal, and who is unruffled in success and failure—such a doer is said to be of the nature of Sattva.

रागी कर्मफलप्रेप्सुर्लुब्धो हिंसात्मकोऽशुचिः ।
हर्षशोकान्वितः कर्ता राजसः परिकीर्तितः ॥ 27 ॥

Rāgī karma-phala-prepsur lubdho hiṁs'ātmako'śuciḥ /
harṣa-śok'ānvitaḥ kartā rājasaḥ parikīrtitaḥ //27//

Rāgī : One who is swayed by passion *karma-phala-prepsuḥ* : one who seeks the fruits of his actions *lubdhaḥ* : covetous *hiṁsātmakaḥ* : cruel *aśuciḥ* : impure *harṣa-sokānvitaḥ* : subject to elation and depression *kartā* : doer *rājasaḥ* : as endowed with Rājas *parikīrtitaḥ*: is declared.

27. A 'doer' who is swayed by passion, who is keen on the fruits of his actions, who is covetuous, cruel and impure at heart, and who is subject to elation and depression in success and failure—such a doer is said to be of the nature of Rajas.

अयुक्तः प्राकृतः स्तब्धः शठो नैष्कृतिकोऽलसः ।
विषादी दीर्घसूत्री च कर्ता तामस उच्यते ॥ 28 ॥

Ayuktaḥ prākṛtaḥ stabdhaḥ śaṭho naiṣkṛtiko'lasaḥ /
viṣādī dīrgha-sūtrī ca kartā tāmasa ucyate //28//

Ayuktaḥ : Unsteady *prākṛtaḥ* : vulgar *stabdhaḥ* : arrogant *śaṭhaḥ* : deceitful *naiskṛtikaḥ* : malicious *alasaḥ* : indolent *viṣādī* : despondent *dīrghasūtrī*: procrastinating *ca* : and *kartā* : doer *tāmasaḥ* : of the nature of Tamas *ucyate* : is said to be.

28. And a 'doer' who is unsteady, vulgar, arrogant, deceitful, malicious, indolent, despondent, and procrastinating—such a doer is said to be of the nature of Tamas.

बुद्धेर्भेदं धृतेश्चैव गुणतस्त्रिविधं शृणु ।
प्रोच्यमानमशेषेण पृथक्त्वेन धनञ्जय ॥ 29 ॥

Buddher bhedaṁ dhṛteś'caiva guṇatas tri-vidhaṁ śṛṇu /
procyamānam aśeṣeṇa pṛthaktvena dhanañjaya //29//

Dhanañjaya : O Arjuna! *buddheḥ* : of the intellect, understanding *dhṛteḥ* : of the power of determination *ca* : and *eva* : also *guṇataḥ* : according to Nature's dispositions *trividham* : threefold *bhedam* : distinction *aśeṣeṇa* : wholly *pṛthaktvena* : severally *procyamānam* : what is being declared *śṛṇu* : hear.

29. Hear now, O Arjuna, of the threefold division of the intellect and of the power of determination on the basis of their constituent Guṇas—hear of them severally and in their totality.

प्रवृत्तिं च निवृत्तिं च कार्याकार्यं भयाभये ।
बन्धं मोक्षं च या वेत्ति बुद्धिः सा पार्थ सात्त्विकी ॥ 30 ॥

Pravṛttiṁ ca nivṛttiṁ ca kāry'ākārye bhay'ābhaye /
bandhaṁ mokṣaṁ ca yā vetti buddhiḥ sā Pārtha sāttvikī //30/

Pārtha : O son of Pṛthā! *pravṛttim ca* : self-centred activity, worldliness *nivṛttim ca* reunciation *kāryākārye*: what should be done and what should not be done i.e what is the moral and what is the immoral *bhayābhaye:* what is to be feared and not feared *bandhaṁ mokṣamca:* bondage and freedom *yā:* which *buddhiḥ:* intellect *vetti:* knows, *sā* : that (*buddhiḥ* : intellect) *sāttvikī* : is of the nature of Sattva.

30. O son of Pṛthā! That intellect is said to be of the nature of Sattva which grasps the distinction between worldliness and renunciation, between the moral and the immoral, between what should be feared and what should not be, and between knowledge and freedom.

यया धर्ममधर्मं च कार्यं चाकार्यमेव च ।
अयथावत्प्रजानाति बुद्धिः सा पार्थ राजसी ॥ 31 ॥

Yayā dharmam adharmaṁ ca kāryaṁ c'ākāryam eva ca
ayathāvat prajānāti buddhiḥ sā Pārtha rājasī //31///

Pārtha : O son of Pṛthā! *yayā* : by which *dharmam* : the moral, the right *adharmam* - the immoral, the wrong *ca* : and *kāryam* : what should be done *ca* : and *akāryam* : what should not be done *eva ca* : and also *ayathāvat* : not as they are, in a distorted manner *prajānāti* : understands, *sā buddhiḥ* : that intellect *Rājasī* : is of the nature of Rajas.

31. O son of Pṛthā! That intellect is said to be of the nature of Rajas, which takes a distorted and confused view of the moral and the immoral, of what should be done and what should not be.

अधर्मं धर्ममिति या मन्यते तमसावृता ।
सर्वार्थान्विपरीतांश्च बुद्धिः सा पार्थ तामसी ॥ 32 ॥

Adharmaṁ dharmam iti yā manyate tamasā'vṛtā /
sarv'ārthān viparītāṁś ca buddhiḥ sā Pārtha tāmasī //32//

Pārtha : O son of Pṛthā! *yā* : which *tamasā* : by darkness *āvṛtā* : covered *adharmam* : the immoral *dharmam* : the moral *iti* : as *sarvārthān* : all things *viparītān* : in a contrary manner *ca* : and *manyate* : understands, *sā* : that *buddhiḥ* : intellect *tāmasī* : is of the nature of Tamas.

32. O son of Pṛthā! That intellect is of the nature of Tamas, which, covered by the darkness of ignorance, understands the immoral as the moral and thus reverses all values.

धृत्या यया धारयते मनःप्राणेन्द्रियक्रियाः ।
योगेनाव्यभिचारिण्या धृतिः सा पार्थ सात्त्विकी ॥ 33 ॥

Dhṛtyā yayā dhārayate manaḥ-prāṇ'endriya-kriyāḥ /
yogenā'vyabhicāriṇyā dhṛtiḥ sā Pārtha sāttvikī //33//

Pārtha : O son of Pṛthā! *yogena* : by concentration *avyabhicāriṇyā* : unswerving *yayā* : by which *dhṛtyā* : by power of determination *manaḥ-prāṇ'endriya-kriyāḥ* : the activities of the mind, the vital breaths and the senses *dhārayate* : holds under control, *sā* : that *dhṛtiḥ* : power of determination *sāttvikī* : is of the nature of Sattva.

33. O Son of Pṛthā! That power of determination is of the nature of Sattva, by which the mind, the vital energy and the senses are held in control through unswerving concentration.

यया तु धर्मकामार्थान्धृत्या धारयतेऽर्जुन ।
प्रसङ्गेन फलाकाङ्क्षी धृतिः सा पार्थ राजसी ॥ 34 ॥

Yayā tu dharma-kām' ārthān dhṛtyā dhārayate' rjuna /
prasaṅgena phal' ākāṅkṣī dhṛtiḥ sā Pārtha rājasī //34//

Arjuna: O Arjuna! *yayā* : by which *dhṛtyā* : power of determination *tu* : but *dharma-kām' ārthān* : duty, pleasure and wealth *dhārayate* : holds on to *prasaṅgena* : with passionate attachment *phalākāṅkṣī* : one desirous of fruits, *sā* : that *dhṛtiḥ* : determination *rājasī* : is of Rajas.

34. That power of determination is of the nature of Rajas, by which one holds on to duty, pleasure and wealth with passionate attachment motivated by the desire for their fruits.

यया स्वप्नं भयं शोकं विषादं मदमेव च ।
न विमुञ्चति दुर्मेधा धृतिः सा पार्थ तामसी ॥ 35 ॥

Yayā svapnaṁ bhayaṁ śokaṁ viṣādaṁ madam eva ca /
na vimuñcati durmedhā dhṛtiḥ sā Pārtha tāmasī //35//

Durmedhāḥ: One of perverted intelligence *yayā* : by which *svapnam* : sleep *bhayam* : fear *śokam* : grief *viṣādam* : despondency *madam* : frenzy of sensuous indulgences *eva ca* : and also *na vimuñcati* : does not give up *sā* : that *dhṛtiḥ* : power of determination *tāmasī matā* : is of the nature of Tamas.

35. That power of determination is of the nature of Tamas, due to which one of perverted intelligence does not give up sloth, fear, grief, despondency and frenzy of sense indulgences.

सुखं त्विदानीं त्रिविधं शृणु मे भरतर्षभ ।
अभ्यासाद्रमते यत्र दुःखान्तं च निगच्छति ॥ 36 ॥

यत्तदग्रे विषमिव परिणामेऽमृतोपमम् ।
तत्सुखं सात्त्विकं प्रोक्तमात्मबुद्धिप्रसादजम् ॥ 37 ॥

Sukhaṁ tu idānīṁ tri-vidhaṁ śṛṇu me Bharata'rṣabha /
abhyāsād ramate yatra duḥkh'āntaṁ ca nigacchati //36//

Yat tad agre viṣam iva pariṇāme'mṛt'opamam /
tat sukhaṁ sāttvikaṁ proktam ātma-buddhi-prasāda-jam //37/

Bharatarṣabha : O the greatest in the Bhārata clan! *trividham* : three kinds *sukham* : pleasure *tu* : also *idānīm* : now *me* : from Me *śṛṇu* : hear; *abhyāsāt* : by practice *yatra* : in which *ramate* : comes to rejoice *duḥkhāntam* : end of all sorrows *nigacchati* : attains to *ca* : and, *yat* : which *tat* : that *agre* : in the beginning *viṣam* : poison *iva* : like, *pariṇāme* : in the end *amṛtopamam* : like nectar *ātma-buddhi-prasāda-jam* : born of the serenity arising from consciousness of the Ātman, *tat sukham* : that happiness *sāttvikam*: of Sattva in nature *proktam* : is declared.

36-37. Hear from Me now about the three kinds of pleasures, O the greatest of the Bhārata clan! That pleasure is said to be of the nature of Sattva which is gained by long practice of disciplines, which puts an end to all sorrows that man is heir to, which is like poison in the beginning but nectar-like at the end, and which springs from the serenity arising from the consciousness of the Ātman.

विषयेन्द्रियसंयोगाद्यत्तदग्रेऽमृतोपमम् ।
परिणामे विषमिव तत्सुखं राजसं स्मृतम् ॥ 38 ॥

Viṣay'endriya-saṁyogād yat tad agre'mṛt'opamam /
pariṇāme viṣam iva tat sukhaṁ rājasaṁ smṛtam //38//

Viṣay'endriya-saṁyogāt : By the union of the senses with their objects *yat* : which *tat* : that *agre* : in the beginning *amṛtopamam* : like nectar *pariṇāme* : in the end *viṣam iva* : like poison *tat sukham* : that pleasure *rājasam* : of the nature of Rajas *smṛtam* : is declared.

38. That pleasure is declared to be of the nature of Rajas, which is born of the union of the senses with their objects, which seems nectar-like in the beginning but turns to be poison in the end.

यदग्रे चानुबन्धे च सुखं मोहनमात्मनः ।
निद्रालस्यप्रमादोत्थं तत्तामसमुदाहृतम् ॥ 39 ॥

Yad agre c'ānubandhe ca sukhaṁ mohanam ātmanaḥ /
nidr'ālasya-pramād'otthaṁ tat tāmasam udāhṛtam //39//

Yat : Which *sukham* : pleasure *nidr'ālasya-pramād'ottham* : which springs from sleepiness, sloth and heedlessness, ***agre ca:*** in the beginning *anubandhe* : in the end *ca* : and *ātmanaḥ* : of the Ātman *mohanam* : delusive, *tat* : that *tāmasam* : born of Tamas *udāhṛtam* : is declared.

39. That pleasure is of the nature of Tamas, which springs from sleepiness, sloth and heedlessness, and which is delusive in its effect on the spirit from beginning to end.

न तदस्ति पृथिव्यां वा दिवि देवेषु वा पुनः ।
सत्त्वं प्रकृतिजैर्मुक्तं यदेभिः स्यात्त्रिभिर्गुणैः ॥ 40 ॥

Na tad asti pṛthivyāṁ vā divi deveṣu vā punaḥ /
sattvaṁ prakṛti-jair muktaṁ yad ebhiḥ syāt tribhir guṇaiḥ //40//

Prakṛtijaiḥ : born of Prakṛti *ebhiḥ* : by these *tribhiḥ* : three *guṇaiḥ* : Guṇas *muktam* : free from *sattvam* : being *yat* : which *syāt* : exists, *tat* : that *pṛthivyām* : on the earth *vā* : or *divi* : in the heavens *deveṣu* : among Devas *vā* : or *punaḥ* : again *na asti* : does not exist.

40. Nowhere, be it in this world or in the heavenly regions of the Devas, is there any being who is free from these three Guṇas of Nature (Prakṛti).

ब्राह्मणक्षत्रियविशां शूद्राणां च परंतप ।
कर्माणि प्रविभक्तानि स्वभावप्रभवैर्गुणैः ॥ 41 ॥

Brāhmaṇa-kṣatriya-viśām śūdrāṇāṁ ca paraṁtapa /
karmāṇi pravibhaktāni svabhāva-prabhavair-guṇaih //41//

Paraṁtapa : O great hero! *brāhmaṇa-kṣatriya-viśām* : of Brāhmaṇas, Kṣatriyas and Vaiśyas *śūdrāṇām* : of Sūdras *ca* : and *karmāṇi* : duties *svabhāva-prabhavaiḥ guṇaiḥ* : according to qualities born of their own nature *pravibhaktāni* : have been divided.

41. O great hero! The duties of Brāhmaṇas, Kṣatriyas, Vaiśyas and also of Sūdras have been divided according to the qualities born of their own nature.[5]

शमो दमस्तपः शौचं क्षान्तिरार्जवमेव च ।
ज्ञानं विज्ञानमास्तिक्यं ब्रह्मकर्म स्वभावजम् ॥ 42 ॥

Śamo damas-tapaḥ śaucaṁ kṣāntir-ārjavam eva ca /
jñānaṁ vijñānam āstikyaṁ brahma-karma svabhāva-jam //42//

Śamaḥ : Serenity *damaḥ* : control of the senses *tapaḥ* : austerity *śaucam* : purity *kṣāntiḥ* : forbearance *ārjavam* : straightforwardness *eva* : also *ca* : and *jñānam* : knowledge *vijñānam* : insight *āstikyam*: faith in a Supreme Being *svabhāvajam* : born of one's own nature *brahmakarma* : the duties of a Brāhmaṇa.

42. Serenity, control of the senses, austerity, purity, straightforwardness, knowledge, insight, and faith in the Supreme Being—these are a Brāhmaṇa's duties born of his own nature.

शौर्यं तेजो धृतिर्दाक्ष्यं युद्धे चाप्यपलायनम् ।
दानमीश्वरभावश्च क्षात्रं कर्म स्वभावजम् ॥ 43 ॥

Śauryaṁ tejo dhṛtir dākṣyaṁ yuddhe c'āpyapalāyanam /
dānam īsvara-bhāvaś ca kṣātraṁ karma svabhāva-jam //43//

Śauryam : Prowess *tejaḥ* : splendour of personality *dhṛtiḥ* : unfailing courage *dākṣyam* : resourcefulness *yuddhe apalāyanam* : not fleeing (dauntlessness) in battle *api* : also *ca* : and *dānam* : generosity *īsvarabhāvam* : lordliness, leadership *ca* : and *svabhāvajam* : born of one's own nature *kṣātram* : pertaining to a Kṣatriya *karma* : duty.

43. Prowess, splendour of personality, unfailing courage, resourcefulness, dauntlessness in battle, generosity, leadership—these are a Kṣatriya's duties born of his specific nature.

कृषिगौरक्ष्यवाणिज्यं वैश्यकर्म स्वभावजम् ।
परिचर्यात्मकं कर्म शूद्रस्यापि स्वभावजम् ॥ 44 ॥

Kṛṣi-gaurakṣya-vāṇijyaṁ vaiśya-karma svabhāva-jam /
paricary'ātmakaṁ karma śūdrasy'āpi svabhāva-jam //44//

Kṛṣi-gaurakṣya-vāṇijyam : Agriculture, cattle-rearing, and trade *svabhāvajam* : born of one's nature *vaiśya-karma*: duty of a Vaiśya; *paricaryātmakam* : subordinate service *śūdrasya* : of the Śūdra *api* : also *svabhāvajam* : born of one's nature.

44. Agriculture, cattle-rearing and trade form the duty of the Vaiśya springing from his own nature, while the natural duty of a Sūdra consists in subordinate service under others.

स्वे स्वे कर्मण्यभिरतः संसिद्धिं लभते नरः ।
स्वकर्मनिरतः सिद्धिं यथा विन्दति तच्छृणु ॥ 45 ॥

Sve sve karmaṇy abhirataḥ saṁsiddhiṁ labhate naraḥ /
sva-karma-nirataḥ siddhiṁ yathā vindati tac-chṛṇu //45//

Sve sve karmaṇi : In one's own (natural) duty *abhirataḥ* : devoted *naraḥ* : man *saṁsiddhim* : spiritual competency *labhate* : attains to; *svadharma-nirataḥ* : one devoted to one's own natural duty *yathā* : how *siddhim* : spiritual competency *vindati* : acquires, *tat* : that *śṛṇu* : hear.

45. By being devoted to one's own natural duty, man attains to spiritual competency. Now hear how devotion to one's own natural duty generates spiritual competency.[6]

यतः प्रवृत्तिर्भूतानां येन सर्वमिदं ततम् ।
स्वकर्मणा तमभ्यर्च्य सिद्धिं विन्दति मानवः ॥ 46 ॥

Yataḥ pravṛttir bhūtānāṁ yena sarvaṁ idaṁ tatam /
sva-karmaṇā tam abhyarcya siddhiṁ vindati mānavaḥ //46//

Yataḥ : From whom *bhūtānām* : of beings *pravṛttiḥ* : emanation, *yena* : by whom *idam* : this *sarvam* : all *tatam* : is pervaded, *tam* : Him *mānavaḥ* : man *svakarmaṇā* : by his own duty *abhyarcya* : worshipping *siddhim* : spiritual competency *vindati* : attains.

46. From whom all beings have emanated and by whom all this universe is pervaded—by worshipping Him through the dedicated performance of one's duty, man attains to spiritual competency (Siddhi).

श्रेयान्स्वधर्मो विगुणः परधर्मात्स्वनुष्ठितात् ।
स्वभावनियतं कर्म कुर्वन्नाप्नोति किल्बिषम् ॥ 47 ॥

Śreyān sva-dharmo viguṇaḥ para-dharmāt svanuṣṭhitāt /
svabhāva-niyataṁ karma kurvan n'āpnoti kilbiṣam //47//

Svanuṣṭhitāt : Than the well-performed *paradharmāt* : duty of another *viguṇaḥ* : without excellence *svadharmaḥ* : one's own duty *śreyān* : is more meritorious; *svabhāvaniyatam* : ordained according to one's nature *karma* : work *kurvan* : doing *kilbiṣam* : sin *na* : does not *āpnoti* : incur.

47. One's own duty, even if without excellence (i.e. inferio. in the scale of worldly values), is more meritorious spiritually than the apparently well-performed duty of another. For, no sin is incurred by one doing works ordained according to one's nature, (that is, in consonance with one's own natural evolution.)[7]

सहजं कर्म कौन्तेय सदोषमपि न त्यजेत् ।
सर्वारम्भा हि दोषेण धूमेनाग्निरिवावृताः ॥ 48 ॥

Sahajaṁ karma Kaunteya sadoṣam api na tyajet /
sarv'ārambhā hi doṣeṇa dhumen'āgnir iv'āvṛtāḥ //48//

Kaunteya : O son of Kuntī! *sahajam* : born with oneself *karma* : work *sadoṣam api* : even if attended with imperfections *na* : do not *tyajet* : abandon; *sarvārambhāḥ* : all undertakings *dhūmena* : by smoke *agniḥ* : fire *iva* : as *doṣeṇa* : by imperfections *āvṛtaḥ* : covered *hi* : indeed.

48. O son of Kuntī! Do not abandon the duty that is natural to you, even if some imperfections are incidental to it. For there is no undertaking without some imperfections, even as there is no fire without a covering of smoke.

असक्तबुद्धिः सर्वत्र जितात्मा विगतस्पृहः ।
नैष्कर्म्यसिद्धिं परमां संन्यासेनाधिगच्छति ॥ 49 ॥

Asakta-buddhiḥ sarvatra jit'ātmā vigata-spṛhaḥ /
naiṣkarmya-siddhiṁ paramāṁ saṁnyāsen'ādhigacchati //49//

Sarvatra : Everywhere *asaktabuddhiḥ* : with mind unattached *jitātmā* : self-subdued *vigataspṛhaḥ* : with all desires abandoned *saṁnyāsena* : by renunciation *paramām* : supreme *naiṣkarmya-siddhim* : perfection of transcendence of work *adhigacchati* : attains.

49. Completely non-attached, self-subdued, and desireless, an aspirant attains the supreme perfection of transcendence of work through renunciation.[8]

सिद्धिं प्राप्तो यथा ब्रह्म तथाप्नोति निबोध मे ।
समासेनैव कौन्तेय निष्ठा ज्ञानस्य या परा ॥ 50 ॥

Siddhiṁ prāpto yathā brahma tath'āpnoti nibodha me /
samāsenaiva Kaunteya niṣṭhā jñānasya yā parā //50//

Siddhim : Perfection in transcendence of work *prāptaḥ* : one who has attained to *yā* : which *jñānasya* : of knowledge *parā* : highest *niṣṭhā* : consummation *brahma* : Brahma *yathā* : how *āpnoti* : attains, *tathā* : that *samāsena* : in brief *eva* : even *me* : from Me *nibodha* : learn.

50. Now hear from Me in brief how one who is established in the perfection of transcendence of work attains to Brahma, the highest consummation of knowledge.

बुद्ध्या विशुद्धया युक्तो धृत्यात्मानं नियम्य च ।
शब्दादीन्विषयांस्त्यक्त्वा रागद्वेषौ व्युदस्य च ॥ 51 ॥

विविक्तसेवी लघ्वाशी यतवाक्कायमानसः ।
ध्यानयोगपरो नित्यं वैराग्यं समुपाश्रितः ॥ 52 ॥

अहंकारं बलं दर्पं कामं क्रोधं परिग्रहम् ।
विमुच्य निर्ममः शान्तो ब्रह्मभूयाय कल्पते ॥ 53 ॥

Buddhyā viśuddhayā yukto dhṛtyā'tmānaṁ niyamya ca /
sabdādīn viṣayāṁs tyaktvā rāga-dveṣau vyudasya ca //51//

Vivikta-sevī laghvāśī yata-vāk-kāya-mānasaḥ /
dhyāna-yoga-paro nityaṁ vairāgyaṁ samupāśritaḥ //52//

Ahaṁkāraṁ balaṁ darpaṁ kāmaṁ krodhaṁ parigraham /
vimucya nirmamaḥ śānto brahma-bhūyāya kalpate //53//

Viśuddhayā : With purified *buddhyā* : intelligence *yuktaḥ* : endowed with, *dhṛtyā* : by firmness *ātmānam* : the self *niyamya* : controlling *ca* : and, *sabdādīn viṣayān* : sensations like sound and the rest *tyaktvā* : abandoning, *rāga-dveṣau* : attachments and antagonisms *vyudasya* : having abandoned *ca* : and, *viviktasevī* : resorting to solitary places *laghvāśī* : eating sparingly, *yata-vākkāyamānasaḥ* : having speech, body and mind under control, *nityam* : always *dhyānayogaparaḥ* : devoted to meditation, *vairāyam* : dispassion *samupāśritaḥ* : depending on, i.e. established in, *ahaṁkāram* : egoism, conceit *balam* : strength, violence *darpam* : arrogance *kāmam* : lust *krodham* : anger *parigraham* : property, possessiveness *vimucya* : abandoning *nirmamaḥ* : selfless *śāntaḥ* : tranquil *brahma-bhūyāya* : for attainment of Brahma-nature (Ātman consciousness) *kalpate* : becomes fit.

51-53. Endowed with a purifed intellect, established in self-control, abandoning the life of the senses as also attachments and antagonisms; frequenting solitary places; reducing food to the minimum; having speech, body and mind under control; ever meditative; endued with dispassion; abandoning conceit, violence, lust, anger and possessiveness; self-less and tranquil, he becomes fit for beatification in Brahman-consciousness (Ātman-consciousness.).[9]

ब्रह्मभूतः प्रसन्नात्मा न शोचति न काङ्क्षति ।
समः सर्वेषु भूतेषु मद्भक्तिं लभते पराम् ॥ 54 ॥

Brahma-bhūtaḥ prasannātmā na śocati na kāṅkṣati /
samaḥ sarveṣu bhūteṣu mad-bhaktiṁ labhate parām //54//

Brahmabhūtaḥ : Brahma-become *prasannātmā* : tranquil in spirit, ***na śocati na kāṅkṣati***: neither grieves nor desires; ***sarveṣu bhūteṣu*** : to all beings *samaḥ* : alike *parām* : the supreme *madbhaktim* : devotion to Me *labhate* : obtains.

54. Brahma-become (established in Ātman-Consciousness), tranquil in spirit, free from grief and passions, and regarding all beings alike, he attains supreme devotion to Me.

भक्त्या मामभिजानाति यावान्यश्चास्मि तत्त्वतः ।
ततो मां तत्त्वतो ज्ञात्वा विशते तदनन्तरम् ॥ 55 ॥

Bhaktyā mām abhijānāti yāvān yaś c'āsmi tattvataḥ /
tato māṁ tattvato jñātvā viśate tad-anantaram //55//

Bhaktyā : By devotion *mām* : Me : *yāvān* : how much, what *yaḥ* : who *ca* : and *asmi* : I am, *tattvataḥ* : in truth and in reality *abhijānāti* : he knows; *tataḥ* : then *mām* : Me *tattvataḥ* : in truth and in reality *jñātvā* : knowing, *tad-anantaram* : forthwith or at once *viśate* : enters into Me.

55. By devotion does he come to know Me—both my extent and My essence. Knowing Me thus in truth and in reality. he enters into Me at once.

सर्वकर्माण्यपि सदा कुर्वाणो मद्व्यपाश्रयः ।
मत्प्रसादादवाप्नोति शाश्वतं पदमव्ययम् ॥ 56 ॥

Sarva-karmāṇy api sadā kurvāṇo mad-vyapāśrayaḥ /
mat-prasādād avāpnoti śāśvataṁ padam avyayam //56//

Sarvakarmāṇi : All kinds of work *api* : also *sadā* : always *kurvāṇaḥ* : performing, *madvyapāśrayaḥ* : he who has taken refuge in Me *matprasādāt* : by My grace *śāśvatam* : eternal *avyayam* : indestructible *padam* : state *avāpnoti* : obtains.

56. Though performing every kind of work always, he who has taken refuge in Me shall, by My grace, attain to the eternal and indestructible state of Mokṣa (spiritual liberation).[10]

चेतसा सर्वकर्माणि मयि संन्यस्य मत्परः ।
बुद्धियोगमुपाश्रित्य मच्चित्तः सततं भव ॥ 57 ॥

Cetasā sarva-karmāṇi mayi saṁnyasya mat-paraḥ /
buddhi-yogam upāśritya mac-cittaḥ satataṁ bhava //57//

Cetasā : With the mind *sarva-karmāṇi* : all actions *mayi* : in Me *saṁnyasya* : resigning, *mat-paraḥ* : intensely devoted to Me *buddhi-yogam* : communion of intellectual love *upāśritya* : adopting, *mac-cittaḥ* : mind constantly fixed in Me, *satatam:* always *bhava:* be

57. Mentally resigning all actions to Me (in respect of their fruits and agency), devoting yourself intensely to Me, and ever practising the communion of intellectual love, be you ever established in the thought of Me.

मच्चित्तः सर्वदुर्गाणि मत्प्रसादात्तरिष्यसि ।
अथ चेत्त्वमहंकारान्न श्रोष्यसि विनङ्क्ष्यसि ॥ 58 ॥

Mac-cittaḥ sarva-durgāṇi mat-prasādāt tariṣyasi /
atha cet tvam ahaṁkārān na śroṣyasi vinaṅkṣyasi //58//

Maccittaḥ : Established in My thought *tvam* : you *mat-prasādāt* : by My grace *sarva durgāṇi: all* obstacles *tariṣyasi:* will overcome; *atha* : but *tvam* : you *ahaṅkārāt* : due to self-conceit *na* : not *śroṣyasi* : listen *cet* : if *vinaṅkṣyasi* : you will perish.

58. If you are thus ever in communion with Me in mind, you will overcome every obstacle. But if, out of self-conceit, you do not listen to Me, destruction will be your fate.

यदहंकारमाश्रित्य न योत्स्य इति मन्यसे ।
मिथ्यैष व्यवसायस्ते प्रकृतिस्त्वां नियोक्ष्यति ॥ 59 ॥

Yad ahaṁkāram āśritya na yotsya iti manyase
mithy'aiṣa vyavasāyas te prakṛtis tvāṁ niyokṣyati //59//

Ahaṁkāram : Self-conceit *āśritya* : taking recourse to *na yotsye* : I will not fight *iti* : thus *yat* : which *manyase* : think. *eṣah* : this *te* : your *vyavasāyaḥ* : resolution *mithyā* : vain; *prakṛtiḥ* : Nature *tvām* : you *niyokṣyati* ; will compel.

59. Vain is your resolve not to fight, born as it is of self-conceit. Nature will compel you.

स्वभावजेन कौन्तेय निबद्धः स्वेन कर्मणा ।
कर्तुं नेच्छसि यन्मोहात्करिष्यस्यवशोऽपि तत् ॥ 60 ॥

Svabhāva-jena Kaunteya nibaddhaḥ svena karmaṇā /
kartuṁ n'ecchasi yan mohāt kariṣyasyavaśo'pi tat //60//

Kaunteya : O son of Kuntī! *svabhāva-jena* : sprung from one's own nature *svena karmaṇā* : by duties natural to one *nibaddhaḥ* : fettered, *mohāt* : out of delusion *yat* : which *na* : not *icchasi* : do not desire, *tat* : that *api* : even *avaśaḥ* : helplessly *kariṣyasi* : you will do.

60. O son of Kuntī! Duties which your natural tendencies have imposed upon you, but which out of delusion you refuse to do, even them you will have to perform by the compulsion of Nature.

ईश्वरः सर्वभूतानां हृद्देशेऽर्जुन तिष्ठति ।
भ्रामयन्सर्वभूतानि यन्त्रारूढानि मायया ॥ 61 ॥

Iśvaraḥ sarva-bhūtānāṁ hṛd-deśe'rjuna tiṣṭhati /
bhrāmayan sarva-bhūtāni yantr'ārūḍhāni māyayā //61//

Arjuna : O Arjuna! *yantrārūḍhāni* : mounted on a wheel *sarva-bhūtāni* : all beings *māyayā* : by his mysterious power : *bhrāmayan* : revolving, *īśvaraḥ* : the Lord *sarva-bhūtānām* : of all beings *hṛddeśe* : in the heart *tiṣṭhati* : dwells.

61. O Arjuna! The Lord dwells in the heart of all beings revolving them all by His mysterious Power Māyā, as if they were objects mounted on a machine.

तमेव शरणं गच्छ सर्वभावेन भारत ।
तत्प्रसादात्परां शान्तिं स्थानं प्राप्स्यसि शाश्वतम् ॥ 62 ॥

Tam eva śaraṇaṁ gaccha sarva-bhāvena Bhārata /
tat-prasādāt parāṁ śāntiṁ sthānaṁ prāpsyasi śāśvatam //62//

Bhārata : O scion of Bharata's clan *sarvabhāvena* : with your whole being *tam* : Him *eva* : even *śaraṇam* : as refuge *gaccha* : go to; *tatprasādāt* : by His grace *parām* : supreme *śāntim* : peace *śāśvatam* : everlasting *sthānam* : abode *prāpsyasi* : will attain.

62. O scion of Bhārata's clan! Seek refuge in Him, making a total surrender of your being—body, mind and soul. By His grace you shall attain to supreme peace and the everlasting abode.

इति ते ज्ञानमाख्यातं गुह्याद्गुह्यतरं मया ।
विमृश्यैतदशेषेण यथेच्छसि तथा कुरु ॥ 63 ॥

Iti te jñānam ākhyātaṁ guhyād guhyataraṁ mayā /
vimṛśy'aitad aśeṣeṇa yath'ecchasi tathā kuru //63//

Iti : Thus *guhyāt* : than any secret *guhyataram* : more secret *jñānam* : wisdom *mayā* : by Me *te* : to you *ākhyātam* : has been imparted; *etat* : this *aśeṣeṇa* : in its entirety *vimṛśya* : having reflected upon *yathā* : as *icchasi* : wish, think fit *tathā* : so *kuru* : do.

63. Thus have I imparted to you wisdom which is more secret (profound) than all that is secret (profound). Reflecting over this whole teaching, do as you think fit.[11]

सर्वगुह्यतमं भूयः शृणु मे परमं वचः ।
इष्टोऽसि मे दृढमिति ततो वक्ष्यामि ते हितम् ॥ 64 ॥

Sarva-guhyatamaṁ bhūyaḥ śṛṇu me paramam vacaḥ /
iṣṭo'si me dṛḍham iti tato vakṣyāmi te hitam //64//

Sarva-guhyatamam : The profoundest spiritual wisdom *me* : My *paramam* : supreme *vacaḥ* : word *bhūyaḥ* : again *śṛṇu* : hear; *me* My *dṛḍham* : firm *iṣṭah* : beloved *asi* : you are; *iti* : thus *tataḥ* : therefore *te* : your *hitam* : what is beneficial *vakṣyāmi* : I shall speak.

64. Listen again to My supreme word, the profoundest of all spiritual teachings. You are well beloved of Me; and so I shall tell you what is beneficial to you.[12]

मन्मना भव मद्भक्तो मद्याजी मां नमस्कुरु ।
मामेवैष्यसि सत्यं ते प्रतिजाने प्रियोऽसि मे ॥ 65 ॥

Man-manā bhava mad-bhakto mad-yājī māṁ namas-kuru /
mām ev'aiṣyasi satyaṁ te pratijāne priyo'si me //65//

Manmanāḥ : With mind absorbed in Me *bhava* : be, *madbhaktaḥ* : be My devotee, *madyājī* : be my worshipper; *mām* : Me *namaskuru* : salute, prostrate, be resigned; *mām eva* : Me alone *eṣyasi* : you shall come to ; *te* : to you *satyam* : in truth *pratijāne* : I promise; *me* : of Me *priyaḥ* : beloved *asi* : you are.

65. Let your mind be engrossed in Me. Be devoted to Me. Offer worship to Me. Be resigned to Me. Beloved as you are of me, I pledge in troth you shall come to Me alone.

सर्वधर्मान्परित्यज्य मामेकं शरणं व्रज ।
अहं त्वा सर्वपापेभ्यो मोक्षयिष्यामि मा शुचः ॥ 66 ॥

Sarva-dharmān parityajya mām ekaṁ śaraṇaṁ vraja /
ahaṁ tvā sarva-pāpebhyo mokṣayiṣyāmi mā śucaḥ //66//

Sarvadharmān : All Dharmas *parityajya* : abandoning, *mām* : to Me *ekam* : the One (or only) *śaraṇam* : refuge *vraja* : take; *aham* : I *tvām* : you *sarva-pāpebhyaḥ* : from all sins *mokṣayiṣyāmi* : will free; *mā* : do not *śucaḥ* : grieve.

66. Abandoning dependence on all Dharmas (or on human efforts at moral and spiritual upliftment), come to Me as the only Refuge. Grieve not; I will deliver you from all sins.

इदं ते नातपस्काय नाभक्ताय कदाचन ।
न चाशुश्रूषवे वाच्यं न च मां योऽभ्यसूयति ॥ 67 ॥

Idaṁ te n'ātapaskāya n'ābhaktāya kadācana /
na c'āśuśrūṣave vācyaṁ na ca māṁ yo'bhyasūyati //67//

Idam : This knowledge *atapaskāya* : to one who is not austere in life *kadācana* : at any time *te* : by you *na vācyam* : not to be spoken; *abhaktāya na ca* : not to one devoid of devotion ; *aśuśrūṣave na ca* : nor to one who has not rendered service; *yaḥ* : who *mām* : Me *abhyasūyati* : cavils *na ca* : and not.

67. This should on no account be imparted to those who do not practise austere living, who have no devotion to Me, who cavil at Me, and are devoid of the discipline of service.[13]

य इदं परमं गुह्यं मद्भक्तेष्वभिधास्यति ।
भक्तिं मयि परां कृत्वा मामेवैष्यत्यसंशयः ॥ 68 ॥

Ya idam paramaṁ guhyaṁ mad-bhakteṣv abhidhāsyati /
bhaktiṁ mayi parāṁ kṛtvā mām ev'aiṣyaty asaṁśayaḥ //68//

Paramam guhyam : Supremely profound doctrine *idam* : this *madbhakteṣu* : among My devotees *yaḥ* : who *abhidhāsyati* : imparts *saḥ* : he *mayi* : in Me *parām* : supreme *bhaktim* : devotion, loving service *kṛtvā* : having done or practised *asamśayaḥ* : undoubtedly *mām* : Me *eva* : even *eṣyati* : shall reach.

68. He who teaches this supremely profound doctrine among men devoted to Me, having thereby offered to Me the highest form of loving service, shall undoubtedly come to Me alone.

न च तस्मान्मनुष्येषु कश्चिन्मे प्रियकृत्तमः ।
भविता न च मे तस्मादन्यः प्रियतरो भुवि ॥ 69 ॥

Na ca tasmān manuṣyeṣu kaścin me priya-kṛttamaḥ /
bhavitā na ca me tasmād anyaḥ priyataro bhuvi //69//

Tasmāt : Than him *me* : to Me *priyakṛttamaḥ* : one who performs a service more pleasing *manuṣyeṣu* : among men *kaścit* : any one *na ca* : not and; *me* : to Me *tasmāt* : than Him *priyataraḥ* : more dear *anyaḥ* : another *bhuvi* : in the world *bhavitā* : shall be *na ca* : and not.

69. No man can do anything more pleasing to Me than he, and nor shall any one on earth be dearer to Me than he.

अध्येष्यते च य इमं धर्म्यं संवादमावयोः ।
ज्ञानयज्ञेन तेनाहमिष्टः स्यामिति मे मतिः ॥ 70 ॥

Adhyeṣyate ca ya imaṁ dharmyaṁ samvādam āvayoḥ /
jñāna-yajñena tenā'ham iṣṭaḥ syām iti me matiḥ //70//

Āvayoḥ : Of us both *dharmyam* : sacred *imam* : this *samvādam* : conversation *yaḥ* : who *ca* : and *adhyeṣyate* : shall study, *tena* : by him *aham* : I *jñānayajñena* : by the sacrifice of knowledge *iṣṭaḥ* : worshipped *syām* : I shall have been *iti* : thus *me* : My *matiḥ* : view.

70. It is My view that he who studies this conversation between us should be regarded as adoring Me with a sacrifice of knowledge.

श्रद्धावाननसूयश्च श‍ृणुयादपि यो नरः ।
सोऽपि मुक्तः शुभाँल्लोकान्प्राप्नुयात्पुण्यकर्मणाम् ॥ 71 ॥

Śraddhāvān anasūyaś-ca srṇuyād api yo naraḥ /
so'pi muktaḥ śubhān lokān prāpnuyāt puṇya-karmaṇām //71//

Yaḥ : Whichever *naraḥ* : man *śraddhāvān* : having faith *anasūyaḥ* : without fault-finding *ca* : and *sṛṇuyāt* : will hear *api* : even *saḥ* : he *api* : even *muktaḥ* : being liberated, *puṇyakarmaṇām* : of those performing righteous deeds *śubhān* : happy *lokān* : regions *prāpnuyāt* : shall attain.

71. Even a man who listens to this holy conversation between us, with deep faith and receptiveness, shall atain to liberation and the happy regions open to righteous men.

कच्चिदेतत् श्रुतं पार्थ त्वयैकाग्रेण चेतसा ।
कच्चिदज्ञानसंमोहः प्रनष्टस्ते धनंजय ॥ 72 ॥

Kaccid etac chrutaṁ Pārtha tvay'aik'āgreṇa cetasā /
kaccid ajñāna-saṁmohaḥ praṇaṣṭas te dhanaṁjaya //72//

Pārtha : O son of Pṛthā! *etat* : this *tvayā* : by you *ekāgreṇa* : with concentrated *cetasā* : mind *śrutam* : heard, *kaccid* : whether *dhanaṁjaya* : O Dhanaṁjaya or O Arjuna! *te* : your *ajñānasaṁmohaḥ* : delusion born of ignorance *praṇaṣṭaḥ* : destroyed *kaccid* : whether.

72. Has this teaching been heard by you, O Arjuna, with a concentrated mind? Has all delusion born of ignorance been dispelled from you, O Dhananjaya?

अर्जुन उवाच

नष्टो मोहः स्मृतिर्लब्धा त्वत्प्रसादान्मयाच्युत ।
स्थितोऽस्मि गतसन्देहः करिष्ये वचनं तव ॥ 73 ॥

Arjuna uvāca:

Naṣṭo mohaḥ smṛtir labdhā tvat-prasādān may'ācyuta /
sthito'smi gata-sandehaḥ kariṣye vacanaṁ tava //73//

Acyuta : O undecaying one! *tvatprasādāt* : by Thy grace *mohaḥ* : delusion *naṣṭaḥ* : is destroyed; *smritiḥ* : memory of one's nature as the Ātman *mayā* : by me *labdhā* : obtained; *gata-sandehaḥ* : with doubts dispelled *sthitaḥ* : firm *asmi* : I am; *tava* : Thy *vacanam* : words *kariṣye* : I will do.

Arjuna said:

73. My delusion has been dispelled and my memory restored by Thy grace, O Undecaying Lord! I now stand firm, with all my doubts cleared, ready to execute Thy command.

संजय उवाच

इत्यहं वासुदेवस्य पार्थस्य च महात्मनः ।
संवादमिममश्रौषमद्भुतं रोमहर्षणम् ॥ ७४ ॥

Sañjaya uvāca

Ity ahaṁ Vāsudevasya pārthasya ca mahātmanaḥ /
saṁvādam imam aśrauṣam adbhutaṁ roma-harṣaṇam //74//

Iti : Thus *aham* : I *vāsudevasya* : of Vāsudeva, Kṛṣṇa *mahātmanaḥ pārthasya* : of the high-souled Pārtha *ca* : and *adbhutam* : wonderful *roma-harṣaṇam* : causing hair to stand on end *imam* : this *saṁvādam* : conversation *aśrauṣam* : have heard.

Sañjaya said:

74. Thus have I heard, with my hair standing on end, this wonderful conversation between Kṛṣṇa and the high-souled son of Pṛthā.

व्यासप्रसादात् श्रुतवानेतद्गुह्यमहं परम् ।
योगं योगेश्वरात्कृष्णात्साक्षात्कथयतः स्वयम् ॥ ७५ ॥

Vyāsa-prasādāc chrutavān etad guhyam ahaṁ param /
yogaṁ yog'eśvarāt kṛṣṇāt sākṣāt kathayataḥ svayam //75//

Vyāsa-prasādāt : By the grace of sage Vyāsa *guhyam* : profound *param* : supreme *etat* : this *yogam* : Yoga *svayam* : himself *kathayataḥ* : teaching *yogeśvarāt* : from the Lord of Yoga *Kṛṣṇāt* : from Kṛṣṇa *aham* : I *sākṣāt* : directly *śrutavān* : heard.

75. Thus did I, by Vyāsa's grace, directly hear Kṛṣṇa, the Lord of Yoga, Himself teaching this Yoga, profound and supreme.

राजन्संस्मृत्य संस्मृत्य संवादमिममद्‌भुतम् ।
केशवार्जुनयोः पुण्यं हृष्यामि च मुहुर्मुहुः ॥ 76 ॥

Rājan saṁsmṛtya-saṁsmṛtya saṁvādam imam adbhutam /
Keśav'ārjunayoḥ puṇyaṁ hṛṣyāmi ca muhur muhuḥ //76//

Rājan : O King! *Keśav'ārjunayoḥ* : of Kṛṣṇa and Arjuna *adbhutam* : astounding *puṇyam* : sacred *imam* : this *saṁvādam* : dialogue *saṁsmṛtya saṁsmṛtya* : remembering again and again *muhuḥ muhuḥ ca* : again and again *hṛṣyāmi* : rejoice.

76. Again and again, O king, does the memory of that sacred and astounding dialogue between Keśava and Arjuna come to my mind, causing no end of joy.

तच्च संस्मृत्य संस्मृत्य रूपमत्यद्‌भुतं हरेः ।
विस्मयो मे महान्राजन्हृष्यामि च पुनः पुनः ॥ 77 ॥

Tac ca saṁsmṛtya saṁsmṛtya rūpam atyadbhutaṁ Hareḥ /
vismayo me mahān rājan hṛṣyāmi ca punaḥ-punaḥ //77//

Rājan : O King! *Hareḥ* : of Hari *atyadbhutam* : most marvellous *tat:* that *ca:* and *rūpam:* form *saṁsmṛtya saṁsmṛtya:* remembering and remembering *me* : my *vismayaḥ* : wonder *mahān* : is great *punaḥ punaḥ* : again and again *hṛṣyāmi* : I rejoice *ca* : and

77. Again and again does that most wondrous form of Hari arise to my mind, generating great astonishment and endless thrills of joy.

यत्र योगेश्वरः कृष्णो यत्र पार्थो धनुर्धरः ।
तत्र श्रीर्विजयो भूतिर्ध्रुवा नीतिर्मतिर्मम ॥ 78 ॥

Yatra yog'eśvaraḥ Kṛṣṇo yatra Pārtho dhanur-dharaḥ /
tatra śrīr vijayo bhūtir dhrūvā nītir matir mama //78//

Yatra : where *yogeśvaraḥ* : the Lord of Yoga *kṛṣṇaḥ* : Kṛṣṇa, *yatra* : where *dhanurdharaḥ* : armed with bow *pārthaḥ* : Arjuna, *tatra* : there *śrīḥ*: good fortune *vijayaḥ* : victory *bhūtiḥ* : prosperity *dhruvā* : enduring, sound *nītiḥ* : policy, *mama* : my *matiḥ* : conviction.

78. Wherever there is Kṛṣṇa, the Lord of Yoga, accompanied by Arjuna wielding the bow—there reign good fortune, victory, prosperity and sound policy. Such is my conviction.

ओं तत्सदिति श्रीमद्भगवद्गीतासूपनिषत्सु ब्रह्मविद्यायां
योगशास्त्रे श्रीकृष्णार्जुनसंवादे मोक्षसंन्यासयोगो
नामाष्टादशोऽध्यायः ॥ 18 ॥

श्रीकृष्णार्पणमस्तु

NOTES

1. *Vrs.*1-7: *Saṁnyāsa* and *Tyāga* are words meaning more or less the same. Here the distinction between them is said to consist in this: *Saṁnyāsa* is the abandonment of works that are generally done for the sake of rewards accruing in this world and the next. *Tyāga* is the abandonment of fruits of all actions i.e., continuing in the sphere of actions without any claim to the fruits of actions. The first of these expressions seems to have special reference to Vedic ritualism which prescribes many ritualistic actions promising ample rewards in the heareafter.

Among the followers of *Saṁnyāsa,* the Lord now points to some who maintain that all actions, whether with fruits or without fruits, are causes of bondage, and therefore form an evil that deserves to be abandoned. The Lord differs from this view and maintains that His final view regarding abandonment is that only desire-prompted works need be abandoned, and that devotional and altruistic works like worship, austerity, and service through charity should be done by all, because they are holy and sanctifying.

It is clear from the final assertion of the Lord in verse 6 that the Gītā teaching requires all, whether they are men of knowledge or otherwise, to do worship of God and service of fellow-beings.

It is maintained by some schools of thought that this assertion of the Lord in favour of work has reference only to men in ignorance and to the Yogins, whereas the Sāṁkhyas (knowing ones) are free from every kind of works and are free also from the compulsion of duty. There is however nothing in the context to support such a view restricting it to the ignorant only. While the Gītā does not object or criticise the pure Sāṁkhyan view of abandonment of every form of work accompanied with knowledge or even as a preparatory discipline, its preference is for all aspirants undertaking some works of the nature of worship and philanthropy, as also of the nature of duty, at all stages of spiritual development. *Niṣkāma-karma* or unselfish work is an all-pervasive doctrine of the Gītā. The aspirant abandons all the fruits to the Lord, and the enlightened one abandons the sense of agency also to Him, seeing the Divine Will working through the wills of all. The enlightened one is free from the promptings of the ego in all work he undertakes.

2. *Vr.*11: This verse confirms what was said earlier that man at all stages of spiritual development should engage in works of the nature of worship and service of fellow beings. The clinching argument given in support of it is that no one who has got a body can live without any work. There is no living being without a body, including the enlightened Sāṁkhya. So the expression has to be interpreted, as 'one with body-consciousness.' Every one except one merged in perpetual Samadhi has body-consciousness. It therefore means that work is a universal law binding all men. So the best an aspirant can do is to offer to the Lord the fruits of works and the sense of agency.

3. *Vr.*12: The word '*Saṁnyāsin*' is a special term applied to those who have taken to the fourth stage of life. The expression '*Saṁnyāsins*', as used here, includes those of the fourth Order who eschew all work after enlightenment, as well as others who continue to work, whether they be *Saṁnyāsins* in the Āśrama sense or are persons without the emblems of *Saṁnyāsa*, provided they resign the fruits of work and the sense of agency to the Lord. In other words according to the Gītā workless *Saṁnyāsins* with knowledge, as also working *Saṁnyāsins* and non-*Saṁnyāsins* who offer the fruits of work and sense of agency to the Lord—all alike are eligible for liberation.

4. *Vrs.*13-17: The five factors mentioned as involved in work are all aspects of Prakṛti, and as such distinct from the Ātman. Ignorance is the state in which the Ātman, who is distinct from the conglomeration of these five factors, identifies himself with this conglomeration and feels himself to be the performer of its activities. This identification is experienced as the I-sense. If this false identification is overcome, there is none to own an act and its consequence, beyond the unconscious elements of Prakṛti. This is the experience of the knowing one; all his so-called actions, whether good or bad, are amoral, as there is no 'I' to own them. The act of killing is mentioned here only because the teaching is in the context of battle. It only means that actions in general become amoral in the case of a knowing one, and not that a licence is given to him for all kinds of unethical acts. If however, in the fulfilment of the world-mission, a knowing one happens to do actions that look unethical from the ordinary point of view, it has no such effect on him; they are amoral just like any event in Nature, because there is no ego behind such actions. Sri Ramakrishna compares the actions of knowing ones to a burnt rope. In shape it looks like a rope even after burning, but it has lost the power of binding.

5. *Vrs.*41-44: A great doctrine of the social philosophy of ancient India, regarding the fourfold class system, is here propounded. There has been no doctrine so much misapplied, misunderstood and misrepresented as this doctrine. The four *Varṇas* of Brāhmaṇa, Kṣatriya, Vaiśya and Śūdra are today and for a long time past, understood as four hereditary castes. But the Varṇas, as understood by the best Indian thinkers, are not castes based on birth in particular groups, but character types based on the domination of the *Sāttvika, Rājasika* and *Tāmasika* elements entering into the constitution of their body-mind, and this is determined by their evolution in their past lives. At least such is the Gītā view. To have identified character types with endogamous social groups is nothing but an aberration. It is in regard to the fourfold class based on character that the Lord says in 4.13 *Cāturvarṇyam mayā sṛṣṭam*—the Order of four classes is My creation. Here also (verse 41) he speaks of duties pertaining to them as born of the constituents of Nature forming their body-mind. See also Notes on Gītā 4.18.

These four character types are universal all the world over

and the prosperity of a society will depend on the man of the right nature and character being put to the right type of duty. For the individuals also doing the duty that is natural to his psycho-physical constitution, is the way of higher evolution.

6. *Vr*.45-46: These two great verses of the Gītā link man's social duties with spiritual discipline. By cultivating a special attitude towards work, work is turned into worship, and the distance between the shrine room and the work-spot disappears. This philosophy is based upon a fundamental faith that this world and the progress of life in it are all under the guidance of a Supreme Intelligence, who is the master of it all, and whose will is expressed in all its movements. If man has got this faith, man ceases to be self-centred. He comes to view himself as a worker of God, and all that he does comes to be done with a sense of dedication to Him. Such work as accrues to one according to one's nature and is done with a spirit of dedication, is called *Svadharma,* one's natural duty. This outlook on one's work makes a man free from corruption and negligence, and induces him to put his best effort into his work. If an attitude of this type were accepted in a society as a whole, it will be the best social philosophy, besides being a spiritual doctrine. It will secure the social good as also bring about the individual's spiritual evolution.

A natural objection to this way of understanding *Cāturvarṇya* (the society with fourfold division) is that all commentators understood the four Varṇas as endogamous groups called castes, and the 'natural duty' (Svadharma) of theirs as the profession that was traditionally and scripturally alloted to those groups under the four distinctive names. Such interpretations of the Gītā were given at a time when these endogamous caste groups were a recognised feature of Indian society, and thinkers considered birth in a group as tantamount to character type. The mistake of such identification was obvious to many thinkers of the past. So some of them have made some kind of amends for it by admitting that if great disparity in quality is found in the actual quality of a Kṣatriya with the traditionally ascribed qualities, he can become a Brāhmaṇa. But all rationality seems to have been neutralised by the very strong prejudice in favour of endogamy.

Stratification into four classes of the priests, the nobility, agriculturists and traders, and serfs existed in all ancient societies, and even among the modern European races, until industrialisation, quick travel, and the modern idea of a welfare State whittled down the importance and practicability of endogamous social groups. But in Indian society with a tradition of more than ten thousand years perhaps, social systems got crystallised into rigid forms, and classes lost their fluidity and became organised as rigid castes. Consequently class duties came to be considered as identical with the caste duties of particular hereditary groups, and consequently all the shortcomings of the modern caste system of Indian society came into vogue.

But what the Lord speaks of here as *Cāturvarṇya* should never be identified with castes, because the *Varṇa* is said to be solely dependent on character formed by the Guṇas of Prakṛti. It is only an ideal grouping based on psychological principle and not on rigid hereditary basis.

Besides, the Gītā is a universal Gospel addressed to all mankind, for all time, and not merely to the Indian society of a particular age. In no part of the world except in India, caste system strictly based on birth seems to have existed. Loose classes there have been, but not rigid castes with unchangeable duties and occupations for subsistence. So the old commentators have done great injustice to Sri Kṛṣṇa in watering down the significance of his message as relevent only to members of the rigid Indian social system.

The only practical way of applying the Gītā teaching in this respect today is to consider the duty to which one is called, as one's Svadharma. Strictly Svadharma is work according to one's nature. But until an ideal and efficient social system comes into vogue, it may not be possibe to give every one a work for which he is suited by his character type. What could be done today, if one's duty is not according to one's nature, is to change it for a more suitable one, considering the former as *Paradharma,* the duty of another type of character. But today most men are found seeking not a duty temperamentally suitable to them, but what will bring them the maximum income. When a duty is valued solely for the income it fetches, it ceases to be a pursuit of a Dharma or a spiritual value. Receiving remuneration for services is unavoidable for man in the world, but what is unspiritual is to value the work only for its remuneration, forgetting that the work he does is an offering to God, irrespective of the remuneration he gets.

It is said in Verse 46 that when one's duty is discharged with the attitude that it is an offering to the Supreme Being, who is the creator and master of the worlds, then in the long run the man who practises such a discipline attains *Siddhi*—spiritual competency. The word *Siddhi* is used in many senses in the Gītā. Its general meaning is the 'attainment of the end in view of an undertaking'. In occultism the word is used to indicate attainment of psychic powers. It is used to mean spiritual perfection as also the physical enlightened person.

Here it cannot mean ultimate perfection. For, further stages of development are given hereafter. What is meant is that one devoted to Svadharma reaches an advanced stage of development through the dedicated performance of it. But if the proper attitude of dedication is to be maintained towards work, intensive practice of meditation and worship is simultaneously necessary. Discharge of Svardharma then ceases to be mere work, but work-cum-intensive worship, integrated into a single discipline.

Whether this combination should be continued throughout the higher stages of development, or whether works are to be abandoned at an advanced stage in preference to an exclusive contemplative life, is a moot question on which commentators have differed. The Advaitins maintain that all works have to be abandoned at this stage. Where the Gītā passages seem to imply otherwise and to advocate a kind of spiritual perfection in which dedicated and disinterested work is given a place at all stages of spiritual life—this school painstakingly interprets such passages as favouring their doctrine of total cessation from works.

What we have tried to maintain in this study is that the Gītā gives a place for both these types—the pure Sāṁkhya who excludes all work and follows the way of the Absolute described as Akṣara and Avyakta, as also the Yogin who combines dedicated work and devotion, and devotes himself to the God of love. Both attain to the identical goal of spiritual illumination, which is described hereafter. Only the follower of the path of love has the help and support of the God of love who reveals His absolute nature to him in the course of his spiritual maturity, while the follower of the Akṣara and Avyakta has to depend on his own strength. This topic has been discussed in Chapter 12.

7. *Vr*.47-48: These verses, which were easy for our ancients to understand, pose great difficulty for us today. So long as Varṇa was identified with the endogamous caste, and valid texts ascribed particular works to each caste (See verse 41—45 of this chapter), it was easy to find out one's Svadharma, and if one had a will, to perform it too. That a priest's son should be a priest, a soldier's son a soldier, a merchant's son a merchant, an agriculturist's son an agriculturist, a serf's son a serf—is an arrangement that could be practised to some extent in the old feudal society when educational opportunities were restricted, when there was no choice in following professions, when social contacts were limited, and when the validity of the system was accepted by the people in general. But today such an idea of Svadharma hereditarily determined, is impossible of practice. Society and professions have become competitive. The imparting of education without any restriction imposed by caste, has helped the shuffling of professional abilities among all members of society, setting aside hereditary factors. So it has become honourable for any one to follow any profession, and the determination of Svadharma based on birth as in a caste-based economy, has become impractical and impossible, and also undesirable. In a democratic society, the same kind of education is open to all, and every one is eligible, according to one's qualification and capacity, to positions of power, prestige and high income. In these days of national armies every able-bodied citizen has the eligibility to be recruited—he may even be conscripted—in the armed forces of the country. In such a milieu, if the Gītā idea of Svadharma is accepted as caste-based, as it was understood a few generations back, and as it used to be interpreted by old commentators, then it has become thoroughly outmoded and will be rejected by every section of society in India and outside.

But, as already pointed out, the wording of the Gītā about *Cāturvarṇya*, except as interpreted by old commentators, does not in itself mean endogamous castes, but the four psychological types. If this is accepted, Svadharma would mean only work that springs out of one's nature and therefore adapted to one's natural development. But how to recognise these types and how to provide them with work suited to their nature—is a problem that cannot be solved. We have to leave work based on psychological type as an ideal arrangement in a more rationally organised society of the future. There is no other way today but to understand Svadharma as the duty devolving on oneself in society, inclusive of the profession one follows. If that is done well with God in view, and not merely for remuneration or with a worldly master in view, then one may be said to follow Svadharma.

A still greater difficulty is involved in understanding the next propositions: 1) To do one's *Svadharma,* even if it be without much merit, is better than well-performed *Paradharma* (or duty alien to oneself). (2) Do not leave a duty that is *sahajam* (born with you or natural with you), even if it involves some evil, because every enterprise in this world has some baneful feature about it, just as smoke is a universal feature of fire.

The difficulty consists in this that in a competitive society there is no way to determine what is Paradharma and what is Svadharma. When Svadharma was interpreted as the caste duty, hereditarily determined, the matter was over-simplified; but it violates the fundamental psychological principle on which the Gītā recognises the division into Varṇas. For, heredity is a very uncertain criterion of aptitude and competence. And besides, under the conditions in which life is organised today, free competition determines the work one is required to do. The only way left for individuals to follow the Gītā teaching is to make a self-estimate of one's own disposition, character and aptitude, and consciously select, as far as it is possible, a profession that is in agreement with one's nature as conceived in this scripture. But the conditions of competitive life are so compelling that one may find it very difficult to follow this rule, even if one can find out one's Varṇa by self-analysis. Under these circumstances, the idea contained in the 47th verse, that Svadharma should not be abandoned in favour of Paradharma, becomes otiose from a practical point of view, however true it might be in an ideal society.

These are the difficulties in interpreting the principle of Svadharma in terms of out-dated social ideologies. We can, however, find much relevancy in it if we adopt an entirely different meaning for the word Svadharma or one's own Dharma in this context.

In the light of the Gītā teaching, to work is the Svadharma or discipline contributing to one's evolution in the case of almost all men. To abstain from work under the cloak of some high-sounding philosophy or an ethical alibi of evil involved in all works, and thus to relapse into worklessness, as Arjuna wanted to do, is Paradharma —the duty of another i.e. of one who has overcome body-consciousness and established himself in the sense of being the uninvolved and unaffectable Ātman. One may apparently be seen to be successfully following the life of workless asceticism externally, but in fact one would only be degenerating into Tamas or inertia in the long run.

Man being thus under the compulsion of work as duty, whatever it be, he rises above the meritorious and evil effects of duty, if he maintains the devotional attitude advocated by the Gītā—namely offering all the fruits of his action to the Lord, and being fully established in the attitude that he is a servant of God, discharging the duties He has entrusted him with.

Work being thus integral with the nature of man, he cannot give it up on the ground that it involves one in some actions one dislikes or has an adverse effect on others. What Arjuna sought to do in the field of battle was to give up his duty on such a plea and take to workless asceticism. He fortunately had a friend and adviser in Kṛṣṇa to disabuse him of this delusion and make him understand that what he egotistically refused to do, he would be compelled to undertake by the force of Nature.

It is not that the Gītā wants one to stick on to some hereditary work, fearing that if he takes to some other kind of work, he will be following Paradharma. For, even hereditary work, if it does not suit one's disposition, becomes Paradharma. If by self-analysis or the advice of a wise teacher, a particular work is not found to be suited to one's evolution, it should be changed by a conscientious person who has a high spiritual ideal. But unfortunately most men are for works that will fetch them the highest remuneration and not for what will contribute to their spiritual advancement.

Besides, professions too are not to be had according to one's choice. Many of the professions today are so technical that it requires years of preparation, and changing them will be practically impossible. A still more complicating factor is that in a democratic State certain duties like taking up arms for the defence of the country become every man's duty. So also democratic processes like forming parties, formation of governments, the electioneering processes etc., are matters of universal concern, thus making a political orientation of society inevitable. The spread of universal education, the technical nature of works and the acceptance of democratic rights for all—these and several features of modern life have made a simple hereditary determination of Svadharma absurd. But the psychological truth contained in the conception of Svadharma stands for all time.

Under the existing circumstances any duty that one is called to, has to be accepted as Svadharma, with freedom to change it if it is found to be a Paradharma (not according to one's nature).

8. *Vrs.*49-50: In verse 46, it was declared that man attains to *Siddhi*, by adoring the Supreme Being with his Svadharma. What sort of '*Siddhi*' or perfection is it? It can only mean an advanced state of spiritual competency (cf. Note 6), and not final perfection. Now in verse 50 he is again spoken of as attaining '*Siddhi*', which is described in verse 49 as *Naiṣkarmya-siddhi*, which we have translated as supreme 'perfection of transcendence of work'. *Naiṣkarmya* or worklessness, is not the physical inactivity but the recognition of oneself as the Ātman who is unaffected and uninvolved in the movements of the body-mind. This state is attained by Saṁnyāsa which is essentially the abandonment of the fruits of action and the sense of agency. Some may give up all work externally also. Such a state is attained by an aspirant who has reached the earlier Siddhi described in verse 46, consisting in purity of mind and powerful aspiration gained through the grace of God, which comes to one adoring Him for long with the performance of his Svadharma in a dedicated manner. This second Siddhi of *Naiṣkarmya* also does not seem to be the end. So it is said in Vrs. 49-50 and those succeeding how one, who is established in this *Naiṣkarmya-siddhi*, attains to 'Brahman' which attainment is declared as the highest consummation of knowledge—*niṣṭhā Jñānasya yā parā.* In the succeeding verses the way to that consummation is given. Thus it must be noted that the Gītā speaks of three types of Siddhi as stages of perfection.

The first is purity of mind and strong aspiration, the second *naiṣkarmya-siddhi* here described and the final consisting in the perfection of Jñāna-bhakti that will be described hereafter.

9. *Vr*.51-55: After the attainment of the second Siddhi, the disciplines one should adopt and the course of one's development are stated in these verses. The description given is of an introvert and ascetic living in solitude absorbed in meditation, having nothing to do with the outside world or with any work. He is workless mentally and physically. By this discipline he attains to what is called here *Brahma-bhūyam* — Brahman-becoming. That even this is not the final state of perfection but only the stepping stone to it, is clear from the verses which follow describing the final state of spiritual attainment.

So *Brahma-bhūyam* is the third stage of perfection or Siddhi, the others being Siddhi resulting from the discharge of Svadharma in a dedicated manner, and the *Naiṣkarmya-siddhi* or realisation that one is not the body but the Ātman above all change.

Thus *Brahma-bhūyam* is the third Siddhi. It is the same as what is spoken of as *Brāhmī-sthiti* in Ch. 2.72. It occurs also in Ch. 14.26. A detailed note on the significance of the expression is given on that verse as Note 6 of Chapter 14. Reference may be made to that Note, as it deals with the present context also.

A person who has reached the state of *Brahma-bhūyam* has not attained to the spiritual summit. His attainment is described in verse 54 as "Tranquil in spirit, free from grief and passions and regarding all beings as alike." This state of tranquillity is also the state of a *Sthita-prajña*—one of steady wisdom described at the close of Chapter 2. He next passes on to the last stage of spiritual perfection consisting in the attainment of transcendent devotion (Parām Bhaktim). It is not the ordinary devotion based on the Guṇas of Prakṛti, but what is called in the Bhāgavata as *Nirguṇa-Bhakti*—spontaneous love of the Lord stimulated not by any body-based passions but by the direct attraction of the Lord as of iron by the magnet. Here Bhakti and Jñāna go together, they being like the obverse and the reverse of the same coin. So it is said "By Bhakti he knows Me—both My extent and My essence." His 'extent' is his transcendence (*Paratva*) and his 'essence' is love (*Saulabhya*). And loving and knowing Him most intimately, the Jīva enters into the Divine Life—which is the acme of spiritual attainment. The Gītā stops there and does not split hairs, unlike the Ācharyas discussing the ontological significance of an attainment that defies all intellectual categories. Whether in this final attainment the Jīva becomes one with the Supreme Being as a river becomes one with the ocean, or whether the Jīva retains a modicum of individuality or refined personality so as to practise eternal love and service of the Divine—are moot points on which theologians and philosophers have argued and speculated for centuries without coming to any agreed solution. The one clear pronouncement that the Gītā makes on this moot question is: "A part of Mine has become the eternal Jīva in the sphere of Jīvas" (15.7). So it is better to maintain that the Jīva can become one with Him, as a part can become one with the whole, or if the Jīva prefers, the Jīva can maintain his Jīvahood absorbed in the service of the Lord.

10. *Vr*.56-62: Till the end of the previous verse 55, the ideal of an absolute contemplative, who, abandoning all works, has retired into solitude, and is engaged in meditation leading to illumination is described. Immediately after, in verse 56, the text seeks to describe an entirely different type of aspirant who is fully engaged in work—of one who performs 'every kind of work always'. It will be highly arbitrary to take it as a continuation of the same topic or to say that it refers to the earliest Siddhi of attaining purity through dedicated work. It has to be interpreted as the beginning of a new topic, namely, the spiritual progress of those who continue to do work by way of service of the Lord as both the way to salvation, and the end to be achieved through it.

From the start itself the Gītā has divided aspirants into two types—the Sāṁkhyas who abandon all work and follow a life of contemplation, and the Yogins who continue to work as a service of the Lord in absolute surrender of fruits of works and agency to Him. Do they represent two independent paths, or is the latter only the preparatory stage for gaining competency for the former? The Kevalādvaita commentaries of the Gītā generally hold that the second alternative is the correct interpretation. Some qualified aspirants may abandon all work from the beginning itself, and the others may do so when they come to a certain maturity through performance of Svadharma as dedicated works, which is called Siddhi in verse 46 of this chapter. The subsequent discipline of introspection and worklessness has been described in verses 51-55, and that topic closes with verse 55 and a new topic begins with the next verse. For, the succeeding verses deal with aspirants engaged in work. That there is such a division of the subject here is accepted even by a great Advaitic commentator like Madhusūdana Sarasvati.

The discipline and spiritual progress of the Yogins, who combine dedicated work and deep devotion throughout their spiritual life is next taken up from verse 55. That kind of discipline was described earlier in Chapter II from Verse 39 onward, in Chapter III from verse 3 onward and in Chapter XII. Aspirants of this type who have absolute faith and resignation to the Lord, are spoken of here as 'doing all kinds of work', but attaining to the eternal state by 'My grace'. The operation of this divine grace is the most important factor in the life of such devotees. In verse 62 the Lord tells them: 'Seek refuge in Him alone with all your being, with all love. By His grace you will attain the eternal state, the highest peace." This factor of grace in the case of such a devotee is emphasised in several passages. It is stated: "I become their uplifter from the ocean of recurring death." (12.7); "Of those who devote themselves to Me entirely without deviation, I shall preserve what they have (their worldly interests) and secure them what they have not, that is 'salvation.'" (9.22); "For those who are ever devoted to Me and worship Me with love, I bestow that illumination of intelligence by which they come to Me. Out of compassion for them, I destroy in them the darkness of ignorance by My presence in their innermost core as the shining lamp of wisdom" (10.10-11); "Of those who surrender all their actions to Me and meditate on Me with exclusive devotion, soon shall I be their uplifter from the ocean of death—of them whose minds are absorbed in Me" (12.6-7) etc. Above all there is the concluding verse of the Gītā: "Abandoning all other Dharma (rites and practices) seek shelter in Me alone. I shall release you from the hold of sin. Do not grieve." (18-66). The verse under comment also conveys the same idea. It says: "Though performing every kind of work always, he who has taken refuge in Me shall, by My grace, attain to the eternal and indestructible state of Mokṣa."

From this it is clear that the Gītā accommodates within its teaching a type of aspirants who practise devotion to the God of Love, combining work with meditation till the end, first as means for realisation and afterward as its consummation. Though they may be practising devotional disciplines, they depend for salvation not on their efforts but on divine grace got through total self-surrender as declared in Gītā verse 18.66.

It is in all respects an independent path in itself, in which divine grace plays the most important part. The followers of this path also attain to that Divine state which the work-renouncing Sāṁkhyas (Saṁnyāsins) are said to attain in verse 55 of this chapter.

In olden days those belonging to monastic Orders had to abandon works of all kinds, and so the work-abandoning aspirants spoken of here, used to be Saṁnyāsins only. The aspirants belonging to the second category—the Yogins who combine work with devotion—were necessarily householders. But in the modern age after the advent of Swami Vivekananda, the conception of Saṁnyāsa has changed. A member of an Order of Saṁnyāsins, according to Swami Vivekananda, can also do works, provided they are not for one's own purpose or profit, but for *Lokasaṁgraha*—the good of the society or rather the service of God in man. Thus this category of aspirants who do not abandon all works, about whom the Gītā speaks from verse 56 onwards, can include such Saṁnyāsins also. The old conception of Saṁnyāsa, according to which man abandons all works, has necessarily got to be confined to a very small circle of people who have largely overcome body-consciousness and about whom for that reason it can no longer be said: "Duties which your natural tendencies have imposed upon you, but which out of delusion you refuse to do, even that you will have to perform by the compulsion of Nature" (18-6). If Saṁnyāsa on the other hand is to be a state of life applicable to a larger circle of people, it has to include works of a dedicated nature also among its disciplines.

Thus the teaching of the Gītā, while it accepts the doctrine of workless Saṁnyāsa leading to illumination for the few, also accepts, as equally valid and independent, the path of Bhakti combined with dedicated work, enlightenment being an accompaniment of it by the grace of God, which He bestows on all devoted servants of His. The *Bhāgavata* puts this uniqueness of higher Bhakti very effectively when it says that just like a ball of rice eaten satisfies hunger, brings strength and gives joy, all together, Bhakti gives illumination, bliss and liberation at one stroke. It is not a mere handmaid of any other discipline.

In fact in the Gītā, Bhakti and Jñāna are one and the same at their highest reaches, each perfecting the other. So it is said in 18.35, "By Bhakti he comes to know Me (*abhijānāti*)—both My extent and My essence"; and again in 18.68 he speaks of this doctrine of love and self-surrender, which forms the essence of Bhakti that He taught in the earlier verses, as "*Iti te jñānam ākhyātaṁ*— thus have I imparted to you that profound wisdom."

11. *Vr.*63: The conclusion of this verse, which is also the near conclusion of the whole teaching, is remarkable for the freedom that the teacher gives the disciple in the statement, "Reflecting over this whole teaching, do as you think fit." An enlightened teacher never imposes any teaching on a worthy disciple.

12. *Vrs.* 64-66: The essence of the Gītā teaching is clinched in the verses 65 and 66. While the Gītā teaching has a place for the renunciation of all actions by aspirants who have attained to purity of mind, its main thrust is to recommend the renunciation not of works but of their fruits and the sense of agency. In verse 66 an aspirant is asked to abandon all Dharma. Dharma is interpreted by some schools of thought as Karmas. If by Karma is meant all Vedic ritualism and ego-centred work for selfish gains, the equation of Dharma with Karma is all right. But it cannot be of works done as pure acts of devotion and service. For the immediately previous verse says: "Let your mind be engrossed in Me. Be resigned to Me. Offer worship to Me." etc. So works of the nature of Bhakti discipline should always be performed. These disciplines are in the words of the *Bhāgavata Purāṇa*—*Śravaṇam* (hearing about God), *Kīrtanam* (chanting His name and praises), *Smaraṇam* (remembering Him through repetition of the Name etc.), *Pādasevanam* (performing all duties as His service), *Arcanam* (worship of Him in images), *Vandanam* (saluting Him in all beings), *Dāsyam* (cultivating the attitude of a servant of His), *Sakhyam* (feeling the intimacy of comradeship with Him), and *Ātmanivedanam* (self-dedication to Him).

Even in the performance of these devotional activities, there is a form of renunciation to be practised. There is a tendency among spiritual aspirants to feel that they have done so much of Sādhana and nothing has happened or that they are entitled to the Lord's grace because they have done so much of spiritual practices. There is nothing so stupid and unspiritual as this kind of mentality. The Infinite Being cannot be purchased for any price of limited commodities. A true aspirant abandons the fruits of all his Sādhanas to Him. The Lord's grace is bestowed according to His will; man's duty is only to pray for it and wait in patience. He is to have the abiding faith that "The Lord dwells in the hearts of all beings, revolving these by his mysterious power Māyā, as one would do objects mounted on a machine" (18-61). His are the fruits and His the agency. The surrender of the fruits and the sense of agency in regard to all one's spiritual practices even, besides the abandonment of all non-spiritual activities, is included in the idea of giving up all Dharma. And with this attitude of mind, an aspirant must abide in the faith that the Lord is his only support, his only redeemer, the only determiner of his destiny.

According to Madhusūdana Sarasvati, this surrender takes three forms determined by the maturity of Sādhana.

1. *Tasyaivāham mamaivāsau sa evāham iti tridhā* |
bhagavac-charaṇatvam syād sādhanābhyāsa pākataḥ ||

That is: first, there is the attitude 'I am His', second is the attitude 'He is mine', and third, there is the experience 'He is I'. Surrender takes these three forms according to one's spiritual maturity.

In explanation of these, he quotes as the example of the first attitude:

Satyapi bhedāpagame nātha tavāham na māmakīnastvam
sāmudro hi taraṅgaḥ kva ca na sāmudro hi tārangaḥ

That is, "When the sense of difference subsides, I am, O Lord, Thy appendage, and not You mine. It is the wave that belongs to the ocean, and never the ocean to the wave."

2. The second stage is represented by the attitude:

Hastam utkṣipya yātosi Balakṛsna! kimadbhutam
Hṛdayād yadi niryāsi pauruṣaṃ gaṇayāmi te

That is, "Well, Kṛṣṇa, Thou art forcibly snatching Thyself away from me physically. How strange! I shall only praise Thy valour if Thou art able to extricate Thyself out of my heart also." Here the devotee's sense of 'myness' with regard to the Lord is so great that he feels that He can never separate Himself from him (the devotee).

3. The third and the highest stage of surrender is represented by the realisation embodied in the verse addressed by Yama to his emissaries in the Viṣṇupurāṇa.

Sakalam idamiham ca vāsudevaḥ paramapumān paramesvaraḥ sa ekaḥ |
iti matiracalā bhavatyanante hṛdayagate vraja tān vihāya dūrāt||

"Do not approach those in whom has arisen the firm conviction that all that exists is Vāsudeva, the one Supreme Lord and Master of all, dwelling within the heart." Here the 'I' has disappeared in the 'He', and there is only He.

One who resorts to Him absolutely, He offers to deliver from all sins. Sins must be understood in a comprehensive sense, namely the effects of all Karma, present and past, good and bad, which lead to repeated births and deaths. Even the effects of good Karma can be called 'sin', as they also lead to repeated births and deaths. In other words, the Lord promises to bestow His grace, and to light in one's heart the lamp of wisdom that removes the darkness of Ignorance, which is the cause of all sin. Individual sins may be absolved by atonements (***prāyascitta***) but sins or sinful tendency can be effaced only by *Haritoṣaṇam*—by securing the grace of the Lord.

13. *Vrs.*67-71: Several of these verses of the Gītā may cause surprise in the minds of many modern readers, because in contrast to the modern idea of giving wide publicity to a spiritual message, the Gītā is prohibiting the preaching of it to persons who do not practise austere living, who have no devotion and no spirit of

service. Its teaching should be confined to devotees of God. The idea behind this prohibition is that perverse people will misinterpret and abuse many of these great teachings to suit their own nefarious purposes. For example, take a teaching contained in 2.10, "He who thinks the self can be a slayer and who thinks it can be the slain—both have no right knowledge. For the self does not slay, nor is the self slain." This can be used by a murderer to justify his anti-social act. The teaching that all beings are like objects mounted on a wheel which the Lord is turning, may be used to justify fatalism, lethargy and anti-social acts. Man can shift the moral responsibility for his actions to God, and thus make a noble teaching ridiculous. People with anti-social tendencies can easily misunderstand and misapply these doctrines. So it should be imparted only to genuine spiritual seekers with sound moral foundations. While accepting the validity of such objection, Gītā lovers will be for preaching this doctrine to a wide circle, justifying their act on the ground that all who come voluntarily to hear or study this text and its exposition, have a spiritual bent of mind, actual or potential, in them.

It is also noteworthy that Kṛṣṇa thinks that preaching of the Gītā to deserving persons is doing the highest form of adoration of Him, a form of service that is most pleasing to Him. He calls the study of the Gītā and its teaching, which is only an extension of study, as Jñāna-yajña, sacrifice of Knowledge. It is a mental form of sacrifice, as contrasted with the ritualistic.

14. *Vr.*73 : The restoration of Smṛti or memory spoken of here is the consciousness of one's being the Immortal Atman and not the perishable body-mind. Arjuna's initial shrinking from the discharge of his duty is the result of the feeling that all the persons arrayed for battle, ready to cause mutual destruction, are his own kith and kin. The identification of man with the perishable body-mind in place of the immortal Spirit is the root cause of this delusion and dereliction of duty. Kṛṣna's instruction now restores to him consciousness of man being the Immortal Spirit.

END

APPENDIX 1

The Samkhya and the Bhagavad Gita

THE Gītā is accepted by all the great Ācāryas of India as one of the three source books (*Prasthāna-traya*) of the Vedānta philosophy. But it will surprise a reader to note that while the Gītā refers to its thought as Sāṁkhya five times (cf. II 39; III 3; V 4-5; XIII 24; and XVIII 13), it speaks of itself as Vedānta only once (cf. XV 15). The surprise arises from two perceptions. First, by Sāṁkhya we usually understand the Darśana or philosophy of that name, included in the six Darśanas or systems of Indian philosophy, and based on Īśvarakṛṣṇa's Sāṁkhya Kārika. The system as given there is atheistic and it is devastatingly criticised by the great Vedāntic Ācāryas including Śaṅkara, in their commentaries on the Vedānta Sūtras. Next, even while it is so, we find the term Sāṁkhya frequently occurring in the Gītā, which is admittedly a great Vedāntic text.

This discrepancy seems to be noticed to some extent at least by Śaṅkara who, while commenting on *eṣā te abhihitā Sāṁkhye* (cf. II39), interprets the word Sāṁkhya as *paramārtha vastu viṣaye* i.e., 'in regard to the Supreme Truth'. In other words, he takes it to mean only as 'metaphysical reality' and not as a reference to Īśvarakṛṣṇa's or Kapila's system of thought. The very context compels him to do so. But when he comments on *procyate guṇa saṁkhyāne* i.e. 'is said in the science of enumeration of Guṇas' (cf. XVIII 19), he interprets *guṇasaṁkyāna* as a reference to the system of Kapila, meaning the classical Sāṁkhya of the Kārika, which is atheistic. Realising the inconsistency of it, perhaps, he immediately says: "This Śāstra is a valid source of knowledge about the constituents (Guṇas) and the Jīvas who experience. Though it contradicts in respect of the non-duality of the metaphysically real or Brahman, the followers of Kapila are adepts as regards constituents and their operation." It is also to be noted that the Ācārya is not at all puzzled when Kṛṣṇa in Vibhūti Yoga, describes Himself to be the Muni Kapila among Siddhas (perfect ones). If Kapila were the atheistic philosopher referred to in the comment on XVIII. 19, how does Kṛṣṇa call him 'a perfect one' (Siddha)?

This confusion arises out of a lack of historical perspective. Kapila, unless the account of him given in the Bhāgavata is taken as history, is a very shadowy figure. The Śvetāśvatara Upaniṣad (5.2) refers to a Ṛiṣi Kapila. The reference, in that context, may be to the 'golden coloured one', the Hiraṇya-garbha. It is often interpreted so by commentators. No one knows what exactly Kapila taught, as he has left no work behind him. *Sāṁkhya-pravacanasūtra* attributed to him must have originated so late as the 15th century A.D., as we do not find any writer of an earlier date referring to it. The Sāṁkhya tradition is said to have been transmitted by Kapila to Āsuri, by him to Pancaśikha and by him to others afterwards. The earliest systematic account of the teachings of Sāṁkhya philosophy is to be got only in the Sāṁkhya-Kārika of Īśvarakṛṣṇa, whose date is supposed to be between the first half of the second century A.D. and the 5th century A.D. *Śaṣṭi-tantra,* a supposed earlier work, is not now extant. For the great Vedāntic Ācāryas, therefore, Sāṁkhya Philosophy meant the system as formulated in the Sāṁkhya Kārikā. The philosophy expounded therein is characterised by its pluralistic dualism, its absolute realism, its thorough rationalism and its pronounced atheism, while being at the same time a gospel of spiritual redemption.

It is only in our times, thanks to the valuable research work of scholars both Indian and western, that the historical background of the Sāṁkhya system has been clarified. As a consequence we can have an understanding of why the Gītā calls its teachings Sāṁkhya. The fact is that at the time when the Upaniṣads and the Gītā came into existence, there was practically no hard and fast difference between the Sāṁkhya and the Vedānta as in later classical times. Many of what are considered the special features of the Sāṁkhya philosophy like the concepts of the Puruṣa, of Prakṛti, of the three Guṇas, of different categories being evolved out of Prakṛti with their corresponding counterparts in the human personality, of the effect subsisting in the cause, of the attainment of freedom by the Puruṣa from the hold of Prakṛti, etc., are all in some form ideologies of the Upaniṣads too. Some of the Upaniṣads use the words Sāṁkhya and Vedānta indiscriminately to denote their teachings. Thus the Śvetāśvatara refers in one place (cf. 6. 12) to the Supreme Truth as *Sāṁkhya-yogādhi-gamyam* —i.e., 'What can be attained through Sāṁkhya and Yoga.' And a few lines after (cf. 6. 22) it speaks of that Supreme Truth as *Vedānta pracoditaṁ paramaṁ guhyam*—'the highest mysticism taught in the Vedānta.'

This tendency of making no hard and fast distinction between Sāṁkhya and Vedānta is seen in a still more marked degree in the Gītā. As we have mentioned already, there is only one reference to the term Vedānta in the Gītā, and that is when the Lord calls Himself Vedāntakṛt or the maker of the Vedānta (cf. XV. 15). As against this, there are five places where He calls His teachings as Sāṁkhya and Yoga—'discriminative wisdom and non-attached action.' The theory of the three Guṇas and the part they play in life by their permutations and combinations are described perhaps in greater detail in the Gītā, chapter fourteen onwards, than in any Sāṁkhyan text proper. The distinction between Puruṣa and Prakṛti is discussed in chapter thirteen. But all this is done from the theistic point of view, and the supremacy of Īśvara over Puruṣa and Prakṛti is maintained all through.

In the Mahābhārata too, in the Mokṣa-Dharma section of its Śānti-parva, the Sāṁkhya is not treated as a hostile system subject to the philosophic criticism, which it receives later at the hands of Vedāntic Ācāryas. The Sāṁkhyans are spoken of therein with great respect as philosophers and believers in the doctrine of the Ātman. They are also described as theists accepting a Supreme Being under whose control the individual Puruṣas and Nature function. He is the 26th principle, the Puruṣottama (Īśvara), in addition to the twentyfour categories evolved out of Prakṛti and the Puruṣa the 25th, recognised by classical Sāṁkhya. And the Puruṣa, though multiple in bondage, becomes one with Īśvara in salvation.

How then the wide gulf of difference between the Sāṁkhya and the Vedānta came about in later times is difficult to trace, because of the absence of any authentic linking literature between the Upaniṣadic and the Gītā Sāṁkhya with the classical Sāṁkhya of Īśvarakṛṣṇa. The Sāṁkhya philosophy, is described as having come from Kapila, through Āruṇi Pañcaśikha, Asita-Devala and Varṣṇaganya to the times when Īśvarakṛṣṇa wrote his Sāṁkhya Kārika, which is plainly atheistic, though propounding a spiritual doctrine. No literature produced by any of these early Sāṁkhya teachers has, however, come down to us, though Īśvarakṛṣṇa claims that he is giving a summary of an extensive literature on the philosophy called Saṣṭi Tantra. No doubt we hear of what must have been a voluminous Sāṁkhya work called by that name and consisting, according to some tradition, of sixty thousand verses, but no such text is now available. Nor does Mahābhārata Śānti-parva, which refers to all philosophers and philosophies known in the pre-classical times, make any mention of such a text. Probably it might not have been one book, but the name for a collection of books, of which the important ones were the product of the Sāṁkhya teachers mentioned before.

Whatever that be, from some discourses found in the Śānti-parva of the Mahābhārata, there is evidence to show that it was with Pañcaśikha that the Sāṁkhya began to take an atheistic turn. Pañcaśikha accepts a soul or a Puruṣa to account for the sense of a continuing individuality, but the soul is not itself a conscious entity. Consciousness, according to him, is a property that comes into existence when the Puruṣa comes into a conglomerated association with the body-mind and Cetana (psychic efficiency), which are all parts of Avyakta or Prakṛti, the ultimate ground of the objective world. Consciousness, being thus a product of the integration of the Puruṣa with a certain aspect of the Avyakta as body-mind, it ceases to exist when this integration ceases at death. Man suffers because he identifies the Puruṣa with this conglomeration of body-mind and considers that conglomeration to be his self. Mukti is got when this identification ceases, but consciousness also ceases with it. But the state of Mukti is not one of ultimate destruction nor of ultimate reality. It is indeterminate and indefinable. It cannot definitely be described as a state of consciousness, as consciousness is not an essential characteristic of the Puruṣa. In bringing about these agglomerations of Avyakta known as body-mind, or in bringing about the identification of the Puruṣa with such agglomerations, or in releasing him, there is no place for a Puruṣottama, a God.

The influence of such thinkers gradually drifted the Sāṁkhya, as represented in the Gītā and the Mokṣa-Dharma of the Śāntiparva of the Mahābhārata, away from its original moorings into the Sāṁkhya of Īśvarakṛṣṇa's Sāṁkhya Kārika, which is characterised by absolute realism, atheism and pluralism. Thus Sāṁkhya, which was one with Vedānta in early times, became the *Pradhana-malla,* the chief opponent, for the Vedāntic Ācāryas of classical times to combat with and refute.

The causes for this drifting apart of Sāṁkhya from Vedānta can only be a matter of guess work . The followers of the Veda always relied on the Vedic text. Not only the ritualists, but also the Vedic philosophers, who came to be called Vedāntins, clung to the Upaniṣadic section of the Vedas to provide them with data to formulate a philosophy of life. Reasoning has an important place in it no doubt, but it is always subject to the authority of the Vedantic texts. It is natural that all thinkers would not agree with this outlook which relies on textual authority, and some of them at least would gradually drift more and more to reliance on reasoning. This must have happened among Indian thinkers in classical times, and Sāṁkhya, 'the pursuit of wisdom,' must have tilted increasingly towards reasoning while continuing to give a lip-allegiance to Vedic authority. The Sāṁkhya thinkers, however, at no time rejected Vedic authority openly and therefore their system continued to be regarded as orthodox and Āstika, in spite of their frank atheism.

At all times in the history of thought, there have been sets of thinkers who felt hesitant to accept an ultimate spiritual principle, which is ordinarily designated by the term God or Īśvara. They have considered Nature as self-explanatory, and brushed aside the idea of a God, who is necessarily unknown, as a gratuitious assumption, serving absolutely no purpose in their world view. But unlike the pure materialists of ancient and modern times, the Sāṁkhyas considered that the functioning of Nature is purposive, indicating the presence of a principle of intelligence somewhere, to serve whose purpose Nature is functioning. They found the purpose-giving principle in the Puruṣa, the individual soul, whose imaginary association with aspects of Prakṛti gives direction to the inherently dynamic Prakṛti in such a way as to subserve the purpose of that Puruṣa. Prakṛti is functioning in order to provide experience to the Puruṣa, until he sees through its wiles, develops complete detachment from it, and gains liberation through the discriminative wisdom. Thus they developed a method of striving for spirituality without a God and scriptural authority.

In the development of such a non-theological philosophy of life with a spiritual import and an emphasis on rationalism, the Sāṁkhyan thinkers might have been influenced by the intellectual milieu brought about by Buddhism, which accepted neither a God nor an individual soul, but none the less presented a highly spiritual pattern of life. There are some people who cannot stand the idea of God, as there are others who swear by Him. It was so then, and it is so today also.

The Sāṁkhya has continued to develop even after Īśvarakṛṣṇa's time and re-capture the theistic spirit, especially in the commentary of Vijñāna-bhikṣu (16th century) on *Sāṁkhya-pravacana-sūtras* attributed to Kapila himself. But the atheistic bent given to it by the Sāṁkhya Karika of Īśvarakṛṣṇa and the acceptance of this as the outlook of that system by the great classical Ācaryas of Vedānta like Bādarāyaṇa and Śaṅkara, have for ever drawn the picture of the Sāṁkhya as an atheistic and pluralistic doctrine in the minds of students of Indian philosophy.

APPPENDIX II

In the Bhagavad Gītā text there are several words of technical importance, whose sense seems to be very fluid, making it very difficult to understand the exact meaning meant. We have selected in the following section a few such words to illustrate the point and to draw the attention of careful readers of the Gītā to this feature of the Text.

BRAHMAN, BRAHMA AND BRAHMĀ

To a student of Vedantic literature today, these words forming the neutral and masculine formations of the same word, convey definite meanings. Brahman and Brahma denote the Supreme Being (the Absolute), and Brahmā is the creator (Demiurge), one of the Trinity. But a student of the Gītā will find that it is not so simple as that. The word is used in diverse senses in the Gītā text, and ascertaining the meaning of it is complicated by the fact that Brahman and Brahmā (both neuter) cannot be distinguished from the creator Brahmā (masculine) except in the nominative and accusative cases, and that in compound words they cannot be distinguished at all.

Etymologically Brahma is derived from the root '*bṛh*' to grow. Some modern scholars conclude from a study of the use of the term in early Vedic literature that originally it conveyed the sense of 'power'—power inherent in the Mantras of the Veda. So the Veda itself came to be called Brahma, as we find in the Gītā verse 3.15 *Karma brahmodbhavam viddhi, brahmā 'kṣara-samudbhavam* (rituals have originated from the Veda or *Brahma,* and *Brahma* i.e. the Veda from the Imperishable). Again it seems to be used in the same sense in 4.32—"*Evam bahuvidhā yajñā vitatā brahmaṇo mukhe* (many such sacrifices are set forth in the 'entrance' of Brahma i.e. the Veda.)

It is used as Eternal Being, as Jiva, as Prakṛti and even as renunciation in other places. In the verse 4.31 that occurs immediately before the above one (4.32), the word Brahman is used in the sense of Eternal Being: *Yajña-śiṣṭām'ṛta bhujo yānti Brahma sanātanam* (those who partake of the nectar, the sacramental remnants of sacrifice, attain to the Eternal Brahman). In this sense of the Eternal or Supreme Being, the word is used in many places. Verse 5.6 says: *Yoga-yukto munir Brahma nacireṇ'ādhigacchati* (the sage accomplished in Yoga attains Brahman in no long time). But Śaṁkara interprcets the word Brahman here as 'renunciation', as it is a means for attaining Brahman. He has to give such a strained interpretation, because according to him *Jñāna* alone constitutes the direct means to lead an aspirant to Brahman and renunciation is an important means to attain that *Jñāna*. This will help one understand the very curiously ambiguaous use made of the word in the Gītā.

In 7.29: *Te Brahma tad viduḥ kṛtsnam* (they know Brahma in entirety), the word is used to denote the Supreme Being. A clear use of it as the Supreme Being is found also in verse 10.12: *Param Brahma param dhāma* (Thou art the Supreme Brahman, the Supreme Abode). It will be noted here that '*param*', supreme, is used to qualify Brahma, as '*kṛtsnam*' is used in the earlier passage. This shows that the Gītā itself is aware that the word Brahma is used in many senses.

In answer to the question (8.1): *Kim tad Brahma* (what is that Brahma?), it is answered: *Akṣaram Brahma paramam* (Supreme Brahman is the Imperishable). Though the reference seems to be to the Supreme Being only, Rāmānuja interprets Brahma here as the true self (Kṣetrajña) i.e. Jivas conceived universally. For him the descriptive epithet *Akṣara* attached to the expression, gives it this meaning.

In 4.24 the word Brahma is used in a very ambiguous way,suggesting many meanings. The verse is "*Brahmārpaṇam ......brahmakarma samādhinā*" By identifying all parts of sacrifice with Brahma, that word is given the meaning of sacrifice. The idea that Brahma is the All, is also suggested i.e. that the Supreme Being is not only transcendent but immanent in everything.

In verse 5-19, *Nirdoṣam hi samam Brahma, tasmād Brahmaṇi* te *sthitāḥ* (Brahma is unsullied and pure; therefore the seers of sameness are said to be established in Brahma), the word Brahma means the Supreme Being. Some modern interpreters like Minor and Zaehner, however, take the words 'established in Brahma' as meaning the state of 'liberated consciousness' or the 'fixed still state of Brahman'. In their predilection to read into the Gītā a kind of personalistic theism, they make a distinction between Brahman and the consciousness of the liberated one and contend that the general use of the word Brahman in the Gītā is to indicate the latter. Monistic Vedanta, however, does not make a distinction between Brahman and the consciousness of the liberated. They are identical according to them. Rāmānuja, who is not Advaitic, explains the passage merely as the 'freedom from the strain of Samsāra.'

In 6.38 occurs the expression, "*Vimūḍho Brahmaṇaḥ pathi*" (lost in the path of Brahma) when the question is asked, "Does one who is unsuccessful in the path of Brahma lose both this world and the hereafter?" The question is asked in the context of the practice of Astāṅga Yoga for gaining absolute concentration of mind. It is not likely that Brahman, the Impersonal Absolute of the Vedānta, is meant here. It can only mean 'the spiritual path and goal' in a general sense. So this seems to be another sense of the word Brahman in the Gītā.

In 8.16 and 8.17 the word Brahma is used in such expressions as "*Ābrahma-bhuvanāl lokāḥ*' (from the world of Brahmā to the earthly sphere), and "*Ahar yad Brahmaṇo viduḥ* (what is known as Brahmā's day)," the word is used in the sense of Brahmā the creator, one of the Trinity, who is only an off-shoot of Viṣṇu. In verse 11.37 occurs the expression "*Brahmaṇo*' *py'ādikartre*' (the originator of even Brahmā). The expression Brahma here can refer to either the masculine Brahmā or the neuter Brahman, as these two words can be distinguished only in the nominative and accusative. In the former case the reference will be to the creator Brahmā. There are, however, modern interpreters like Zaehner who interpret it as 'Impersonal Brahman', as they want to uphold the doctrine that the Impersonal is subordinate to the personal represented by Kṛṣṇa. They support this view by a quotation from the Gītā itself: "*Brahmaṇo hi pratiṣṭhāham* (I, Kṛṣṇa, am the foundation of Brahmā even 14.27)." For a detailed discussion of this obscure passage see the Notes on pp. 374-377. In 11.15 it is clearly used for creator Brahmā in the expression—"*Brahmāṇam īśam kamalasanastham.*"

In 17.23 occurs the expression, "*Om Tat Sad iti nirdeśo Brahmaṇas trividhaḥ smṛtaḥ*" (Om, Tat, Sat—these three are the symbolic designations of Brahma)". Here Brahma can very well mean the Supreme Being. But Rāmānuja interprets it as Veda, as in 3.15, which has already been considered.

In verse 13.12 there is the expression, "*Anādimatparaṁ Brahma.*" The interpretation Śankara gives is: Brahman who is Anādi (beginningless) and Param (supreme). *Mat* is taken as a meaningless suffix used for metrical purposes only. He also gives an alternative interpretation, taking the expression as "*Anādi* and *Matparam*", meaning thereby that Brahman is supreme, and I, Vāsudeva is Brahman's *Parā* or Pre-eminent Power. But Rāmānuja reads quite a different meaning. He splits the word as *Anādi* and *matparam Brahma*, and interprets the expression as "Brahma or Jīva who is without an origin and dependent on Me, Vāsudeva." Thus Brahma here means for him Jīva.

In Verse 13.30 it is said that when one perceives "the manifold as centred in the One etc." he attains to Brahma (*Brahma sampadyate tadā*). Here the word can mean Brahman, the Impersonal Absolute, in the Upaniṣadic sense. But the modern interpreters like Zaener and Minor refuse to accept that Gītā propounds the idea of an Absolute as understood in Advaita Vedānta. So Zaener interprets "*Brahma sampadyate*" as meaning the same as *Brahma-bhūta* in 5.24, and attributes to it the Buddhist sense of "entering a form of existence which is unconditioned by space, time and causation, the very flavour of Nirvāṇa."..Minor remarks about it "Presumbly as used regularly in the Gītā for Kṛṣṇa's state of consciousness."

The word Brahma is used in the sense of Prakṛti, Nature, in 14.3 and 14.7. The verses run—"*Mama yonir mahat Brahma* (The great Brahma, Nature, is my womb)", and "*Teṣām brahma mahat yoniḥ* (Of them i.e. of all beings, Brahma or Nature is the great womb or source). Some modern interpreters are of the view that Brahma is used in the sense of Prakṛti or Nature even in 3.15—"*Karma brahmodbhavam viddhi* (know that Karma or action is born of Brahma or Nature)". The traditional interpretation of the word, as already given earlier, is Veda, which is the basis and therefore the origin of all ritualistic work. It can as well mean Nature, which is the source of all activity.

In 18-50, towards the close of the Gītā, in order to indicate the Supreme Being, the Gītā says: "*Siddhim parapto yathā Brahma tathāpnoti nibodha me*—hear from Me how one who has gained perfection in transcendence of work (*naiṣkarmya-siddiḥ*) attains to Brahma." Here also there is a complication, causing a doubt whether the word really means the Supreme Being or a state of mind that precedes it. For it is said in the verse 53 and 54 that the one who has followed the disciplines described from 50 to 53, becomes only fit to become Brahman (*brahma-bhūyāya*), and that this state of attainment makes him "tranquil in mind and free from grief and passions, alike to all beings and eligible for supreme devotion." This makes it justifiable to think that Brahma referred to in Verse 50 is only this state and not the state of being Brahma. It is supreme devotion that gives him the love and knowledge of the Supreme Being and entry into the Divine Life thereby. It must be for these reasons that Personalistic Vedantins of the old type like Rāmānuja think that attaining Brahma in the Gītā means gaining the Jiva-consciousness i.e. the consciousness that one is the Ātman[1] as distinguished from body-mind which is a part of Prakṛti. It is on this enlarged spirit-consciousness that Bhakti and Jnana of the highest type arise through Divine grace. Modern interpreters of the Gītā also lean towards a similar meaning. These modern views will be given in the next section on *Brahma-bhūya.*

In 5.10 speaking about resignation of all work, it is said, "*Brahmaṇy'ādhāya karmāṇi* (resigning all works in Brahman). Śaṅkara interprets Brahman here as Īśvara i.e. Saguṇa-brahman of the Advaitins. Rāmānuja interprets it as Prakṛti, Nature, the use being parallel to the clear reference in 14.3—"*Mama yonir madhad brahma.*" There is much justification for this latter view from the context. For, in the previous verse (5.7), one is asked to feel that all actions are done by the Indriyas, which are parts of Prakṛti, and not by one's real self. So also, it is said in 3.28: "*Guṇā guṇeṣu vartanta iti matvā na sajjate* (Guṇas or organs which are parts of Prakṛti, work on Guṇas or objects which are also parts of Prakṛti)." Prakṛti is constituted of Guṇas. Apart from the context, the difficulty in fixing the meaning is caused by the fact that except in the nominative and accusative cases Brahman and Brahmā cannot be distinguished. The former is neuter and means the Supreme Being,and the latter, Brahma, is masculine and means the creator Brahmā. But Brahma, also neuter, can mean the Supreme Being, Prakṛti, Veda, Jīva etc., as has been illustrated by several Gītā passages.

COMPOUND WORD FORMATIONS WITH BRAHMA

In the Gītā there are several compound words formed with Brahma as a part of it. These are Brahma-nirvāṇa (2.72: 5.24-26); Brahma-bhūtam (6.27); Brahma-bhūtaḥ (5.24, 18.54); Brahma-bhūyam (14.26; 18.53); Brahma-yoga-yukta (5.21) etc. From an Advaitic point of view, most these expressions signify 'becoming one with Brahman', and that is the way in which a reader of the Gītā usually understands these expressions. But the fact that the word Brahma has, as shown in the previous section, many meanings, should make us exercise much caution in interpreting the word as Supreme Being wherever we come across that word. For a detailed discussion on the various views held on these expressions, the reader may refer to Note 6 on V. 24 (p. 164), Note on. 27 of xiv (p. 374), and Note 7 on 51-55 xviii (p. 474). A scrutiny of the text and the discussions referred to above, will make one feel that Brahma-bhūyam and Brahmī-sthiti do not represent the attainment of the Supreme Being, but are only a stepping stone to it. According to modern scholars these expressions show an attempt, on the part of the Gītā, to accommodate certain current Buddhistic ideologies with its thought, just as it does with Sāṁkhyan ideas as discussed in Appendix I. The acceptance of this modern view is complicated by the difficulty that such an acceptance will imply a post-Buddhistic date to the Text, which is contrary to the Indian tradition that it was revealed at the time of the Mahābhrāata war, shortly before the Kali era began in 3100 B.C. or thereabout. For Rāmānuja, however, it poses no difficulty, because he accepts Ātman or the Jīva also as a meaning of Brahman. To attain to the consciousness that one is a Jiva, a spiritual monad as distinguished from the body-mind,is the stepping stone to the attainment of supreme devotion to, and knowledge of, God.

AKSARA

Derived from the root 'Kṣa', the various dictionary meanings of the word are: Imperishable; unalterable; sword; Siva; Viṣṇu; syllable; Om; letter; vowal; sound; word; final beatitude; religious austerity; sacrifice; water; and speech. In the Gītā it used in some of these different senses as shown below.

1. *Brahmā'kṣara-samudbhavam* 3.15 (Brahma or Veda is born of Akṣara the Imperishable i.e the Supreme Being). Because of the various alternative meanings for Brahma, other meanings also are given for it.

2. *Akṣaram Brahma paramam* 8.3 (Brahman supreme is Akṣara, the Imperishable, higher than all). The word here is equated with the Supreme Being.

3. *Om ity ek'ākṣaraṁ Brahma* 8.13—(Om, the single syllable, is Brahma.)

4. *Girām asmy ekam akṣaram* 10-25 (among utterances I am the mono-syllabled Om).

5. *Yad akṣaram vedavido vadanti...tat te padam* 8.11 (what the knowers of Veda call Akṣara, the Imperishable, of that Status, I shall speak to you). The meaning of the word here is a state of attainment.

6. *Tvam akṣaram paramam veditavyam* 11. 18 (Thou art the Imperishable Being who is the highest goal of wisdom).

7. In 11. 37 occurs *Tvam akṣaram sad-asat tat-param yat* (Thou art the Akṣara, the Immutable, who is both exis-

tance, *sat*, and non-existence, *asat*, and what is beyond that). It can mean that Kṛṣṇa is equated with the Impersonal Absolute or Supreme Being here, or it can also be an adjectival complement describing Kṛṣṇa as one who has no decay like ordinary entities known to us.

8. In 12. 1 occurs the passage: "*Ye c' āpy akṣaram avyaktam* (those who adore or meditate on the Akṣara ,the Imperishable, and the Avyakta, unmanifest or unclear)." From the description of it that follows in 12. 3 and 4 it does not look like the Impersonal Absolute of Vedanta except for the words *acintya* and *kūṭastha.* It is formless but not what is described as Neti Neti.

9. In 8. 21 occurs "*Avyvakto' kṣara ityuktas tam āhuḥ paramām gatim*—what is known as the Unmanifest and as the Imperishable (Akṣara), is called My Supreme State (*Gati*)." The same is the case in the highly controversial verse 15. 16: "*Dvāv imau puruṣau loke kṣaras' c' ākṣara eva ca*—there are two categories, *Puruṣas*, the perishable (*kṣaraḥ*) and the imperishable (*akṣaraḥ*)." Here it is used to describe two kinds of Puruṣas. Whether that second Puruṣa described as Akṣara is Jīva or Māyā-śakti or anything else—is disputed. For discussion on this, see Note 5 on p.39. Anyway, it is not the Impersonal Absolute.

10. In 10.33 occurs "*Akṣarāṇām akāro' smi*—among Akṣaras (letters) I am the letter A." Here the word is used in the same sense as earlier in "*Om ity ekākṣaram Brahma*—the single syllable Om is Brahma. (8.13)".

AVYAKTA

Avyakta is another word of technical importance used very widely in varying senses in different contexts. The common meaning of the word is "anything that is not clear." Probably basing on this meaning it has been used in the Gītā in the following senses: unclear, Ātman, Prakṛti, the Impersonal Absolute, and the Supreme Abode. The use of the word in these verying meanings may be, as in the case of the other words considered, because of the attempt made by the Gītā to synthesise various systems of thought or due to the fluidity of the meanings of these words at the time when the Gītā came into existence.

1. "*Avyakt'ādīni bhūtani* 2.28—The origin of beings is unclear (*avyakta*)". 2.A little earlier (2.25) the word has been used to describe the Ātman: "*Avyakto' yam, acintyo' yam*—the Ātman is Avyakta (not manifest to the senses)". This seems to be contrary in a way to the classical Advaitic idea that the Atman is *svatas-siddha* or self-revealed. Probably a reconciliation might be effected on the consideration that unclearness is only on the sense level and not in the intuitive sense. 3. In 8.18 occurs, "*Avyaktād vyaktayaḥ sarvāḥ* etc. i.e. from the *Avyakta*, i.e. Prakṛti or Root Nature in unmanifested condition, all things come into manifestation etc." Avyakta is a common equivalent of Prakṛti in the unmanifest condition in the Sāṁkhya system. The Gītā adopts the same meaning for it here. So the swing of the meaning of the word from the soul to Prakṛti may be noted. 4. In 7.24 it is said referring to the view of the ignorant about the Incarnation, "*Avyaktam vyaktim āpannam manyante mām* etc—the ignorant think of Me as *Avyakta* (unmanifest) come into manifestation. Here it can mean the Sāṁkhyan Prakṛti in contrast to its manifestation. Or it may have no technical sense, but that the ignorant hold the Incarnation too as just a man as referred to in 3.21. 5. In 12.1 the word *Avyakta* is used in a very ambiguous manner. The passage is "*Evam satatayuktā ye... ye cā-pyakṣaram avyaktam*—which of these have greater understanding of Yoga, those who are devotees of the Personal or those devoted to that which is Akṣaram and Avyaktam (the imperishable and the unclear)?" Śaṅkara interprets these words as meaning the adjunctless and the unclear (i,e. attributeless and not visible to the senses). In other words, it refers to the Impersonal Absolute (*Nirviśeṣa Brahman*). For Rāmānuja it means the individual self (*Pratyagātmā*). Shortly after the quoted verse, the word comes again in 12.5 "*Avyakt'āsakta cetasām* (of those who are devoted to the Avyakta)". In the context of the Gītā, it is very difficult to say to what this word Avyakta here refers. For, in the previous chapter the cosmic form of the Lord was described and it was declared that its experience can be had only by supreme Bhakti. So the contrast drawn here is

between Bhakti and another discipline. This second alternative discipline must be what is contained in some earlier chapter, say, as in 8.3—*Akṣaram Brahma paramam* etc. or in 2.72—*Eṣā Brāhmī-sthitiḥ* etc. It is described by several other epithets also in verse 3 of this 12th chapter itself by words like *anirdeśa, acintya, avyakta, kūṭastha,* etc., which indicate it to be Impersonal. Rāmānuja, however interprets all these words to mean soul or Atman-consciousness. In that case, it has to be explained how even they, the latter type of aspirants, attain to 'Me'—*te prāpnuvanti mām eva.* The explanation is perhaps found in 8.21 and 22. There the Supreme Abode is described as Avyakta, Akṣara etc., and it is also added that the Supreme Being (*Puruṣaḥ paraḥ*) is obtained through supreme and exclusive Bhakti (*bhaktyā labhyas tv' ananyayā*). So it means even those who follow the path of the Akṣara, be it the Impersonal Absolute or soul consciousness, attain supreme devotion and consequently Divine grace, and thereby only they are lifted up from Samsāra. But their path is difficult according to the Gītā.

In 13.5 the word Avyakta means Prakṛti, the stuff of Nature, as in the Sāṁkhya philosophy. The passage is: *Mabā-bhūtāny ahamkāro buddhir avyaktam eva ca,*" Here it is to be noted that the same word, meaning the Impersonal Absolute and the soul consciousness in other contexts, is used in the Gītā in the Sāṁkhyan sense as Prakṛti. Now these two entirely different meanings of the word are brought clearly side by side in 8.20 and 21. "*Paras tasmāt tu bhavo' nyo vyakto' vyaktāt sanātanaḥ, yaḥ sarveṣu bhūteṣu naśyatsu na vinaśyati*—different from the undifferentiated state of Prakṛti (Avyakta), there is another, the Supreme and Eternal Avyakta or Unmanifested who remains unaffected even when everything is destroyed." For full explanation see Note 4 on p. 231.

PURUSA

This is another important word used in different senses in the Gītā. Its common non-technical sense is, a man, a person. Coming from the root '*Puru*' meaning 'man', its dictionary meanings are: a male, a person, officer, attendant, esrvant, follower of the Sāṁkhya philosophy, representative of a race, Primeval Man who is the source of the universe; identified with Śiva, Viṣṇu, Brahmā and Durgā; the personal animating principle; soul of the universe; the conscious principle of the Sāṁkhyas; a prince etc.

In 2.21 it is used in the sense of a man or person. It runs: *Katham sa puruṣaḥ Pārtha kam ghātayati hanti kam*—how and whom can that person kill, how and whom can he cause to be killed. In the same sense it is used in 3.4 and 3.36.

A totally different use occurs in a later chapter (8.4): "*Puruṣas c'ādhidaivatam*—Puruṣa is what refers to Divinities. Puruṣa here means the indwelling spirit. Śaṅkara interprets Puruṣa here as '*pūrṇam anena sarvam iti; puria yanāt vā puruṣaḥ*' (what infills all or what reclines in the city of the body). This, according to him, is Hiraṇyagarbha (the cosmic soul) installed in the sun, who is the protector of all the Indriyas (instruments of cognition and action). Indriyas are called Devas. It may be described as the pervading spiritual essence in the individual. That it is not Kṛṣṇa, the Supreme Being,is sure from the last line of the verse which says, "I am the Adhiyajña, the recipient of all worship in all bodies".

Later in the same Chapter (8.22) the word Puruṣa with the adjective 'Paraḥ' (supreme) is used to indicate the Supreme Being—*Puruṣaḥ sa paraḥ*. In the same sense it is used in 11.18 with a different descriptive epithet '*Sanātanaḥ*'(eternal)—'*Sanātanas tvam puruṣaḥ*. In the same sense the word is used in 11.38: "*Tvam ādi devaḥ puruṣaḥ purāṇaḥ*—Thou art the Puruṣa, the first of all divinities and the most ancient.' However it looks that the meaning of the other epithet '*Adhidaivatam*' in 8.4 is here reflected in a way; for Brahmā is the first of the Devas. But the context and the later descriptive epithets show that it means the Supreme Being and not Hiraṇyagarbha Brahmā. It only reveals the fluidity of the meaning of the word.

The same fluidity in the meaning of the word *Puruṣa* is revealed in its use in Verses 19—22 of the 13th Chp. At first it is used in the pure Sāṁkhyan sense of 'a monad of consciousness' as distinct from the purely insentient and unconscious Nature (Prakṛti). For example "*Prakṛtim puruṣam c'aiva viddhy anādī ubhāvapi*—know both Prakṛti and Puruṣa to be beginningless eternal verities. In the few succeeding verses the word is used in the same sense, but coming to the 22nd verse, the meaning is changed by adding the descriptive epithets *paraḥ* and others to it. It becomes '*Puruṣaḥ paraḥ*'—the supreme Self or Iśvara as the indweller.

But the most confusing use of the word occurs in verses 16 to 18 of Chap. 15. For a detailed discussion of it reference may be made to Note 5 of chapter 15. Here the word Puruṣa is used for Kṛṣṇa, for the changing manifestations of Prakṛti as body-minds and also for what the text calls *Kūṭastha* and *Akṣara,*—words that are interpreted in different ways. The ordinary meaning of these words is'firmly set'and 'undecaying' What the entity meant is anybody's guess. Many commentators feel that it denotes Prakṛti. In that case Prakṛti also becomes 'Puruṣa'. The Supreme Being is distinguished from these Puruṣas as Puruṣottama and Paramātmā—the highest Puruṣa or the Supreme Spirit. In these contexts the word Puruṣa seems to mean only a 'category'. The fluidity of the meaning of the word is astonishing.

A recent research work of Prof. P.M. Modi entitled 'Akṣara' has got something very interesting and novel to say on these words with fluid meanings. He studies the words Akṣara, Puruṣa, Avyakta and Brahman in the light of the various contexts in the Gītā and also in relation to their use in the later poetical Upaniṣads and the Śāntiparva of the Mahābhārata, and arrives at the following conclusion in regard to the significance of these words in the Gītā.

The Gītā, according to him, does not indentify Brahman with the Supreme Being. The Supreme Being is Puruṣa who is identical with Kṛṣṇa. Brahman is only a power dependent on Kṛṣṇa, as it is put in 14.27 of the Gītā: 'I (Kṛṣṇa) am the foundation or support of Brahman'.

The Puruṣa (i.e Kṛṣṇa) has two Powers or Natures—the higher and the lower. The higher Nature is Akṣara, (also called Sanātana Avyakta) and the lower Nature Brahman (also called Avyakta). Akṣara is the higher Nature that sustains(*dharyate*) the lower Nature or Brahman which, through the activity ofKarma, becomes the cause of creation. The relation of these two Natures to the Puruṣa or Kṛṣṇa is one of Dharma and Dharmī, attribute and substance.

That is why Kṛṣṇa says that even those who adore Akṣara reach Him, in Gītā 13.1 to 4.

Prof. Modi puts all these in a very confused way, though he gives quotations and references to his conclusions. It is not, however, convincing enough as a final conclusion, but it, confirms the idea that all these technical expressions are fluid in their meanings in the Gītā, not having received their definite fixed meanings as in the Vedanta philosophy, of which it is a fundamental text.

Index